Valery V. Matveev, Vladimir V. Matveev

The Noo Logistics

The Short Description

This is translation from Russian by authors of original book "Матвеев В. В., Матвеев Вл. В. Ноо Логистика. Краткое описание. ISBN 978-83-949046-0-9. Электронная книга, формат Windows eBook, 15,6 Мб. http://www.noologistics.ru, 04.09.2017. — 401 с."

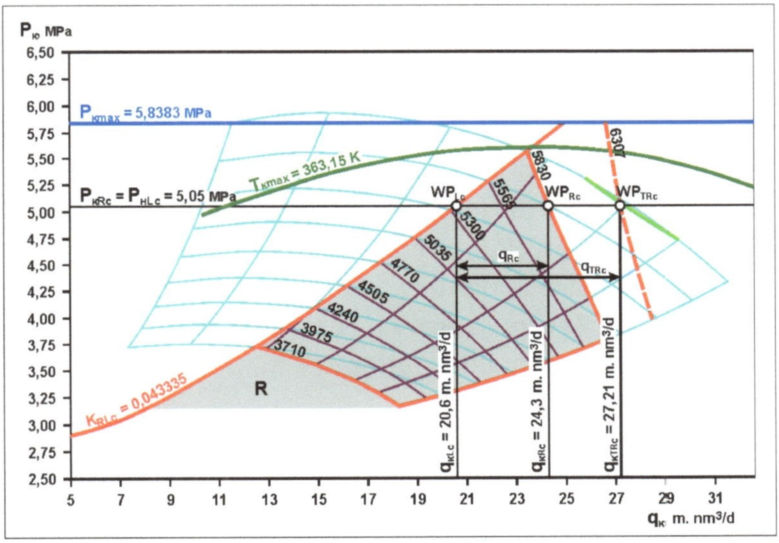

ISBN 978-83-949046-1-6

9 788394 904616

ISBN 978-83-949046-1-6

Kaliningrad
2018

Content

The Introduction

Each **person** has their own individual **needs**. He uses something material or informational to satisfy each of **needs**, which is of **value** to it in terms of its ability to satisfy it. The movement or change of **value** occurs in the satisfaction process of a concrete **need**. This movement or change is hereinafter referred to as **the value flow**.

It is well known that the whole set of **needs** of any **person** may be divided into two types: **primary** (final) and **secondary** (infinite). His physiological **needs** for food, clothing, housing, the renewal of nature, security, the rejection of waste products, etc. are attributed to his **primary needs**. The process of immediate satisfaction of **primary needs** is necessarily included in **provision his existence** (**life support**), and their termination leads to its death or to the termination of its kind. The flows of **secondary values** by which it meets its **secondary needs** are also part of the **life support** of each **person**. Nomenclature, quantitative and qualitative parameters of **values** and their **flows** contained in the **life support** of each **person** are known and amenable to logical and mathematical processing – see **examples formalization of their description**.

The current flows of material and informational values mentioned above are the only form of interaction of people with their **habitats** and to other people. These **flows** are divided into three types: **current flows of consumption**, **of creation**, and **of rejection the values**. It follows from the above that for each **person** one of the main **goals** is **the reasonable management of the current flows of values**, otherwise it will not be able to achieve the **goals** of his existence.

The limited physical, intellectual and psychological capabilities of an **person**, as well as the **values** available to him / her in his / her individual **habitat**, determine the existence of two interrelated forms of human relations: mutual assistance and competition. They are the basis for uniting people into groups with common **goals**, which provides a synergetic effect, expressed in a more effective expansion of their common **habitat**, as well as in increasing the nomenclature, size and quality of **the current flows of values** that make up their individual **life support**. By joining together in a group, people hope that meeting their **primary needs** will be one of the primary and most important of its overall **goals**.

Differences in property, physical, intellectual and psychological qualities of people cause obligatory hierarchy of their relationships in the group. **Hierarchy** stability is provided by its **rules**, which are divided into three types: **laws of nature**, **individual** and **group ones**. **The laws of nature** are determined by **science**. **Individual rules** are determined by genes (inheritance), property, physical, intellectual, psychological qualities of each **person**, as well as qualities acquired by them in the process of education. **Group rules** determine the way of forming the overall **goal** of **the hierarchy**, **principles**, **criteria of reasonableness**, **means** and **technology** of achieving them, as well as the difference in the parameters of individual **life supports** and **habitats** of people who are members of it at different levels of its management.

Despite the complexity, great variety and a large amount of **group rules**, they may be presented for any **hierarchy** in the form of **reasonable control system** that contains a lot of **information pyramids**. Each **pyramid** describes the structure of the distribution of the total **current flow of some value** between its people in accordance to their positions in **the hierarchy** and the forms of relationships between them. The mathematical and logical apparatus used to develop **reasonable management solutions** and calculate the corresponding **control actions** in this distribution is extremely simple because it contains only four arithmetic actions (+ , -, * and /) and the simplest logical functions (AND, OR, IF and NOT) – see examples of **the calculation of non-indexed information pyramids**.

The development of **reasonable management solutions** and the calculation of the magnitudes of **reasonable control actions**, taking into account **the laws of nature** in the management of **hierarchies**, for example, in goal to minimize the impact on **the habitat**, requires the use of mathematical devices from the relevant **Sciences** – see examples of **the calculation of indexed information pyramids**.

A feature of the **life support** is an obvious **need** to maintain its parameters at the current time (i.e. the **PRESENT**) in such a way as to achieve set **goal** in the **FUTURE**. To develop **reasonable management solutions** and the calculation of **reasonable management actions** that support such **life support**, a specially developed **technology of forecast calculation in the PRESENT**. The joint use of formal descriptions of the **life support**, **habitat** and **goal**, **technology of calculation of the information pyramids**, **technology of forecast calculation in the PRESENT**, etc. has led to the formation of the aggregate **goal** of any **hierarchy** based on the individual **goals** of all its people in real time.

Each **person**, each group of interacting people and all mankind as a whole always aspired to manage reasonably the **life support**. To do this, they have been using **Logistics** Since ancient times (Greek λογιστική, eng. Logistics), which has been formed to date as a science of optimal management of interconnected flows of goods, money and information to meet their **needs**. These flows are varieties of **value flows** and constitute only part of the flows totality contained in **life support**. The subject of commodity-money **Logistics** is their optimization to achieve the **goals** that **person** set for using it. **Logistics** has become an important component of the modern **Economy**, regulating commodity-money relations between people, in the extreme manifestation of which money has turned from the equivalent of quantity, quality, utility and importance of goods into an independent **value**, and the world (According to K. Marx) began to rule the social **need** in the form of material and economic interests. The obvious fact is that the commodity-money **Economy**, which declares the maximum satisfaction of human **needs** multitude as its main **goal**, in reality dedicated to the achievement of a single **goal** – to maximize profits in monetary terms.

It is well known that people within their **habitat** interact to other species of beings which showing signs of mind, having their own individual **life supports**, **habitats** and **goals**, for example, to animals. These interactions are also carried out through **current flows of material and information values**, from which cash flows are excluded. They have a hierarchical structure and the same two forms: mutual aid and competition. This identity of relationships allows to combine the management of **a hierarchy** consisting of people and other intelligent beings into a single process under the overall **goals** and to use for it the above-mentioned **technologies for calculating information pyramids**, **forecast in the PRESENT**, etc.

The possibility of such joint management was first expressed by the outstanding Russian scientist Vladimir Ivanovich Vernadsky more than a hundred years ago. He first introduced the concept of "**noosphere**" (from the Greek νόος – the mind and σφαῖρα – the ball) as the interaction of **intelligent beings** to each other and to nature across the planet.

It has been shown above that the only form of interaction of intelligent beings to each other and to their **habitat** is **the current flows of material and informational values** between them. Thus, the **noosphere** is physically the aggregate of all **current flows of material and informational values** between all intelligent beings on the planet, as well as between them and the planet, for example, the Earth. Therefore, it is possible not only to make a nomenclature of all these flows, to measure their density and quality parameters, but also to manage them reasonably to achieve their **goals**. The management technology for that is described below.

V. I. Vernadsky noted **Logistics** as one of the mathematical Sciences, which carries "the immutability and binding of properly derived scientific truths for any human person". Science about **reasonable (noo) managing** (hereafter **noo** is from the Greek νόος – the mind) of **life support**, hereafter is called "**Noo Logistics**" or "**Noologistics**" by analogy to the name "**Logistics**". Accordingly, **Noologistics** is an important component of **Nooeconomy** regulating of **the value relationship** between intelligent beings, and also between them and their **habitat** and the vital necessity in the form of **reasonable (noo) needs** rules the world in accordance to it.

In **Noologistics** along to the concept of "**noosphere**" is used and other similarly-formed names for the relevant scope of its application, including: **noogalaxy**, **noocluster of stars**, **nooconstellation**, **noonebula**, **noouniverse**, etc.

The aim of this research was the clarification the concepts of "**life support**", "**habitat**", "**noosphere**", "**noogalaxy**", "**noouniverse**", etc. in terms that allow to use **Noologistics** in daily practice for a **reasonable (noo)** meet **the needs** of any **persons**, for example, of all mankind, to find ways and means is **reasonable (noo)** control the process of meeting them, providing the possibility of forming their parameters. The following tasks were solved to achieve this goal:

- the essence of the concept "**person**" as a reasonable being interacting to other intelligent beings, **habitat** and **environment** is defined;
- the essence of the concept of "**life support**", "**habitat**", "**noosphere**", "**noogalaxy**", "**noouniverse**", etc. as sets of persons interactions to other intelligent beings, the **habitat** and **environment** is defined;
- the essence of the concept of "**habitat**" as the place of existence of the **person** (reasonable existence) is defined;
- the essence of the concept of "**environment**" as a place of existence of a set of mutual-acting **persons** (intelligent beings) is defined;
- the description of the **person** is formalized, thus providing the possibility of mathematical processing of his parameters;
- the descriptions of the **person** interactions are formalized, thus providing the possibility of mathematical processing of their parameters;
- the descriptions of the "**life support**", "**noosphere**", "**noogalaxy**", "**noouniverse**", etc. are formalized, thus providing the possibility of mathematical processing of their parameters;
- the descriptions of the "**habitat**" and "**environment**" are formalized, thus providing the possibility of mathematical processing of their parameters;
- was developed a set of **principles the noo management** of **the life support**, **noosphere**, **noogalaxy**, **noouniverse**, etc.;
- was developed a set of **criteria noo management** of **the life support**, **noosphere**, **noogalaxy**, **noouniverse**, etc., and formation of **habitat** and **environment**;
- was created a universal mathematical apparatus that provides:

- taking into account the real situation in the **habitat** and **environment** in the **PRESENT**;
- taking into account the parameters of the real state of each **control object** in the **PRESENT**;
- calculation of the magnitudes of **noo control actions** in the **PRESENT**;
- taking into account the real status of each **person** in relations to other **persons**, to **habitat** and to **environment** in the **PRESENT**;
- taking into account the real **relative subjectivities** and **forms of interaction** of each **person** in relations to other **persons** in the **PRESENT**;
- **noo** formation of the overall **goal** of all interacting **persons** of entire **the hierarchy**;
- **noo** formation of **the life support**, **noosphere**, **noogalaxy**, **noouniverse**, etc., as well as **habitat** and **environment** to achieve overall **goal** of all interacting **persons**.

The object of the research are all forms of interaction between the **person**, **habitat** and **environment** that constitute **the life support**, **noosphere**, **noogalaxy**, **noouniverse**, etc. The subject of research is process **reasonable (noo)** formation of **habitat**, **environment**, **noosphere**, **noogalaxy**, **noouniverse**, etc. to achieve overall **goal** of all interacting **persons**.

Ideas and hypotheses of **Noologistics** on the basis of which were the research:

- **the person** is any being who shows signs of intelligence who is interacting to other intelligent beings, to **habitat** and to **environment** (a virus, a microorganism, a cell of the organism of a being, plant, animal, robot, man, alien, god, etc.) and their union (strain, colony, thickets, flock, tribe, collective, State, UN, host, and so on);
- each **person** has only three types of needs **to consume the values**, **to create the values** and **to reject the values**;
- each **person** has the own individual **goal**;

- each **person** has the own individual scale of importance the **noo needs** and **noo values**, which defines the sequence (priority) of satisfying them according to ability to meet **current needs**, including the separation of them to **primary** and **secondary** (high);
- finiteness of **primary needs** and infinity of **secondary needs**;
- competition between **persons** up to antagonism and mutual aid between them up to self-sacrifice in achieving **the goal**;
- the desire of **persons** to unite in **a hierarchy** for synergetic improvement of the parameters of their **habitat**, **life support** and **goal**;
- **hierarchy** between the **persons** is determined by the relevant **rules**, which contain a formalized description of the degree of inequality (**subjectivity**) in the formation of a common **goal** and meet their individual **needs**;
- harmonization of relations between **the persons** implies minimization of antagonistic competition between them due to application of **reasonable (noo)** combination of magnitudes of **status coefficients**, of **forms of interaction** and of **relative subjectivities**;
- the defining role of **persons** in the formation of the **noosphere**, **noogalaxy**, **noouniverse**, etc. as a set of their **life supports**, which satisfying their **needs** and are means of achieving their **goals**;
- formalization of the concepts of **the person**, **value**, **goal**, **noosphere**, **noogalaxy**, **noouniverse**, **habitat**, **environment**, **life support**, etc.;
- application of the universal mathematical apparatus and algorithms to produce **the noo management solutions** and for calculating **the noo control actions** in the formation of the **habitat**, **environment**, **noosphere**, **noogalaxy**, **noouniverse**, etc. while achieving set **goal**;
- the possibility of expanding the scope of **persons** relationship beyond the **noosphere**, for example, to **noogalaxy**, **noouniverse** and beyond.

General scientific methods of research were used in the process of solving the problems posed above, including methods of formalization, generalization, abstraction, deduction, experiment, ascent from the abstract to the concrete, idealization, etc. Methods of the system approach, economic-mathematical modeling, control object simulation, etc. referred to the special research methods used.

The scientific novelty of the research consists in the development of the theory, methodology and practice of **noologistical management**, in the refinement and development of the notion of the **noosphere**, in the addition of concepts of the **noogalaxy**, **noouniverse**, etc., in the representation of them as a set of interaction of sentient beings between themselves, and to the **habitat** and **environment** in the scale of the planets, galaxies, the universe, etc., respectively. The use of logistics as a management tool for the first time was expanded beyond the commodity-money **Economy**.

The scientific novelty of the research is also in the development of the theoretical foundations of a new science containing objective, systematically organized and grounded knowledge about the management of the **noosphere**, **noogalaxy**, **noouniverse**, etc. and of the formation of the **environment** which **persons** use to achieve their **goals**. The nature of the management **objects** (**current flows of material and information noo values**) and its field of knowledge (**logistics**, **noosphere**, **noogalaxy**, **noouniverse**, etc.) were the basis to call it the **Noologistics**.

The definitions of the set of concepts pertaining to an objectively existing reality are given for the first time in **Noologistics**. This allowed to form its conceptual apparatus as a science. The description of each of its concepts is formalized and contains a definition, structure, parameters and, if necessary, a mathematical apparatus and an algorithm for its use in the processes of developing **noo management solutions** and calculating the magnitudes of **noo control actions**. These include descriptions of the concepts of the **person**, **hierarchy**, its **rules**, **noo values**, **goal**, **status coefficients**, **relative subjectivities**, **forms of interaction**, **object**, **life support**, **habitat**, **noosphere**, **noogalaxy**, **noouniverse**, **environment**, etc. The objective necessity are justified for a gradual transition from commodity-money **Economy** to **Nooeconomy** and from representative democracy to direct democracy, regulating **value relations**, whose main **goal** is to satisfy the **needs** of its **persons**, the rational management of **noosphere**, **noogalaxy**, **noouniverse**, etc., as well as the formation of the **environment**, and not just getting the maximum profit. The technical possibility of transition from representative democracy to direct democracy is also justified.

The descriptions of calculation technologies were first presented in **Noologistics**, which provides the solution of all the above management tasks, including:

- **The Technology of Forecast Calculation in the PRESENT**;
- **The Technology of Calculating the Indexed Noologistical Area of Possible Operating Modes**;
- **The Technology of Calculating Information Pyramids**, including:
    - **The Technology of Calculation of the Upward Non-indexed Information Pyramid**;
    - **The Technology of Calculation of the Upward Indexed Information Pyramid**;
    - **The Technology of Calculation of the Downward Non-indexed Information Pyramid**;
    - **The Technology of Calculation of the Downward Indexed Information Pyramid**.

Descriptions of scientific provisions, which are set out in the sections listed in the content, are based on generally known facts, phenomena, laws of nature and mathematical relationships. Almost all calculation technologies are presented in detailed examples of calculations due concretely magnitudes obtained from real **objects**, except when the calculations are performed using methods known to the relevant experts, and specific values are not of fundamental importance. Such abbreviations were used to reduce the volume of the description.

Noologistics proceeds from the obvious fact that the main form of mutual relations between the **persons** that make up an individual or common **provision for their existence (life support)**, **noosphere**, **noogalaxy**, **noouniverse**, etc., as well as of any **persons** to the **environment** are not commodity-money, but **value relationships**. This allows us to move to the post-commodity-money economy, which is named above as **Nooeconomy**, the organic part of which is the modern commodity-money **Economy**. It may be extended to any **hierarchy** of **persons**, for example, to the Ivanov family and be called **the Ivanovs Nooeconomy**, to OJSC Gazprom and to be called **the Gazprom Nooeconomy**, to any country and be called, for example, **the Russian Federation Nooeconomy**, to any continent and called, for example, **the Europe Nooeconomy**, on any planet and be called **the Global Nooeconomy**, on any galaxy and be called **the Galactic Nooeconomy**, the Universe and be called **the Universe Nooeconomy**.

It is obvious that indicators of the **Nooeconomy** development of a specific **hierarchy** of **persons** will not only be the magnitudes of its internal and external commodity turnover expressed in monetary form, the amount of money in its budget and the amount of its assets and liabilities in cash, but, first and foremost, individual, average, gross, normative and other types of parameters for **life support**, **the habitat** of its **persons** and **goals**, which characterizing the degree of satisfaction of **current primary and secondary needs** of **the persons** in it and possible the achievement of their assigned individual and collective **goals**, expressed in kind.

It follows from the description of **Noologistics** that from the point of view of any of its **person**, the **Nooeconomy** indicators of the **reasonableness** (justice, honesty, equality, freedom, equality, etc.) of the **rules** of its specific **hierarchy** will be the specific magnitudes of its personal **status coefficients**, **relative subjectivities** and **forms of interaction** in it in comparison to its other **persons**. It is these indicators that determine the parameters of his **life support**, **habitat** and the possibility of achieving its individual **goals**, and not the form of its social and political structure, for example, "slave", "monarchical", "feudal", "socialist", "democratic", "capitalist", "communist", "theocratic", "unitary", "confederation", "totalitarian", "fascist", etc. The most effective form of participation of each **person** in his **hierarchy** from the point of view of **Noologistics** is direct democracy, which is ensured by the organization of **a permanent referendum**.

Another aspect of the practical significance of the application of **Noologistics** is the possibility of constantly support in the **PRESENT** the any **criteria of reasonableness** control which set the **person**, the magnitude of which may be expressed by a numerical value and measured, or any compromise between any number of **criteria** in the management of any **equipment unit**, of a group of jointly operating **equipment units** or the entire its **grid** of any complexity, any scale, any equipment type, with any number of levels of management, etc. **Noologistics** provides observance of the criterion of reasonableness of management set by a **person** primarily by automatic control of the operating mode of each **equipment unit** and additionally by changing the magnitudes of individual **status coefficients**, **relative subjectivities** and **forms of interaction** of **persons** of the corresponding **hierarchy**, if it is stipulated by its **rules**.

Noologistics provides preliminary modeling the formation of parameters of any **goals** and **noo management solutions**, which allows the **persons** to avoid mistakes in their implementation.

The above-described properties of **Noologistics** allow interacting **persons** to use it to form and maintain the **environment**, **noosphere**, **noogalaxy**, **noouniverse**, etc., in a state corresponding to their **needs** and **goals**, regardless of their worldview (instinctive, mythological, religious, philosophical, scientific and / or any other). Thus, **Noologistics** is politically neutral and implies that the world is ruled by **the current needs** of the **persons** and their **goals**, which are extremely diverse, constantly changing and may be harmonized by improving **the rules** of their relationship.

The main difference of **Noologistics** from traditional **Logistics** is **reasonable (noo) management** of "here and now" precisely the course of **current continuous and intermittent technology processes** in solving all types of its tasks (procurement, production, marketing, storage, stocks, transportation, customs, information, financial, trade, etc.) in logistics systems of any complexity, scale and purpose. For example, its application in water, gas, product and energy **grids** transforms them into smart grids. Other traditional logistical systems of a continuous production process (chemical, oil refining, etc.) may be converted in a similar way, as well as of an intermittent ones. Continuous optimization from the beginning to the end of the course of any intermittent process provides its integral optimum at the moment of completion.

Noologistics will qualitatively change the meaning of creating a "digital (electronic) economy": it will provide the exact satisfaction of **the current needs** of all its **persons** in accordance with the laws of nature and the **rules** of their **hierarchy** (laws, traditions, instructions, sacred writings, etc.) currently available resources and current environmental parameters. It will also provide the transition from environmental protection to its formation.

Practical examples of the implementation of Noologistics contain materials of research carried out by authors on real **objects** of gas industries in Russia, Poland, Bulgaria, Azerbaijan, etc. The current level of development of industry, science, computer technology, communications, and relative ease of implementation provide an opportunity to disseminate this knowledge and experience everywhere, for example, in the form of universal ("boxed") software products built into existing control systems and adapted to specific **control objects**.

Special attention is given **reasonable (noo) management** of **equipment units** working together at all levels of **large - scale grids** of gas and electricity that contains gas wells, gas-compressor units (GCU), gas air coolers (GAC), installations of preparation of gas to transportation, steam boilers, multistage steam turbines, pumps, heat exchangers, pipelines, condensers, shut-off valves, etc., including:

- the calculation of a **noo** redistribution of the total load between the steam turbine stages due to the change of the steam extraction magnitudes from them;
- the calculation of a **noo** combination of operating modes and the positions of elements of all **equipment units** (steam boiler, multistage steam turbine, heat exchangers, pumps, condenser, pipelines, shut-off valve, etc.) as a part of the power unit;
- the calculation of the **noo** combination of operating modes and the positions of elements of all **equipment units** into the power station;
- the calculation of the **noo** combination of operating modes and the positions of elements of all **equipment units** into the district of power supply;

- the calculation of the **noo** combination of operating modes and the positions of elements of all **equipment units** into the **large - scale grid** of power supply;
- the calculation **noo** combinations of extraction or injection magnitudes of all gas wells in the composition of their group;
- the calculation **noo** combinations of extraction or injection magnitudes of all gas wells, of operation of the gas treatment unit and of booster compressor station in the composition of gas field or of station of underground gas storage;
- the calculation of the **noo** combination of operating modes for all GCU that parallel working in the compression stage of the compressor station;
- the calculation of the **noo** combinations of operation modes and the positions of all elements of GAC which are controlled by change in the number of included fans and the speeds of its rotation, by the provisions of the input, output and by-pass shutters;
- the calculation of the **noo** combinations of modes and provisions of the elements of GCU and GAC into the all compression stages which sequentially operating in a compressor station;
- the calculation of the **noo** combination of operating modes and the positions of all elements of all **equipment units** into the section of the main gas pipeline;
- the calculation of the **noo** combination of operating modes and the positions of all elements of all **equipment units** into the **large - scale grid** of gas supply.

There are no analogues in the world described in the book method of managing **large - scale grids**, moreover, currently many of the described in it is considered to be technically not feasible. For example, the mathematical apparatus and algorithms of development of **noo management solutions**, and also calculation of **noo control actions** which are presented in it, provided for the first time the theoretical and technical opportunity to create "smart grid" for entire OJSC Gazprom, for entire RAO UES of Russia and for entire any other **large - scale grid**. In the field of social relations, the described method of management of any **hierarchy** allows to move to direct democracy.

The practical significance of the application of **Noologistics** is also the possibility of overcoming the well-known systemic crises inherent in modernity.

One of these systemic crises is due to the contradiction between the level of development of the productive forces of mankind and commodity-money relations. Its reason is the reduction of jobs due to the increasing use of so-called "technologies without people" and, accordingly, the exclusion of an increasing number of people from commodity-money relations. Thus, commodity-money relations at a certain level of development of the productive forces of mankind begin to destroy themselves because an increasing number of people are pushed out from them forcibly. At the same time, there are many facts of overproduction of goods (**values**), which show that the real possibilities of the productive forces of mankind are able to satisfy almost all of its **primary needs** due to their finality. However, it is impossible to fully meet the **secondary needs** of mankind because of their infinity. It is this contradiction that should be the main impetus for the development of mankind.

Overcoming this crisis is provided in **Noologistics** by moving the process of meet **the primary needs** of each **person** from the commodity-money relations to **the value relationship**. That is proposed in **the hierarchy rules** set assessment, planning and meeting individual **primary needs** of each **person** only in physical terms and to be excluded the money from these processes. This does not mean giving up a commodity-money relationship because it may be used to assess, plan, and meet the aggregate **needs** of hierarchies, as well as the individual **secondary needs** of people.

The second systemic crisis is caused by the contradiction between the ever-increasing **needs** of people (humanity) and their **habitat**. It is caused by discrepancy of the nomenclature, quantitative and qualitative parameters of flows of goods, money and information used in commodity-money relationship between people, in comparison to **the current flows of the material and information values** used by them in the relations to their **habitat**. Because the money is in the interaction of people with their **habitat** can't fulfill the role that they play in relations between people. Overcoming this crisis in **Noologistics** provided by the fixing in **the rules of hierarchy** the priority **the value relationship** above the commodity-money relations in the development of **the noo management decisions**, calculation and implementation of **noo control actions**.

The third systemic crisis is caused by inequality of people at different levels of **hierarchy** management. In any known **hierarchy**, even in the most democratic one, the common **goal** of the whole **hierarchy**, the **principles**, **criteria of reasonableness**, ways and means of achieving it are determined either solely or by a narrow circle of people at the highest level of its management, according to **the rules** formulated by themselves. They themselves set also their responsible for the results of their rule in this **rules**. Therefore, it is enough in one way or another to take the top level of governance in **the hierarchy** to realize their individual **goals** and **needs**, democratically presenting them socially necessary or despotically openly ignoring the **goals** and **needs** of other people.

Therefore, there is no example in human history where people who, as a result of elections, revolutions or coups, have taken the upper levels of **hierarchy** management would have fulfilled their promises in full. And the coming to power of new people does not change anything – they also do not fulfill their promises. Overcoming this crisis is to set in **the rules of hierarchy**, the obligation to make **the permanent (constant) referendum** and to realize its results, possibility of which provides **the technology of Noologistics**. Its essence consists in giving to each person the opportunity to express his opinion on any problem of management **the hierarchy** at any time and to account of his opinion at development of **noo management solutions**, calculation and realization of the corresponding **noo control actions**. Unfortunately **Noologistics** not able to provide for all absolute justice, fairness, equality, freedom, equality, etc., which are a utopia.

Based on the opinions expressed in **the permanent referendum** in accordance to **the rules of hierarchy**, the development of the current situation is modeled, **noo management solutions** are developed, the **noo control actions** are calculated and implemented. It is **the rules of hierarchy** that determine the **principles** and **criteria** for its management, as well as the means used for it: they may completely ignore the **Noologistics**, use it partially, for example, to create a "smart grids" in individual industries, or use it completely, i.e., in the totality of the relations of all intelligent beings to each other and to **the environment**. The creation of **a system of Noologistics** may be the main meaning of the so-called "electronic economy".

The presented materials may be of interest to specialists and researchers working in any field: **production**, **Economics**, **Logistics**, **ecology**, **forecasting**, **environmental protection**, **politics**, etc., as well as for teachers, postgraduates and students of all specialties. They may be of interest to employees of various government structures that control **hierarchies** (firms, regional, state, interstate organizations, etc.). They give the opportunity not only to develop **goals**, plans and recommendations for the **FUTURE** and to evaluate **PAST** performance, but also achieve in the **PRESENT** the extremely size of any known **criterion of reasonableness**, for example, **minimum CO2 emissions, minimum costs**, **maximum profit**, **maximum meet the needs**, etc., or any **compromise** between any **criteria of reasonableness** in the whole **object** and in any element thereof.

The phrase "Brief description" in the title of the book means that the materials contained therein contain a minimum of information and consist of **definitions** of basic concepts, formalized descriptions of their parameters and structures of their relations to other concepts of **Noologistics**. If necessary, this information is supplemented by a simplified description of the mathematical apparatus and algorithm, showing the technology of the use of this particular concept. This amount of information in the opinion of the authors is sufficient to represent the General structure of the theory of **Noologistics**, its most general **concepts** and capabilities. The presentation of the entire amount of information accumulated by the authors during its creation will require readers to spend too much time to study it. For example, only the description of the mathematical apparatus and algorithm of its use in **the system of Noologistics** of **booster compressor station of the Komsomolsk gas field** occupies about two thousand pages and contains many specific details, which cannot be applied, for example, in **noologistcal control** of nuclear power plant, religious ceremonies, educational or medical institutions.

The authors reserve the right to eliminate errors and typographical errors noted in the book, as well as are continuing work on this scientific direction - preparing the second edition of the book, which will take into account the wishes of readers.

1. The Base of Noologistics

1.1. The Essence and Definition of Noologistics

A lot of **creatures with signs of mind** known to mankind which interact to each other and to **the environment** as **persons** to achieve their **goals**. Obviously, each of these **persons** is guided by their **needs**, which they consider reasonable, in collaboration to other stakeholders and **the environment**. Therefore, the word "**noo**" is used here and below to refer to all that the **person** makes even if for other **persons** it is unreasonable or unacceptable. It is derived from the Greek "νόος" - the mind. The **person** uses the appropriate **noo value** to satisfy each of its **noo need**. The set of **noo values** available for **person**, is called its **habitat**.

Each **person** interacts to other **persons** and their **habitat** by his own **rules** through the **current flows of noo values**, and manages its parameters under his own evaluation system of importance the entire totality set of their quantitative and qualitative magnitudes. These **rules** contain reasonable from his point of view, the set of governance **principles** and **the criteria of reasonableness** for which he intends to take responsibility in relations with other **persons**. The set of the **current flows of noo values** that the considering **person** uses in interaction to other **persons** and his **habitat**, called by **the providing of his existence** (**life support**). Description of the process of reasonable management by **the person** of his own **providing of existence** (**life support**) is called by **Noologistics** (in short – **NL**) and has the following definition:

Noologistics is the science of the reasonable (**noo**) **management** by **person** the **provision his existence** (**life support**) in the **PRESENT** according to the **rules**, containing from his point of view a reasonable set of **principles of management** and **criteria** that he uses to achieve the **goal** set by him in the **FUTURE**.

The set of interactions of all entities on Earth to each other and with **the environment** is called **the noosphere**. Extrapolation of the description of the mentioned interactions in the Galaxy, Universe and beyond, enables to spread the **Noologistics** to the **noogalaxy**, **noouniverse**, etc.

Based on the definition **Noologistics**, it is a science **reasonable** (**noo**) **management** of the **noosphere**, **noogalaxy**, **noouniverse**, etc., the **goal** of it is formation and maintenance them in a state corresponding to **the needs** of the interacting **persons**. It uses the concepts that are the similar to the conventional **control theory**.

Fundamental concepts in **control theory** are the notions of **person**, **object**, **subject**, **goal of management**, **management solution**, **control action**, and other related notions, which together existing needs, knowledge, opportunities and **environmental** conditions of **the person** in a single management process. This conceptual framework is used to formulate the basic concepts of **Noologistics**, including:

The person – it is the physical, legal, social, or other **person** (a specific **person**, group of people, organization or group of people, organizations, etc.) that identifies the **object**, **subject** and **goals** of management, generating a **management solution** which calculates and implements appropriate **control action** on **the control object** to achieve management **goals**. The specific content of this concept in **Noologistics** – reflected in the section "**2.2. The Person of Noologistics**".

The object – an umbrella term referring to objectively existing **object**, **device**, **process**, **relationships**, **needs**, tastes, group of people, mechanism, **material flow**, **informational flow**, **financial flow**, **impacts flow** on the **environment**, etc., as well as their combination, dynamic state (functioning, behavior, mode, direction, magnitude, efficiency, optimality, impact on other objects, etc.) that changes and/or supports the **person** of management in accordance with **management goals**

established by him. The specific content of this concept in **Noologistics** – reflected in the section "**2.3. The Object of Noologistics**".

The subject – a generic term signifying the relationship between the **person** and **object** of management. The specific content of this concept in **Noologistics** – reflected in the section "**2.4. The Subject of Noologistics**".

The goal is the ideal final result, which **person** strives to achieve through the modification or maintenance of the dynamic state of **the control object**. The specific content of this concept in **Noologistics** – reflected in the section "**2.5. The Goal of Noologistics**".

Management solution – a generic term indicating the end of the process of the description of such set of objectively existing interrelated technologies used to provide dynamic state of the control object (operation, behavior, work, direction, magnitude, best magnitude for money, impact on other object, for calculating the control action, etc.), control parameters and their magnitudes, which developed by technology management established by **the person of management**, and which meets the **goals** of the control. The specific content of this concept in **Noologistics** – reflected in the section "**2.13. The Noo Management Solution**".

The dynamic state of the control object is an umbrella term referring to objectively existing in the **control object** the totality of **control parameters** and their magnitudes at a particular point in time. The specific content of this concept in **Noologistics** – reflected in the section "**2.3. The Object of Noologistics**".

The control parameters are the characteristics of **the dynamic state of the control object**, the list of which is established **the person of management** to determine the accuracy of achieving **the goals** of the control. The specific content of this concept in **Noologistics** – reflected in the section "**2.3. The Object of Noologistics**".

The control action is an umbrella term for the process of the forced change or maintaining no change of **the control parameters**, in accordance to the developed **control solution** to achieve **the goals** of the control which were set by **the person** of management. The specific content of this concept in **Noologistics** – reflected in the section "**2.14. The Noo Control Action**".

The control system is a combination of **control theory**, **control technology** and **means of its realization**, which provides the achievement of management **goals** which were set by **the person of management**. Description of the application of this concept in **Noologistics** – see section "**2.11. The System of Noologistics**".

The technology of control is a scientific, technical and normative description of a set of interrelated methods, processes, operations, principles, optimality criteria, mathematical apparatus, algorithms, **control parameters** and their magnitudes, and the means of its realization to achieve the management **goals** set by **the person** of management. The specific content of this concept in **Noologistics** – reflected in the section "**3.1. The Structure of Noologistics Technology**".

The means of realization of control technology is the combination of personnel, real estate, equipment, finances, regulatory documents, organizational activities, current material flows, energy flows, financial flows, information flows and service flows and impacts on the environment, which is used in accordance to **the technology of control** and provides the achievement of **management goals** which were set by **the person** of management. The specific content of this concept in **Noologistics** – reflected in the section "**2.10. The Grid of Noologistics**".

The prefix "**noo**" in the name of any concept means that it refers to **Noologistics**, meets the **needs**, **values**, and **rules** its **persons**, implies observance of **the principles** and **specific criteria of reasonableness**, and the use of its **technology**. It is obvious that the concept of "**noo**" (reasonable), which reflects a logical relationship between **the needs** and **actions** of a specific **person** is not synonymous of "fair", which reflects the equivalence relations between the **persons** in accordance of their position in **the hierarchy**.

The formalization of the descriptions of the above concepts in **Noologistics** provides possibility of application of its **technology**, which is a set of **mathematics and formal logic**. Under **the formalization of the descriptions of concepts** refers to the provision of information about them in the form of a simple structure containing a certain range of parameters, reflecting their quantitative and qualitative characteristics in numerical terms, and the ratio between them in the form of mathematical expressions and logical functions. **Formal descriptions of concepts** may be represented by tables, theory that consists mathematical and logical functions, by databases such "**Foreign Economic Activity Commodity Nomenclature (FEACN)**", etc. depending on the scope of application, the type of tasks the control and preferences of the **person**.

Noologistics provides to **the person** the solving of the following tasks of **reasonable control** of **the object** in achieving the **goals**:

- Update, storage, verification, supply and visualization of information;
- Development of **the noo management solution** that meets the **goal**;
- The calculation of **noo control actions** on **the objects of Noologistics**, i.e. appropriate to the developed **noo management solution**;
- Execution of **the noo control actions** on **the objects of Noologistics**, etc.

Noologistics provides control of both continuous and intermittent processes of **providing the existence (life support)** for any length of time because it automatically starts and ends simultaneously with the beginning and end of the process.

The **person** may provide limited use of the elements **Noologistics** one sector, territory, activity, needs, criteria of reasonableness, principles and give her an appropriate name:

Noologistics – when using its **technology** without restriction;

Green logistics – when using **technology of Noologistics** for the solution of management tasks in the protection of **the environment**, i.e. the maintenance of the **extremum** of one of the given **ecological criteria of reasonableness**, or **compromise** between the several given **ecological criteria of reasonableness**;

Logistics – when using **technology of Noologistics** for solving problems of management in the commodity-money **Economy**, i.e. the maintenance of the **extremum** of one of the given **economic criteria of reasonableness**, or **compromise** between the several given **economic criteria of reasonableness**;

Economic Ecological Logistics – when using **technology of Noologistics** for the solution of management tasks in the **Economy** in combination with **environmental protection**, i.e. the maintenance of **compromise** between the several given **economic and ecological criteria of reasonableness**;

Energy Ecological Logistics – when using **technology of Noologistics** for the solution of management tasks in the energy sector in combination with **environmental** protection in it, etc.

The person may use **technology of Noologistics** for any task management at its sole discretion, including for: monitoring, promoting, organizing, planning, modeling, forecasting, execution, etc. For example, the use of **Noologistics** in the electricity, gas, water supply etc. converts them into the **Smart Grid**. And its application in the Digital Economy allows you to start a gradual transition of **persons** to qualitatively other relations that are called **relations of value**. They affect all types of relationships of **persons** in any state, and between States that are governed by administrative, labor, criminal, family, civil and international law.

1.2. The Main Principles of Noologistics

The analysis of the principles of management applied in various spheres of human activity, set out in the **available sources**, was carried out to create a list of **principles of Noologistics**, including:

- universal principles in control theory;
- principles of production management;
- principles of energy management;
- principles of gas transportation system management;
- management principles of traditional (commodity-money) **Logistics**;
- the principles that were elaborated in the introduction of **noologistical elements** to real **objects**;
- principles of governance, etc.

A set of 16 interrelated basic **principles of Noologistics** was formed as a result of the analysis, including:

1. **Noo principle** (principle of reasonableness);
2. **Principle of sustainability**;
3. **The principle of adaptability**;
4. **The principle of sufficiency**;
5. **The principle of minimization of information flows**;
6. **The principle of information protection**;
7. **The principle of accessibility of information**;
8. **The principle of control in real-time**;
9. **The principle of forecasting**;
10. **The principle of synchronization**;
11. **The principle of minimizing impacts to the environment**;
12. **Principle of objectivity** (scientific character);
13. **The principle of subjectivity**;
14. **The principle of sociality**;
15. **The principle of totality**;
16. **The principle of systematicity**.

A brief description of the nature and manner in which each principle is provided is shown below.

1. Noo principle (principle of reasonableness)

Noologistics provides that each of its **persons** in interaction with other **persons** and **the environment** is guided by their **needs**, which he considers acceptable and **reasonable**, even if other entities considered that is unreasonable or unacceptable.

Compliance with **the principle of reasonableness** in **Noologistics** in the management of **the object** means that any **management solutions** and implementing its **control actions** relating to the parameters of his **provision of existence** (**life support**) and **habitat**, provide or extreme magnitudes of one particular **criterion of reasonableness** from the set of their possible ones, or the compromise between the extremes of the magnitudes of their particular set, which was set by **the person** setting its **goal**.

Compliance with the above-mentioned **extremum or compromise** in the development of **management solutions**, calculation and implementation of the relevant **control actions** provides a specially created **technology**.

Numerous automatic control systems, controls and regulators in which there is a function of automatic observance of the set limits of regulation of parameters of **provision of existence** (**life support**) and **habitat**, for example, density of the current flows of **consumption of values**, **creation of values**, **rejection of values**, pressure, temperature, turns, current, power, radiation and other parameters of **the current technological processes** belong to technical means which provide **the noo principles of management** of **object** and **the grid**.

Functions of control of the set limits of their operating modes, corresponding to **the noo principles** and the elimination of emerging complications are provided by the work of the relevant systems at **PRESENT**. Systems of fire automation, gas pollution control, technical diagnostics of equipment, emergency stop of **the object** and **the grid** belong to them. Requirements that meet **the noo principles** of these control systems, are specified obviously in the standard requirements for their design, creation, installation, commissioning and operation and are observed by **the person**.

2. Principle of sustainability

Compliance with **the principle of stability** means in **Noologistics** that each **management solution** and implementing corresponding **control actions** by **the person** must to **provide his existence** (**life support**) and **habitat** under certain boundary conditions.

Stability of **the object** and **the grid** provide usually by normative documents, technical means, organizational measures and means of control. Laws, standards, instructions, etc. are normative documents. The technical means include: the creation of reserves in the facility and the network, the use of duplicating elements in automatic control systems and controllers, the use of special-purpose equipment that has passed the necessary tests. Organizational arrangements are ensured by compliance with the rules of trouble-free operation. The means of control include the system of Instrumentation and automation, automation, ACS, etc.

Stability requirements are necessarily specified in the standard requirements for the creation of control systems of **the object** and **the grid** and are observed by **the person** in their design, creation, installation, commissioning and operation.

3. The principle of adaptability

Compliance with **the principle of adaptability** in **Noologistics** in the management of **the object** means that in the development of any **management solution**, the calculation and implementation of the relevant **control actions**, take into account all the current changes in **the person**, in **the environment**, **habitat**, **providing his existence** (**life support**), **the object** and **the grid** occurring at the time of completion of all relevant **control actions**, including:

- current movements of **the person** in space;
- current changes in the magnitudes of the parameters of **the current flows** of **consumption of values**, **creation of values**, **rejection of values**, including their spatial distribution;
- current changes in **the environment** at each location the current place of each element of **object** and **grid**;
- changes of **the current indexed noologistical areas of the possible operating modes** of each unit of the facility equipment due to wear, contamination of work surfaces, deposits in pipelines, hydrate plugs, etc.;
- changes in **the current flows** of **consumption of values**, **creation of values**, **rejection of values** in each unit of the equipment of **the object** under to changes in the parameters of their operating modes;

- current changes to **the rules of hierarchy** between **the persons** (taxes, guarantees, preferences, privileges, restrictions, punishment, development plans, etc.);
- current changes in scientific knowledge and technical capabilities related to **the environment**, **habitat**, **providing of existence** (**life support**), **object** and **grid**;
- the duration of the cycle of **management solution** - making, calculation and implementation of the relevant **control actions**, etc.

The taking into account all these factors provides by **a technology** specially created for this purpose.

4. The principle of sufficiency

Compliance with **the principle of sufficiency** in **Noologistics** means that the development and implementation of any **management solution** is based on the presence of the necessary combination of **environmental** parameters with the technical ability to maintain the necessary parameters to **providing of existence** (**life support**) and **the rules** that are observed by **the person**, for example, due current financing, energy supply, logistics, etc. by nomenclature, volume, timing and sources.

5. The principle of minimization of information flows

It is well known that the physiological ability of **the person** to perceive information is quite limited and evaluated in units of data per second, they were determined and are: when the proofreading work - 18 units, when reading aloud - 30 units, reading "Pro themselves" – 45 units; the largest amount of data that he may perceive by ear, is about 8 units per second. For example, a radio listener loses the ability to perceive information if it is transmitted at a speed of more than 180 words per minute. In television broadcasting, the average rate is 103 words per minute, which is optimal for the transmission of text material accompanied by an image. These figures impose severe restrictions on other operations with information, which are complicated by the lack of time and lack of attention of **the person** in obtaining information.

It is experimentally established that the human brain is able to perceive and accurately process information at a speed of no more than 25 bits per second.

There is a situation when the excessive amount of information received may suppress the **person**'s ability to analyze, make **solutions** and, accordingly, execute them, due to the strict need to make urgent, current, even unimportant decisions in conditions of time deficit.

Thus, compliance with **the principle of minimizing information flows** means that the amount of information provided to **the person** at the current moment of time for the development of **management solutions**, calculation and implementation of the relevant **control actions** should not exceed its physiological and/or technical capabilities.

In addition, large amounts of information require large capacities from management systems for their processing and, accordingly, high costs for their creation and operation.

The principle of minimization of information flows in **Noologistics** provides by the use mainly of the current (operational) information in the loop under the algorithm "to collect information, to check its reliability, to develop **a managerial solution**, to calculate **the control actions**, performed **the control action**, to remove information".

Really achieved a reduction in density of information flow in several orders of magnitude confirms the following comparative calculation, which is executed according to test results of **Noologistics system** elements in the control system of **booster compressor station of the Komsomolsk gas field** (**BCS KGF**).

Source data:

The total number of analog and discrete signals are receiving by **the system of Noologistics** from the **BCS KGF** in each cycle of the development of a set of **control actions** is $\mathbf{CIF}_{in}$ = 4073 signals;

The total number of analog and discrete signals supplied to the **BCS KGF** from **the system of Noologistics** in each calculation cycle of **the control actions** set is **CIF_{out}** = 701 signals;

The period of the cycle of information gathering is T_c = 2 minutes;

The minimum period for collecting statistical information used in traditional **Logistics** is N_{ymin} = 1 year.

Calculation:

1. The total number of signals **CIF**, which contained in the current information flow and are used by **the system of Noologistics** in each calculation cycle of the set of the control actions, is calculated by the formula:

$$CIF = CIF_{in} + CIF_{out} = 4073 + 701 = 4774 \text{ signals},$$

here are CIF_{in} and CIF_{out} – see above.

2. The minimum number of cycles of collection of statistical information contained in databases is calculated by the formula:

$$N_c = N_{ymin} * N_d * N_h * N_m / T_c = 1 * 365 * 24 * 60 / 2 = 262\,800 \text{ cycles},$$

here are:

N_{ymin} and T_c – see above;

N_d – the number of days in a year;

N_h – number of hours per day;

N_m – the number of minutes in an hour.

3. The minimum number of IF_{sd} signals stored in statistical databases is calculated by the formula:

$$IF_{sd} = CIF * N_c = 4774 * 262800 = 1\,254\,607\,200 \text{ signals},$$

here are CIF and N_c – see above.

4. The minimum number of signals IF used in the calculation of a set of control actions based on statistical information is calculated by the formula:

$IF = CIF + IF_{sd} = 4774 + 1254607200 = 1\,254\,611\,974$ signals,

here are CIF and IF_{sd} – see above.

5. The comparison shows how many times the magnitude of IF is greater than the magnitude of CIF due magnitudes of T_c and N_{ymin}:

$IF / CIF = 1254611974 / 4774 = 262\,801 \approx 2{,}63 * 10^5$ times.

The above calculations show that the use of elements of **the technology of Noologistics** reduces the amount of processed information by at least five orders (2,63*105 times) in comparison to traditional technology that uses arrays of statistical information. However, there are reasons to increase this ratio by a few more orders of magnitude because **the system of Noologistics** itself is able to process the above-mentioned CIF containing 4774 signals for a period of time T_{SN} < 2 seconds, the value of T_c = 2 minutes was set for the information collection cycle of the then existing automated control system **BCS KGF**, which, in addition, stored the collected statistical information for a period of time N_y > 3 years. Therefore, a similar calculation is given below for comparison, in which N_{ymin} = 1 year and T_c = 2 minutes are replaced by N_y = 3 years and T_{SN} = 2 seconds respectively.

6. The number of cycles of collecting statistical information N_{cSN} contained in the databases at T_{SN} and N_y, is calculated by the formula:

$N_{cSN} = N_y * N_d * N_h * N_m * N_s / T_{SN} = 3 * 365 * 24 * 60 * 60 / 2 = 15\,768\,000$ cycles,

here are:

N_y, N_d, N_h, N_m and T_{US} – see above;

N_s – the number of seconds in a minute.

7. The number of signals IF_{sdSN} stored in databases at T_{SN} and N_y is calculated by the formula:

IF_{sdSN} = CIF * N_{cSN} = 4774 * 15768000 = 75 276 432 000 signals,

here are CIF and N_{cSN} – see above.

8. The number of signals IF_{SN} contained in the statistics and used to calculate the set of control actions due magnitudes of T_{SN} and N_y, is calculated by the formula:

IF_{SN} = CIF + IF_{sdSN} = 4774 + 75 276 432 000 = 75 276 436 774 signals,

here are CIF and IF_{sdSN} – see above.

9. The comparison shows how many times the magnitude of IF_{SN} is greater than the magnitude of CIF due magnitudes of T_{SN} and N_y:

IF_{SN} / CIF = 75276436774 / 4774 = 15 768 001 ≈ 1,58 * 10^7 times.

The calculations performed in the example above, show that the application of elements of **the technology of Noologistics** only at the expense of abandoning the use of statistical information, reduces the amount of information processed from five to seven orders of times (of 2,63*10^5 to 1,58*10^7 times) in comparison with the traditional technology that uses arrays of statistical information.

The use of **the technology of calculation information pyramids** is the second method to reduce the density of information flow in **Noologistics** that reduces it magnitude additionally in several orders of times depending on the number of management levels.

The purpose of calculating information pyramids is to process the current flow of information in transferring from each lower level to each next higher level, that reduces its density from 10 to 15 times or more.

Real large-scale **objects**, for example, the power supply system of the entire EU, have 15 and more levels of management. Consequently, at the 15th level of management, the density of the current information flow in the energy supply system of the whole EU will decrease from ≈ 10^{14} to more than ≈ $2{,}92*10^{16}$ times (i.e. from ≈ $10^{(15-1)}$ to ≈ $15^{(15-1)}$ and more times) compared to its density at the 1st level.

After multiplying the magnitude IF / CIF ≈ $2{,}63*10^{5}$ times (see above p. 5) and the magnitude ≈ 10^{14} times we get that the reduction ratio of the density of the current information flow at 15 level control of an **object** in comparison with the magnitude of the current flow of information on the first level is equal of ≈ $2{,}63*10^{19}$ times. After multiplying the magnitude IF_{SN} / CIF ≈ $1{,}58*10^{7}$ times (see above p. 9) and the magnitude ≈$2{,}92*10^{16}$ times we get that the reduction ratio of the density of the current information flow at 15 level control of an **object** in comparison with the magnitude of the current flow of information on the first level is equal of ≈$4{,}61*10^{23}$ times.

Thus, the total decrease in the density of the current flow of information at the 15th control level of a large-scale **object** in comparison with the density of the current flow of information at its 1st control level may be more than twenty orders of magnitude.

6. The principle of information protection

The principle of protection of information used in **the technology of Noologistics** is provided in two directions:

- **by protection of data** against access and influence of outsiders;
- **by the protection of information from errors and omissions** arising in the course of its conversion, transfer and storage on the path from the source of its origin and to the place of use.

These directions of **information protection** are provided by a large number of normative documents contained in **the rules** of the relevant **person**, for example, **hierarchy**, some of which are given in **the sources of information**.

The principle of information protection in accordance with the above-mentioned normative documents provide standard organizational measures and technical means, including:

- by duplication of information;
- by increase of fault tolerance of control systems;
- through opposition to overload and "freezes" of control systems;
- by using strictly defined software core in control systems;
- through control of information integrity in control systems;
- by special regulation of maintenance processes and software improvements in control systems;
- due the implementation of a set of anti-virus measures, etc.

The peculiarity of **Noologistics** is the maximum use of the management systems already existing in **the object** and the addition to them only those functions and processes that convert them into **a system of Noologistics**. Therefore, **the system of Noologistics** complies with all regulatory documents that provide **the principle of information protection** in **the object** which correspond to control systems that are used in it.

Automatic verification of information is an additional means of **protecting information** from distortion. It is not mentioned in the normative documents, but necessarily used in **the system of Noologistics**. It is carried out for each set of parameters, before the beginning of each cycle of development of **the management solution**, calculation and implementation of a set of **control actions**, according to the following universal algorithm:

1. Perform verification of a set of information, including stages:

- Check a presence all of parameters included in the kit;
- Check that the magnitude of each parameter corresponds to the range of its possible magnitudes;
- Check the conformity of a ratio of magnitudes of the parameters between themselves;

- Check the conformity of a ratio of magnitudes of the parameters to the combinations of work characteristics, physical, chemical, thermodynamic, gas dynamic and other processes occurring in **the object**.

2. If the set of information has been successfully verified according to claim 1, **the system of Noologistics** performs a cycle of **the management solution**, calculation and implementation of a set of **control actions**.

3. If again the set of information does not pass any of the stages of verification listed in paragraph 1, **the system of Noologistics**:

- does not accept this set of parameters for development of **the management solution**, calculation and realization of the set of **control actions**;
- determines the possible reason for the deviation of the set of parameters from the norm;
- informs the staff about the detected deviations in the set of parameters and recommendations for their elimination.

4. Starts a new cycle from step 1 (see above).

7. The principle of accessibility of information

Compliance with **the principle of accessibility of information** in **Noologistics** in the control of **the object** means that the processes of development of **management solutions**, calculation and implementation of a set of **control actions** should be provided with all the necessary information.

The accessibility of information determines a large number of regulations contained in **the rules** of the relevant **person**, such as **hierarchy**, some of which are given in **the sources of information**.

The principle of accessibility of information in accordance to the above-mentioned normative documents is provided by appropriate organizational measures and technical means that determine the requirements for:

- to methods of show information;
- to data carriers;
- to methods of information transfer;
- to frequency of updating of the provided information;
- to the magnitudes of the flows of submitted information, etc.

The peculiarity of **Noologistics** is the maximum use of the management systems already existing in **the object** and the addition to them only those functions and processes that convert them into **a system of Noologistics**. Therefore, **the system of Noologistics** complies with all regulatory documents that provide **the principle of accessibility of information** in **the object** which correspond to control systems that are used in it.

Information on **the areas of possible modes of operation** and on **the noologistical areas of possible modes of operation** for individual units of the equipment of **the object**, and for the whole **object** is an additional means of providing **the principle of accessibility of information**. They are not mentioned in normative documents, but necessarily used in **the system of Noologistics**.

The above-mentioned **areas** concentrate and provide all the information necessary for the staff in the most convenient and understandable form to, almost at a glance, assess the current situation as in the manual or semi-automatic control of **the object**. In addition, their use provides information for the processes of **management solution** - making, calculation and implementation of a set of **control actions** in the automatic control of **the object**.

8. The principle of control in real-time

Typically, the control system is called a real-time system, if the accuracy of **the control actions** calculated by it provide not only by logical correctness of calculations and the magnitude of the resulting control error, but also the time for which they are calculated and implemented. That is, for each **control action** in such a system, the moment of completion of its calculation and implementation is as important as the logical correctness of the calculations used in its development and the minimum control error.

By ensuring the logical correctness of the management of **the object** mean the calculation and implementation of such **management solutions** and **control actions** that meet **the principles, criteria of reasonableness** and other parameters set by **the person** in his **goal**.

The principle of real-time control in **Noologistics** is provided by a specially developed **technology of forecast calculation in the PRESENT** to control the object in real time.

Compliance with **the principle of control in real time** means that the execution of all **control actions** on all **objects** is provided by the speeds of the Executive elements of their regulators, the magnitude of which is synchronized in **the PRESENT** from the condition of achieving **the goal** in **the FUTURE**.

9. The principle of forecasting

Compliance with the principle of forecasting in **Noologistics** means the using any known method of highly specialized and focused research the future development of **providing of existence** (**life-support**), **habitat, noosphere, noogalaxy, noouniverse, environment** and of any phenomena and events in the form of the development of the forecast for any interest term of the person in the **FUTURE** on the basis of information obtained in the **PAST**.

In addition, **the principle of forecasting** is provided by the **technology of forecast calculation in the PRESENT**, analogues of which until now did not exist.

10. The principle of synchronization

The essence of the providing **the principle of synchronization** in **Noologistics** consists in applying the set of mathematical apparatus and algorithm that provides the parametric unity in time and space data and processes of **system of Noologistics** to the phenomena and events that occur into the **providing of existence** (**life-support**), **habitat, noosphere, noogalaxy, noouniverse, environment**, etc.

The following **well-known techniques** are used for synchronization:

1. Obeying the rules of the technological sequence of execution of operations on **objects**. They are contained in the accompanying documentation of the equipment of each **object** and are automatically executed by the appropriate automatic control systems, which are included in **the system of Noologistics**.

2. Synchronization of the AC frequency, which is produced by each generator, to the frequency of the network. This synchronization is automatically carried out by special systems that are installed in each generator.

3. Take into account the fact that the impact of specific phenomena and events of the various elements of the **providing of existence** (**life-support**), **habitat**, **noosphere**, **noogalaxy**, **noouniverse**, **environment**, etc. may not occur simultaneously, for example due to their distance from each other. For example, the velocity of propagation of expansion or compression waves in liquids and gases is equal to the sum or difference of the values of the velocity of sound propagation in them and the velocity of their flows, depending on the coincidence or mismatch of the vectors of these velocities. And the velocity and propagation vector of the chemical composition change in the flows of liquids and gases are equal to the velocity and vector of the corresponding flow.

Special methods of synchronization, typical for **Noologistics** are described in its **technology**.

11. The principle of minimizing impacts to the environment

Compliance with the principle of impacts minimization to the environmental means that the implementation of any control shall be accompanied by a minimum change into it, if the its change is not the goal of the person. **Noologistics** provides to its **person** the many variants of options to impact on **the environment**. For example, it could be **a minimum of CO_2 emissions**, **a minimum of acoustic exposure**, **a minimum of heat release**, and any other **extreme of the**

reasonableness criterion for the many types of impacts that are established by **environmental regulations**. It provides the required ratio between magnitudes extremes of a particular set of impacts on **the environment**, i.e. **the compromise** between the two. Moreover, this setting may be set as a separate for certain areas, separately for each **person** at all levels of **the hierarchy**, as for any unit of equipment of **the object**, and for the whole **object**, for example, globally. The setting may allow the automatic transition from the one type of magnitude extreme of impact or compromise to another magnitude extreme over time or when the specified magnitude of any other parameter is reached.

Thus, **the minimization of environmental impacts** in **Noologistics** means that **control action** to each unit of the facility equipment provides to the extreme of one of the many criteria of reasonableness or a compromise between them, which is set by the person by setting the parameters of his goal. The set of methods and means to achieve this is described in section "**2.11. The System of Noologistics**".

12. Principle of objectivity (scientific character)

Observance of the principle of objectivity is ensured by the use in **the system of Noologistics** only of those methods and means that contain scientifically based mathematical laws between the values of parameters determined by the fundamental Sciences (astronomy, physics, chemistry, biology, mathematics, etc.), the reliability of which may be tested scientifically based methods and means of measurement.

13. The principle of subjectivity (of the freedom)

Observance of **the principle of subjectivity** (**freedom**) in **Noologistics** is provided by the free choice by each **person** to use it in full, partially or to abandon its use in **the PRESENT** in the formation and achievement of **the goal** of his existence in **the environment** in **the FUTURE**.

14. The principle of sociality

Observance of **the principle of sociality** in **Noologistics** is ensured by providing each **person** the technical ability to form the parameters of his **goal**, taking into account the parameters of the **goals** of other **persons** included in the same **hierarchy** on the basis of their current **rules**. **System of Noologistics** gives each entity the ability to pre-simulate changes of parameters of **habitat** and **providing of existence** (**life support**) depending on changes of parameters of the **General goal** of his **hierarchy**, and also corresponding change of magnitudes of parameters impacts on **providing of existence** (**life-support**), **habitat**, **noosphere**, **noogalaxy**, **noouniverse**, **environment**, etc. It also provides each person the opportunity to pre-model changes in **the rules** of his **hierarchy** to change his own **habitat** and **providing of existence** (**life-support**), and that part of the social **habitat** and **providing of existence** (**life-support**), which he uses, as well as – the corresponding change in the values of the parameters of impacts on the **environment**, **noosphere**, **noogalaxy** and **noouniverse**.

Achieving consensus between stakeholders in **the hierarchy** technically provides **a permanent referendum** used in **Noologistics** for the formation of its **General goal**.

15. The principle of totality

Ensuring **the principle of totality** is based on the objective of the inter-relationships of all processes in the **noosphere**, **noogalaxy**, **noouniverse**, **environment**, etc., as well as on the provision to **persons** of science-based opportunities to provide a reasonable balance between the parameters of their **providing of existence** (**life-support**), **habitat**, **noosphere**, **noogalaxy**, **noouniverse**, **environment**, etc.

16. The principle of systematicity

Observance of **the principle of systematicity** in **Noologistics** in developing **management solutions**, calculation and implementation of appropriate **control actions** has three aspects:

- any **management solution** and **control action** is distributed on interconnected **providing of existence (life-support)**, **habitat, noosphere, noogalaxy, noouniverse, environment**, etc;
- any **management solution** and **control action** shall be made on the basis of **the rules**, subject to all **the principles** and **reasonableness criteria** specified above that are established in correspondent **goals**;
- any **management solution** and **control action** is distributed on elements of the object, taking into account their interaction with each other.

System of Noologistics is built to comply with **the principle of systematicity** under the properties inherent in complex systems, which include:

1. **Integrity**, which means that all its parts work as a whole, realizing the potential ability to the association and to work together.
2. **The interrelatedness of the elements**, which means that between the elements of **the system of Noologistics**, there are certain connections as an organizational (including contractual) and technological, industrial, economic, environmental, and other, larger, than to objects outside of this system.
3. **The orderliness of the set of elements**, which means that the potential of the elements of **the system of Noologistics** to form relationships and unite into a single whole are embodied in the real system, if to these elements will be applied to certain organizing actions, aimed at achieving integrity.
4. **Synergy** (the sum effect is greater than the sum of effects), which means that **the system of Noologistics**, manifests qualities that are more than the sum of qualities of its all individual elements.
5. **Complexity**, which is characterized by such basic features as the presence of a large number of elements in **the system of Noologistics**; multifactorial nature of the interaction between its individual elements; the content of functions performed by **the system of Noologistics**; the structure of the organized management; the impact on **the system of Noologistics** an unknown number of stochastic environmental factors.
6. **Hierarchical pattern**, which means subordination of elements of **the system of Noologistics** of a lower level (order, rank) to elements of a higher level, which concerns both linear and functional management.

7. **Emergence**, which means that all purposes, principles, criteria of reasonableness and rules are able to realize only by **the system of Noologistics** as a whole, and not its individual elements.
8. **Structuredness**, which means the presence of a certain organization structure of **the system of Noologistics**, consisting of interrelated elements and providing its decomposition.

Technology of Noologistics was developed to implement these **principles** in a single process the **noo** governance. It contains a generic mathematical tools and algorithms, the description of which is given below in the relevant sections.

1.3. The Criteria of Reasonableness of Noologistics

To create a list of criteria for the reasonableness of the **Noologistics**, an analysis was made of the criteria for the optimality used in various fields of human activity, outlined in **accessible sources**, including:

universal criteria for optimality, set out in the theory of management;
criteria for optimality of production management;
criteria for optimality of energy management;
criteria for optimality of management the gas transport system;
criteria for optimality of economic (commodity-money) **Logistics**;
criteria for optimality of medic management;
criteria for optimality of ecology management;
optimality criteria developed during the creation of the **Noologistics** system;
criteria for the optimality of state management, etc.

The genesis of scientific and other literature reflecting the development of the notion of the **criterion** made it possible to establish that there is no single nomenclature of **criteria** for **the reasonableness of management** and their magnitudes because the concept of **reasonability** is subjective and is constantly changing under a variety of reasons. **Noologistics** means the providing an extreme value of the density of the current flow of **consumption**, **creation** and **rejection** of **value** into **provision the existence** (**life-support**) of any

person of **Noologistics**, as well as a direction of change both to the decreasing and increasing its current quantity in his **habitat**.

Therefore, the **criterion of reasonableness** in **Noologistics** is named the extremum of the value of any parameter characterizing the magnitude or quality the flow of **consumption**, **creation** and **rejection** of **value** in **provision their existence** (**life support**), and also the limit of its quantity in its **habitat**, which was established by the **person** for the **FUTURE** in his **goals** in accordance his **principles** and **rules**.

The compromise of the criteria of reasonableness in **Noologistics** is named any combination of the extremums of the magnitudes of any parameters characterizing the quantities or qualities the flows of **consumption**, **creation** and **rejection** of **value** in **provision their existence** (**life support**), the combination of the limits of their quantities in their **habitat**, any nomenclature, their parameters, etc., the achievement of which in the **FUTURE** has been established by the **person** in his **goal** in accordance his **principles** and **rules**.

For example, if the **person** establishes in his **goal** the need to maintain a minimum of CO_2 emissions, then his **system of Noologistics** will control his **object** in such a way that at each current time the magnitude of the flux density of the total CO_2 emissions from it to the **environment** is maintained at the lowest possible level. If the **person** establishes in his **goal** the need to maintain a 50% minimum of total costs of all kinds in cash, a 30% minimum of total energy costs of all types expressed in MW, and a 20% minimum of total CO_2 emissions, then his **system of Noologistics** will maintain a minimum density of the current flow of total monetary costs of 50%, energy costs of 30% and CO_2 emissions of 20% part of **equipment units** into its **object**. Obviously, in order to comply with such a **compromise**, the interpretation of the notion of these % and densities of current flows should be determined by the current **rules**. It is also obvious that the **rules** may determine the countless other variants of **compromise** that the **system of Noologistics** will provide.

Analysis of the **criteria** most often discussed by the **persons** allows them to be grouped into any groups, for example, into economic, environmental, energy, etc. A brief description of some of these groups is below:

The economic (commodity-money)

They are characterized by providing the extreme value of the density the one of the many types of **current flows** of **consumption** and the **creation** of values, as well as the sizes of their quantities during the reporting period, or the ratio between them maintained at the current time, including:

- The current maximum gross output;
- The current minimum of gross costs;
- The current maximum gross revenue;
- The current maximum gross profit;
- The current minimum of the average selling price;
- The current trade-off between the values of density of any current flows of consumption and the creation of values;
- Gross output;
- Gross costs;
- Gross revenue;
- Gross profit, etc.;
- Compromise between all listed economic criteria.

Efficiency of any process is defined in the (commodity-money) Economy as the ratio of "results-costs" according to the formula:

$E = R / C$,
Here are:
E – economic efficiency;
R – economic results determined by accounting records;
C – economic costs determined by accounting records.

The current economic efficiency of any process is defined in **Noologistics** in a similar way instead of economic efficiency by the ratio "current results - current costs" according to the formula:

$CE = CR / CC$,
Here are:

CE – current economic efficiency;

CR – the current density of the current economic result determined by current instrument readings and price;

CC – current density of current economic costs, determined by current instrument readings and price.

However, this current indicator is very general, since it characterizes the current efficiency of all current aggregate costs, which fall, for example, on the current output of a unit of production. Therefore, a system of specific current indicators is used in **Noologistics** to determine the current effective use of each factor of production separately, for example: current labor productivity, current labor intensity, current capital output, current capital intensity, current material output, current material intensity, current energy intensity, and so on.

So, the level and dynamics of current labor productivity are estimated by different indicators, for example:

The current productivity of labor is the current capacity for work. It is defined on the microlevel as the ratio of the density of the current flow of produced products to the density of the current flow of the man-hours being worked at the current time by the formula:

Current Labor Productivity = Current Flow Of Produced Products / Density Of The Current Flow Of The Man-Hours;

The current labor productivity at the macro level is defined as the ratio of the density of the current flow of the gross domestic product (GDP) or the density of the current flow of net national income (NNI) to the density of the current flow of man-hours being worked at the current time by the formula:

Current Labor Productivity = Current Flow Of Gross Domestic Product (GDP) / Density Of The Current Flow Of The Man-Hours;

Current labor intensity is the current indicator, the inverse of current labor productivity, which determines the current value of living labor expended on the current production of a unit of output at the current time by the formula:

Current Labor Intensity = Density Of The Current Flow Of The Value Of Living Labor Expended / Density Of The Current Flow Of The Cost The Products;

Current capital productivity is the current indicator that characterizes the current efficiency of using fixed capital (means of labor). It is calculated as the ratio of the density of the current output flow of the value to the density of the current flow of the value of fixed capital at the current time by the formula:

Current Capital Productivity = Density Of The Current Output Flow Of The Value / Density Of The Current Flow Of The Value Of Fixed Capital;

Current capital intensity is the inverse measure of the current capital productivity, which shows the current value of the cost of fixed capital per unit of output at the current time using the formula:

Current Capital Intensity = Density Of The Current Flow Of The Value Of Fixed Capital / = Density Of The Current Output Flow Of The Value;

The current material return characterizes the current efficiency of the use of labor items, that is, it shows how much production is produced from the material resources consumed at the current time (raw materials, materials, fuel, etc.). It is calculated as the ratio of the density of the current flow of products to the density of the current flow of consumable material resources at the current time by the formula:

Current Material Return = Density Of The Current Flow Of Products / Density Of The Current Flow Of Consumable Material Resources;

Current material consumption is the reverse index of current material return, which characterizes the cost of material resources spent per unit of output at the current time using the formula:

Current Material Consumption = Density Of The Current Flow Of Consumable Material Resources / Density Of The Current Flow Of Products;

The current energy intensity characterizes the expenditure of energy resources per unit of output at the current time using the formula:

Current Energy Intensity = Density Of The Current Energy Cost Flow / Density Of The Current Flow Of Production Costs;

etc.

Environmental

They are characterized by a minimum amount of the density of one of the types of current flows of **consumed values** from the **environment** and **rejected** them by emission into **environment**, as well as by the nomenclature of it's composition and by the relationship between them are maintained by the **person** while **provision the existence** (**life-support**) at the current time, for example:

- The minimum density of the **current flow of consumption value** of any solid, liquid or gaseous **value** from the **environment**;
- The minimum density of the **current flow of the rejected value** of any kind: solid, liquid, gaseous, or radiated emission of it into the **environment**;
- The minimum of the greenhouse effect at the current time;
- Minimum depletion of the ozone layer at the current time;
- The minimum of acid rain at the current time.

A compromise between the minima of the values of any types of **current flows of consumption values** from the **environment** and of **rejected values** by their emission into it, including:

- gas extracted from deposits;
- oil extracted from deposits;
- cookery, potassium and other salts extracted from deposits;
- coal extracted from deposits;
- ores of metals extracted from deposits;
- air taken from the atmosphere;
- water taken from open reservoirs and underground sources;
- carbon dioxide emitted from equipment facilities;
- toxic substances (mercury, organophosphorus compounds, chlorinated hydrocarbons, etc.), emitted from equipment facilities;
- irritating substances (acids, alkalis, chlorine, fluorine, sulfur and nitrogen containing compounds, pesticides, mineral fertilizers, etc.), emitted from equipment facilities;
- sensitizing substances (aldehydes, solvents and lacquers based on nitro compounds, soffit, nimrod, sumicidin, etc.), emitted from equipment facilities;
- carcinogenic substances (asbestos, arsenic, areozine, diureen, calcium arsenate, etc.), emitted from equipment facilities;
- mutagenic substances (lead, manganese, etaleamine, maneb, benemyl, cyrram, dichlorvos, etc.), emitted from equipment facilities;
- industrial dust of vegetable, animal, mineral, and also mixed origin, allocated from the equipment of objects;
- electromagnetic emissions from equipment facilities;
- acoustic emissions from equipment facilities;
- electric fields of industrial frequency from equipment facilities;
- infrared radiation from equipment facilities;
- ultraviolet radiation from equipment facilities;
- ionizing radiation from equipment facilities
- etc.

Thus, if the extremum of the amount the (commodity-money) economic **criterion** or a compromise between them is chosen as a **criterion**, then such a **Noologistics** may be called Economic Logistics, when choosing the environmental **criteria** - Environmental Logistics, and when choosing a trade-off between economic and environmental **criteria** - Economic Ecologistics.

The application of any combination of the above **criteria** in the energy sector may be called Energy Ecologistics, in gas supply - by Gas Logistics, in the chemical industry - by Chemical Ecologistics, etc. Therefore, the appearance of many varieties of logistic names associated with certain industries and ecology is possible.

A unified mathematical apparatus and algorithms are applied in the **technology of Noologistics** described below, to provide an magnitude extremum of any of the known **criteria**, and also to ensure a **compromise** between them in the object of any industry, of any size, complexity, territorial, global, galactic, universal, and other placement.

Noologistics provides for the possibility of appointing for any **objects** and their elements any individual **criteria**, methods for calculating them, and preparing all the information necessary for this by the **persons** themselves.

2. The Characteristics of the Basic Elements of the Noologistics Conceptual Apparatus

2.1. The Definitions of the Basic Elements of the Conceptual Apparatus

Nooeconomy (activity) is the joint activity of interconnected beings that show signs of reason and are its **persons**, aimed at **provision of their existence** (ie, their **life-support**), as well as the totality of their relations to each other and to the **environment** that form in the process **creation**, **consumption** and **rejection** of **values** in the formation and achievement of the **goal** of their existence.

Nooeconomy (science) is a set of sciences that study the **creation**, **consumption** and **rejection** of **values**, as well as the formation and achievement by its **persons** of the **goal** of their existence.

Nooeconomy (system) is a set of systemically interconnected the **value relations** of its **persons** to each other and to the **environment** (i.e., provision of their existence in their **habitat**,

noosphere, **noogalaxy**, **noouniverse**, etc.), its **rules** (i.e. science, laws, sacred writings, traditions, etc.) and the theory of rational management of them (ie, **Noologistics**), applied by its **persons** for the formation and achievement of the **goal** of its existence.

Noologistics is the science of the **reasonable (noo) management** by **person** the **provision of his existence (life support)** in the **PRESENT** according to the **rules**, containing from his point of view a reasonable set of **principles of management** and **criteria** that he uses to achieve the **goal** set by him in the **FUTURE**.

The formalization of the descriptions of the concepts of **Noologistics** is the presentation of information about them in the form of a strict structure containing a certain nomenclature of parameters that reflect their quantitative and qualitative characteristics in a numerical expression, as well as the relationships between them in the form of mathematical expressions and logical functions.

Observance of the **principle of reasonableness** in the **Noologistics** in the management of an **object** means that any **management solution** and implementing **control actions** relating to the parameters of **provision of his existence** (**life support**) and **habitat** provide either an extreme of the magnitude of that one particular **criterion** of reasonableness from the set of their possible, or that compromise between the extremums of the magnitudes of their particular set, which was set by the **person** when setting his **goal**.

Observance of **the principle of sustainability** in **Noologistics** means that every **managerial solution** of the **person** and the corresponding **control actions** must **provision of his existence** (**life support**) under certain boundary conditions.

Adherence to **the principle of adaptability** in **Noologistics** in the management of an **object** means that in the development of any **managerial solution**, the calculation and implementation of the relevant **control actions**, should be taken into account all current changes in the **person**, in the **environment**, **habitat**, **provision of his existence** (**life support**), **object** and **grids**, occurring in the moment of execution of all relevant **control actions**.

Compliance **the principle of sufficiency** in **Noologistics** means that the development and implementation of any **management solution** is based on the availability of the necessary combination of parameters of the **habitat** and the technical ability to maintain the necessary parameters for **provision of his existence** (**life support**) and **rules** that the **person** supports, for example, through the current financing, energy supply, technical supply, etc. in the nomenclature, magnitudes, terms and sources.

Observance of **the principle of minimization of information flows** means that the amount of information provided to the **person** at the current time for the development of a **management solution**, calculation and implementation of the relevant **control actions** should not exceed his physiological and / or technical capabilities.

The principle of protection of information used in **the technology of Noologistics** is provided in two ways:

- protection of information from access and exposure to unauthorized **persons**;
- protection of information from distortions arising in the process of its transformation, transmission and storage on the way from the source of its occurrence and to the place of use.

Observance of **the principle of accessibility of information** in the **Noologistics** at the **object management** means that the processes of development of **the management solution**, calculation and implementation of the set of **control actions** should be provided with all necessary information.

Realization of **the principle of control in real time** means that the execution of all **control actions** on all **objects** is ensured by the speeds of the actuators of their regulators, the magnitudes of which is synchronized in the **PRESENT** under the condition of achieving the set goal in the **FUTURE**.

Observance of **the principle of forecasting** in **Noologistics** means the use of any known method of highly specialized and purposeful scientific research of the future development of **life**

support, **habitat**, **noosphere**, **noogalaxy**, **noouniverse**, **environment**, etc., as well as of any phenomena and events in them, in form the development of the forecast for any future moment that was the subject of interest in the **FUTURE** based on the information obtained in the **PAST**.

The essence of provision **the principle of synchronization** in **Noologistics** is the application of a set of mathematical apparatus and algorithms that ensure the parametric unity in time and space of data and processes of **the system of Noologistics** to phenomena and events occurring in **provision of existence** (**life support**), **habitat**, **noosphere**, **noogalaxy**, **noouniverse**, **environment**, **object**, and so on.

Compliance with **the principle of minimizing environmental actions** means that the implementation of any **control action** must be accompanied by a minimal change in it, if the change is not the **goal** of the **person**.

Observance of **the principle of objectivity** is ensured by using in **the system of Noologistics** only those methods and means that contain scientifically grounded mathematical regularities between the magnitudes of parameters determined by fundamental sciences (astronomy, physics, chemistry, biology, mathematics, etc.), the reliability of which may be verified by scientifically grounded methods and means of measurement.

Observance of **the principle of subjectivity** (**freedom**) in **Noologistics** is ensured by the freedom of choice by each **person** to use or to abandon it in the **PRESENT** in shaping and achieving the **goal** of its **existence** in the **environment** in the **FUTURE**.

Observance of **the principle of sociality** in **Noologistics** is ensured by giving each **person** the technical ability to formulate the parameters of his **goal** and the process of achieving them, taking into account the parameters of the **goals** and processes of their achievement by other **persons** that are in the same **hierarchy** and based on the **rules** in it.

The provision of **the principle of universality** is based on the objectively existing interrelationship of all processes in **noosphere**, **noogalaxy**, **noouniverse**, **environment**, etc., and also by providing **persons** a scientifically grounded ability to provide a reasonable balance between the parameters of their **habitat**, their **existence** (**life support**), **noosphere**, **noogalaxy**, **noouniverse**, **environment**, and so on.

The observance of **the principle of systematic** in **Noologistics** in the development of **management solutions**, the calculation and implementation of the appropriate **control actions** contains three aspects:

- any **managerial solution** and **control action** extends to interconnected **habitats**, **provision of existences** (**life supports**), **noosphere**, **noogalaxy**, **noouniverse**, **environment**, etc.;
- any **managerial solution** and **control action** are developed on the basis of **rules**, under all its **principles** and **criteria of reasonableness** specified in the relevant **goals**;
- any **managerial solution** and **control action** extends to all elements of the **object** taking into account their interaction to each other.

The criterion of reasonableness in **Noologistics** is the extremum of the size of any parameter characterizing the magnitude or quality of the **flow** of the **consumption**, **creation** or **rejection** of **value** into **the provision of his existence** (**life support**), and also the limit of its quantity in his **habitat**, the achievement of which in the **FUTURE** the **person** has established in his **goal** in accordance to his **principles** and **rules**.

The compromise of the criteria of reasonableness in **Noologistics** is any combination of the extremums of the magnitudes of any parameters characterizing the quantities or qualities the **flows of consumption**, **creation** or **rejection of values** in **the provision of their existence** (**life support**), the combination of the limits of their quantities in their **habitat**, any nomenclature, their parameters, etc., the achievement of which in the **FUTURE** has been established by the **person** in his **goal** in accordance to his **principles** and **rules**.

Person of Noologistics is any being who shows signs of intelligence (a virus, a microorganism, a cell of the organism of a being, plant, animal, robot, man, alien, god, etc.) and their union (strain, colony, thickets, flock, tribe, collective, State, UN, host, and so on), who is interacting in **PRESENT** to other intelligent beings and **the environment**, and also uses **Noologistics** то manage **the provision of his existence** (**life support**) in **environment** to achieve his **goal** in the **FUTURE**.

The **noo value** of the **person** is called the part of **environment**, which he highlights from it informatically under its ability to meet his specific **need**.

Provision of the existence (**life support**) of the **person of Noologistics** is the totality of the **current flows of consumption**, **creation** and **rejection** of **current noo values** between him and other **persons**, and between him and his **habitat**, by which he meets his **needs** in the **PRESENT** to achieve his **goal** in the **FUTURE**.

Noo habitat of **the person** is the part of **the environment**, which is a set of **noo values** (**V_v**), which **the person** considered allocated by information from it to the category used for satisfaction of his **noo needs** (**N_v**) to achieve his **goal** in **the FUTURE**.

Hierarchy (the ancient Greek ἱεραρχία, from ἱερός "sacred" and ἀρχή "rule") is a management principle characterized by the subordination of the lower elements to the higher and organizing them into a structure such as the roots of a tree.

The hierarchy of persons is a stable set of relationships in their group, that is organized into a tree-type structure and characterized by the established inequality between them in the individual parameters of their **provision of the existence** (**life support**) and the **habitat** which they receive from their common **existence** (**life support**) and **habitat**.

The rules of hierarchy of persons are the set of **principles**, **criteria of reasonableness**, **priorities of needs**, magnitudes of the **status coefficients**, **forms of interaction**, **laws of nature**, **laws of**

society, etc., which they keep in relations to other **persons** and to **the environment** and install into their general **goal**.

Value relationships are the relationships between **persons**, and also between them and the **environment**, based on the use of **current flows of consumption**, **creation** and **rejection of values**.

The ideal object of management of a **person** of **Noologistics** is **the provision of his existence** (**life support**), represented in it by a set of interconnected **current flows of consumption**, **creation** and **rejection of values** between him, other **persons** and his **habitat** in **PRESENT** for achieving in the **FUTURE** the **goal** set by him.

The real (technological) object of management of the **person** of **Noologistics** is the totality of his **grids**, in which he supports the **current flows of consumption**, **creation** and **rejection of values**, and also controls flows in the **PRESENT** by affecting the **units of their equipment**.

The object of management of **the person of Noologistics** is the totality of its **ideal** and **real objects of management**.

The subject of Noologistics is the formation by **person** the **noo** (reasonable) **provision of his existence** (**life support**), which he uses in the **PRESENT** to achieve the **goal** set by him in the **FUTURE**.

The **goal** of **the person of Noologistics** is that ideal **provision of his existence** (**life support)**, which it seeks to achieve in the **FUTURE** through the reasonable management of **the provision of his existence** (**life support**) in the **PRESENT**.

A permanent referendum in **Noologistics** is the process of automatic formation of a common **goal** and the process of its achievement of the whole **hierarchy** in the **PRESENT** according to its **rules** on the basis of individual **goals** and the processes of their reaching the constituent **persons**.

The current conditional-variable flow of consumption of noo value is the process of using it by the **person** of **Noologistics** in the **PRESENT** by means of satisfying his **need** for achieving the set **goal**.

The current conditional-fixed flow of consumption of noo value is the depreciation (amortization) of the amount of the consumed **noo value** by the **person** in the **PAST** to the consumed or created **noo value** in the **PRESENT**.

The current total consumption flow of noo value is the sum of **the current conditional-variable flow of consumption noo value** and **the current conditional-fixed flow of consumption noo value** in the **PRESENT**.

The current flow of creation the noo value is called the process of orderly transformation into it by **the person of Noologistics** of other **noo values**, under satisfying his **needs** in the **PRESENT** to achieve in the **FUTURE** the **goal** set by him.

The current conditional-variable flow of rejection of noo value is the process of orderly allocation (emission) it by **person of Noologistics** into his **habitat** by means of satisfying his **needs** in the **PRESENT** to achieve in the **FUTURE** the **goal** set by him.

The current conditional-fixed flow of rejection of noo value is the depreciation (amortization) of the amount of **noo value** rejected by the **person** to its **habitat** in the **PAST** to the consumed or created **noo value** in the **PRESENT**.

The current total rejection flow of noo value is the sum of the **current conditional-variable flow of rejection of noo value** and the **current conditional-fixed flow of rejection of noo value** in the **PRESENT**.

The noosphere is the totality of the current flows of **consumption**, **creation** and **rejection** of the **values** used by the aggregate **person** of **Noologistics** within his joint **habitat** - the planet, in the **PRESENT** to achieve in the **FUTURE** of his aggregate **goal**.

The noogalaxy is the totality of the **current flows of consumption**, **creation** and **rejection of the values** used by the cumulative **person of Noologistics** within its cumulative **habitat** - the Galaxy, in the **PRESENT** to achieve in the **FUTURE** of its aggregate **goal**.

The noouniverse is the totality of the **current flows of consumption**, **creation** and **rejection of the values** used by the cumulative **person of Noologistics** within its cumulative **habitat** - the Universe, in the **PRESENT** to achieve in the **FUTURE** of its aggregate **goal**.

The environment is a set of **values** known to the cumulative **person of Noologistics** in **PRESENT** and projected in the **FUTURE**.

The grid of Noologistics is the aggregate of interconnected **noo values**, that its **person** highlights from the environment into the information category of **the real control object**, which is the limits (boundaries) of **the ideal control object** that moves within it, which is the current flow of **noo value** or their totality, and by which he **reasonable (noo) manages** in the **PRESENT** under the use of its **theory** and **technology** to achieve in the **FUTURE** its **goal**.

The unit of the equipment is a part **the grid of Noologistics**, that contains one controller with a logical, physical, chemical, mathematical or any other dependence known to the **person** between the magnitude of the **control action** on it, for example, the magnitude of the movement speed of its actuator and the corresponding change in the parameter magnitude of an ideal control object , for example, the magnitude of the rate of change in the density of the current flow of fuel consumption, and which the **person** uses in the **PRESENT** as a means of controlling it.

The system of Noologistics is called the totality the theory of **Noologistics**, its **technologies** and means of its implementation in the form of, for example, the appropriate **grid** that its **person** uses in the **PRESENT** within management of **the provision of his existence** (**life support**) in order to achieve its **goal** in the **FUTURE**.

The current technological process in **Noologistics** is a set of control actions of its **person** in accordance its technology to determine, maintain or change the state of his **object** in the **PRESENT**, provision of the achievement in the **FUTURE** the **goal** set by him.

Noo management solution is a generalization term denoting the completion by **the person of Noologistics** in the **PRESENT** the process change of its management **rules** for **provision of his existence** (**life support**) or the abandonment to change in order to achieve in the **FUTURE** the **goal** set by him.

Noo control action is a generalized term that designates a forced changing or not changing by the **person of Noologistics** the state the actuator of the regulator of the **equipment unit** in the **PRESENT**, for example, the speed of its movement, providing the achievement of its **goal** in the **FUTURE**, in accordance its **rules**, **principles** and **criteria of reasonableness**.

The technology of Noologistics is the totality of methods and technical means of reasonable management by its **person the provision of his existence** (**life support**) in the **PRESENT**, which he uses to achieve in the **FUTURE** the **goal** set by him.

The PRESENT is the conditional dividing line between **FUTURE** and **PAST**, through which the former "flows" into the second by the generally accepted theory of forecasting.

Real-time control mode ("**real time**") in **Noologistics** refers to such a mode of information processing, in which forecasting is provided at the current time, i.e. - in the **PRESENT**.

The PAST in **Noologistics** are the aggregates magnitudes of the parameters that characterize stochastic phenomena and events, **the provision of existence** (**life support**), **the habitat**, **noo management solutions**, **noo control actions**, **objects** of management, **actors**, **persons**, **environment**, **noosphere**, **noogalaxy**, **noouniverse**, etc., in the past time moments.

PRESENT in **Noologistics** is aggregate the magnitudes of the current parameters characterizing stochastic phenomena and events, **the provision of the existence (life support), habitat, noo management solutions, noo control actions, objects** of management, **actors, persons, environment, noosphere, noogalaxy, noouniverse,** etc., at the current time moment.

The FUTURE in **Noologistics** is the aggregate of the expected magnitudes of the parameters characterizing stochastic phenomena and events, **the provision of the existence (life support), habitat, noo management solutions, noo control actions, objects** of management, **actors, persons, environment, noosphere, noogalaxy, noouniverse,** etc., at **moments of forecasting time.**

Forecast in **Noologistics** is the calculated magnitude of the current parameter or a set of them that characterizes the expected quantitative and / or qualitative state of a stochastic phenomenon or events, **the provision of the existence (life support), habitat, noo management solutions, noo control actions, objects** of management, **actors, persons, environment, noosphere, noogalaxy, noouniverse,** etc., at **moments of forecasting time.**

Forecasting is the process of calculating **the forecast.**

The forecasting period (pre-forecast period, forecast generation period, forecast range, forecast horizon) is the time period for which **the forecast** is calculated.

The moment of forecasting time is the time of completion of **the forecasting period.**

The current parameter is a magnitude that qualitatively or quantitatively characterizes the properties of a stochastic phenomenon or event, **the provision of the existence (life support), habitat, noo management solutions, noo control actions, objects** of management, **actors, persons, environment, noosphere, noogalaxy, noouniverse,** etc., and which the **person** measures or calculates using **the technology of calculating the forecast in the PRESENT** at the current time.

The history of changes is the totality of the measured magnitudes of **the current parameter** of a stochastic phenomenon or event, **the provision of the existence** (**life support**), **habitat**, **noo management solutions**, **noo control actions**, **objects** of management, **actors**, **persons**, **environment**, **noosphere**, **noogalaxy**, **noouniverse**, etc., or a set of **current parameters**, as well as - the moments of their measurement.

The trend line is a time-ordered set of a set of predicted intermediate magnitudes of the current parameter characterizing a stochastic phenomenon or event, **the provision of the existence** (**life support**), **habitat**, **noo management solutions**, **noo control actions**, **objects** of management, **actors**, **persons**, **environment**, **noosphere**, **noogalaxy**, **noouniverse**, etc., or **sets** of current parameters calculated with a given step during **the forecasting period** at **the moment of forecasting time**.

A step is a given interval of time between the intermediate magnitudes when forming a **history of changes** and calculating **a trend line**.

A set is a collection of stochastic phenomena or events, as well as the magnitudes of **the current parameters** characterizing a stochastic phenomenon or event, **the provision of the existence** (**life support**), **habitat**, **noo management solutions**, **noo control actions**, **objects** of management, **actors**, **persons**, **environment**, **noosphere**, **noogalaxy**, **noouniverse**, etc., which fully ensures the application of **technology for calculating the forecast in the PRESENT**.

Synchronization in **the technology of forecast calculation in the PRESENT** means that the calculation of all magnitudes of **the current parameters** is performed at the current time (in the **PRESENT**), fixed by a single chronometer at arbitrarily predetermined **moments of forecasting time**, the number of **steps**, the magnitudes of the **forecasting period** and **steps**.

The current mode is **a set** of magnitudes of **the current parameters** of the operation of the control **object**, which quantitatively and qualitatively characterizes its current state in the

PRESENT and separates it from a bunch of possible states, described, for example, by its **current noologistical area of possible operating modes**.

The technology of forecast calculation in PRESENT is called the scientifically grounded calculation of the **set** of changing magnitudes of the current parameters characterizing **a set** of stochastic phenomena and events that affect the current mode of operation of the control **object** and also the calculation and realization of a synchronized **set** of magnitudes of **noo control actions** on it in **PRESENT**, providing in the **FUTURE** the achievement of the **goal** set by the **person**.

The technology of calculating the information pyramid in **Noologistics** is the processing of current information flows in accordance the rules of the person, which reduces their total density in the direction from the lower to the upper levels of **the information pyramid** and increases it in the opposite direction.

The status coefficients in **Noologistics** are the magnitudes established by the **hierarchy rules** that are used in the formation of **upward** and **downward non-indexed information pyramids** and which determine the inequality of the **persons** in the **hierarchy** when they form an individual **provision of their existence** (**life support**) and **habitat** from the common **provision of their existence** (**life support**) of the entire **hierarchy** and from its common **habitat**.

The technology for calculating an upward non-indexed information pyramid is of the summation of a set of magnitudes expressed by the same **units** of measure and related to the same **noo value**, for example, measured in the **PAST**, measured in the **PRESENT** or projected in the **FUTURE**, and also - in combining the nomenclature of quantities of **noo values** and / or **densities** of their flows contained in **formalized descriptions** of elements of complex structure, for example, in descriptions of **persons**, **hierarchies**, **habitats**, **provision of their existence** (**life support**), **objects**, **goals**, **noo management solutions**, **environment**, **noosphere**, **noogalaxy**, **noouniverse**, etc. It is performed taking into account of **the status coefficients** established in the relevant **rules**, starting with the lowest level element of said elements of complicated structure to its uppermost level.

The technology of calculating the upward indexed information pyramid is to summarize the **set** of **indexed noologistical areas of possible modes of operation** of **real objects** working together in one group that are previously calculated in the same coordinates with respect to the same their **noologistic values**, starting from the elements of the lowest level of **real object** of management up to elements of its highest level. The summation is performed on the points at which the magnitudes of the indices of **the criteria of reasonableness** are equal or are the closest in magnitude.

The technology of calculating the downward non-indexed information pyramid consists in the separation (distribution) of one magnitude of a certain parameter characterizing the total quantity or total flow density of a certain **noo value** defined in the **PAST**, defined in the **PRESENT** or projected in the **FUTURE**, and also in the division (distribution) of one nomenclature of **the noo values** and / or their flows contained in a **formalized description** of a complex structure, for example, **hierarchies**, **habitats**, **provision of their existence** (**life support**), **objects**, **goals**, **noo management solutions**, **environment**, **noosphere**, **noogalaxy**, **noouniverse**, etc., between the elements of this complex structure. It is carried out beginning with the elements of the highest level of the complex structure mentioned, to the elements of its lowest level, taking into account **the status coefficients** established in the relevant **rules**.

The technology of calculating the downward indexed information pyramid consists in the separation (distribution) of one magnitude of a certain parameter characterizing the total quantity or total flow density of a certain **noologistical value** in the complex structure of the real **object** for which was calculated in the **PAST**, calculating in **PRESENT** or forecast in the **FUTURE** the total **indexed noologistical area possible modes of operation**, for example, between elements of a complex network of any **hierarchy**. Separation (distribution) is performed from the elements of the highest level to the **equipment units** of its lowest level on the points of **indexed noologistical areas of possible modes of operation** of elements in which the magnitudes of the indices of **the criteria of reasonableness** are equal or the closest in magnitude.

2.2. The Person of Noologistics

The concept of the origin and development of **the noosphere** expressed by the prominent Russian scientist V. I. Vernadsky and developed in the writings of Edouard Le Roy, Pierre Teilhard de Chardin and his followers sees it as a special condition of the biosphere, in which the key role belongs to the human mind. Humanity has received many evidences of the signs of intelligence in other **living beings** (briefly – **LB**) parallel to the development of this concept, for example, individual viruses, microorganisms, cells, organisms, living creatures, the whole of living organisms plants, animals, people, and also their associations (strains, of the colonies, thickets, flocks, groups, States, etc.). The main sign of intelligence in them is the ability to manage **the provision of their existence** (briefly – **SP**) in a constantly changing **environment**, allowing them to keep their life in competition to other living beings due to, including, and mutual assistance between them. The term "**the provision of existence**" refers to the combination of **current material** and **information flows** between the **living beings** and its **habitats** (briefly – **PH**), whom them meets their **needs** (briefly – **N**) in the current time, i.e. in **the PRESENT**.

In addition, there is a lot facts not explained by science which some people take as signs of the existence of other minds, for example, aliens, deities, etc. Moreover, there are situations in which people are showing less intelligence than some other **living beings**. This means that humanity must be prepared for what may eventually be detected another mind, which may be in development not below human, and which may have its own concept of **the noosphere**.

Only **living beings** that make up mankind of all known beings that have at present such information technology, which provide the ability to gather information, verify, protect, store, modify, destroy, give, visualize and pass it on to other generations, not pass it through DNA. It may be assumed that in the future mankind will learn the recording of information in the DNA of **living beings**, which will reduce the time cost for training and education of their new generations. The absence of other **living beings** of information technologies, similar to those that has humanity, complicates reasonable (**noo**) relationship to them and forcing humanity to take on the function of leader.

Thus, all the above mentioned **living beings** and their associations interact to each other and to their **habitats**, thereby participating in the formation of **the noosphere**. All **living beings** and their enterprises show signs of **personality** in this interaction and therefore belong to the category of **person of Noologistics** (briefly – **P**).

The main signs of the **personality** of the **living being** in **Noologistics** are accepted the presence of abilities and opportunity to develop **the managerial solutions**, to calculate and implement **the control actions**, as well as the presence of **needs**, **values**, **goals**, **habitats**, **provision of existence**, **rules**, **control object**, **criteria of rationality** and **principles of management**. Beings having artificial intelligence, for example, the robots and beings, about interaction to which some people inform (deities, aliens, spirits, ghosts, evil spirits, etc.) also possess the signs of personality. They, as living beings who are able and have the opportunity to develop **the managerial solutions**, to calculate and implement **the control actions**, as well as the presence of **needs**, **values**, **goals**, **habitats**, **provision of existence**, **rules**, **control object**, **criteria of rationality** and **principles of management**.

Based on the above was definition of the **person of Noologistics**, which reads as follows:

Person of Noologistics is any being who shows signs of intelligence (a virus, a microorganism, a cell of the organism of a being, plant, animal, robot, man, alien, god, etc.) and their union (strain, colony, thickets, flock, tribe, collective, State, UN, host, and so on), who is interacting in **PRESENT** to other intelligent beings and **the environment**, and also uses **Noologistics** то manage **the provision his existence** (**life support**) in **environment** to achieve his **goal** in the **FUTURE**.

Thus, this definition provides that a global **person of Noologistics** is the totality of all beings, showing signs of intelligence on planet Earth (live, artificial intelligence, etc), a galactic one – all beings showing signs of intelligence in the Galaxy, a universe one – all beings showing signs of intelligence in the Universe, etc.

One of the main signs of the **personality** of every being is the presence of needs and abilities to manage the process to meet them. It is accepted in **Noologistics** that in this process each **person of Noologistics** selects from the **environment** by information those parts of it which are of different degrees on the ability to meet the relevant **need** in **the PRESENT**: the maximum degree has that part which fully meets the **primary**, i.e. the most important **need**, and minimum – maximally prevents its satisfaction. Every part of **the environment** which the **person** selects from **the environment** by information under its ability to satisfy his specific **need** is call by his **value** (briefly – **V**) in the future.

Biological, physical, technical, informational, social, etc. similarity of **the persons** known at the present time determines the similarity of their **needs**, how they use and interact in the process of meeting them, as well as the similarity of the **values**, their sources and receivers of **rejected values**.

The analysis of the needs of any **person** shows that they may be divided into three groups: t**o consume the values** (briefly – N_C), **to creation the values** (briefly – N_M) and **to reject the values** (briefly – N_S).

Thus, every subject due information divides his values into three groups corresponding to satisfy their needs: **consumption value** (briefly – V_C), **creation values** (briefly – V_M) and **rejected values** (briefly – V_S).

Each **person** has his own system (i.e. a set of method, technology, tools, and a set of criteria) to assess the extent of the each value: **consumed**, **creation** and **reject** ones, which characterize the number of (briefly respectively – Q_C, Q_M and Q_S) and quality parameters (briefly accordingly – QP_C, QP_M and QP_S).

It follows from the above that each **subject** selects from **the environment** by information the set of **values**, which has any impact (from provision to the limitations) to meet his **needs** in **the PRESENT**.

This set of **values** is called in **Noologistics** by his **habitat**. Obviously, that formalized description of **the habitat** of any **person** contains the whole nomenclature of his **values** (the list of their names), their amounts (briefly – $\mathbf{Q_C}$, $\mathbf{Q_M}$ and $\mathbf{Q_S}$), their allocations (briefly – $\mathbf{LV_C}$, $\mathbf{LV_M}$ and $\mathbf{LV_S}$) in **the environment**, their distributions (briefly – $\mathbf{AV_C}$, $\mathbf{AV_M}$ and $\mathbf{AV_S}$) in **the environment** and the quality parameters (briefly – $\mathbf{QP_C}$, $\mathbf{QP_M}$ and $\mathbf{QP_S}$) each of them. It is also clear that for **the person** is vital to the combined nomenclature, quantity and quality of the values contained in **the environment**, corresponded to a particular standard, in which **the persons** may reasonably meet their **needs** within a certain period of time in **the FUTURE**.

The process of satisfaction of every **need** through the use of appropriate **value** is, in fact, creating and maintaining its **current flow** (briefly – **F**). The presence of each **person** in **PRESENT** a totality of many types of interrelated **needs** necessitated the creation and maintenance of the appropriate aggregate of a plurality of types of current interconnected **flows of values**, including **the current flows** of **values consumption**, of **creation of values** and of **rejecting the values**, aggregate of which is called below as **the provision of their existence (life support)**. Formalized description of **the provision the existence** (**life support**) of any of **the person** contains the entire nomenclature of its constituent flows (list of their names), the sizes of their current densities, the names of **values** carried by them, the parameters of their quality, their location in **the environment**, the predicted **FUTURE** duration of its use (briefly – $\mathbf{DU_C}$, $\mathbf{DU_M}$ and $\mathbf{DU_S}$), etc.

The term "**the provision the person's existence** (**life support**)" in **Noologistics** mean the aggregate of current material and information flows between him and other **persons**, as well as between him and his **environment** through which he meets his **needs** in **the PRESENT**.

It is obvious that for **the person** is vital to the combined nomenclature of current flows contain in **the provision the his existence** (**life support**), magnitudes of their densities and quality parameters corresponded to a well–defined standard, in which the **person** is reasonably meets his **needs** in **the PRESENT** given the formation and maintenance of a reasonable living **environment** for the forecast period in **the FUTURE**.

The values of **the person** may be divided conditionally into two types: material **values** and information **values**. The conventionality of this division is that the term "**material value**" in **Noologistics** means **the information** (!) about the part of **the environment**, the specific parameters of which estimates in **the PRESENT** as **material value** by the mentioned above system of evaluation (i.e., through set of methods, technologies, means and criteria). All other types of **values** in **Noologistics** belong to the category of "**information values**", even if they contain information which in **the PAST** was obtained from the same part of **the environment** in the form of "**material value**" and saved available of **the person** method, for example, in the genes, organs of higher nervous activity, books, computers, etc.

It is accepted in **Noologistics** that the relationship between the **persons** in their interaction are unequal and formed according to **the rules of hierarchy of the persons** (briefly – **RP** or **rules**).

Hierarchy (the ancient Greek ἱесбсчЯб, from ἱесьт "sacred" and ἀсчЮ "rule") is a management principle characterized by the subordination of the lower elements to the higher and organizing them into a structure such as the roots of a tree.

The hierarchy of persons is a stable set of relationships in their group, that is organized into a tree-type structure and characterized by the established inequality between them in the individual parameters of their **provision the existence** (**life support**) and the **habitat** which they receive from their common **provision the existence** (**life support**) and **habitat**.

This inequality is reflected in the ratio of the magnitudes of **the status coefficients** established by the rules of the **hierarchy of persons** in **upward and downward unindexed information pyramids** in each **hierarchy**. It is the ratio of **status coefficients** magnitudes determines the degree of "justice", "democracy", "equality", "honesty" and other subjective assessments of **the hierarchy** by persons from the point of **Noologistics** view.

The rules of hierarchy of persons are the set of **principles**, **criteria of reasonableness**, **priorities of needs**, magnitudes of **the status coefficients**, **forms of interaction**, **laws of nature**, **laws of society**, etc., which they keep in relations to other **persons** and to **the environment** and install into their general **goal**.

The basic gist of **the rules** is to determine that ratio of **the status coefficients magnitudes** and **forms of inter–action** of all its **persons**, which will provide the sustainability of its existence and development.

Decisive role in the formation of **the rules hierarchy** (i.e. in the purpose of the magnitudes **the status coefficients** and **forms of interaction**) performs one of its **person**, which is able to force other **persons** to comply to them. He formalizes **rules** for those of its **persons** who interact to **the environment**, but may not do that, for example, due to insufficient development of the mind, lack of understanding (due an another way of communication – telepathy instead of the audio signals and gestures), the different concept of the **noosphere**, **noogalaxy**, **noouniverse**.

Self-determination of **relative subjectivity** (briefly – **Sb**) in the formation **rules** take into account between the interacting actors and their modes of interaction (briefly – **FI**). Each **person** may formally assess his **relative subjectivity** to another **person** by the numeric magnitude in the range from -1 to +1, for example:

If **Sb** = -1, then **the person** perceives himself as standing above in **a hierarchy**;
If **Sb** = 0, then **the person** perceives himself as an equal in **a hierarchy**;
If **Sb** = +1, then **the person** perceives himself as a subordinate in **a hierarchy**.

Each **person** may formally evaluate the actual form of its **interaction to another person** by numerical ranging from -1 to +1, for example:

If **FI** = -1, then he competes to that **person**;

If **FI** = 0, then he found a compromise to that **person**;

If **FI** = +1, then his relationships with that **person** are based on mutual help.

A set of magnitudes of **person's relative subjectivity** and **forms of interaction** determines his status in **hierarchy** and is used in the formation of its **rules**, for example, in the form of **the status coefficients** magnitudes.

The concrete impacts of **persons** to each other in their pairs established in **the hierarchy rules** at different combinations of magnitudes of **relative subjectivity** and **forms of interaction** depending on **hierarchy** type (food, social, economic, production, cultural, religious or any other), for example: using as food, compulsory elimination, unquestioning obedience, avoidance of contact, counter-attack, cooperation, help, self sacrifice, etc. It is obvious that the **persons** take into account this wide variety of their impact to each other during the formation of the concrete **information pyramids**.

The base of **rules**, obviously, is contained in the DNA of **the persons** that performing the function of permanent memory, they are manifested in the instincts, are reflected in the bodies of higher nervous activity, performing the functions of operating memory and are changed in it under the influence of **the environment** and other **persons** (through education, training, self-training, competition, etc.). Because every **living being** is involved in several types of **hierarchies** (forced or by his choice), he has a few own **rules** of his participation in them.

Confirmation of the existence of different **rules** in the DNA of **the persons** to participate in various **hierarchies** and available a various **rules** for their choice are present in the Internet, for example, through the description of relationship between the tiger Amur and the goat Timur. Both animals have their own rules for participation in the food and social **hierarchies**, in which each of them relative to the other is a quite concrete combination of the degree of **relative subjectivity** and **forms of interaction**, for example:

The degree of **relative subjectivity** that is set in **the rules** of the tiger Amur to participate in the food **hierarchy** in relation to any smaller ungulate, for example, to the goat Timur is the $\mathbf{Sb_{A\text{-}T}}$ = - 1, i.e. Amur considers himself above Timur;

A form of interaction that is set in the same **rules** of the tiger Amur to participate in the food **hierarchy** in relation to any smaller ungulate, for example, to the goat Timur is the $\mathbf{FI_{A\text{-}T}}$ = - 1, i.e. Amur considers Timur as a food;

The degree of **relative subjectivity** that is set in **the rules** of the tiger Amur to participate in the social **hierarchy** in relation to any smaller animal, for example, to the goat Timur is the $\mathbf{Sb_{A\text{-}T}}$ = - 1, i.e. Amur considers himself above Timur;

A form of interaction that is set in the same **rules** of the tiger Amur to participate in the social **hierarchy** in relation to any smaller animal, for example, to the goat Timur is the $FI_{A\text{-}T}$ = + 1, i.e. Amur not considers Timur a competitor in the hierarchy and satisfy their secondary needs of communication and power, and he impacts to Timur if it bothers him;

The degree of **relative subjectivity** that is set in **the rules** of the mentioned goat Timur to participate in the food **hierarchy** in relation to any significant size prey animal, for example, to the tiger Amur is the $\mathbf{Sb_{T\text{-}A}}$ = + 1, i.e. Timur considers himself lower Amur;

A form of interaction that is set in the same **rules** of the goat Timur to participate in the food **hierarchy** in relation to any significant size prey animal, for example, to the tiger Amur is the $\mathbf{FI_{T\text{-}A}}$ = - 1, i.e. Timur considers Amur of life-threatening;

The degree of **relative subjectivity** that is set in **the rules** of the goat Timur to participate in the social **hierarchy** in relation to any significant in size and physically stronger animal, for example, the tiger Amur is the $\mathbf{Sb_{T\text{-}A}}$ = - 1, i.e. Timur considers himself lower Amur;

A form of interaction that is set in the same **rules** of the goat Timur for participation in the social **hierarchy** in relation to any sizeable animal, for example, to the tiger Amur is the $\mathbf{FI_{T\text{-}A}} = +1$, i.e. Timur considers Amur's as a rival in the **hierarchy** and satisfies his own **secondary needs** in communication and power by sometimes trying to assert itself through physically actions to the Amur.

Both animals described in example, as **persons** in relationship to each other, took **a noo management solution** to use **the rules** of the social **hierarchy** because of the tiger Amur hadn't his **primary need** to satisfy his hunger thanks the efforts of the workers of the Primorsky Safari Park. This circumstance saved the lives of goat Timur and has allowed both animals to satisfy their **secondary need** for communication and power.

The above-described social hierarchy, **the persons** of which were the tiger Amur and the goat Timur, represented one general **person** from the point of view **Noologistics**, which had their habitat and their **provision the existence** (**life support**), whose parameters were able to describe formally the staff of the Safari Park much the same way the model descriptions, which are presented below. They also may perform the calculation of formalized descriptions of general **habitat** and general **provision the existence** (**life support**) of the Amur and Timur by **the technology of calculating information pyramids** based on their individual descriptions.

Many examples of union the different **living beings** in **the hierarchy** are shown in the Internet. Ii is set in **Noologistics** that union of **persons** into **the hierarchy** gives synergistic changes of the parameters of their **environment**, of **provision the existence** (**life support**) and of **goal**, as well as the ways and means of achieving it. Obviously, the more different **the persons** have in **the hierarchy** by biology, physiology, psychology, communications, intelligence, sociality, values, and other properties, the more synergistic effect they take from combining them.

The actual leadership of humanity in relations to other **living beings** is evident in his desire to define **the rules** that observe to other kinds of **living beings**, and to use relations to them in accordance to people's **needs**. The lack of humanity of the ability to establish an accurate exchange of information to other kinds of **living beings** forced to study their **habitat**, **provision the existences** (**life supports**), instincts, **goals** and ways to achieve them. The results of their study are given in the form of scientific and religious **rules**. Scientific **rules** recognize the leadership of mankind, and religious – leadership of one God or multitude of gods. For example, biology allows us to develop **rules** for union of all types of **living beings** (viruses, bacteria, cells, organisms, plants, animals, strains, colonies, thickets, flocks, etc.) in **the hierarchy** with people.

The persons are located on the upper levels of **the hierarchy**, usually get the maximum synergetic effect from the merger because they formulate its **rules** in accordance to their own **needs** and **goals**, monitor and force other **persons** to follow them.

The above-described relationship between **persons** and also between them and **the environment** based on the use of **current flows of values**, are universal because are used not only by humanity but also by other **living beings**, and further referred to as **value relations**.

Value relationships are the relationships between **persons**, and also between them and the **environment**, based on the use of **current flows of consumption**, **creation** and **rejection of values**.

The set of **value relations** of all **the persons** in the scale of the planet forms **the noosphere**. Commodity-money relations are a form of **value relations** between people, and (commodity-money) **Economy** is part of **the noosphere** that are specific only to humanity, which it involved other types of **persons** as **consumed**, **created** and **rejected values**, **objects**, **means** of achieving **goals**, etc. A sign that the commodity-money **Economy** is part of the **noosphere**, is many times repeated in all the sources of information statement on its main **goal** – ensuring the needs of people, the maintenance and continuation of life. A sign that the commodity-money Economy is part of the **noosphere**, is the repeat in many times in all the sources of information statement that its main **goal** is providing **the needs** of people, the maintenance and continuation of their life. Because from the above it follows that **the needs** of the people are extremely diverse and to meet each of them, they use well-defined **values**, then, following the basic logic, the whole commodity-money **Economy** should be devoted to the specific **needs** of specific individuals and their corresponding **values**. However, the analysis of commodity-money **Economy** shows that it mainly considers **the needs** of people in the money, which are a universal **values**, i.e. that they replace any other **values**.

Commodity-money relations people in their hierarchies, the main motivating incentive which is the profit for a long period of time, effectively promoted the development of the productive forces of humanity, and thus give the improvement of the parameters of **provision the existence** (**life support**) and **habitat** of human. Currently they have developed to such a level that enables to satisfy **the primary needs** of all people according to **A. Maslow** – see below. Further its development goes towards reducing the number of jobs. As a result vacated able-bodied people lose the opportunity to receive money in exchange for their labor and thus partially excluded from the commodity-money relations. Incapable people (children, invalids, pensioners etc.) are also partially excluded from the commodity-money relations. **Environment** and other types of **persons** (viruses, microorganisms, cells, organisms, plants, animals, strains, colonies, clumps, flocks, etc.) is completely excluded from the commodity-money relations. Obviously, all the above mentioned **persons** as being in the commodity-money relations between themselves and partially or entirely excluded from them, always had, have and will have between themselves and to **the environment** the constant **value relations** but the commodity-money relations are just the kind that humanity uses to develop its productive forces often to the detriment of the people themselves, other actors and **the environment**. Thus, the **value relations** are the more natural ones between people, other **persons** and **the environment**, rather than commodity-money relations.

The above-described circumstances give reason to assume that the commodity-money relations between people, after the fulfilling his mission of development of the productive forces of mankind will be gradually converted into another kind of **value relations**, for example: the post commodity-money, cultural, environmental, moral, humanitarian, ethical, etc. Therefore, humanity will be to increase the share of post commodity-money relations and change they in the direction of a fully **value relations** after a certain stage of productive forces development which will increase the share of people excluded from the commodity-money relations, because humanity has failed to establish commodity-money relations to other **persons** and to **the environment**.

One of the innumerable possible variants of transition from commodity-money to the value relations may be a gradual change in the rules of hierarchy with the development of their productive forces through a phased transfer the meeting all the needs of every person in it to the free base, starting from the lowest level of **the pyramid of needs A. Maslow**. But a particular **management solution** always remains to **the persons** who are in the appropriate **hierarchy**, which may establish in its **rules**, for example, as a unhelpful all of people living on margins of commodity-money relations (excess, losers, outsiders, parasites, etc.) and to eliminate them physically as they arise using, including **technology of Noologistics**: such an approach was repeatedly used in practice and theoretically substantiated, for example, **the Malthusian theory**.

An important step in the transition from commodity-money relations to **value relations** will be moving from the assessment of all indicators characterizing the quantitative and qualitative parameters of **environment**, **provision the existence** (**life support**), **habitat** and **goal** of every **hierarchy**, from monetary units to physical ones.

Technology of Noologistics provides the formalization of the description of the parameters of **the person**, his **needs**, **values**, **provision the existence** (**life support**), **habitat**, **hierarchies**, etc., a possible example of which is shown below.

The symbol in the form of the Latin letter P, as well as identification number in subscript is used to identify any **person**, including:

$\mathbf{P_{ip}}$ – it is the conditional designation of **the person**, which is one **living being** manifesting symptoms of the mind, for example, a man in which "**ip**" is the conditional designation of the identification number that was derived from the **I**nternet **P**rotocol Address of **the person** and is written in lowercase letters. Attention! not to confuse it to an IP which is written with a capital (uppercase) letters and is conditional designation of **the information pyramids**;

P_{ih} – it is the conditional designation of **the person**, which is a **hierarchy** that combines several interacting **living beings** exhibiting signs of mind in which "**ih**" is the conditional designation of the identification number that was derived from the **hierarchy of persons**;

P_{il} – it is the conditional designation of **the person**, which is a local **hierarchy** that combines several interacting **hierarchies of living beings** exhibiting signs of mind in which "**il**" is the conditional designation of the **i**dentification number that was derived from **the local hierarchy**;

P_{iw} – it is the conditional designation of **the person**, which is a wide-scale **hierarchy** that combines several interacting local **hierarchies of living beings** exhibiting signs of mind in which "**iw**" is the conditional designation of the **i**dentification number that was derived from **the wide-scale hierarchy**;

P_{ib} – it is the conditional designation of **the person**, which is a global **hierarchy** that combines interacting at the scale of one planet **living beings** exhibiting signs of mind in which "**ib**" is the conditional designation of the **i**dentification number that was derived from **the global hierarchy**;

P_{ig} – it is the conditional designation of **the person**, which is a galaxy **hierarchy** that combines interacting at the scale of one galaxy **living beings** exhibiting signs of mind in which "**ig**" is the conditional designation of the **i**dentification number that was formed from **the galaxy hierarchy**;

P_{im} – it is the conditional designation of **the person**, which is a macrocosm **hierarchy** that combines interacting at the scale of macrocosm **living beings** exhibiting signs of mind in which "**im**" is the conditional designation of the **i**dentification number that was derived from **the macrocosm hierarchy**, etc.

The mentioned above conditional designations «$_{ip}$», «$_{ih}$», «$_{il}$», «$_{iw}$», «$_{ib}$», «$_{ig}$», «$_{im}$», etc., are also used in the lower indices of the conditional designations of **the signs of subjectivity** and all parameters of relevant **persons**.

Formalized information about any of the above-mentioned **person** may be represented by the database, interrelated by «$_{ip}$», «$_{ih}$», «$_{il}$», «$_{iw}$», «$_{ib}$», «$_{ig}$», «$_{im}$», etc. The formalized description $\mathbf{P_{ip}}$ may contain, for example, the following information:

- **Requisites of $\mathbf{P_{ip}}$**;
- **Noo habitat of $\mathbf{P_{ip}}$** (briefly – $\mathbf{PH_{ip.v}}$);
- **Current noo habitat of $\mathbf{P_{ip}}$** (briefly – $\mathbf{PH_{ip.c}}$);
- **Noologistical habitat of $\mathbf{P_{ip}}$** (briefly – $\mathbf{PH_{ip.h}}$);
- **Current noologistical habitat of $\mathbf{P_{ip}}$** (briefly – $\mathbf{PH_{ip.l}}$);
- **Noo provision the** P_{ip}'s **existence** (**life support**) (briefly – $\mathbf{SP_{ip.c}}$);
- **Noologistical provision the** P_{ip}'s **existence** (**life support**) (briefly – $\mathbf{SP_{ip.l}}$);
- **The $\mathbf{P_{ip}}$'s rules** (briefly – $\mathbf{RP_{ip}}$);
- **The $\mathbf{P_{ip}}$'s goal** (briefly – $\mathbf{A_{ip}}$);
- **The $\mathbf{P_{ip}}$'s object** (briefly – $\mathbf{Ot_{ip}}$);
- **The $\mathbf{P_{ip}}$'s technological process** (briefly – $\mathbf{TP_{ip}}$).

The conditional designations relating to the **persons** and used in the formalization of information about them in **Noologistics** are given below.

One of **the signs of subjectivity** is the ability to group their **needs** by importance, which determines the order in which they are used, for example, to divide them into **primary** and **secondary** according to **Maslow's hierarchy of needs**:

The primary needs of persons (briefly – $\mathbf{N_1}$) – physiological (food, clothing, housing, etc.), safety and security (care, protection, medicine, etc.), social (education, training, etc.) for the $\mathbf{P_{ip}}$, $\mathbf{P_{ih}}$, $\mathbf{P_{il}}$, $\mathbf{P_{iw}}$, $\mathbf{P_{ib}}$, $\mathbf{P_{ig}}$, $\mathbf{P_{im}}$ have the conditional designations $\mathbf{N_{1.ip}}$, $\mathbf{N_{1.ih}}$, $\mathbf{N_{1.il}}$, $\mathbf{N_{1.iw}}$, $\mathbf{N_{1.ib}}$, $\mathbf{N_{1.ig}}$, $\mathbf{N_{1.im}}$ accordingly and are the ultimate;

The secondary needs of persons (briefly – N_2) – social (belonging, love, respect, worship, etc.), spiritual (cognitive, aesthetic, self-actualization, etc.) for the $\mathbf{P_{ip}}$, $\mathbf{P_{ih}}$, $\mathbf{P_{il}}$, $\mathbf{P_{iw}}$, $\mathbf{P_{ib}}$, $\mathbf{P_{ig}}$, $\mathbf{P_{im}}$ have the conditional designations $\mathbf{N_{2.ip}}$, $\mathbf{N_{2.ih}}$, $\mathbf{N_{2.il}}$, $\mathbf{N_{2.iw}}$, $\mathbf{N_{2.ig}}$, $\mathbf{N_{2.im}}$ accordingly and are the endless.

A feature of **the primary needs** is their finality, i.e. they may be, ultimately, fully satisfied except when the **person** puts them into the category of **secondary needs**, which are endless.

The **values** by which the **person** meets their **primary needs**, are referred below by his **primary values** that for $\mathbf{P_{ip}}$, $\mathbf{P_{ih}}$, $\mathbf{P_{il}}$, $\mathbf{P_{iw}}$, $\mathbf{P_{ib}}$, $\mathbf{P_{ig}}$, $\mathbf{P_{im}}$ have the conditional designations respectively: $\mathbf{V_{1.ip}}$, $\mathbf{V_{1.ih}}$, $\mathbf{V_{1.il}}$, $\mathbf{V_{1.iw}}$, $\mathbf{V_{1.ig}}$, $\mathbf{V_{1.im}}$, and those of ones by which he satisfies his **secondary needs** are referred below by his **secondary values** that have the conditional designations respectively: $\mathbf{V_{2.ip}}$, $\mathbf{V_{2.ih}}$, $\mathbf{V_{2.il}}$, $\mathbf{V_{2.iw}}$, $\mathbf{V_{2.ig}}$, $\mathbf{V_{2.im}}$.

Many types of values used by **persons** to meet their **needs**, have different properties which are taken into account in the formalization of the description of the above-mentioned **signs of subjectivity**. However, many of them have not yet amenable to direct mathematical treatment. Such usually include **secondary values** that characterize, for example, the ethical quality of decisions, revealing the laws of **the environment**, national languages, mathematics, texts, methods of making management decisions and calculate their corresponding **control actions**, and more, for example, **the Bible**, **the Economy**, the political theory of a society, etc. At the same time there are many kinds of **values** which have a full set of parameters is mathematically processed by **the technology of Noologistics**. These include, for example, **a primary values**, to provide **the primary needs** (food, clothing, shelter, energy, healthcare, transport, etc.), as well as the impact on **the environment** (emission of gaseous, liquid, solids, radiation, etc.). Therefore here all the **values** are divided into homogeneous categories for which the following conventions are used:

$\mathbf{V_v}$ – it is the conditional designation of any well-known **noo value**, in which small Latin letter "**v**" in the subscript denotes an individual identification number of its registration into **a formalized description of the environment**, for example:

$\mathbf{V_{C.ip.v}}$ – it is the conditional designation of **noo value**, which was consumed, is consumed or will be consumed by the **person** that is denoted as $\mathbf{P_{ip}}$;

$V_{M.iw.v}$ – it is the conditional designation of **noo value**, which was created, is created or will be created by the **person** that is denoted as P_{iw};

$V_{S.il.v}$ – it is the conditional designation of **noo value**, which was rejected, is rejected or will be rejected by the **person** that is denoted as P_{il}, etc.

V_c – it is the conditional designation of any well-known **current noo value** that any **person** uses in **the PRESENT** to meet his **current needs** and in which small Latin letter "c" in the subscript denotes an individual identification number of its registration into **a formalized description of the environment**, for example:

$V_{C.ip.c}$ – it is the conditional designation of **noo value** that the **person** denoted as P_{ip}, consumes in **the PRESENT**;

$V_{M.iw.c}$ – it is the conditional designation of **noo value** that the **person** denoted as P_{iw}, creates in **the PRESENT**;

$V_{S.il.c}$ – it is the conditional designation of **noo value** that the **person** denoted as P_{il}, rejects in **the PRESENT**, etc.

V_h – it is the conditional designation of those **noologistical values** which have a set of parameters that are suitable for mathematical processing by **the technology of calculation the indexed information pyramids**, in which small Latin letter "h" in subscript denotes an individual identification number of its registration in **a formalized description of the environment**, for example:

$V_{C.ip.h}$ – it is the conditional designation of **noologistical value**, which was consumed, is consumed or will be consumed by the **person** that is denoted as P_{ip};

$V_{M.iw.h}$ – it is the conditional designation of **noologistical value**, which was created, is created or will be created by the **person** that is denoted as P_{iw};

$V_{S.il.h}$ – it is the conditional designation of **noologistical value**, which was rejected, is rejected or will be rejected by the **person** that is denoted as P_{il}, etc.

V_l – it is the conditional designation of any **noologistical values** that any **person** uses in **the PRESENT** to meet their **current needs** and in which small Latin letter "l" in the subscript denotes an individual identification number of its registration in **a formalized description of the environment**, for example:

$\mathbf{V_{C.ip.l}}$ – it is the conditional designation of **noologistical value** that the **person** denoted as $\mathbf{P_{ip}}$, consumes in **the PRESENT**;

$\mathbf{V_{M.iw.l}}$ – it is the conditional designation of **noologistical value** that the **person** denoted as $\mathbf{P_{iw}}$, creates in **the PRESENT**;

$\mathbf{V_{S.il.l}}$ – it is the conditional designation of **noologistical value** that the **person** denoted as $\mathbf{P_{il}}$, rejects in **the PRESENT**, etc.

The same symbols are used in the lower indices of the conditional designations for **the signs of subjectivity** in their formalized description mentioned above, which applied the following conventions:

$\mathbf{PH_v}$ – it is the conditional designation of **the noo habitat** of any of the foregoing **person**, which has the following definition:

Noo habitat of **the person** is the part of **the environment**, which is a set of **noo values** ($\mathbf{V_v}$), which **the person** considered allocated by information from it to the category used for satisfaction of his **noo needs** ($\mathbf{N_v}$) to achieve his **goal** in **the FUTURE**.

A description of **noo habitat** ($\mathbf{PH_v}$) of each of the foregoing types of **persons** is formalized – see below an example of the description for the $\mathbf{P_{ip}}$ called "**Noo habitat of $\mathbf{P_{ip}}$ ($\mathbf{PH_{ip.v}}$)**" which contains the parameters for all of his $\mathbf{V_{ip.v}}$. The same conditional designations are used for other types of **persons** ($\mathbf{P_{ih}}$, $\mathbf{P_{il}}$, $\mathbf{P_{iw}}$, $\mathbf{P_{ib}}$, $\mathbf{P_{ig}}$, $\mathbf{P_{im}}$, etc.), for example: $\mathbf{PH_{ih.v}}$, $\mathbf{PH_{il.v}}$, $\mathbf{PH_{iw.v}}$, $\mathbf{PH_{ig.v}}$, $\mathbf{PH_{im.v}}$, etc.

$\mathbf{PH_c}$ – it is the conditional designation of **the current noo habitat** of any of the foregoing **person**, which has the following definition:

The current noo habitat of **the person** is the part of his **noo habitat**, which is a set of **current noo values** ($\mathbf{V_c}$), which **the person** considered uses in **PRESENT** for satisfaction of his **current noo needs** ($\mathbf{N_c}$) to achieve his **goal**.

A description of **the current noo habitat** (**PH_c**) of each of the foregoing types of **persons** is formalized – see below an example of the description for the **P_{ip}** called "**Current noo habitat of P_{ip} ($PH_{ip.c}$)**" which contains the parameters for all of his **$V_{ip.c}$**. The same conditional designations are used for other types of **persons** (**P_{ih}**, **P_{il}**, **P_{iw}**, **P_{ib}**, **P_{ig}**, **P_{im}**, etc.), for example: **$PH_{ih.c}$**, **$PH_{il.c}$**, **$PH_{iw.c}$**, **$PH_{ig.c}$**, **$PH_{im.c}$**, etc.

PH_h – it is the conditional designation of **the noologistical habitat** of any of the foregoing **person**, which has the following definition:

Noologistical habitat of **the person** is the part of **the environment**, which is a set of **noologistical values** (**V_h**), which **the person** considered allocated by information from it to the category used for satisfaction of his **noologistical needs** (**N_h**) to achieve his **goal** in **the FUTURE**.

A description of **noologistical habitat** (**PH_h**) of each of the foregoing types of **persons** is formalized – see below an example of the description for the **P_{ip}** called "**Noologistical habitat of P_{ip} ($PH_{ip.h}$)**" which contains the parameters for all of his **$V_{ip.h}$**. The same conditional designations are used for other types of **persons** (**P_{ih}**, **P_{il}**, **P_{iw}**, **P_{ib}**, **P_{ig}**, **P_{im}**, etc.), for example: **$PH_{ih.h}$**, **$PH_{il.h}$**, **$PH_{iw.h}$**, **$PH_{ig.h}$**, **$PH_{im.h}$**, etc.

PH_l – it is the conditional designation of **the current noologistical habitat** of any of the foregoing **person**, which has the following definition:

The current noologistical habitat of **the person** is the part of his **noologistical habitat**, which is a set of **current noologistical values** (**V_l**), which **the person** considered uses in **PRESENT** for satisfaction of his **current noologistical needs** (**N_l**) to achieve his **goal**.

A description of **the current noologistical habitat** (**PH_l**) of each of the foregoing types of **persons** is formalized – see below an example of the description for the **P_{ip}** called "**Current noologistical habitat of P_{ip} ($PH_{ip.l}$)**" which contains the parameters for all of his **$V_{ip.l}$**. The same conditional designations are used for other types of **persons** (**P_{ih}**, **P_{il}**,

P_{iw}, P_{ib}, P_{ig}, P_{im}, etc.), for example: $\mathbf{PH_{ih.l}}$, $\mathbf{PH_{il.l}}$, $\mathbf{PH_{iw.l}}$, $\mathbf{PH_{ig.l}}$, $\mathbf{PH_{im.l}}$, etc.

$\mathbf{SP_c}$ – it is the conditional designation of **the noo provision the existence** (**life support**) of any of the foregoing **person**, which has the following definition:

Noo provision the existence (life support) of the **person of Noologistics** is the totality of **current noo flows of consumption** ($F_{C.c}$), **creation** ($F_{M.c}$) and **rejection** ($F_{S.c}$) **of current noo values** (V_c) between him and other **persons**, and between him and his **noo habitat**, by which he meets his **noo needs** ($N_{C.c}$, $N_{M.c}$ and $N_{S.c}$) in the **PRESENT** to achieve his **goal** in the **FUTURE**.

A description of **noo provision the existence (life support)** of each of the foregoing types of **persons** is formalized – see below an example of the description for the P_{ip} called "**Noo provision the P_{ip}'s existence (life support)** ($\mathbf{SP_{ip.c}}$)" which contains the parameters for all of his $F_{C.ip.c}$, $F_{M.ip.c}$ and $F_{S.ip.c}$. The same conditional designations are used for other types of **persons** (P_{ih}, P_{il}, P_{iw}, P_{ib}, P_{ig}, P_{im}, etc.), for example: $\mathbf{SP_{ih.c}}$, $\mathbf{SP_{il.c}}$, $\mathbf{SP_{iw.c}}$, $\mathbf{SP_{ig.c}}$, $\mathbf{SP_{im.c}}$, etc.

$\mathbf{SP_l}$ – it is the conditional designation of **the noologistical provision the existence** (**life support**) of any of the foregoing **person**, which has the following definition:

Noologistical provision the existence (life support) of the **person of Noologistics** is the totality of **current noologistical flows of consumption** ($F_{C.l}$), **creation** ($F_{M.l}$) and **rejection** ($F_{S.l}$) **of current noologistical values** (V_l) between him and other **persons**, and between him and his **noologistical habitat**, by which he meets his **noologistical needs** ($N_{C.l}$, $N_{M.l}$ and $N_{S.l}$) in the **PRESENT** to achieve his **goal** in the **FUTURE**.

A description of **noologistical provision the existence (life support)** of each of the foregoing types of **persons** is formalized – see below an example of the description for the P_{ip} called "**Noologistical provision the P_{ip}'s existence (life support)** ($\mathbf{SP_{ip.l}}$)" which contains the parameters for all of his $F_{C.ip.l}$, $F_{M.ip.l}$ and $F_{S.ip.l}$. The same conditional designations are used for other types of **persons** (**P_{ih}, P_{il}, P_{iw}, P_{ib}, P_{ig}, P_{im}**, etc.), for example: **$SP_{ih.l}$, $SP_{il.l}$, $SP_{iw.l}$, $SP_{ig.l}$, $SP_{im.l}$**, etc.

The number of formalized descriptions and their contents in the specific case of the use of **technology of Noologistics** may differ from the presented here examples for many reasons. A brief descriptions of their contents are given below for **P_{ip}**, which, between other things, intended to visualize them. Therefore, some types of information in different descriptions are repeated for the convenience of users. Each **person** contributes his own information the formal descriptions according to his own **rules** (**RP**), based on his **goal** of the purpose of his **existence** in **the environment**. The person takes a special decision on the priority of the **RP_{ip}** or **RP_{ih}, RP_{il}, RP_{iw}, RP_{ig}, RP_{im}**, etc. in cases where its own rules (**RP_{ip}**) contrary to the rules of hierarchy (**RP_{ih}, RP_{il}, RP_{iw}, RP_{ig}, RP_{im}**, etc.) that include it. All other information entered into formal descriptions automatically.

The formalized description of the requisites of the **P_{ip}** may to contain the following information:

Requisites of P_{ip}

The description contains:

- The name and identification number of the **P_{ip}**, for example, **ip**;
- E-mail and other addresses of the **P_{ip}**;
- Bank requisites of the **P_{ip}**;
- Taxpayer identification number (TIN) of the **P_{ip}**;
- The location of the **P_{ip}** in **Ev_{ip}**, for example, the current coordinates of its location in the geo information system;
- Nomenclature of hierarchies **P_{ip}** (**P_{ih}, P_{il}, P_{iw}, P_{ib}, P_{ig}, P_{im}**, etc.), which contains a list of the names of those hierarchies, in which is **P_{ip}**, and their identification numbers, for example, ih, iw, il, ig, im, etc.;
- His **Sb** and **FI** to other **P_{ip}, P_{ih}, P_{il}, P_{iw}, P_{ib}, P_{ig}, P_{im}**, etc. in each **hierarchy**;
- A link to the description of **Noo habitat of P_{ip}** (**$PH_{ip.v}$**), see below;

- A link to the description of **Current noo habitat of P_{ip}** (**$PH_{ip.c}$**), see below;
- A link to the description of **Noologistical habitat of P_{ip}** (**$PH_{ip.h}$**), see below;
- A link to the description of **Current noologistical habitat of P_{ip}** (**$PH_{ip.l}$**), see below;
- A link to the description of **Noo provision the P_{ip}**'s **existence** (**life support**) (**$SP_{ip.c}$**), see below;
- A link to the description of **Noologistical provision the P_{ip}**'s **existence** (**life support**) (**$SP_{ip.l}$**), see below;
- A link to the description of **The P_{ip}'s rules** (**RP_{ip}**), see below;
- A link to the description of **The P_{ip}'s goal** (**A_{ip}**), see below;
- A link to the description of **The P_{ip}'s object** (**Ot_{ip}**), see below;
- A link to the description of **The P_{ip}'s technological process** (**TP_{ip}**), see below, etc.

The structures of the **Ev_{ip}**, **$PH_{ip.v}$**, **$PH_{ip.c}$**, **$PH_{ip.h}$** and **$PH_{ip.l}$** l for **P_{ip}**, which follow from the above descriptions and definitions are shown in Fig. P 1.

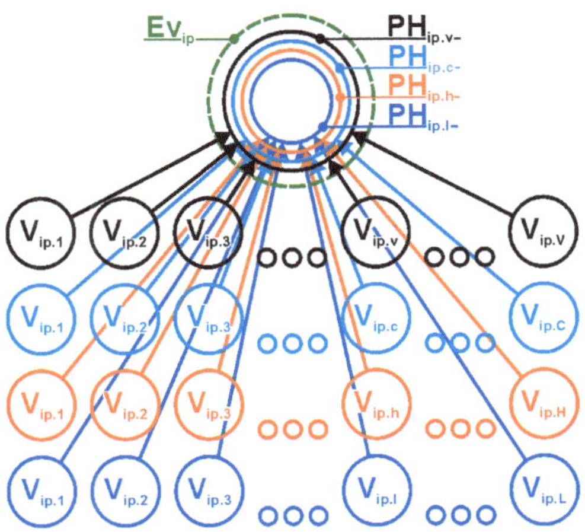

Fig. P 1

The conditional designation on the Fig. P 1:

Ev_{ip} – it is environment of the **P_{ip}**;

arrows show the formation of **$PH_{ip.v}$**, **$PH_{ip.c}$**, **$PH_{ip.h}$** and **$PH_{ip.l}$** from, respectively, the **$V_{ip.v}$**, **$V_{ip.c}$**, **$V_{ip.h}$** and **$V_{ip.l}$**;

the rest – see above.

Formalized description of **the noo habitat of P_{ip}** may contain the following information:

Noo habitat of P_{ip} ($PH_{ip.v}$)

The description contains:

The name «**Noo habitat of P_{ip}**» and identification number of the P_{ip}, for example, **ip**;

Nomenclature all of $V_{ip.v}$, between them:

v = 1, 2, 3, …, V – it is an individual identification number of its registration into **a formalized description of the environment**;

The list of $V_{ip.v}$ names and its conditional designations ($V_{ip.v}$);

Description of the contents of each $V_{ip.v}$;

Indication of $N_{C.ip}$, $N_{M.ip}$ and $N_{S.ip}$, which satisfies the corresponding $V_{ip.v}$;

The scale of priorities the $N_{C.ip}$, $N_{M.ip}$ and $N_{S.ip}$;

The scale of importance the $V_{ip.v}$, etc.

Formalized description of **the current noo habitat of P_{ip}** may contain the following information:

Current noo habitat of P_{ip} ($PH_{ip.c}$)

The description contains:

The name «**Current noo habitat of P_{ip}**» and identification number of the P_{ip}, for example, **ip**;

Nomenclature all of $V_{ip.c}$, between them:

c = 1, 2, 3, …, C – it is an individual identification number of its registration into **a formalized description of the environment**;

The list of $V_{ip.c}$ names and its conditional designations ($V_{ip.c}$);

Description of the contents of each $V_{ip.c}$;

Indication of $N_{C.ip}$, $N_{M.ip}$ and $N_{S.ip}$, which satisfies the corresponding $V_{ip.c}$;

The scale of priorities the $N_{C.ip}$, $N_{M.ip}$ and $N_{S.ip}$;

The scale of importance the $\mathbf{V}_{ip.c}$, etc.

Formalized description of **the noological habitat of $\mathbf{P}_{ip}$** may contain the following information:

Noological habitat of $\mathbf{P}_{ip}$ ($\mathbf{PH}_{ip.h}$)

The description contains:

The name «**Noological habitat of $\mathbf{P}_{ip}$**» and identification number of the $\mathbf{P}_{ip}$, for example, **ip**;

Nomenclature all of $\mathbf{V}_{ip.h}$, between them:

h = 1, 2, 3, ..., H – it is an individual identification number of its registration into **a formalized description of the environment**;

The list of $\mathbf{V}_{ip.h}$ names and its conditional designations ($\mathbf{V}_{ip.h}$);

Description of the contents of each $\mathbf{V}_{ip.h}$, between them:

Unit of measurement the quantity of the $\mathbf{Q}_{ip.h}$, the best magnitude of the $\mathbf{Q}_{ip.h}$ for the $\mathbf{P}_{ip}$, i. e. corresponding to his **goal** $\mathbf{A}_{ip.h}$ (briefly – $\mathbf{BQ}_{ip.h}$), the worst magnitude of the $\mathbf{Q}_{ip.h}$ (briefly – $\mathbf{WQ}_{ip.h}$), the P_{ip}'s actual own magnitude of the $\mathbf{Q}_{ip.h}$ (briefly – $\mathbf{OQ}_{ip.h}$), the part of common $\mathbf{Q}_{ih.h}$ in P_{ip}'s using (briefly – $\mathbf{CQ}_{ip.h}$), the P_{ip}'s actual $\mathbf{Q}_{ip.h}$ (briefly – $\mathbf{RQ}_{ip.h}$), equal to the sum $\mathbf{OQ}_{ip.h}$ and $\mathbf{CQ}_{ip.h}$, the highest $\mathbf{Q}_{ip.h}$ guaranteed for P_{ip} in P_{ih} (briefly – $\mathbf{HQ}_{ip.h}$) on his status in the $\mathbf{P}_{ih}$, the lowest $\mathbf{Q}_{ih.h}$ guaranteed for P_{ip} in P_{ih} (briefly – $\mathbf{LQ}_{ip.h}$) on his status in the $\mathbf{P}_{ih}$, the magnitude of the $\mathbf{Q}_{ih.h}$ corresponds to $\mathbf{A}_{ih.h}$ (briefly – $\mathbf{QA}_{ip.h}$) on his status in the $\mathbf{P}_{ih}$, the projected duration of $\mathbf{V}_{ip.h}$'s **u**se (briefly – $\mathbf{DU}_{ip.h}$) in **FUTURE**, etc.;

The locations (briefly – $\mathbf{LV}_C$, $\mathbf{LV}_M$ and $\mathbf{LV}_S$) and allocations (briefly – $\mathbf{AV}_C$, $\mathbf{AV}_M$ and $\mathbf{AV}_S$) each of the $\mathbf{Q}_{ip.h}$ in the $\mathbf{Ev}_{ip}$, for example, by the coordinates of the geo information system;

The nomenclature of parameters that characterize the quality (briefly – $\mathbf{QP}_C$, $\mathbf{QP}_M$ and $\mathbf{QP}_S$) each of the $\mathbf{V}_{ip.h}$;

Units of measurement and numerical magnitudes of the parameters that characterize the quality each of the $\mathbf{V}_{ip.h}$ (briefly – $\mathbf{QP}_C$, $\mathbf{QP}_M$ and $\mathbf{QP}_S$), etc.

Each P_{ip} performs a formal description by the his own **rules**, on the basis of $A_{ip.h}$ of his existence in Ev_{ip} and of analysis the current situation in it.

The structure information is shown in Fig. P 2, which follows from the formal description, entitled "**Noologistical habitat of P_{ip}**".

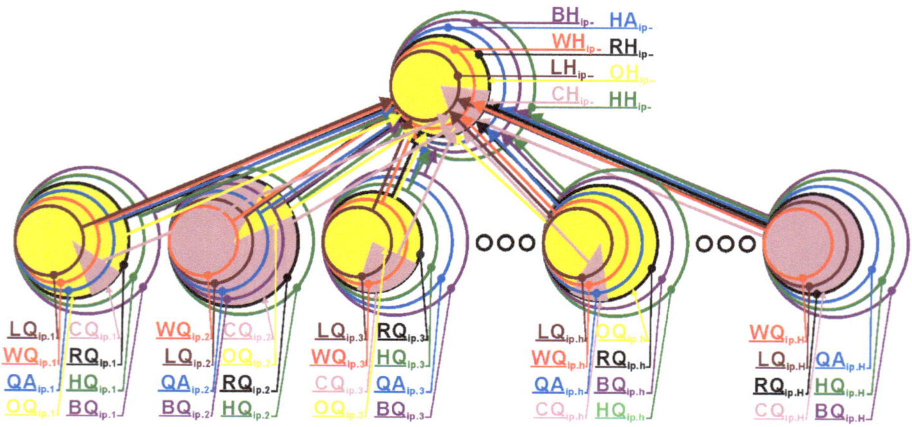

Fig. P 2

The conditional designation on the Fig. P 2:

BH_{ip} – it is the best **noologistical habitat for the P_{ip}**, that is the set of the **$BQ_{ip.h}$**, corresponds to his **$A_{ip.h}$**;

WH_{ip} – it is the worst **noologistical habitat for the P_{ip}**, that is the set of the **$WQ_{ip.h}$**;

OH_{ip} – it is **P_{ip}**'s private part of the **$PH_{ip.h}$**, that is the set of the **$OQ_{ip.h}$**;

CH_{ip} – it is the common part of the **$PH_{ip.h}$** in P_{ip}'s using, that is the set of the **$CQ_{ip.h}$**;

RH_{ip} – it is the whole actual **noologistical habitat** of the **P_{ip}**, that is the sum of the **OH_{ip}** and **CH_{ip}**, and is the set of the **$RQ_{ip.h}$** also;

HH_{ip} – it is the highest **noologistical habitat for the P_{ip}**, guaranteed to him in the **P_{ih}** on his status in the **P_{ih}**, that is the set of the **$HQ_{ip.h}$**;

LH_{ip} – it is lowest **noologistical habitat for the P_{ip}**, guaranteed to him in the **P_{ih}** on his status in the **P_{ih}**, that is the set of the **$LQ_{ip.h}$**;

HA_{ip} – it is the **noologistical habitat of the P_{ip}**, corresponds to **A_{ih}** on his status in the **P_{ih}**, that is the set of the **$QA_{ip.h}$**;

arrows show the formation of **BH_{ip}**, **WH_{ip}**, **$OH_{ip.h}$**, **CH_{ip}**, **RH_{ip}**, **HH_{ip}**, **LH_{ip}** and **HA_{ip}** by union in correspond set of magnitudes of the **$BQ_{ip.h}$**, **$WQ_{ip.h}$**, **$OQ_{ip.h}$**, **$CQ_{ip.h}$**, **$RQ_{ip.h}$**, **$HQ_{ip.h}$**, **$LQ_{ip.h}$** and **$QA_{ip.h}$**;

the rest – see above.

Calculation of magnitudes **$RQ_{ip.h}$** for b-th **technology processes** (**$TP_{ip.b}$**) that were completed in **the PAST** is performed according to a standard formula, for example:

$$RQ_{ip.h} = Q_{ip.h} - \sum_{b=1}^{B} \int_{t_н}^{t_к} D_{C.ip.h.b}(t) * dt + \sum_{b=1}^{B} \int_{t_н}^{t_к} D_{M.ip.h.b}(t) * dt - \sum_{b=1}^{B} \int_{t_н}^{t_к} D_{S.ip.h.b}(t) * dt \text{ ,}$$

here are:

$Q_{ip.h}$ – it is actual quantity of the **$V_{ip.h}$**, is used by **P_{ip}** on start of completed **$TP_{ip.b}$**, that was calculated by the rules of **$RP_{ip.h}$**;

t – it is current time of **$TP_{ip.b}$**, measured according to the **$RP_{ip.h}$**, for example, according to the testimony of standard time;

$t_Н$ – it is current time at the beginning of the completed period of the **$TP_{ip.b}$**;

$t_К$ – it is current time at the end of the counting of completed period the **$TP_{ip.b}$**;

b = 1, 2, 3, ..., B – it is identification number of completed or not completed the **$TP_{ip.b}$**;

$D_{C.ip.h.b}$ – it is actual density of consumption flow of **$V_{ip.h}$** (**$F_{C.ip.h.b}$**), which was been measured during the **$TP_{ip.b}$** by **the rules** of the **$RP_{ip.h}$**;

$D_{M.ip.h.b}$ – it is actual density of creation flow of **$V_{ip.h}$** (**$F_{M.ip.h.b}$**), which was been measured during the **$TP_{ip.b}$** by **the rules** of the **$RP_{ip.h}$**;

$D_{S.ip.h.b}$ – it is actual density of rejection flow of **$V_{ip.h}$** (**$F_{S.ip.h.b}$**), which was been measured during the **$TP_{ip.b}$** by **the rules** of the **$RP_{ip.h}$**;

the rest – see above.

Calculation of magnitudes **$BQ_{ip.h}$** and **$QA_{ip.h}$** for b-th **technology processes** (**$TP_{ip.b}$**) that were completed in **the PAST** is performed according to a standard formulas, for example:

$$BQ_{ip.h} = Q_{p.h} - \sum_{b=1}^{B} \int_{t_н}^{t_к} BD_{C.ip.h.b}(t) * dt + \sum_{b=1}^{B} \int_{t_н}^{t_к} BD_{M.ip.h.b}(t) * dt - \sum_{b=1}^{B} \int_{t_н}^{t_к} BD_{S.ip.h.b}(t) * dt,$$

here are:

$BD_{C.ip.h.b}$ – it is the best density of **$F_{C.ip.h.b}$** for **P_{ip}**, which was determined during the **$TP_{ip.b}$** by **the rules** of the **$RP_{ip.h}$**, for example, by **the technology of Noologistics**;

$BD_{M.ip.h.b}$ – it is the best density of **$F_{M.ip.h.b}$** for **P_{ip}**, which was determined during the **$TP_{ip.b}$** by **the rules** of the **$RP_{ip.h}$**, for example, by **the technology of Noologistics**;

$BD_{S.ip.h.b}$ – it is the best density of **$F_{S.ip.h.b}$** for **P_{ip}**, which was determined during the **$TP_{ip.b}$** by **the rules** of the **$RP_{ip.h}$**, for example, by **the technology of Noologistics**;

the rest – see above.

$$QA_{ip.h} = Q_{ip.h} - \sum_{b=1}^{B} \int_{t_н}^{t_к} DA_{C.ip.h.b}(t) * dt + \sum_{b=1}^{B} \int_{t_н}^{t_к} DA_{M.ip.h.b}(t) * dt - \sum_{b=1}^{B} \int_{t_н}^{t_к} DA_{S.ip.h.b}(t) * dt,$$

here are:

$DA_{C.ip.h.b}$ – it is the density of **$F_{C.ip.h.b}$**, which was calculated during the **$TP_{ip.b}$** according to the **$RP_{ih.h}$** under condition to achievement the **$A_{ih.h}$**, for example, by **the technology of Noologistics**;

$DA_{M.ip.h.b}$ – it is the density of **$F_{M.ip.h.b}$**, which was calculated during the **$TP_{ip.b}$** according to the **$RP_{ih.h}$** under condition to achievement the **$A_{ih.h}$**, for example, by **the technology of Noologistics**;

$DA_{S.ip.h.b}$ – it is the density of **$F_{S.ip.h.b}$**, which was calculated during the **$TP_{ip.b}$** according to the **$RP_{ih.h}$** under condition to achievement the **$A_{ih.h}$**, for example, by **the technology of Noologistics**;

the rest – see above.

Calculation of magnitudes **$WQ_{ip.h}$**, **$OQ_{ip.h}$**, **$CQ_{ip.h}$**, **$HQ_{ip.h}$** and **$LQ_{ip.h}$** for b-th **technology processes** (**$TP_{ip.b}$**) that were completed in **the PAST** is performed according to a **$RP_{ip.h}$** and **$RP_{ih.h}$**.

Calculation of magnitudes **$RQ_{ip.h}$** for b-th **current technology processes** **$CTP_{ip.l.b}$** that were not completed in **PRESENT** and are selected below to second version of the formalized description under the name of the "**Current noo habitat of P_{ip}**" under the symbols $\mathbf{RQ_{ip.l}}$, is performed according to a standard formula, for example:

$$RQ_{ip.h} = RQ_{ip.l} = Q_{ip.l} - \sum_{b=1}^{B} \int_{t_н}^{t} D_{C.ip.l.b}(t) * dt + \sum_{b=1}^{B} \int_{t_н}^{t} D_{M.ip.l.b}(t) * dt - \sum_{b=1}^{B} \int_{t_н}^{t} D_{S.ip.l.b}(t) * dt,$$

here are:

$\mathbf{Q_{ip.l}}$ – it is actual quantity of $\mathbf{V_{ip.l}}$ was used by the $\mathbf{P_{ip}}$ in the beginning of the $\mathbf{CTP_{ip.l.b}}$, that was calculated by the $\mathbf{RP_{ip.l}}$;

$\mathbf{D_{C.ip.l.b}}$ – it is actual density of current consumption flow of $\mathbf{V_{ip.l}}$ ($\mathbf{F_{C.ip.l.b}}$), that is measuring in **PRESENT** in the в b-th $\mathbf{CTP_{ip.l.b}}$ by the $\mathbf{RP_{ip.l}}$;

$\mathbf{D_{M.ip.l.b}}$ – it is actual density of current creation flow of $\mathbf{V_{ip.l}}$ ($\mathbf{F_{M.ip.l.b}}$), that is measuring in **PRESENT** in the в b-th $\mathbf{CTP_{ip.l.b}}$ by the $\mathbf{RP_{ip.l}}$;

$\mathbf{D_{S.ip.l.b}}$ – it is actual density of current rejection flow of $\mathbf{V_{ip.l}}$ ($\mathbf{F_{S.ip.l.b}}$), that is measuring in **PRESENT** in the в b-th $\mathbf{CTP_{ip.l.b}}$ by the $\mathbf{RP_{ip.l}}$;

the rest – see above.

Calculation of magnitudees $\mathbf{BQ_{ip.l}}$ and $\mathbf{QA_{ip.l}}$ for b-th technology processes ($\mathbf{TP_{ip.b}}$) that were not completed in **the PRESENT** is performed according to a standard formulas, for example:

$$BQ_{ip.h} = Q_{p.h} - \sum_{b=1}^{B} \int_{t_н}^{t_к} BD_{C.ip.h.b}(t) * dt + \sum_{b=1}^{B} \int_{t_н}^{t_к} BD_{M.ip.h.b}(t) * dt - \sum_{b=1}^{B} \int_{t_н}^{t_к} BD_{S.ip.h.b}(t) * dt,$$

here are:

$\mathbf{BD_{C.ip.l.b}}$ – it is the best density of $\mathbf{F_{C.ip.l.b}}$ for $\mathbf{P_{ip}}$, which is determining during the $\mathbf{CTP_{ip.l.b}}$ in **PRESENT** under condition to achievement the $\mathbf{A_{ih.l}}$ by **the** $\mathbf{RP_{ih.l}}$, for example, by **the technology of Noologistics;**

$\mathbf{BD_{M.ip.l.b}}$ – it is the best density of $\mathbf{F_{M.ip.l.b}}$ for $\mathbf{P_{ip}}$, which is determining during the $\mathbf{CTP_{ip.l.b}}$ in **PRESENT** under condition to achievement the $\mathbf{A_{ih.l}}$ by **the** $\mathbf{RP_{ih.l}}$, for example, by **the technology of Noologistics;**

$BD_{S.ip.l.b}$ – it is the best density of $F_{S.ip.l.b}$ for P_{ip}, which is determining during the $CTP_{ip.l.b}$ in **PRESENT** under condition to achievement the $A_{ih.l}$ by **the** $RP_{ih.l}$, for example, by **the technology of Noologistics;**

the rest – see above.

$$QA_{ip.h} = Q_{ip.h} - \sum_{b=1}^{B} \int_{t_н}^{t_к} DA_{C.ip.h.b}(t) * dt + \sum_{b=1}^{B} \int_{t_н}^{t_к} DA_{M.ip.h.b}(t) * dt - \sum_{b=1}^{B} \int_{t_н}^{t_к} DA_{S.ip.h.b}(t) * dt ,$$

here are:

$DA_{C.ip.l.b}$ – it is the density of $F_{C.ip.l.b}$, which is determining during the $CTP_{ip.l.b}$ in **PRESENT** under condition to achievement the $A_{ih.l}$ by **the** $RP_{ih.l}$, for example, by **the technology of Noologistics**;

$DA_{M.ip.l.b}$ – it is the density of $F_{M.ip.l.b}$, which is determining during the $CTP_{ip.l.b}$ in **PRESENT** under condition to achievement the $A_{ih.l}$ by **the** $RP_{ih.l}$, for example, by **the technology of Noologistics**;

$DA_{S.ip.l.b}$ – it is the density of $F_{S.ip.l.b}$, which is determining during the $CTP_{ip.l.b}$ in **PRESENT** under condition to achievement the $A_{ih.l}$ by **the** $RP_{ih.l}$, for example, by **the technology of Noologistics**;

the rest – see above.

Calculation of magnitude $DU_{ip.h}$ for each $V_{ip.h}$ is performed according to a standard formula, for example:

$DU_{ip.h} = DU_{C.ip.l}$, $DU_{ip.h} = DU_{M.ip.l}$ or $DU_{ip.h} = DU_{S.ip.l}$,

in which conditional designations $DU_{C.ip.l}$, $DU_{M.ip.l}$ and $DU_{S.ip.l}$ – see below.

Calculation of magnitudes $WQ_{ip.l}$, $OQ_{ip.l}$, $CQ_{ip.l}$, $HQ_{ip.l}$ and $LQ_{ip.l}$ is performed in **PRESENT** according to a RP_{ip} and RP_{ih}.

The formalized description of **the current noologistical habitat of** P_{ip} may contain the following information:

Current noologistical habitat of P_{ip} ($PH_{ip.l}$)

The description contains:

The name «**Current noologistical habitat of P_{ip}**» and identification number of the P_{ip}, for example, **ip**;

Nomenclature all of $V_{ip.l}$, between them:

l = 1, 2, 3, ..., L – it is an individual identification number of its registration into **a formalized description of the environment**;
The list of $V_{ip.l}$ names and its conditional designations ($V_{ip.l}$);
Description of the contents of each $V_{ip.l}$, between them:

Unit of measurement the quantity of the $Q_{ip.l}$, the best magnitude of the $Q_{ip.l}$ for the P_{ip}, i. e. corresponding to his **goal** $A_{ip.l}$ (briefly – $BQ_{ip.l}$), the worst magnitude of the $Q_{ip.l}$ (briefly – $WQ_{ip.l}$), the P_{ip}'s actual own magnitude of $Q_{ip.l}$ (briefly – $OQ_{ip.l}$), the part of common $Q_{ih.l}$ in P_{ip}'s using (briefly – $CQ_{ip.l}$), the P_{ip}'s actual $Q_{ip.l}$ (briefly – $RQ_{ip.l}$), equal to the sum $OQ_{ip.l}$ and $CQ_{ip.l}$, the highest $Q_{ip.l}$ guaranteed for P_{ip} in P_{ih} (briefly – $HQ_{ip.l}$) on his status in the P_{ih}, the lowest $Q_{ih.l}$ guaranteed for P_{ip} in P_{ih} (briefly – $LQ_{ip.l}$) on his status in the P_{ih}, the magnitude of the $Q_{ih.l}$ corresponds to $A_{ih.l}$ (briefly – $QA_{ip.l}$) on his status in the P_{ih}, etc.;
The locations (briefly – LV_C, LV_M and LV_S) and alocations (briefly – AV_C, AV_M and AV_S) each of the $Q_{ip.l}$ in the Ev_{ip}, for example, by the coordinates of the geo information system;
The nomenclature of parameters that characterize the quality (briefly – QP_C, QP_M and QP_S) each of the $V_{ip.l}$;
Units of measurement and numerical magnitudes of the parameters that characterize the quality each of the $V_{ip.l}$ (briefly – QP_C, QP_M and QP_S), etc.

Each P_{ip} performs a formal description by the his own rules, on the basis of $A_{ip.l}$ of his existence in Ev_{ip} and of analysis the current situation in it.

The structure information is shown in Fig. P 3, which follows from the formal description, entitled "**Current noologistical habitat of P_{ip}**".

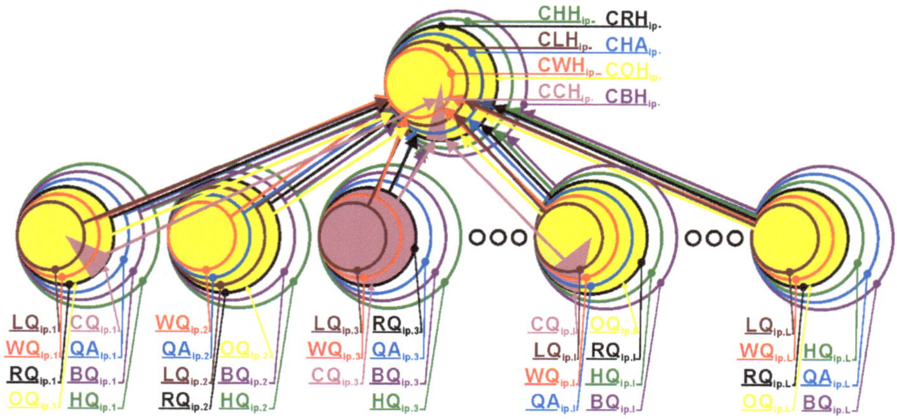

Fig. P 3

The conditional designation on the Fig. P 3:

CBH_{ip} – it is the best **current noologistical habitat for the P_{ip}**, that is the set of the **$BQ_{ip.l}$**, corresponds to his **$A_{ip.l}$**;

CWH_{ip} – it is it is the worst **current noologistical habitat for the P_{ip}**, that is the set of the **$WQ_{ip.l}$**;

COH$_{ip}$ – it is **P_{ip}**'s private part of the **$PH_{ip.l}$**, that is the set of the **$OQ_{ip.l}$**;

CCH_{ip} – it is the common part of the **$PH_{ip.l}$** in P_{ip}'s using, that is the set of the **$CQ_{ip.l}$**;

CRH_{ip} – it is the whole actual **current noologistical habitat** of the **P_{ip}**, that is the sum of the **COH_{ip}** and **CCH_{ip}**, and is the set of the **$RQ_{ip.l}$** also;

$CHH_{ip.l}$ – it is the highest **current noologistical habitat for the P_{ip}**, guaranteed to him in the **P_{ih}** on his status in the **P_{ih}**, that is the set of the **$HQ_{ip.l}$**;

CLH_{ip} – it is lowest **current noologistical habitat for the P_{ip}**, guaranteed to him in the **P_{ih}** on his status in the **P_{ih}**, that is the set of the **$LQ_{ip.l}$**;

CHA_{ip} – it is the **current noologistical habitat of the P_{ip}**, corresponds to **A_{ih}** on his status in the **P_{ih}**, that is the set of the **$QA_{ip.l}$**;

arrows show the formation of **CBH_{ip}**, **CWH_{ip}**, **COH_{ip}**, **CCH_{ip}**, **CRH_{ip}**, **CHH_{ip}**, **CLH_{ip}** and **CHA_{ip}** by union in correspond set of magnitudes of the **$BQ_{ip.l}$**, **$WQ_{ip.l}$**, **$OQ_{ip.l}$**, **$CQ_{ip.l}$**, **$RQ_{ip.l}$**, **$HQ_{ip.l}$**, **$LQ_{ip.l}$** and **$QA_{ip.l}$**;

the rest – see above.

Calculation of magnitudes $\mathbf{BQ_{ip.l}}$, $\mathbf{WQ_{ip.l}}$, $\mathbf{OQ_{ip.l}}$, $\mathbf{CQ_{ip.l}}$, $\mathbf{RQ_{ip.l}}$, $\mathbf{HQ_{ip.l}}$, $\mathbf{LQ_{ip.l}}$ and $\mathbf{QA_{ip.l}}$ is performed according to above given standard formulas, used in formalized description «**Noologistical habitat of P_{ip}**».

Formalized description of **the noo provision the existence** (**life support**) **of P_{ip}** may contain the following information:

Noo provision the P_{ip}'s existence (life support) ($SP_{ip.c}$)

The description may consist of three parts: «**Noo provision the P_{ip}'s existence (life support) by consumption of the $V_{C.ip.c}$**», «**Noo provision the P_{ip}'s existence (life support) by creation of the $V_{M.ip.c}$**» and «**Noo provision the P_{ip}'s existence (life support) by rejection of the $V_{S.ip.c}$**», that are put on display separately or together:

The first part of the description contains:

The name «**Noo provision the P_{ip}'s existence (life support) by consumption of the $V_{C.ip.c}$**», its conditional designation $\mathbf{SP_{C.ip.c}}$ and identification number of the $\mathbf{P_{ip}}$, for example, **ip**;

Nomenclature all of $\mathbf{F_{C.ip.c.b}}$ from b-th $\mathbf{CTP_{ip.l.b}}$, between them:

The list of $\mathbf{F_{C.ip.c.b}}$ names and its conditional designations ($\mathbf{F_{C.ip.c.b}}$);

Identification number **«c»** each of the $\mathbf{V_{C.ip.c}}$, that is the base of the correspond $\mathbf{F_{C.ip.c.b}}$ from **formalized description of the environment**;

Parameters each of $\mathbf{F_{C.ip.c.b}}$, between them:

Unit of measurement the magnitude of **density the current consumption flow of $V_{C.ip.c}$** (briefly – $\mathbf{D_{C.ip.c.b}}$) in the b-th $\mathbf{CTP_{ip.l.b}}$, the best magnitude of the **current $D_{C.ip.c.b}$** for the $\mathbf{P_{ip}}$, i. e. corresponding to his **goal $A_{ip.c}$** (briefly – $\mathbf{BD_{C.ip.c.b}}$) – see above, the worst magnitude of the **current $D_{C.ip.c.b}$** for the $\mathbf{P_{ip}}$ (briefly – $\mathbf{WD_{C.ip.c.b}}$), the P_{ip}'s actual own magnitude of the **current $D_{C.ip.c.b}$** from his own $\mathbf{PH_{ip.c}}$ (briefly – $\mathbf{OD_{C.ip.c.b}}$), the actual magnitude of the **current $D_{C.ip.c.b}$** from common $\mathbf{PH_{ih.c}}$ (briefly – $\mathbf{CD_{C.ip.c.b}}$), the actual magnitude of the **current $D_{C.ip.c.b}$** used by the $\mathbf{P_{ip}}$ (briefly – $\mathbf{RD_{C.ip.c.b}}$), equal to the sum $\mathbf{OD_{C.ip.c.b}}$ and $\mathbf{CD_{C.ip.c.b}}$, the highest magnitude of the **current $D_{C.ip.c.b}$**, guaranteed for P_{ip} in P_{ih}

(briefly – $\mathbf{HD_{C.ip.c.b}}$) on his status in the $\mathbf{P_{ih}}$, the lowest magnitude of the **current** $\mathbf{D_{C.ip.c.b}}$, guaranteed for P_{ip} in P_{ih} (briefly – $\mathbf{LD_{C.ip.c.b}}$) on his status in the $\mathbf{P_{ih}}$, the magnitude of the **current** $\mathbf{D_{C.ip.c.b}}$, corresponds to $\mathbf{A_{ih.c}}$ (briefly – $\mathbf{DA_{C.ip.c.b}}$) on his status in the $\mathbf{P_{ih}}$, the projected duration each of $\mathbf{V_{C.ip.c}}$'s **u**se (briefly – $\mathbf{DU_{C.ip.c}}$) in **FUTURE**, etc.

Link to the $\mathbf{CTP_{ip.l.b}}$, in which the $\mathbf{F_{C.ip.c.b}}$ is used.

The second part of the description contains:

The name «**Noo provision the** $\mathbf{P_{ip}}$'s **existence** (**life support**) **by creation of the** $\mathbf{V_{M.ip.c}}$», its conditional designation $\mathbf{SP_{M.ip.c}}$ and identification number of the $\mathbf{P_{ip}}$, for example, **ip**;

Nomenclature all of $\mathbf{F_{M.ip.c.b}}$ from b-th $\mathbf{CTP_{ip.l.b}}$, between them:

The list of $\mathbf{F_{M.ip.c.b}}$ names and its conditional designations ($\mathbf{F_{M.ip.c.b}}$);

Identification number **«c»** each of the $\mathbf{V_{M.ip.c}}$, that is the base of the correspond $\mathbf{F_{M.ip.c.b}}$ from **formalized description of the environment**;

Parameters each of $\mathbf{F_{M.ip.c.b}}$, between them:

Unit of measurement the magnitude of **density the current creation flow of** $\mathbf{V_{M.ip.c}}$ (briefly – $\mathbf{D_{M.ip.c.b}}$) in the b-th $\mathbf{CTP_{ip.l.b}}$, the best magnitude of the **current** $\mathbf{D_{M.ip.c.b}}$ for the $\mathbf{P_{ip}}$, i. e. corresponding to his **goal** $\mathbf{A_{ip.c}}$ (briefly – $\mathbf{BD_{M.ip.c.b}}$) – see above, the worst magnitude of the **current** $\mathbf{D_{M.ip.c.b}}$ for the $\mathbf{P_{ip}}$ (briefly – $\mathbf{WD_{M.ip.c.b}}$), the P_{ip}'s actual own magnitude of the **current** $\mathbf{D_{M.ip.c.b}}$ from his own $\mathbf{PH_{ip.c}}$ (briefly – $\mathbf{OD_{M.ip.c.b}}$), the actual magnitude of the **current** $\mathbf{D_{M.ip.c.b}}$ from common $\mathbf{PH_{ih.c}}$ (briefly – $\mathbf{CD_{M.ip.c.b}}$), the actual magnitude of the **current** $\mathbf{D_{M.ip.c.b}}$ used by the $\mathbf{P_{ip}}$ (briefly – $\mathbf{RD_{M.ip.c.b}}$), equal to the sum $\mathbf{OD_{M.ip.c.b}}$ and $\mathbf{CD_{M.ip.c.b}}$, the highest magnitude of the **current** $\mathbf{D_{M.ip.c.b}}$, guaranteed for P_{ip} in P_{ih} (briefly – $\mathbf{HD_{M.ip.c.b}}$) on his status in the $\mathbf{P_{ih}}$, the lowest magnitude of the **current** $\mathbf{D_{M.ip.c.b}}$, guaranteed for P_{ip} in P_{ih} (briefly – $\mathbf{LD_{M.ip.c.b}}$) on his status in the $\mathbf{P_{ih}}$, the magnitude of the **current** $\mathbf{D_{M.ip.c.b}}$, corresponds to $\mathbf{A_{ih.c}}$ (briefly – $\mathbf{DA_{M.ip.c.b}}$) on his status in the $\mathbf{P_{ih}}$, the projected duration each of $\mathbf{V_{M.ip.c}}$'s **u**se (briefly – $\mathbf{DU_{M.ip.c}}$) in **FUTURE**, etc.

Link to the **CTP**$_{ip.l.b}$, in which the **F**$_{M.ip.c.b}$ is created.

The third part of the description contains:

The name «**Noo provision the P**$_{ip}$**'s existence (life support) by rejection of the V**$_{S.ip.c}$», its conditional designation **SP**$_{S.ip.c}$ and identification number of the **P**$_{ip}$, for example, **ip**;

Nomenclature all of **F**$_{S.ip.c.b}$ from b-th **CTP**$_{ip.l.b}$, between them:

The list of **F**$_{S.ip.c.b}$ names and its conditional designations (**F**$_{S.ip.c.b}$);

Identification number **«c»** each of the **V**$_{S.ip.c}$, that is the base of the correspond **F**$_{S.ip.c.b}$ from **formalized description of the environment**;

Parameters each of **F**$_{S.ip.c.b}$, between them:

Unit of measurement the magnitude of **density the current rejection flow of V**$_{S.ip.c}$ (briefly – **D**$_{S.ip.c.b}$) in the b-th **CTP**$_{ip.l.b}$, the best magnitude of the **current D**$_{S.ip.c.b}$ for the **P**$_{ip}$, i. e. corresponding to his **goal A**$_{ip.c}$ (briefly – **BD**$_{S.ip.c.b}$) – see above, the worst magnitude of the **current D**$_{S.ip.c.b}$ for the **P**$_{ip}$ (briefly – **WD**$_{S.ip.c.b}$), the P_{ip}'s actual own magnitude of the **current D**$_{S.ip.c.b}$ from his own **PH**$_{ip.c}$ (briefly – **OD**$_{S.ip.c.b}$), the actual magnitude of the **current D**$_{S.ip.c.b}$ from common **PH**$_{ih.c}$ (briefly – **CD**$_{S.ip.c.b}$), the actual magnitude of the **current D**$_{S.ip.c.b}$ used by the **P**$_{ip}$ (briefly – **RD**$_{S.ip.c.b}$), equal to the sum **OD**$_{S.ip.c.b}$ and **CD**$_{S.ip.c.b}$, the highest magnitude of the **current D**$_{S.ip.c.b}$, guaranteed for P_{ip} in P_{ih} (briefly – **HD**$_{S.ip.c.b}$) on his status in the **P**$_{ih}$, the lowest magnitude of the **current D**$_{S.ip.c.b}$, guaranteed for P_{ip} in P_{ih} (briefly – **LD**$_{S.ip.c.b}$) on his status in the **P**$_{ih}$, the magnitude of the **current D**$_{S.ip.c.b}$, corresponds to **A**$_{ih.c}$ (briefly – **DA**$_{S.ip.c.b}$) on his status in the **P**$_{ih}$, the projected duration each of **V**$_{S.ip.c}$'s use (briefly – **DU**$_{S.ip.c}$) in **FUTURE**, etc.

Link to the **CTP**$_{ip.l.b}$, from which the **F**$_{S.ip.c.b}$ is rejected.

Formalized description of **the noologistical provision the existence (life support) of P**$_{ip}$ may contain the following information:

Noologistical provision the P_{ip}'s existence (life support) ($SP_{ip.l}$)

The description may consist of three parts: «**Noologistical provision the P_{ip}'s existence (life support) by consumption of the $V_{C.ip.l}$**», «**Noologistical provision the P_{ip}'s existence (life support) by creation of the $V_{M.ip.l}$**» and «**Noologistical provision the P_{ip}'s existence (life support) by rejection of the $V_{S.ip.l}$**», that are put on display separately or together:

The first part of the description contains:

The name «**Noologistical provision the P_{ip}'s existence (life support) by consumption of the $V_{C.ip.l}$**», its conditional designation $SP_{C.ip.l}$ and identification number of the P_{ip}, for example, **ip**;

Nomenclature all of $F_{C.ip.l.b}$ from b-th $CTP_{ip.l.b}$, between them:

The list of $F_{C.ip.l.b}$ names and its conditional designations ($F_{C.ip.l.b}$);

Identification number **«l»** each of the $V_{C.ip.l}$, that is the base of the correspond $F_{C.ip.l.b}$ from **formalized description of the environment**;

Parameters each of $F_{C.ip.l.b}$, between them:

Unit of measurement the magnitude of **density the current consumption flow of $V_{C.ip.l}$** (briefly – $D_{C.ip.l.b}$) in the b-th $CTP_{ip.l.b}$, the best magnitude of the **current** $D_{C.ip.l.b}$ for the P_{ip}, i. e. corresponding to his **goal** $A_{ip.l}$ (briefly – $BD_{C.ip.l.b}$) – see above, the worst magnitude of the **current** $D_{C.ip.l.b}$ for the P_{ip} (briefly – $WD_{C.ip.l.b}$), the P_{ip}'s actual own magnitude of the **current** $D_{C.ip.l.b}$ from his own $PH_{ip.l}$ (briefly – $OD_{C.ip.l.b}$), the actual magnitude of the **current** $D_{C.ip.l.b}$ from common $PH_{ih.l}$ (briefly – $CD_{C.ip.l.b}$), the actual magnitude of the **current** $D_{C.ip.l.b}$ used by the P_{ip} (briefly – $RD_{C.ip.l.b}$), equal to the sum $OD_{C.ip.l.b}$ and $CD_{C.ip.l.b}$, the highest magnitude of the **current** $D_{C.ip.l.b}$, guaranteed for P_{ip} in P_{ih} (briefly – $HD_{C.ip.l.b}$) on his status in the P_{ih}, the lowest magnitude of the **current** $D_{C.ip.l.b}$, guaranteed for P_{ip} in P_{ih} (briefly – $LD_{C.ip.l.b}$) on his status in the P_{ih}, the magnitude of the **current** $D_{C.ip.l.b}$, corresponds to his $A_{ih.l}$ (briefly – $DA_{C.ip.l.b}$) on his status in the P_{ih}, the projected duration each of $V_{C.ip.l}$'s use (briefly – $DU_{C.ip.l}$) in **FUTURE**, etc.

Link to the $\mathbf{CTP_{ip.l.b}}$, in which the $\mathbf{F_{C.ip.l.b}}$ is used.

The structure information is shown in Fig. P 4, which follows from the formal description, entitled "**Noologistical provision the $\mathbf{P_{ip}}$**'s **existence** (**life support**) **by consumption of the $\mathbf{V_{C.ip.l}}$** ".

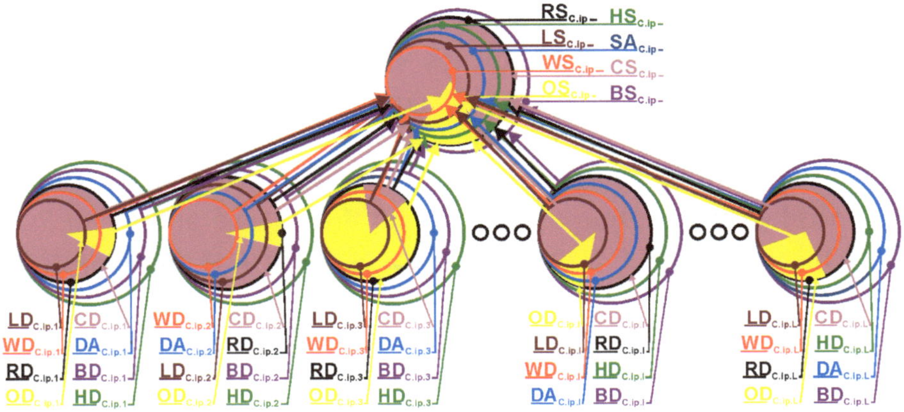

Fig. P 4

The conditional designation on the Fig. P 4:

$\mathbf{BS_{C.ip}}$ – it is the best **noologistical provision the existence** (**life support**) **by consumption of the $\mathbf{V_{C.ip.l}}$** for the $\mathbf{P_{ip}}$ that corresponds to his $\mathbf{A_{ip.l}}$, and is the set of the best for the $\mathbf{P_{ip}}$ total densities of **the consumption flows** of the $\mathbf{V_{C.ip.l}}$, the calculation formula of which is given below;

$\mathbf{WS_{C.ip}}$ – it is the worst **noologistical provision the existence** (**life support**) **by consumption of the $\mathbf{V_{C.ip.l}}$** for the $\mathbf{P_{ip}}$ and is the set of the worst for the $\mathbf{P_{ip}}$ total densities of **the consumption flows** of the $\mathbf{V_{C.ip.l}}$, the calculation formula of which is given below;

$\mathbf{OS_{C.ip}}$ – it is the actual **noologistical provision the existence** (**life support**) **by consumption of the $\mathbf{V_{C.ip.l}}$** by the $\mathbf{P_{ip}}$ from his own $\mathbf{Q_{ip.l}}$, that is the set of the total densities of **the consumption flows** of the $\mathbf{V_{C.ip.l}}$ from his own $\mathbf{Q_{ip.l}}$, the calculation formula of which is given below;

$\mathbf{CS_{C.ip}}$ – it is the actual **noologistical provision the existence** (**life support**) **by consumption of the $\mathbf{V_{C.ip.l}}$** by the $\mathbf{P_{ip}}$ from the common $\mathbf{Q_{ih.l}}$, that is the set of the total densities of **the consumption flows** of the

$\mathbf{V_{C.ip.l}}$ from the common $\mathbf{Q_{ih.l}}$, the calculation formula of which is given below;

$\mathbf{RS_{C.ip}}$ – it is the actual total **noologistical provision the existence (life support) by consumption of the** $\mathbf{V_{C.ip.l}}$ by the $\mathbf{P_{ip}}$, that is the sum of the $\mathbf{OS_{C.ip}}$ and $\mathbf{CS_{C.ip}}$;

$\mathbf{HS_{C.ip}}$ – it is highest **noologistical provision the existence** (**life support**) **by consumption of the** $\mathbf{V_{C.ip.l}}$ for the $\mathbf{P_{ip}}$, guaranteed for P_{ip} in P_{ih} on his **status** in the $\mathbf{P_{ih}}$ that is the sum of **the highest densities of the consumption flows of** $\mathbf{V_{C.ip.l}}$, guaranteed for him in P_{ih}, the calculation formula of which is given below;

$\mathbf{LS_{C.ip}}$ – it is lowest **noologistical provision the existence** (**life support**) **by consumption of the** $\mathbf{V_{C.ip.l}}$ for the $\mathbf{P_{ip}}$, guaranteed for P_{ip} in P_{ih} on his **status** in the $\mathbf{P_{ih}}$ that is the sum of **the lowest densities of the consumption flows of** $\mathbf{V_{C.ip.l}}$, guaranteed for him in P_{ih}, the calculation formula of which is given below;

$\mathbf{SA_{C.ip}}$ – it is **noologistical provision the existence** (**life support**) **by consumption of the** $\mathbf{V_{C.ip.l}}$ for the $\mathbf{P_{ip}}$, corresponds to his $\mathbf{A_{ih.l}}$ on his **status** in the $\mathbf{P_{ih}}$, that is the sum of **the densities of the consumption flows of** $\mathbf{V_{C.ip.l}}$, corresponds to his $\mathbf{A_{ih.l}}$, the calculation formula of which is given below;

arrows show the formation of $\mathbf{BS_{C.ip}}$, $\mathbf{WS_{C.ip}}$, $\mathbf{OS_{C.ip}}$, $\mathbf{CS_{C.ip}}$ $\mathbf{RS_{C.ip}}$, $\mathbf{HS_{C.ip}}$, $\mathbf{LS_{C.ip}}$ and $\mathbf{SA_{C.ip}}$ by union in correspond set of magnitudes of the $\mathbf{BD_{C.ip.l}}$, $\mathbf{WD_{C.ip.l}}$, $\mathbf{OD_{C.ip.l}}$, $\mathbf{CD_{C.ip.l}}$, $\mathbf{RD_{C.ip.l}}$, $\mathbf{HD_{C.ip.l}}$, $\mathbf{LD_{C.ip.l}}$ and $\mathbf{DA_{C.ip.l}}$;

the rest – see above.

Calculation of magnitudes $\mathbf{BD_{C.ip.l}}$, $\mathbf{WD_{C.ip.l}}$, $\mathbf{OD_{C.ip.l}}$, $\mathbf{CD_{C.ip.l}}$, $\mathbf{RD_{C.ip.l}}$, $\mathbf{HD_{C.ip.l}}$, $\mathbf{LD_{C.ip.l}}$ and $\mathbf{DA_{C.ip.l}}$ is performed according to above given standard formulas:

$$BD_{C.ip.l} = \sum_{b=1}^{B} BD_{C.ip.l.b}, \qquad WD_{C.ip.l} = \sum_{b=1}^{B} WD_{C.ip.l.b},$$

$$OD_{C.ip.l} = \sum_{b=1}^{B} OD_{C.ip.l.b}, \qquad CD_{C.ip.l} = \sum_{b=1}^{B} CD_{C.ip.l.b},$$

$$RD_{C.ip.l} = \sum_{b=1}^{B} D_{C.ip.l.b} = OD_{C.ip.l} + CD_{C.ip.l}, \qquad HD_{C.ip.l} = \sum_{b=1}^{B} HD_{C.ip.l.b},$$

$$LD_{C.ip.l} = \sum_{b=1}^{B} LD_{C.ip.l.b}, \; DA_{C.ip.l} = \sum_{b=1}^{B} DA_{C.ip.l.b},$$

here are:

$\mathbf{BD_{C.ip.l.b}}$ – it is the best density of the $\mathbf{F_{C.ip.l.b}}$ for the $\mathbf{P_{ip}}$ in b-th $\mathbf{CTP_{ip.l.b}}$ in **PRESENT**, which is determined from the condition of achieving his $\mathbf{A_{ig.l}}$, for example, by **the technology of Noologistics**;

$\mathbf{WD_{C.ip.l.b}}$ – it is the worst density of the $\mathbf{F_{C.ip.l.b}}$ for the $\mathbf{P_{ip}}$ in b-th $\mathbf{CTP_{ip.l.b}}$ in **PRESENT**, which is determined by the $\mathbf{RP_{ip.l}}$;

$\mathbf{OD_{C.ip.l.b}}$ – it is the actual density of the $\mathbf{F_{C.ip.l.b}}$ from the $\mathbf{OQ_{C.ip.l}}$, used in b-th $\mathbf{CTP_{ip.l.b}}$ in **PRESENT**, which is measured by the $\mathbf{RP_{ip.l}}$;

$\mathbf{CD_{C.ip.l.b}}$ – it is the actual density of the $\mathbf{F_{C.ip.l.b}}$ from the $\mathbf{CQ_{C.ip.l}}$, used in b-th $\mathbf{CTP_{ip.l.b}}$ in **PRESENT**, which is measured by the $\mathbf{RP_{ip.l}}$;

$\mathbf{D_{C.ip.l.b}}$ – it is the actual density of the $\mathbf{F_{C.ip.l.b}}$, used in b-th $\mathbf{CTP_{ip.l.b}}$ in **PRESENT**, which is measured by the $\mathbf{RP_{ip}}$;

$\mathbf{HD_{C.ip.l.b}}$ – it is highest density of the $\mathbf{F_{C.ip.l.b}}$, guaranteed for P_{ip} in P_{ih} in b-th $\mathbf{CTP_{ip.l.b}}$ in **PRESENT** on his status in the $\mathbf{P_{ih}}$, which is determined by the $\mathbf{RP_{ih.l}}$;

$\mathbf{LD_{C.ip.l.b}}$ – it is lowest density of the $\mathbf{F_{C.ip.l.b}}$, guaranteed for P_{ip} in P_{ih} in b-th $\mathbf{CTP_{ip.l.b}}$ in **PRESENT** on his status in the $\mathbf{P_{ih}}$, which is determined by the $\mathbf{RP_{ih.l}}$;

$\mathbf{DA_{C.ip.l.b}}$ – it is density of the $\mathbf{F_{C.ip.l.b}}$ in b-th $\mathbf{CTP_{ip.l.b}}$ in **PRESENT**, which is determined from the condition of achieving his $\mathbf{A_{ih.l}}$, for example, by **the technology of Noologistics**;

the rest – see above.

Calculation of magnitude $\mathbf{DU_{C.ip.l}}$ for each $\mathbf{V_{C.ip.h}}$ is performed according to a standard formula, for example:

$$DU_{C.ip.l} = \frac{QA_{ip.h}}{\sum_{b=1}^{B}\int_{t_н}^{t} DA_{C.ip.l.b}(t) * dt},$$

in which all conditional designations – see above.

The second part of the description contains:

The name «**Noologistical provision the P_{ip}'s existence (life support) by creation of the $V_{M.ip.l}$**», its conditional designation $\mathbf{SP_{M.ip.l}}$ and identification number of the $\mathbf{P_{ip}}$, for example, **ip**;

Nomenclature all of $\mathbf{F_{M.ip.l.b}}$ from b-th $\mathbf{CTP_{ip.l.b}}$, between them:

The list of $\mathbf{F_{M.ip.l.b}}$ names and its conditional designations ($\mathbf{F_{M.ip.l.b}}$);

Identification number **«l»** each of the $\mathbf{V_{M.ip.l}}$, that is the base of the correspond $\mathbf{F_{M.ip.l.b}}$ from **formalized description of the environment**;

Parameters each of $\mathbf{F_{M.ip.l.b}}$, between them:

Unit of measurement the magnitude of **density the current creation flow of** $\mathbf{V_{M.ip.l}}$ (briefly – $\mathbf{D_{M.ip.l.b}}$) in the b-th $\mathbf{CTP_{ip.l.b}}$, the best magnitude of the **current** $\mathbf{D_{M.ip.l.b}}$ for the $\mathbf{P_{ip}}$, i. e. corresponding to his **goal** $\mathbf{A_{ip.l}}$ (briefly – $\mathbf{BD_{M.ip.l.b}}$) – see above, the worst magnitude of the **current** $\mathbf{D_{M.ip.l.b}}$ for the $\mathbf{P_{ip}}$ (briefly – $\mathbf{WD_{M.ip.l.b}}$), the P_{ip}'s actual own magnitude of the **current** $\mathbf{D_{M.ip.l.b}}$ from his own $\mathbf{PH_{ip.l}}$ (briefly – $\mathbf{OD_{M.ip.l.b}}$), the actual magnitude of the **current** $\mathbf{D_{M.ip.l.b}}$ from common $\mathbf{PH_{ih.l}}$ (briefly – $\mathbf{CD_{M.ip.l.b}}$), the actual magnitude of the **current** $\mathbf{D_{M.ip.l.b}}$ used by the $\mathbf{P_{ip}}$ (briefly – $\mathbf{RD_{M.ip.l.b}}$), equal to the sum $\mathbf{OD_{M.ip.l.b}}$ and $\mathbf{CD_{M.ip.l.b}}$, the highest magnitude of the **current** $\mathbf{D_{M.ip.l.b}}$**,** guaranteed for P_{ip} in P_{ih} (briefly – $\mathbf{HD_{M.ip.l.b}}$) on his status in the $\mathbf{P_{ih}}$, the lowest magnitude of the **current** $\mathbf{D_{M.ip.l.b}}$**,** guaranteed for P_{ip} in P_{ih} (briefly – $\mathbf{LD_{M.ip.l.b}}$) on his status in the $\mathbf{P_{ih}}$, the magnitude of the **current** $\mathbf{D_{M.ip.l.b}}$**,** corresponds to his $\mathbf{A_{ih.l}}$ (briefly – $\mathbf{DA_{M.ip.l.b}}$) on his status in the $\mathbf{P_{ih}}$, the projected duration each of $\mathbf{V_{M.ip.l}}$'s **u**se (briefly – $\mathbf{DU_{M.ip.l}}$) in **FUTURE**, etc.

Link to the $\mathbf{CTP_{ip.l.b}}$, in which the $\mathbf{F_{M.ip.l.b}}$ is created.

The structure information is shown in Fig. P 5, which follows from the formal description, entitled "**Noologistical provision the** $\mathbf{P_{ip}}$'s **existence** (**life support**) **by creation of the** $V_{M.ip.l}$ ".

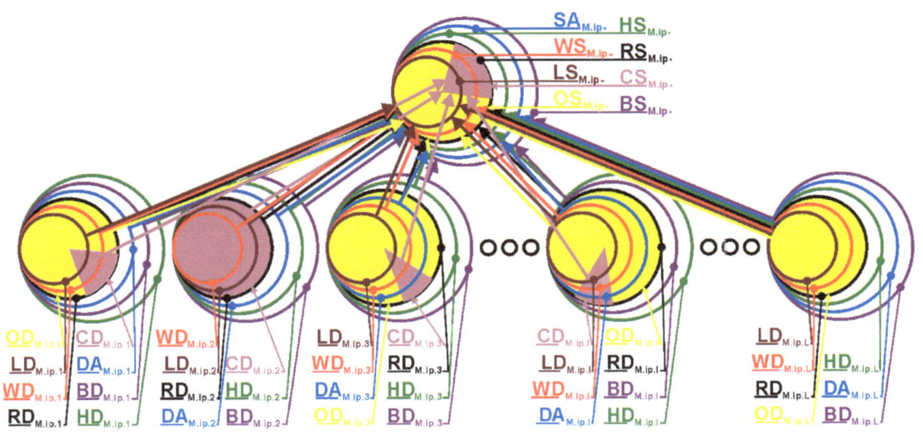

Fig. P 5

The conditional designation on the Fig. P 5:

$BS_{M.ip}$ – it is the best **noologistical provision the existence** (**life support**) **by creation of the $V_{M.ip.l}$** for the **P_{ip}** that corresponds to his **$A_{ip.l}$**, and is the set of the best for the **P_{ip}** total densities of **the creation flows** of the **$V_{M.ip.l}$**, the calculation formula of which is given below;

$WS_{M.ip}$ – it is the worst **noologistical provision the existence** (**life support**) **by creation of the $V_{M.ip.l}$** for the **P_{ip}** and is the set of the worst for the **P_{ip}** total densities of **the creation flows** of the **$V_{M.ip.l}$**, the calculation formula of which is given below;

$OS_{M.ip}$ – it is the **noologistical provision the existence** (**life support**) **by creation of the $V_{M.ip.l}$** by the **P_{ip}** from his own **$Q_{ip.l}$**, that is the set of the total densities of **the creation flows** of the **$V_{M.ip.l}$** from his own **$Q_{ip.l}$**, the calculation formula of which is given below;

$CS_{M.ip}$ – it is the actual **noologistical provision the existence** (**life support**) **by creation of the $V_{M.ip.l}$** by the **P_{ip}** from the common **$Q_{ih.l}$**, that is the set of the total densities of **the creation flows** of the **$V_{M.ip.l}$** from the common **$Q_{ih.l}$**, the calculation formula of which is given below;

$RS_{M.ip}$ – it is the actual total **noologistical provision the existence** (**life support**) **by creation of the $V_{C.ip.l}$** by the **P_{ip}**, that is the sum of the **$OS_{M.ip}$** and **$CS_{M.ip}$**;

$HS_{M.ip}$ – it is highest **noologistical provision the existence** (**life support**) **by creation of the $V_{M.ip.l}$** for the **P_{ip}**, guaranteed for P_{ip} in P_{ih} on his **status** in the **P_{ih}** that is the sum of **the highest densities of the**

creation flows of $V_{M.ip.l}$, guaranteed for him in P_{ih}, the calculation formula of which is given below;

$LS_{M.ip}$ – it is lowest **noologistical provision the existence** (**life support**) **by creation of the** $V_{M.ip.l}$ for the **P_{ip}**, guaranteed for P_{ip} in P_{ih} on his **status** in the **P_{ih}** that is the sum of **the lowest densities of the creation flows of $V_{M.ip.l}$**, guaranteed for him in P_{ih}, the calculation formula of which is given below;

$SA_{M.ip}$ – it is **noologistical provision the existence** (**life support**) **by creation of the** $V_{M.ip.l}$ for the **P_{ip}**, corresponds to his **$A_{ih.l}$** on his **status** in the **P_{ih}**, that is the sum of **the densities of the creation flows of $V_{C.ip.l}$**, corresponds to his **$A_{ih.l}$**, the calculation formula of which is given below;

arrows show the formation of **$BS_{M.ip}$**, **$WS_{M.ip}$**, **$OS_{M.ip}$**, **$CS_{M.ip}$**, **$RS_{M.ip}$**, **$HS_{M.ip}$**, **$LS_{M.ip}$** and **$SA_{M.ip}$** by union in correspond set of magnitudes of the **$BD_{M.ip.l}$**, **$WD_{M.ip.l}$**, **$OD_{M.ip.l}$**, **$CD_{M.ip.l}$**, **$RD_{M.ip.l}$**, **$HD_{M.ip.l}$**, **$LD_{M.ip.l}$** and **$DA_{M.ip.l}$**;

the rest – see above.

Calculation of magnitudes **$BD_{M.ip.l}$**, **$WD_{M.ip.l}$**, **$OD_{M.ip.l}$**, **$CD_{M.ip.l}$**, **$RD_{M.ip.l}$**, **$HD_{M.ip.l}$**, **$LD_{M.ip.l}$** and **$DA_{M.ip.l}$** is performed according to above given standard formulas:

$$BD_{M.ip.l} = \sum_{b=1}^{B} BD_{M.ip.l.b}, \qquad WD_{M.ip.l} = \sum_{b=1}^{B} WD_{M.ip.l.b},$$

$$OD_{M.ip.l} = \sum_{b=1}^{B} OD_{M.ip.l.b}, \qquad CD_{M.ip.l} = \sum_{b=1}^{B} CD_{M.ip.l.b},$$

$$RD_{M.ip.l} = \sum_{b=1}^{B} D_{M.ip.l.b} = OD_{M.ip.l} + CD_{M.ip.l}, \qquad HD_{M.ip.l} = \sum_{b=1}^{B} HD_{M.ip.l.b},$$

$$LD_{M.ip.l} = \sum_{b=1}^{B} LD_{M.ip.l.b}, \quad DA_{M.ip.l} = \sum_{b=1}^{B} DA_{M.ip.l.b},$$

here are:

$BD_{M.ip.l.b}$ – it is the best density of the **$F_{M.ip.l.b}$** for the **P_{ip}** in b-th **$CTP_{ip.l.b}$** in **PRESENT**, which is determined from the condition of achieving his **$A_{ip.l}$**, for example, by **the technology of Noologistics**;

$WD_{M.ip.l.b}$ – it is the worst density of the **$F_{M.ip.l.b}$** for the **P_{ip}** in b-th **$CTP_{ip.l.b}$** in **PRESENT**, which is determined by the **$RP_{ip.l}$**;

$OD_{M.ip.l.b}$ – it is the actual density of the **$F_{M.ip.l.b}$** from the **$OQ_{C.ip.l}$**, used in b-th **$CTP_{ip.l.b}$** in **PRESENT**, which is measured by the **$RP_{ip.l}$**;

$CD_{M.ip.l.b}$ – it is the actual density of the **$F_{M.ip.l.b}$** from the **$CQ_{M.ip.l}$**, used in b-th **$CTP_{ip.l.b}$** in **PRESENT**, which is measured by the **$RP_{ip.l}$**;

$D_{M.ip.l.b}$ – it is the actual density of the **$F_{M.ip.l.b}$**, used in b-th **$CTP_{ip.l.b}$** in **PRESENT**, which is measured by the **RP_{ip}**;

$HD_{M.ip.l.b}$ – it is highest density of the **$F_{M.ip.l.b}$**, guaranteed for P_{ip} in P_{ih} in b-th **$CTP_{ip.l.b}$** in **PRESENT** on his status in the **P_{ih}**, which is determined by the **$RP_{ih.l}$**;

$LD_{M.ip.l.b}$ – it is lowest density of the **$F_{M.ip.l.b}$**, guaranteed for P_{ip} in P_{ih} in b-th **$CTP_{ip.l.b}$** in **PRESENT** on his status in the **P_{ih}**, which is determined by the **$RP_{ih.l}$**;

$DA_{M.ip.l.b}$ – it is density of the **$F_{M.ip.l.b}$** in b-th **$CTP_{ip.l.b}$** in **PRESENT**, which is determined from the condition of achieving his **$A_{ih.l}$**, for example, by **the technology of Noologistics**;

the rest – see above.

Calculation of magnitude **$DU_{M.ip.l}$** for each **$V_{M.ip.h}$** is performed according to a standard formula, for example:

$$DU_{M.ip.l} = \frac{QA_{ip.h}}{\sum_{b=1}^{B} \int_{t_н}^{t} DA_{M.ip.l.b}(t) * dt},$$

in which all conditional designations – see above.

The third part of the description contains:

The name «**Noologistical provision the P_{ip}'s existence** (**life support**) **by rejection of the $V_{S.ip.l}$**», its conditional designation **$SP_{S.ip.l}$** and identification number of the **P_{ip}**, for example, **ip**;

Nomenclature all of **$F_{S.ip.l.b}$** from b-th **$CTP_{ip.l.b}$**, between them:

The list of **$F_{S.ip.l.b}$** names and its conditional designations (**$F_{S.ip.l.b}$**);

Identification number **«l»** each of the **$V_{S.ip.l}$**, that is the base of the correspond **$F_{S.ip.l.b}$** from **formalized description of the environment**;

Parameters each of $\mathbf{F_{S.ip.l.b}}$, between them:

Unit of measurement the magnitude of **density the current rejection flow of** $\mathbf{V_{S.ip.l}}$ (briefly – $\mathbf{D_{S.ip.l.b}}$) from the b-th $\mathbf{CTP_{ip.l.b}}$, the best magnitude of the **current** $\mathbf{D_{S.ip.l.b}}$ for the $\mathbf{P_{ip}}$, i. e. corresponding to his **goal** $\mathbf{A_{ip.l}}$ (briefly – $\mathbf{BD_{S.ip.l.b}}$) – see above, the worst magnitude of the **current** $\mathbf{D_{S.ip.l.b}}$ for the $\mathbf{P_{ip}}$ (briefly – $\mathbf{WD_{S.ip.l.b}}$), the P_{ip}'s actual own magnitude of the **current** $\mathbf{D_{S.ip.l.b}}$ from his own $\mathbf{PH_{ip.l}}$ (briefly – $\mathbf{OD_{S.ip.l.b}}$), the actual magnitude of the **current** $\mathbf{D_{S.ip.l.b}}$ from common $\mathbf{PH_{ih.l}}$ (briefly – $\mathbf{CD_{S.ip.l.b}}$), the actual magnitude of the **current** $\mathbf{D_{S.ip.l.b}}$ used by the $\mathbf{P_{ip}}$ (briefly – $\mathbf{RD_{S.ip.l.b}}$), equal to the sum $\mathbf{OD_{S.ip.l.b}}$ and $\mathbf{CD_{S.ip.l.b}}$, the highest magnitude of the **current** $\mathbf{D_{S.ip.l.b}}$, guaranteed for P_{ip} in P_{ih} (briefly – $\mathbf{HD_{S.ip.l.b}}$) on his status in the $\mathbf{P_{ih}}$, the lowest magnitude of the **current** $\mathbf{D_{S.ip.l.b}}$, guaranteed for P_{ip} in P_{ih} (briefly – $\mathbf{LD_{S.ip.l.b}}$) on his status in the $\mathbf{P_{ih}}$, the magnitude of the **current** $\mathbf{D_{S.ip.l.b}}$, corresponds to his $\mathbf{A_{ih.l}}$ (briefly – $\mathbf{DA_{S.ip.l.b}}$) on his status in the $\mathbf{P_{ih}}$, the projected duration each of $\mathbf{V_{S.ip.l}}$'s **u**se (briefly – $\mathbf{DU_{S.ip.l}}$) in **FUTURE**, etc.

Link to the $\mathbf{CTP_{ip.l.b}}$, from which the $\mathbf{F_{S.ip.l.b}}$ is rejected.

The structure information is shown in Fig. P 6, which follows from the formal description, entitled "**Noologistical provision the** $\mathbf{P_{ip}}$'**s existence** (**life support**) **by rejection of the** $\mathbf{V_{S.ip.l}}$".

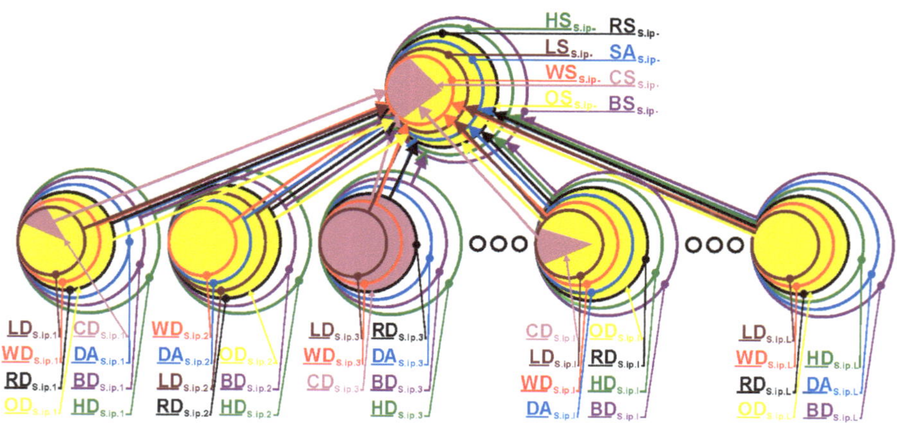

Fig. P 6

The conditional designation on the Fig. P 6:

$BS_{S.ip}$ – it is the best **noological provision the existence** (**life support**) **by rejection of the $V_{S.ip.l}$** for the **P_{ip}** that corresponds to his **$A_{ip.l}$**, and is the set of the best for the **P_{ip}** total densities of **the rejection flows** of the **$V_{S.ip.l}$**, the calculation formula of which is given below;

$WS_{S.ip}$ – it is the worst **noological provision the existence** (**life support**) **by rejection of the $V_{S.ip.l}$** for the **P_{ip}** and is the set of the worst for the **P_{ip}** total densities of **the rejection flows** of the **$V_{C.ip.l}$**, the calculation formula of which is given below;

$OS_{S.ip}$ – it is the **noological provision the existence** (**life support**) **by rejection of the $V_{S.ip.l}$** by the **P_{ip}** to his own **$Q_{ip.l}$**, that is the set of the total densities of **the rejection flows** of the **$V_{S.ip.l}$** to his own **$Q_{ip.l}$**, the calculation formula of which is given below;

$CS_{S.ip}$ – it is the actual **noological provision the existence** (**life support**) **by rejection of the $V_{S.ip.l}$** by the **P_{ip}** to the common **$Q_{ih.l}$**, that is the set of the total densities of **the rejection flows** of the **$V_{S.ip.l}$** to the common **$Q_{ih.l}$**, the calculation formula of which is given below;

$RS_{S.ip}$ – it is the actual total **noological provision the existence** (**life support**) **by rejection of the $V_{S.ip.l}$** by the **P_{ip}**, that is the sum of the **$OS_{S.ip}$** and **$CS_{S.ip}$**;

$HS_{S.ip}$ – it is highest **noological provision the existence** (**life support**) **by rejection of the $V_{S.ip.l}$** for the **P_{ip}**, guaranteed for P_{ip} in P_{ih} on his **status** in the **P_{ih}** that is the sum of **the highest densities of the rejection flows of $V_{S.ip.l}$**, guaranteed for him in P_{ih}, the calculation formula of which is given below;

$LS_{S.ip}$ – it is lowest **noological provision the existence** (**life support**) **by rejection of the $V_{S.ip.l}$** for the **P_{ip}**, guaranteed for P_{ip} in P_{ih} on his **status** in the **P_{ih}** that is the sum of **the lowest densities of the rejection flows of $V_{S.ip.l}$**, guaranteed for him in P_{ih}, the calculation formula of which is given below;

$SA_{S.ip}$ – it is **noological provision the existence** (**life support**) **by rejection of the $V_{S.ip.l}$** for the **P_{ip}**, corresponds to his **$A_{ih.l}$** on his **status** in the **P_{ih}**, that is the sum of **the densities of the rejection flows of $V_{S.ip.l}$**, corresponds to his **$A_{ih.l}$**, the calculation formula of which is given below;

arrows show the formation of **$BS_{S.ip}$**, **$WS_{S.ip}$**, **$OS_{S.ip}$**, **$CS_{S.ip}$**, **$RS_{S.ip}$**, **$HS_{S.ip}$**, **$LS_{S.ip}$** and **$SA_{S.ip}$** by union in correspond set of magnitudes of the **$BD_{S.ip.l}$**, **$WD_{S.ip.l}$**, **$OD_{S.ip.l}$**, **$CD_{S.ip.l}$**, **$RD_{S.ip.l}$**, **$HD_{S.ip.l}$**, **$LD_{S.ip.l}$** and **$DA_{S.ip.l}$**;

the rest – see above.

Calculation of magnitudes $\mathbf{BD_{S.ip.l}}$, $\mathbf{WD_{S.ip.l}}$, $\mathbf{OD_{S.ip.l}}$, $\mathbf{CD_{S.ip.l}}$, $\mathbf{RD_{S.ip.l}}$, $\mathbf{HD_{S.ip.l}}$, $\mathbf{LD_{S.ip.l}}$ and $\mathbf{DA_{S.ip.l}}$ is performed according to above given standard formulas:

$$BD_{S.ip.l} = \sum_{b=1}^{B} BD_{S.ip.l.b}, \qquad WD_{S.ip.l} = \sum_{b=1}^{B} WD_{S.ip.l.b},$$

$$OD_{S.ip.l} = \sum_{b=1}^{B} OD_{S.ip.l.b}, \qquad CD_{S.ip.l} = \sum_{b=1}^{B} CD_{S.ip.l.b},$$

$$RD_{S.ip.l} = \sum_{b=1}^{B} D_{S.ip.l.b} = OD_{S.ip.l} + CD_{S.ip.l}, \qquad HD_{S.ip.l} = \sum_{b=1}^{B} HD_{S.ip.l.b},$$

$$LD_{S.ip.l} = \sum_{b=1}^{B} LD_{S.ip.l.b}, \; DA_{S.ip.l} = \sum_{b=1}^{B} DA_{S.ip.l.b},$$

here are:

$\mathbf{BD_{S.ip.l.b}}$ – it is the best density of the $\mathbf{F_{S.ip.l.b}}$ for the $\mathbf{P_{ip}}$ from b-th $\mathbf{CTP_{ip.l.b}}$ in **PRESENT**, which is determined from the condition of achieving his $\mathbf{A_{ip.l}}$, for example, by **the technology of Noologistics**;

$\mathbf{WD_{S.ip.l.b}}$ – it is the worst density of the $\mathbf{F_{S.ip.l.b}}$ for the $\mathbf{P_{ip}}$ from b-th $\mathbf{CTP_{ip.l.b}}$ in **PRESENT**, which is determined by the $\mathbf{RP_{ip.l}}$;

$\mathbf{OD_{S.ip.l.b}}$ – it is the actual density of the $\mathbf{F_{S.ip.l.b}}$ to the $\mathbf{OQ_{S.ip.l}}$, used in b-th $\mathbf{CTP_{ip.l.b}}$ in **PRESENT**, which is measured by the $\mathbf{RP_{ip.l}}$;

$\mathbf{CD_{S.ip.l.b}}$ – it is the actual density of the $\mathbf{F_{S.ip.l.b}}$ to the $\mathbf{CQ_{S.ip.l}}$, used in b-th $\mathbf{CTP_{ip.l.b}}$ in **PRESENT**, which is measured by the $\mathbf{RP_{ip.l}}$;

$\mathbf{D_{S.ip.l.b}}$ – it is the actual density of the $\mathbf{F_{S.ip.l.b}}$, used in b-th $\mathbf{CTP_{ip.l.b}}$ in **PRESENT**, which is measured by the $\mathbf{RP_{ip}}$;

$\mathbf{HD_{S.ip.l.b}}$ – it is highest density of the $\mathbf{F_{S.ip.l.b}}$, guaranteed for P_{ip} in P_{ih} in b-th $\mathbf{CTP_{ip.l.b}}$ in **PRESENT** on his status in the $\mathbf{P_{ih}}$, which is determined by the $\mathbf{RP_{ih.l}}$;

$\mathbf{LD_{S.ip.l.b}}$ – it is lowest density of the $\mathbf{F_{S.ip.l.b}}$, guaranteed for P_{ip} in P_{ih} in b-th $\mathbf{CTP_{ip.l.b}}$ in **PRESENT** on his status in the $\mathbf{P_{ih}}$, which is determined by the $\mathbf{RP_{ih.l}}$;

$\mathbf{DA_{S.ip.l.b}}$ – it is density of the $\mathbf{F_{S.ip.l.b}}$ from b-th $\mathbf{CTP_{ip.l.b}}$ in **PRESENT**, which is determined from the condition of achieving his $\mathbf{A_{ih.l}}$, for example, by **the technology of Noologistics**;

the rest – see above.

Calculation of magnitude $\mathbf{DU_{S.ip.l}}$ for each $\mathbf{V_{S.ip.h}}$ is performed according to a standard formula, for example:

$$DU_{S.ip.l} = \frac{QA_{ip.h}}{\sum_{b=1}^{B} \int_{t_н}^{t} DA_{S.ip.l.b}(t) * dt},$$

in which all conditional designations – see above.

The structure information is shown in Fig. P 7, which follows from the formal description, entitled "**Noologistical provision the $\mathbf{P_{ip}}$'s existence (life support)**".

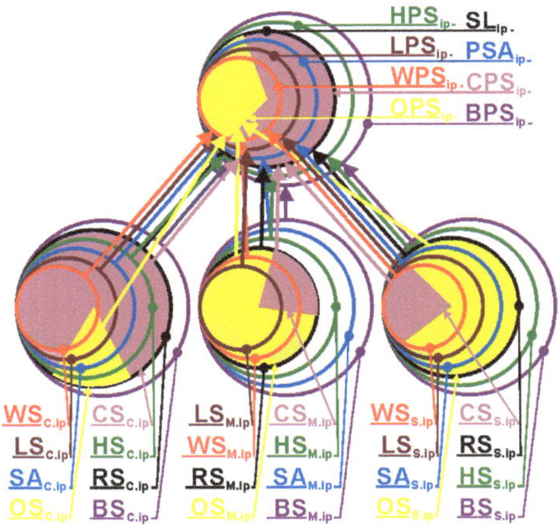

Fig. P 7

The conditional designation on the Fig. P 7:

$\mathbf{BPS_{ip}}$ – it is the best **noologistical provision the existence (life support)** for the $\mathbf{P_{ip}}$ that is the set of $\mathbf{BS_{C.ip}}$, $\mathbf{BS_{M.ip}}$ and $\mathbf{BS_{S.ip}}$;

$\mathbf{WPS_{ip}}$ – it is the worst **noologistical provision the existence (life support)** for the $\mathbf{P_{ip}}$ that is the set of the $\mathbf{WS_{C.ip}}$, $\mathbf{WS_{M.ip}}$ and $\mathbf{WS_{S.ip}}$;

$\mathbf{OPS_{ip}}$ – it is the actual **noologistical provision the existence (life support)** of the $\mathbf{P_{ip}}$ on base of his own $\mathbf{Q_{ip.l}}$, that is the set of the $\mathbf{OS_{C.ip}}$, $\mathbf{OS_{M.ip}}$ and $\mathbf{OS_{S.ip}}$;

CPS_{ip} – it is the actual **noologistical provision the existence** (**life support**) of the the **P_{ip}** on base of common **$Q_{ih.l}$**, that is the set **$CS_{C.ip}$**, **$CS_{M.ip}$** and **$CS_{S.ip}$**;

SP_{ip} – it is the actual total **noologistical provision the existence** (**life support**) of the the **P_{ip}**, that is the sum of the **OPS_{ip}** and **CPS_{ip}** and is the sum of the **$RS_{C.ip}$**, **$RS_{M.ip}$** and **$RS_{S.ip}$** also;

PS_{ip} – it is highest **noologistical provision the existence** (**life support**) of the the **P_{ip}**, guaranteed for P_{ip} in P_{ih} on his **status** in the **P_{ih}**, guaranteed for him in P_{ih}, that is the sum of the **$HS_{C.ip}$**, **$HS_{M.ip}$** and **$HS_{S.ip}$**;

LPS_{ip} – it is lowest **noologistical provision the existence** (**life support**) of the **P_{ip}**, guaranteed for P_{ip} in P_{ih} on his **status** in the **P_{ih}**, guaranteed for him in P_{ih}, that is the sum of the **$LS_{C.ip}$**, **$LS_{M.ip}$** and **$LS_{S.ip}$**;

PSA_{ip} – it is **noologistical provision the existence** (**life support**) for the **P_{ip}**, corresponds to his **$A_{ih.l}$** on his **status** in the **P_{ih}**, that is the sum of **the $SA_{C.ip}$**, **$SA_{M.ip}$** and **$SA_{S.ip}$**;

arrows show the formation of **BPS_{ip}**, **WPS_{ip}**, **OPS_{ip}**, **CPS_{ip}**, **SP_{ip}**, **PS_{ip}**, **LPS_{ip}** and **$PSA_{S.ip}$** by union in correspond set of magnitudes of the **$BS_{C.ip}$**, **$BS_{M.ip}$**, **$BS_{S.ip}$**, **$WS_{C.ip}$**, **$WS_{M.ip}$**, **$WS_{S.ip}$**, **$OS_{C.ip}$**, **$OS_{M.ip}$**, **$OS_{S.ip}$**, **$CS_{C.ip}$**, **$CS_{M.ip}$**, **$CS_{S.ip}$**, **$RS_{C.ip}$**, **$RS_{M.ip}$**, **$RS_{S.ip}$**, **$HS_{C.ip}$**, **$HS_{M.ip}$**, **$HS_{S.ip}$**, **$LS_{C.ip}$**, **$LS_{M.ip}$**, **$LS_{S.ip}$**, **$SA_{C.ip}$**, **$SA_{M.ip}$** and **$SA_{S.ip}$**;

the rest – see above.

Formalized description of **the rules of P_{ip}** may contain the following information:

The P_{ip}'s rules (RP_{ip})

The content of the formalized description of "**the P_{ip}'s rules** " (briefly – **RP_{ip}**) reflects the meaning of the existence of the **P_{ip}** in **Ev** and is determined by a variety of well-defined, but constantly changing objective circumstances, which have parameters that may be measured and modified at will of the **P_{ip}**, as well as its **subjective principles** and **criteria of rationality** that articulate approaches to the search for the meaning of life **P_{ip}** in **Ev**. The ratio magnitude of **Sb** and **FI** to other **P_{ip}** and **P_{ih}**, which is reflected in the **RP_{ip}** on the one hand, is stored in his DNA (congenital), and, on the other hand, was changed under the influence of **Ev**, education and training. The some such specific, but constantly changing objective circumstances are listed below:

- the nomenclature of $\mathbf{N_{ip}}$ and their **priorities**;
- the rules of $\mathbf{P_{ih}}$, $\mathbf{P_{il}}$, $\mathbf{P_{iw}}$, $\mathbf{P_{ig}}$, etc. (briefly – $\mathbf{RP_{ih}}$, $\mathbf{RP_{il}}$, $\mathbf{RP_{iw}}$, $\mathbf{RP_{ig}}$, etc.);
- the work characteristics and current modes of operation of the technological equipment available to the $\mathbf{P_{ip}}$;
- the technologies available to the $\mathbf{P_{ip}}$;
- his economic possibilities;
- his economic interests;
- his cultural interests;
- its moral and ethical attitudes;
- the laws of nature and advanced technology known to him;
- the situation in **Ev**, the nature and intensity of his impacts to it;
- the magnitudes of his **Sb** and **Fl** to other $\mathbf{P_{ip}}$, $\mathbf{P_{ih}}$, $\mathbf{P_{iw}}$, $\mathbf{P_{ig}}$, etc.;
- his previous experience;
- his forecast for the development of the current situation in **Ev** and of the relations to other $\mathbf{P_{ip}}$, $\mathbf{P_{ih}}$, $\mathbf{P_{iw}}$, $\mathbf{P_{ig}}$, etc. in **FUTURE**;
- the need for control of current parameters characterizing the object $\mathbf{Ot_{ip}}$;
- his submission on **the criteria of reasonableness** to all of the above;
- his **principles**, etc.

The letter **R** with a subscript that contains the identification number "ir" (briefly – $\mathbf{R_{ir}}$) is applied to identify a single specific regulations as shown below. All regulations are combined into one unified description for each $\mathbf{P_{ip}}$, that marked as $\mathbf{RP_{ip}}$ and contains:

- The name of the $\mathbf{RP_{ip}}$ and the name of $\mathbf{P_{ip}}$ for which to apply these rules, his **ip** and the conditional designation;
- Sections of the $\mathbf{RP_{ip}}$: $\mathbf{RP_{ip.v}}$, $\mathbf{RP_{ip.c}}$, $\mathbf{RP_{ip.h}}$ and $\mathbf{RP_{ip.l}}$ or $\mathbf{RP_{1.ip}}$ ($\mathbf{RP_{1.ip.v}}$, $\mathbf{RP_{1.ip.c}}$, $\mathbf{RP_{1.ip.h}}$ and $\mathbf{RP_{1.ip.l}}$) and $\mathbf{RP_2}$ ($\mathbf{RP_{2.ip.v}}$, $\mathbf{RP_{2.ip.c}}$, $\mathbf{RP_{2.ip.h}}$ and $\mathbf{RP_{2.ip.l}}$);
- Nomenclature of the $\mathbf{R_{ir}}$, that consisting of their names, their **ir** and conditional designations;
- His **Sb** and **Fl** to other $\mathbf{P_{ip}}$, $\mathbf{P_{ih}}$, $\mathbf{P_{iw}}$, $\mathbf{P_{ig}}$, etc.;
- Requisites of all formalized descriptions used in **Noologistics**;
- The originator of every description, storage, providing of the information contained therein;

- Description of mathematical apparatus and algorithm of calculation of each parameter represented into each formalized description;
- The scale of the importance of the $\mathbf{N_{ip}}$ (the sequence of their satisfaction), etc.

An example of a formalized description of the subjectivity $\mathbf{P_{ih}}$ is presented below.

A universal image pyramid, which is shown in Fig. P 8, is used to formalize the structure of any $\mathbf{P_{ih}}$ in **Noologistics**.

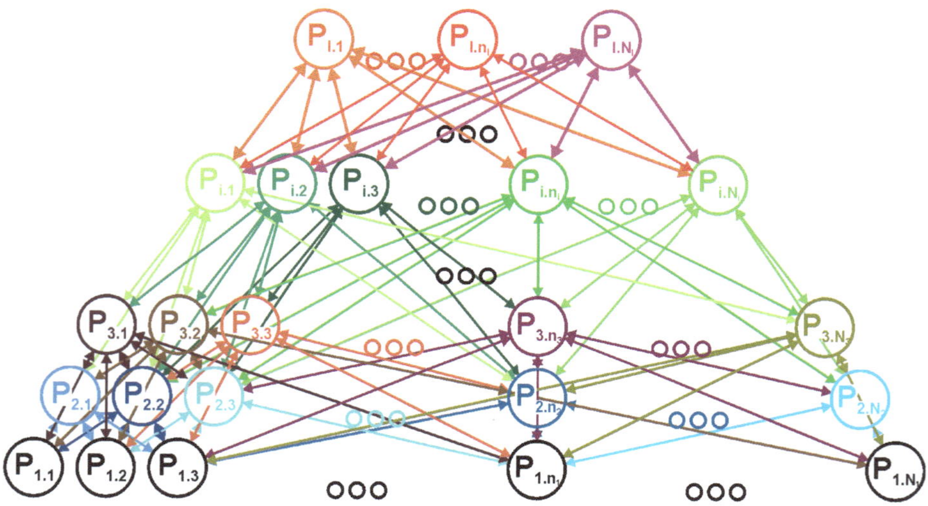

Fig. P 8

The conditional designation on the Fig. P 8:

$\mathbf{P_{1.1}}$, $\mathbf{P_{1.2}}$, $\mathbf{P_{1.3}}$, ..., $\mathbf{P_{i.ni}}$, ..., $\mathbf{P_{I.NI}}$ – it are the persons of P_{ih}, which may be as described above $\mathbf{P_{ip}}$, and the other $\mathbf{P_{ih}}$;

I – it is the number of top-level of $\mathbf{P_{ih}}$ equal to the quantity of levels in it;

i = 1, 2, 3, ..., **I** – it is the identification number of the level of $\mathbf{P_{ih}}$;

N_i – it is the total quantity of $\mathbf{P_{i.n}}$ in the i-th level of $\mathbf{P_{ih}}$;

n_i = 1, 2, 3, ..., N_i – it is the identification number of $\mathbf{P_{i.n}}$, located in the i-th level of $\mathbf{P_{ih}}$, associated to his **ip** and other **signs of subjectivity** described above;

if $N_l > 1$ at the topmost level, the highest governing body of $\mathbf{P_{ih}}$ is collegial;

if $N_l = 1$ at the topmost level, the highest governing body of $\mathbf{P_{ih}}$ is sole;

the rest – see above.

Structures of $\mathbf{Ev_{ih}}$, $\mathbf{PH_{ih.v}}$, $\mathbf{PH_{ih.c}}$, $\mathbf{PH_{ih.h}}$ and $\mathbf{PH_{ih.l}}$, which follow from the above descriptions and definitions, are shown in Fig. P 9.

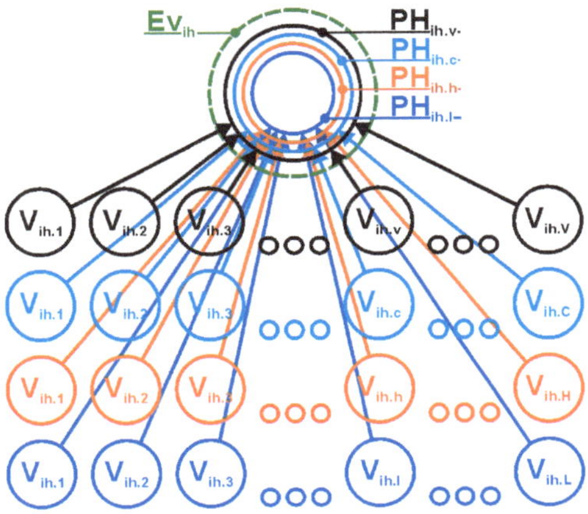

Fig. P 9

The conditional designation on the Fig. P 9:

$\mathbf{Ev_{ih}}$ – it is environment of the $\mathbf{P_{ih}}$;

arrows show the formation of $\mathbf{PH_{ih.v}}$, $\mathbf{PH_{ih.c}}$, $\mathbf{PH_{ih.h}}$ and $\mathbf{PH_{ih.l}}$ from, respectively, the $\mathbf{V_{ih.v}}$, $\mathbf{V_{ih.c}}$, $\mathbf{V_{ih.h}}$ and $\mathbf{V_{ih.l}}$;

the rest – see above.

Signs of $\mathbf{P_{ih}}$**'s subjectivity** in **Noologistics** may be represented by a database containing interrelated by ih formalized descriptions of the characteristics of subjectivity of $\mathbf{P_{ih}}$, including:

Requisites of $\mathbf{P_{ih}}$;
Noo habitat of $\mathbf{P_{ih}}$ (briefly – $\mathbf{PH_{ih.v}}$);
Current noo habitat of $\mathbf{P_{ih}}$ (briefly – $\mathbf{PH_{ih.c}}$);
Noologistical habitat of $\mathbf{P_{ih}}$ (briefly – $\mathbf{PH_{ih.h}}$);
Current noologistical habitat of $\mathbf{P_{ih}}$ (briefly – $\mathbf{PH_{ih.l}}$);

Noo provision the P_{ih}'s existence (life support) (briefly – **$SP_{ih.c}$**);

Noological provision the P_{ih}'s existence (life support) (briefly – **$SP_{ih.l}$**);

The P_{ih}'s rules (briefly – **RP_{ih}**);

The P_{ih}'s goal (briefly – **A_{ih}**);

The P_{ih}'s object (briefly – **Ot_{ih}**);

The P_{ih}'s technological process (briefly – **TP_{ih}**).

The formalized description of the requisites of the **P_{ih}** may to contain the following information:

Requisites of P_{ih}

The description contains:

The name and identification number of the **P_{ih}**, for example, **ih**;

E-mail and other addresses of the **P_{ih}**;

Bank requisites of the **P_{ih}**;

Taxpayer identification number (TIN) of the **P_{ih}**;

The location of the **P_{ih}** in **Ev_{ih}**, for example, the current coordinates of its location in the geo information system;

Nomenclature of hierarchies **P_{ip}** (**P_{il}**, **P_{iw}**, **P_{ib}**, **P_{ig}**, **P_{im}**, etc.), which contains a list of the names of those hierarchies, in which is **P_{ih}**, and their identification numbers, for example, iw, il, ig, im, etc.;

Its **Sb** and **Fl** to other **P_{ip}**, **P_{ih}**, **P_{il}**, **P_{iw}**, **P_{ib}**, **P_{ig}**, **P_{im}**, etc. in each **hierarchy**;

A link to the description of **Noo habitat of P_{ih}** (**$PH_{ih.v}$**), see below;

A link to the description of **Current noo habitat of P_{ih}** (**$PH_{ih.c}$**), see below;

A link to the description of **Noological habitat of P_{ih}** (**$PH_{ih.h}$**), see below;

A link to the description of **Current noological habitat of P_{ih}** (**$PH_{ih.l}$**), see below;

A link to the description of **Noo provision the P_{ih}'s existence (life support)** (**$SP_{ih.c}$**), see below;

A link to the description of **Noological provision the P_{ih}'s existence (life support)** (**$SP_{ih.l}$**), see below;

A link to the description of **The P_{ih}'s rules** (**RP_{ih}**), see below;

A link to the description of **The P_{ih}'s goal** (**A_{ih}**), see below;

A link to the description of **The P_{ih}'s object** (Ot_{ih}), see below;

A link to the description of **The P_{ih}'s technological process (TP_{ih})**, see below, etc.

Formalized description of **the noo habitat of P_{ih}** may contain the following information:

Noo habitat of P_{ih} ($PH_{ih.v}$)

The description contains:

The name «**Noo habitat of P_{ih}**» and identification number of the P_{ih}, for example, **ih**;

Nomenclature all of $V_{ih.v}$, between them:

v = 1, 2, 3, ..., V – it is an individual identification number of its registration into **a formalized description of the environment**;

The list of $V_{ih.v}$ names and its conditional designations ($V_{ih.v}$);

Description of the contents of each $V_{ih.v}$;

Indication of $N_{C.ih}$, $N_{M.ih}$ and $N_{S.ih}$, which satisfies the corresponding $V_{ih.v}$;

The scale of priorities the $N_{C.ih}$, $N_{M.ih}$ and $N_{S.ih}$;

The scale of importance the $V_{ih.v}$, etc.

Formalized description of **the current noo habitat of P_{ih}** may contain the following information:

Current noo habitat of P_{ih} ($PH_{ih.c}$)

The description contains:

The name «**Current noo habitat of P_{ih}**» and identification number of the P_{ih}, for example, **ih**;

Nomenclature all of $V_{ih.c}$, between them:

c = 1, 2, 3, ..., C – it is an individual identification number of its registration into **a formalized description of the environment**;

The list of $V_{ih.c}$ names and its conditional designations ($V_{ih.c}$);

Description of the contents of each $V_{ih.c}$;

Indication of $\mathbf{N_{C.ih}}$, $\mathbf{N_{M.ih}}$ and $\mathbf{N_{S.ih}}$, which satisfies the corresponding $\mathbf{V_{ih.c}}$;

The scale of priorities the $\mathbf{N_{C.ih}}$, $\mathbf{N_{M.ih}}$ and $\mathbf{N_{S.ih}}$;

The scale of importance the $\mathbf{V_{ih.c}}$, etc.

Formalized description of **the noological habitat of $\mathbf{P_{ih}}$** may contain the following information:

Noologistical habitat of $\mathbf{P_{ih}}$ ($\mathbf{PH_{ih.h}}$)

The description contains:

The name «**Noologistical habitat of $\mathbf{P_{ih}}$**» and identification number of the $\mathbf{P_{ih}}$, for example, **ih**;

Nomenclature all of $\mathbf{V_{ih.h}}$, between them:

h = 1, 2, 3, ..., H – it is an individual identification number of its registration into **a formalized description of the environment**;

The list of $\mathbf{V_{ih.h}}$ names and its conditional designations ($\mathbf{V_{ih.h}}$);

Description of the contents of each $\mathbf{V_{ih.h}}$, between them:

Unit of measurement the quantity of the $\mathbf{Q_{ih.h}}$, the best magnitude of the $\mathbf{Q_{ih.h}}$ for the $\mathbf{P_{ih}}$, i. e. corresponding to his **goal** $\mathbf{A_{ih.h}}$ (briefly – $\mathbf{BQ_{ih.h}}$), the worst magnitude of the $\mathbf{Q_{ih.h}}$ (briefly – $\mathbf{WQ_{ih.h}}$), the P_{ih}'s actual own magnitude of the $\mathbf{Q_{ih.h}}$ (briefly – $\mathbf{OQ_{ih.h}}$), the part of common $\mathbf{Q_{iw.h}}$ in P_{ih}'s using (briefly – $\mathbf{CQ_{ih.h}}$), the P_{ih}'s actual $\mathbf{Q_{ih.h}}$ (briefly – $\mathbf{RQ_{ih.h}}$), equal to the sum $\mathbf{OQ_{ih.h}}$ and $\mathbf{CQ_{ih.h}}$, the highest $\mathbf{Q_{ip.h}}$ guaranteed for P_{ih} in P_{iw} (briefly – $\mathbf{HQ_{ih.h}}$) on his status in the $\mathbf{P_{iw}}$, the lowest $\mathbf{Q_{iw.h}}$ guaranteed for P_{ih} in P_{iw} (briefly – $\mathbf{LQ_{ih.h}}$) on his status in the $\mathbf{P_{iw}}$, the magnitude of the $\mathbf{Q_{iw.h}}$ corresponds to $\mathbf{A_{iw.h}}$ (briefly – $\mathbf{QA_{ih.h}}$) on his status in the $\mathbf{P_{iw}}$, the projected duration of $\mathbf{V_{ih.h}}$'s **u**se (briefly – $\mathbf{DU}_{ih.h}$) in **FUTURE**, etc.;

The locations (briefly – $\mathbf{LV_C}$, $\mathbf{LV_M}$ and $\mathbf{LV_S}$) and allocations (briefly – $\mathbf{AV_C}$, $\mathbf{AV_M}$ and $\mathbf{AV_S}$) each of the $\mathbf{Q_{ih.h}}$ in the $\mathbf{Ev_{ih}}$, for example, by the coordinates of the geo information system;

The nomenclature of parameters that characterize the quality (briefly – $\mathbf{QP_C}$, $\mathbf{QP_M}$ and $\mathbf{QP_S}$) each of the $\mathbf{V_{ih.h}}$;

Units of measurement and numerical magnitudes of the parameters that characterize the quality each of the $\mathbf{V_{ip.l}}$ (briefly – $\mathbf{QP_C}$, $\mathbf{QP_M}$ and $\mathbf{QP_S}$), etc.

Each $\mathbf{P_{ih}}$ performs a formal description by the his own rules, on the basis of $A_{ih.l}$ of his existence in $\mathbf{Ev_{ih}}$ and of analysis the current situation in it.

The structure information is shown in Fig. P 10, which follows from the formal description, entitled "**Noological habitat of** $\mathbf{P_{ih}}$".

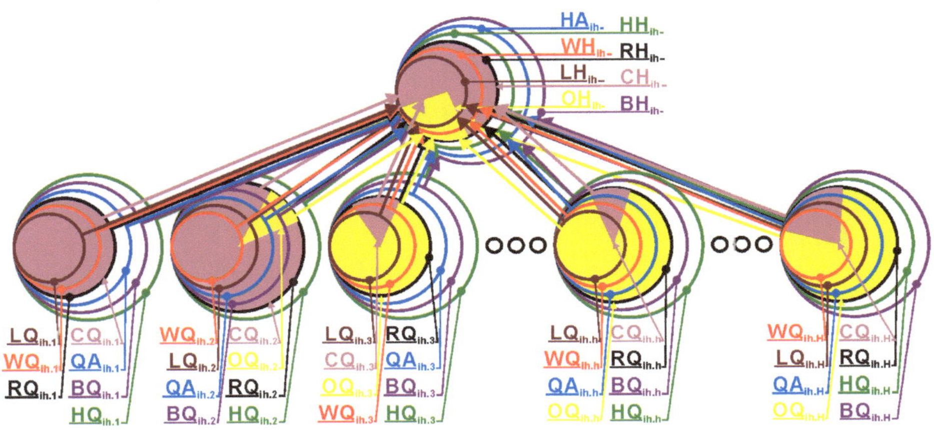

Fig. P 10

The conditional designation on the Fig. P 10:

$\mathbf{BH_{ih}}$ – it is the best **noological habitat for the** $\mathbf{P_{ih}}$, that is the set of the $\mathbf{BQ_{ih.h}}$, corresponds to his $\mathbf{A_{ih.h}}$;

$\mathbf{WH_{ih}}$ – it is the worst **noological habitat for the** $\mathbf{P_{ih}}$, that is the set of the $\mathbf{WQ_{ih.h}}$;

$\mathbf{OH_{ih}}$ – it is $\mathbf{P_{ih}}$'s private part of the $\mathbf{PH_{ih.h}}$, that is the set of the $\mathbf{OQ_{ih.h}}$;

$\mathbf{CH_{ih}}$ – it is the common part of the $\mathbf{PH_{ih.h}}$ in P_{ih}'s using, that is the set of the $\mathbf{CQ_{ih.h}}$;

$\mathbf{RH_{ih}}$ – it is the whole actual **noological habitat** of the $\mathbf{P_{ih}}$, that is the sum of the $\mathbf{OH_{ih}}$ and $\mathbf{CH_{ih}}$, and is the set of the $\mathbf{RQ_{ih.h}}$ also;

HH_{ih} – it is the highest **noologistical habitat for the P_{ih}**, guaranteed to him in the **P_{iw}** on his status in the **P_{iw}**, that is the set of the **$HQ_{ih.h}$**;

LH_{ih} – it is lowest **noologistical habitat for the P_{ih}**, guaranteed to him in the **P_{iw}** on his status in the **P_{iw}**, that is the set of the **$LQ_{ih.h}$**;

HA_{ih} – it is the **noologistical habitat of the P_{ih}**, corresponds to **A_{iw}** on his status in the **P_{iw}**, that is the set of the **$QA_{ih.h}$**;

arrows show the formation of **BH_{ih}**, **WH_{ih}**, **$OH_{ih.h}$**, **CH_{ih}**, **RH_{ih}**, **HH_{ih}**, **LH_{ih}** and **HA_{ih}** by union in correspond set of magnitudes of the **$BQ_{ih.h}$**, **$WQ_{ih.h}$**, **$OQ_{ih.h}$**, **$CQ_{ih.h}$**, **$RQ_{ih.h}$**, **$HQ_{ih.h}$**, **$LQ_{ih.h}$** and **$QA_{ih.h}$**;

the rest – see above.

Calculation of magnitudes **$RQ_{ih.h}$** for b-th **technology processes** (**$TP_{ih.b}$**) that were completed in **the PAST** is performed according to a standard formula, for example:

$$\mathbf{RQ_{ih.h}} = \mathbf{Q_{ih.h}} - \sum_{b=1}^{B}\int_{t_н}^{t_к} D_{C.ih.h.b}(t)*dt + \sum_{b=1}^{B}\int_{t_н}^{t_к} D_{M.ih.h.b}(t)*dt - \sum_{b=1}^{B}\int_{t_н}^{t_к} D_{S.ih.h.b}(t)*dt\ ,$$

here are:

$Q_{ih.h}$ – it is actual quantity of the **$V_{ih.h}$**, is used by **P_{ih}** on start of completed **$TP_{ih.b}$**, that was calculated by the rules of **$RP_{ih.h}$**;

t – it is current time of **$TP_{ih.b}$**, measured according to the **$RP_{ih.h}$**, for example, according to the testimony of standard time;

$t_Н$ – it is current time at the beginning of the completed period of the **$TP_{ih.b}$**;

$t_К$ – it is current time at the end of the counting of completed period the **$TP_{ih.b}$**;

b = 1, 2, 3, ..., B – it is identification number of completed or not completed the **$TP_{ih.b}$**;

$D_{C.ih.h.b}$ – it is actual density of consumption flow of **$V_{ih.h}$** (**$F_{C.ih.h.b}$**), which was been measured during the **$TP_{ih.b}$** by **the rules** of the **$RP_{ih.h}$**;

$D_{M.ih.h.b}$ – it is actual density of creation flow of **$V_{ih.h}$** (**$F_{M.ih.h.b}$**), which was been measured during the **$TP_{ih.b}$** by **the rules** of the **$RP_{ih.h}$**;

D$_{S.ih.h.b}$ – it is actual density of rejection flow of **V**$_{ih.h}$ (**F**$_{S.ih.h.b}$), which was been measured during the **TP**$_{ih.b}$ by **the rules** of the **RP**$_{ih.h}$;

the rest – see above.

Calculation of magnitudes **BQ**$_{ih.h}$ and **QA**$_{ih.h}$ for b-th technology processes (**TP**$_{ih.b}$) that were completed in **the PAST** is performed according to a standard formulas, for example:

$$\mathbf{BQ}_{ih.h} = \mathbf{Q}_{ih.h} - \sum_{b=1}^{B}\int_{t_н}^{t_к} BD_{C.ih.h.b}(t) * dt + \sum_{b=1}^{B}\int_{t_н}^{t_к} BD_{M.ih.h.b}(t) * dt - \sum_{b=1}^{B}\int_{t_н}^{t_к} BD_{S.ih.h.b}(t) * dt ,$$

here are:

BD$_{C.ih.h.b}$ – it is the best density of **F**$_{C.ih.h.b}$ for **P**$_{ih}$, which was determined during the **TP**$_{ih.b}$ by **the rules** of the **RP**$_{ih.h}$, for example, by **the technology of Noologistics**;

BD$_{M.ih.h.b}$ – it is the best density of **F**$_{M.ih.h.b}$ for **P**$_{ih}$, which was determined during the **TP**$_{ih.b}$ by **the rules** of the **RP**$_{ih.h}$, for example, by **the technology of Noologistics**;

BD$_{S.ih.h.b}$ – it is the best density of **F**$_{S.ih.h.b}$ for **P**$_{ih}$, which was determined during the **TP**$_{ih.b}$ by **the rules** of the **RP**$_{ih.h}$, for example, by **the technology of Noologistics**;

the rest – see above.

$$\mathbf{QA}_{ih.h} = \mathbf{Q}_{ih.h} - \sum_{b=1}^{B}\int_{t_н}^{t_к} DA_{C.ih.h.b}(t) * dt + \sum_{b=1}^{B}\int_{t_н}^{t_к} DA_{M.ih.h.b}(t) * dt - \sum_{b=1}^{B}\int_{t_н}^{t_к} DA_{S.ih.h.b}(t) * dt ,$$

here are:

DA$_{C.ih.h.b}$ – it is the density of **F**$_{C.ih.h.b}$, which was calculated during the **TP**$_{ih.b}$ according to the **RP**$_{iw.h}$ under condition to achievement the **A**$_{iw.h}$, for example, by **the technology of Noologistics**;

$DA_{M.ih.h.b}$ – it is the density of **$F_{M.ih.h.b}$**, which was calculated during the **$TP_{ih.b}$** according to the **$RP_{iw.h}$** under condition to achievement the **$A_{iw.h}$**, for example, by **the technology of Noologistics**;

$DA_{S.ih.h.b}$ – it is the density of **$F_{S.ih.h.b}$**, which was calculated during the **$TP_{ih.b}$** according to the **$RP_{iw.h}$** under condition to achievement the **$A_{iw.h}$**, for example, by **the technology of Noologistics**;

the rest – see above.

Calculation of magnitudes **$WQ_{ih.h}$**, **$OQ_{ih.h}$**, **$CQ_{ih.h}$**, **$HQ_{ih.h}$** and **$LQ_{ih.h}$** for b-th **technology processes** (**$TP_{ih.b}$**) that were completed in **the PAST** is performed according to a **$RP_{ih.h}$** and **$RP_{iw.h}$**.

Calculation of magnitudes **$RQ_{ih.h}$** for b-th **current technology processes $CTP_{ih.l.b}$** that were not completed in **PRESENT** and are selected below to second version of the formalized description under the name of the "**Current noo habitat of P_{ih}**" under the symbols **$RQ_{ih.l}$**, is performed according to a standard formula, for example:

$$RQ_{ih.h} = RQ_{ih.l} = Q_{ih.l} - \sum_{b=1}^{B}\int_{t_н}^{t} D_{C.ih.l.b}(t)*dt + \sum_{b=1}^{B}\int_{t_н}^{t} D_{M.ih.l.b}(t)*dt - \sum_{b=1}^{B}\int_{t_н}^{t} D_{S.ih.l.b}(t)*dt,$$

here are:

$Q_{ih.l}$ – it is actual quantity of **$V_{ih.l}$** was used by the **P_{ih}** in the beginning of the **$CTP_{ih.l.b}$**, that was calculated by the **$RP_{ih.l}$**;

$D_{C.ih.l.b}$ – it is actual density of current consumption flow of **$V_{ih.l}$** (**$F_{C.ih.l.b}$**), that is measuring in **PRESENT** in the в b-th **$CTP_{ih.l.b}$** by the **$RP_{ih.l}$**;

$D_{M.ih.l.b}$ – it is actual density of current creation flow of **$V_{ih.l}$** (**$F_{M.ih.l.b}$**), that is measuring in **PRESENT** in the в b-th **$CTP_{ih.l.b}$** by the **$RP_{ih.l}$**;

$D_{S.ih.l.b}$ – it is actual density of current rejection flow of **$V_{ih.l}$** (**$F_{S.ih.l.b}$**), that is measuring in **PRESENT** in the в b-th **$CTP_{ih.l.b}$** by the **$RP_{ih.l}$**;

the rest – see above.

Calculation of magnitudes $\mathbf{BQ_{ih.l}}$ and $\mathbf{QA_{ih.l}}$ for b-th **current technology processes** $\mathbf{CTP_{ih.l.b}}$ that were not completed in **the PRESENT** is performed according to a standard formulas, for example:

$$\mathbf{BQ_{ih.l}} = \mathbf{Q_{ih.l}} - \sum_{b=1}^{B}\int_{t_н}^{t} BD_{C.ih.l.b}(t)*dt + \sum_{b=1}^{B}\int_{t_н}^{t} BD_{M.ih.l.b}(t)*dt - \sum_{b=1}^{B}\int_{t_н}^{t} BD_{S.ih.l.b}(t)*dt,$$

here are:

$\mathbf{BD_{C.ih.l.b}}$ – it is the best density of $\mathbf{F_{C.ih.l.b}}$ for $\mathbf{P_{ih}}$, which is determining during the $\mathbf{CTP_{ih.l.b}}$ by **the** $\mathbf{RP_{iw.l}}$, for example, by **the technology of Noologistics;**

$\mathbf{BD_{M.ih.l.b}}$ – it is the best density of $\mathbf{F_{M.ih.l.b}}$ for $\mathbf{P_{ih}}$, which is determining during the $\mathbf{CTP_{ih.l.b}}$ by **the** $\mathbf{RP_{iw.l}}$, for example, by **the technology of Noologistics;**

$\mathbf{BD_{S.ih.l.b}}$ – it is the best density of $\mathbf{F_{S.ih.l.b}}$ for $\mathbf{P_{ih}}$, which is determining during the $\mathbf{CTP_{ih.l.b}}$ by **the** $\mathbf{RP_{iw.l}}$, for example, by **the technology of Noologistics;**

the rest – see above.

$$\mathbf{QA_{ih.l}} = \mathbf{Q_{ih.l}} - \sum_{b=1}^{B}\int_{t_н}^{t} DA_{C.ih.l.b}(t)*dt + \sum_{b=1}^{B}\int_{t_н}^{t} DA_{M.ih.l.b}(t)*dt - \sum_{b=1}^{B}\int_{t_н}^{t} DA_{S.ih.l.b}(t)*dt,$$

here are:

$\mathbf{DA_{C.ih.l.b}}$ – it is the density of $\mathbf{F_{C.ih.l.b}}$, which is determining during the $\mathbf{CTP_{ih.l.b}}$ in **the PRESENT** under condition to achievement the $\mathbf{A_{iw.l}}$ by **the** $\mathbf{RP_{iw.l}}$, for example, by **the technology of Noologistics**;

$\mathbf{DA_{M.ih.l.b}}$ – it is the density of $\mathbf{F_{M.ih.l.b}}$, which is determining during the $\mathbf{CTP_{ih.l.b}}$ in **the PRESENT** under condition to achievement the $\mathbf{A_{iw.l}}$ by **the** $\mathbf{RP_{iw.l}}$, for example, by **the technology of Noologistics**;

$DA_{S.ih.l.b}$ – it is the density of **$F_{S.ih.l.b}$**, which is determining during the **$CTP_{ih.l.b}$** in **the PRESENT** under condition to achievement the **$A_{iw.l}$** by **the $RP_{iw.l}$**, for example, by **the technology of Noologistics**;

the rest – see above.

Calculation of magnitude **$DU_{ih.h}$** for each **$V_{ih.h}$** is performed according to a standard formula, for example:

$DU_{ih.h} = DU_{C.ih.l}$, $DU_{ih.h} = DU_{M.ih.l}$ or **$DU_{ih.h} = DU_{S.ih.l}$**,

in which conditional designations **$DU_{C.ih.l}$**, **$DU_{M.ih.l}$** and **$DU_{S.ih.l}$** – see below.

Calculation of magnitudes $WQ_{ih.l}$, $OQ_{ih.l}$, $CQ_{ih.l}$, $HQ_{ih.l}$ and $LQ_{ih.l}$ is performed in **the PRESENT** according to a RP_{ih} and RP_{iw}.

The formalized description of **the current noological habitat of P_{ih}** may contain the following information:

Current noological habitat of P_{ih} ($PH_{ih.l}$)

The description contains:

The name «**Current noological habitat of P_{ih}**» and identification number of the **P_{ih}**, for example, **ih**;

Nomenclature all of **$V_{ih.l}$**, between them:

l = 1, 2, 3, ..., L – it is an individual identification number of its registration into **a formalized description of the environment**;

The list of **$V_{ih.l}$** names and its conditional designations (**$V_{ih.l}$**);

Description of the contents of each **$V_{ih.l}$**, between them:

Unit of measurement the quantity of the **$Q_{ih.l}$**, the best magnitude of the **$Q_{ih.l}$** for the **P_{ih}**, i. e. corresponding to his **goal $A_{ih.l}$** (briefly – **$BQ_{ih.l}$**), the worst magnitude of the **$Q_{ih.l}$** (briefly – **$WQ_{ih.l}$**), the P_{ih}'s actual own magnitude of **$Q_{ih.l}$** (briefly – **$OQ_{ih.l}$**), the part of common **$Q_{iw.l}$** in P_{ih}'s using (briefly – **$CQ_{ih.l}$**), the P_{ih}'s actual **$Q_{ih.l}$** (briefly – **$RQ_{ih.l}$**), equal to the sum **$OQ_{ih.l}$** and **$CQ_{ih.l}$**, the highest **$Q_{ip.l}$** guaranteed for P_{ih} in P_{iw} (briefly – **$HQ_{ih.l}$**) on his status in the **P_{iw}**, the lowest **$Q_{iw.l}$**

guaranteed for P_{ih} in P_{iw} (briefly – $\mathbf{LQ_{ih.l}}$) on his status in the $\mathbf{P_{iw}}$, the magnitude of the $\mathbf{Q_{iw.l}}$ corresponds to $\mathbf{A_{iw.l}}$ (briefly – $\mathbf{QA_{ih.l}}$) on his status in the $\mathbf{P_{iw}}$, etc.;

The locations (briefly – $\mathbf{LV_C}$, $\mathbf{LV_M}$ and $\mathbf{LV_S}$) and allocations (briefly – $\mathbf{AV_C}$, $\mathbf{AV_M}$ and $\mathbf{AV_S}$) each of the $\mathbf{Q_{ih.l}}$ in the $\mathbf{Ev_{ih}}$, for example, by the coordinates of the geo information system;

The nomenclature of parameters that characterize the quality (briefly – $\mathbf{QP_C}$, $\mathbf{QP_M}$ and $\mathbf{QP_S}$) each of the $\mathbf{V_{ih.l}}$;

Units of measurement and numerical magnitudes of the parameters that characterize the quality each of the $\mathbf{V_{ih.l}}$ (briefly – $\mathbf{QP_C}$, $\mathbf{QP_M}$ and $\mathbf{QP_S}$), etc.

Each $\mathbf{P_{ih}}$ performs a formal description by the his own rules, on the basis of $\mathbf{A_{ih.l}}$ of his existence in $\mathbf{Ev_{ih}}$ and of analysis the current situation in it.

The structure information is shown in Fig. P 11, which follows from the formal description, entitled "**Current noologistical habitat of** $\mathbf{P_{ih}}$".

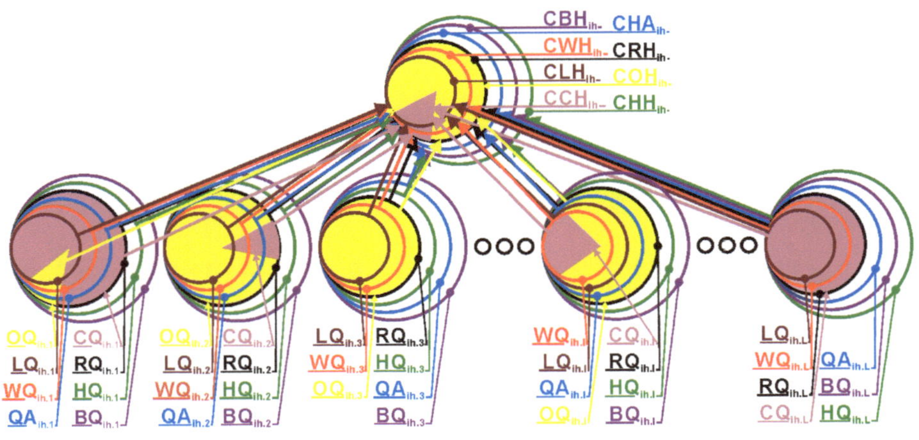

Fig. P 11

The conditional designation on the Fig. P 11:

$\mathbf{CBH_{ih}}$ – it is the best **current noologistical habitat for the** $\mathbf{P_{ih}}$, that is the set of the $\mathbf{BQ_{ih.l}}$, corresponds to his $\mathbf{A_{ih.l}}$;

CWH_{ih} – it is it is the worst **current noologistical habitat for the P_{ih}**, that is the set of the **$WQ_{ih.l}$**;

COH_{ih} – it is **P_{ih}**'s private part of the **$PH_{ih.l}$**, that is the set of the **$OQ_{ih.l}$**;

CCH_{ih} – it is the common part of the **$PH_{ih.l}$** in P_{ih}'s using, that is the set of the **$CQ_{ih.l}$**;

CRH_{ih} – it is the whole actual **current noologistical habitat** of the **P_{ih}**, that is the sum of the **COH_{ih}** and **CCH_{ih}**, and is the set of the **$RQ_{ih.l}$** also;

$CHH_{ih.l}$ – it is the highest **current noologistical habitat for the P_{ih}**, guaranteed to him in the **P_{iw}** on his status in the **P_{iw}**, that is the set of the **$HQ_{ih.l}$**;

CLH_{ih} – it is lowest **current noologistical habitat for the P_{ih}**, guaranteed to him in the **P_{iw}** on his status in the **P_{iw}**, that is the set of the **$LQ_{ih.l}$**;

CHA_{ih} – it is the **current noologistical habitat of the P_{ih}**, corresponds to **A_{iw}** on his status in the **P_{iw}**, that is the set of the **$QA_{ih.l}$**;

arrows show the formation of **CBH_{ih}**, **CWH_{ih}**, **COH_{ih}**, **CCH_{ih}**, **CRH_{ih}**, **CHH_{ih}**, **CLH_{ih}** and **CHA_{ih}** by union in correspond set of magnitudes of the **$BQ_{ih.l}$**, **$WQ_{ih.l}$**, **$OQ_{ih.l}$**, **$CQ_{ih.l}$**, **$RQ_{ih.l}$**, **$HQ_{ih.l}$**, **$LQ_{ih.l}$** and **$QA_{ih.l}$**;

the rest – see above.

Calculation of magnitudes **$BQ_{ih.l}$**, **$WQ_{ih.l}$**, **$OQ_{ih.l}$**, **$CQ_{ih.l}$**, **$RQ_{ih.l}$**, **$HQ_{ih.l}$**, **$LQ_{ih.l}$** and **$QA_{ih.l}$** is performed according to above given standard formulas, used in formalized description «**Noologistical habitat of P_{ih}**».

Formalized description of **the noo provision the existence** (**life support**) **of P_{ih}** may contain the following information:

Noo provision the P_{ih}'s **existence** (**life support**) (**$SP_{ih.c}$**)

The description may consist of three parts: «**Noo provision the P_{ih}**'s **existence** (**life support**) **by consumption of the** $V_{C.ih.c}$», «**Noo provision the P_{ih}**'s **existence** (**life support**) **by creation of the** $V_{M.ih.c}$» and «**Noo provision the P_{ih}**'s **existence** (**life support**) **by rejection of the** $V_{S.ih.c}$», that are put on display separately or together:

The first part of the description contains:

The name «**Noo provision the P_{ih}'s existence** (**life support**) **by consumption of the $V_{C.ih.c}$**», its conditional designation **$SP_{C.ih.c}$** and identification number of the **P_{ih}**, for example, **ih**;

Nomenclature all of **$F_{C.ih.c.b}$** from b-th **$CTP_{ih.c.b}$**, between them:

The list of **$F_{C.ih.c.b}$** names and its conditional designations (**$F_{C.ih.c.b}$**);

Identification number **«c»** each of the **$V_{C.ih.c}$**, that is the base of the correspond **$F_{C.ih.c.b}$** from **formalized description of the environment**;

Parameters each of **$F_{C.ih.c.b}$**, between them:

Unit of measurement the magnitude of **density the current consumption flow of $V_{C.ih.c}$** (briefly – **$D_{C.ih.c.b}$**) in the b-th **$CTP_{ih.c.b}$**, the best magnitude of the **current $D_{C.ih.c.b}$** for the **P_{ih}**, i. e. corresponding to his **goal $A_{ih.c}$** (briefly – **$BD_{C.ih.c.b}$**) – see above, the worst magnitude of the **current $D_{C.ih.c.b}$** for the **P_{ih}** (briefly – **$WD_{C.ih.c.b}$**), the P_{ih}'s actual own magnitude of the **current $D_{C.ih.c.b}$** from his own **$PH_{ih.c}$** (briefly – **$OD_{C.ih.c.b}$**), the actual magnitude of the **current $D_{C.ih.c.b}$** from common **$PH_{iw.c}$** (briefly – **$CD_{C.ih.c.b}$**), the actual magnitude of the **current $D_{C.ih.c.b}$** used by the **P_{ih}** (briefly – **$RD_{C.ih.c.b}$**), equal to the sum **$OD_{C.ih.c.b}$** and **$CD_{C.ih.c.b}$**, the highest magnitude of the **current $D_{C.ih.c.b}$**, guaranteed for P_{ih} in P_{iw} (briefly – **$HD_{C.ih.c.b}$**) on his status in the **P_{iw}**, the lowest magnitude of the **current $D_{C.ih.c.b}$**, guaranteed for P_{ih} in P_{iw} (briefly – **$LD_{C.ih.c.b}$**) on his status in the **P_{iw}**, the magnitude of the **current $D_{C.ih.c.b}$**, corresponds to **$A_{iw.c}$** (briefly – **$DA_{C.ih.c.b}$**) on his status in the **P_{iw}**, the projected duration each of **$V_{C.ih.c}$**'s **use** (briefly – **$DU_{C.ih.c}$**) in **FUTURE**, etc.

Link to the **$CTP_{ih.c.b}$**, in which the **$F_{C.ih.c.b}$** is used.

The second part of the description contains:

The name «**Noo provision the P_{ih}'s existence** (**life support**) **by creation of the $V_{M.ih.c}$**», its conditional designation **$SP_{M.ih.c}$** and identification number of the **P_{ih}**, for example, **ih**;

Nomenclature all of **$F_{M.ih.c.b}$** from b-th **$CTP_{ih.c.b}$**, between them:

The list of **$F_{M.ih.c.b}$** names and its conditional designations (**$F_{M.ih.c.b}$**);

Identification number **«c»** each of the $\mathbf{V_{M.ih.c}}$, that is the base of the correspond $\mathbf{F_{M.ih.c.b}}$ from **formalized description of the environment**;

Parameters each of $\mathbf{F_{M.ih.c.b}}$, between them:

Unit of measurement the magnitude of **density the current creation flow of** $\mathbf{V_{M.ih.c}}$ (briefly – $\mathbf{D_{M.ih.c.b}}$) in the b-th $\mathbf{CTP_{ih.c.b}}$, the best magnitude of the **current** $\mathbf{D_{M.ih.c.b}}$ for the $\mathbf{P_{ih}}$, i. e. corresponding to his **goal** $\mathbf{A_{ih.c}}$ (briefly – $\mathbf{BD_{M.ih.c.b}}$) – see above, the worst magnitude of the **current** $\mathbf{D_{M.ih.c.b}}$ for the $\mathbf{P_{ih}}$ (briefly – $\mathbf{WD_{M.ih.c.b}}$), the P_{ih}'s actual own magnitude of the **current** $\mathbf{D_{M.ih.c.b}}$ from his own $\mathbf{PH_{ih.c}}$ (briefly – $\mathbf{OD_{M.ih.c.b}}$), the actual magnitude of the **current** $\mathbf{D_{M.ih.c.b}}$ from common $\mathbf{PH_{iw.c}}$ (briefly – $\mathbf{CD_{M.ih.c.b}}$), the actual magnitude of the **current** $\mathbf{D_{M.ih.c.b}}$ used by the $\mathbf{P_{ih}}$ (briefly – $\mathbf{RD_{M.ih.c.b}}$), equal to the sum $\mathbf{OD_{M.ih.c.b}}$ and $\mathbf{CD_{M.ih.c.b}}$, the highest magnitude of the **current** $\mathbf{D_{M.ih.c.b}}$, guaranteed for P_{ih} in P_{iw} (briefly – $\mathbf{HD_{M.ih.c.b}}$) on his status in the $\mathbf{P_{iw}}$, the lowest magnitude of the **current** $\mathbf{D_{M.ih.c.b}}$, guaranteed for P_{ih} in P_{iw} (briefly – $\mathbf{LD_{M.ih.c.b}}$) on his status in the $\mathbf{P_{iw}}$, the magnitude of the **current** $\mathbf{D_{M.ih.c.b}}$, corresponds to $\mathbf{A_{iw.c}}$ (briefly – $\mathbf{DA_{M.ih.c.b}}$) on his status in the $\mathbf{P_{iw}}$, the projected duration each of $\mathbf{V_{M.ih.c}}$'s **u**se (briefly – $\mathbf{DU_{M.ih.c}}$) in **FUTURE**, etc.

Link to the $\mathbf{CTP_{ih.c.b}}$, in which the $\mathbf{F_{M.ih.c.b}}$ is created.

The third part of the description contains:

The name «**Noo provision the** $\mathbf{P_{ih}}$'s **existence** (**life support**) **by rejection of the** $\mathbf{V_{S.ih.c}}$», its conditional designation $\mathbf{SP_{S.ih.c}}$ and identification number of the $\mathbf{P_{ih}}$, for example, **ih**;

Nomenclature all of $\mathbf{F_{S.ih.c.b}}$ from b-th $\mathbf{CTP_{ih.c.b}}$, between them:

The list of $\mathbf{F_{S.ih.c.b}}$ names and its conditional designations ($\mathbf{F_{S.ih.c.b}}$);

Identification number **«c»** each of the $\mathbf{V_{S.ih.c}}$, that is the base of the correspond $\mathbf{F_{S.ih.c.b}}$ from **formalized description of the environment**;

Parameters each of $\mathbf{F_{S.ih.c.b}}$, between them:

Unit of measurement the magnitude of **density the current rejection flow of** $\mathbf{V_{S.ih.c}}$ (briefly – $\mathbf{D_{S.ih.c.b}}$) in the b-th $\mathbf{CTP_{ih.c.b}}$, the best magnitude of the **current** $D_{S.ih.c.b}$ for the P_{ih}, i. e. corresponding to his **goal** $A_{ih.c}$ (briefly – $BD_{S.ih.c.b}$) – see above, the worst magnitude of the **current** $D_{S.ih.c.b}$ for the P_{ih} (briefly – $WD_{S.ih.c.b}$), the P_{ih}'s actual own magnitude of the **current** $D_{S.ih.c.b}$ from his own $PH_{ih.c}$ (briefly – $OD_{S.ih.c.b}$), the actual magnitude of the **current** $D_{S.ih.c.b}$ from common $PH_{iw.c}$ (briefly – $CD_{S.ih.c.b}$), the actual magnitude of the **current** $D_{S.ih.c.b}$ used by the P_{ih} (briefly – $RD_{S.ih.c.b}$), equal to the sum $OD_{S.ih.c.b}$ and $CD_{S.ih.c.b}$, the highest magnitude of the **current** $D_{S.ih.c.b}$, guaranteed for P_{ih} in P_{iw} (briefly – $HD_{S.ih.c.b}$) on his status in the P_{iw}, the lowest magnitude of the **current** $D_{S.ih.c.b}$, guaranteed for P_{ih} in P_{iw} (briefly – $LD_{S.ih.c.b}$) on his status in the P_{iw}, the magnitude of the **current** $D_{S.ih.c.b}$, corresponds to $A_{iw.c}$ (briefly – $DA_{S.ih.c.b}$) on his status in the P_{iw}, the projected duration each of $V_{S.ih.c}$'s use (briefly – $DU_{S.ih.c}$) in **FUTURE**, etc.

Link to the $CTP_{ih.c.b}$, from which the $F_{S.ih.c.b}$ is rejected.

Formalized description of **the noologistical provision the existence (life support) of** P_{ih} may contain the following information:

Noological provision the P_{ih}**'s existence (life support) (**$SP_{ih.l}$**)**

The description may consist of three parts: «**Noologistical provision the** P_{ih}**'s existence (life support) by consumption of the** $V_{C.ih.l}$», «**Noologistical provision the** P_{ih}**'s existence (life support) by creation of the** $V_{M.ih.l}$» and «**Noologistical provision the** P_{ih}**'s existence (life support) by rejection of the** $V_{S.ih.l}$», that are put on display separately or together:

The first part of the description contains:

The name «**Noologistical provision the** P_{ih}**'s existence (life support) by consumption of the** $V_{C.ih.l}$», its conditional designation $SP_{C.ih.l}$ and identification number of the P_{ih}, for example, **ih**;

Nomenclature all of $F_{C.ih.l.b}$ from b-th $CTP_{ih.l.b}$, between them:

The list of $F_{C.ih.l.b}$ names and its conditional designations ($F_{C.ih.l.b}$);

Identification number **«l»** each of the $V_{C.ih.l}$, that is the base of the correspond $F_{C.ih.l.b}$ from **formalized description of the environment**;

Parameters each of $F_{C.ih.l.b}$, between them:

Unit of measurement the magnitude of **density the current consumption flow of $V_{C.ih.l}$** (briefly – $D_{C.ih.l.b}$) in the b-th **$CTP_{ih.l.b}$**, the best magnitude of the **current $D_{C.ih.l.b}$** for the **P_{ih}**, i. e. corresponding to his **goal $A_{ih.l}$** (briefly – **$BD_{C.ih.l.b}$**) – see above, the worst magnitude of the **current $D_{C.ih.l.b}$** for the **P_{ih}** (briefly – **$WD_{C.ih.l.b}$**), the P_{ih}'s actual own magnitude of the **current $D_{C.ih.l.b}$** from his own **$PH_{ih.l}$** (briefly – **$OD_{C.ih.l.b}$**), the actual magnitude of the **current $D_{C.ih.l.b}$** from common **$PH_{iw.l}$** (briefly – **$CD_{C.ih.l.b}$**), the actual magnitude of the **current $D_{C.ih.l.b}$** used by the **P_{ih}** (briefly – **$RD_{C.ih.l.b}$**), equal to the sum **$OD_{C.ih.l.b}$** and **$CD_{C.ih.l.b}$**, the highest magnitude of the **current $D_{C.ih.l.b}$**, guaranteed for P_{ih} in P_{iw} (briefly – **$HD_{C.ih.l.b}$**) on his status in the **P_{iw}**, the lowest magnitude of the **current $D_{C.ih.l.b}$**, guaranteed for P_{ih} in P_{iw} (briefly – **$LD_{C.ih.l.b}$**) on his status in the **P_{iw}**, the magnitude of the **current $D_{C.ih.l.b}$**, corresponds to his **$A_{iw.l}$** (briefly – **$DA_{C.ih.l.b}$**) on his status in the **P_{iw}**, the projected duration each of **$V_{C.ih.l}$**'s **use** (briefly – **$DU_{C.ih.l}$**) in **FUTURE**, etc.

Link to the **$CTP_{ih.l.b}$**, in which the **$F_{C.ih.l.b}$** is used.

The structure information is shown in Fig. P 12, which follows from the formal description, entitled "**Noological provision the P_{ih}'s existence** (**life support**) **by consumption of the $V_{C.ih.l}$** ".

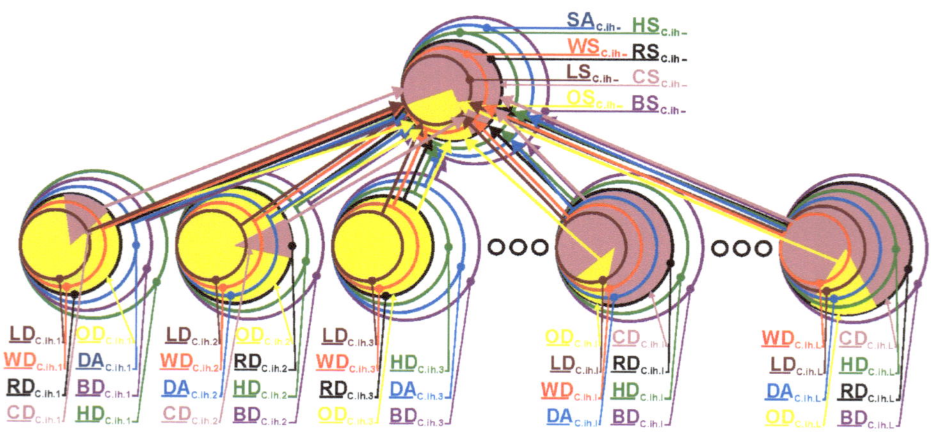

Fig. P 12

The conditional designation on the Fig. P 12:

$BS_{C.ih}$ – it is the best **noologistical provision the existence** (**life support**) **by consumption of the $V_{C.ih.l}$** for the **P_{ih}** that corresponds to his $\mathbf{A}_{ih.l}$, and is the set of the best for the $\mathbf{P}_{ih}$ total densities of **the consumption flows** of the $\mathbf{V}_{C.ih.l}$, the calculation formula of which is given below;

WS$_{C.ih}$ – it is the worst **noologistical provision the existence (life support) by consumption of the** $\mathbf{V}_{C.ih.l}$ for the $\mathbf{P}_{ih}$ and is the set of the worst for the $\mathbf{P}_{ih}$ total densities of **the consumption flows** of the $\mathbf{V}_{C.ih.l}$, the calculation formula of which is given below;

OS$_{C.ih}$ – it is the actual **noologistical provision the existence (life support) by consumption of the** $\mathbf{V}_{C.ih.l}$ by the $\mathbf{P}_{ih}$ from his own $\mathbf{Q}_{ih.l}$, that is the set of the total densities of **the consumption flows** of the $\mathbf{V}_{C.ih.l}$ from his own $\mathbf{Q}_{ih.l}$, the calculation formula of which is given below;

CS$_{C.ih}$ – it is the actual **noologistical provision the existence** (**life support**) **by consumption of the** $\mathbf{V}_{C.ih.l}$ by the $\mathbf{P}_{ih}$ from the common $\mathbf{Q}_{iw.l}$, that is the set of the total densities of **the consumption flows** of the $\mathbf{V}_{C.ih.l}$ from the common $\mathbf{Q}_{iw.l}$, the calculation formula of which is given below;

RS$_{C.ih}$ – it is the actual total **noologistical provision the existence** (**life support**) **by consumption of the** $\mathbf{V}_{C.ih.l}$ by the $\mathbf{P}_{ih}$, that is the sum of the **OS**$_{C.ih}$ and **CS**$_{C.ih}$;

HS$_{C.ih}$ – it is highest **noologistical provision the existence** (**life support**) **by consumption of the** $\mathbf{V}_{C.ih.l}$ for the $\mathbf{P}_{ih}$, guaranteed for P_{ih} in P_{iw} on his **status** in the $\mathbf{P}_{iw}$ that is the sum of **the highest densities of the consumption flows of** $\mathbf{V}_{C.ih.l}$, guaranteed for him in P_{iw}, the calculation formula of which is given below;

LS$_{C.ih}$ – it is lowest **noologistical provision the existence** (**life support**) **by consumption of the** $\mathbf{V}_{C.ih.l}$ for the $\mathbf{P}_{ih}$, guaranteed for P_{ih} in P_{iw} on his **status** in the $\mathbf{P}_{iw}$ that is the sum of **the lowest densities of the consumption flows of** $\mathbf{V}_{C.ih.l}$, guaranteed for him in P_{iw}, the calculation formula of which is given below;

SA$_{C.ih}$ – it is **noologistical provision the existence** (**life support**) **by consumption of the** $\mathbf{V}_{C.ih.l}$ for the $\mathbf{P}_{ih}$, corresponds to his $\mathbf{A}_{iw.l}$ on his **status** in the $\mathbf{P}_{iw}$, that is the sum of **the densities of the consumption flows of** $\mathbf{V}_{C.ih.l}$, corresponds to his $\mathbf{A}_{iw.l}$, the calculation formula of which is given below;

arrows show the formation of **BS**$_{C.ih}$, **WS**$_{C.ih}$, **OS**$_{C.ih}$, **CS**$_{C.ih}$ **RS**$_{C.ih}$, **HS**$_{C.ih}$, **LS**$_{C.ih}$ and **SA**$_{C.ih}$ by union in correspond set of magnitudes of the **BD**$_{C.ih.l}$, **WD**$_{C.ih.l}$, **OD**$_{C.ih.l}$, **CD**$_{C.ih.l}$, **RD**$_{C.ih.l}$, **HD**$_{C.ih.l}$, **LD**$_{C.ih.l}$ and **DA**$_{C.ih.l}$;

the rest – see above.

Calculation of magnitudes $\mathbf{BD_{C.ih.l}}$, $\mathbf{WD_{C.ih.l}}$, $\mathbf{OD_{C.ih.l}}$, $\mathbf{CD_{C.ih.l}}$, $\mathbf{RD_{C.ih.l}}$, $\mathbf{HD_{C.ih.l}}$, $\mathbf{LD_{C.ih.l}}$ and $\mathbf{DA_{C.ih.l}}$ is performed according to above given standard formulas:

$$BD_{C.ih.l} = \sum_{b=1}^{B} BD_{C.ih.l.b}, \qquad WD_{C.ih.l} = \sum_{b=1}^{B} WD_{C.ih.l.b},$$

$$OD_{C.ih.l} = \sum_{b=1}^{B} OD_{C.ih.l.b}, \qquad CD_{C.ih.l} = \sum_{b=1}^{B} CD_{C.ih.l.b},$$

$$RD_{C.ih.l} = \sum_{b=1}^{B} D_{C.ih.l.b} = OD_{C.ih.l} + CD_{C.ih.l}, \qquad HD_{C.ih.l} = \sum_{b=1}^{B} HD_{C.ih.l.b},$$

$$LD_{C.ih.l} = \sum_{b=1}^{B} LD_{C.ih.l.b}, \; DA_{C.ih.l} = \sum_{b=1}^{B} DA_{C.ih.l.b},$$

here are:

$\mathbf{BD_{C.ih.l.b}}$ – it is the best density of the $\mathbf{F_{C.ih.l.b}}$ for the $\mathbf{P_{ih}}$ in b-th $\mathbf{CTP_{ih.l.b}}$ in **PRESENT**, which is determined from the condition of achieving his $\mathbf{A_{ih.l}}$, for example, by **the technology of Noologistics**;

$\mathbf{WD_{C.ih.l.b}}$ – it is the worst density of the $\mathbf{F_{C.ih.l.b}}$ for the $\mathbf{P_{ih}}$ in b-th $\mathbf{CTP_{ih.l.b}}$ in **PRESENT**, which is determined by the $\mathbf{RP_{ih.l}}$;

$\mathbf{OD_{C.ih.l.b}}$ – it is the actual density of the $\mathbf{F_{C.ih.l.b}}$ from the $\mathbf{OQ_{C.ih.l}}$, used in b-th $\mathbf{CTP_{ih.l.b}}$ in **PRESENT**, which is measured by the $\mathbf{RP_{ih.l}}$;

$\mathbf{CD_{C.ih.l.b}}$ – it is the actual density of the $\mathbf{F_{C.ih.l.b}}$ from the $\mathbf{CQ_{C.ih.l}}$, used in b-th $\mathbf{CTP_{ih.l.b}}$ in **PRESENT**, which is measured by the $\mathbf{RP_{ih.l}}$;

$\mathbf{D_{C.ih.l.b}}$ – it is the actual density of the $\mathbf{F_{C.ih.l.b}}$, used in b-th $\mathbf{CTP_{ih.l.b}}$ in **PRESENT**, which is measured by the $\mathbf{RP_{ih}}$;

$\mathbf{HD_{C.ih.l.b}}$ – it is highest density of the $\mathbf{F_{C.ih.l.b}}$, guaranteed for P_{ih} in P_{iw} in b-th $\mathbf{CTP_{ih.l.b}}$ in **PRESENT** on his status in the $\mathbf{P_{iw}}$, which is determined by the $\mathbf{RP_{iw.l}}$;

$\mathbf{LD_{C.ih.l.b}}$ – it is lowest density of the $\mathbf{F_{C.ih.l.b}}$, guaranteed for P_{ih} in P_{iw} in b-th $\mathbf{CTP_{ih.l.b}}$ in **PRESENT** on his status in the $\mathbf{P_{iw}}$, which is determined by the $\mathbf{RP_{iw.l}}$;

$\mathbf{DA_{C.ih.l.b}}$ – it is density of the $\mathbf{F_{C.ih.l.b}}$ in b-th $\mathbf{CTP_{ih.l.b}}$ in **PRESENT**, which is determined from the condition of achieving his $\mathbf{A_{iw.l}}$, for example, by **the technology of Noologistics**;

the rest – see above.

Calculation of magnitude $\mathbf{DU_{C.ih.l}}$ for each $\mathbf{V_{C.ih.h}}$ is performed according to a standard formula, for example:

$$DU_{C.ih.l} = \frac{QA_{ih.h}}{\sum_{b=1}^{B} \int_{t_н}^{t} DA_{C.ih.l.b}(t) * dt},$$

in which all conditional designations – see above.

The second part of the description contains:

The name «**Noologistical provision the $\mathbf{P_{ih}}$'s existence** (**life support**) **by creation of the $\mathbf{V_{M.ih.l}}$**», its conditional designation $\mathbf{SP_{M.ih.l}}$ and identification number of the $\mathbf{P_{ih}}$, for example, **ih**;

Nomenclature all of $\mathbf{F_{M.ih.l.b}}$ from b-th $\mathbf{CTP_{ih.l.b}}$, between them:

The list of $\mathbf{F_{M.ih.l.b}}$ names and its conditional designations ($\mathbf{F_{M.ih.l.b}}$);

Identification number **«l»** each of the $\mathbf{V_{M.ih.l}}$, that is the base of the correspond $\mathbf{F_{M.ih.l.b}}$ from **formalized description of the environment**;

Parameters each of $\mathbf{F_{M.ih.l.b}}$, between them:

Unit of measurement the magnitude of **density the current creation flow of $\mathbf{V_{M.ih.l}}$** (briefly – $\mathbf{D_{M.ih.l.b}}$) in the b-th $\mathbf{CTP_{ih.l.b}}$, the best magnitude of the **current $\mathbf{D_{M.ih.l.b}}$** for the $\mathbf{P_{ih}}$, i. e. corresponding to his **goal $\mathbf{A_{ih.l}}$** (briefly – $\mathbf{BD_{M.ih.l.b}}$) – see above, the worst magnitude of the **current $\mathbf{D_{M.ih.l.b}}$** for the $\mathbf{P_{ih}}$ (briefly – $\mathbf{WD_{M.ih.l.b}}$), the P_{ih}'s actual own magnitude of the **current $\mathbf{D_{M.ih.l.b}}$** from his own $\mathbf{PH_{ih.l}}$ (briefly – $\mathbf{OD_{M.ih.l.b}}$), the actual magnitude of the **current $\mathbf{D_{M.ih.l.b}}$** from common $\mathbf{PH_{iw.l}}$ (briefly – $\mathbf{CD_{M.ih.l.b}}$), the actual magnitude of the **current $\mathbf{D_{M.ih.l.b}}$** used by the $\mathbf{P_{ih}}$ (briefly – $\mathbf{RD_{M.ih.l.b}}$), equal to the sum $\mathbf{OD_{M.ih.l.b}}$ and $\mathbf{CD_{M.ih.l.b}}$, the highest magnitude of the **current $\mathbf{D_{M.ih.l.b}}$**, guaranteed for P_{ih} in P_{iw} (briefly – $\mathbf{HD_{M.ih.l.b}}$) on his status in the $\mathbf{P_{iw}}$, the lowest magnitude of the **current $\mathbf{D_{M.ih.l.b}}$**, guaranteed for P_{ih} in P_{iw} (briefly – $\mathbf{LD_{M.ih.l.b}}$) on his status in the $\mathbf{P_{iw}}$, the magnitude of the **current $\mathbf{D_{M.ih.l.b}}$**, corresponds to his $\mathbf{A_{iw.l}}$ (briefly – $\mathbf{DA_{M.ih.l.b}}$) on his status in the $\mathbf{P_{iw}}$, the projected duration each of $V_{M.ih.l}$'s use (briefly – $DU_{M.ih.l}$) in **FUTURE**, etc.

Link to the $CTP_{ih.l.b}$, in which the $F_{M.ih.l.b}$ is created.

The structure information is shown in Fig. P 13, which follows from the formal description, entitled "**Noological provision the P_{ih}'s existence (life support) by creation of the $V_{M.ih.l}$** ".

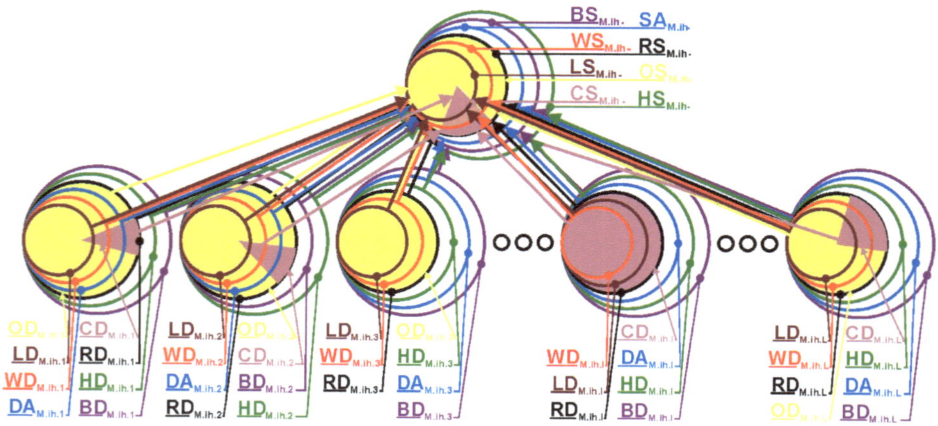

Fig. P 13

The conditional designation on the Fig. P 13:

$BS_{M.ih}$ – it is the best **noological provision the existence (life support) by creation of the $V_{M.ih.l}$** for the P_{ih} that corresponds to his $A_{ih.l}$, and is the set of the best for the P_{ih} total densities of **the creation flows** of the $V_{M.ih.l}$, the calculation formula of which is given below;

$WS_{M.ih}$ – it is the worst **noological provision the existence (life support) by creation of the $V_{M.ih.l}$** for the P_{ih} and is the set of the worst for the P_{ih} total densities of **the creation flows** of the $V_{M.ih.l}$, the calculation formula of which is given below;

$OS_{M.ih}$ – it is the **noological provision the existence (life support) by creation of the $V_{M.ih.l}$** by the P_{ih} from his own $Q_{ih.l}$, that is the set of the total densities of **the creation flows** of the $V_{M.ih.l}$ from his own $Q_{ih.l}$, the calculation formula of which is given below;

$CS_{M.ih}$ – it is the actual **noological provision the existence (life support) by creation of the $V_{M.ih.l}$** by the P_{ih} from the common

$Q_{iw.l}$, that is the set of the total densities of **the creation flows** of the **$V_{M.ih.l}$** from the common **$Q_{iw.l}$**, the calculation formula of which is given below;

$RS_{M.ih}$ – it is the actual total **noologistical provision the existence** (**life support**) **by creation of the $V_{C.ih.l}$** by the **P_{ih}**, that is the sum of the **$OS_{M.ih}$** and **$CS_{M.ih}$**;

$HS_{M.ih}$ – it is highest **noologistical provision the existence** (**life support**) **by creation of the $V_{M.ih.l}$** for the **P_{ih}**, guaranteed for P_{ih} in P_{iw} on his **status** in the **P_{iw}** that is the sum of **the highest densities of the creation flows of $V_{M.ih.l}$**, guaranteed for him in P_{iw}, the calculation formula of which is given below;

$LS_{M.ih}$ – it is lowest **noologistical provision the existence** (**life support**) **by creation of the $V_{M.ih.l}$** for the **P_{ih}**, guaranteed for P_{ih} in P_{iw} on his **status** in the **P_{iw}** that is the sum of **the lowest densities of the creation flows of $V_{M.ih.l}$**, guaranteed for him in P_{iw}, the calculation formula of which is given below;

$SA_{M.ih}$ – it is **noologistical provision the existence** (**life support**) **by creation of the $V_{M.ih.l}$** for the **P_{ih}**, corresponds to his **$A_{iw.l}$** on his **status** in the **P_{iw}**, that is the sum of **the densities of the creation flows of $V_{C.ih.l}$**, corresponds to his **$A_{iw.l}$**, the calculation formula of which is given below;

arrows show the formation of **$BS_{M.ih}$**, **$WS_{M.ih}$**, **$OS_{M.ih}$**, **$CS_{M.ih}$**, **$RS_{M.ih}$**, **$HS_{M.ih}$**, **$LS_{M.ih}$** and **$SA_{M.ih}$** by union in correspond set of magnitudes of the **$BD_{M.ih.l}$**, **$WD_{M.ih.l}$**, **$OD_{M.ih.l}$**, **$CD_{M.ih.l}$**, **$RD_{M.ih.l}$**, **$HD_{M.ih.l}$**, **$LD_{M.ih.l}$** and **$DA_{M.ih.l}$**;

the rest – see above.

Calculation of magnitudes **$BD_{M.ih.l}$**, **$WD_{M.ih.l}$**, **$OD_{M.ih.l}$**, **$CD_{M.ih.l}$**, **$RD_{M.ih.l}$**, **$HD_{M.ih.l}$**, **$LD_{M.ih.l}$** and **$DA_{M.ih.l}$** is performed according to above given standard formulas:

$$BD_{M.ih.l} = \sum_{b=1}^{B} BD_{M.ih.l.b}, \qquad WD_{M.ih.l} = \sum_{b=1}^{B} WD_{M.ih.l.b},$$

$$OD_{M.ih.l} = \sum_{b=1}^{B} OD_{M.ih.l.b}, \qquad CD_{M.ih.l} = \sum_{b=1}^{B} CD_{M.ih.l.b},$$

$$RD_{M.ih.l} = \sum_{b=1}^{B} D_{M.ih.l.b} = OD_{M.ih.l} + CD_{M.ih.l}, \qquad HD_{M.ih.l} = \sum_{b=1}^{B} HD_{M.ih.l.b},$$

$$LD_{M.ih.l} = \sum_{b=1}^{B} LD_{M.ih.l.b}, \quad DA_{M.ih.l} = \sum_{b=1}^{B} DA_{M.ih.l.b},$$

here are:

$BD_{M.ih.l.b}$ – it is the best density of the **$F_{M.ih.l.b}$** for the **P_{ih}** in b-th **$CTP_{ih.l.b}$** in **PRESENT**, which is determined from the condition of achieving his **$A_{ih.l}$**, for example, by **the technology of Noologistics**;

$WD_{M.ih.l.b}$ – it is the worst density of the **$F_{M.ih.l.b}$** for the **P_{ih}** in b-th **$CTP_{ih.l.b}$** in **PRESENT**, which is determined by the **$RP_{ih.l}$**;

$OD_{M.ih.l.b}$ – it is the actual density of the **$F_{M.ih.l.b}$** from the **$OQ_{C.ih.l}$**, used in b-th **$CTP_{ih.l.b}$** in **PRESENT**, which is measured by the **$RP_{ih.l}$**;

$CD_{M.ih.l.b}$ – it is the actual density of the **$F_{M.ih.l.b}$** from the **$CQ_{M.ih.l}$**, used in b-th **$CTP_{ih.l.b}$** in **PRESENT**, which is measured by the **$RP_{ih.l}$**;

$D_{M.ih.l.b}$ – it is the actual density of the **$F_{M.ih.l.b}$**, used in b-th **$CTP_{ih.l.b}$** in **PRESENT**, which is measured by the **RP_{ih}**;

$HD_{M.ih.l.b}$ – it is highest density of the **$F_{M.ih.l.b}$**, guaranteed for P_{ih} in P_{iw} in b-th **$CTP_{ih.l.b}$** in **PRESENT** on his status in the **P_{iw}**, which is determined by the **$RP_{iw.l}$**;

$LD_{M.ih.l.b}$ – it is lowest density of the **$F_{M.ih.l.b}$**, guaranteed for P_{ih} in P_{iw} in b-th **$CTP_{ih.l.b}$** in **PRESENT** on his status in the **P_{iw}**, which is determined by the **$RP_{iw.l}$**;

$DA_{M.ih.l.b}$ – it is density of the **$F_{M.ih.l.b}$** in b-th **$CTP_{ih.l.b}$** in **PRESENT**, which is determined from the condition of achieving his **$A_{iw.l}$**, for example, by **the technology of Noologistics**;

the rest – see above.

Calculation of magnitude **$DU_{M.ih.l}$** for each **$V_{M.ih.h}$** is performed according to a standard formula, for example:

$$DU_{M.ih.l} = \frac{QA_{ih.h}}{\sum_{b=1}^{B} \int_{t_н}^{t} DA_{M.ih.l.b}(t) * dt},$$

in which all conditional designations – see above.

The third part of the description contains:

The name «**Noologistical provision the** P_{ih}'s **existence** (**life support**) **by rejection of the** $V_{S.ih.l}$», its conditional designation **$SP_{S.ih.l}$** and identification number of the **P_{ih}**, for example, **ih**;

Nomenclature all of $F_{S.ih.l.b}$ from b-th **$CTP_{ih.l.b}$**, between them:

The list of $F_{S.ih.l.b}$ names and its conditional designations ($F_{S.ih.l.b}$);

Identification number **«l»** each of the $V_{S.ih.l}$, that is the base of the correspond $F_{S.ih.l.b}$ from **formalized description of the environment**;

Parameters each of $F_{S.ih.l.b}$, between them:

Unit of measurement the magnitude of **density the current rejection flow of** $V_{S.ih.l}$ (briefly – $D_{S.ih.l.b}$) from the b-th **$CTP_{ih.l.b}$**, the best magnitude of the **current** $D_{S.ih.l.b}$ for the P_{ih}, i. e. corresponding to his **goal** $A_{ih.l}$ (briefly – **$BD_{S.ih.l.b}$**) – see above, the worst magnitude of the **current** $D_{S.ih.l.b}$ for the P_{ih} (briefly – **$WD_{S.ih.l.b}$**), the P_{ih}'s actual own magnitude of the **current** $D_{S.ih.l.b}$ from his own **$PH_{ih.l}$** (briefly – **$OD_{S.ih.l.b}$**), the actual magnitude of the **current** $D_{S.ih.l.b}$ from common **$PH_{iw.l}$** (briefly – **$CD_{S.ih.l.b}$**), the actual magnitude of the **current** $D_{S.ih.l.b}$ used by the P_{ih} (briefly – **$RD_{S.ih.l.b}$**), equal to the sum **$OD_{S.ih.l.b}$** and **$CD_{S.ih.l.b}$**, the highest magnitude of the **current** $D_{S.ih.l.b}$, guaranteed for P_{ih} in P_{iw} (briefly – **$HD_{S.ih.l.b}$**) on his status in the P_{iw}, the lowest magnitude of the **current** $D_{S.ih.l.b}$, guaranteed for P_{ih} in P_{iw} (briefly – **$LD_{S.ih.l.b}$**) on his status in the P_{iw}, the magnitude of the **current** $D_{S.ih.l.b}$, corresponds to his $A_{iw.l}$ (briefly – **$DA_{S.ih.l.b}$**) on his status in the P_{iw}, the projected duration each of $V_{S.ih.l}$'s use (briefly – **$DU_{S.ih.l}$**) in **FUTURE**, etc.

Link to the **$CTP_{ih.l.b}$**, from which the $F_{S.ih.l.b}$ is rejected.

The structure information is shown in Fig. P 14, which follows from the formal description, entitled "**Noologistical provision the** P_{ih}'s **existence** (**life support**) **by rejection of the** $V_{S.ih.l}$".

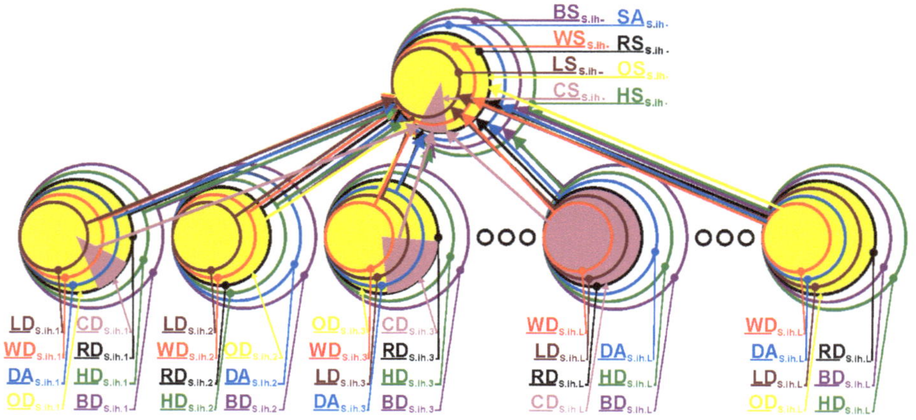

Fig. P 14

The conditional designation on the Fig. P 14:

$BS_{S.ih}$ – it is the best **noological provision the existence** (**life support**) **by rejection of the $V_{S.ih.l}$** for the **P_{ih}** that corresponds to his **$A_{ih.l}$**, and is the set of the best for the **P_{ih}** total densities of **the rejection flows** of the **$V_{S.ih.l}$**, the calculation formula of which is given below;

$WS_{S.ih}$ – it is the worst **noologistical provision the existence** (**life support**) **by rejection of the $V_{S.ih.l}$** for the **P_{ih}** and is the set of the worst for the **P_{ih}** total densities of **the rejection flows** of the **$V_{C.ih.l}$**, the calculation formula of which is given below;

$OS_{S.ih}$ – it is the **noologistical provision the existence** (**life support**) **by rejection of the $V_{S.ih.l}$** by the **P_{ih}** to his own **$Q_{ih.l}$**, that is the set of the total densities of **the rejection flows** of the **$V_{S.ih.l}$** to his own **$Q_{ih.l}$**, the calculation formula of which is given below;

$CS_{S.ih}$ – it is the actual **noologistical provision the existence** (**life support**) **by rejection of the $V_{S.ih.l}$** by the **P_{ih}** to the common **$Q_{iw.l}$**, that is the set of the total densities of **the rejection flows** of the **$V_{S.ih.l}$** to the common **$Q_{iw.l}$**, the calculation formula of which is given below;

$RS_{S.ih}$ – it is the actual total **noologistical provision the existence** (**life support**) **by rejection of the $V_{S.ih.l}$** by the **P_{ih}**, that is the sum of the **$OS_{S.ih}$** and **$CS_{S.ih}$**;

$HS_{S.ih}$ – it is highest **noologistical provision the existence** (**life support**) **by rejection of the $V_{S.ih.l}$** for the **P_{ih}**, guaranteed for P_{ih} in P_{iw} on his **status** in the **P_{iw}** that is the sum of **the highest densities of the rejection flows of $V_{S.ih.l}$**, guaranteed for him in P_{iw}, the calculation formula of which is given below;

$LS_{S.ih}$ – it is lowest **noologistical provision the existence** (**life support**) **by rejection of the $V_{S.ih.l}$** for the **P_{ih}**, guaranteed for P_{ih} in P_{iw} on his **status** in the **P_{iw}** that is the sum of **the lowest densities of the rejection flows of $V_{S.ih.l}$**, guaranteed for him in P_{iw}, the calculation formula of which is given below;

$SA_{S.ih}$ – it is **noologistical provision the existence** (**life support**) **by rejection of the $V_{S.ih.l}$** for the **P_{ih}**, corresponds to his **$A_{iw.l}$** on his **status** in the **P_{iw}**, that is the sum of **the densities of the rejection flows of $V_{S.ih.l}$**, corresponds to his **$A_{iw.l}$**, the calculation formula of which is given below;

arrows show the formation of **$BS_{S.ih}$**, **$WS_{S.ih}$**, **$OS_{S.ih}$**, **$CS_{S.ih}$**, **$RS_{S.ih}$**, **$HS_{S.ih}$**, **$LS_{S.ih}$** and **$SA_{S.ih}$** by union in correspond set of magnitudes of the **$BD_{S.ih.l}$**, **$WD_{S.ih.l}$**, **$OD_{S.ih.l}$**, **$CD_{S.ih.l}$**, **$RD_{S.ih.l}$**, **$HD_{S.ih.l}$**, **$LD_{S.ih.l}$** and **$DA_{S.ih.l}$**;

the rest – see above.

Calculation of magnitudes **$BD_{S.ih.l}$**, **$WD_{S.ih.l}$**, **$OD_{S.ih.l}$**, **$CD_{S.ih.l}$**, **$RD_{S.ih.l}$**, **$HD_{S.ih.l}$**, **$LD_{S.ih.l}$** and **$DA_{S.ih.l}$** is performed according to above given standard formulas:

$$BD_{S.ih.l} = \sum_{b=1}^{B} BD_{S.ih.l.b}, \qquad WD_{S.ih.l} = \sum_{b=1}^{B} WD_{S.ih.l.b},$$

$$OD_{S.ih.l} = \sum_{b=1}^{B} OD_{S.ih.l.b}, \qquad CD_{S.ih.l} = \sum_{b=1}^{B} CD_{S.ih.l.b},$$

$$RD_{S.ih.l} = \sum_{b=1}^{B} D_{S.ih.l.b} = OD_{S.ih.l} + CD_{S.ih.l}, \qquad HD_{S.ih.l} = \sum_{b=1}^{B} HD_{S.ih.l.b},$$

$$LD_{S.ih.l} = \sum_{b=1}^{B} LD_{S.ih.l.b}, \; DA_{S.ih.l} = \sum_{b=1}^{B} DA_{S.ih.l.b},$$

here are:

$BD_{S.ih.l.b}$ – it is the best density of the **$F_{S.ih.l.b}$** for the **P_{ih}** from b-th **$CTP_{ih.l.b}$** in **PRESENT**, which is determined from the condition of achieving his **$A_{ih.l}$**, for example, by **the technology of Noologistics**;

$WD_{S.ih.l.b}$ – it is the worst density of the **$F_{S.ih.l.b}$** for the **P_{ih}** from b-th **$CTP_{ih.l.b}$** in **PRESENT**, which is determined by the **$RP_{ih.l}$**;

$OD_{S.ih.l.b}$ – it is the actual density of the **$F_{S.ih.l.b}$** to the **$OQ_{S.ih.l}$**, used in b-th **$CTP_{ih.l.b}$** in **PRESENT**, which is measured by the **$RP_{ih.l}$**;

$CD_{S.ih.l.b}$ – it is the actual density of the **$F_{S.ih.l.b}$** to the **$CQ_{S.ih.l}$**, used in b-th **$CTP_{ih.l.b}$** in **PRESENT**, which is measured by the **$RP_{ih.l}$**;

$\mathbf{D_{S.ih.l.b}}$ – it is the actual density of the $\mathbf{F_{S.ih.l.b}}$, used in b-th $\mathbf{CTP_{ih.l.b}}$ in **PRESENT**, which is measured by the $\mathbf{RP_{ih}}$;

$\mathbf{HD_{S.ih.l.b}}$ – it is highest density of the $\mathbf{F_{S.ih.l.b}}$, guaranteed for P_{ih} in P_{iw} in b-th $\mathbf{CTP_{ih.l.b}}$ in **PRESENT** on his status in the $\mathbf{P_{iw}}$, which is determined by the $\mathbf{RP_{iw.l}}$;

$\mathbf{LD_{S.ih.l.b}}$ – it is lowest density of the $\mathbf{F_{S.ih.l.b}}$, guaranteed for P_{ih} in P_{iw} in b-th $\mathbf{CTP_{ih.l.b}}$ in **PRESENT** on his status in the $\mathbf{P_{iw}}$, which is determined by the $\mathbf{RP_{iw.l}}$;

$\mathbf{DA_{S.ih.l.b}}$ – it is density of the $\mathbf{F_{S.ih.l.b}}$ from b-th $\mathbf{CTP_{ih.l.b}}$ in **PRESENT**, which is determined from the condition of achieving his $\mathbf{A_{iw.l}}$, for example, by **the technology of Noologistics**;

the rest – see above.

Calculation of magnitude $\mathbf{DU_{S.ih.l}}$ for each $\mathbf{V_{S.ih.h}}$ is performed according to a standard formula, for example:

$$DU_{S.ih.l} = \frac{QA_{ih.h}}{\sum_{b=1}^{B} \int_{t_н}^{t} DA_{S.ih.l.b}(t) * dt},$$

in which all conditional designations – see above.

The structure information is shown in Fig. P 15, which follows from the formal description, entitled "**Noologistical provision the P_{ih}'s existence (life support)**".

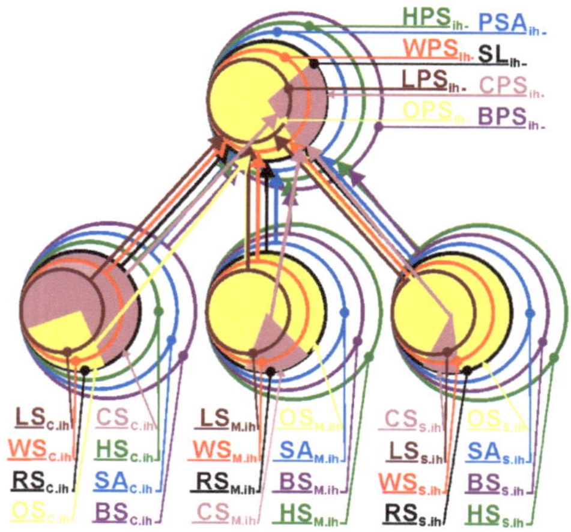

Fig. P 15

The conditional designation on the Fig. P 15:

BPS_{ih} – it is the best **noologistical provision the existence** (**life support**) for the **P_{ih}** that is the set of **$BS_{C.ih}$**, **$BS_{M.ih}$** and **$BS_{S.ih}$**;

WPS_{ih} – it is the worst **noologistical provision the existence** (**life support**) for the **P_{ih}** that is the set of the **$WS_{C.ih}$**, **$WS_{M.ih}$** and **$WS_{S.ih}$**;

OPS_{ih} – it is the actual **noologistical provision the existence** (**life support**) of the **P_{ih}** on base of his own **$Q_{ih.l}$**, that is the set of the **$OS_{C.ih}$**, **$OS_{M.ih}$** and **$OS_{S.ih}$**;

CPS_{ih} – it is the actual **noologistical provision the existence** (**life support**) of the the **P_{ih}** on base of common **$Q_{iw.l}$**, that is the set **$CS_{C.ih}$**, **$CS_{M.ih}$** and **$CS_{S.ih}$**;

SP_{ih} – it is the actual total **noologistical provision the existence** (**life support**) of the the **P_{ih}**, that is the sum of the **OPS_{ih}** and **CPS_{ih}** and is the sum of the **$RS_{C.ih}$**, **$RS_{M.ih}$** and **$RS_{S.ih}$** also;

PS_{ih} – it is highest **noologistical provision the existence** (**life support**) of the the **P_{ih}**, guaranteed for P_{ih} in P_{iw} on his **status** in the **P_{iw}**, guaranteed for him in P_{iw}, that is the sum of the **$HS_{C.ih}$**, **$HS_{M.ih}$** and **$HS_{S.ih}$**;

LPS_{ih} – it is lowest **noologistical provision the existence** (**life support**) of the **P_{ih}**, guaranteed for P_{ih} in P_{iw} on his **status** in the **P_{iw}**, guaranteed for him in P_{iw}, that is the sum of the **$LS_{C.ih}$**, **$LS_{M.ih}$** and **$LS_{S.ih}$**;

PSA_{ih} – it is **noologistical provision the existence** (**life support**) for the **P_{ih}**, corresponds to his **$A_{iw.l}$** on his **status** in the **P_{iw}**, that is the sum of **the $SA_{C.ih}$**, **$SA_{M.ih}$** and **$SA_{S.ih}$**;

arrows show the formation of **BPS_{ih}**, **WPS_{ih}**, **OPS_{ih}**, **CPS_{ih}**, **SP_{ih}**, **PS_{ih}**, **LPS_{ih}** and **$PSA_{S.ih}$** by union in correspond set of magnitudes of the **$BS_{C.ih}$**, **$BS_{M.ih}$**, **$BS_{S.ih}$**, **$WS_{C.ih}$**, **$WS_{M.ih}$**, **$WS_{S.ih}$**, **$OS_{C.ih}$**, **$OS_{M.ih}$**, **$OS_{S.ih}$**, **$CS_{C.ih}$**, **$CS_{M.ih}$**, **$CS_{S.ih}$**, **$RS_{C.ih}$**, **$RS_{M.ih}$**, **$RS_{S.ih}$**, **$HS_{C.ih}$**, **$HS_{M.ih}$**, **$HS_{S.ih}$**, **$LS_{C.ih}$**, **$LS_{M.ih}$**, **$LS_{S.ih}$**, **$SA_{C.ih}$**, **$SA_{M.ih}$** and **$SA_{S.ih}$**;

the rest – see above.

Formalized description of **the rules of P_{ih}** may contain the following information:

The P_{ih}'s rules (RP_{ih})

The content of the formalized description of "**the P_{ih}'s rules** " (briefly – **RP_{ih}**) reflects the meaning of the existence of the **P_{ih}** in **Ev** and is determined by a variety of well-defined, but constantly changing objective circumstances, which have parameters that may be measured and modified at will of the **P_{ih}**, as well as its **subjective**

principles and **criteria of rationality** that articulate approaches to the search for the meaning of life P_{ih} in **Ev**. The ratio magnitude of **Sb** and **Fl** to other P_{ih} and P_{iw}, which is reflected in the RP_{ih} on the one hand, is stored in his DNA (congenital), and, on the other hand, was changed under the influence of **Ev**, education and training. The some such specific, but constantly changing objective circumstances are listed below:

- the nomenclature of N_{ip} and their **priorities**;
- the **rules** of P_{il}, P_{iw}, P_{ib}, P_{ig}, P_{im}, etc. (briefly – RP_{il}, RP_{iw}, RP_{ib}, RP_{ig}, RP_{im}, etc.);
- the work characteristics and current modes of operation of the technological equipment available to the P_{ip};
- the technologies available to the P_{ip};
- his economic possibilities;
- his economic interests;
- his cultural interests;
- its moral and ethical attitudes;
- the laws of nature and advanced technology known to him;
- the situation in **Ev**, the nature and intensity of his impacts to it;
- the magnitudes of his **Sb** and **Fl** to other P_{ip}, P_{ih}, P_{il}, P_{iw}, P_{ib}, P_{ig}, P_{im}, etc.;
- his previous experience;
- his forecast for the development of the current situation in **Ev** and of the relations to other P_{ip}, P_{ih}, P_{il}, P_{iw}, P_{ib}, P_{ig}, P_{im}, etc. in **FUTURE**;
- the need for control of current parameters characterizing the object Ot_{ih};
- his submission on **the criteria of reasonableness** to all of the above;
- his **principles**, etc.

The letter **R** with a subscript that contains the identification number "ir" (briefly – R_{ir}) is applied to identify a single specific regulations as shown below. All regulations are combined into one unified description for each P_{ih}, that marked as RP_{ih} and contains:

- The name of the RP_{ih} and the name of P_{ih} for which to apply these rules, his **ih** and the conditional designation;

- Sections of the $\mathbf{RP_{ih}}$: $\mathbf{RP_{ip.v}}$, $\mathbf{RP_{ip.c}}$, $\mathbf{RP_{ip.h}}$ and $\mathbf{RP_{ip.l}}$ or $\mathbf{RP_{1.ip}}$ ($\mathbf{RP_{1.ip.v}}$, $\mathbf{RP_{1.ip.c}}$, $\mathbf{RP_{1.ip.h}}$ and $\mathbf{RP_{1.ip.l}}$) and $\mathbf{RP_2}$ ($\mathbf{RP_{2.ip.v}}$, $\mathbf{RP_{2.ip.c}}$, $\mathbf{RP_{2.ip.h}}$ and $\mathbf{RP_{2.ip.l}}$);
- Nomenclature of the $\mathbf{R_{ir}}$, that consisting of their names, their **ir** and conditional designations;
- His **Sb** and **Fl** to other $\mathbf{P_{ip}}$, $\mathbf{P_{ih}}$, $\mathbf{P_{iw}}$, $\mathbf{P_{ig}}$, etc.;
- Requisites of all formalized descriptions used in **Noologistics**;
- The originator of every description, storage, providing of the information contained therein;
- Description of mathematical apparatus and algorithm of calculation of each parameter represented into each formalized description;
- the scale of the importance of the $\mathbf{N_{ih}}$ (the sequence of their satisfaction), etc.

Formalized descriptions of $\mathbf{P_{il}}$, $\mathbf{P_{iw}}$, $\mathbf{P_{ib}}$, $\mathbf{P_{ig}}$, $\mathbf{P_{im}}$, etc., and their structures are similar to that given above for $\mathbf{P_{ih}}$, and it is not shown here to reduce the volume of description.

Summing up the description of the total **person** of **Noologistics** we may conclude that he is in the final form represents the totality of all **beings**, showing signs of intelligence, including all of humanity, which are united in of different hierarchies of **persons** ($\mathbf{P_{ih}}$, $\mathbf{P_{il}}$, $\mathbf{P_{iw}}$, $\mathbf{P_{ib}}$, $\mathbf{P_{ig}}$, $\mathbf{P_{im}}$, etc.) with a complex structure, consisting of specific **persons** ($\mathbf{P_{1.1}}$, $\mathbf{P_{1.2}}$, $\mathbf{P_{1.3}}$, ..., $\mathbf{P_{i.n}}$, ..., $\mathbf{P_{I.N}}$), located in them at various levels. The nomenclature of **noo values** ($\mathbf{V_{ih.v}}$, $\mathbf{V_{il.v}}$, $\mathbf{V_{iw.v}}$, $\mathbf{V_{ig.v}}$, etc.) which contained in the relevant formalized descriptions of **noo habitats** ($\mathbf{PH_{ih.v}}$, $\mathbf{PH_{il.v}}$, $\mathbf{PH_{iw.v}}$, $\mathbf{PH_{ig.v}}$, etc.) should be created in ideal by the simple automatic summation of nomenclatures the **noo values** ($\mathbf{V_{ip.v}}$) from the **noo habitats** ($\mathbf{PH_{ip}}$) all of **the persons** and their quantities ($\mathbf{Q_{ih.v}}$, $\mathbf{Q_{il.v}}$, $\mathbf{Q_{iw.v}}$, $\mathbf{Q_{ig.v}}$, etc.) are calculated by simple summation of the quantities ($\mathbf{Q_{ip.v}}$) of the respective $\mathbf{V_{ip.v}}$ which contain in all of **noo habitats** ($\mathbf{PH_{ip.v}}$) all member $\mathbf{P_{ip}}$. Similarly, would be formed in ideal:

The nomenclatures and quantities of **the current noo values** ($\mathbf{V_{ih.c}}$, $\mathbf{V_{il.c}}$, $\mathbf{V_{iw.c}}$, $\mathbf{V_{ig.c}}$, etc.) in the relevant formalized descriptions of the **current noo habitats** ($\mathbf{PH_{ih.c}}$, $\mathbf{PH_{il.c}}$, $\mathbf{PH_{iw.c}}$, $\mathbf{PH_{ig.c}}$, etc.) of **persons**;

The nomenclatures and quantities of **the noological values** (**$V_{ih.h}$**, **$V_{il.h}$**, **$V_{iw.h}$**, **$V_{ig.h}$**, etc.) in the relevant formalized descriptions of **the noological habitats** (**$PH_{ih.h}$**, **$PH_{il.h}$**, **$PH_{iw.h}$**, **$PH_{ig.h}$**, etc.) of **persons**;

The nomenclatures and quantities of **the current noological values** (**$V_{ih.l}$**, **$V_{il.l}$**, **$V_{iw.l}$**, **$V_{ig.l}$**, etc.) in the relevant formalized descriptions of **the current noological habitats** (**$PH_{ih.l}$**, **$PH_{il.l}$**, **$PH_{iw.l}$**, **$PH_{ig.l}$**, etc.) of **persons**;

The nomenclatures and magnitudes of **densities the current flows of consumption** (**$F_{C.ih.c}$, $F_{C.il.c}$, $F_{C.iw.c}$, $F_{C.ig.c}$, etc.**), **creation** (**$F_{M.ih.c}$, $F_{M.il.c}$, $F_{M.iw.c}$, $F_{M.ig.c}$, etc.**) and **rejection** (**$F_{S.ih.c}$, $F_{S.il.c}$, $F_{S.iw.c}$, $F_{S.ig.c}$, etc.**) **of current noo values** (**$V_{ih.c}$**, **$V_{il.c}$**, **$V_{iw.c}$**, **$V_{ig.c}$**, etc.) in relevant formalized descriptions of **noo provisions the existences** (**life supports**) (**$SP_{ih.c}$**, **$SP_{il.c}$**, **$SP_{iw.c}$**, **$SP_{ig.c}$**, etc.) of **persons**;

The nomenclatures and magnitudes of **densities the current flows of consumption** (**$F_{C.ih.l}$, $F_{C.il.l}$, $F_{C.iw.l}$, $F_{C.ig.l}$, etc.**), **creation** (**$F_{M.ih.l}$, $F_{M.il.l}$, $F_{M.iw.l}$, $F_{M.ig.l}$, etc.**) and **rejection** (**$F_{S.ih.l}$, $F_{S.il.l}$, $F_{S.iw.l}$, $F_{S.ig.l}$, etc.**) **of current noological values** (**$V_{ih.l}$**, **$V_{il.l}$**, **$V_{iw.l}$**, **$V_{ig.l}$**, etc.) in relevant formalized descriptions of **noological provisions the existences** (**life supports**) (**$SP_{ih.l}$**, **$SP_{il.l}$**, **$SP_{iw.l}$**, **$SP_{ig.l}$**, etc.) of **persons**.

The real creation of nomenclatures and quantities the **values** in the structures of **habitats**, as well as the nomenclatures and magnitudes of **densities of the current flows** in **the provision of existence** (**life support**) may significantly differ from the above-described **noo** ideal and depend on **the rules** (**RP**) adopted by **persons**, which may reflect some form of model of development of **the hierarchy**: strain, mycelium, the body of a living being, thickets, flock, family, primitive communal, slave, feudal, capitalist, socialist, Communist, post-industrial, post commodity-money, etc. Therefore, **the information pyramids** are used in **Noologistics** to formalize real **habitats** and **provisions of existence** (**life support**), which account for the specific **status** of the relevant **persons** in accordance to **the rules** of their **hierarchies**.

Two spheres of relationship exists between persons (**P_{ip}**, **P_{ih}**, **P_{il}**, **P_{iw}**, **P_{ib}**, **P_{ig}**, **P_{im}**, etc.) from the point of view **Noologistics**, which are characterized by different categories of **needs**: **primary** (N_1) and the **secondary** (N_2):

The primary sphere of relations between the **persons** (briefly – **S1**) is connected to the satisfaction of their **primary noo needs** (N_1) through the use of **primary noo** ($V_{1.v}$ and $V_{1.c}$) and **noologistical values** ($V_{1.h}$ and $V_{1.l}$). **Primary sphere of relations** (**S1**) of different **persons** (P_{ip}, P_{ih}, P_{il}, P_{iw}, P_{ib}, P_{ig}, P_{im}, etc.) conventionally denoted by $S1_{ip}$, $S1_{ih}$, $S1_{il}$, $S1_{iw}$, $S1_{ig}$, etc. Their formalization is making automatically by forming a set of formalized descriptions of the **primary habitats** (PH_1) and **provision the existences (life supports)** (SP_1) of **persons** by **the technology of calculation the information pyramid**, including:

Formalized description of **the primary noo habitat** of **the person** (briefly – $PH_{1.v}$ or $PH_{1.ip.v}$, $PH_{1.ih.v}$, $PH_{1.il.v}$, $PH_{1.iw.v}$, $PH_{1.ig.v}$, etc.);

Formalized description of **the current primary noo habitat** of **the person** (briefly – $PH_{1.c}$ or $PH_{1.ip.c}$, $PH_{1.ih.c}$, $PH_{1.il.c}$, $PH_{1.iw.c}$, $PH_{1.ig.c}$, etc.);

Formalized description of **the primary noologistical habitat** of **the person** (briefly – $PH_{1.h}$ or $PH_{1.ip.h}$, $PH_{1.ih.h}$, $PH_{1.il.h}$, $PH_{1.iw.h}$, $PH_{1.ig.h}$, etc.);

Formalized description of **the current primary noologistical habitat** of **the person** (briefly – $PH_{1.l}$ or $PH_{1.ip.l}$, $PH_{1.ih.l}$, $PH_{1.il.l}$, $PH_{1.iw.l}$, $PH_{1.ig.l}$, etc.);

Formalized description of **the primary noo provisions the existence (life support)** of **the person** (briefly – $SP_{1.c}$ or $SP_{1.ip.c}$, $SP_{1.ih.c}$, $SP_{1.il.c}$, $SP_{1.iw.c}$, $SP_{1.ig.c}$, etc.);

Formalized description of **the primary noologistical provisions the existence (life support)** of **the person** (briefly – $SP_{1.l}$ or $SP_{1.ip.l}$, $SP_{1.ih.l}$, $SP_{1.il.l}$, $SP_{1.iw.l}$, $SP_{1.ig.l}$, etc.).

The contents of formalized descriptions of the $PH_{1.v}$, $PH_{1.c}$, $PH_{1.h}$, $PH_{1.l}$, $SP_{1.c}$ and $SP_{1.c}$ is analog to the content of formalized descriptions the PH_v, PH_c, PH_h, PH_l, SP_c and SP_l, but is different by subscripts in the conditional designations. They are not shown here to reduce description.

The secondary sphere of relations between the **persons** (briefly – **S2**) is connected to the satisfaction of their **secondary noo needs** (N_2) through the use of **secondary noo** ($V_{2.v}$ and $V_{2.c}$) and **noologistical values** ($V_{2.h}$ and $V_{2.l}$). **Secondary sphere of relations** (**S2**) of different **persons** (P_{ip}, P_{ih}, P_{il}, P_{iw}, P_{ib}, P_{ig}, P_{im}, etc.) conventionally denoted by **$S2_{ip}$, $S2_{ih}$, $S2_{il}$, $S2_{iw}$, $S2_{ig}$**, etc. Their formalization is making automatically by forming a set of formalized descriptions of the **secondary habitats** (**PH_2**) and **provision the existences (life supports)** (**SP_2**) of **persons** by **the technology of calculation the information pyramid**, including:

Formalized description of **the secondary noo habitat** of **the person** (briefly – **$PH_{2.v}$** or **$PH_{2.ip.v}$, $PH_{2.ih.v}$, $PH_{2.il.v}$, $PH_{2.iw.v}$, $PH_{2.ig.v}$**, etc.);

Formalized description of **the current secondary noo habitat** of **the person** (briefly – **$PH_{2.c}$** or **$PH_{2.ip.c}$, $PH_{2.ih.c}$, $PH_{2.il.c}$, $PH_{2.iw.c}$, $PH_{2.ig.c}$**, etc.);

Formalized description of **the secondary noologistical habitat** of **the person** (briefly – **$PH_{2.h}$** or **$PH_{2.ip.h}$, $PH_{2.ih.h}$, $PH_{2.il.h}$, $PH_{2.iw.h}$, $PH_{2.ig.h}$**, etc.);

Formalized description of **the current secondary noologistical habitat** of **the person** (briefly – **$PH_{2.l}$** or **$PH_{2.ip.l}$, $PH_{2.ih.l}$, $PH_{2.il.l}$, $PH_{2.iw.l}$, $PH_{2.ig.l}$**, etc.);

Formalized description of **the secondary noo provisions the existence** (**life support**) of **the person** (briefly – **$SP_{2.c}$** or **$SP_{2.ip.c}$, $SP_{2.ih.c}$, $SP_{2.il.c}$, $SP_{2.iw.c}$, $SP_{2.ig.c}$**, etc.);

Formalized description of **the secondary noologistical provisions the existence** (**life support**) of **the person** (briefly – **$SP_{2.l}$** or **$SP_{2.ip.l}$, $SP_{2.ih.l}$, $SP_{2.il.l}$, $SP_{2.iw.l}$, $SP_{2.ig.l}$**, etc.).

The aforementioned formalized descriptions of the **$PH_{2.v}$, $PH_{2.c}$, $PH_{2.h}$** and **$PH_{2.l}$** are created by an exception the **primary noo** (**$V_{1.v}$** and **$V_{1.c}$**) and **noologistical** (**$V_{1.h}$** and **$V_{1.l}$**) **values** from the above-described formalized descriptions **PH_v, PH_c, PH_h** and **PH_l**, and formalized descriptions of the **$SP_{2.c}$** and **$SP_{2.l}$** – by an exception of the respective **current flows** of **consumption** (**$F_{1.C.c}$** and **$F_{1.C.l}$**), **creation** (**$F_{1.M.c}$** and **$F_{1.M.l}$**) and **rejection** (**$F_{1.S.c}$** and **$F_{1.S.l}$**) of **primary noo** (**$V_{1.v}$** and **$V_{1.c}$**) and **noologistical values** (**$V_{1.h}$** and **$V_{1.l}$**) from the above-described formalized descriptions of the **SP_c** and **SP_l**. The contents of formalized descriptions of the **$PH_{2.v}$, $PH_{2.c}$, $PH_{2.h}$, $PH_{2.l}$, $SP_{2.c}$** and **$SP_{2.c}$** is analog to the content of formalized descriptions the **$PH_{1.v}$, $PH_{1.c}$, $PH_{1.h}$, $PH_{1.l}$, $SP_{1.c}$** and **$SP_{1.c}$**, but is different by subscripts in the conditional designations. They are not shown here to reduce description.

Persons automatically control parameters given above in the formalized descriptions, by the existing devices, systems, power automation, automated control systems, etc. that they have, and use thus obtained information to generate **the noo management solutions**, calculation and execution of **the noo control actions** when solving problems of **the current noo management** of his **objects**, forecasting, planning, provisioning, repair, modeling, design, and other.

Remark. The above structure of information the $\mathbf{P_{1.1}}$, $\mathbf{P_{1.2}}$, $\mathbf{P_{1.3}}$, ..., $\mathbf{P_{i.ni}}$, ..., $\mathbf{P_{I.NI}}$ and $\mathbf{P_{ip}}$, as well as the form and content of the relevant pages given for demonstration of the ability to form the universal databases of information are necessary for the application of **the technology of Noologistics**. Any other names of parameters, structure and formal descriptions are possible in reality, which depend on many specific conditions – see section **4. The Practical Examples of Noologistics Implementation**.

2.3. The Object of Noologistics

The concept of "**control Object**" is a General term in **General management theory**, indicate objectively existing thing, device, process, relationships, needs, tastes, group of people, mechanism, material, information and financial flow, the flow impacts on the environment, etc., as well as their combination, dynamic state (functioning, behavior, mode, direction, magnitude, efficiency, optimality, impact on other objects, etc.) which is changed and/or supported by the **person** of management in accordance to goal given by him.

It follows from the definition of **Noologistics** that **the ideal object of control** (briefly - **IO**) of **person** is **the provision of his existence (life support)**, which is represented in **Noologistics** through a set of interrelated **current flows of consumption**, **creation** and **rejection** of **values** between him, other **persons** and his **habitat** in **the PRESENT** to achieve in **the FUTURE a goal** set by him.

It is known that managing the set of **current flows of consumption**, **creation** and **rejection** of **values** is realized trough the impact on the equipment appropriate **set of grids** in which these **flows** are supported by the **person**. This **set of grids** is their **real** (technological) **object of control** (briefly - **RO**).

Therefore, the real (technological) **object of Noologistics** is the combination of **person's grids** in which he supports the **current flows of consumption**, **creation** and **rejection** of **values**, and controls flows in **the PRESENT** by impacting to **the units of equipment**.

As mentioned above **the ideal** (**IO**) and **real** (**RO**) **objects** exist inseparably from each other in the future under the concept "**object** (briefly - **Ot**)" means the aggregate of them, i.e. Ot = Σ(IO, RO).

Classification of **objects** is established in **Noologistics** in accordance to the classification of types of **persons** and **values**, **current flows** of which form the **provision of their existence**. It is reflected in the subscript of **objects** notations, for example:

Noo object (briefly - $\mathbf{Ot_c}$) – is an aggregate of **the current flows of noo values** ($\mathbf{V_c}$) and related **grids** ($\mathbf{G_c}$), i.e. $Ot_c = \Sigma(\mathbf{IO_c}, \mathbf{RO_c})$;

Noologistical object (briefly – $\mathbf{Ot_l}$) – is an aggregate of **the current flows of noologistical values** ($\mathbf{V_l}$) and related **grids** ($\mathbf{G_l}$), i.e. $Ot_c = \Sigma(\mathbf{IO_l}, \mathbf{RO_l})$;

The primary noo object (briefly - $\mathbf{Ot_{1.c}}$) – is an aggregate of **the current flows of primary noo values** ($\mathbf{V_{1.c}}$) and related **grids** ($\mathbf{G_{1.c}}$), i.e. $Ot_{1.c} = \Sigma(\mathbf{IO_{1.c}}, \mathbf{RO_{1.c}})$;

The secondary noo object (briefly - $\mathbf{Ot_{2.c}}$) – is an aggregate of **the current flows of secondary noo values** ($\mathbf{V_{2.c}}$) and related **grids** ($\mathbf{G_{2.c}}$), i.e. $Ot_{2.c} = \Sigma(\mathbf{IO_{2.c}}, \mathbf{RO_{2.c}})$;

The primary noologistical object (briefly - $\mathbf{Ot_{1.l}}$) – is an aggregate of **the current flows of primary noologistical values** ($\mathbf{V_{1.l}}$) and related **grids** ($\mathbf{G_{1.l}}$), i.e. $Ot_{1.l} = \Sigma(\mathbf{IO_{1.l}}, \mathbf{RO_{1.l}})$;

The secondary noologistical object (briefly - $\mathbf{Ot_{2.l}}$) – is an aggregate of **the current flows of secondary noologistical values** ($\mathbf{V_{2.l}}$) and related **grids** ($\mathbf{G_{2.l}}$), i.e. $Ot_{2.l} = \Sigma(\mathbf{IO_{2.l}}, \mathbf{RO_{2.l}})$, etc.

Formal descriptions of the above types of **objects** are contained in formalized descriptions of **the provisions of existences** (**life supports**) and of **grids**. These formalized descriptions for the persons located at upper levels of hierarchies, are formed by **the technology of calculating information pyramids**.

If the totality of all beings on Earth which have attributes of the mind, taken as a total **person**, his **ideal object** shall be the **noosphere** because it is a combination of **the provisions of their existences** (**life supports**), and its **real object** – the totality of technical means, such as **grids**, which he uses to impact the **noosphere**. The totality of the **noosphere** and the corresponding **grids** on the planet Earth, from the point of view **Noologistics** is a global **control object**. **The control objects** in level of galaxy and universe may be formed similarly.

2.4. The Subject of Noologistics

Subject of Noologistics (briefly - **SNL**) - it is a generalizing term, indicating the relationship between its **person** and **the object**, the brief definition of which has the form:

The subject of Noologistics is the formation of the **noo (reasonable) providing of own existence** (**life support**), which **the person** uses in **the PRESENT** to achieve his **goal** in **the FUTURE**.

Since **the providing of own existence** (**life support**) of any **person** consists of a set of interconnected **current flows of consumption of values**, **creation of values** and **rejection of values** to other **persons** and his **habitat**, reasonable systematical formation of **life support** is the essence of its activity within **the rules** that determine the degree of competition and mutual assistance in relations to other **persons** and his **habitat**, as well as **the principles** and **criteria of reasonableness** in the formation and achievement of his **goal**.

Any collection of interacting **persons** forms a **hierarchy**, which itself is a single **person** with a single **providing of his existence** (**life support**) and the single common **habitat**, from the point of view **Noologistics**. It follows that the subject of **Noologistics** for the totality of all interacting **persons** within the planet Earth and any other planet is the formation of the **noosphere**, within any Galaxy - formation **noogalaxy** and within the Universe – the formation of **noouniverse**, etc.

2.5. The Goal of Noologistics Person

In the general management theory, the concept of "management goal" is a general term denoting an ideal end result, which the **person** of management aspires to achieve by changing or maintaining the dynamic state of his control object.

Noo Logistics (**Noologistics**) provides for each of its persons their individual **goal** as one of the main signs of his **personality**.

The definition of the concept «**the goal** of **the person of Noologistics**» that is given below was formulated on the basis of the above and the description of the **object of Noologistics**:

The **goal** of **the person of Noologistics** is that ideal **provision of his existence** (**life support**), which it seeks to achieve in the **FUTURE** through the **reasonable management** of **the provision of his existence** (**life support**) in the **PRESENT**.

The abbreviated designations of **goal** concepts form in **Noologistics** the addition of the letter "A" after the abbreviated notations of other similar concepts, as shown below:

$\mathbf{VA_v}$ – the conventional designation of any of the **noo values** contained in the description of **the goal**, in which the Latin small letter "v" in the lower index denotes an individual identification number of it's registration in **a formalized description of environment**, for example:

$\mathbf{VA_{C.ip.v}}$ – the conventional designation of any of the **noo values** contained in the description of **the goal** that the **person** designated by $\mathbf{P_{ip}}$ is planning to consume;

$VA_{M.ip.v}$ – the conventional designation of any of the **noo values** contained in the description of **the goal** that the **person** designated by **P_{ip}** is planning to creation;

$VA_{S.ip.v}$ – the conventional designation of any of the **noo values** contained in the description of **the goal** that the **person** designated by **P_{ip}** is planning to reject;

$DA_{C.ip.v}$ – conventional designation of the flow density of consumption the **noo values** contained in the description of **the goal** that the **person** designated by **P_{ip}** is planning to consume;

$DA_{M.iw.v}$ – the conventional designation of the flow density of creation the **noo values** contained in the description of **the goal** that the **person** designated by **P_{iw}** is planning to creation;

$DA_{S.il.v}$ – the conventional designation of the flow density of rejecting the **noo values** contained in the description of **the goal** that the **person** designated by **P_{il}** is planning to reject;

PHA – the conventional designation of the **noo habitat** corresponding to the description of the **goal** formulated by the **person**;

SPA – the conventional designation of the **provision the existence** (**life support**) corresponding to the description of the **goal** formulated by the **person**, and so on.

The classification of **goals** is provided for in **Noologistics**, which is reflected in the lower index of their conventional designations in accordance with the classification of types of **persons** and **values**, for example:

A_v – **noo goal** contains the quantities and densities of flows of **goal's noo values (VA_v)**;

A_h – **noologistical goal** contains the quantities and densities of flows of **goal's noologistical values (VA_h)**;

$A_{1.v}$ – **primary noo goal** contains the quantities and densities of flows of **goal's primary noo values ($VA_{1.c}$)**;

$A_{2.ip.h}$ – **secondary noologistical goal** contains the quantities and densities of flows of **goal's secondary noologistical values ($VA_{2.ip.h}$)**;

$A_{1.ip.h}$ – **primary noologistical goal** contains the quantities and densities of flows of **goal's primary noologistical values ($VA_{1.ip.h}$)**, and so on.

It is accepted in **Noologistics** that each **person** knows the nomenclature and ideal parameters of his **goal**, of each his **noo value** (**VA**), the ideal parameters and structure of his flows of **consumed**, **creation** and **rejected values**, which are designed to meet his **goal's noo needs**. He has the ability to set in its **goal** not only the parameters that characterize the **goal's provision his existence** (**life support**) in the **FUTURE**, but also the parameters characterizing his **goal's habitat** in the **FUTURE**. The values of these parameters are recalculated into each other using the same formulas used to recalculate similar parameters for **provision his existence** (**life support**) and **habitat** in the **PRESENT**.

All the types of **goals** of any **person** mentioned above may be presented by him in a formalized form by means of the corresponding uniform formalized descriptions. Below are examples of such typical descriptions for a **person** having the conventional designation **P_{ip}**, which are intended not only for the generation of **noo (NCS_{IP})** and **noologistical (NCS_{ip}) management solutions** in the **PRESENT**, as well as for calculating the simulated parameters of the **goal's noo ($NCA_{ip.v}$)** and the **noologistical ($NCA_{ip.h}$) control actions** in the **FUTURE** but also to visualize the process of **noo management**. Therefore, some types of information in different descriptions are repeated for the convenience of **P_{ip}**.

Each **person** writes into the formalized descriptions of his **goals** only that information that is absent in the **system of Noologistics**, according to his own **rules**, based on his **goal needs** and analysis of the current situation in the **habitat**. All other information is automatically entered. When manually filling each parameter in a formalized description, its possible minimum and maximum limit is automatically displayed, and its verification is also performed, which prevents the setting of values beyond its biological limits, **rules** and technical capabilities of the equipment of the **real object**.

Below are given examples of the content of formalized descriptions of the **goals** of the **person** having the conventional designation **P_{ip}**, including:

The Noo Goal of P_{ip} ($A_{ip.v}$)

The description may contain four parts: **«The goal** - **to provide the noo existence (life support) of P_{ip} by consuming the $VA_{C.ip.v}$»**, **«The goal - to provide the noo existence (life support) of P_{ip} by creation the $VA_{M.ip.v}$»**, «**The goal - to provide the noo existence (life support) of P_{ip} by rejecting the $VA_{S.ip.v}$**» and «**The goal – the noo habitat of P_{ip}**», provided for review separately or together, including:

The first part of the description contains:

Name **«The goal** - **to provide the noo existence (life support) of P_{ip} by consuming the $VA_{C.ip.v}$»**, the conventional designation **$SPA_{C.ip.v}$** and personal identification number **P_{ip}**, for example, **ip**;

nomenclature of all **flows of $VA_{C.ip.v}$ ($FA_{C.ip.v}$)** including:

nomenclature of names **$FA_{C.ip.v}$** and its conventional designations (**$FA_{C.ip.v}$**);

individual identification number **v** of each **$VA_{C.ip.v}$** from formalized description of the **environment** that forms the basis of correspond **$FA_{C.ip.v}$**;

parameters of each **$FA_{C.ip.v}$** including:

unit of measure density of **$FA_{C.ip.v}$** (**$DA_{C.ip.v}$**), the size of the proper part of **$DA_{C.ip.v}$** is at the disposal of a **P_{ip}** (**$ODA_{C.ip.v}$**), the size of common part of **$DA_{C.ip.v}$** is at the disposal of a **P_{ip}** (**$CDA_{C.ip.v}$**), the **goal's size** of **$DA_{C.ip.v}$** is equal to the sum **$ODA_{C.ip.v}$** plus **$CDA_{C.ip.v}$** (**$RDA_{C.ip.v}$**), the **highest size** of **$DA_{C.ip.v}$** guaranteed for **P_{ip}** in **P_{ih}** (**$HDA_{C.ip.v}$**) under his status in **P_{ih}**, the **lowest size** of **$DA_{C.ip.v}$**, guaranteed for **P_{ip}** in **P_{ih}** (**$LDA_{C.ip.v}$**) under his status in **P_{ih}**, the **size** of **$DA_{C.ip.v}$** corresponds to **goals** of **P_{ih}** (**$DAA_{C.ip.v}$**) under his status in **P_{ih}**, etc.

The second part of the description contains:

Name «**The goal - to provide the noo existence (life support) of P_{ip} by creation the $VA_{M.ip.v}$**», the conventional designation **$SPA_{M.ip.v}$** and personal identification number **P_{ip}**, for example, **ip**;

nomenclature of all **flows of $VA_{M.ip.v}$** (**$FA_{M.ip.v}$**) including:

nomenclature of names $\mathbf{FA_{M.ip.v}}$ and its conventional designations ($\mathbf{FA_{M.ip.v}}$);

individual identification number **v** of each $\mathbf{VA_{M.ip.v}}$ from formalized description of the **environment** that forms the basis of correspond $\mathbf{FA_{M.ip.v}}$;

parameters of each $\mathbf{FA_{M.ip.v}}$ including:

unit of measure density of $\mathbf{FA_{M.ip.v}}$ ($\mathbf{DA_{M.ip.v}}$), the size of the proper part of $\mathbf{DA_{M.ip.v}}$ is at the disposal of a $\mathbf{P_{ip}}$ ($\mathbf{ODA_{M.ip.v}}$), the size of common part of $\mathbf{DA_{M.ip.v}}$ is at the disposal of a $\mathbf{P_{ip}}$ ($\mathbf{CDA_{M.ip.v}}$), the **goal's size** of $\mathbf{DA_{M.ip.v}}$ is equal to the sum $\mathbf{ODA_{M.ip.v}}$ plus $\mathbf{CDA_{M.ip.v}}$ ($\mathbf{RDA_{M.ip.v}}$), the **highest size** of $\mathbf{DA_{M.ip.v}}$ guaranteed for $\mathbf{P_{ip}}$ in $\mathbf{P_{ih}}$ ($\mathbf{HDA_{M.ip.v}}$) under his status in $\mathbf{P_{ih}}$, the **lowest size** of $\mathbf{DA_{M.ip.v}}$ guaranteed for $\mathbf{P_{ip}}$ in $\mathbf{P_{ih}}$ ($\mathbf{LDA_{M.ip.v}}$) under his status in $\mathbf{P_{ih}}$, the **size** of $\mathbf{DA_{M.ip.v}}$ corresponds to goals of $\mathbf{P_{ih}}$ ($\mathbf{DAA_{M.ip.v}}$) under his status in $\mathbf{P_{ih}}$, etc.

The third part of the description contains:

Name «**The goal - to provide the noo existence (life support) of $\mathbf{P_{ip}}$ by rejecting the $\mathbf{VA_{S.ip.v}}$**», the conventional designation $\mathbf{SPA_{S.ip.v}}$ and personal identification number $\mathbf{P_{ip}}$, for example, **ip**;

nomenclature of all **flows of $\mathbf{VA_{S.ip.v}}$** ($\mathbf{FA_{S.ip.v}}$) including:

nomenclature of names $\mathbf{FA_{S.ip.v}}$ and its conventional designations ($\mathbf{FA_{S.ip.v}}$);

individual identification number **v** of each $\mathbf{VA_{S.ip.v}}$ from formalized description of the **environment** that forms the basis of correspond $\mathbf{FA_{S.ip.v}}$;

parameters of each $\mathbf{FA_{S.ip.v}}$ including:

unit of measure density of $\mathbf{FA_{S.ip.v}}$ **($\mathbf{DA_{S.ip.v}}$)**, the size of the proper part of $\mathbf{DA_{S.ip.v}}$ is at the disposal of a $\mathbf{P_{ip}}$ ($\mathbf{ODA_{S.ip.v}}$), the size of common part of $\mathbf{DA_{S.ip.v}}$ is at the disposal of a $\mathbf{P_{ip}}$ ($\mathbf{CDA_{S.ip.v}}$), the **goal's size** of $\mathbf{DA_{S.ip.v}}$ is equal to the sum $\mathbf{ODA_{S.ip.v}}$ plus $\mathbf{CDA_{S.ip.v}}$ ($\mathbf{RDA_{S.ip.v}}$), the **highest size** of $\mathbf{DA_{S.ip.v}}$ guaranteed for $\mathbf{P_{ip}}$ in $\mathbf{P_{ih}}$ ($\mathbf{HDA_{S.ip.v}}$) under his status in $\mathbf{P_{ih}}$, the **lowest size** of $\mathbf{DA_{S.ip.v}}$ guaranteed for $\mathbf{P_{ip}}$ in $\mathbf{P_{ih}}$ ($\mathbf{LDA_{S.ip.v}}$) under his status in $\mathbf{P_{ih}}$, the **size** of $\mathbf{DA_{S.ip.v}}$ corresponds to goals of $\mathbf{P_{ih}}$ ($\mathbf{DAA_{S.ip.v}}$) under his status in $\mathbf{P_{ih}}$, etc.

The fourth part of the description contains:

Name «**The goal – the noo habitat of P_{ip}**», the conventional designation **$PHA_{ip.v}$** and personal identification number **P_{ip}**, for example, **ip**;

nomenclature of all **volums** (**$VA_{ip.v}$**) including:

nomenclature of names **$VA_{ip.v}$** and its conventional designations (**$VA_{ip.v}$**);

individual identification number **v** of each **$VA_{ip.v}$** from **formalized description of the environment**;

parameters of each **$VA_{ip.v}$** including:

unit of measure quantity of **$VA_{ip.v}$ ($QA_{ip.v}$)**, the size of the proper part of **$QA_{ip.v}$** is at the disposal of a **P_{ip}** (**$OQA_{ip.v}$**), the size of common part of **$QA_{ip.v}$** is at the disposal of a **P_{ip}** (**$CQA_{ip.v}$**), the **goal's size** of **$QA_{ip.v}$** is equal to the sum **$OQA_{ip.v}$** plus **$CQA_{ip.v}$** (**$RQA_{ip.v}$**), the **highest size** of **$QA_{ip.v}$** guaranteed for **P_{ip}** in **P_{ih}** (**$HQA_{ip.v}$**) under his status in **P_{ih}**, the **lowest size** of **$QA_{ip.v}$** guaranteed for **P_{ip}** in **P_{ih}** (**$LQA_{ip.v}$**) under his status in **P_{ih}**, the **size** of **$QA_{ip.v}$** corresponds to goals of **P_{ih}** (**$QAA_{ip.v}$**) under his status in **P_{ih}**, wished duration of **$VA_{ip.v}$** 's use at future (**$DUA_{ip.v}$**), etc.

General parameters for the whole **goal**:

A reasonable compromise between the 50% minimum of conditionally fixed costs in monetary terms, 30% minimum fuel consumption - energy resources in kWh equivalent and 20% minimum CO_2 emission;

Reasonable priority scale of **$VA_{C.ip.v}$**, **$VA_{M.ip.v}$** and **$VA_{S.ip.v}$**;

Reasonable scale of **$VA_{ip.v}$** importance, etc.

The Noologistical Goal of P_{ip} ($A_{ip.h}$)

The description may contain four parts: «**The goal - to provide the noologistical existence (life support) of P_{ip} by consuming the $VA_{C.ip.h}$**», «**The goal - to provide the noologistical existence (life support) of P_{ip} by creation the $VA_{M.ip.h}$**», «**The goal - to provide the noologistical existence (life support) of P_{ip} by rejecting the $VA_{S.ip.h}$**»

and «**The goal – the noologistical habitat of P_{ip}**», provided for review separately or together, including:

The first part of the description contains:

Name «**The goal - to provide the noologistical existence (life support) of P_{ip} by consuming the $VA_{C.ip.h}$**», the conventional designation **$SPA_{C.ip.h}$** and personal identification number **P_{ip}**, for example, **ip**;

nomenclature of all **flows of $VA_{C.ip.h}$** (**$FA_{C.ip.h}$**) including:

nomenclature of names **$FA_{C.ip.h}$** and its conventional designations (**$FA_{C.ip.h}$**);

individual identification number **h** of each **$VA_{C.ip.h}$** from **formalized description of the environment** that forms the basis of correspond **$FA_{C.ip.h}$**;

parameters of each **$FA_{C.ip.h}$** including:

unit of measure density of **$FA_{C.ip.h}$** (**$DA_{C.ip.h}$**), the size of the proper part of **$DA_{C.ip.h}$** is at the disposal of a **P_{ip}** (**$ODA_{C.ip.h}$**), the size of common part of **$DA_{C.ip.h}$** is at the disposal of a **P_{ip}** (**$CDA_{C.ip.h}$**), the **goal's size** of **$DA_{C.ip.h}$** is equal to the sum **$ODA_{C.ip.h}$** plus **$CDA_{C.ip.h}$** (**$RDA_{C.ip.h}$**), the **highest size** of **$DA_{C.ip.h}$** guaranteed for **P_{ip}** in **P_{ih}** (**$HDA_{C.ip.h}$**) under his status in **P_{ih}**, the **lowest size** of **$DA_{C.ip.h}$**, guaranteed for **P_{ip}** in **P_{ih}** (**$LDA_{C.ip.h}$**) under his status in **P_{ih}**, the **size** of **$DA_{C.ip.h}$** corresponds to goals of **P_{ih}** **(**$DAA_{C.ip.h}$**)** under his status in **P_{ih}**, etc.

The second part of the description contains:

Name «**The goal - to provide the noologistical existence (life support) of P_{ip} by creation the $VA_{M.ip.h}$**», the conventional designation **$SPA_{M.ip.h}$** and personal identification number **P_{ip}**, for example, **ip**;

nomenclature of all **flows of $VA_{M.ip.h}$** (**$FA_{M.ip.h}$**) including:

nomenclature of names **$FA_{M.ip.h}$** and its conventional designations (**$FA_{M.ip.h}$**);

individual identification number **h** of each **$VA_{M.ip.h}$** from **formalized description of the environment** that forms the basis of correspond **$FA_{M.ip.h}$**;

parameters of each **$FA_{M.ip.h}$** including:

unit of measure density of **$FA_{M.ip.h}$** (**$DA_{M.ip.h}$**), the size of the proper part of **$DA_{M.ip.h}$** is at the disposal of a **P_{ip}** (**$ODA_{M.ip.h}$**), the size of common part of **$DA_{M.ip.h}$** is at the disposal of a **P_{ip}** (**$CDA_{M.ip.h}$**), the **goal's size** of **$DA_{M.ip.h}$** is equal to the sum **$ODA_{M.ip.h}$** plus **$CDA_{M.ip.h}$** (**$RDA_{M.ip.h}$**), the **highest size** of **$DA_{M.ip.h}$** guaranteed for **P_{ip}** in **P_{ih}** (**$HDA_{M.ip.h}$**) under his status in **P_{ih}**, the **lowest size** of **$DA_{M.ip.h}$** guaranteed for **P_{ip}** in **P_{ih}** (**$LDA_{M.ip.h}$**) under his status in **P_{ih}**, the **size** of **$DA_{M.ip.h}$** corresponds to goals of **P_{ih}** (**$DAA_{M.ip.h}$**) under his status in **P_{ih}**, etc.

The third part of the description contains:

Name «**The goal - to provide the noological existence (life support) of P_{ip} by rejecting the $VA_{S.ip.h}$**», the conventional designation **$SPA_{S.ip.h}$** and personal identification number **P_{ip}**, for example, **ip**;

nomenclature of all **flows of $VA_{S.ip.h}$** (**$FA_{S.ip.h}$**) including:

nomenclature of names **$FA_{S.ip.h}$** and its conventional designations (**$FA_{S.ip.h}$**);

individual identification number **h** of each **$FA_{S.ip.h}$** from **formalized description of the environment** that forms the basis of correspond **$FA_{S.ip.h}$**;

parameters of each **$FA_{S.ip.h}$** including:

unit of measure density of **$FA_{S.ip.h}$** (**$DA_{S.ip.h}$**), the size of the proper part of **$DA_{S.ip.h}$** is at the disposal of a **P_{ip}** (**$ODA_{S.ip.h}$**), the size of common part of **$DA_{S.ip.h}$** is at the disposal of a **P_{ip}** (**$CDA_{S.ip.h}$**), the **goal's size** of **$DA_{S.ip.h}$** is equal to the sum **$ODA_{S.ip.h}$** plus **$CDA_{S.ip.h}$** (**$RDA_{S.ip.h}$**), the **highest size** of **$DA_{S.ip.h}$** guaranteed for **P_{ip}** in **P_{ih}** (**$HDA_{S.ip.h}$**) under his status in **P_{ih}**, the **lowest size** of **$DA_{S.ip.h}$** guaranteed for **P_{ip}** in **P_{ih}** (**$LDA_{S.ip.h}$**) under his status in **P_{ih}**, the **size** of **$DA_{S.ip.h}$** corresponds to goals of **P_{ih}** (**$DAA_{S.ip.h}$**) under his status in **P_{ih}**, etc.

The fourth part of the description contains:

Name «**The goal – the noological habitat of P_{ip}**», the conventional designation **$PHA_{ip.h}$** and personal identification number **P_{ip}**, for example, **ip**;

nomenclature of all **volums** (**$VA_{ip.h}$**) including:

nomenclature of names **$VA_{ip.h}$** and its conventional designations (**$VA_{ip.h}$**);

individual identification number **h** of each **$VA_{ip.h}$** from **formalized description of the environment**;

parameters of each **$VA_{ip.h}$** including:

unit of measure quantity of **$VA_{ip.h}$** **(**$QA_{ip.h}$**)**, the size of the proper part of **$QA_{ip.h}$** is at the disposal of a **P_{ip}** (**$OQA_{ip.h}$**), the size of common part of **$QA_{ip.h}$** is at the disposal of a **P_{ip}** (**$CQA_{ip.h}$**), the **goal's size** of **$QA_{ip.h}$** is equal to the sum **$OQA_{ip.h}$** plus **$CQA_{ip.h}$** (**$RQA_{ip.h}$**), the **highest size** of **$QA_{ip.h}$** guaranteed for **P_{ip}** in **P_{ih}** (**$HQA_{ip.h}$**) under his status in **P_{ih}**, the **lowest size** of **$QA_{ip.h}$** guaranteed for **P_{ip}** in **P_{ih}** (**$LQA_{ip.h}$**) under his status in **P_{ih}**, the **size** of **$QA_{ip.h}$** corresponds to goals of **P_{ih}** (**$QAA_{ip.h}$**) under his status in **P_{ih}**, wished duration of **$VA_{ip.h}$**'s use at future (**$DUA_{ip.h}$**), etc.

General parameters for the whole **goal**:

A reasonable compromise between the 50% minimum of conditionally fixed costs in monetary terms, 30% minimum fuel consumption - energy resources in kWh equivalent and 20% minimum CO_2 emission;

Reasonable priority scale of **$VA_{C.ip.h}$**, **$VA_{M.ip.h}$** and **$VA_{S.ip.h}$**;

Reasonable scale of **$VA_{ip.h}$** importance, etc.

The technology of Noologistics provides an automatic calculation of a formalized description containing the target parameters of any **hierarchy P** (**P_{ih}, P_{il}, P_{iw}, P_{ig}, etc.**) from formalized descriptions of its constituent entities using **the technology of calculating information pyramids (IP)** under **the rules** of this **hierarchy**. Openness, justice, liberalism, democracy, equality, humanity, environmental friendliness and other subjective assessments of relations between **persons** in the relevant **hierarchy**, as well as **environmental** action and relations to other **persons** depend on the content of these **rules** and on the correlation of the values of **the status coefficients** contained in them for each **person**.

Mankind knows many kinds of **hierarchies**, which were given different names, for example, food, primitive communal, slave-owning, feudal, capitalist, socialist, communist, democratic, liberal, multicultural, theocratic, post-industrial, people's capitalism, humane, etc. It is obvious that each of them is a person and therefore unconsciously (ie, instinctively) or consciously (that is, reasonably) somehow shapes its common **goal**, taking into account, to some extent or other, the **goals** of the **persons** entering into them. History shows that very often those **hierarchies** that ideologically positioned themselves as the most progressive established in their **rules** such relationships of the magnitudes of **status coefficients** for the constituent entities that hampered their development and unreasonably maintained the parameters of **life support** and the **habitats** of many of them at a level that was lower than that of **the persons** of backward **hierarchies**. The main reason for this discrepancy was the ignoring of the individual **goals** of most of their **persons** when forming the common **goal** of the whole **hierarchy**. This ignoring in the **Noologistics** is mathematically expressed in the zeroing out of the values of the individual **status coefficients** of these **persons** in the **rules** that describe the principles and criteria of the reasonableness of the formation of the overall **goal** of **the hierarchy** on the basis of the individual **goals** of **the persons** entering into it.

Obviously, the above method of forming a **noo** (ie, reasonable) **goal** will provide compliance to the rules of any of the **hierarchies** listed above, taking into account the desired action on the **environment** and relations to other entities.

For example, any **person** has the opportunity to establish money in the nomenclature of his **goal values** (**VA**), as well as the condition for reaching the maximum amount of them as a criterion of the reasonableness of managing his **object** and interaction with other entities, and also achieving the extremum of any other **criterion** of economic efficiency. Thus, the above method of forming of the **noo goal** completely provides commodity-money relations between the **persons**. However, it is obvious that commodity-money relations constitute an insignificant part of the **noosphere**, are fully characteristic only for a certain part of people and the share of such people will decrease as the productive forces of mankind develop. At the same time, the only universal form of relations in the **noosphere** is the **value relationship**.

The method described above also allows any person to establish any **values** in the nomenclature of their **goal values** (**VA**), as well as the condition for achieving a reasonable combination between the parameters of **provision their existence** (**life support**) and **habitat** in the **FUTURE**. Thus, the above method of forming the goal completely provides the value relations of the persons to each other and to the environment and provides an opportunity for mankind to gradually move to the post of commodity-money model of the development of society. This model provides for the voluntary formation of any **hierarchy** of **persons** that have a common **goal**, automatically is formed in real time on the basis of a compromise between the individual **goals** of all its participants. Such a method of forming a **hierarchy** and his **noo goal** may be called a **permanent referendum**, which designates a model for the voluntary formation of **a hierarchy** of **persons**. The transition to the post of the commodity-money model of the development of mankind may be smooth by gradually, by consciously changing the **hierarchy rules** in the direction of free satisfaction of the people's **primary needs**.

A permanent referendum in **Noologistics** is named the process of automatically forming the common goal of the whole hierarchy in the **PRESENT** according to its **rules** on the basis of the individual goals of its constituent **persons**. **The technology of calculating the upward non-indexed information pyramid** and **the status coefficients** set in the **rules** of the **hierarchy** is used for it's realization.

The current level of development of science and technology is already technically able to provide a permanent referendum thanks to the use of personal electronic devices, augmented reality, cloud information technologies, neural computer networks, mechanization and automation of production, industrial robots, etc. It is obvious that its total application will be a sign of the completion of the transition from representative to direct democracy.

2.6. The Current Flow of Noo Value Consumption

Each **person of Noologistics** supports **the provision of his existence** (**life support**) in the **PRESENT**, an integral part of which is his process of consumption of **values**. It consists in extracting a particular **value** directly from the **habitat** or receiving it from another **person** and in using it to meet a specific **need** to achieve his **goal**. To implement the above-mentioned process, the **person** uses either his own organism, or **unit equipment** of **grid**, or his entire **grid**, thereby forming a flow of **noo value**, which according to the classification of **Noologistics** is categorized as the **current conditional-variable flow of his consumption** (briefly - $\mathbf{F_C}$), which has the following definition:

The current conditional-variable flow of consumption of noo value is the process of using it by the **person** of **Noologistics** in the **PRESENT** by means of satisfying his **need** for achieving the set **goal**.

This flow is called conditional variables by analogy with the terminology of the commodity-money **Economy** because its magnitude depends on the productivity of the process in which it is used. Each **person** usually uses several types of **current conditional-variable consumption flows** at the same time: some of them satisfy their **primary needs** that directly support his biological existence, while others use it to meet their **secondary needs** at a higher level. Between the many types of **current conditional-variable consumption flows**, the persons also highlight information, which is based on **current noologistical values** and which it may use to develop **noologistical managerial solutions** and calculate the corresponding **noologistical control actions** on their **real control objects**.

Persons use formalized information about the simplest **current conditional variable consumption flows** when solving various management tasks that are supported by their organisms, as well as the b-th **unit of his equipment** used by them at the current time. **Persons** form the rest of his species, the name and notations of these most simple types of their designation depends on many factors. An example of the formalization of such a simple form of **the current conditional-variable flow of consumption** of the l-th **noologistical**

value in the b-th **unit of the grid equipment** of the **person** that has the notation P_{ip} is shown below. The notation of this flow is $F_{C.ip.l.b}$, the notation of **unit of the grid equipment** by which he manages this flow is $G_{C.ip.l.b}$, the notation of the **current technological process** in it is $CTP_{C.ip.l.b}$, and the notation for his **grid** - $G_{ip.l.b}$. The most frequently used parameters in **Noologistics** when formalizing such simplest types of **current conditional-variable consumption flows** are the following ones:

$D_{C.ip.l.b}$ – it is the notation of the density of the $F_{C.ip.l.b}$, which is called the density of **the current conditional-variable flow** of l-st **noologistical value consumption** in $G_{C.ip.l.b}$ and which **the system of Noologistics** measures in the **PRESENT** (at the current time) by the corresponding device according to the **rules** it observes, for example, a counter, a flowmeter, a monitoring system, and so on.

$Q_{C.ip.l.b}$ – it is the notation of the **current quantity** of l-st **consumed noological value** ($V_{C.ip.l.b}$) in $G_{C.ip.l.b}$ in a given period of time, for example, from the moment of its start to the current moment, which **the system of Noologistics** calculates in the **PRESENT** (at the current time) according to the **rules** it observes, for example, by the formula:

$$Q_{C.ip.l.b} = \int_{t_н}^{t} D_{C.ip.l.b}(t) * dt ,$$

here are:

t – it is the notation of the current time the $G_{C.ip.l.b}$'s working which **the system of Noologistics** measures from it's start according to the **rules** it observes, for example, by the time etalon;

t – it is the notation of the current time at the start moment of $G_{C.ip.l.b}$'s work on the same etalon of time, other – see above.

$D_{S.ip.l.b}$ – it is the notation of the density of the $F_{S.ip.l.b}$, which is called the density of **the current flow of conditional-variable noologistical value reject** of l-st **noologistical value** ($V_{S.ip.l.b}$) from $G_{C.ip.l.b}$ and which **the system of Noologistics** measures in the **PRESENT** (at the current time) by the corresponding device according to the **rules** it observes, for example, a counter, a flow meter, a monitoring system, and so on;

$QP_{C.ip.l.b}$ and **$QP_{S.ip.l.b}$** – it are the notations of the **current quality parameters** of l-st **noologistical values** (**$V_{C.ip.l.b}$** and **$V_{S.ip.l.b}$**) which **the system of Noologistics** measures in the **PRESENT** (at the current time) by the corresponding device according to the **rules** it observes, for example, a thermometer, a gas analyzer, a monitoring system, and so on;

$LF_{C.ip.l.b}$ and **$LF_{S.ip.l.b}$** – it are the notations of the **current location** of **$F_{C.ip.l.b}$** and **$F_{S.ip.l.b}$** in the **environment** which **the system of Noologistics** measures in the **PRESENT** (at the current time) by the corresponding device according to the **rules** it observes, for example, by the **geoinformation system**;

$AF_{C.ip.l.b}$ and **$AF_{S.ip.l.b}$** – it are the notations of the **current allocation** of **$F_{C.ip.l.b}$** and **$F_{S.ip.l.b}$** in the **environment** which **the system of Noologistics** calculates in the **PRESENT** (at the current time) by the corresponding device according to the **rules** it observes, for example, by the **geoinformation system**.

The system of Noologistics calculates the parameters of the flows that describe prehistory of the **$F_{C.ip.l.b}$** in accordance to the **criteria of reasonableness** that were given by **person** in his **goal,** except for the parameters directly listed at the moment. **The current conditional-fixed flow of consumption the noo value** (shortly – **FF_C**) and **current total flow of consumption the noo value** (shortly – **TF_C**) are referred to them, which have the following definitions:

The current conditional-fixed flow of consumption of noo value is the depreciation (amortization) of the quantities of the consumed **noo value** in the **PAST** to the consumed or created **noo value** in the **PRESENT**.

The current total flow of consumption of noo value (**TF_C**) is the sum of **the current conditional-variable flow of consumption the noo**

value (F_C) and **the current conditional-fixed flow of consumption the noo value** (FF_C) in the **PRESENT**.

These flows have the following notations in this example:

The current conditional-fixed flow of consumption of the $\mathbf{V_{C.ip.l.b}}$ in $\mathbf{G_{C.ip.l.b}}$ has the notation $\mathbf{FF_{C.ip.l.b}}$.

The current total flow of consumption of the $\mathbf{V_{C.ip.l.b}}$ in $\mathbf{G_{C.ip.l.b}}$ has the notation $\mathbf{TF_{C.ip.l.b}}$.

The current conditional-fixed flow of rejection of the $\mathbf{V_{S.ip.l.b}}$ from $\mathbf{G_{C.ip.l.b}}$ has the notation $\mathbf{FF_{S.ip.l.b}}$.

The current total flow of rejection of the $\mathbf{V_{S.ip.l.b}}$ from $\mathbf{G_{C.ip.l.b}}$ has the notation $\mathbf{TF_{S.ip.l.b}}$.

Parameters of the $\mathbf{FF_{C.ip.l.b}}$, $\mathbf{TF_{C.ip.l.b}}$, $\mathbf{FF_{S.ip.l.b}}$ and $\mathbf{TF_{S.ip.l.b}}$ are used for the depreciation of the consumed $\mathbf{V_{C.ip.l.b}}$ quantities from the environment and rejected $\mathbf{V_{S.ip.l.b}}$ quantities to it in the **PAST** to the consumed $\mathbf{V_{C.ip.l.b}}$ and created $\mathbf{V_{M.ip.l.b}}$ in the **PRESENT** in the processes of their extraction, creation, storage, transport, servicing, rejection, etc. Such a reference is used in the (commodity-money) Economy and is called depreciation (amortization). The main difference between **noologistic** depreciation and the used in (commodity-money) **Economy** is that:

- it is depreciated not only to previously consumed **values**, but also to **values** previously rejected to the **environment**;
- not only money is used as a depreciable **value**, but also any other types of **values** that are set by the **person** in his **goal** as **criteria for the reasonableness of management**.

Parameters of the above-mentioned simplest types of the $\mathbf{FF_{C.ip.l.b}}$, $\mathbf{TF_{C.ip.l.b}}$, $\mathbf{FF_{S.ip.l.b}}$ and $\mathbf{TF_{S.ip.l.b}}$ are used in **Noologistics** to formalize information as a basis for further calculations, including:

$\mathbf{FD_{C.ip.l.b}}$ – it is the notation of the density of the $\mathbf{FF_{C.ip.l.b}}$, which is called the density of **the current conditional-fixed flow** of the $\mathbf{V_{C.ip.l.b}}$ in $\mathbf{G_{C.ip.l.b}}$;

$\mathbf{FQ_{C.ip.l.b}}$ – it is the notation of the **current quantity** of the $\mathbf{V_{C.ip.l.b}}$ was consumed in $\mathbf{G_{C.ip.l.b}}$ in the processes of extraction, creation, storage, transport, servicing, rejection, etc. which **the system of Noologistics** amortizes in the **PRESENT** (at the current time) according to the **rules** it observes, for example, through accounting;

$SFD_{C.ip.l.b}$ – it is the notation of the **current specified fixed density of consumption flow** of the **$V_{C.ip.l.b}$** in **$G_{C.ip.l.b}$**, which shows the total amount of previously expended **$V_{C.ip.l.b}$** per unit of quantity consumed by **$V_{C.ip.l.b}$** in **$G_{C.ip.l.b}$** and which the **system of Noologistics** is amortizing at the current time according to the **rules** it observes, for example, by the formula:

$$SFD_{C.ip.l.b} = FQ_{C.ip.l.b}/Q_{C.ip.l.b},$$

in which the notations of all quantities - see above;

$TD_{C.ip.l.b}$ – it is the notation of the density of the **$FF_{C.ip.l.b}$**, which is called **current total density of consumption flow** of the **$V_{C.ip.l.b}$** in **$G_{C.ip.l.b}$**, which the **system of Noologistics** is amortizing at the current time according to the **rules** it observes, for example, by the formula:

$$TD_{C.ip.l.b} = D_{C.ip.l.b} + FD_{C.ip.l.b},$$

in which the notations of all quantities - see above;

$TQ_{C.ip.l.b}$ – it is the notation of the **current total quantity** of the **$V_{C.ip.l.b}$** was consumed in **$G_{C.ip.l.b}$** in the processes of extraction, creation, storage, transport, servicing, rejection, etc. which **the system of Noologistics** amortizes in the **PRESENT** (at the current time) according to the **rules** it observes, for example, by the formula:

$$TQ_{C.ip.l.b} = Q_{C.ip.l.b} + FQ_{C.ip.l.b},$$

in which the conventional designations of all quantities - see above;

$FD_{S.ip.l.b}$ – it is the notation of the density of the **$FF_{S.ip.l.b}$**;

$FQ_{S.ip.l.b}$ – it is the notation of the **current conditional-fixed quantity** of the **$V_{S.ip.l.b}$**;

$\mathbf{SFD_{S.ip.l.b}}$ – it is the notation of the **specified density** of the $\mathbf{FF_{S.ip.l.b}}$;

$\mathbf{TD_{S.ip.l.b}}$ – it is the notation of the density of the $\mathbf{TF_{S.ip.l.b}}$;

$\mathbf{TQ_{S.ip.l.b}}$ – it is the notation of the **total quantity** of the $\mathbf{V_{S.ip.l.b}}$.

The system of Noologistics determines the magnitudes of the parameters only for those species whose parameters are specified in **person's goal** as **criteria of reasonableness**. For example, if **the criterion of reasonableness** in the **goal** is a compromise between 40% of the minimum cost in money terms, 30% of the minimum fuel consumption - energy resources in kWh equivalent and 30% minimum CO_2 emissions, then their nomenclature in the formal description $\mathbf{F_{C.ip.l.b}}$ will contain the following items:

$\mathbf{FD_{C.ip.Mn.b}}$ – it is the notation of the density of the $\mathbf{FF_{C.ip.Mn.b}}$ in **PRESENT** which the **system of Noologistics** is amortizing at the current time according to the **rules** it observes, for example, by the accounting due the formulas:

$$\mathbf{FD_{C.ip.Mn.b} = FQ_{C.ip.Mn.b} / T_{A.ip.Mn.b}}$$

or

$$\mathbf{FD_{C.ip.Mn.b} = SFD_{C.ip.Mn.b} * D_{C.ip.l.b}},$$

here are:

$\mathbf{T_{A.ip.Mn.b}}$ – this is the duration of the depreciation period of the $\mathbf{FQ_{C.ip.l.b}}$, which is established in the **rules**, for example, in accounting;

$\mathbf{SFD_{C.ip.Mn.b}}$ – it is the notation of the **current specified fixed density of** $\mathbf{FF_{C.ip.Mn.b}}$, which shows its price, i.e., the total amount of previously spent of $\mathbf{V_{C.ip.Mn.b}}$, occurring at the current time per unit of quantity consumed by $\mathbf{V_{C.ip.Mn.b}}$ in $\mathbf{G_{C.ip.l.b}}$, and is calculated by the **rules**, for example, of accounting - see description of $\mathbf{F_{M.ip.l.b}}$;

other – see above.

$TD_{C.ip.Mn.b}$ – it is the notation of the density of the **$TF_{C.ip.Mn.b}$** ie the total current costs corresponding to **$F_{C.ip.l.b}$** in the **PRESENT**, which is calculated according to the **rules**, for example, of accounting using the formula:

$$TD_{C.ip.Mn.b} = D_{C.ip.Mn.b} + FD_{C.ip.Mn.b},$$

in which the notations of all quantities - see above;

$FD_{C.ip.Vth.b}$ – it is the notation of the current density of the conditionally-fixed flow of costs in the **PRESENT**, which is calculated by the **rules**, for example, of energy audit according to the formula:

$$FD_{C.ip.Vth.b} = SFD_{C.ip.Vth.b} * D_{C.ip.l.b},$$

in which the notations of all quantities - see above;

$TD_{C.ip.Vth.b}$ – it is the notation of the density of the **$TF_{C.ip.Vth.b}$** ie the total current costs corresponding to **$F_{C.ip.l.b}$** in the **PRESENT**, which is calculated according to the **rules**, for example, of energy audit using the formula:

$$TD_{C.ip.Vth.b} = D_{C.ip.Vth.b} + FD_{C.ip.Vth.b},$$

in which the notations of all quantities - see above;

$FD_{S.ip.CO2.b}$ – it is the notation of the current density of the conditionally-fixed flow of CO_2 emissions in the **PRESENT**, which is calculated by the **rules**, for example, according to the rules of environmental protection according to the formula:

$$FD_{S.ip.CO2.b} = SFD_{S.ip.CO2.b} * D_{C.ip.l.b},$$

here are:

$SFD_{S.ip.CO2.b}$ – it is the notation of the **current specified conditionally-fixed density of $FF_{S.ip.CO2.b}$,** which shows the total previous CO_2 emissions in the **PAST** that are currently at the unit of the amount of **$V_{M.ip.l.b}$** created in **$G_{C.ip.l.b}$** in the **PRESENT**, calculated, for example, by the **rules** of environmental protection - see description $\mathbf{F_{M.ip.I.b}}$;

other – see above.

$\mathbf{TD_{S.ip.CO2.b}}$ – it is the notation of the **density of $\mathbf{TF_{S.ip.CO2.b}}$** ie the total current CO_2 emission in the **PRESENT** corresponding to $\mathbf{F_{C.ip.I.b}}$, which is calculated, for example, by the **rules** of environmental protection according to the formula:

$$\mathbf{TD_{S.ip.CO2.b} = D_{S.ip.CO2.b} + FD_{S.ip.CO2.b}},$$

in which the notations of all quantities - see above.

If the magnitudes of the current conditional-variable, conditionally-constant and total quantities $\mathbf{V_{C.ip.Mn.b}}$, $\mathbf{V_{C.ip.Vth.b}}$ and $\mathbf{V_{S.ip.CO2.b}}$ in $\mathbf{G_{C.ip.CO2.b}}$ corresponding to the calculated $\mathbf{F_{C.ip.CO2.b}}$ in the **PRESENT** from the moment of its operation start are required for developing a **management solution** and calculating the appropriate **control actions**, the **system of Noologistics** automatically calculates them according to the **rules**, for example, according to the formulas:

$$Q_{C.ip.Mn.b} = \int_{t_н}^{t} D_{C.ip.Mn.b}(t)*dt, \quad Q_{C.ip.Vth.b} = \int_{t_н}^{t} D_{C.ip.Vth.b}(t)*dt$$ and

$Q_{C.ip.CO2.b} = \int_{t_н}^{t} D_{S.ip.CO2.b}(t)*dt$ - these are formulas for calculating the conditional-variable magnitudes of the current quantities the $\mathbf{V_{C.ip.Mn.b}}$, $\mathbf{V_{C.ip.Vth.b}}$ and $\mathbf{V_{S.ip.CO2.b}}$,

$$FQ_{C.ip.Mn.b} = \int_{t_н}^{t} FD_{C.ip.Mn.b}(t)*dt, \quad FQ_{C.ip.Vth.b} = \int_{t_н}^{t} FD_{C.ip.Vth.b}(t)*dt$$

and $FQ_{C.ip.CO2.b} = \int_{t_н}^{t} FD_{S.ip.CO2.b}(t)*dt$ - these are formulas for calculating the conditional-fixed magnitudes of the current quantities the $\mathbf{V_{C.ip.Mn.b}}$, $\mathbf{V_{C.ip.Vth.b}}$ and $\mathbf{V_{S.ip.CO2.b}}$,

$$TQ_{C.ip.Mn.b} = \int_{t_н}^{t} TD_{C.ip.Mn.b}(t)*dt\ ,\ TQ_{C.ip.Vth.b} = \int_{t_н}^{t} TD_{C.ip.Vth.b}(t)*dt$$ and

$TQ_{C.ip.CO2.b} = \int_{t_н}^{t} TD_{S.ip.CO2.b}(t)*dt$ - these are formulas for calculating the total magnitudes of the current quantities the $\mathbf{V_{C.ip.Mn.b}}$, $\mathbf{V_{C.ip.Vth.b}}$ and $\mathbf{V_{S.ip.CO2.b}}$,

in which the notations of all quantities - see above.

The formalized description of any $\mathbf{F_{C.ip.l.b}}$ may have the name "**Current consumption flow of $\mathbf{V_{C.ip.l.b}}$ in $\mathbf{G_{C.ip.l.b}}$**" and contain the following information:

Current consumption flow of $\mathbf{V_{C.ip.l.b}}$ in $\mathbf{G_{C.ip.l.b}}$ ($\mathbf{F_{C.ip.l.b}}$)

Description contains:

The name «**Current consumption flow of $\mathbf{V_{C.ip.l.b}}$ in $\mathbf{G_{C.ip.l.b}}$**»;

The name, notation of $\mathbf{V_{C.ip.l.b}}$ and its unique number l from **the formalized description of the environment**;

unique ip for $\mathbf{P_{ip}}$;

Individual number b for $\mathbf{G_{C.ip.l.b}}$ from **the formalized description of equipment unit** ($\mathbf{G_b}$);

parameters of $\mathbf{F_{C.ip.l.b}}$, including:

The names of $\mathbf{D_{C.ip.l.b}}$, $\mathbf{FD_{C.ip.l.b}}$, $\mathbf{TD_{C.ip.l.b}}$, $\mathbf{QP_{C.ip.l.b}}$, $\mathbf{LF_{C.ip.l.b}}$, $\mathbf{AF_{C.ip.l.b}}$, $\mathbf{t_н}$ and $\mathbf{Q_{C.ip.l.b}}$, their notations, units of measure, magnitudes, etc.

The nomenclature and parameters of the $\mathbf{F_{C.ip.l.b}}$, $\mathbf{FF_{C.ip.l.b}}$, $\mathbf{TF_{C.ip.l.b}}$, $\mathbf{F_{S.ip.l.b}}$, $\mathbf{FF_{S.ip.l.b}}$ and $\mathbf{TF_{S.ip.l.b}}$, amortized on the $\mathbf{F_{C.ip.l.b}}$, including:

The notations of $\mathbf{V_{C.ip.l.b}}$, $\mathbf{V_{S.ip.l.b}}$ and their unique numbers l from **the formalized description of the environment**, names of $\mathbf{D_{C.ip.l.b}}$, $\mathbf{FD_{C.ip.l.b}}$, $\mathbf{TD_{C.ip.l.b}}$, $\mathbf{FQ_{C.ip.l.b}}$, $\mathbf{SD_{C.ip.l.b}}$, $\mathbf{SFD_{C.ip.l.b}}$, $\mathbf{STD_{C.ip.l.b}}$, $\mathbf{D_{S.ip.l.b}}$, $\mathbf{FD_{S.ip.l.b}}$, $\mathbf{TD_{S.ip.l.b}}$, $\mathbf{FQ_{S.ip.l.b}}$, $\mathbf{SD_{S.ip.l.b}}$, $\mathbf{SFD_{S.ip.l.b}}$, $\mathbf{STD_{S.ip.l.b}}$, their notations, units of measure, magnitudes, etc.

It follows from the formalized description of **current values** (V_c) that the parameters of some of their species are not subject to use in **noologistic** calculations, so when formalizing the description of **the current consumption flow** of such $V_{C.ip.c.b}$ ($F_{C.ip.c.b}$), **the person** (P_{ip}) uses the formalized information only about $F_{C.ip.l.b}$, $FF_{C.ip.l.b}$, $TF_{C.ip.l.b}$, $F_{S.ip.l.b}$, $FF_{S.ip.l.b}$ and $TF_{S.ip.l.b}$, related to the existence of $F_{C.ip.c.b}$ in **PRESENT**, the formalized description of which is similar to the way it was shown above, for example:

Current consumption flow of $V_{C.ip.c.b}$ in $G_{C.ip.c.b}$ ($F_{C.ip.c.b}$)

Description contains:

The name «**Current consumption flow of $V_{C.ip.c.b}$ in $G_{C.ip.c.b}$**»;
The name, notation of $V_{C.ip.c.b}$ and its unique number l from **the formalized description of the environment**;
unique ip for P_{ip};
parameters of $F_{C.ip.c.b}$, including:

The names of $F_{C.ip.c.b}$, $D_{C.ip.c.b}$, $QP_{C.ip.c.b}$, $LF_{C.ip.c.b}$, $AF_{C.ip.c.b}$, t_H and $Q_{C.ip.c.b}$, their notations, units of measure, magnitudes, etc.

The nomenclature and parameters of the $F_{C.ip.l.b}$, $FF_{C.ip.l.b}$, $TF_{C.ip.l.b}$, $F_{S.ip.l.b}$, $FF_{S.ip.l.b}$ and $TF_{S.ip.l.b}$, amortized on the $F_{C.ip.c.b}$, including:

The notation of $V_{C.ip.l.b}$, $V_{S.ip.l.b}$ and their unique numbers l from **the formalized description of the environment**, names of $D_{C.ip.l.b}$, $FD_{C.ip.l.b}$, $TD_{C.ip.l.b}$, $FQ_{C.ip.l.b}$, $SD_{C.ip.l.b}$, $SFD_{C.ip.l.b}$, $STD_{C.ip.l.b}$, $D_{S.ip.l.b}$, $FD_{S.ip.l.b}$, $TD_{S.ip.l.b}$, $FQ_{S.ip.l.b}$, $SD_{S.ip.l.b}$, $SFD_{S.ip.l.b}$, $STD_{S.ip.l.b}$, their notations, units of measure, magnitudes, etc.

It is envisaged to use in **Noologistics** the set of corresponding types of $F_{C.l}$ and $F_{C.c}$ in accordance with the type of the control task to be solved, which are reflected in the lower indexes of their notations, for example:

$F_{C.ip.l.b}$, $F_{C.ih.l.b}$, $F_{C.il.l.b}$, $F_{C.iw.l.b}$, $F_{C.ib.l.b}$, $F_{C.ig.l.b}$, $F_{C.im.l.b}$, etc. – it is notations of **current conditional-variable consumption flows** of **l-th noologistical value** ($V_{C.l}$) in b-th **equipment units (**$G_{C.ip.l.b}$, $G_{C.ih.l.b}$, $G_{C.il.l.b}$,

$G_{C.iw.l.b}$, $G_{C.ib.l.b}$, $G_{C.ig.l.b}$, $G_{C.im.l.b}$, etc.) of **persons (P_{ip}, P_{ih}, P_{il}, P_{iw}, P_{ib}, P_{ig}, P_{im}, etc.)**;

$F_{1.C.ip.l.b}$, $F_{1.C.ih.l.b}$, $F_{1.C.il.l.b}$, $F_{1.C.iw.l.b}$, $F_{1.C.ib.l.b}$, $F_{1.C.ig.l.b}$, $F_{1.C.im.l.b}$, etc. – it is notations of **current conditional-variable consumption flows** of **l-th primary noologistical value** (**$V_{1.C.l}$**) in b-th **equipment units ($G_{1.C.ip.l.b}$, $G_{1.C.ih.l.b}$, $G_{1.C.il.l.b}$, $G_{1.C.iw.l.b}$, $G_{1.C.ib.l.b}$, $G_{1.C.ig.l.b}$, $G_{1.C.im.l.b}$, etc.)** of **persons (P_{ip}, P_{ih}, P_{il}, P_{iw}, P_{ib}, P_{ig}, P_{im}, etc.)**;

$F_{C.ip.l}$, $F_{C.ih.l}$, $F_{C.il.l}$, $F_{C.iw.l}$, $F_{C.ib.l}$, $F_{C.ig.l}$, $F_{C.im.l}$, etc. – it is notations of sum **current conditional-variable consumption flows** of **l-th noologistical value** (**$V_{C.l}$**) in **grids ($G_{C.ip.l}$, $G_{C.ih.l}$, $G_{C.il.l}$, $G_{C.iw.l}$, $G_{C.ib.l}$, $G_{C.ig.l}$, $G_{C.im.l}$, etc.)** of **persons (P_{ip}, P_{ih}, P_{il}, P_{iw}, P_{ib}, P_{ig}, P_{im}, etc.)**;

$F_{2.C.ip.c}$, $F_{2.C.ih.c}$, $F_{2.C.il.c}$, $F_{2.C.iw.c}$, $F_{2.C.ib.c}$, $F_{2.C.ig.c}$, $F_{2.C.im.c}$, etc. – it is notations of sum **current conditional-variable consumption flows** of **c-th secondary noo value** (**$V_{2.C.c}$**) in **grids ($G_{2.C.ip.c}$, $G_{2.C.ih.c}$, $G_{2.C.il.c}$, $G_{2.C.iw.c}$, $G_{2.C.ib.c}$, $G_{2.C.ig.c}$, $G_{2.C.im.c}$, etc.)** of **persons (P_{ip}, P_{ih}, P_{il}, P_{iw}, P_{ib}, P_{ig}, P_{im}, etc.)**;

$F_{C.ib.l}$ – it is notation of sum **current conditional-variable consumption flow** of **l-th noologistical value** (**$V_{C.ib.l}$**) entire the **noosphere**.

$F_{C.ip.c}$, $F_{C.ih.c}$, $F_{C.il.c}$, $F_{C.iw.c}$, $F_{C.ib.c}$, $F_{C.ig.c}$, $F_{C.im.c}$, etc. – it is notations of sum **current conditional-variable consumption flows** of **c-th noo value** (**$V_{C.c}$**) of several **persons (P_{ip}, P_{ih}, P_{il}, P_{iw}, P_{ib}, P_{ig}, P_{im}, etc.)**;

$F_{1.C.ip.c}$, $F_{1.C.ih.c}$, $F_{1.C.il.c}$, $F_{1.C.iw.c}$, $F_{1.C.ib.c}$, $F_{1.C.ig.c}$, $F_{1.C.im.c}$, etc. – it is notations of sum **current conditional-variable consumption flows** of **c-th primary noo value** (**$V_{1.C.c}$**) of several **persons (P_{ip}, P_{ih}, P_{il}, P_{iw}, P_{ib}, P_{ig}, P_{im}, etc.)**;

$F_{C.ib.c}$ – it is notation of sum **current conditional-variable consumption flow** of **c-th noo value** (**$V_{C.ib.c}$**) entire the **noosphere**, etc.

Examples of the current conditional-variable consumption flows of the l-th **primary noological value** (**$V_{1.C.l}$**) are flows (**$F_{1.C.ip.l.b}$**), which, with the minimum magnitude of their density, are provided only by the biological existence of the **person**, are current flows of consumed atmospheric air, food, clothing, housing, heat, water, sunlight, etc., used by him at the current time. Examples of current conditional-variable consumption flows of the c-th **secondary noo value** (**$V_{1.C.l}$**) are flows (**$F_{2.C.ip.c}$**) of consumed entertainments, art objects, foreign languages, rules of subject's relations, results of scientific activity, religious rites, etc.

Parameters of the total current conditional-variable consumption flows of any $\mathbf{V_{C.l}}$ and $\mathbf{V_{C.c}}$ by any **person ($\mathbf{P_{ip}}$, $\mathbf{P_{ih}}$, $\mathbf{P_{il}}$, $\mathbf{P_{iw}}$, $\mathbf{P_{ib}}$, $\mathbf{P_{ig}}$, $\mathbf{P_{im}}$, etc.)**, in the entire **grid** of each of them, in **provision the existence** (**life support**), by all of them in the **noosphere**, etc., are calculated using **the technology of calculating information pyramids**. Information from the corresponding formalized descriptions of the flows of **persons** located at their lower levels is used for these calculations. The results of these calculations may be presented in the form of corresponding descriptions, the content of which is similar to the content of the above formalized descriptions "Current consumption flow $\mathbf{V_{C.ip.l.b}}$ in $\mathbf{G_{C.ip.l.b}}$ ($\mathbf{F_{C.ip.l.b}}$)" and "Current consumption flow $\mathbf{V_{C.ip.c.b}}$ in $\mathbf{G_{C.ip.c.b}}$ ($\mathbf{F_{C.ip.c.b}}$)".

2.7. The Current Flow of Noo Value Creation

Each **person of Noologistics** supports **the provision of his existence** (**life support**) in the **PRESENT**, an integral part of which is his process of **creation the values**. It consists in transforming by him of the one or more specific **current flows of value consumption** into **a flow of the value** that satisfies his need to creation it. To implement the above process, the **person** uses either his own organism or **unit of grid equipment** or his entire **grid**, thereby forming a flow of **noo value**, which according to the classification of **Noologistics** is classified as the current flow of its creation ($\mathbf{F_M}$), which has the following definition:

The current flow of creation the noo value is called the process of orderly transformation into it by **the person of Noologistics** of other **noo values**, under satisfying his **needs** in the **PRESENT** to achieve in the **FUTURE** the **goal** set by him. When solving various management tasks, the **persons** use formalized information about the simplest **current creation flows** that are supported by their organisms, as well as the b-th **units of grid equipment** used by them at the current time. From these most simple types, they form the rest of their species, the name and notations of which depends on many factors. An example of the formalization of such a simple type of **the current flow of creation**

the l-th **noological value** in the b-th unit of the grid equipment of person which has the notation $\mathbf{P_{ip}}$ is shown below. The notation of this flow is $\mathbf{F_{M.ip.l.b}}$, the notation **the unit of the grid equipment** by means of which it controls this flow is $\mathbf{G_{M.ip.l.b}}$, the notation of **the current technological process** in it is $\mathbf{CTP_{M.ip.l.b}}$, and the notation for his grid is $\mathbf{G_{ip.l.b}=\Sigma(G_{C.ip.l.b}, G_{M.ip.l.b}}$ **and** $\mathbf{G_{S.ip.l.b})}$. The most commonly used parameters in **Noologistics** when formalizing these most simple types of current creation flows are:

$\mathbf{D_{M.ip.l.b}}$ – it is the notation of the density of the $\mathbf{F_{M.ip.l.b}}$, which is called the density of **the current flow of creation the noogistical value** in $\mathbf{G_{ip.l.b}}$ and which **the system of Noologistics** measures in the **PRESENT** (at the current time) by the corresponding device according to **the rules** it observes, for example, a counter, a flowmeter, a control system, etc.

$\mathbf{Q_{M.ip.l.b}}$ – it is the notation of the **current quantity** of l-st **creation noologistical value** ($\mathbf{V_{M.ip.l.b}}$) in $\mathbf{G_{ip.l.b}}$ in a given period of time, for example, from the moment of its start to the current moment, which **the system of Noologistics** calculates in the **PRESENT** (at the current time) according to the **rules** it observes, for example, by the formula:

$$Q_{M.ip.l.b} = \int_{t_н}^{t} D_{M.ip.l.b}(t) * dt ,$$

here are:

t – it is the notation of the current time the $\mathbf{G_{ip.l.b}}$'s working which **the system of Noologistics** measures from it's start according to the **rules** it observes, for example, by the time etalon;

t – it is the notation of the current time at the start moment of $\mathbf{G_{ip.l.b}}$'s work on the same etalon of time, other – see above.

$\mathbf{D_{C.ip.l.b}}$ – it is the notation of the density of the $\mathbf{F_{C.ip.l.b}}$, which is called the density of **the current flow of conditional-variable noologistical value consumption** of l-st **noologistical value** ($\mathbf{V_{C.ip.l.b}}$) in $\mathbf{G_{ip.l.b}}$, in which it is spent on the creation the $\mathbf{F_{M.ip.l.b}}$ and which **the system of Noologistics** measures in the **PRESENT** (at the current time) by the corresponding device according to the **rules** it observes, for example, a counter, a flow meter, a monitoring system, and so on;

$\mathbf{D_{S.ip.l.b}}$ – it is the notation of the density of the $\mathbf{F_{S.ip.l.b}}$, which is called the density of **the current flow of conditional-variable noologistical value reject** of l-st **noologistical value** ($\mathbf{V_{S.ip.l.b}}$) from $\mathbf{G_{ip.l.b}}$ due the creation the $\mathbf{F_{M.ip.l.b}}$ and which **the system of Noologistics** measures in the **PRESENT** (at the current time) by the corresponding device according to the **rules** it observes, for example, a counter, a flow meter, a monitoring system, and so on;

$\mathbf{QP_{C.ip.l.b}}$, $\mathbf{QP_{M.ip.l.b}}$ and $\mathbf{QP_{S.ip.l.b}}$ – it is the notations of the **current quality parameters** of l-st **noologistical values** ($\mathbf{V_{C.ip.l.b}}$, $\mathbf{V_{M.ip.l.b}}$ and $\mathbf{V_{S.ip.l.b}}$) which **the system of Noologistics** measures in the **PRESENT** (at the current time) by the corresponding device according to the **rules** it observes, for example, a thermometer, a gas analyzer, a monitoring system, and so on;

$\mathbf{LF_{C.ip.l.b}}$, $\mathbf{LF_{M.ip.l.b}}$ and $\mathbf{LF_{S.ip.l.b}}$ – it is the notations of the **current location** of $\mathbf{F_{C.ip.l.b}}$, $\mathbf{F_{M.ip.l.b}}$ and $\mathbf{F_{S.ip.l.b}}$ in the **environment** which **the system of Noologistics** measures in the **PRESENT** (at the current time) by the corresponding device according to the **rules** it observes, for example, by the **geoinformation system**;

$\mathbf{AF_{C.ip.l.b}}$, $\mathbf{AF_{M.ip.l.b}}$ and $\mathbf{AF_{S.ip.l.b}}$ – it is the notations of the **current allocation** of $\mathbf{F_{C.ip.l.b}}$, $\mathbf{F_{M.ip.l.b}}$ and $\mathbf{F_{S.ip.l.b}}$ in the **environment** which **the system of Noologistics** calculates in the **PRESENT** (at the current time) by the corresponding device according to the **rules** it observes, for example, by the **geoinformation system**.

The system of Noologistics calculates the parameters of the flows that describe prehistory of the $\mathbf{F_{C.ip.l.b}}$ in accordance to the **criteria of reasonableness** that were given by **person** in his **goal**, except for the parameters directly listed at the moment. Such flows include:

The current conditional-fixed flow of consumption of the $\mathbf{V_{C.ip.l.b}}$ in $\mathbf{G_{ip.l.b}}$ has the notation $\mathbf{FF_{C.ip.l.b}}$.

The current total flow of consumption of the $\mathbf{V_{C.ip.l.b}}$ in $\mathbf{G_{ip.l.b}}$ has the notation $\mathbf{TF_{C.ip.l.b}}$.

The current conditional-fixed flow of rejection of the $\mathbf{V_{S.ip.l.b}}$ from $\mathbf{G_{ip.l.b}}$ has the notation $\mathbf{FF_{S.ip.l.b}}$.

The current total flow of rejection of the $\mathbf{V_{S.ip.l.b}}$ from $\mathbf{G_{ip.l.b}}$ has the notation $\mathbf{TF_{S.ip.l.b}}$.

Parameters of the $\mathbf{FF_{C.ip.l.b}}$, $\mathbf{TF_{C.ip.l.b}}$, $\mathbf{FF_{S.ip.l.b}}$ and $\mathbf{TF_{S.ip.l.b}}$ are used for the depreciation of the consumed $\mathbf{V_{C.ip.l.b}}$ quantities from the environment and rejected $\mathbf{V_{S.ip.l.b}}$ quantities to it in the **PAST** to the consumed $\mathbf{V_{C.ip.l.b}}$ and created $\mathbf{V_{M.ip.l.b}}$ in the **PRESENT** in the processes of their extraction, creation, storage, transport, servicing, rejection, etc. Such a reference is used in the (commodity-money) Economy and is called depreciation (amortization). The main difference between **noologistic** depreciation and the used in (commodity-money) **Economy** is that:

- it is depreciated not only to previously consumed **values**, but also to **values** previously rejected to the **environment**;
- not only money is used as a depreciable **values**, but also any other types of **values** that are set by the **person** in his **goal** as **criteria for the reasonableness of management**.

Parameters of the above-mentioned simplest types of the $\mathbf{FF_{C.ip.l.b}}$, $\mathbf{TF_{C.ip.l.b}}$, $\mathbf{FF_{S.ip.l.b}}$ and $\mathbf{TF_{S.ip.l.b}}$ are used in **Noologistics** to formalize information as a basis for further calculations, including:

$\mathbf{FD_{C.ip.l.b}}$ – it is the notation of the density of the $\mathbf{FF_{C.ip.l.b}}$ amortized in the **PRESENT**;

$\mathbf{FQ_{C.ip.l.b}}$ – it is the notation of the **quantity** of the $\mathbf{V_{C.ip.l.b}}$ consumed in the **PAST**;

$\mathbf{SFD_{C.ip.l.b}}$ – it is the notation of the **specified density** of the $\mathbf{FF_{C.ip.l.b}}$ amortized in the **PRESENT**;

$\mathbf{TD_{C.ip.l.b}}$ – it is the notation of the density of the $\mathbf{TF_{C.ip.l.b}}$ calculated in the **PAST**;

$\mathbf{TQ_{C.ip.l.b}}$ – it is the notation of the **total quantity** of the $\mathbf{V_{C.ip.l.b}}$ calculated in the **PRESENT**;

$\mathbf{FD_{S.ip.l.b}}$ – it is the notation of the density of the $\mathbf{FF_{S.ip.l.b}}$, calculated in the **PRESENT**;

$FQ_{S.ip.l.b}$ – it is the notation of the **quantity** of the **$V_{S.ip.l.b}$** rejected in the **PAST**;

$SFD_{S.ip.l.b}$ – it is the notation of the **specified density** of the **$FF_{S.ip.l.b}$** amortized in the **PRESENT**;

$TD_{S.ip.l.b}$ – it is the notation of the density of the **$TF_{S.ip.l.b}$**, calculated in the **PRESENT**;

$TQ_{S.ip.l.b}$ – it is the notation of the **total quantity** of the **$V_{S.ip.l.b}$** calculated in the **PRESENT**.

The magnitudes of the specific density above mentioned types of **$F_{C.ip.l.b}$**, **$FF_{C.ip.l.b}$**, **$TF_{C.ip.l.b}$**, **$F_{S.ip.l.b}$**, **$FF_{S.ip.l.b}$** and **$TF_{S.ip.l.b}$** are used to calculate the **indexed noologistical area of possible operating modes** any **unit of equipment** the mathematical apparatus of which is given below.

$SD_{C.ip.l.b}$ – it is the notation of the **specified density of the current conditional-variable consumption flow** of the **$V_{C.ip.l.b}$** in **$G_{ip.l.b}$** (**$F_{C.ip.l.b}$**), which is spent on maintaining **$F_{M.ip.l.b}$** and is called **current specific density of conditional-variable consumption flow $V_{C.ip.l.b}$** in **$G_{ip.l.b}$**. It is calculated in the **PRESENT** according to the **rules** of the **person**, for example, according to the formula:

$$SD_{C.ip.l.b} = D_{C.ip.l.b} / D_{M.ip.l.b},$$

in which the notations of all quantities - see above.

$SFD_{C.ip.l.b}$ – it is the notation of the **current specified density of conditionally-fixed consumption flow** of the **$V_{C.ip.l.b}$** in **$G_{ip.l.b}$** (**$FF_{C.ip.l.b}$**), which is spent on maintaining **$F_{M.ip.l.b}$** and is called **current specific density of conditional- fixed consumption flow $V_{C.ip.l.b}$** in **$G_{ip.l.b}$**. It is calculated in the **PRESENT** according to the **rules** of the **person**, for example, according to the formula:

$$SFD_{C.ip.l.b} = \Sigma FD_{C.ip.l.b} / D_{M.ip.l.b},$$

here are:

$\Sigma FD_{C.ip.l.b}$ – it is the sum of the magnitudes of all **$FD_{C.ip.l.b}$** spent on supporting all **$F_{C.ip.l.b}$** before their arrival in **$G_{ip.l.b}$**, for example, on the creation of their **$V_{C.ip.l.b}$** components, their storage, preparation, transport, etc.;

other – see above.

$STD_{C.ip.l.b}$ – it is the notation of the **current specified density of total consumption flow** of the **$V_{C.ip.l.b}$** in **$G_{ip.l.b}$** (**$TF_{C.ip.l.b}$**), which is spent on maintaining **$F_{M.ip.l.b}$** and is called **current specific density of total consumption flow $V_{C.ip.l.b}$** in **$G_{ip.l.b}$**. It is calculated in the **PRESENT** according to the **rules** of the **person**, for example, according to the formula:

$$STD_{C.ip.l.b} = (D_{C.ip.l.b} + \Sigma FD_{C.ip.l.b}) / D_{M.ip.l.b},$$

in which the notations of all quantities - see above.

$SD_{S.ip.l.b}$ – it is the notation of the **specified density of the current conditional-variable rejection flow** of the **$V_{S.ip.l.b}$** from **$G_{ip.l.b}$** (**$F_{S.ip.l.b}$**), which is spent on maintaining **$F_{M.ip.l.b}$** and is called **current specific density of conditional-variable rejection flow $V_{S.ip.l.b}$** from **$G_{ip.l.b}$**. It is calculated in the **PRESENT** according to the **rules** of the **person**, for example, according to the formula:

$$SD_{S.ip.l.b} = D_{S.ip.l.b} / D_{M.ip.l.b},$$

in which the notations of all quantities - see above.

$SFD_{S.ip.l.b}$ – it is the notation of the **current specified density of total conditional-fixed rejection flow** of the **$V_{S.ip.l.b}$** from **$G_{ip.l.b}$** (**$FF_{S.ip.l.b}$**), which is spent on maintaining **$F_{M.ip.l.b}$** and is called **current specific density of total conditional-fixed rejection flow $V_{S.ip.l.b}$** from **$G_{ip.l.b}$**. It is calculated in the **PRESENT** according to the **rules** of the **person**, for example, according to the formula:

$$SFD_{S.ip.l.b} = \Sigma FD_{S.ip.l.b} / D_{M.ip.l.b},$$

here are:

$\Sigma FD_{S.ip.l.b}$ – it is the sum of the magnitudes of all **$FD_{S.ip.l.b}$** spent on supporting all **$F_{C.ip.l.b}$** before their arrival in **$G_{ip.l.b}$**, for example, on the creation of their **$V_{C.ip.l.b}$** components, their storage, preparation, transport, etc.;

other – see above.

$STD_{S.ip.l.b}$ – it is the notation of the **current specified density of total rejection flow** of the **$V_{S.ip.l.b}$** from **$G_{ip.l.b}$** (**$TF_{S.ip.l.b}$**), which is spent on maintaining **$F_{M.ip.l.b}$** and is called **current specific density of total rejection flow $V_{S.ip.l.b}$** from **$G_{ip.l.b}$**. It is calculated in the **PRESENT** according to the **rules** of the **person**, for example, according to the formula:

$$STD_{S.ip.l.b} = (D_{S.ip.l.b} + TD_{S.ip.l.b}) / D_{M.ip.l.b},$$

in which the notations of all quantities - see above.

The system of Noologistics determines the magnitudes of the parameters the **$FF_{C.ip.l.b}$**, **$TF_{C.ip.l.b}$**, **$FF_{S.ip.l.b}$** and **$TF_{S.ip.l.b}$** only for those species whose parameters are specified in **person's goal** as **criteria of reasonableness**. For example, from the point of view of **Noologistics**, a formalized description of the flow of water (**$F_{M.ip.H2O.b}$**), pumped by a pump driven by a gasoline engine (**$G_{ip.H2O.b}$**), provides for the introduction into the appropriate formalized description of the nomenclature of the set of **current conditional-variables consumption flows** (**$\Sigma FD_{C.ip.l.b}$**): gasoline, engine oil, maintenance workers, pump life, maintenance costs and much more, as well as many **current conditional-variable rejection flows** (**$\Sigma FD_{S.ip.l.b}$**): electromagnetic radiation, heat, mechanical vibrations, waste oil, CO_2 and much more. The parameters of some of the listed **$F_{C.ip.l.b}$** and **$F_{S.ip.l.b}$** may be indicated by the **person** in whose **grid** the pump in question is located, as **criteria of the reasonableness** of control over it.

For example, if **the criterion of reasonableness** in the **goal** is a compromise between 40% of the minimum cost in money terms, 30% of the minimum fuel consumption - energy resources in kWh equivalent and 30% minimum CO_2 emissions, then their nomenclature in the formal description $F_{M.ip.l.b}$ will necessarily contain the nomenclatures of **the current conditional-variable cost flows** in monetary terms ($\Sigma F_{C.ip.Mn.b}$), the current conditional variable energy cost flows in kWh equivalent ($\Sigma F_{C.ip.Vth.b}$) and the current conditional variable CO_2 emission flows ($\Sigma F_{C.ip.CO2.b}$).

The formal description of $F_{M.ip.l.b}$ is defined in the relevant **rules** of the **person** and may be represented in the formal description by the name "**Current flow of creation the $V_{M.ip.l.b}$ in $G_{ip.l.b}$**" and "**Current flow of creation the $V_{M.ip.c.b}$ in $G_{ip.c.b}$**", the content of which satisfies the management tasks solved by the **person**, for example:

Current flow of creation the $V_{M.ip.l.b}$ in $G_{ip.l.b}$ ($F_{M.ip.l.b}$)

Description contains:

The name «**Current flow of creation the $V_{M.ip.l.b}$ in $G_{ip.l.b}$**»;
The name, notation of $V_{Mip.l.b}$ and its unique number l from **the formalized description of the environment**;
unique ip for P_{ip};
Individual number b for $G_{ip.l.b}$ from **the formalized description of equipment unit** (G_b);
parameters of $F_{M.ip.l.b}$, including:

The names of $F_{M.ip.l.b}$, $D_{M.ip.l.b}$, $QP_{M.ip.l.b}$, $LF_{M.ip.l.b}$, $AF_{M.ip.l.b}$, $V_{M.ip.l.b}$, t_H and $Q_{M.ip.l.b}$, their notations, units of measure, magnitudes, etc.

The nomenclature and parameters of the $F_{C.ip.l.b}$, $FF_{C.ip.l.b}$, $TF_{C.ip.l.b}$, $F_{S.ip.l.b}$, $FF_{S.ip.l.b}$ and $TF_{S.ip.l.b}$, amortized on the $F_{M.ip.l.b}$, including:

The notation of $V_{C.ip.l.b}$, $V_{S.ip.l.b}$ and their unique numbers l from **the formalized description of the environment**, names of $D_{C.ip.l.b}$, $FD_{C.ip.l.b}$, $TD_{C.ip.l.b}$, $FQ_{C.ip.l.b}$, $SD_{C.ip.l.b}$, $SFD_{C.ip.l.b}$, $STD_{C.ip.l.b}$, $D_{S.ip.l.b}$, $FD_{S.ip.l.b}$, $TD_{S.ip.l.b}$, $FQ_{S.ip.l.b}$, $SD_{S.ip.l.b}$, $SFD_{S.ip.l.b}$, $STD_{S.ip.l.b}$, their notations, units of measure, magnitudes, etc.

It follows from the formalized description of **current values** (V_c) that the parameters of some of their species are not subject to use in

noologistic calculations, so when formalizing the description of **the current consumption flow** of such $V_{C.ip.l.b}$ ($F_{C.ip.l.b}$), **the person** (P_{ip}) uses the formalized information only about $FF_{C.ip.l.b}$, $TF_{C.ip.l.b}$, $FF_{S.ip.l.b}$ and $TF_{S.ip.l.b}$, related to the existence of $F_{M.ip.c.b}$ in **PRESENT**, the formalized description of which is similar to the way it was shown above, for example:

Current flow of creation the $V_{M.ip.c.b}$ in $G_{ip.c.b}$ ($F_{M.ip.c.b}$)

Description contains:

The name «**Current flow of creation the $V_{M.ip.c.b}$ in $G_{ip.c.b}$**»;

The name, notation of $V_{Mip.c.b}$ and its unique number l from **the formalized description of the environment**;

unique ip for P_{ip};

Individual number b for $G_{ip.c.b}$ from **the formalized description of equipment unit** (G_b);

parameters of $F_{M.ip.c.b}$, including:

The names of $F_{M.ip.c.b}$, $D_{M.ip.c.b}$, $QP_{M.ip.c.b}$, $LF_{M.ip.c.b}$, $AF_{M.ip.c.b}$, $V_{M.ip.c.b}$, t_H and $Q_{M.ip.c.b}$, their notations, units of measure, magnitudes, etc.

The nomenclature and parameters of the $F_{C.ip.l.b}$, $FF_{C.ip.l.b}$, $TF_{C.ip.l.b}$, $F_{S.ip.l.b}$, $FF_{S.ip.l.b}$ and $TF_{S.ip.l.b}$, amortized on the $F_{M.ip.c.b}$, including:

The notation of $V_{C.ip.l.b}$, $V_{S.ip.l.b}$ and their unique numbers l from **the formalized description of the environment**, names of $D_{C.ip.l.b}$, $FD_{C.ip.l.b}$, $TD_{C.ip.l.b}$, $FQ_{C.ip.l.b}$, $SD_{C.ip.l.b}$, $SFD_{C.ip.l.b}$, $STD_{C.ip.l.b}$, $D_{S.ip.l.b}$, $FD_{S.ip.l.b}$, $TD_{S.ip.l.b}$, $FQ_{S.ip.l.b}$, $SD_{S.ip.l.b}$, $SFD_{S.ip.l.b}$, $STD_{S.ip.l.b}$, their notations, units of measure, magnitudes, etc.

It is envisaged to use in **Noologistics** the set of corresponding types of $F_{M.l}$ and $F_{M.c}$ in accordance with the type of the control task to be solved, which are reflected in the lower indexes of their notations, for example:

$F_{M.ip.l.b}$, $F_{M.ih.l.b}$, $F_{M.il.l.b}$, $F_{M.iw.l.b}$, $F_{M.ib.l.b}$, $F_{M.ig.l.b}$, $F_{M.im.l.b}$, etc. – it is notations of **current conditional-variable creation flows** of **l-th noologistical value** ($V_{C.l}$) in b-th **equipment units** (**$G_{ip.l.b}$, $G_{ih.l.b}$, $G_{il.l.b}$,**

$G_{iw.l.b}$, $G_{ib.l.b}$, $G_{ig.l.b}$, $G_{im.l.b}$, **etc.)** of **persons** **(P_{ip}, P_{ih}, P_{il}, P_{iw}, P_{ib}, P_{ig}, P_{im}, etc.)**;

$F_{1.M.ip.l.b}$, $F_{1.M.ih.l.b}$, $F_{1.M.il.l.b}$, $F_{1.M.iw.l.b}$, $F_{1.M.ib.l.b}$, $F_{1.M.ig.l.b}$, $F_{1.M.im.l.b}$, etc. – it is notations of **current conditional-variable creation flows** of **l-th primary noologistical value** ($V_{1.M.l}$) in b-th **equipment units** **($G_{1.ip.l.b}$, $G_{1.ih.l.b}$, $G_{1.il.l.b}$, $G_{1.iw.l.b}$, $G_{1.ib.l.b}$, $G_{1.ig.l.b}$, $G_{1.im.l.b}$, etc.)** of **persons** **(P_{ip}, P_{ih}, P_{il}, P_{iw}, P_{ib}, P_{ig}, P_{im}, etc.)**;

$F_{M.ip.l}$, $F_{M.ih.l}$, $F_{M.il.l}$, $F_{M.iw.l}$, $F_{M.ib.l}$, $F_{M.ig.l}$, $F_{M.im.l}$, etc. – it is notations of sum **current conditional-variable creation flows** of **l-th noologistical value** ($V_{M.l}$) in **grids** **($G_{ip.l}$, $G_{ih.l}$, $G_{il.l}$, $G_{iw.l}$, $G_{ib.l}$, $G_{ig.l}$, $G_{im.l}$, etc.)** of **persons** **(P_{ip}, P_{ih}, P_{il}, P_{iw}, P_{ib}, P_{ig}, P_{im}, etc.)**;

$F_{2.M.ip.c}$, $F_{2.M.ih.c}$, $F_{2.M.il.c}$, $F_{2.M.iw.c}$, $F_{2.M.ib.c}$, $F_{2.M.ig.c}$, $F_{2.M.im.c}$, etc. – it is notations of sum **current conditional-variable creation flows** of **c-th secondary noo value** ($V_{2.M.c}$) in **grids** **($G_{2.ip.c}$, $G_{2.ih.c}$, $G_{2.il.c}$, $G_{2.iw.c}$, $G_{2.ib.c}$, $G_{2.ig.c}$, $G_{2.im.c}$, etc.)** of **persons** **(P_{ip}, P_{ih}, P_{il}, P_{iw}, P_{ib}, P_{ig}, P_{im}, etc.)**;

$F_{M.ib.l}$ – it is notation of sum **current conditional-variable creation flow** of **l-th noologistical value** ($V_{M.ib.l}$) entire the **noosphere**.

$F_{M.ip.c}$, $F_{M.ih.c}$, $F_{M.il.c}$, $F_{M.iw.c}$, $F_{M.ib.c}$, $F_{M.ig.c}$, $F_{M.im.c}$, etc. – it is notations of sum **current conditional-variable creation flows** of **c-th noo value** ($V_{M.c}$) of several **persons** **(P_{ip}, P_{ih}, P_{il}, P_{iw}, P_{ib}, P_{ig}, P_{im}, etc.)**;

$F_{1.M.ip.c}$, $F_{1.M.ih.c}$, $F_{1.M.il.c}$, $F_{1.M.iw.c}$, $F_{1.M.ib.c}$, $F_{1.M.ig.c}$, $F_{1.M.im.c}$, etc. – it is notations of sum **current conditional-variable creation flows** of **c-th primary noo value** ($V_{1.M.c}$) of several **persons** **(P_{ip}, P_{ih}, P_{il}, P_{iw}, P_{ib}, P_{ig}, P_{im}, etc.)**;

$F_{M.ib.c}$ – it is notation of sum **current conditional-variable creation flow** of **c-th noo value** ($V_{M.ib.c}$) entire the **noosphere**.

Examples of the current conditional-variable creation flows of the l-th **primary noological value** ($V_{1.M.l}$) are flows ($F_{1.M.ip.l.b}$), which, with the minimum magnitude of their density, are provided only by the biological existence of the **person**, are current flows of food, clothing, housing, heat, water, sunlight, etc., used by him at the current time. Examples of current conditional-variable creation flows of the c-th **secondary noo value** ($V_{2.M.c}$) are flows ($F_{2.M.ip.c}$) of creation entertainments, art objects, foreign languages, rules of subjects' relations, results of scientific activity, religious rites, etc.

Parameters of the total current conditional-variable creation flows of any $V_{M.l}$ and $V_{M.c}$ by any **person** **(P_{ip}, P_{ih}, P_{il}, P_{iw}, P_{ib}, P_{ig}, P_{im},**

etc.), in the entire **grid** of each of them, in **provision the existence** (**life support**), by all of them in the **noosphere**, etc., are calculated using **the technology of calculating information pyramids**. Information from the corresponding formalized descriptions of **the flows** of **persons** located at their lower levels is used for these calculations. The results of these calculations may be presented in the form of corresponding descriptions, the content of which is similar to the content of the above formalized descriptions "Current creation flow $\mathbf{V_{M.ip.l.b}}$ in $\mathbf{G_{ip.l.b}}$ ($\mathbf{F_{M.ip.l.b}}$)" and "Current creation flow $\mathbf{V_{M.ip.c.b}}$ in $\mathbf{G_{ip.c.b}}$ ($\mathbf{F_{M.ip.c.b}}$)".

2.8. The Current Flow of Noo Value Reject

Each **person of Noologistics** supports **the provision of his existence** (**life support**) in the **PRESENT**, an integral part of which is his process of rejection of **values**. It consists in the emission directly to his **habitat** of that **value**, which prevents the satisfaction of his specific **needs** in process to achieve his **goal**. To implement the above-mentioned process, the **person** uses either his own organism, or **unit equipment** of **grid**, or his entire **grid**, thereby forming a flow of **noo value**, which according to the classification of **Noologistics** is categorized as the **current conditional-variable flow of its reject** (briefly – $\mathbf{F_S}$), which has the following definition:

The current conditional-variable flow of rejection of noo value is the process of orderly allocation (emission) it by **person of Noologistics** into his **habitat** by means of satisfying his **needs** in the **PRESENT** to achieve in the **FUTURE** the **goal** set by him.

This flow is called conditional variables by analogy with the terminology of the commodity-money **Economy** because its magnitude depends on the productivity of the process in which it is used. Each **person** usually uses several types of **current conditional-variable flows of rejection** at the same time: some of them satisfy their **primary needs** that directly support his biological existence, while others use it to meet their **secondary needs** at a higher level. Between the many types of **current conditional-variable flows of rejection**, the persons also highlight information, which is based on **current noological values** and which it may use to develop **noologistical**

managerial solutions and calculate the corresponding **noologistical control actions** on their **real control objects**.

Persons use formalized information about the simplest **current conditional variable flows of rejection** when solving various management tasks that are supported by their organisms, as well as the b-th **unit of his equipment** used by them at the current time. **Persons** form the rest of his species, the name and notations of these most simple types of their designation depends on many factors. An example of the formalization of such a simple form of **the current conditional-variable flow of rejection** of the l-th **noologistical value** from the b-th **unit of the grid equipment** of the **person** that has the notation $\mathbf{P_{ip}}$ is shown below. The notation of this flow is $\mathbf{F_{S.ip.l.b}}$, the notation of **unit of the grid equipment** by which he manages this flow is $\mathbf{G_{S.ip.l.b}}$, the notation of the **current technological process** in it is $\mathbf{CTP_{S.ip.l.b}}$, and the notation for his **grid** – $\mathbf{G_{S.ip.l.b}}$. The most frequently used parameters in **Noologistics** when formalizing such simplest types of **current conditional-variable flows of rejection** are the following ones:

$\mathbf{D_{S.ip.l.b}}$ – it is the notation of the density of the $\mathbf{F_{S.ip.l.b}}$, which is called the density of **the current conditional-variable flow** of l-st **noologistical value rejection** from $\mathbf{G_{S.ip.l.b}}$ and which **the system of Noologistics** measures in the **PRESENT** (at the current time) by the corresponding device according to the **rules** it observes, for example, a counter, a flowmeter, a monitoring system, and so on.

$\mathbf{Q_{S.ip.l.b}}$ – it is the notation of the **current quantity** of l-st **rejected noologistical value** ($\mathbf{V_{S.ip.l.b}}$) from $\mathbf{G_{S.ip.l.b}}$ in a given period of time, for example, from the moment of its start to the current moment, which **the system of Noologistics** calculates in the **PRESENT** (at the current time) according to the **rules** it observes, for example, by the formula:

$$Q_{S.ip.l.b} = \int_{t_н}^{t} D_{S.ip.l.b}(t) * dt \quad ,$$

here are:

t – it is the notation of the current time the $\mathbf{G_{S.ip.l.b}}$'s working which **the system of Noologistics** measures from it's start according to the **rules** it observes, for example, by the time etalon;

t – it is the notation of the current time at the start moment of $G_{S.ip.l.b}$'s work on the same etalon of time, other – see above.

$CS_{S.ip.l.b}$ – it is a notation of the current concentration value $V_{S.ip.l.b}$ in the **habitat** of the **person**, which **the system of Noologistics** measures in the **PRESENT** (at the current time) by the appropriate device according to the **rules** it observes, for example, according to **the environmental protection**;

$CS_{S.l}$ – it is a notation of the current concentration value $V_{S.l}$ in the **environment**, which **the system of Noologistics** measures in the **PRESENT** (at the current time) by the appropriate device according to the **rules** it observes, for example, according to **the environmental protection**;

$MPC_{S.l}$ – it is a notation of the magnitude of the maximum permissible concentration the $V_{S.l}$ in the **environment**, which is set at the current time in the **rules**, for example, by **environmental protection**;

$QP_{S.ip.l.b}$ – it is the notation of the **current quality parameters** of l-st **noologistical value** ($V_{S.ip.l.b}$) which **the system of Noologistics** measures in the **PRESENT** (at the current time) by the corresponding device according to the **rules** it observes, for example, a thermometer, a gas analyzer, a monitoring system, and so on;

$LF_{S.ip.l.b}$ – it is the notation of the **current location** of $F_{S.ip.l.b}$ in the **environment** which **the system of Noologistics** measures in the **PRESENT** (at the current time) by the corresponding device according to the **rules** it observes, for example, by the **geoinformation system**;

$AF_{S.ip.l.b}$ – it is the notation of the **current allocation** of $F_{S.ip.l.b}$ in the **environment** which **the system of Noologistics** calculates in the **PRESENT** (at the current time) by the corresponding device according to the **rules** it observes, for example, by the **geoinformation system**.

The system of Noologistics calculates the parameters of the flows that describe prehistory of the $F_{S.ip.l.b}$ in accordance to the **criteria of reasonableness** that were given by **person** in his **goal**, except for the parameters directly listed at the moment. **The current conditional-fixed flow of noo value reject** (shortly – FF_S) and **current total flow of noo value reject** (shortly – TF_S) are referred to them, which have the following definitions:

The current conditional-fixed flow of rejection (FF_S) **the noo value** is the depreciation (amortization) of the quantities of the rejected **noo value** in the **PAST** to the consumed or created **noo value** in the **PRESENT**.

The current total flow of rejection (TF_S) **the noo value** is the sum of **the current conditional-variable flow of rejection** (F_S) **the noo value** and **the current conditional-fixed flow of rejection** (FF_S) **the noo value** in the **PRESENT**.

These flows have the following notations in this example:

The current conditional-fixed flow of rejection the $V_{S.ip.l.b}$ from $G_{S.ip.l.b}$ has the notation $FF_{S.ip.l.b}$.

The current total flow of rejection the $V_{S.ip.l.b}$ from $G_{S.ip.l.b}$ has the notation $TF_{S.ip.l.b}$.

Parameters of the $FF_{S.ip.l.b}$ and $TF_{S.ip.l.b}$ are used for the depreciation of the rejected $V_{S.ip.l.b}$ quantities to it in the **PAST** to the consumed $V_{C.ip.l.b}$ and created $V_{M.ip.l.b}$ in the **PRESENT** in the processes of their extraction, creation, storage, transport, servicing, rejection, etc. Such a reference is used in the (commodity-money) **Economy** and is called depreciation (amortization). The main difference between **noologistic** depreciation and the used in (commodity-money) **Economy** is that:

- it is depreciated not only to previously consumed **values**, but also to **values** previously rejected to the **environment**;
- not only money is used as a depreciable **value**, but also any other types of **values** that are set by the **person** in his **goal** as **criteria for the reasonableness of management**.

Parameters of the above-mentioned simplest types of the $FF_{S.ip.l.b}$ and $TF_{S.ip.l.b}$ are used in **Noologistics** to formalize information as a basis for further calculations, including:

$FD_{S.ip.l.b}$ – it is the notation of the density of the $FF_{S.ip.l.b}$, which is called the density of **the current conditional-fixed flow of rejection** the $V_{S.ip.l.b}$ from $G_{S.ip.l.b}$;

$FQ_{S.ip.l.b}$ – it is the notation of the **current quantity** of the $V_{S.ip.l.b}$ was emitted from $G_{S.ip.l.b}$ in the processes of extraction, creation, storage, transport, servicing, rejection, etc. which **the system of**

Noologistics amortizes in the **PRESENT** (at the current time) according to the **rules** it observes, for example, through accounting;

$\mathbf{TD_{S.ip.l.b}}$ – it is the notation of the density of the $\mathbf{TF_{S.ip.l.b}}$, which is called the density of **the current total flow of rejection** the $\mathbf{V_{S.ip.l.b}}$ from $\mathbf{G_{S.ip.l.b}}$.

The system of Noologistics determines the magnitudes of the parameters only for those species whose parameters are specified in **person's goal** as **criteria of reasonableness**. For example, if **the criterion of reasonableness** in the **goal** is a compromise between 40% of the minimum cost in money terms, 30% of the minimum fuel consumption - energy resources in kWh equivalent and 30% minimum CO_2 emissions, then their nomenclature in the formal description $\mathbf{F_{S.ip.l.b}}$ will contain the following items:

$\mathbf{D_{S.ip.CO2.b}}$ – it is the notation of the density **the current conditional-variable flow of rejection** the CO_2 from $\mathbf{G_{S.ip.l.b}}$ and which measured by the **rules**, for example, of **the environmental protection**;

$\mathbf{FD_{S.ip.CO2.b}}$ – it is the notation of the density **the current conditional-fixed flow of rejection** the CO_2 from $\mathbf{G_{S.ip.l.b}}$ and which calculated, for example, by the formula:

$$\mathbf{FD_{S.ip.CO2.b} = SFD_{S.ip.CO2.b} * D_{M.ip.l.b}},$$

here are:

$\mathbf{SFD_{S.ip.CO2.b}}$ – it is the notation of the **specified density** of the $\mathbf{FF_{S.ip.CO2.b}}$, see description of $\mathbf{F_{M.ip.l.b}}$;

other – see above.

$\mathbf{TD_{S.ip.CO2.b}}$ – it is the notation of the density **the current total flow of rejection** the CO_2 from $\mathbf{G_{S.ip.l.b}}$ and which calculated, for example, by the formula:

$$\mathbf{TD_{S.ip.CO2.b} = D_{S.ip.CO2.b} + FD_{S.ip.CO2.b}},$$

in which the notations of all quantities - see above;

If the magnitudes of the current conditional-variable, conditionally-fixed and total quantities of $\mathbf{V_{S.ip.CO2.b}}$ from $\mathbf{G_{S.ip.CO2.b}}$ from the moment of its operation start are required for developing a **management solution** and calculating the appropriate **control actions**, the **system of Noologistics** automatically calculates them according to the **rules**, for example, according to the formulas:

$$Q_{S.ip.CO2.b} = \int_{t_н}^{t} D_{S.ip.CO2.b}(t)*dt$$

- it is formula for calculating the conditional-variable magnitude of the current quantity the $\mathbf{V_{S.ip.CO2.b}}$,

$$FQ_{S.ip.CO2.b} = \int_{t_н}^{t} FD_{S.ip.CO2.b}(t)*dt$$

- it is formula for calculating the conditional-fixed magnitude of the current quantity the $\mathbf{V_{S.ip.CO2.b}}$,

$$TQ_{S.ip.CO2.b} = \int_{t_н}^{t} TD_{S.ip.CO2.b}(t)*dt$$

- it is formula for calculating the total magnitude of the current quantity the $\mathbf{V_{S.ip.CO2.b}}$,

in which the notations of all quantities - see above;

The formalized description of any $\mathbf{F_{S.ip.l.b}}$ may have the name "**Current flow of rejection** the $\mathbf{V_{S.ip.l.b}}$ **from** $\mathbf{G_{S.ip.l.b}}$ **(**$\mathbf{F_{S.ip.l.b}}$**)**" and contain the following information:

Current flow of rejection the $\mathbf{V_{S.ip.l.b}}$ **from** $\mathbf{G_{S.ip.l.b}}$ **(**$\mathbf{F_{S.ip.l.b}}$**)**

Description contains:

The name «**Current flow of rejection** the $\mathbf{V_{S.ip.l.b}}$ **from** $\mathbf{G_{S.ip.l.b}}$»;

The name, notation of $\mathbf{V_{S.ip.l.b}}$ and its unique number l from **the formalized description of the environment**;

unique ip for $\mathbf{P_{ip}}$;

Individual number b for $\mathbf{G_{S.ip.l.b}}$ from **the formalized description of equipment unit** (**$\mathbf{G_b}$**);

parameters of $\mathbf{F_{S.ip.l.b}}$, including:

The names of $\mathbf{D_{S.ip.l.b}}$, $\mathbf{CS_{S.ip.l.b}}$, $\mathbf{CS_{S.l}}$, $\mathbf{MPC_{S.ip.l}}$, $\mathbf{Q_{S.ip.l.b}}$, $\mathbf{QP_{S.ip.l.b}}$, $\mathbf{LF_{S.ip.l.b}}$, $\mathbf{AF_{S.ip.l.b}}$, $\mathbf{FD_{S.ip.l.b}}$, $\mathbf{TD_{S.ip.l.b}}$, $\mathbf{SFD_{S.ip.l.b}}$ and $\mathbf{t_H}$, their notations, units of measure, magnitudes, etc.

The nomenclature and parameters of the $\mathbf{FF_{S.ip.l.b}}$, amortized on the $\mathbf{F_{S.ip.l.b}}$, including:

The notations of $\mathbf{V_{S.ip.l.b}}$ and their unique numbers l from **the formalized description of the environment**, names of $\mathbf{FD_{S.ip.l.b}}$, $\mathbf{FQ_{S.ip.l.b}}$, $\mathbf{SFD_{S.ip.l.b}}$, their notations, units of measure, magnitudes, etc.

It is envisaged to use in **Noologistics** the set of corresponding types of $\mathbf{F_S}$ in accordance with the type of the control task to be solved, which are reflected in the lower indexes of their notations, for example:

$\mathbf{F_{S.ip.l.b}}$, $\mathbf{F_{S.ih.l.b}}$, $\mathbf{F_{S.il.l.b}}$, $\mathbf{F_{S.iw.l.b}}$, $\mathbf{F_{S.ib.l.b}}$, $\mathbf{F_{S.ig.l.b}}$, $\mathbf{F_{S.im.l.b}}$, etc. – it is notations of **current conditional-variable flows of rejection the l-th noologistical value** ($\mathbf{V_{S.l}}$) from b-th **equipment units (**$\mathbf{G_{S.ip.l.b}}$, $\mathbf{G_{S.ih.l.b}}$, $\mathbf{G_{S.il.l.b}}$, $\mathbf{G_{S.iw.l.b}}$, $\mathbf{G_{S.ib.l.b}}$, $\mathbf{G_{S.ig.l.b}}$, $\mathbf{G_{S.im.l.b}}$, **etc.)** of **persons (**$\mathbf{P_{ip}}$, $\mathbf{P_{ih}}$, $\mathbf{P_{il}}$, $\mathbf{P_{iw}}$, $\mathbf{P_{ib}}$, $\mathbf{P_{ig}}$, $\mathbf{P_{im}}$, **etc.)**;

$\mathbf{F_{1.S.ip.l.b}}$, $\mathbf{F_{1.S.ih.l.b}}$, $\mathbf{F_{1.S.il.l.b}}$, $\mathbf{F_{1.S.iw.l.b}}$, $\mathbf{F_{1.S.ib.l.b}}$, $\mathbf{F_{1.S.ig.l.b}}$, $\mathbf{F_{1.S.im.l.b}}$, etc. – it is notations of **current conditional-variable flows of rejection the l-th primary noologistical value** ($\mathbf{V_{1.S.l}}$) from b-th **equipment units (**$\mathbf{G_{1.S.ip.l.b}}$, $\mathbf{G_{1.S.ih.l.b}}$, $\mathbf{G_{1.S.il.l.b}}$, $\mathbf{G_{1.S.iw.l.b}}$, $\mathbf{G_{1.S.ib.l.b}}$, $\mathbf{G_{1.S.ig.l.b}}$, $\mathbf{G_{1.S.im.l.b}}$, **etc.)** of **persons (**$\mathbf{P_{ip}}$, $\mathbf{P_{ih}}$, $\mathbf{P_{il}}$, $\mathbf{P_{iw}}$, $\mathbf{P_{ib}}$, $\mathbf{P_{ig}}$, $\mathbf{P_{im}}$, **etc.)**;

$\mathbf{F_{S.ip.l}}$, $\mathbf{F_{S.ih.l}}$, $\mathbf{F_{S.il.l}}$, $\mathbf{F_{S.iw.l}}$, $\mathbf{F_{S.ib.l}}$, $\mathbf{F_{S.ig.l}}$, $\mathbf{F_{S.im.l}}$, etc. – it is notations of sum **current conditional-variable flows of rejection the l-th noologistical value** ($\mathbf{V_{S.l}}$) from **grids (**$\mathbf{G_{S.ip.l}}$, $\mathbf{G_{S.ih.l}}$, $\mathbf{G_{S.il.l}}$, $\mathbf{G_{S.iw.l}}$, $\mathbf{G_{S.ib.l}}$, $\mathbf{G_{S.ig.l}}$, $\mathbf{G_{S.im.l}}$, **etc.)** of **persons (**$\mathbf{P_{ip}}$, $\mathbf{P_{ih}}$, $\mathbf{P_{il}}$, $\mathbf{P_{iw}}$, $\mathbf{P_{ib}}$, $\mathbf{P_{ig}}$, $\mathbf{P_{im}}$, **etc.)**;

$\mathbf{F_{2.S.ip.c}}$, $\mathbf{F_{2.S.ih.c}}$, $\mathbf{F_{2.S.il.c}}$, $\mathbf{F_{2.S.iw.c}}$, $\mathbf{F_{2.S.ib.c}}$, $\mathbf{F_{2.S.ig.c}}$, $\mathbf{F_{2.S.im.c}}$, etc. – it is notations of sum **current conditional-variable flows of rejection the c-th secondary noo value** ($\mathbf{V_{2.S.c}}$) from **grids (**$\mathbf{G_{2.S.ip.c}}$, $\mathbf{G_{2.S.ih.c}}$, $\mathbf{G_{2.S.il.c}}$, $\mathbf{G_{2.S.iw.c}}$, $\mathbf{G_{2.S.ib.c}}$, $\mathbf{G_{2.S.ig.c}}$, $\mathbf{G_{2.S.im.c}}$, **etc.)** of **persons (**$\mathbf{P_{ip}}$, $\mathbf{P_{ih}}$, $\mathbf{P_{il}}$, $\mathbf{P_{iw}}$, $\mathbf{P_{ib}}$, $\mathbf{P_{ig}}$, $\mathbf{P_{im}}$, **etc.)**;

$\mathbf{F_{S.ib.l}}$ – it is notation of sum **current conditional-variable flows of rejection the l-th noologistical value** ($\mathbf{V_{S.ib.l}}$) entire the **noosphere**.

$\mathbf{F_{S.ip.c}}$, $\mathbf{F_{S.ih.c}}$, $\mathbf{F_{S.il.c}}$, $\mathbf{F_{S.iw.c}}$, $\mathbf{F_{S.ib.c}}$, $\mathbf{F_{S.ig.c}}$, $\mathbf{F_{S.im.c}}$, etc. – it is notations of sum **current conditional-variable flows of rejection the c-th noo value** ($\mathbf{V_{S.c}}$) of several **persons (**$\mathbf{P_{ip}}$, $\mathbf{P_{ih}}$, $\mathbf{P_{il}}$, $\mathbf{P_{iw}}$, $\mathbf{P_{ib}}$, $\mathbf{P_{ig}}$, $\mathbf{P_{im}}$, **etc.)** to the **environment**;

$\mathbf{F_{1.S.ip.c}}$, $\mathbf{F_{1.S.ih.c}}$, $\mathbf{F_{1.S.il.c}}$, $\mathbf{F_{1.S.iw.c}}$, $\mathbf{F_{1.S.ib.c}}$, $\mathbf{F_{1.S.ig.c}}$, $\mathbf{F_{1.S.im.c}}$, etc. – it is notations of sum **current conditional-variable flows of rejection the c-th primary noo value** ($V_{1.S.c}$) of several **persons** ($\mathbf{P_{ip}}$, $\mathbf{P_{ih}}$, $\mathbf{P_{il}}$, $\mathbf{P_{iw}}$, $\mathbf{P_{ib}}$, $\mathbf{P_{ig}}$, $\mathbf{P_{im}}$, **etc.**);

$\mathbf{F_{S.ib.c}}$ – it is notation of sum **current conditional-variable flows of rejection the c-th noo value** ($V_{S.ib.c}$) entire the **noosphere**.

Examples of **current conditional-variable flows of rejection** ($\mathbf{F_{S.ip.l.b}}$) **the** l-th **noological values** ($\mathbf{V_{S.l}}$), which are characterized, for example, by emission into the **environment** carbon dioxide, general toxic substances (mercury, organophosphorus compounds, chlorinated hydrocarbons, etc.); irritants (acids, alkalis, chlorine, fluorine, sulfur and nitrogen containing compounds, pesticides, mineral fertilizers, etc.); sensitizing substances (aldehydes, solvents and lacquers based on nitro compounds, soffit, nimrod, sumicidin, etc.); carcinogenic substances (asbestos, arsenic, arezine, diureth, calcium arsenate, etc.); mutagenic substances (lead, manganese, etaleamine, maneb, benemyl, cyrram, dichlorvos, etc.); industrial dust of plant, animal, mineral, as well as mixed origin.

Each specific **person** separats of the above mentioned set **of current conditional-variable flows of rejection** into primary ones ($\mathbf{F_{1S.l}}$ and $\mathbf{F_{1S.c}}$), which provide, for example, his biological existence, and secondary ($\mathbf{F_{2S.l}}$ and $\mathbf{F_{2S.c}}$) that satisfy his **higher needs**. The **primary current conditional-variable flows of rejection** are those that it uses to meet his **primary needs**, and secondary ones to meet **secondary needs**.

Parameters of **the total current conditional-variable flows of rejection** of any $\mathbf{V_{S.l}}$ and $\mathbf{V_{S.c}}$ by any **person** ($\mathbf{P_{ip}}$, $\mathbf{P_{ih}}$, $\mathbf{P_{il}}$, $\mathbf{P_{iw}}$, $\mathbf{P_{ib}}$, $\mathbf{P_{ig}}$, $\mathbf{P_{im}}$, **etc.**), from the whole **grid** of each of them, in **provision the existence** (**life support**), by all of them in the **noosphere**, etc., are calculated using **the technology of calculating information pyramids**. Information from the corresponding formalized descriptions of **the flows** of **persons** located at their lower levels is used for these calculations. The results of these calculations may be presented in the form of corresponding descriptions, the content of which is similar to the content of the above formalized description "**Current flow of rejection** the $\mathbf{V_{S.ip.l.b}}$ **from** $\mathbf{G_{S.ip.l.b}}$ ($\mathbf{F_{S.ip.l.b}}$)".

2.9. The Environment, Noosphere, Noogalaxy, Noouniverce ...

An outstanding Russian scientist Vladimir Ivanovich Vernadsky is the author of the concept of "**Noosphere**" (from the Greek νόος – the mind and σφαῖρα – sphere, short – **Nsp**). He meant by this term the totality of the reasonable interactions of multiple creatures to each other in **the environment** (short – **Ev**) as **persons** in the process of achieving their **goals**.

It was shown in the description of the **person of Noologistics** that the only formalized mode of interactions of multiple intelligences to each other and to the environment is to provide his own existence, as living sentient beings – their own livelihood and it is their only means of achieving the given **goals**.

Noologistics offers to mankind a theoretical possibility to unite all sentient beings in a total entity by a combined **goal** and, accordingly, under **the providing their united existence** (**life support**) and the total **habitat**. A comparison of the Vernadsky concept of "**noosphere**" described above and the concept of "**providing common existence** (**life support**)" all of sentient beings, for example, on planet Earth, allows to assert that their content are identical, if the planet is accepted as the σφαῖρα – sphere in it.

This approach is the basis for the **noologistical** formulation the definition of "**noosphere**":

The noosphere is the totality of the current flows of **consumption**, **creation** and **rejection** of **the values** used by the aggregate **person of Noologistics** within his joint **habitat** - the planet, in **the PRESENT** to achieve in **the FUTURE** of his aggregate **goal**.

A formal approach similarly allows to formulate the notion of "**noogalaxy**", (short – **Ngl**), "**noouniverse**", (short – **Nun**), etc.:

The noogalaxy is the totality of the current flows of **consumption**, **creation** and **rejection** of **the values** used by the aggregate **person of Noologistics** within his joint **habitat** - the Galaxy, in **the PRESENT** to achieve in **the FUTURE** of his aggregate **goal**.

The noocluster of stars is the totality of the current flows of **consumption**, **creation** and **rejection** of **the values** used by the aggregate **person of Noologistics** within his joint **habitat** - the star cluster, in **the PRESENT** to achieve in **the FUTURE** of his aggregate **goal**.

The nooconstellation is the totality of the current flows of **consumption**, **creation** and **rejection** of **the values** used by the aggregate **person of Noologistics** within his joint **habitat** - the constellation, in **the PRESENT** to achieve in **the FUTURE** of his aggregate **goal**.

The noonebula is the totality of the current flows of **consumption**, **creation** and **rejection** of **the values** used by the aggregate **person of Noologistics** within his joint **habitat** - the stellar nebula, in **the PRESENT** to achieve in **the FUTURE** of his aggregate **goal**.

The noouniverse is the totality of the current flows of **consumption**, **creation** and **rejection** of **the values** used by the aggregate **person of Noologistics** within his joint **habitat** - the universe, in **the PRESENT** to achieve in **the FUTURE** of his aggregate **goal**.

It is assumed in **Noologistics** that every **person** knows and may formalize the following information:

- the nomenclature of available **values** in **the PRESENT**, and also the size of their quantitative and qualitative parameters, the totality of which is a formalized description of his **habitat**;
- forecast nomenclature available **values** in **the FUTURE**, and – magnitudes of their quantitative and qualitative parameters, which he uses for setting his **goal**;
- the nomenclature of **values** that are unavailable in **the PRESENT**, as well as the magnitudes of their quantitative and qualitative parameters that characterize his potential possibilities to meet the new **needs**;
- forecast nomenclature of **values** that are not available in **the FUTURE** as well as the magnitudes of their quantitative and

qualitative parameters which characterize the limits of his **environment**.

Technical capabilities of mankind allow him to combine all of the above nomenclatures of **values** are available, unavailable and predicted ones and their parameters in single formal description. This aggregate nomenclature from the point of view of any **person** describes the entire limits of what is known the combined **person** in **the PRESENT** and what he expects in **the FUTURE**. These limits in **Noologistics** are the formalized description of the total **environment** of the **aggregate person's habitats** who is considered and the set of **environments** of all the **persons**, for example, on planet Earth, is their common **environment**. It is obvious that the total **environment** of the united **person** the entire planet Earth at least equal to the Universe due to scientific and educational activities of mankind. The **noologistical** concept of "**environment**" are formulated on the basis of the above:

The environment is a set of **values** known to the cumulative **person of Noologistics** in **PRESENT** and projected in the **FUTURE**.

As stated above the **noologistical** concepts of the **noosphere**, **noogalaxy**, **noouniverse** and **the environment** mean that every **person** that is part of the total entity, has their own ideas and definitions for them based on information received in the genes, in teaching, from his own experience, from scientific sources, intuition, faith, forecast, etc. They do not contradict any of the known definitions, give to the aggregate **persons** the opportunity to formalize their options and to manage reasonably (**noo**) by aggregate **provision of their existence** (**live support**), i.e. **the noosphere**, **noogalaxy**, **noouniverse**, etc., to achieve their aggregate **goals**.

Examples of their possible formal descriptions is given below for the aggregate **person** having the symbol $\mathbf{P_{ib}}$, the **habitat** of which is, for example, the planet Earth. They presented in a formalized information that is pertinent to the application **the technology of Noologistics** and are named of "**The Noosphere**", "**The Noogalaxy**", "**The Noocluster**", "**The Nooconstellation**", "**The Noonebula**", "**The Noouniverse**", "**The Environment**", etc. The content of the information in these formalized descriptions depend on the management tasks that are solved by the corresponding aggregate **person**, for example:

The Noosphere

Formalized description contains information about **the current flows of consumption** ($F_{C.ib.c}$), **of creation** ($F_{M.ib.c}$) and **of rejection** ($F_{S.ib.c}$) of the corresponding **noo values** ($V_{C.ib.c}$, $V_{M.ib.c}$ and $V_{S.ib.c}$) supported by P_{ib} in **the PRESENT**, including:

the nomenclature (list, table) of all $F_{C.ib.c}$, $F_{M.ib.c}$ and $F_{S.ib.c}$, consisting of their names and notations, and also a set of parameters to each of them defining its type (the flow of information, rituals, actions, works of art, laws, rules, energy, gas, liquid, solids, etc.), names and notations of their densities (briefly - $D_{C.ib.c}$, $D_{M.ib.c}$ and $D_{S.ib.c}$), and also their measurement units (PCs/min, m^3/h, kg/sec, l/day, W, etc.) and their numerical magnitudes, the nomenclature of quality parameters (briefly - $QP_{C.ib.c}$, $QP_{M.ib.c}$ and $QP_{S.ib.c}$) of each flow, consisting of the name of each parameter (hardness, viscosity, temperature, brightness, chemical composition, etc.), their measurement units (the hardness on HB and HRC, the viscosity of the in St, the temperature in °C and °K, brightness in LM, share in %, etc.) and their numerical values, their current location (briefly - $AF_{C.ib.c}$, $AF_{M.ib.c}$ and $AF_{S.ib.c}$) in **the habitat**, for example, in the coordinates of the geographic information system, etc.

Small Latin letter "c" in subscript the above notation is the registration number of the current **noo value** (V_c) in the example below of the information composition in a formalized description of **the environment**.

Formal description also contains information about **the current flows of consumption** ($F_{C.ib.l}$), **of creation** ($F_{M.ib.l}$) and **of rejection** ($F_{S.ib.l}$) of the corresponding **noological values** ($V_{C.ib.l}$, $V_{M.ib.l}$ and $V_{S.ib.l}$) that are supported by the P_{ib} in **the PRESENT**, including:

the nomenclature (list, table) of all $F_{C.ib.l}$, $F_{M.ib.l}$ and $F_{S.ib.l}$, consisting of their names and notations, and also a set of parameters to each of them defining its type (the flow of information, rituals, actions, works of art, laws, rules, energy, gas, liquid, solids, etc.), names and notations of their densities (briefly - $\mathbf{D_{C.ib.l}}$, $\mathbf{D_{M.ib.l}}$ and $\mathbf{D_{S.ib.l}}$), and also their measurement units (PCs/min, m^3/h, kg/sec, l/day, W, etc.) and their numerical magnitudes, the nomenclature of quality parameters (briefly - $\mathbf{QP_{C.ib.l}}$, $\mathbf{QP_{M.ib.l}}$ and $\mathbf{QP_{S.ib.l}}$) of each flow, consisting of the name of each parameter (hardness, viscosity, temperature, brightness, chemical composition, etc.), their measurement units (the hardness on HB and HRC, the viscosity of the in St, the temperature in °C and °K, brightness in LM, share in %, etc.) and their numerical magnitudes, their current location (briefly - $\mathbf{AF_{C.ib.l}}$, $\mathbf{AF_{M.ib.l}}$ and $\mathbf{AF_{S.ib.l}}$) in **the habitat**, for example, in the coordinates of the geographic information system, etc.

Small Latin letter "l" in subscript the above notation is the registration number of the current **noologistical value** ($\mathbf{V_l}$) in the example below of the information composition in a formalized description of **the environment**.

The formalized descriptions of **noogalaxy**, **noouniverse**, etc., may contain the similar information.

The Environment of $\mathbf{P_{ib}}$

Each of **noo value** in its register in a formalized description of **environment** assign a unique number, which is placed in the lower index legend. These unique registration number divided into types that have a considerable impact for the use **the technology of Noologistics**, including:

Small Latin letter "v" in the lower index is a unique identity number for the initial registration of each **noo value** ($\mathbf{V_{ib.v}}$), which then retain, even if is given other numbers;

Small Latin letter "c" in lower index indicates that this **noo value** ($\mathbf{V_{ib.c}}$) used in **the PRESENT** only in **the technology of calculation of non-indexed information pyramids**;

Small Latin letter "h" in lower index indicates that this **noo value** ($\mathbf{V_{ib.h}}$) is **noologistical** and is intended for use in **the technology of calculation of indexed information pyramids**;

Small Latin letter "l" in lower index indicates that this **noologistical value** ($V_{ib.l}$) is used in the **PRESENT** in **the technology of calculation of indexed information pyramids**;

Small Latin letter "f" in the lower index shows that the use of this **noo values** ($V_{ib.f}$) is predicted in **the FUTURE**.

Formalized description of **environment** contains a single register of all **the noo values** used in **the PAST**, are using in **the PRESENT** and projected for **FUTURE** using by all **persons** within the aggregate **person**, including:

the nomenclature (list, table) all **noo values** (briefly - $V_{ib.v}$, $V_{ib.c}$, $V_{ib.h}$, $V_{ib.l}$ and $V_{ib.f}$) consisting of their names and notations, and also a set of parameters to each of them defining its type (information, rituals, actions, works of art, laws, rules, energy, gas, liquid, solids, etc.), names and notations of their quantities (briefly - $Q_{ib.v}$, $Q_{ib.c}$, $Q_{ib.h}$, $Q_{ib.l}$ and $Q_{ib.f}$), units of their measurement (PCs, m, kg, l, WHr, etc.) and their numerical magnitudes, the nomenclature of quality parameters (briefly - $QP_{ib.v}$, $QP_{ib.c}$, $QP_{ib.h}$, $QP_{ib.l}$ and $QP_{ib.f}$) each of them, consisting of the name of each parameter (hardness, viscosity, temperature, brightness, chemical composition, etc.) and their numerical magnitudes, their measurement units (the hardness on HB and HRC, the viscosity of the in St, the temperature in ^{o}C and ^{o}K, brightness in LM, share in %, etc.) and their numerical magnitudes, their current location (briefly - $AV_{ib.v}$, $AV_{ib.c}$, $AV_{ib.h}$, $AV_{ib.l}$ and $AV_{ib.f}$) in **the habitat** each of $V_{ib.v}$, $V_{ib.c}$, $V_{ib.h}$, $V_{ib.l}$ and $V_{ib.f}$, for example, in the coordinates of the geographic information system, etc.

Methods of combining nomenclatures and calculation of parameters used in the formalized descriptions of **noosphere**, **noogalaxy**, **noouniverse**, **environment**, etc. based on **the technologies of calculation of information pyramids**. **Persons** calculate them similarly to formalized descriptions of **habitats** and of **provisions the existence** (**life supports**) of **hierarchies** using the information from formalized descriptions of constituent **persons**. Aggregate **persons** describe Specific details of using **the technology of calculation of the upward non-indexed information pyramid** in their **rules**.

It follows From the above that **Noologistics** gives to **persons** the opportunity not only reasonable (**noo**) to manage **the provision of their existence (live support)**, but also to shape the **environmental** parameters in accordance to their stated **goals**. These changes are achieved by reasonable (**noo**) control **the current flows of consumption** ($F_{C.ib}$), **of creation** ($F_{M.ib}$) and **of rejection** ($F_{S.ib}$) of the corresponding **noo values** (V_{ib}) in **the PRESENT**, including:

- **current conditional variables flows of extraction** the natural gas, oil, sodium chloride, potassium, etc. salts, coal, ores of metals, air, water, building materials, solid, liquid, gaseous substances, energy, radiation, etc. from environmental;
- **current creation flows of a primary or secondary noo values**;
- **the current conditional variables flows of rejection** to **the environment** of carbon dioxide, toxic substances (mercury, organophosphorus compounds, chlorinated hydrocarbons, etc.); of irritants (acids, alkalis, chlorine-, fluorine-, sulphur - and nitrogen compounds, pesticides, fertilizers, etc.); of sensitizing substances (aldehydes, solvents, and lacquers based on nitro compounds, soffit, Nimrod, sumicidin, etc.); of carcinogenic substances (asbestos, arsenic, arezina, diurea, arsenate of calcium, etc.); of mutagenic substances (lead, manganese, italiamia, manaba, benimeli, ziram, dichlorvos, etc.); of product dust of vegetable, animal, mineral, and mixed origin; of electromagnetic, acoustic, infrared, ultraviolet and ionizing radiation; of electric, magnetic, gravitational and other fields, etc.

2.10. The Grid of Noologistics

The set of physically existing interconnected objects, which the **person** highlights from objectively existing reality in the information category of limits (boundaries) for objects and their collections moving within it to achieve his **goal**, is called **the grid** in the general form, and the objects and their totality moving within **the grid** is called **the flow** of them.

It follows from this definition that **the grid** and **the flow** existing in it are interrelated. It is obvious that physically any **grid** consists of a set of interconnected objects of real estate, equipment for consumption, creation and rejection of flows, means of their transportation, technical means for managing equipment and transport, including instrumentation and automatic, collection, storage, verification, transmission, visualization and processing of information, etc., the action on which is transferred to **the flows** within it. Therefore, **the grid** is **a real control object**.

The technical ability to upgrade any known **grid** and manage it exists in **Noologistics** using its **technology**. **The grid** that has been modernized in this way becomes a technical means of realization its theory and technology, forming in conjunction of them **a system of Noologistics**. A particular definition for **the grid of Noologistics** (shortly - **G**) is formulated below on the basis of the above:

The grid of Noologistics is the aggregate of interconnected **noo values**, that its **person** highlights from the environment into the information category of **the real control object**, which is the limits (boundaries) of **the ideal control object** that moves within it, which is the current flow of **noo value** or their totality, and by which he reasonable (**noo**) manages in the **PRESENT** under the use of its **theory** and **technology** to achieve in the **FUTURE** its **goal**.

It is accepted in **Noologistics** that each of the set of its **persons** has his own **grid**, for example:

The grid of Noologistics of a **person** bearing the notation $\mathbf{P_{ip}}$ has the notation $\mathbf{G_{ip}}$;

The grid of Noologistics of a **hierarchy** bearing the notation $\mathbf{P_{ih}}$ has the notation $\mathbf{G_{ih}}$;

The grid of Noologistics of a **hierarchy** bearing the notation $\mathbf{P_{il}}$ has the notation $\mathbf{G_{il}}$;

The grid of Noologistics of a **hierarchy** bearing the notation $\mathbf{P_{iw}}$ has the notation $\mathbf{G_{iw}}$;

The grid of Noologistics of a **hierarchy** bearing the notation $\mathbf{P_{ib}}$ has the notation $\mathbf{G_{ib}}$;

The grid of Noologistics of a **hierarchy** bearing the notation $\mathbf{P_{ig}}$ has the notation $\mathbf{G_{ig}}$;

The grid of Noologistics of a **hierarchy** bearing the notation $\mathbf{P_{im}}$ has the notation $\mathbf{G_{im}}$, etc.

Symbols indicating for the satisfaction of which need is used this grid, may be added in the lower index of it notation, for example:

$G_{1.M.ih.NG}$ - to satisfy the **primary (1) need** of the **hierarchy** having the notation P_{ih}, to creation (**M**) the flow of natural gas (**NG**);

$G_{2.C.ih.Mn}$ - to satisfy the **secondary (2) need** of the **person** having the notation P_{ih}, to consume (**C**) the flow of money (**Mn**), etc.

The management structure of any **grid of Noologistics** may be represented in the form of an **information pyramid**, in the lowest level of which there are its elements, which here are called b-th **units of equipment** (briefly - $G_{ip.b}$, $G_{ih.b}$, $G_{il.b}$, $G_{iw.b}$, $G_{ig.b}$, etc.) and are indicated by the symbol "b" at the end of the lower index. The individual number, indicated above by the symbol b, is used through for **the equipment units** of all $G_{ip.b}$, $G_{ih.b}$, $G_{il.b}$, $G_{iw.b}$, $G_{ig.b}$, etc. and is not tied to any of them. This makes it possible to combine **the units of equipment** into a single formalized description called "**Equipment Units** (G_b)" (see below), in which they appear under the symbols G_b. The symbol **b** is also added to the end of the lower index in the notation of all parameters characterizing G_b, and the remaining symbols in the lower index of its designation correspond to **the grid of Noologistics**, in which it is included by the **person** in solving a particular control task, for example: $G_{C.ih.NG.b}$, $G_{1.M.ig.Mn.b}$, $G_{1.S.il.CO2.b}$, $G_{1.M.ih.NG}$, $G_{2.M.iw.Vth.b}$ and the like.

The main signs that give a basis to the person to allocate some of his noo values to the category of equipment are:

- use of its by the **person** as a means of control action on another **noo value**, which is called of his **ideal object of management**;
- the presence in it's composition of a single regulator, which allows **the person** to change the magnitude of this **control action**;
- the presence of logical, physical, chemical, mathematical or any other dependence between the magnitude of the **control action** and the corresponding change in **the ideal control object**.

To unify the description of parts of organisms and whole organisms of **persons** that participate in the current technological (biological) processes of creating and maintaining current consumption flows, creation and rejecting **the noo values** are taken for individual **units of equipment**.

The unit is referred to the grid equipment, if contains one controller with a logical, physical, chemical, mathematical or any other known to the **person** dependence between the **control** magnitude on it, for example, the magnitude of the speed of its actuator movement, and the corresponding change in the parameter magnitude of the **ideal control object**, for example, the magnitude of the rate of change the density of the current flow of fuel consumption, and which the **person** uses as a means of controlling it in **PRESENT**.

An example of the content of a formalized description **the units of equipment** is shown below.

Equipment Units (G_b)

Description contains:

The name «**Equipment Units** (G_b)»;

the nomenclature of all **units of equipment**, the parameters of which are currently known, including:

list of names of equipment items and their notations (G_b);

individual number **b** for each G_b;

individual number v, c, h and l, taken from **the formalized description of the environment**, since each **unit of equipment** is also **the noo value**;

passport (nominal) parameters, including: the technological scheme of its inclusion in **the grid of Noologistics** relative to other **units of equipment** (sequentially or in parallel in the group), the period of amortization $T_{A.b}$, the **rules** of creation, delivery, installation, commissioning, operation, repair, etc., the nomenclature of **the conditionally-fixed costs** of each type of **consumed** and **rejected values**, spent for its creation, delivery, installation, commissioning, repair, etc.: the unit of measure for each parameter, the quantity, and so on;

passport work characteristics describing the mathematical relationship between the magnitudes of the density of consumption, the creation, rejection flows of **noo values**, the parameters of the operating conditions (**environment**) and the modes of its operation;

established limits of its operating modes;

current parameters (in PRESENT), including: individual number of ip, ih, il, iw, ib, ig, im, etc., used by person, taken from his formalized description; current location in the coordinates of the geographic information system; current state: in work, in hot standby, in reserve, in repair, in installation, in creation and in transportation, the technological scheme of its inclusion in the grid of Noologistics in relation to other units of equipment (in series or in parallel in the group), the quantity of the developed resource, the nomenclature of current flows of consumed, created and rejected values, related to its current state: the name and unit of measurement of each parameter that characterizes its properties; parameters of operating conditions (environment) and operating modes, etc.

All the current parameters of **the units of equipment** listed in the above-mentioned formalized description are measured by the appropriate monitoring instruments or are calculated at the current time on the basis of their magnitudes using the mathematical apparatus described in the relevant sections **the technology of Noologistics**.

The formalized description of any **grid of Noologistics** (**G_{ip}, G_{ih}, G_{il}, G_{iw}, G_{ib}, G_{ig}, G_{im}**, etc.) is formed according to **the technology of calculating the upward information pyramids** in accordance to the **rules** of the **persons** by unifying the parameters of **the equipment units** included in them.

Description of examples of implementation of **Noologistics** shows the possibility of upgrading any grid available at the disposal of the person to **the grid of Noologistics**, with the maximum use of the available technical means at his disposal.

2.11. The System of Noologistics

The System of Noologistics (briefly – **SN**) is a set (Σ) of theory of **Noologistics**, its **technology** and means of its realization in the form of, for example, the matching **grid**, which **the person** uses **the PRESENT** when managing the **providing of his existence (life support**) to achieve in **the FUTURE** his **goal**.

Briefly, the structure of any **System of Noologistics** may be described by equation SN = Σ(**NL**, **TN** and **G**), in which **NL** denotes the theory of **Noologistics**, **TN** – its **technology** and **G** – the corresponding **grid**. Due to the large number of types of **persons** (P_{ip}, P_{ih}, P_{il}, P_{iw}, P_{ib}, P_{ig}, P_{im}, **etc.**) in **Noologistics**, each of them has its own **System of Noologistics**, including:

System of Noologistics of **a person** having a symbol P_{ip} (briefly – SN_{ip}): $SN_{ip} = \Sigma(NL, TN_{ip}$ and $G_{ip})$;

System of Noologistics of **a hierarchy** having a symbol P_{ih} (briefly – SN_{ih}): $SN_{ih} = \Sigma(NL, TN_{ih}$ and $G_{ih})$;

System of Noologistics of **a hierarchy** having a symbol P_{il} (briefly – SN_{il}): $SN_{il} = \Sigma(NL, TN_{il}$ and $G_{il})$;

System of Noologistics of **a hierarchy** having a symbol P_{iw} (briefly – SN_{iw}): $SN_{iw} = \Sigma(NL, TN_{iw}$ and $G_{iw})$;

System of Noologistics of **a hierarchy** having a symbol P_{ib} (briefly – SN_{ib}): $SN_{ib} = \Sigma(NL, TN_{ib}$ and $G_{ib})$;

System of Noologistics of **a hierarchy** having a symbol P_{ig} (briefly – SN_{ig}): $SN_{ig} = \Sigma(NL, TN_{ig}$ and $G_{ig})$;

System of Noologistics of **a hierarchy** having a symbol P_{im} (briefly – SN_{im}): $SN_{im} = \Sigma(NL, TN_{im}$ and $G_{im})$, etc.

The absence of a short descriptions of details of **System of Noologistics** for different types of **persons** in the above subscript legend **NL**, shows that the theory of **Noologistics** is universal and available to each of them and the rest of its elements require clarification in accordance to **the goals** and **objects** of specific **persons**.

The **System of Noologistics** of any **hierarchy** is formed in accordance to his **rules** on **the technology of calculating information**

pyramid as a set of **Systems of Noologistics** of its constituent entities.

2.12. The Current Technological Process

The current technological process in **Noologistics** is a set of control actions of its **person** in accordance his technology to determine, maintain or change the state of his **object** in the **PRESENT**, provision the achievement in the **FUTURE** of the **goal** set by him.

It follows from this definition that the **current technological process** is the implementation of **Noologistics technology** in the **PRESENT** (at the current time).

The term "**technological process**" (**TP**) used in the description of the **Noologistics technology** is a set of descriptions of the **noo control actions** of its **person** on his **object** in the **PAST** or predicted in the **FUTURE**.

Biological processes that occur in parts of organisms and whole organisms of living entities, creating and sustaining current flows of **consumption**, **creating** and **rejecting** the **noo values**, are categorized as their personal **current technological processes** for unifying description.

Classification of **current technological processes** is used in **Noologistics**, that is reflected in the lower index of their conventional designations and corresponds to the classification of types of it's **persons** and **noo values**, for example:

Current Technological Process in **P_{ip}'s b^{st} unit of equipment** has conventional designations **$CTP_{ip.b}$**;

Current Technological Process in **b^{st} unit of equipment** of **hierarchy P_{ih}** has conventional designations **$CTP_{ih.b}$**;

Current Technological Process in **grid** of **hierarchy P_{il}** has conventional designations **CTP_{il}**;

Current Technological Process in **grid** of **hierarchy P_{iw}** has conventional designations **CTP_{iw}**;

Current Technological Process in **grid** of **hierarchy P_{ib}** has conventional designations **CTP_{ih}**;

Current Technological Process in **grid** of **hierarchy** $\mathbf{P_{ig}}$ has conventional designations $\mathbf{CTP_{ig}}$;

Current Technological Process in **grid** of **hierarchy** $\mathbf{P_{im}}$ has conventional designations $\mathbf{CTP_{im}}$, etc.

Symbols may be added in the lower index of conventional designations the **Current Technological Process** that specifying what **needs** they satisfy, for example:

$\mathbf{CTP_{1.M.ih.NG.b}}$ – to satisfy the **primary (1) need** of **hierarchy** $\mathbf{P_{ih}}$ to create (M) the current flow of natural gas (NG) in **b**[st] **unit of equipment**;

$\mathbf{CTP_{2.C.ip.Mn.b}}$ – to satisfy the **secondary (2) need** of the **person** $\mathbf{P_{ip}}$ to consume (C) the current flow of money (Mn) in **b**[st] **unit of equipment**, etc.

Formalized descriptions of **current technological processes** are used for mathematical processing of their parameters, an example of the possible content of such a description is shown below under the heading "**Current Technological Process** in $\mathbf{G_{ip.l.b}}$ ($\mathbf{CTP_{ip.l.b}}$)".

Current Technological Process in $\mathbf{G_{ip.l.b}}$ ($\mathbf{CTP_{ip.l.b}}$)

The formalized description contains:

The heading «**Current Technological Process** in $\mathbf{G_{ip.l.b}}$» and personal identification number $\mathbf{P_{ip}}$, for example, **ip**;

b - the identification number of the b-th **equipment unit** used in it and a link to its formal description;

nomenclature and parameters of the **current conditional variables**, **conditionally constant** and **gross consumption flows** of **noo and noologictical values**, including: the names and conventional designations of constituent them the **noo and noologistical values**, the names and conventional designations of their flows ($\mathbf{F_{C.ip.c.b}}$, $\mathbf{FF_{C.ip.c.b}}$, $\mathbf{TF_{C.ip.c.b}}$, $\mathbf{F_{C.ip.l.b}}$, $\mathbf{FF_{C.ip.l.b}}$ and $\mathbf{TF_{C.ip.l.b}}$), unit of measurement and the magnitudes of their densities ($\mathbf{D_{C.ip.c.b}}$, $\mathbf{FD_{C.ip.c.b}}$, $\mathbf{TD_{C.ip.c.b}}$, $\mathbf{D_{C.ip.l.b}}$, $\mathbf{FD_{C.ip.l.b}}$ and $\mathbf{TD_{C.ip.l.b}}$), names, units of measure and the magnitudes of their qualitative parameters - temperature, chemical composition, specific gravity, viscosity, color, currency type, etc.;

nomenclature and parameters of the **current conditional variables**, **conditionally constant** and **gross consumption flows** of **noo and noologictical values**, including: the names and conventional designations of constituent them the **noo and noologistical values**, the names and conventional designations of their flows ($\mathbf{F_{M.ip.c.b}}$ and $\mathbf{F_{M.ip.L.b}}$), unit of measurement and the magnitudes of their densities ($\mathbf{D_{M.ip.c.b}}$ and $\mathbf{D_{M.ip.L.b}}$), names, units of measure and the magnitudes of their qualitative parameters - temperature, chemical composition, specific gravity, viscosity, color, currency type, etc.;

nomenclature and parameters of the **current conditional variables**, **conditionally constant** and **gross rejection flows** of **noo and noologictical values**, including: the names and conventional designations of constituent them the **noo and noologistical values**, the names and conventional designations of their flows ($\mathbf{F_{S.ip.c.b}}$, $\mathbf{FF_{S.ip.c.b}}$, $\mathbf{TF_{S.ip.c.b}}$, $\mathbf{F_{S.ip.l.b}}$, $\mathbf{FF_{S.ip.l.b}}$ and $\mathbf{TF_{S.ip.l.b}}$), unit of measurement and the magnitudes of their densities ($\mathbf{D_{S.ip.c.b}}$, $\mathbf{FD_{S.ip.c.b}}$, $\mathbf{TD_{S.ip.c.b}}$, $\mathbf{D_{S.ip.l.b}}$, $\mathbf{FD_{S.ip.l.b}}$ and $\mathbf{TD_{S.ip.l.b}}$), names, units of measure and the magnitudes of their qualitative parameters - temperature, chemical composition, specific gravity, viscosity, color, currency type, etc.

The concrete content of the formalized description and its design are set by the respective **persons** in their **rules**, depending, for example, on the type of task being solved, the **equipment unit**, the **object**, the **person**, etc.

The description of the **current technological process** of each of the **hierarchies** mentioned above is formalized in accordance his **rules** and is formed using **the technology of calculating information pyramids**, from the formalized descriptions of **current technological processes** of **equipment units** of **grids** of all its constituent **persons**, including:

The formalized description of the current technological process of the **grid** of a **person** $\mathbf{P_{ip}}$ ($\mathbf{CTP_{ip}}$) is formed according to his **rules** as a set (**Σ**) of formalized descriptions of **current technological processes** of all b-th constituents of his **equipment units** ($\mathbf{CTP_{ip.b}}$): $\mathbf{CTP_{ip} = \Sigma(CTP_{ip.b})}$;

The formalized description of the current technological process of the **grid** of the **person** P_{ih} (CTP_{ih}) is formed according to his **rules** as a set of (**Σ**) of formalized descriptions of the **current technological processes** of all his b-th **equipment units** ($CTP_{ih.b}$) or **grids** of its constituent **persons** (CTP_{ip}): $CTP_{ih} = \Sigma(CTP_{ih.b}) = \Sigma(CTP_{ip})$;

The formalized description of the current technological process of the **grid** of the **person** P_{il} (CTP_{il}) is formed according to his **rules** as a set of (Σ) of formalized descriptions of the current technological processes of all his b-th **equipment units** ($CTP_{il.b}$) or **grids** of its constituent **persons** (CTP_{ip}, CTP_{ih}): $CTP_{il} = \Sigma(CTP_{il.b}) = \Sigma(CTP_{ip}, CTP_{ih})$;

The formalized description of the current technological process of the **grid** of the **person** P_{iw} (CTP_{iw}) is formed according to his **rules** as a set of (Σ) of formalized descriptions of the current technological processes of all his b-th **equipment units** ($CTP_{iw.b}$) or **grids** of its constituent **persons** (CTP_{ip}, CTP_{ih}, CTP_{il}): $CTP_{iw} = \Sigma(CTP_{iw.b}) = \Sigma(CTP_{ip}, CTP_{ih}, CTP_{il})$, etc.

2.13. The Noo Management Solution

The following definition of a **management solution** from **control theory** was adopted as a model for the concept of "**noo management solution**" (shortly - **NCS**):

Management solution – a generic term indicating the end of the process of the description of such set of objectively existing interrelated technologies used to provide dynamic state of the **control object** (operation, behavior, work, direction, magnitude, best magnitude for money, impact on other **objects**, for calculating **the control actions**, etc.), control parameters and their magnitudes, which developed by technology management established by **the person** of management, and which meets the **goals** of the control.

The concept of "**Noo Management Solution**" formulated on its basis:

Noo management solution is a generalization term denoting the completion by **the person of Noologistics** in the **PRESENT** the process change of his management **rules** for **provision of his existence** (**life support**) or the abandonment to change in order to achieve in the **FUTURE** the **goal** set by him.

Person of Noologistics one way or another mention in his **rules** all **the values** in **the environment** that they know. Therefore, the use of various types of **noo management solutions** provided in **Noologistics**, which are reflected in the lower indices of the notations, for example:

$NCS_{1.C.ip.l.b}$, $NCS_{1.C.ih.l.b}$, $NCS_{1.C.il.l.b}$, $NCS_{1.C.iw.l.b}$, $NCS_{1.C.ib.l.b}$, $NCS_{1.C.ig.l.b}$, $NCS_{1.C.im.l.b}$, etc. – this are the notations of **noologistical management solutions** of **persons (P_{ip}, P_{ih}, P_{il}, P_{iw}, P_{ib}, P_{ig}, P_{im}, etc.)** to their **current flows of consumption the l-th primary noologistical value** ($V_{1.C.l}$) in their **b-th units of equipment ($G_{1.C.ip.l.b}$, $G_{1.C.ih.l.b}$, $G_{1.C.il.l.b}$, $G_{1.C.iw.l.b}$, $G_{1.C.ib.l.b}$, $G_{1.C.ig.l.b}$, $G_{1.C.im.l.b}$, etc.)** and apply directly to their actual **units of equipment**.

$NCS_{M.ip.l}$, $NCS_{M.ih.l}$, $NCS_{M.il.l}$, $NCS_{M.iw.l}$, $NCS_{M.ib.l}$, $NCS_{M.ig.l}$, $NCS_{M.im.l}$, etc. – this are the notations of **noologistical management solutions** of **persons (P_{ip}, P_{ih}, P_{il}, P_{iw}, P_{ib}, P_{ig}, P_{im}, etc.)** to their **current flows of creation the l-th noologistical value** ($V_{M.l}$) in their **grids ($G_{M.ip.l}$, $G_{M.ih.l}$, $G_{M.il.l}$, $G_{M.iw.l}$, $G_{M.ib.l}$, $G_{M.ig.l}$, $G_{M.im.l}$, etc.)** and apply directly to their actual **grids**;

$NCS_{S.ip.l.b}$, $NCS_{S.ih.l.b}$, $NCS_{S.il.l.b}$, $NCS_{S.iw.l.b}$, $NCS_{S.ib.l.b}$, $NCS_{S.ig.l.b}$, $NCS_{S.im.l.b}$, etc. – this are the notations of **noologistical management solutions** of **persons (P_{ip}, P_{ih}, P_{il}, P_{iw}, P_{ib}, P_{ig}, P_{im}, etc.)** to their **current flows of rejection the l-th noologistical value** ($V_{S.l}$) to **the environment** from their **b-the units of equipment** (**$G_{S.ip.l.b}$, $G_{S.ih.l.b}$, $G_{S.il.l.b}$, $G_{S.iw.l.b}$, $G_{S.ib.l.b}$, $G_{S.ig.l.b}$, $G_{S.im.l.b}$, etc.**) and apply directly to their actual **units of equipment**;

$NCS_{2.C.ip.c}$, $NCS_{2.C.ih.c}$, $NCS_{2.C.il.c}$, $NCS_{2.C.iw.c}$, $NCS_{2.C.ib.c}$, $NCS_{2.C.ig.c}$, $NCS_{2.C.im.c}$, etc. – this are the notations of **noo management solutions** of **persons (P_{ip}, P_{ih}, P_{il}, P_{iw}, P_{ib}, P_{ig}, P_{im}, etc.)** to their **current flows of consumption the c-th secondary noo value** ($V_{2.C.c}$) in their **grids ($G_{2.C.ip.c}$, $G_{2.C.ih.c}$, $G_{2.C.il.c}$, $G_{2.C.iw.c}$, $G_{2.C.ib.c}$, $G_{2.C.ig.c}$, $G_{2.C.im.c}$, etc.)** and apply directly to their actual **grids**;

$NCS_{C.ib.c}$ – this is the notation of sum **noo management solution** of **person** (**P_{ip}**) to his sum **current flow of consumption the c-th noo value** (**$V_{C.ib.c}$**) in his **grid** (**$G_{C.ib.c}$**) and apply directly to his actual **grid;**

$NCS_{S.ip.c}$, $NCS_{S.ih.c}$, $NCS_{S.il.c}$, $NCS_{S.iw.c}$, $NCS_{S.ib.c}$, $NCS_{S.ig.c}$, $NCS_{S.im.c}$, etc. – this are the notations of **noo management solutions** of **persons** **(P_{ip}, P_{ih}, P_{il}, P_{iw}, P_{ib}, P_{ig}, P_{im}, etc.)** to their **current flows of rejection the c-th noo value** (**$V_{S.c}$**) to **the environment** from their **grids** **($G_{S.ip.c}$, $G_{S.ih.c}$, $G_{S.il.c}$, $G_{S.iw.c}$, $G_{S.ib.c}$, $G_{S.ig.c}$, $G_{S.im.c}$, etc.)** and apply directly to their actual **grids**;

$NCS_{1.M.ip.c}$, $NCS_{1.M.ih.c}$, $NCS_{1.M.il.c}$, $NCS_{1.M.iw.c}$, $NCS_{1.M.ib.c}$, $NCS_{1.M.ig.c}$, $NCS_{1.M.im.c}$, etc. – this are the notations of **noo management solutions** of **persons** **(P_{ip}, P_{ih}, P_{il}, P_{iw}, P_{ib}, P_{ig}, P_{im}, etc.)** to their **current flows of creation the c-th primary noo value** (**$V_{1.M.c}$**) in their **grids** **($G_{1.M.ip.c}$, $G_{1.M.ih.c}$, $G_{1.M.il.c}$, $G_{1.M.iw.c}$, $G_{1.M.ib.c}$, $G_{1.M.ig.c}$, $G_{1.M.im.c}$, etc.)** and apply directly to their actual **grids**;

$NCS_{S.im.c}$ – this is the notation of sum **noo management solution** of **person** (**P_{im}**) to his sum **current flow of rejection the c-th noo value** (**$V_{S.im.c}$**) to **the environment** from his **grid** (**$G_{S.im.c}$**) and apply directly to his actual **grid**.

The above notations of **noo** management solutions are applied for their uniformity in theoretical description of **Noologistics**. But it is more convenient to use the names and notations adopted by **the persons** in the relevant areas of science and technology in the control of **real objects**, as shown in **the practical examples of Noologistics implementation**.

Specific examples of rule changes in the PAST is given, for example, in the section "**5. The List of Used Information Sources**". The present description is an example of the process of their creation in **the FUTURE**. They relate to changes in preferences, aggravations, punishment, scales of remuneration the table of ranks, taxes, boundaries, rights, descriptions of laws of nature, regulations of primary needs and a lot that contain sets of laws, criminal, civil, procedural codes, traditions, Scriptures, research results, etc. The inclusion of these changes in **technology of Noologistics** is usually expressed as four arithmetic operations (+, -, *, :), as in the algorithm of calculations - the simplest of logical operations (IF, AND, OR, TRUE, FALSE, NO). Mathematical statement of fact scientific studies of natural phenomena, which often contain complex mathematical calculations are derived in **technology of Noologistics** entirely directly from **the relevant sections of science**.

2.14. The Noo Control Action

The definition of the control action from **control theory** it is accepted as a counterpart of the concept of **noo control action**:

The control action is a generalized that designates a forced changing or not changing of the control parameters, in accordance the developed **control solution** to achieve the management **goals** set by the **person** of management.

The concept of "**Noo Control Action**" formulated on its basis:

The noo control action is a generalized term that designates a forced changing or not changing by the **person of Noologistics** the state the actuator of the regulator of the **equipment unit** in the **PRESENT**, for example, the speed of its movement, providing the achievement of his **goal** in the **FUTURE**, in accordance his **rules**, **principles** and **criteria of reasonableness**.

It is known from the description of **providing the existence** (**life support**) that it is **the ideal object** of management by **the person of Noologistics** directly related to the satisfaction of his **needs**, to which he usually is not able to perform direct **noo control action**. **The persons** realize their **noo control actions** to their **ideal objects** through **the real objects** for this reason. They use for this as **a real objects** the available **units of equipment**, as well as **grids** consisting of many interconnected **units of equipment** of any kind working together.

The essence of each **noo control action** on the affected **unit of equipment** is the forced displacement of its Executive body of the controller in **the PRESENT** (i.e. current time) at a speed which provides in **the FUTURE** the achievement of the **goals** set by the entity including compliance to his **rules**, **principles** and **criteria of reasonableness**. Moreover, the speed of movement of the Executive body of each **unit of equipment** in the network in **the PRESENT** synchronized to the speed of movement of the Executive bodies of other **units of equipment** in it according **to the technology forecast in the PRESENT**.

The technology of Noologistics containing **the technology of forecast calculation in the PRESENT**, **the technology of calculating the indexed noologistical area of possible operating modes** and **the technology of calculating information pyramids** are used for calculating **the noo control actions**. The combination of these technologies provides a mathematically precise achievement of **the goals** set by **the person**.

The use of various types of **noo control actions** provided in **Noologistics**, which are reflected in the lower indices of the notations in accordance of **the person**, of **the unit of equipment**, of the satisfied **needs**, of the management tasks, etc., for example:

$NCA_{1.C.ip.l.b}$, $NCA_{1.C.ih.l.b}$, $NCA_{1.C.il.l.b}$, $NCA_{1.C.iw.l.b}$, $NCA_{1.C.ib.l.b}$, $NCA_{1.C.ig.l.b}$, $NCA_{1.C.im.l.b}$, etc. – this are the notations of **noologistical control actions** of **persons (P_{ip}, P_{ih}, P_{il}, P_{iw}, P_{ib}, P_{ig}, P_{im}, etc.)** to the **b-th units of equipment ($G_{1.C.ip.l.b}$, $G_{1.C.ih.l.b}$, $G_{1.C.il.l.b}$, $G_{1.C.iw.l.b}$, $G_{1.C.ib.l.b}$, $G_{1.C.ig.l.b}$, $G_{1.C.im.l.b}$, etc.)** to change or not change their **current flows of consumption the l-th primary noologistical value** ($V_{1.C.l}$);

$NCA_{M.ip.l}$, $NCA_{M.ih.l}$, $NCA_{M.il.l}$, $NCA_{M.iw.l}$, $NCA_{M.ib.l}$, $NCA_{M.ig.l}$, $NCA_{M.im.l}$, etc. – this are the notations of **noologistical control actions** of **persons (P_{ip}, P_{ih}, P_{il}, P_{iw}, P_{ib}, P_{ig}, P_{im}, etc.)** to the **grids ($G_{M.ip.l}$, $G_{M.ih.l}$, $G_{M.il.l}$, $G_{M.iw.l}$, $G_{M.ib.l}$, $G_{M.ig.l}$, $G_{M.im.l}$, etc.)** to change or not change their **current flows of creation the l-th noologistical value** ($V_{M.l}$);

$NCA_{S.ip.l.b}$, $NCA_{S.ih.l.b}$, $NCA_{S.il.l.b}$, $NCA_{S.iw.l.b}$, $NCA_{S.ib.l.b}$, $NCA_{S.ig.l.b}$, $NCA_{S.im.l.b}$, etc. – this are the notations of **noologistical control actions** of **persons (P_{ip}, P_{ih}, P_{il}, P_{iw}, P_{ib}, P_{ig}, P_{im}, etc.)** to the **b-th units of equipment ($G_{S.ip.l.b}$, $G_{S.ih.l.b}$, $G_{S.il.l.b}$, $G_{S.iw.l.b}$, $G_{S.ib.l.b}$, $G_{S.ig.l.b}$, $G_{S.im.l.b}$, etc.)** to change or not change their **current flows of rejection the l-th noologistical value** ($V_{S.l}$) to **the environment**;

$NCA_{2.C.ip.c}$, $NCA_{2.C.ih.c}$, $NCA_{2.C.il.c}$, $NCA_{2.C.iw.c}$, $NCA_{2.C.ib.c}$, $NCA_{2.C.ig.c}$, $NCA_{2.C.im.c}$, etc. – this are the notations of **noo control actions** of **persons (P_{ip}, P_{ih}, P_{il}, P_{iw}, P_{ib}, P_{ig}, P_{im}, etc.)** to the **grids** ($G_{2.C.ip.c}$, $G_{2.C.ih.c}$, $G_{2.C.il.c}$, $G_{2.C.iw.c}$, $G_{2.C.ib.c}$, $G_{2.C.ig.c}$, $G_{2.C.im.c}$, **etc.)** to change or not change their **current flows of consumption the c-th secondary noo value** ($V_{2.C.c}$);

$NCA_{C.ib.c}$ – this is the notation of sum **noo control action** of **person** (**P_{ib}**) to the **grid** (**$G_{C.ib.c}$**) to change or not change his **current flow of consumption the c-th noo value** ($V_{C.ib.c}$);

$NCA_{S.ip.c}$, $NCA_{S.ih.c}$, $NCA_{S.il.c}$, $NCA_{S.iw.c}$, $NCA_{S.ib.c}$, $NCA_{S.ig.c}$, $NCA_{S.im.c}$, etc. – this are the notations of **noo control actions** of **persons (**P_{ip}, P_{ih}, P_{il}, P_{iw}, P_{ib}, P_{ig}, P_{im}**, etc.)** to the **grids (**$G_{S.ip.c}$, $G_{S.ih.c}$, $G_{S.il.c}$, $G_{S.iw.c}$, $G_{S.ib.c}$, $G_{S.ig.c}$, $G_{S.im.c}$**, etc.)** to change or not change their **current flows of rejection the c-th noo value** ($V_{S.c}$) to **the environment**;

$NCA_{1.M.ip.c}$, $NCA_{1.M.ih.c}$, $NCA_{1.M.il.c}$, $NCA_{1.M.iw.c}$, $NCA_{1.M.ib.c}$, $NCA_{1.M.ig.c}$, $NCA_{1.M.i1M.c}$, etc. – this are the notations of **noo control actions** of **persons (**P_{ip}, P_{ih}, P_{il}, P_{iw}, P_{ib}, P_{ig}, P_{im}**, etc.)** to the **grids (**$G_{1.M.ip.c}$, $G_{1.M.ih.c}$, $G_{1.M.il.c}$, $G_{1.M.iw.c}$, $G_{1.M.ib.c}$, $G_{1.M.ig.c}$, $G_{1.M.i1M.c}$**, etc.)** to change or not change their **current flows of creation the c-th primary noo value** ($V_{1.M.c}$);

$NCA_{S.im.c}$ – this is the notation of sum **noo control action** of **person** (**P_{im}**) to the **grid** (**$G_{S.im.c}$**) to change or not change his sum **current flow of rejection the c-th noo value** ($V_{S.im.c}$) to **the environment**.

The above notations of **noo control actions** are applied for their uniformity in theoretical description of **Noologistics**. But it is more convenient to use the names and notations adopted by **the persons** in the relevant areas of science and technology in the control of **real objects**, as shown in **the practical examples of Noologistics implementation**.

3. The Technology of Noologistics

3.1. The Structure of Noologistics Technology

The technology of Noologistics (briefly – **TN**) is a set of methods and technical means of reasonable (**noo**) management of **provision of owned existence** (**life support**) in **the PRESENT**, which **person** uses to achieve in **the FUTURE** his **goal**.

TN combines many **known technologies** ($\sum$**T**) which **the person** yet is not know of **Noologistics** uses to **provision of his existence** (**life support**) and interconnected universal technologies **of calculation of**

the forecast in the PRESENT (**TCF**), **calculating the current indexed noologistical possible modes of operation** (**RPM**) and **calculation of the information pyramid** (**IP**), which together form **the technology of Noologistics**. **The person** uses this **set of technologies** to a reasonable (**noo**) control **the provision of his existence** (**life support**) and **the environment** in **the PRESENT**. Furthermore, **the person** uses this set for scheduling, reserving, forecasting, repair, modernization, simulation, bottlenecks, etc. in **the FUTURE**.

Brief the structure of **technology of Noologistics** may be described by the equation **TN** = **Σ(ΣT**, **TCF**, **RPM** and **IP**), in which **ΣT** denotes the set of **known technologies**, which uses any given **person** regardless of whether he uses **Noologistics**, **TCF** denotes **the technology of forecast calculation in the PRESENT**, **RPM** denotes **the technology of calculating the indexed noologistical area of possible operating modes** of **the real object** and **IP** denotes **the technology of calculating information pyramids**. Due to the large number of types of **persons** (**P_{ip}, P_{ih}, P_{il}, P_{iw}, P_{ib}, P_{ig}, P_{im}, etc.**) in **Noologistics**, each of them has its own **technology of Noologistics**, including:

The technology of Noologistics of **a person** having a symbol **P_{ip}** (briefly – **TN_{ip}**): **TN_{ip}** = Σ(**ΣT_{ip}**, **TCF**, **RPM** and **IP**);

The technology of Noologistics of **a hierarchy** having a symbol **P_{ih}** (briefly – **TN_{ih}**): **TN_{ih}** = Σ(**ΣT_{ih}**, **TCF**, **RPM** and **IP**);

The technology of Noologistics of **a hierarchy** having a symbol **P_{il}** (briefly – **TN_{il}**): **TN_{il}** = Σ(**ΣT_{il}**, **TCF**, **RPM** and **IP**);

The technology of Noologistics of **a hierarchy** having a symbol **P_{iw}** (briefly – **TN_{iw}**): **TN_{iw}** = Σ(**ΣT_{iw}**, **TCF**, **RPM** and **IP**);

The technology of Noologistics of **a hierarchy** having a symbol **P_{ib}** (briefly – **TN_{ib}**): **TN_{ib}** = Σ(**ΣT_{ib}**, **TCF**, **RPM** and **IP**);

The technology of Noologistics of **a hierarchy** having a symbol **P_{ig}** (briefly – **TN_{ig}**): **TN_{ig}** = Σ(**ΣT_{ig}**, **TCF**, **RPM** and **IP**);

The technology of Noologistics of **a hierarchy** having a symbol **P_{im}** (briefly – **TN_{im}**): **TN_{im}** = Σ(**ΣT_{im}**, **TCF**, **RPM** and **IP**), etc.

The technology of Noologistics of any **hierarchy** is the set of on **the technologies of Noologistics** of its constituent entities are united on **the technology of calculating information pyramids**.

Some of the countless possible variants the technology of **Noologistics** are presented in **the practical examples of Noologistics implementation**.

3.2. The Technology of Forecast Calculation in the PRESENT

The mode of information processing, in which the interaction of its processing system to external processes in relation to it is provided at a rate commensurate under the speed of these processes, is called the control mode "real time" in **the generally accepted theory of management**.

Experts believe that in the prediction there are only two kinds of time: **PAST** and **FUTURE**: "In a sense, we may talk almost not about the past, present and future, but only about the past and future, of which the second continuously "flows" into the first through the conditional dividing line, called the present. Modern science may deal either with the past (that dealt historical Sciences, including the history of physics, chemistry, biology, and other Sciences) or with a future that is more or less actively "invading " the present to soon become the past (what physical, chemical, medical, philosophical, economic, pedagogical, legal, philological, military, and other Sciences are doing, thus having to constantly go beyond the "present" in the narrow sense of the concept).)» (I. V. Bestuzhev-Lada). **PRESENT** from the point of view of **the conventional theory of forecasting** is the current moment of time in which **the FUTURE** passes into **the PAST**.

The above quote in fact denies the possibility to determine what is necessary and sufficient to do **the person** at the moment to achieve in **the FUTURE the goal** set by him, using the experience of **the PAST**. Thus, the authors of **the conventional theory of forecasting** recognize **the person** as a outside observer for how **the FUTURE** is more or less actively "invading" **the PRESENT** in order to soon become **the PAST**.

Nevertheless, the obvious fact is that each **person** constantly in real time, i.e. in **the PRESENT**, develops and realizes **noo control actions** on **the objects** of management, using the previous experience, experience of other **persons** known to him and intuition, and also hoping for the help of higher forces (i.e. other **persons**) and good luck. Thus each **person** in **the PRESENT** is constantly involved himself in shaping **the FUTURE**, using **PAST** experience, on the basis of his **goal**.

It is well known that **the PAST** never happen again in **the PRESENT** and forecast **the FUTURE** will always be different from **the PRESENT**, when it comes time. Therefore, it is extremely important for **a person** for order to achieve his **goal**, to develop **a management solution** and calculate a set of appropriate **control actions** in this very moment.

Therefore, the control mode in "real time" is called from the point of view of a **Noologistics** a that mode of information processing, which provides forecasting at the current time, i.e. – in **the PRESENT**.

The mathematical apparatus and algorithm of its application are shown below for the **noo** calculation of the "flow" of any **stochastic phenomenon or event** through a conditional dividing line, called **the PRESENT**, from **the FUTURE** to **the PAST**. The set of operations to calculate the parameters of the above process of "flow" is called here **The Technology of Forecast Calculation in the PRESENT** (briefly – **TCF**). The essence of **TCF** is, first, the calculation of the current rate of change of each predicted current parameter of each **stochastic phenomenon or event**, which affects the process of achieving **the goal** set by **the person**, and, secondly, the calculation of the current rate of change in the position of the Executive body of each regulator in its **control object** in **the PRESENT** from the condition of achieving this **goal** in **the FUTURE**.

The phenomena and events are related to the category of **stochastic phenomena and events**, if to calculate the predicted magnitudes of their current parameters in **Noologistics** are used **the conventional predict theory** a universal mathematical tools and algorithms for treatment based on their **history of changes** in **the PAST**. The main difference in their application into **TCF** that is considered here is the prediction on the conditional line between **FUTURE** and **PAST**, referred to as **PRESENT**, which was excluded from the prediction in the above quotation I. V. Bestuzhev-Lada.

The following concepts were used to describe the **TCF**:

The PAST - it is the set of magnitudes of the parameters characterizing **the stochastic phenomena and events, providing the existence** (**life support**), **habitat, noo management solutions, control actions, noo control objects, persons, goals, environment, noosphere, noogalaxy, noouniverce**, etc. at the past time moments.

The PRESENT - it is the set of magnitudes of the parameters characterizing **the stochastic phenomena and events, providing the existence** (**life support**), **habitat, noo management solutions, control actions, noo control objects, persons, goals, environment, noosphere, noogalaxy, noouniverce**, etc. at the current time moment.

The FUTURE is the aggregate of the expected magnitudes of the parameters characterizing **the stochastic phenomena and events, providing the existence** (**life support**), **habitat, noo management solutions, control actions, noo control objects, persons, goals, environment, noosphere, noogalaxy, noouniverce**, etc. at **moments of forecasting time**.

Forecast in **Noologistics** is the calculated magnitude of the current parameter or a set of them that characterizes the expected quantitative and / or qualitative state of **the stochastic phenomena and events, providing the existence** (**life support**), **habitat, noo management solutions, control actions, noo control objects, persons, goals, environment, noosphere, noogalaxy, noouniverce**, etc. at **the moments of forecasting time**.

Forecasting is the process of calculating **the forecast**.

The forecasting period (pre-forecast period, forecast generation period, forecast range, forecast horizon) is the time period for which **the forecast** is calculated.

The moment of forecasting time is the time of completion of **the forecasting period**.

The current parameter is a magnitude that qualitatively or quantitatively characterizes the properties of **the stochastic phenomena and events, providing the existence (life support), habitat, noo management solutions, control actions, noo control objects, persons, goals, environment, noosphere, noogalaxy, noouniverce**, etc., and which the **person** measures or calculates using **the technology of calculating the forecast in the PRESENT** at the current time.

The history of changes is the totality of the measured magnitudes of **the current parameter** of **the stochastic phenomena and events, providing the existence** (**life support**), **habitat, noo management solutions, control actions, noo control objects, persons, goals, environment, noosphere, noogalaxy, noouniverce**, etc., or a set of **current parameters**, as well as - the moments of their measurement.

The trend line is a time-ordered set of a set of predicted intermediate magnitudes of the current parameter characterizing **the stochastic phenomena and events, providing the existence** (**life support**), **habitat, noo management solutions, control actions, noo control objects, persons, goals, environment, noosphere, noogalaxy, noouniverce**, etc., or **sets** of current parameters calculated with a given step during **the forecasting period** at **the moment of forecasting time**.

A step is a given interval of time between the intermediate magnitudes when forming a **history of changes** and calculating **a trend line**.

A set is a collection of stochastic phenomena or events, as well as the magnitudes of **the current parameters** characterizing **the stochastic phenomena and events, providing the existence** (**life support**), **habitat, noo management solutions, control actions, noo control objects, persons, goals, environment, noosphere, noogalaxy, noouniverce**, etc., which fully ensures the application of **technology for calculating the forecast in the PRESENT**.

Synchronization in **the technology of forecast calculation in the PRESENT** means that the calculation of all magnitudes of **the current parameters** is performed at the current time (in the **PRESENT**), fixed by a single chronometer at arbitrarily predetermined **moments of forecasting time**, the number of **steps**, the magnitudes of the **forecasting period** and **steps**.

The current mode is a **set** of magnitudes of **the current parameters** of the operation of the control **object**, which quantitatively and qualitatively characterizes its current state in the **PRESENT** and separates it from a bunch of possible states, described, for example, by its **current noologistical area of possible operating modes**.

The definition of the technology of forecast calculation in **PRESENT** is formulated on the basis of the above:

The technology of forecast calculation in PRESENT is called the scientifically grounded calculation of the **set** of changing magnitudes of the current parameters characterizing a **set** of stochastic phenomena and events that affect the current mode of operation of the control **object** and also the calculation and realization of a synchronized **set** of magnitudes of **noo control actions** on it in **PRESENT**, providing in the **FUTURE** the achievement of the **goal** set by the **person**.

The technology of forecast calculation in PRESENT is an integral part **technology of Noologistics** and is used to calculate the magnitudes of all parameters that are classified in it as **current parameters**.

It is obvious that a set of current **stochastic phenomena and events**, well-known to science and practice, has an impact on **the current mode of operation** of each **object**, which is controlled by **the person** in the process of achieving his **goal**. It is also obvious that the set of current parameters of **the object** depends on its composition, the **current technological processes** used, the mutual influence of its elements on each other, as well as their relationship to **the environment**. All sets of **stochastic phenomena and events** that are important for management and their parameters are specified in the accompanying documentation for each **object** and in **the relevant scientific and technical literature**.

TCF is performed by repeating the same cycles, which may be performed both sequentially and in parallel with the time offset relative to each other. The sequence of their execution, their start and end times are calculated automatically from the condition of their **synchronization**.

Described below one a simplified **TCF** cycle is designed to calculate any of the ith set of magnitudes of **noo control actions** on **the object**. Its structure and character moments are shown in Fig. TCF 1 ... TCF 5. In these figures are not shown other **TCF** cycles, which is performed in a cascading arrangement to described i^{th} **TCF** cycle to provide the continuity of the control process of **object**. When describing and graphically depicting the ith **TCF** cycle, the following symbols of its elements were accepted:

All that belongs to **the PAST** shown in black;
Blue color represents all that relates to **the PRESENT**;
Navy blue color depicts all that relates to **the FUTURE**.

The horizontal line represents the time scale on which the leftward arrow labeled **PAST**, depicts elapsed time, and an arrow with the words **the FUTURE** depicts a future time. Divisions in seconds with minus sign are marked on the scale the **PAST**, and on the scale the **FUTURE** scale - up in seconds.

The vertical line labeled **CURRENT**, shows the current time in **TCF**. From it is counting time in the directions of **PAST** and **FUTURE**.

Vertical lines marked by the letter M with lower indexes indicate **the moments of forecasting time** of the ith **TCF** cycle, including:

$\mathbf{M_{hi.0}}$, $\mathbf{M_{hi.1}}$, $\mathbf{M_{hi.2}}$, ..., $\mathbf{M_{hi.j}}$, ..., $\mathbf{M_{hi.J}}$ – it is j^{th} moments of time of the beginning and end of the steps of collecting of parameters "slices" about the predicted **stochastic phenomenon or event** and filling of the ith stack table of **history of changes** (see below);

j = 1, 2, 3, …, J – it is the moment number in the ith stack table of **history of changes**;

$\mathbf{M_{ci.1}}$ – it is the time moment of completion the calculation step of the set of parameter magnitudes of predicted stochastic phenomena and events in the ith **TCF** cycle;

$M_{ci.2}$ – it is the moment of time of step completion of calculation the set of magnitudes of **the noo control actions** to **the object** in the ith **TCF** cycle;

$\mathbf{M_{ri}}$ – it is **the moment of forecasting time** of the ith **TCF** cycle.

Horizontal lines that denoted by P and S with down indexes denote the time periods of the processes and the **steps** in the ith **TCF** cycle, including:

$\mathbf{P_{hi}}$ – it is the time period (duration) in which **the history of changes** in the ith **TCF** cycle is formed;

$\mathbf{S_{hi.1}}$, $\mathbf{S_{hi.2}}$, $\mathbf{S_{hi.3}}$, …, $\mathbf{S_{hi.j}}$, …, $\mathbf{S_{hi.J}}$ – it is the formation steps the history of changes in the ith **TCF** cycle;

$\mathbf{P_{ci}}$ – it is the time period (duration) of calculating the magnitudes of **noo control actions** at **the object** in the ith **TCF** cycle;

$\mathbf{S_{ci.1}}$ – it is **the step** of calculation of magnitudes sets of predicted parameters of **stochastic phenomenon or event** in the ith **TCF** cycle;

$\mathbf{S_{ci.2}}$ – it is **the step** of calculating the magnitudes set of **noo control actions** at **the object** in the ith **TCF** cycle;

$\mathbf{P_{ri}}$ – it is the period of time (duration) in which the set of **noo control actions** at **the object** calculated in the ith **TCF** cycle is executed.

Comments to figures TCF 1 ... TCF 5 contain a simplified example of the calculation of the ith **TCF** cycle, in which were taken the following numeric magnitudes of its elements:

$\mathbf{M_{hi.0}}$ = April 12, 2016, 04 hours 22 minutes of 15.91 seconds (briefly – $\mathbf{M_{hi.0}}$ = 2016.04.12, 04:22:15,91)

J = 5;

$\mathbf{S_{hi.1}} = \mathbf{S_{hi.2}} = \mathbf{S_{hi.3}} = \mathbf{S_{hi.4}} = \mathbf{S_{hi.5}}$ = 5 s;

$\mathbf{S_{ci.1}}$ = 5 s;

$\mathbf{S_{ci.2}}$ = 2,5 s;

$\mathbf{P_{ri}}$ = 5 s.

The numerical magnitudes of the elements of the ith **TCF** cycle which were accepted here are obtained from the actual operating systems of control **object**, and the magnitude of $\mathbf{P_{ri}}$ is set to the minimum possible to obtain the minimum control error from the condition of the possibility of its technical implementation. The real i^th^ **TCF** cycle is much more complicated than the ith **TCF** cycle described below. Because in it are detailed $\mathbf{P_{ci}}$, $\mathbf{S_{ci.1}}$, $\mathbf{S_{ci.2}}$, $\mathbf{P_{ri}}$, is used the verification of the information gathered, is choose the best dynamic range of the plurality of known, are calibrated results of calculation, etc.

All the above elements of the ith **TCF** cycle, shown in figures TCF 1 ... TCF 5, moving from right to left and continually "flow" from the **FUTURE** into the PAST through the **PRESENT** in accordance to the progress of the current time (the **PRESENT**).

One of character current time of the ith **TCF** cycle, which corresponds, for example, to **the PRESENT** time on April 12, 2016, 04 hours 22 minutes of 15.91 seconds (briefly – Mhi.0 = 2016.04.12, 04:22:15,91), is pictured in Fig. TCF 1.

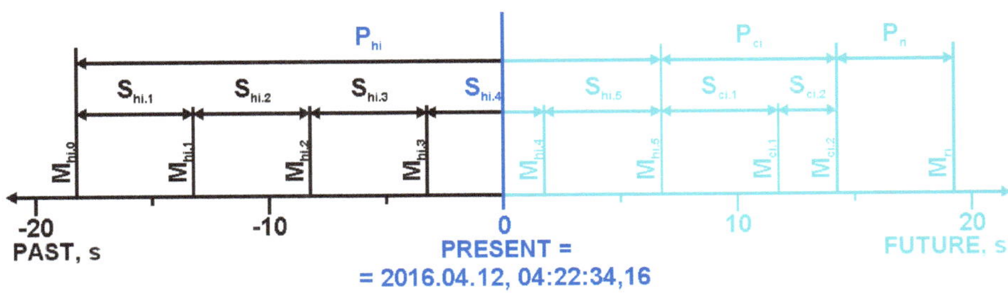

Fig. TCF 1

At the time of the ith **TCF** cycle, which is shown in Fig. TCF 1, **the system of Noologistics** performs $\mathbf{S_{hi.4}}$. It is characterized by the following numerical magnitudes of the cycle elements:

PRESENT = 2016.04.12, 04: 22:34,16 – it is the current system time, constantly measured by **the system of Noologistics** itself;

$M_{hi.0}$ = 2016.04.12, 04:22:15,91 – this **moment of time** has already passed and is stored in a stack table (see below);

$M_{hi.1}$ = 2016.04.12, 04:22:20,91 – this **moment of time** has already passed and is stored in a stack table (see below);

$M_{hi.2}$ = 2016.04.12, 04:22:25,91 – this **moment of time** has already passed and is stored in a stack table (see below);

$M_{hi.3}$ = 2016.04.12, 04:22:30,91 – this **moment of time** has already passed and is stored in a stack table (see below);

$M_{hi.4}$ = **$M_{hi.3}$** + **$S_{hi.4}$** = 2016.04.12, 04:22:30,91 + 5 = 2016.04.12, 04:22:35,91 – this is **the moment of forecasting time** of completion of the **$S_{hi.4}$** and beginning of **$S_{hi.5}$**;

$M_{hi.5}$ = **M_{s4}** + **$S_{hi.5}$** = 2016.04.12, 04:22:35,91 + 5 = 2016.04.12, 04:22:40,91 – this is **the moment of forecasting time** of completion of the **P_{hi}** and beginning of **P_{ci}**;

$M_{ci.1}$ = **$M_{hi.5}$** + **$S_{hi.1}$** = 2016.04.12, 04:22:40,91 + 5 = 2016.04.12, 04:22:45,91 – this is **the moment of forecasting time** of completion of the **$S_{hi.1}$** and beginning of **$S_{hi.2}$**;

$M_{ci.2}$ = **$M_{ci.1}$** + **$S_{hi.2}$** = 2016.04.12, 04:22:45,91 + 2,5 = 2016.04.12, 04:22:48,41 – this is **the moment of forecasting time** of completion of the **P_{ci}** and beginning of **P_{ri}**;

M_{ri} = **$M_{ci.2}$** + **P_{ri}** = 2016.04.12, 04:22:48,41 + 5 = 2016.04.12, 04:22:53,41 – this is the moment of forecasting time of completion of ith **TCF** cycle.

The character current time of the ith **TCF** cycle, which corresponds, for example, to **the PRESENT** = 2016.04.12, 04:22:40,91, is pictured in Fig. TCF 2.

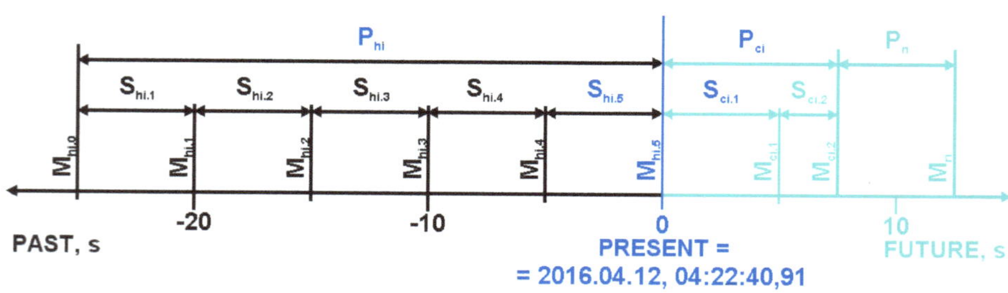

Fig. TCF 2

At the time of the ith **TCF** cycle, which is shown in Fig. TCF 2, **the system of Noologistics** completes $\mathbf{P_{hi}}$ and begins $\mathbf{P_{ci}}$. It is characterized by the following numerical magnitudes of the cycle elements:

PRESENT = 2016.04.12, 04:22:40,91 – it is the current system time, constantly measured by **the system of Noologistics** itself;

$\mathbf{M_{hi.4}}$ = 2016.04.12, 04:22:35,91 – this **moment of time** has already passed and is stored in a stack table (see below);

$\mathbf{M_{hi.5}}$ = 2016.04.12, 04:22:40,91 – **the system of Noologistics** is storing this **current moment of time** in the stock table (see below);

The rest – see comment to Fig. TCF 1.

The **system of Noologistics** was forming a **history of changes** for the ith **TCF** cycle during $\mathbf{P_{hi}}$ at **the moment of time** shown in Fig. TCF 2. It was shown above that the work of any **object** is influenced by a well-known in **science and practice** set of **current stochastic phenomena and events**. The magnitude of the density of **the current conditional variable consumption flow** of natural gas, the satisfaction of which is provided for in **the goal** set by **the person**, is accepted in the considered example of the ith **TCF** cycle as one of the many current parameters of such **stochastic phenomenon**.

The result of the formation of the history of changes in the density of **the current conditional variable consumption flow** of natural gas ($\mathbf{D_{C.iw.NG.i.j}}$) in $\mathbf{P_{hi}}$ at the **PRESENT** = 2016.04.12, 04: 22:40.91 on the principle of the stack (Last Input First Output) for one current parameter is summarized in a stack table:

j	$\mathbf{D_{C.iw.NG.i.j}}$	$\mathbf{M_{hi.j}}$	$\mathbf{S_{hi.j}}$	$\mathbf{P_{hi.j}}$
	nm^3/s	yyyy.mm.dd., hh:mm:ss,00	s	s
1	891,0415	2016.04.12, 04:22:20,91	5	5
2	890,8882	2016.04.12, 04:22:25,91	5	10
3	889,9765	2016.04.12, 04:22:30,91	5	15
4	890,8969	2016.04.12, 04:22:35,91	5	20
5	892,2885	2016.04.12, 04:22:40,91	5	25

The following symbols are accepted in the stack table:

$\mathbf{D_{C.iw.NG.i.j}}$ – it is the density of **the current conditional variable consumption flow** of natural gas, measured at the **moment of time** $\mathbf{M_{hi.j}}$;

$\mathbf{P_{hi.j}}$ – it is the magnitude of the jth time period from $\mathbf{M_{hi.0}}$ = 2016.04.12, 04:22:15,91 in the stack, the calculation of which see below;

the rest – see above.

Similar measurements are performed for the whole set of current stochastic phenomena and events, and their results are entered into the corresponding stack tables.

The magnitudes of $\mathbf{P_{hi.j}}$ recorded in the stack table are calculated by the formula:

$$\mathbf{P_{hi.j} = M_{hi.j} - M_{hi.0}},$$

in which all the symbols – see above.

Calculation example:

$\mathbf{P_{hi.1}} = \mathbf{M_{hi.1}} - \mathbf{M_{hi.0}}$ = 201.04.12, 04:22:20,91 – 2016.04.12, 04:22:15,91 = 5 s,

$\mathbf{P_{hi.2}} = \mathbf{M_{hi.2}} - \mathbf{M_{hi.0}}$ = 2016.04.12, 04:22:25,91 – 2016.04.12, 04:22:15,91 = 10 s,

$\mathbf{P_{hi.3}} = \mathbf{M_{hi.3}} - \mathbf{M_{hi.0}}$ = 2016.04.12, 04:22:30,91 – 2016.04.12, 04:22:15, 91 = 15 s,

$\mathbf{P_{hi.4}} = \mathbf{M_{hi.4}} - \mathbf{M_{hi.0}}$ = 2016.04.12, 04:22:35,91 – 2016.04.12, 04:22:15,91 = 20 s,

$\mathbf{P_{hi.5}} = \mathbf{M_{hi.5}} - \mathbf{M_{hi.0}}$ = 2016.04.12, 04:22:40,91 – 2016.04.12, 04:22:15,91 = 25 s.

The results of these calculations are recorded in the stack table.

The comparison of the results of some the most frequently used time series (linear, polynomial, logarithmic, exponential and power) shows that in this example that the smallest error gives the prediction of the density of **the current conditional variable consumption flow** of natural gas using a linear dynamic series. It is obvious that the $\mathbf{P_{ri}}$ magnitude may be divided into any number of **steps**, for each of which the corresponding sets of **noo control actions** on **the object** in the ith **TCF** cycle will be calculated. The accuracy of forecasting and, accordingly, the control accuracy is higher, the more of these **steps**. In order to reduce the description below, it is accepted that for the considered example, sufficient control accuracy is provided by the implementation of $\mathbf{P_{ri}}$ in one **step**, within which the movement of each Executive body of each regulator of **the object** is performed at a constant speed calculated specifically for it. Therefore, below is a calculation the trend line of density of **the current conditional variable consumption flow** of natural gas, which consists of two projected magnitudes $\mathbf{PD_{C.iw.NG.i.j}}$ in moments of time $\mathbf{M_{ci.2}}$ and $\mathbf{M_{ri}}$.

Predicted density magnitudes of **the current conditional variable consumption flow** of natural gas $\mathbf{PD_{C.iw.NG.i.j}}$ in moments of time $\mathbf{M_{ci.2}}$ and $\mathbf{M_{ri}}$ of the ith **TCF** cycle are calculated by linear regression equation:

$$PD_{C.iw.NG.i.p} = a_i + b_i * P_{i.p},$$

here are:

a_i and b_i – it is the coefficients of the linear regression equation in the ith **TCF** cycle;

$P_{i.p}$ – it is the duration of the time period between the $\mathbf{M_{hi.0}}$ and $\mathbf{M_{ci.2}}$ or $\mathbf{M_{ri}}$;

p – the number of the predicted parameter $\mathbf{PD_{C.iw.NG.i.j}}$ in its trend line: p = 1 for $\mathbf{M_{ci.2}}$ and p = 2 for $\mathbf{M_{ri}}$;

the rest – see above.

The coefficient b_i for the linear regression equation is calculated by the formula:

$$b_i = \frac{J * \sum_{j=1}^{J} P_{hi.j} * D_{C.iw.NG.i.j} - \left(\sum_{i=1}^{J} P_{hi.j}\right) * \left(\sum_{j=1}^{J} D_{C.iw.NG.i.j}\right)}{J * \sum_{j=1}^{J} P_{hi.j}^2 - \left(\sum_{j=1}^{J} P_{hi.j}\right)^2} =$$

$$= \frac{J * (P_{hi.1} * D_{C.iw.NG.i.1} + P_{hi.2} * D_{C.iw.NG.i.2} + P_{hi.3} * D_{C.iw.NG.i.3} + P_{hi.4} * D_{C.iw.NG.i.4} + P_{hi.5} * D_{C.iw.NG.i.5})}{J * (P_{hi.1}^2 + P_{hi.2}^2 + P_{hi.3}^2 + P_{hi.4}^2 + P_{s5}^2) - (P_{hi.1} + P_{hi.2} + P_{hi.3} + P_{hi.4} + P_{hi.5})^2} -$$

$$- \frac{(P_{hi.1} + P_{hi.2} + P_{hi.3} + P_{hi.4} + P_{hi.5}) * (D_{C.iw.NG.i.1} + D_{C.iw.NG.i.2} + D_{C.iw.NG.i.3} + D_{C.iw.NG.i.4} + D_{C.iw.NG.i.5})}{J * (P_{hi.1}^2 + P_{hi.2}^2 + P_{hi.3}^2 + P_{hi.4}^2 + P_{s5}^2) - (P_{hi.1} + P_{hi.2} + P_{hi.3} + P_{hi.4} + P_{hi.5})^2} =$$

$$= \frac{5 * (5 * 891{,}0415 + 10 * 890{,}8882 + 15 * 889{,}9765 + 20 * 890{,}8969 + 25 * 892{,}2885)}{5 * (5^2 + 10^2 + 15^2 + 20^2 + 25^2) - (5 + 10 + 15 + 20 + 25)^2} -$$

$$- \frac{(5 + 10 + 15 + 20 + 25) * (891{,}0415 + 890{,}8882 + 889{,}9765 + 890{,}8969 + 892{,}885)}{5 * (5^2 + 10^2 + 15^2 + 20^2 + 25^2) - (5 + 10 + 15 + 20 + 25)^2}$$

= 0,050054 nm³/s²,

in which all the symbols – see above.

The coefficient a_i for the linear regression equation is calculated by the formula:

$$a_i = \overline{D_{C.iw.NG.i.j}} - b_i * \overline{P_{hi.j}} =$$

$$= \frac{D_{C.iw.NG.i.1} + D_{C.iw.NG.i.2} + D_{C.iw.NG.i.3} + D_{C.iw.NG.i.4} + D_{C.iw.NG.i.5}}{J} - b_f * \frac{P_{hi.1} + P_{hi.2} + P_{hi.3} + P_{hi.4} + P_{hi.5}}{J} =$$

$$= \frac{891{,}0415 + 890{,}8882 + 889{,}9765 + 890{,}8969 + 892{,}885}{5} - 0{,}050054 * \frac{5 + 10 + 15 + 20 + 25}{5}$$

= 890,2675 nm³/s,

in which all the symbols – see above.

Calculation example:

$\mathbf{P_{i.1}} = \mathbf{M_{ci.2}} - \mathbf{M_{hi.0}}$ = 2016.04.12, 04:22:48,41 – 2016.04.12, 04:22:15,91 = 32,5 s,

$\mathbf{P_{i.2}} = \mathbf{M_{ri}} - \mathbf{M_{hi.0}}$ = 2016.04.12, 04:22:53,41 – 2016.04.12, 04:22:15,91 = 37,5 s,

$PD_{C.iw.NG.i.1} = a_i + b_i * P_{i.1} = 890{,}2675 + 0{,}050054 * 32{,}5 = 891{,}89426$ nm³/s,

$PD_{C.iw.NG.i.2} = a_i + b_i * P_{i.2} = 890{,}2675 + 0{,}050054 * 37{,}5 = 892{,}14453$ nm³/s.

The predicted speed of change the density of **the current conditional variable consumption flow** of natural gas in the $\mathbf{P_{ri}}$ in the ith **TCF** cycle are calculated by the formula:

$$VD_{C.iw.NG.i} = \frac{PD_{C.iw.NG.i.2} - PD_{C.iw.NG.i.1}}{P_{i.2} - P_{i.1}} = \frac{892{,}14453 - 891{,}89426}{37{,}5 - 32{,}5} = 0{,}050054$$

nm³/s²,

in which all the symbols – see above.

Predicted density magnitudes of **the current conditional variable consumption flow** of natural gas at any predicted moment of time during the $\mathbf{P_{ri}}$ of the ith **TCF** cycle, is calculated by the formula:

$$PD_{C.iw.NG.i} = a_i + b_i * (PRESENT_i - M_{hi.0}),$$

here are:

$\mathbf{PRESENT_i}$ – any current moment of time during the $\mathbf{P_{ri}}$ of the ith **TCF** cycle;

the rest – see above.

The trend lines of the predicted magnitudes of the parameters of all other **current stochastic phenomena and events** in the ith **TCF** cycle, which will be used in $\mathbf{S_{ci.2}}$ for calculation the set of magnitudes of **noo control actions** on **the object** in the ith **TCF** cycle calculated similarly.

The character current time of the ith **TCF** cycle, which corresponds, for example, to **the PRESENT** = 2016.04.12, 04:22:45,91, is pictured in Fig. TCF 3.

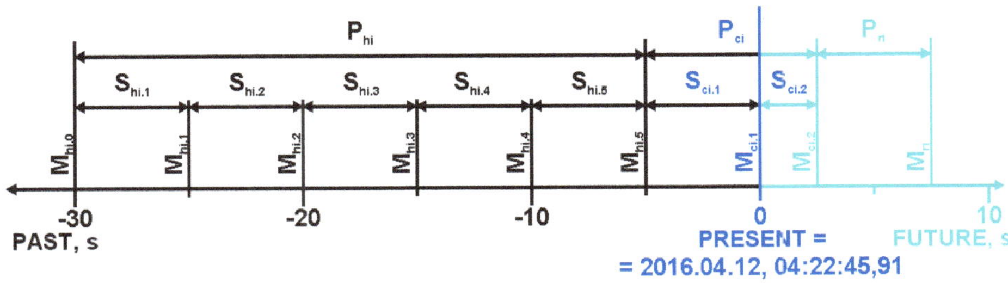

Fig. TCF 3

At the time of the ith **TCF** cycle, which is shown in Fig. TCF 3, **the system of Noologistics** continues to perform the steps into $\mathbf{P_{ci}}$: completes $\mathbf{S_{ci.1}}$ and begins $\mathbf{S_{ci.2}}$. It is characterized by the following numerical magnitudes of the cycle elements:

PRESENT = 2016.04.12, 04: 22:45,91 – it is the current system time, constantly measured by **the system of Noologistics** itself;

$\mathbf{M_{ci.1}}$ = 2016.04.12, 04:22:45,91 – this is **the moment of forecasting time** of completion of the $\mathbf{S_{hi.1}}$ and beginning of $\mathbf{S_{hi.2}}$;

$\mathbf{M_{ci.1}}$ = 2016.04.12, 04:22:45,91 – this moment has come and corresponds to **the PRESENT**;

a set of trend lines of predicted parameters of all stochastic phenomena and events sufficient to calculate a set of **trend lines** of predicted current magnitudes of **noo control actions** on **the object** in the ith **TCF** cycle is calculated;

the rest – see above.

Booster compressor station of the Komsomolsk gas field (**BCS KGF**) is adopted as an example of the calculated **object** in the ith **TCF** cycle. Calculation of a set of **trend lines** of **predicted current magnitudes** of **noo control actions** on it is performed in the following sequence:

A set of trend lines of **predicted indexed noologistical areas of possible modes of operation** is calculated on the basis of **the set of trend lines** of **predicted parameter magnitudes** for all **stochastic phenomena and events** calculated in $\mathbf{S_{ci.1}}$;

A set of trend lines of **the predicted current magnitudes** of **the noo control actions** is calculated using the **technology of calculating indexed information pyramid** based on the above set of **predicted indexed noologistical areas of possible modes of operation** and parameters of **the goal** set by **the person**.

The set containing 701 **trend lines** of **the predicted current magnitudes** of **the noo control actions** is obtained as a result of the above calculations in $\mathbf{S_{ci.2}}$ of the ith **TCF** cycle - one **set** for each **unit of equipment** of **BCS KGF**. **The trend line** of the **predicted reasonable speed of rotation** of the compressor of the **gas pumping unit** (**GCU**)

No. 1 installed in its 1st stage of compression is one of them. It is characterized by the following parameters:

$Pn_{AVth.C1.i.1}$ = 5463,108 rpm – it is the predicted reasonable frequency of rotation of the **GCU** No. 1 compressor at the time moment of **$M_{ci.2}$**;

$Pn_{AVth.C1.i.2}$ = 5467,312 rpm – it is the predicted reasonable frequency of rotation of the **GCU** No. 1 compressor at the time moment of **M_{ri}**;

$Vn_{AVth.C1.i}$ = 0,8408 rpm/s – it is the predicted reasonable speed of change the frequency of rotation of the **GCU** No. 1 compressor in **P_{ri}** of the ith **TCF** cycle;

$Pn_{AVth.C1.i}$ = **$Pn_{AVth.C1.i.1}$** + **$Vn_{AVth.C1.i}$***(**$PRESENT_i$** - **$M_{ci.2}$**) = 5467,312 + 0,8408*(**$PRESENT_i$** - 2016.04.12, 04:22:48,41) – it is the formula for calculating the predicted current reasonable speed of the **GCU** No. 1 compressor at any moment in **P_{ri}** of the ith **TCF** cycle, in which all the symbols – see above.

The character current time of the ith **TCF** cycle, which corresponds, for example, to **the PRESENT** = 2016.04.12, 04:22:48,41, is pictured in Fig. TCF 4.

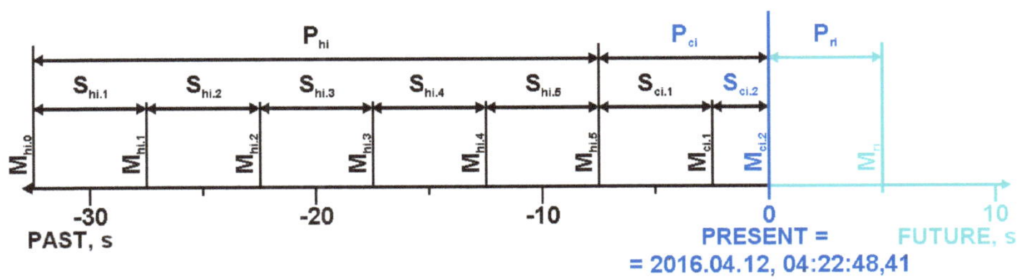

Fig. TCF 4

At the time of the ith **TCF** cycle, which is shown in Fig. TCF 4, **the system of Noologistics** completes **P_{ci}** and begins **P_{ri}**. It is characterized by the following numerical magnitudes of the cycle elements:

PRESENT = 2016.04.12, 04: 22:48,41 – it is the current system time, constantly measured by **the system of Noologistics** itself;

$M_{ci.1}$ = 2016.04.12, 04:22:48,41 – this moment has come and corresponds to **the PRESENT**;

a set of trend lines of predicted magnitudes of **noo control actions** on **the object** in the ith **TCF** cycle is calculated;

the rest – see above.

The system of Noologistics begins to give 701 parallel control signal to the automation system of each **unit of equipment** in **BCS KGF** at the beginning of the process of execution of the P_{ri}, which correspond to the parameters of **a set of trend lines** of predicted magnitudes of **noo control actions** calculated in the ith **TCF** cycle. They include of **trend line** signal to the automation system of **GCU** No. 1 too, which provides a reasonable magnitude of the speed of change of rotation frequency of the **GCU** No. 1 compressor $Vn_{AVth.C1.i}$ = 0,8408 rpm/s. These signals provide the kept of current operating modes of the equipment within reasonable parameters.

One of the many current time points in the P_{ri} execution of the ith **TCF** cycle is shown in figure TCF 5, which corresponds to the PRESENT = 2016.04.12, 04:22: 49,41.

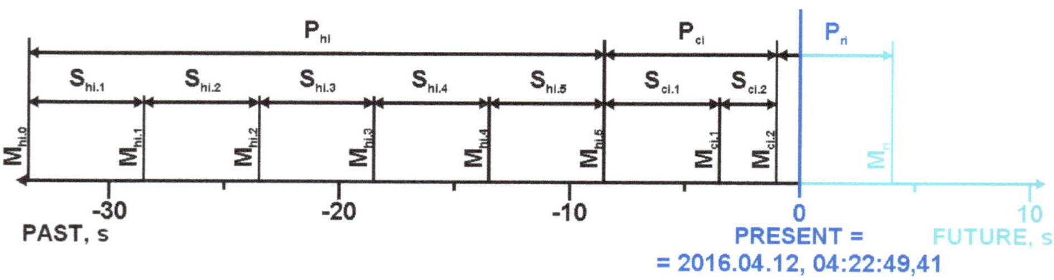

Fig. TCF 5

At the time of the ith **TCF** cycle, which is shown in Fig. TCF 5, **the system of Noologistics** performs P_{ri}. It is characterized by the following numerical magnitudes of the cycle elements:

PRESENT = 2016.04.12, 04: 22:49,41 – it is the current system time, constantly measured by **the system of Noologistics** itself;

The system of Noologistics continues to give 701 parallel control signal to the automation system of each **unit of equipment** in **BCS KGF** at the process is shown in Fig. TCF 5, which correspond to the parameters of **a set of trend lines** of predicted magnitudes of **noo control actions** calculated in the ith **TCF** cycle. They include of **trend**

line signal to the automation system of **GCU** No. 1 too, which provides a reasonable magnitude of rotation frequency of the **GCU** No. 1 compressor $\mathbf{n_{AVth.C1.i}}$ = 5467,312 + 0,8408*(2016.04.12, 04:22:49,41 - 2016.04.12, 04:22:48,41) = 5468,1528 rpm under it's speed of change $\mathbf{Vn_{AVth.C1.i}}$ = 0,8408 rpm/s.

the rest – see above.

A cascade of eight ith **TCF** cycles is shown in figure TCF 6, which corresponds to **the PRESENT** = 2016.04.12, 04:22: 49,41, shown in Fig. TCF 5. It provides continuity of the current management by **the object**.

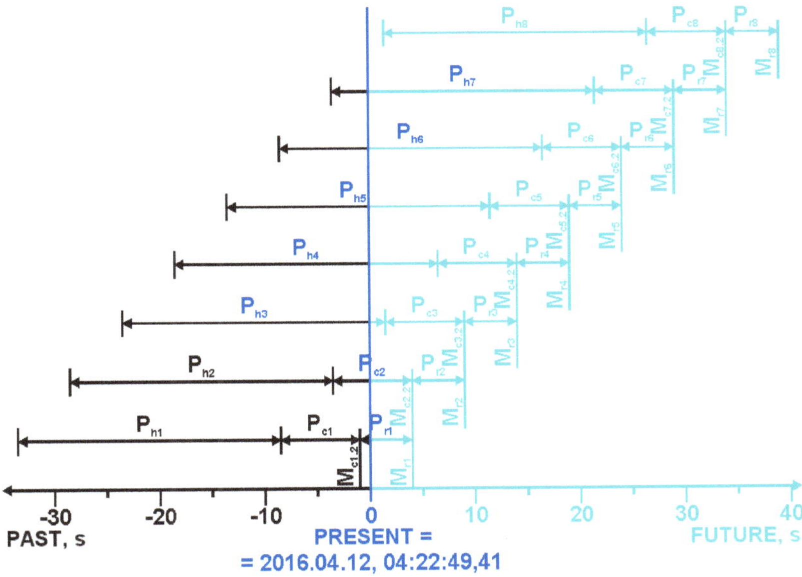

Fig. TCF 6

Images of ith **TCF** cycles in Fig. TCF 6 are simplified in comparison to the image of the ith **TCF** cycle in Fig. TCF 1 ... TCF 5: those elements of them are left on them, which show one of the many possible variants of their mutual synchronization. The time moment PRESENT = 2016.04.12, 04:22:49,41 and the 1st **TCF** cycle in Fig. TCF 6 exactly correspond to the time moment and ith **TCF** cycle in Fig. TCF 5. The remaining cycles (2nd, 3rd, 4th, 5th, 6th, 7th and 8th) shall be performed in such a way that their starting time for the execution of **the noo control action** $M_{c(i+1).2}$ coincided to the time of completion of **the noo control action** in the previous cycle M_{r1}, including:

$M_{c2.2} = M_{r1}$ = 2016.04.12, 04:22:53,41;

$M_{c3.2} = M_{r2}$ = 2016.04.12, 04:22:58,41;
$M_{c4.2} = M_{r3}$ = 2016.04.12, 04:23:03,41;
$M_{c5.2} = M_{r4}$ = 2016.04.12, 04:23:08,41;
$M_{c6.2} = M_{r5}$ = 2016.04.12, 04:23:13,41;
$M_{c7.2} = M_{r6}$ = 2016.04.12, 04:23:18,41;
$M_{c8.2} = M_{r7}$ = 2016.04.12, 04:23:23,41;
etc.

All information about the 1st **TCF** cycle loses relevance for the current management and may be archived or destroyed at the time of completion of P_{r1}, i.e. in M_{r1} = 2016.04.12, 04:22:53,41. The sequence numbers of the remaining yet running **TCF** cycles are reduced per one point at this time moment. This peculiarity is shown in Fig. TCF 7 and TCF 8.

A cascade of eight ith **TCF** cycles is shown in figure. TCF 7, which corresponds to **the PRESENT** = 2016.04.12, 04:22:53,40, i.e. before 0,01 second to removing the information that has lost relevance and changing the sequence numbers of those cycles that continue to perform.

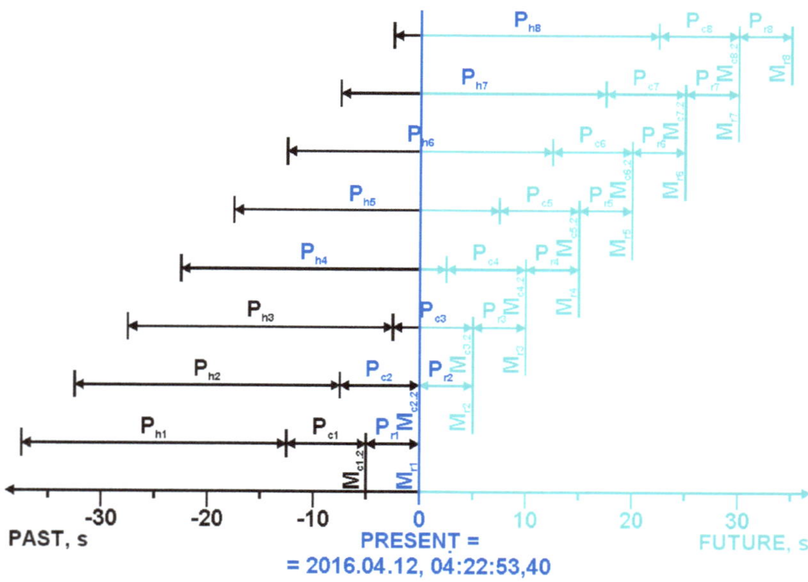

Fig. TCF 7

A cascade of eight i^th^ **TCF** cycles is shown in figure. TCF 8, which corresponds to **the PRESENT** = 2016.04.12, 04:22:53,42, i.e. after 0,01 second of removing the information that has lost relevance and changing the sequence numbers of those cycles that continue to perform.

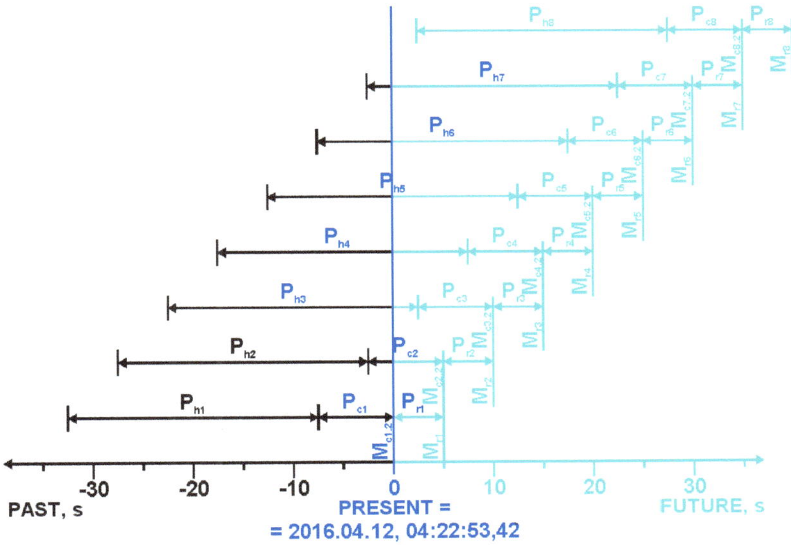

Fig. TCF 8

A cascade of eight i^th^ **TCF** cycles is shown in figure. TCF 9, which corresponds to **the PRESENT** = 2016.04.12, 04:22:54,41, i.e. after 1 second of removing the information that has lost relevance and changing the sequence numbers of those cycles that continue to perform.

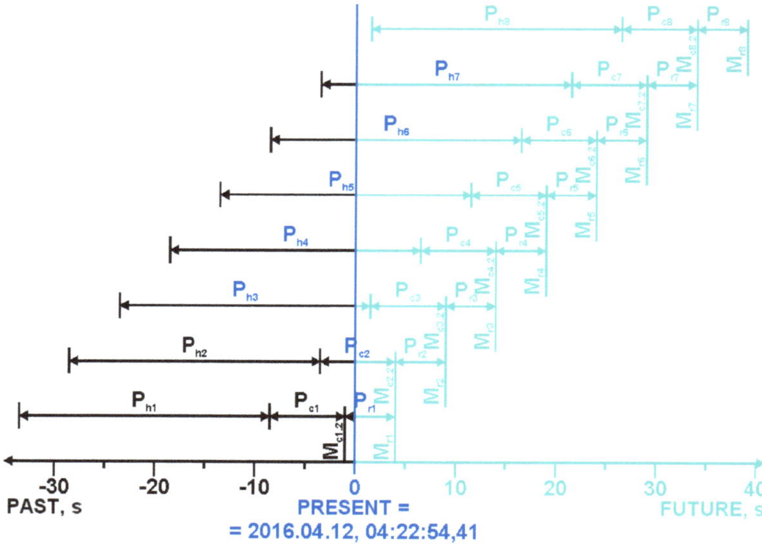

Fig. TCF 9

Comparing the images in figures TCF 6 and TCF 9 shows that they differ only in the time of **the PRESENT**, and thus provide the continuity of current management.

The above simplified mathematical apparatus and algorithm of its application shows the principal possibility of their application in practice. Their advantage is the possibility of synchronization only in the current time, i.e. in **the PRESENT**, which does not require synchronization of individual elements of cycles throughout the entire **system of Noologistics**: it is enough only to provide a condition that for each predicted parameter of each **stochastic phenomenon and event** would be recorded **the history of changes** under the necessary accuracy. There are many opportunities for its improvement that are not described here to reduce the scope of the description.

The software that uses the mathematical apparatus described above and the algorithm of its application may be unified and applied in microprocessors, from which elements for **the system of Noologistics** of any complexity, purpose and scale may be collected.

TCF may be implemented on both analog and digital computing.

3.3. The Technology of Calculating the Indexed Noologistical Area of Possible Operating Modes

Each **person of the Noologistics** manages his **current flows of consumption**, **of creation** and **of rejection the noo values** in the process of reasonable control of **provision of his existence** (**life support**), through **control actions** on **units of equipment** combined in the appropriate **grid**.

The mathematical relationship between the magnitudes of densities of **current flows of consumption**, **of creation** and **of rejection the noo values** and modes of operation of the corresponding **units of equipment** in the entire range of possible modes of operation is established in the form of their **passport performance characteristics** (briefly – **PM**) for some so-called "normal" operating conditions, for example for "normal" **environmental** parameters, for "normal" technical condition (no wear, contamination of work surfaces, ice deposits, etc.), for "normal" parameters of their **flows of consumption**, **of creation** and **of rejection the noo values**, etc. Their characteristic disadvantages are:

- different units of measurement used in passport performance for different types of **equipment units**, which prevents their processing using **the technology of calculating information pyramids** when working together in a single **grid**;
- invariance of **PM** at the current change of **environmental** parameters (temperature, pressure, humidity, precipitation);
- invariance of **PM** at the current change of technical condition (presence of wear, contamination of working surfaces, ice deposits, hydrate plugs in gas pipelines, etc.);
- the immutability of **PM** at the current change in the parameters of **current flows of consumption**, **of creation** and **of rejection the noo values** (deviation of their thermodynamic parameters from the "normal", deviation of the chemical composition from the "normal", deviation of the calorific value of fuel, etc.);
- the absence of a direct mathematical relationship between the parameters of the current operating mode and the

parameters of **current flows of consumption**, **of creation** and **of rejection the noo values** that characterize **the criteria of reasonableness** of management, which **the person** established in his **goal**, which makes it impossible to assess the reasonableness of the current mode of operation of **equipment units**;

- the absence of mathematical links between the current parameters of the operating modes of **the equipment units**, and the extremes of the magnitudes of **the reasonableness criteria** that **the person** has set in his **goal**, which makes it impossible to establish a mode of operation for it, providing an extreme of the magnitude of one **criterion** or a compromise between the extremes of several **criteria**;
- the absence of mathematical relationships between the current parameters of **the current flows of consumption**, **of creation** and **of rejection the noo values** and modes of operation of several **units of equipment**, which take into account their mutual influence when working together in one group of several **units**;
- the absence of a direct mathematical relationship between the parameters of the current operating modes of **equipment units**, of the parameters of **the current flows of consumption**, **of creation** and **of rejection the noo values**, and of the current **rules** that **the person** complies with when achieving the **goal**, etc.

Indexed noologistical areas of possible operating modes (briefly – **RPM**) hardware units are used in **technology of Noologistics** to eliminate these drawbacks. **RPM** are calculated on the basis of **PM** of the **equipment units**, limits their parameters, current operating modes, **the current flows of consumption**, **of creation** and **of rejection the noo values**, of **the environment**, famous mathematical and logical relations, as well as algorithms of calculation set out in the relevant **Sciences**, the applicable **rules of the person**, etc.

It follows from the above that the **RPM** are calculated automatically at the current time individually for each **unit of equipment** in specific operating conditions. For example, in **the practical examples of Noologistics implementation** used **RPM** that **the**

system of Noologistics automatically calculates in **the PRESENT** for water pumps, steam boilers, heat exchangers, steam turbines, piping, condensers, gas wells, centrifugal, axial, reciprocating natural gas compressors, gas turbines, gas-compressor units (briefly – **GCU**), electric motors, gas engines, gas air coolers (briefly – **GAC**), air fan, inlet, outlet and overflow louvers in **GAC**, steam turbines, electric generators, gas treatment plants, etc.

The same sequence of operations is used in the calculation of **RPM** of the above types of **equipment units**, despite their wide variety, which is shown below:

1. To calculate **a current passport performance modes of operation** (briefly – **CPM**) of **equipment unit**. Its **PM**, current **environmental** parameters, set limits of its operating modes, mathematical and logical relationships between the parameters of its operating modes and **the environment**, as well as the calculation algorithms set out in the relevant **Sciences**, are used in this calculation.

2. To calculate **the current actual modes of operation** (briefly – **RM**) of **equipment unit**. **CPM** that was calculated above and the current coefficient of the real technical condition of **the unit of equipment**, which is calculated on the basis of the ratio of the currently measured parameters of its real operating mode and the current parameters of its operating mode for **the current passport characteristics**, mathematical and logical relationships between which are set out in the relevant **Sciences**, used in this calculation.

3. To calculate **the current area of possible modes of operation** (briefly – **CM**) of **equipment unit**. **The RM** calculated above and the current limits of the modes of operation this **equipment unit**, used in calculations which are set out in the relevant **Sciences** and established in the current **rules**.

4. To calculate **the current noologistical areas of the possible operating modes** (briefly – **NM**) of **equipment unit** for each **criterion the reasonableness of control**, which **the person** has set in his **goal**. **The CM**, calculated above, as well as-calculation algorithms and mathematical relationships between its parameters and the parameters that determine **the criteria of reasonableness** set in the current **rules** are used in this calculation. In addition, **the person** has

the ability to calculate two different types of NM: the first – on the basis of the current conditional variables parameters which determine **the criteria of reasonableness of control**, and the second – on the basis of their current gross parameters. Thus, the number of **NM** of **a unit of equipment** may be equal to twice the number of established **criteria**.

5. To calculate **the current noologistical areas of the possible operating modes to specific parameters** (briefly – **NS**) for each **criterion the reasonableness of control**, which **the person** has set in his **goal**. **The NM** calculated above, as well as the mathematical relations established in the current **rules** and the algorithms for calculating the specific parameters defining **the criteria**, are used in this calculation. Thus, the number of **NS** will be equal to the number of **NM**.

6. To calculate **the indexed noologistical areas of the possible operating modes** (briefly – **RPM**) of **equipment unit**. **Summation indices** (briefly – **Ix**) are calculated for this purpose. **The NS** calculated above, and - mathematical tools and algorithms of **Noologistics** specially developed for their calculation, are used in this calculation. **RPM** are formed by applying lines of the **Ix** on the **NM** calculated above. Thus, the number of **RPM** will be equal to the number of **NM**.

All parameters specified here as current ones are calculated by **the technology of forecast calculation in the PRESENT** and are their trend lines. The result of the calculation by p. 1 ... 6 are trend lines consisting of time-ordered sets of lots intermediate predictable **RPM**. A brief description of the mathematical apparatus, algorithm and calculation result of one of these intermediate predicted **RPM**, which is included in the corresponding trend, is shown below in Example 1.

Example 1

The gas-compressor unit #1 (briefly – **GCU #1**) installed in the 1st stage of compression of **the booster compressor station of the Komsomolsk gas field** (briefly – **BKS KGF**) is accepted as **unit of the equipment** for the description of an example of calculation of its **RPM**. This choice is due to the sufficient complexity of the current process in it to demonstrate the possibility of its calculation, the presence of different types of equipment, the presence of several levels of regulation, the presence of both parallel and sequential incorporation of equipment. In addition, the design, fabrication, installation, testing and commissioning of **the system of Noologistics** were made successful in it.

GCU #1 that is calculated here was produced in Sumy NPO im. M. V. Frunze. It is an automated block-container units with gas turbine marine engine DG90L2 and a replaceable centrifugal compressor (replaceable flow part, briefly – RFP) of NC-16/45-1,7 type. It is used in **the current technological process** of the creation of **the current flow** of the transported natural gas, which is conventionally denoted $\mathbf{F_{M.ip.NG.b}}$, so its **passport performance characteristics** labeled as $\mathbf{PM_{M.ip.NG.b}}$. Symbols which located in subscript designate: "**M**" - create, "**ip**" - 1st stage compression in **BKS KGF**, "**NG**" - type of **current noologistical value** (V_l) is created, which is the pumped natural gas, "b" – **unit of the equipment**, which is **GCU #1**, established in the 1st stage of compression in **BKS KGF**. These legend symbols in the lower indexes of any other legend mean the same in Example 1.

Image $\mathbf{PM_{M.ip.NG.b}}$ of calculated **GCU #1** of **BKS KGF** is presented in Fig. RPM 1, RPM 2 and RPM 3.

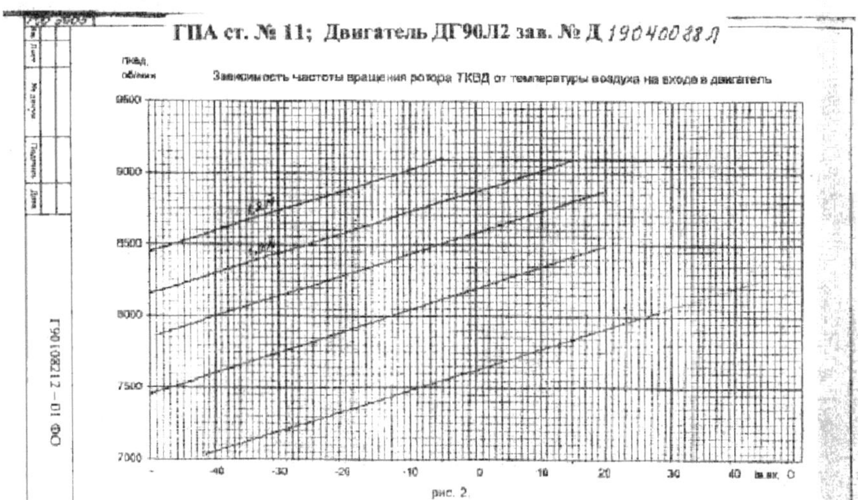

Fig. RPM 1

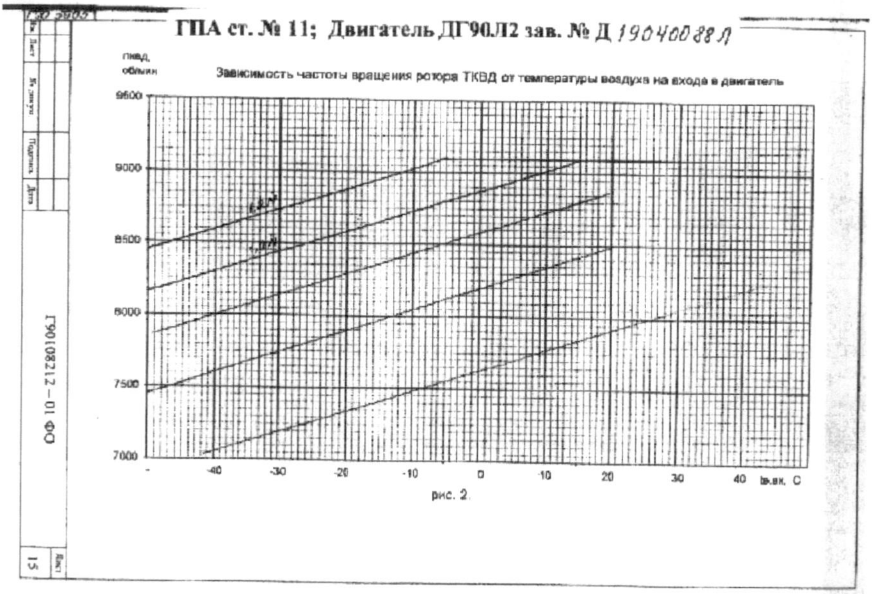

Fig. RPM 2

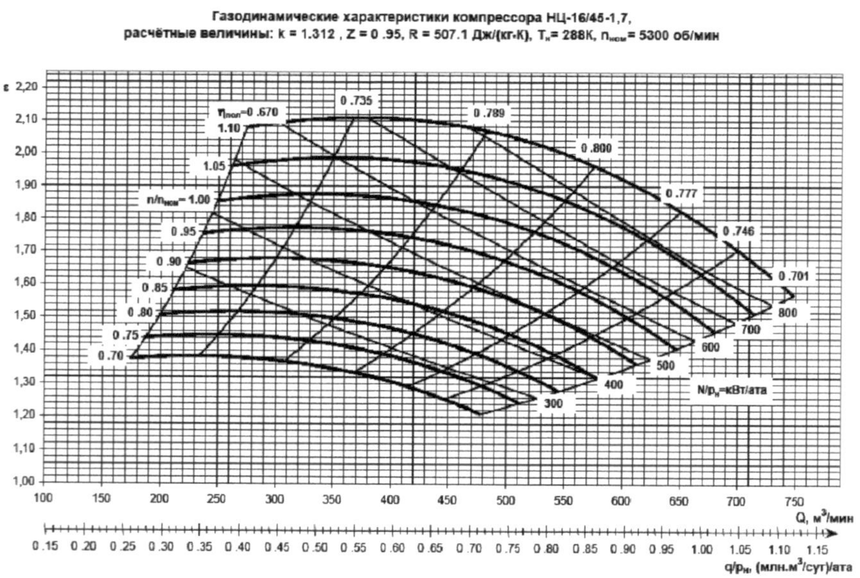

Fig. RPM 3

The parameters of the current operating mode of **GCU**, pumped gas, fuel gas and **the environment** obtained from the existing aggregate automation, as well as the permitted limits of its operating modes, are used in the calculation, including:

The current composition of the pumped gas, which is determined by the appropriate automatic gas analyzer, is presented in Table 1:

The current composition of the pumped gas

Table 1

Name	Chem. formula	Share	Molar mass, kg / mol
Methane	CH_4	0,8924	16,043
Ethane	C_2H_6	0,0224	30,07
Propane	C_3H_8	0,0105	44,097
N-Butane	C_4H_{10}	0,0004	58,123
I-Bhutan	C_4H_{10}	0,0004	58,123
Nitrogen	N_2	0,0004	28,0135
Carbon dioxide	CO_2	0,043	44,01
Hydrogen sulphide	H_2S	0,0305	34,082

The current absolute temperature of the pumped gas at the inlet of the **GCU** compressor is measured by the readings of the corresponding automatic device:

$T_{НС}$ = 279 К (5,85 °С).

The current absolute temperature of the pumped gas at the outlet of the **GCU** compressor is measured by the readings of the corresponding automatic device:

$T_{КС}$ = 337,3 К (64,15 °С).

The current absolute pressure of the pumped gas at the inlet of the **GCU** compressor is measured by the readings of the corresponding automatic device:

$P_{нс}$ = 2,667 MPa (27,2 kg/sm^2).

The current absolute pressure of the pumped gas at the outlet of the **GCU** compressor is measured by the readings of the corresponding automatic device:

$P_{кс}$ = 5,05 MPa (51,5 kg/sm^2).

The current speed of the **GCU** compressor, is measured by the readings of the corresponding automatic device:

n_c = 5340 rpm.

The current commercial productivity of the **GCU** compressor is measured by the readings of the corresponding automatic flow meter:

$q_{кс}$ = 20,6 Mnm^3/day.

The maximum capacity of the gas turbine under standard conditions:

N_{epmax} = 19 MW.

Current conditional-variable cost of the electric power in **GCU** from an external source, are measured by **rules of the person**, for example, on indications of the corresponding automatic electric meter measuring the current power (it is accepted conditionally in example):

$D_{элс}$ = 0,636 kW.

Cost of all types of energy for production, transportation, installation, adjustment and commissioning of GCU, is measured by the rules of the person, for example, by special account similar to accounting (it is accepted conditionally in example):

$FQ_{элс}$ = 18974 MW-h.

Depreciation period of **GCU**, determined by **the rules of the person** (it is accepted conditionally in example):

T_{Ac} = 6 years.

Real current conditional variable consumption of fuel gas, is measured by **the rules of the person**, e.g., by readings of the corresponding meter (it is accepted conditionally in example):

G_{TC} = 3641,233 kg/h.

The real current price of fuel gas, is determined by **the rules of the person**, for example, under the supply contract (it is accepted conditionally in example):

$C_{GT.c}$ = 172 rub./nm^3.

The actual purchase price of the **GCU**, determined by **the rules of the person**, for example, under the supply contract (it is accepted conditionally in example):

FQ_{GCU} = 134428 krub.

The real total current conditionally-variables cost in monetary form on the functioning of the **GCU** except for the actual current conditionally-variables cost in monetary form on the fuel gas, is determined by **the rules of the person**, for example, according to accounting data (these data have been accepted conditionally in example):

$D_{C.ip.T.b}$ = 380,909 krub./h.

The real current conditional-variable specific CO_2 emission from the combustion of 1 kg of fuel gas, calculated in accordance to **the rules of the person**, for example, according to the readings of the corresponding flow meter (it is accepted conditionally in example):

$E_{CO2.c}$ = 2,5547/1000 kg_{CO2}/kg.

The real total conditional variable the current CO_2 emission associated with **GCU** operation, with the exception of the emission from the combustion of fuel gas in it, determined by the rules of the person (it is accepted conditionally in example):

$E_{S.ip.T.b}$ = 4,198 kg_{CO2}/h.

The total amount of CO_2 that was previously allocated in the creation, transportation, installation, commissioning and commissioning of the **GCU**, determined by **the rules of the person**, for example, according to actual data (it is accepted conditionally in example):

FQ_{CO2} = 258273 kg.

The standard temperature of the atmosphere:

T_{an} = 273,15 K (20 °C).

The current temperature of the atmosphere is measured by the readings of the corresponding automatic device:

T_a = 257 K (-16,15 °C).

The current atmospheric pressure is measured by the readings of the corresponding automatic device:

P_a = 0,1013 MPa (1,033 kg/sm^2).

The maximum permitted temperature of the pumped gas at the **GCU** compressor outlet under the conditions of thermal stability of the thermal insulation of the intra-station pipelines is determined by the passport characteristics of the **BKS KGF**:

$T_{кmax}$ = 363,15 K (90 °C).

The maximum permitted excess pressure of the pumped gas from the strength condition of the intra-station pipelines is determined by the passport characteristics of **BKS KGF**:

$P_{\text{кandmax}}$ = 5,737 MPa (58,5 kg/sm^2).

Minimum allowed rotation frequency of the compressor is defined by its passport characteristics:

n_{min} = 3710 rpm.

Nominal rotation frequency of the compressor is defined by its passport characteristics:

n_n = 5300 rpm.

Maximum allowed rotation frequency of the compressor is defined by its passport characteristics:

n_{max} = 5830 rpm.

Lowest heat of fuel gas combustion:

$Q_{н}^{p}$ = 33,8128 MJ/m^3 = 49,7247 MJ/kg.

The mathematical apparatus and algorithms are used in the calculation, which is widely used in the theory and practice of the **GCU**, so references to concrete **sources of information** are not presented here to reduce the volume of the description. Team of **BKS KGF** is its **person (P_{ip})** by classification of **Noologistics** in this example; **BKS KGF** is a set of all his **grids ($G_{C.ip}$, $G_{M.ip}$** and **$G_{S.ip}$)**; the **GCUs** are included in each of them as **an unit of equipment** (**$G_{C.ip}$, $G_{M.ip}$** and **$G_{S.ip}$**) the fuel gas is **a consumed noologistical value** (**$V_{C.ip.NG.b}$**); the pumped gas is **a created noologistical value** (**$V_{M.ip.NG.b}$**), emitted carbon dioxide is **a rejected noologistical value** (**$V_{S.ip.NG.b}$**); a current commercial productivity of **GCU** $q_{кс}$ = 20,6 Mnm^3/day is the density of **the current flow of creation the noologistical value** (**$D_{M.ip.NG.b}$**); the current gross cost in monetary form in rub./day on the functioning of the **GCU** is **the density of the current total flow of consumption the noologistical**

value (**$TD_{C.ip.Mn.b}$**) in monetary form; the current gross energy consumption for the operation of the **GCU** is **the density of the current total flow of consumption the noologistical value** (**$TD_{C.ip.Vth.b}$**) in the form of MW; the current gross CO_2 emission in m^3/day from **GCU** is **the density of the current total flow of rejection the noological value** (**$TD_{S.ip.CO2.b}$**) in CO_2 form.

All calculations are divided into two types in the example. The parameters of the current conditional variables flows **$F_{C.ip.Vth.b}$**, **$F_{C.ip.Mn.b}$**, **$F_{S.ip.CO2.b}$** and current flow **$F_{M.ip.NG.b}$** are used into the first type of calculations. The parameters of the current gross flows **$TF_{C.ip.Vth.b}$**, **$TF_{C.ip.Mn.b}$**, **$TF_{S.ip.CO2.b}$** and current flow **$F_{M.ip.NG.b}$** are used into the second type of calculations. This separation implies that **the person** uses the first type of calculation, for example, to control at the current time, i.e., when calculating the magnitudes of **noologistical control actions** on the installed units of equipment (**$G_{C.ip}$**, **$G_{M.ip}$** and **$G_{S.ip}$**) at **the PRESENT** which are in working order and which **the person** has switched on or off in accordance to his current **needs**. He applies the second type of calculations, for example, to solve the problems of planning, forecasting and modeling in the development of his **goals** parameters and **noologistical management solutions** in **the FUTURE**. This shows the universality of the method described here, and the specific content of the information used and the tasks to be solved is determined by **the person** in accordance to his **needs**.

1. The calculation of **current passport performance modes of operation** (briefly – **$CPM_{M.ip.NG.b}$**) of **GCU** compressor.

1.1. Calculation of thermodynamic parameters of the pumped gas in the current operating mode by its chemical composition, pressure and temperature at the compressor inlet:

- k_c = 1,297 – it is the current ratio of specific heats is calculated according to **the standard equation of gas state** based on the current chemical composition, the current absolute temperature T_{HC} and the current absolute pressure of the pumped gas P_{HC} at the compressor inlet;

- Z_c = 0,941 – it is the current coefficient of compressibility of the pumped gas is calculated according to **the standard equation of gas state** based on the current chemical composition, the current absolute temperature T_{HC} and the current absolute pressure of the pumped gas P_{HC} at the compressor inlet;
- R_c = 509,1 J/(kg*°K) – it is the current gas constant is calculated according to **the standard method** based on the current chemical composition of the pumped gas;
- ρ_{HC} = 19,952 kg/m³ – it is the current density of the gas at the inlet of the compressor is calculated by the **standard method** based on the current chemical composition, the current absolute temperature T_{HC} and the current absolute pressure of the pumped gas P_{HC} at the compressor inlet;
- ρ_{0c} = 0,6804 kg/m³ – it is the current density of the gas at the normal conditions is calculated by the **standard method** based on the current chemical composition, normal temperature T_0 = 288 °K and pressure P_0 = 0,1013 MPa.

1.2. Calculation of **CPM$_{M.ip.NG.b}$** of **GCU** compressor.

For this calculation are used:

- **the PM$_{M.ip.NG.b}$** of **GCU** compressor, that are shown on Fig. RPM 1, RPM 2 and RPM 3 (see above);
- mathematical relationships from **the theory of centrifugal compressors** that link thermodynamic parameters of the pumped gas to the parameters of their operation modes;
- current thermodynamic parameters of the pumped gas (see above).

The calculation itself is made according to the standard methodology set out in the usual **scientific and technical literature**, and therefore is not presented here to reduce the scope of the description. Calculated **CPM$_{M.ip.NG.b}$** of **GCU** compressor is shown in green on Fig. RPM 4 in coordinates that are similar to $\mathbf{PM_{M.ip.NG.b}}$ coordinates (see Fig. RPM 3 above): horizontal coordinate shows the commercial productivity of the **GCU** compressor $q_к$, vertical – pressure at its outlet $P_К$. $\mathbf{PM_{M.ip.NG.b}}$ of the **GCU** compressor from Fig. RPM 3 are shown in black in Fig. RPM 4 for comparison.

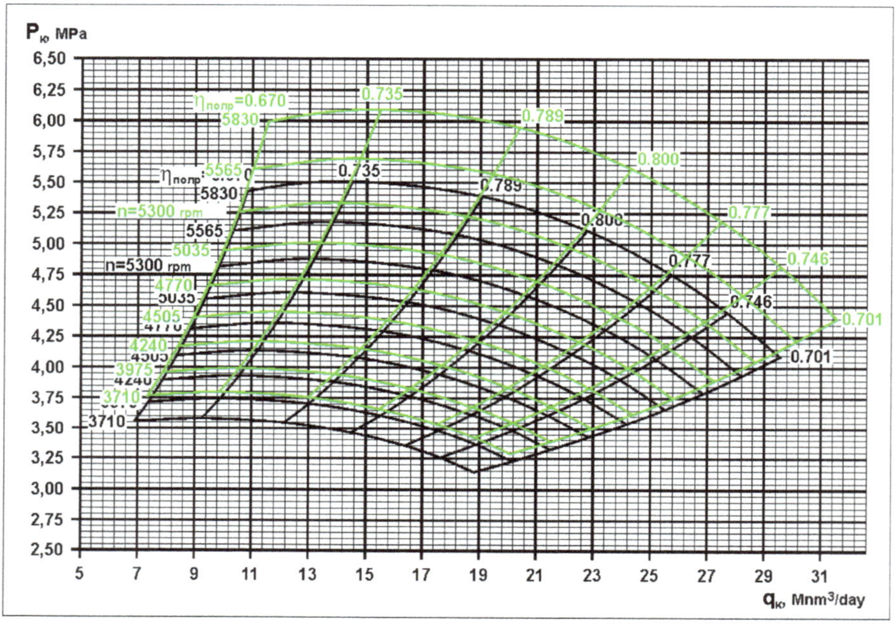

Fig. RPM 4

2. **The current actual modes of operation** (briefly – $\mathbf{RM_{M.ip.NG.b}}$) of **GCU** compressor.

2.1. The point $\mathbf{WP_c}$ of current operating mode of the compressor is added as shown in Fig. RPM 5, on the image of $\mathbf{CPM_{M.ip.NG.b}}$, that was calculated above in section 1.2 and shown in Fig. RPM 4. Its position corresponds to the current productivity of the compressor $q_{кс}$ (see above) and the current pressure at its output $P_{кс}$ (see above).

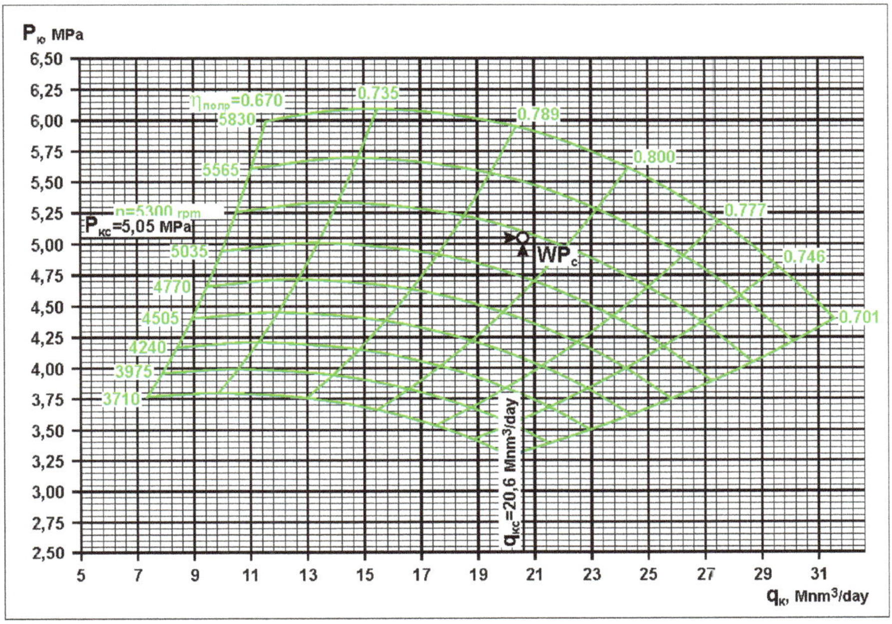

Fig. RPM 5

2.2. The calculation of the passport reduced characteristics of the **GCU** compressor.

The calculation of the passport reduced characteristics are performed on the basis of $\mathbf{PM_{M.ip.NG.b}}$ that are shown in Fig. RPM 3 is based on the standard methodology set out in the usual **scientific and technical literature** and therefore is not presented here to reduce the scope of the description. The result of this calculation is shown in Fig. RPM 6.

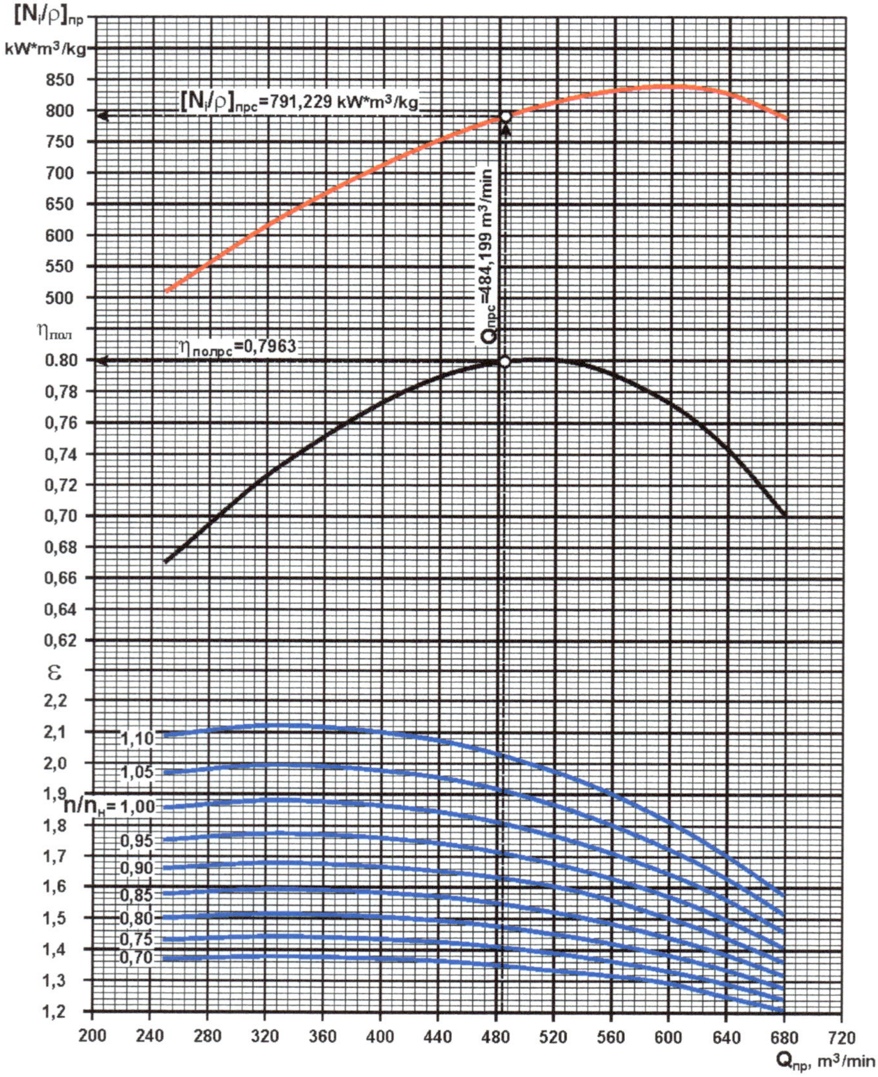

Fig. RPM 6

2.3. The magnitude of the current volumetric productivity of the **GCU** compressor is calculated by the formula:

$$Q_c = q_{кс} * \frac{1000000 * \rho_{0c}}{24 * 60 * \rho_{нс}} = 20{,}6 * \frac{1000000 * 0{,}6804}{24 * 60 * 19{,}952} \quad = \quad 487{,}854$$

m³/min,

in which all magnitudes – see above.

2.4. The magnitude of the current reduced productivity of the **GCU** compressor is calculated by the formula:

$$Q_{прс} = Q_c * \frac{n_п}{n_c} = 487{,}854 * \frac{5300}{5340} = 484{,}199 \text{ m}^3/\text{min},$$

in which all magnitudes – see above.

2.5. The magnitudes of the current reduced relative capacity $[N_i/\rho]_{прс}$ and of the passport efficiency $\eta_{полрс}$ of **GCU** compressor are determined by its **passport reduced characteristics** (see Fig. RPM 6) based on the magnitude of its current reduced productivity $Q_{прс}$ = 484,199 m^3 / min (see above):

$[N_i/\rho]_{прс}$ = 791,229 kW*m^3/kg;

$\eta_{полрс}$ = 0,7963.

2.6. The magnitude of the current pressure ratio in the **GCU** compressor is calculated by the formula:

$\varepsilon_c = P_{кс}/P_{нс}$ = 5,05/2,667 = 1,8935,

in which all magnitudes – see above.

2.7. The magnitude of the current real polytrophic efficiency of the **GCU** compressor is calculated by the formula:

$$\eta_{полс} = \frac{Q_{прс} * Z_c * R_c * T_{нс}}{3600 * [N_i/\rho]_{прс} * \rho_{нс}} * \frac{k_c}{k_c - 1} * \left(\frac{n_п}{n_c}\right)^2 * \left(\varepsilon_c^{\frac{(k_c-1)}{k_c}} - 1\right) =$$

$$= \frac{484{,}199 * 0{,}941 * 509{,}1 * 279}{3600 * 791{,}229 * 19{,}952} * \frac{1{,}297}{1{,}297 - 1} * \left(\frac{5300}{5340}\right)^2 * \left(1{,}8935^{\frac{(1{,}297-1)}{1{,}297}} - 1\right) =$$

0,7712,

in which all magnitudes – see above.

2.8. The magnitude of the current wear factor of the compressor is calculated by the formula:

$K_{andк} = \eta_{полс}/\eta_{полрс}$ = 0,7712/0,7963 = 0,9685,

in which all magnitudes – see above.

The calculated coefficient of wear of compressor $K_{andк}$ is used not only to calculate the **$CPM_{M.ip.NG.b}$**, but also to assess the technical condition when the definition of output of the compressor in the repair and for the appointment order it on and off in the process of calculation **the total indexed noologistical areas of possible modes of operation** of the group together working **GCU** compressors in the first compression stage of **BKS KGF** through **the technology of calculation of the upward indexed information pyramid**.

2.9. The magnitudes of the current real polytropic efficiency of the compressor at the points of the line on its reduced characteristics are calculated by the formula:

$\eta_{полсj} = K_{andк} * \eta_{полрj}$,

here are:

j – it is the serial number of the calculated point on the line of the current real polytropic efficiency of the compressor;

$\eta_{полрj}$ – it is the passport polytropic efficiency of the compressor corresponding to its jth current reduced productivity $Q_{прt}$ in his **reduced characteristics** (see Fig. RPM 3);

$K_{andк}$ – it is the current wear factor of the compressor (see above).

Calculation example:

$\eta_{полс1} = K_{andк} * \eta_{полр1} = 0{,}9685 * 0{,}670 = 0{,}649$,

$\eta_{полс2} = K_{andк} * \eta_{полр2} = 0{,}9685 * 0{,}735 = 0{,}712$,

$\eta_{полс3} = K_{andк} * \eta_{полр3} = 0{,}9685 * 0{,}789 = 0{,}764$,

$\eta_{полс4} = K_{andк} * \eta_{полр4} = 0{,}9685 * 0{,}800 = 0{,}775$,

$\eta_{полс5} = K_{andк} * \eta_{полр5} = 0{,}9685 * 0{,}777 = 0{,}753$,

$\eta_{полс6} = K_{andк} * \eta_{полр6} = 0{,}9685 * 0{,}746 = 0{,}722$,

$\eta_{полс7} = K_{andк} * \eta_{полр7} = 0{,}9685 * 0{,}701 = 0{,}679$.

The result of calculating the line of the current real polytropic efficiency of the compressor is shown in brown in Fig. RPM 7. The passport polytropic efficiency line of the compressor is shown there in black for comparison.

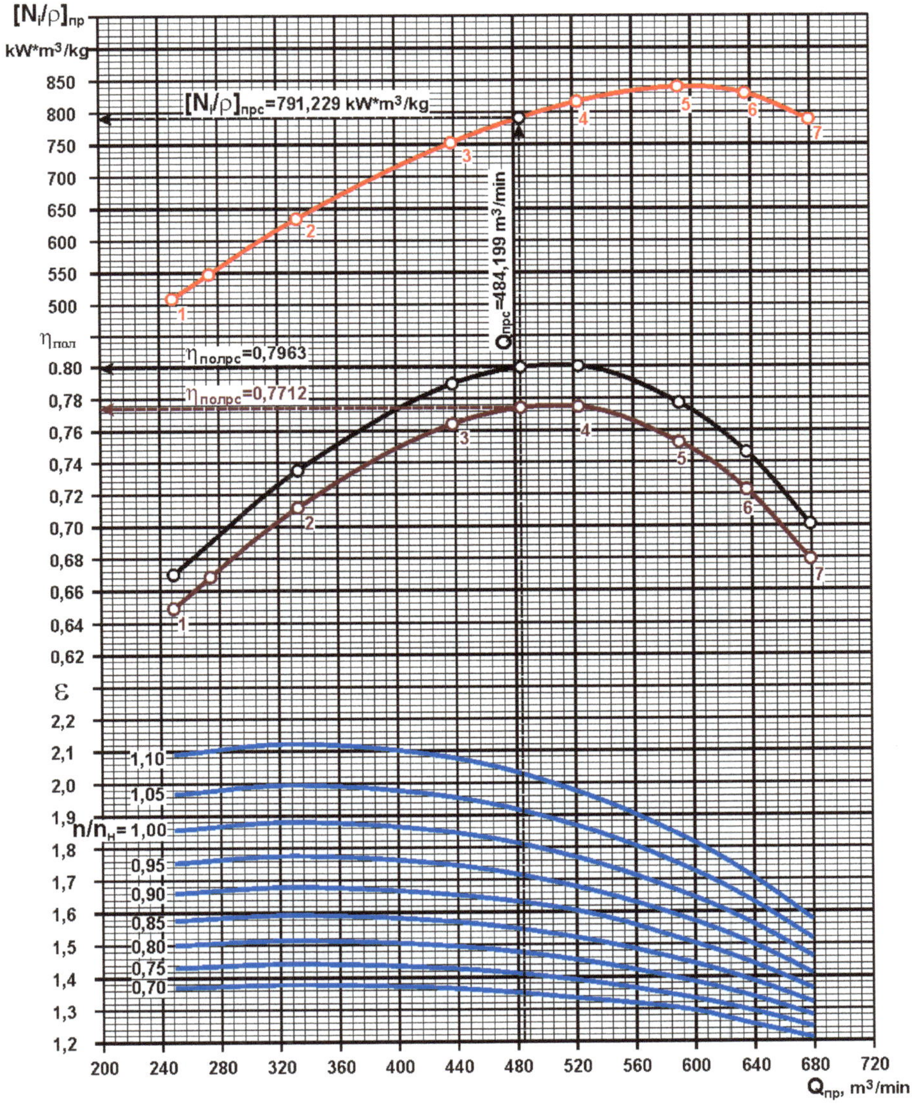

Fig. RPM 7

2.10. The calculation of the $\mathbf{RM_{M.ip.NG.b}}$ of the compressor.

The calculation of $\mathbf{RM_{ip.l.b}}$ is performed according to the standard method based on **the current real reduced characteristics shown** in Fig. RPM 7. The result of the calculation $\mathbf{RM_{ip.l.b}}$ are shown in brown on Fig. RPM 8. Calculated above $\mathbf{CPM_{M.ip.NG.b}}$ of the compressor (see Fig. RPM 5) are shown in this figure for comparison in green.

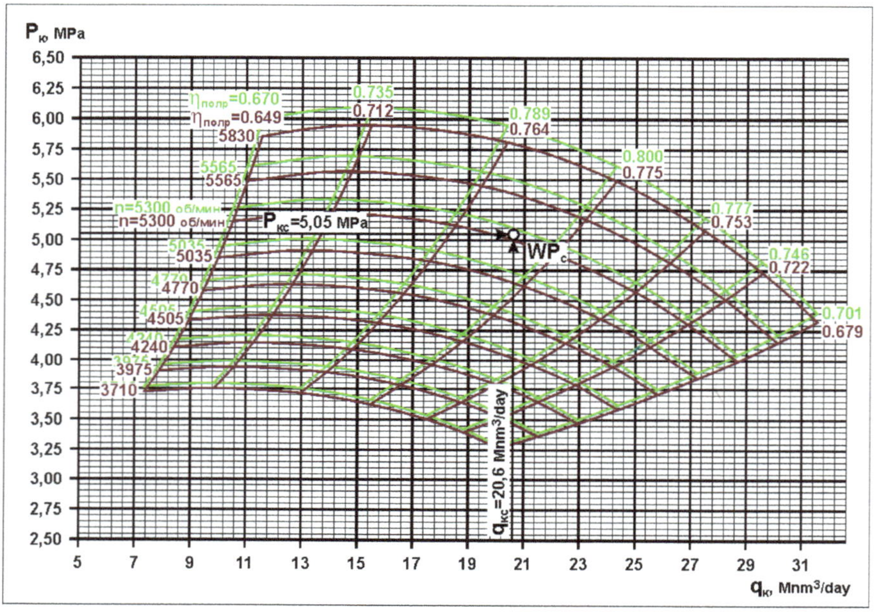

Fig. RPM 8

3. The current area of possible modes of operation (briefly – $\mathbf{CM_{M.ip.NG.b}}$) the **GCU** compressor.

3.1. The compressor minimum speed line n_{min} = const in this example corresponds to the line with the speed n = 3710 rpm (see Fig. RPM 10).

3.2. The compressor maximum speed line n_{max} = const in this example corresponds to the line with the speed n = 5830 rpm (see Fig. RPM 10).

3.3. The line of limitation of absolute pressure at the compressor outlet $P_{кmax}$ = const in this example corresponds to the maximum permissible overpressure at the compressor outlet from the strength condition of the corresponding intra-station pipelines. It is calculated by the formula:

$$P_{кmax} = P_{кandmax} + P_a = 5{,}737 + 0{,}1013 = 5{,}8383 \text{ MPa } (59{,}5 \text{ kg/sm}^2),$$

in which all magnitudes – see above.

3.4. The maximum productivity line of the compressor $q_{кс}$ = max in the example corresponds to the line of constant current polytropic efficiency $\eta_{полс}$ = 0,679 (see Fig. RPM 10).

3.5. The boundary of the pompage in this example is calculated by **the standard method** from the condition of 10% of the compressor productivity deviation from the boundary of stable modes (see red line $q_{кс}$ = min on Fig. RPM 10).

3.6. The line N_{emax} = const in this example is calculated from the actual maximum current effective power that may be provided by **the gas turbine drive unit** (**GTU**) in the current operating conditions, taking into account its actual wear.

3.6.1. The internal power of the compressor in the **WP**$_c$ is calculated by the formula:

$$N_{ic} = 0{,}001 * \left(\frac{n_c}{n_n}\right)^3 * [N_i/\rho]_{npc} * \rho_{нс} = 0{,}001 * \left(\frac{5340}{5300}\right)^3 * 791{,}229 * 19{,}952 =$$

16,147 MW,

in which all magnitudes – see above.

3.6.2. Current effective power of the gas turbine in **WP**$_c$ is calculated by the formula:

$$N_e = N_{ic}/\eta_{мех} = 16{,}147/0{,}99 = 16{,}310 \text{ MW},$$

in which all magnitudes – see above.

3.6.3. Passport fuel consumption in **GTU** in **WP**$_c$ is calculated by the **PM**$_{\mathbf{M.ip.NG.b}}$ (see Fig. RPM 2):

under N_{ec} = 16,310 MW, G_T = 3596,790 kg/h ($G_{Tуд}$ = 220,529 kg/MW-h).

3.6.4. The magnitude of the current wear rate of the **GTU** is calculated by the formula:

$K_{andт}$ = 1 – (G_{Tc} - G_T)/G_T = 1- (3641,233 - 3596,790)/3596,790 = 0,9876,

in which all magnitudes – see above.

The calculated coefficient of wear of **GTU** $K_{andт}$ is used not only to calculate the $\mathbf{CM_{M.ip.NG.b}}$, but also to assess the technical condition when the definition of output of the **GTU** in the repair and for the appointment order it on and off in the process of calculation **the total indexed noologistical areas of possible modes of operation** of the group together working **GCU** compressors in the first compression stage of **BKS KGF** through **the technology of calculation of the upward indexed information pyramid**.

3.6.5. The magnitude of the current real available effective power of **GTU** is calculated by the formula:

$N_{eрасп}$ = $K_{andт}$ * N_{epmax} * (T_{an}/T_a) = 0,9876 * 19 * (297,15/257) = 21,697 MW,

in which all magnitudes – see above.

3.6.6. Calculation of coordinates of points to construct a line N_{imax} on $\mathbf{PM_{M.ip.NG.b}}$ corresponding to the $N_{eрасп}$ = 21,697 MW performed in the following sequence:

a) Calculate the maximum internal power of the compressor N_{imax} corresponding to N_{emax} by the formula:

N_{imax} = $N_{eрасп}$ *$\eta_{мех}$ = 21,697 * 0,99 = 21,480 MW,

in which all magnitudes – see above.

b) Calculate the reduced relative power of the compressor corresponding to the magnitudes of N_{imax} and n_{max} by the formula:

$$[N_i/\rho]_{пр\max} = 1000 * \left(\frac{n_п}{n_{\max}}\right)^3 * N_{i\max}/\rho_{нс} = 1000 * \left(\frac{5300}{5830}\right)^3 * 21{,}480/19{,}952$$

= 808,849 kW,

in which all magnitudes – see above.

c) Determine the parameters of operating modes of the compressor at the calculated points 1, 2, 3, ..., 7, which are uniformly distributed in the interval between 1 and 7 points in the graph $[N_i/\rho]_{пр}$ of the current reduced characteristics – see Fig. RPM 9:

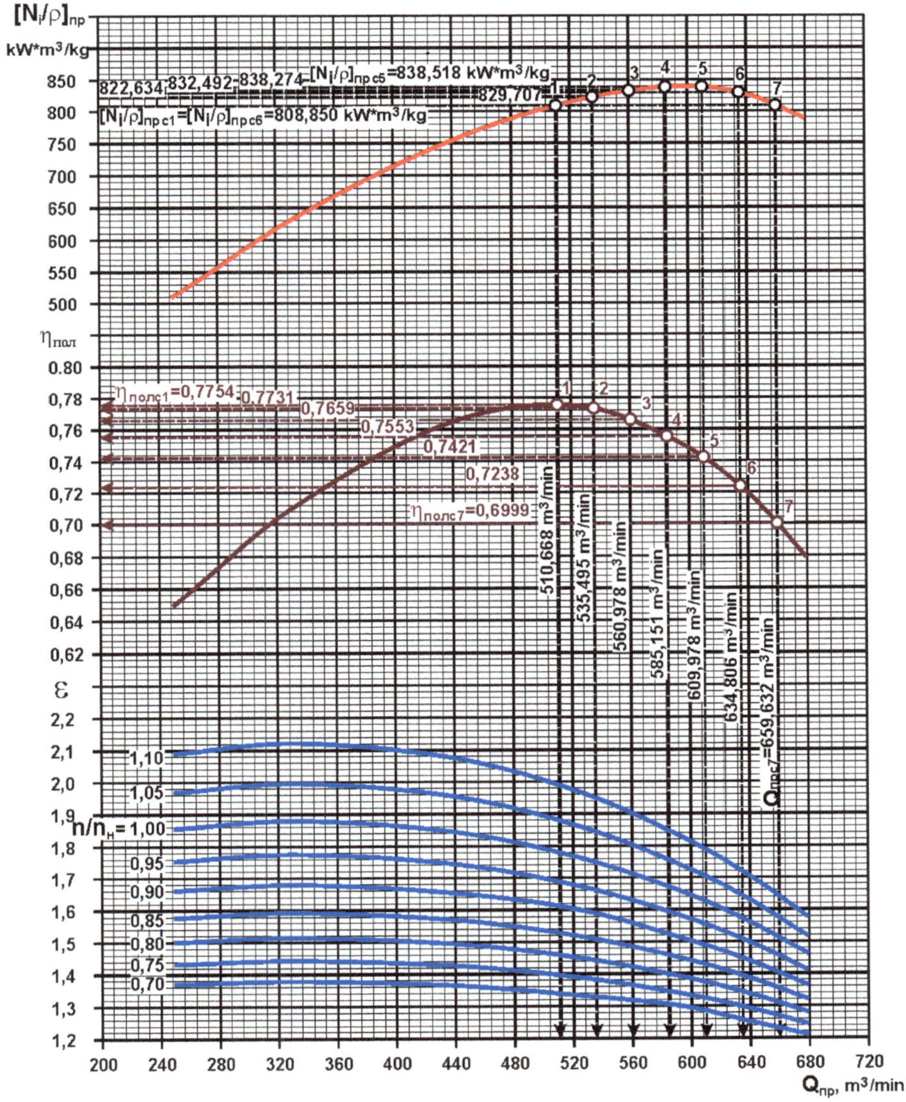

Fig. RPM 9

Parameter magnitudes in the points 1, 2, 3, ..., 7:

$[N_i/\rho]_{пр1}$ = 808,850 kW*m^3/kg, $\eta_{пол1}$ = 0,7754, $Q_{пр1}$ = 510,668 m^3/min;

$[N_i/\rho]_{пр2}$ = 822,634 kW*m^3/kg, $\eta_{пол2}$ = 0,7731, $Q_{пр2}$ = 535,495 m^3/min;

$[N_i/\rho]_{пр3}$ = 832,492 kW*m^3/kg, $\eta_{пол3}$ = 0,7659, $Q_{пр3}$ = 560,323 m^3/min;

$[N_i/\rho]_{пр4}$ = 838,274 kW*m^3/kg, $\eta_{пол4}$ = 0,7553, $Q_{пр4}$ = 585,151 m^3/min;

$[N_i/\rho]_{пр5}$ = 838,518 kW*m^3/kg, $\eta_{пол5}$ = 0,7421, $Q_{пр5}$ = 609,978 m^3/min;

$[N_i/\rho]_{пр6}$ = 829,707 kW*m^3/kg, $\eta_{пол6}$ = 0,7238, $Q_{пр6}$ = 634,806 m^3/min;

$[N_i/\rho]_{пр7}$ = 808,850 kW*m^3/kg, $\eta_{пол7}$ = 0,6999, $Q_{пр7}$ = 659,632 m^3/min.

d) Calculate the frequency of rotation of the compressor in the jth points 1, 2, 3, ..., 7 by the formula:

$$n_j = n_n * \sqrt[3]{\frac{1000 * N_{i\max}}{[N_i/\rho]_{прj} * \rho_{нс}}},$$

here are:

j – it is the sequence number of the calculated point on **the current reduced operating characteristics** of the compressor;

the rest – see above.

Calculation example:

$$n_1 = n_n * \sqrt[3]{\frac{1000 * N_{i\max}}{[N_i/\rho]_{пр1} * \rho_{нс}}} = 5300 * \sqrt[3]{\frac{1000 * 21{,}480}{808{,}850 * 19{,}952}} = 5830 \text{ rpm};$$

$$n_2 = n_n * \sqrt[3]{\frac{1000 * N_{i\max}}{[N_i/\rho]_{пр2} * \rho_{нс}}} = 5300 * \sqrt[3]{\frac{1000 * 21{,}480}{822{,}634 * 19{,}952}} = 5797 \text{ rpm};$$

$$n_3 = n_n * \sqrt[3]{\frac{1000 * N_{i\max}}{[N_i / \rho]_{np3} * \rho_{нс}}} = 5300 * \sqrt[3]{\frac{1000 * 21{,}480}{832{,}496 * 19{,}952}} = 5774 \text{ rpm};$$

$$n_4 = n_n * \sqrt[3]{\frac{1000 * N_{i\max}}{[N_i / \rho]_{np4} * \rho_{нс}}} = 5300 * \sqrt[3]{\frac{1000 * 21{,}480}{838{,}274 * 19{,}952}} = 5761 \text{ rpm};$$

$$n_5 = n_n * \sqrt[3]{\frac{1000 * N_{i\max}}{[N_i / \rho]_{np5} * \rho_{нс}}} = 5300 * \sqrt[3]{\frac{1000 * 21{,}480}{838{,}518 * 19{,}952}} = 5760 \text{ rpm};$$

$$n_6 = n_n * \sqrt[3]{\frac{1000 * N_{i\max}}{[N_i / \rho]_{np6} * \rho_{нс}}} = 5300 * \sqrt[3]{\frac{1000 * 21{,}480}{829{,}707 * 19{,}952}} = 5781 \text{ rpm};$$

$$n_7 = n_n * \sqrt[3]{\frac{1000 * N_{i\max}}{[N_i / \rho]_{np7} * \rho_{нс}}} = 5300 * \sqrt[3]{\frac{1000 * 21{,}480}{808{,}850 * 19{,}952}} = 5830 \text{ rpm}.$$

e) Calculate the pressure at the outlet of the compressor in the jth the points 1, 2, 3, ..., 7 on the line N_{imax} by the formula:

$$P_{кcj} = P_{нс} * \sqrt[\frac{k_c}{(k_c - 1)}]{\eta_{полj} * \frac{3600 * [N_i / \rho]_{npj} * \rho_{нс}}{Q_{npj} * Z_c * R_c * T_{нс}} * \frac{k_c - 1}{k_c} * \left(\frac{n_j}{n_n}\right)^2 + 1},$$

in which all magnitudes – see above.

Calculation example:

$$P_{кс1} = 2{,}667 * \sqrt[\frac{1{,}297}{(1{,}297-1)}]{0{,}7754 * \frac{3600 * 808{,}850 * 19{,}952}{510{,}6 * 0{,}941 * 509{,}1 * 279} * \frac{1{,}297 - 1}{1{,}297} * \left(\frac{5830}{5300}\right)^2 + 1} = 5{,}553$$

MPa;

$$P_{кс2} = 2{,}667 * \sqrt[\frac{1{,}297}{(1{,}297-1)}]{0{,}7731 * \frac{3600 * 822{,}634 * 19{,}952}{535{,}7032 * 0{,}941 * 509{,}1 * 279} * \frac{1{,}297 - 1}{1{,}297} * \left(\frac{5797}{5300}\right)^2 + 1} =$$

5,391 MPa;

$$P_{кс3} = 2{,}667 * \sqrt[\frac{1{,}297}{(1{,}297-1)}]{0{,}7659 * \frac{3600 * 832{,}492 * 19{,}952}{560{,}805 * 0{,}941 * 509{,}1 * 279} * \frac{1{,}297 - 1}{1{,}297} * \left(\frac{5774}{5300}\right)^2 + 1} =$$

5,220 MPa;

$$P_{нс4} = 2{,}667 * \sqrt[\frac{1{,}297}{(1{,}297-1)}]{0{,}7553 * \frac{3600 * 838{,}274 * 19{,}952}{585{,}908 * 0{,}941 * 509{,}1 * 279} * \frac{1{,}297 - 1}{1{,}297} * \left(\frac{5761}{5300}\right)^2 + 1} =$$

5,048 MPa;

$$P_{нс5} = 2{,}667 * \sqrt[\frac{1{,}297}{(1{,}297-1)}]{0{,}7421 * \frac{3600*838{,}518*19{,}952}{611{,}01*0{,}941*509{,}1*279} * \frac{1{,}297-1}{1{,}297} * \left(\frac{5760}{5300}\right)^2 + 1}$$ = 4,878 MPa;

$$P_{нс6} = 2{,}667 * \sqrt[\frac{1{,}297}{(1{,}297-1)}]{0{,}7238 * \frac{3600*829{,}707*19{,}952}{636{,}113*0{,}941*509{,}1*279} * \frac{1{,}297-1}{1{,}297} * \left(\frac{5781}{5300}\right)^2 + 1}$$ = 4,699 MPa;

$$P_{нс7} = 2{,}667 * \sqrt[\frac{1{,}297}{(1{,}297-1)}]{0{,}6999 * \frac{3600*808{,}850*19{,}952}{661{,}214*0{,}941*509{,}1*279} * \frac{1{,}297-1}{1{,}297} * \left(\frac{5830}{5300}\right)^2 + 1}$$ = 4,509 MPa.

f) Calculate the current commercial productivity of the compressor in jth points 1, 2, 3,..., 7 on the N_{imax} line by the formula:

$$q_{кcj} = Q_{npj} * \frac{n_j}{n_n} * \frac{24*60*\rho_{нс}}{1000000*\rho_{0c}},$$

in which all magnitudes – see above.

Calculation example:

$$q_{кc1} = 510{,}668 * \frac{5830}{5300} * \frac{24*60*19{,}952}{1000000*0{,}6804}$$ = 23,720 Mnm³/day;

$$q_{кc2} = 535{,}495 * \frac{5797}{5300} * \frac{24*60*19{,}952}{1000000*0{,}6804}$$ = 24,733 Mnm³/day;

$$q_{кc3} = 560{,}323 * \frac{5774}{5300} * \frac{24*60*19{,}952}{1000000*0{,}6804}$$ = 25,777 Mnm³/day;

$$q_{кc4} = 585{,}151 * \frac{5761}{5300} * \frac{24*60*19{,}952}{1000000*0{,}6804}$$ = 26,857 Mnm³/day;

$$q_{кc5} = 609{,}978 * \frac{5760}{5300} * \frac{24*60*19{,}952}{1000000*0{,}6804}$$ = 27,994 Mnm³/day;

$$q_{кc6} = 634{,}806 * \frac{5781}{5300} * \frac{24*60*19{,}952}{1000000*0{,}6804}$$ = 29,236 Mnm³/day;

$$q_{кc7} = 659{,}632 * \frac{5830}{5300} * \frac{24*60*19{,}952}{1000000*0{,}6804}$$ = 30,639 Mnm³/day.

g) A line N_{emax} = const was built based on the results of the calculations in 3.6.6.(e) and 3.6.6.f) that is shown in light green on Fig. RPM 10.

3.7. The line of the current maximum permitted temperature of the pumped gas at the outlet of the compressor $T_{кmax}$ = const is calculated by the conditions of thermal stability of the insulation of the intra-station pipelines. The pressure of the pumped gas at the compressor outlet corresponding to the maximum permitted temperature $T_{кmax}$ is calculated by the formula:

$$P_{кT\max i} = P_{нс} * \left(\frac{T_{к\max}}{T_{нс}} \right)^{\frac{k_c * \eta_{полі}}{k_c - 1}},$$

here are:

i – it is the sequence number of the design point on the current line of the maximum permitted temperature of the pumped gas at the compressor outlet;

$\eta_{полсі}$ – it is the current reduced efficiency of the compressor (see above p. 2.9.);

the rest – see above.

Calculation example:

$$P_{кT\max 1} = 2{,}667 * \left(\frac{363{,}15}{279} \right)^{\frac{1{,}297*0{,}6489}{1{,}297-1}} = 5{,}629 \text{ MPa};$$

$$P_{кT\max 2} = 2{,}667 * \left(\frac{363{,}15}{279} \right)^{\frac{1{,}297*0{,}7118}{1{,}297-1}} = 6{,}052 \text{ MPa};$$

$$P_{кT\max 3} = 2{,}667 * \left(\frac{363{,}15}{279} \right)^{\frac{1{,}297*0{,}7641}{1{,}297-1}} = 6{,}428 \text{ MPa};$$

$$P_{кT\max 4} = 2{,}667 * \left(\frac{363{,}15}{279} \right)^{\frac{1{,}297*0{,}7748}{1{,}297-1}} = 6{,}507 \text{ MPa};$$

$$P_{\kappa T\max 5} = 2{,}667 * \left(\frac{363{,}15}{279}\right)^{\frac{1{,}297*0{,}7525}{1{,}297-1}} = 6{,}342 \text{ MPa};$$

$$P_{\kappa T\max 6} = 2{,}667 * \left(\frac{363{,}15}{279}\right)^{\frac{1{,}297*0{,}7225}{1{,}297-1}} = 6{,}127 \text{ MPa};$$

$$P_{\kappa T\max 7} = 2{,}667 * \left(\frac{363{,}15}{279}\right)^{\frac{1{,}297*0{,}6789}{1{,}297-1}} = 5{,}827 \text{ MPa}.$$

Line $T_{\kappa max}$ = const build on the basis of calculations. It passes through the points of intersection of horizontal lines $P_{\kappa Tmaxi}$ = const and the top points of the lines of constant efficiency $\eta_{полсі}$ = const. This line is shown in dark green on Fig. RPM 10.

3.8. Build **CM**$_{\mathbf{M.ip.NG.b}}$ on the results of the calculations.

Impose calculated above lines, which are boundaries of the **CM**$_{\mathbf{M.ip.NG.b}}$, on the **RM**$_{\mathbf{M.ip.NG.b}}$, which are shown above in Fig. RPM 8, to build it – see Fig. RPM 10:

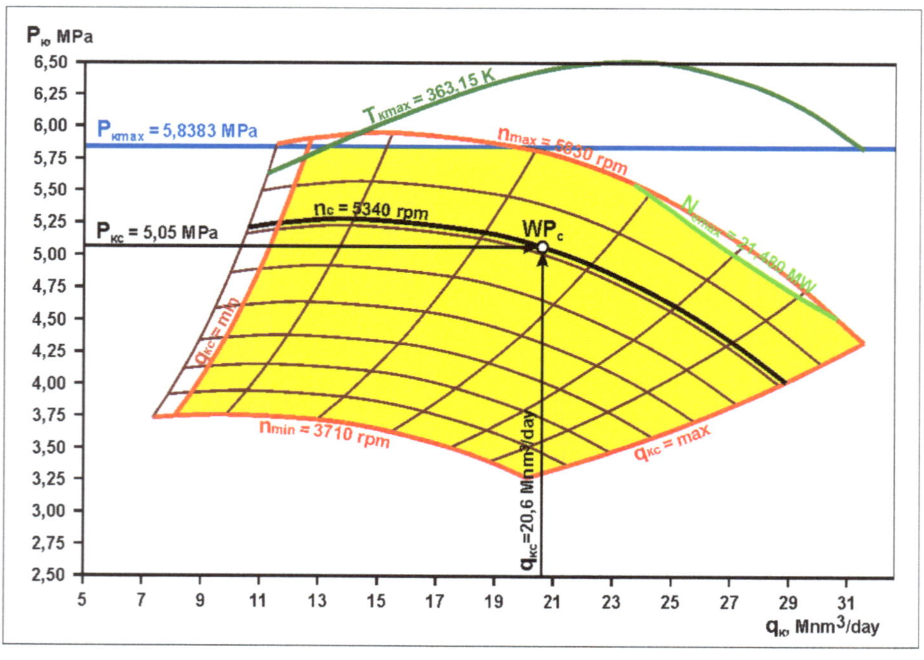

Fig. RPM 10

$\mathbf{CM_{M.ip.NG.b}}$ is shown on Fig. RPM 10 in yellow.

It is obvious that:

any current mode of the **GCU**, if its operating point $\mathbf{WP_c}$ is located inside $\mathbf{CM_{M.ip.NG.b}}$, may be implemented in the current time reliably, sustainably and safely. Therefore, the staff may go not into the details of the current or projected operating mode of the compressor: just one look at the Fig. RPM 10 to make sure that its working point is located inside $\mathbf{CM_{M.ip.NG.b}}$ and sufficiently far of its boundaries;
any change in the **GCU's** current operating conditions or wear and tear will alter the shape and location of the $\mathbf{CM_{M.ip.NG.b}}$ on its $\mathbf{RM_{M.ip.NG.b}}$;
$\mathbf{RM_{M.ip.NG.b}}$ and $\mathbf{CM_{M.ip.NG.b}}$ of other **GCU** of the same type, operating in that stage or that compressor shop, in parallel, discussed above, are typically different from those shown in Fig. RPM 10. This difference arises from, for example, different levels of wear, contamination of work surfaces, accuracy of creation, etc.

4. The calculation of **the current noologistical areas of the possible operating modes** (briefly – $\mathbf{NM_{C.ip.Vth.b}}$, $\mathbf{NM_{C.ip.Mn.b}}$ and $\mathbf{NM_{S.ip.CO2.b}}$).

4.1. The calculation of **the** $\mathbf{NM_{C.ip.Vth.b}}$.

4.1.1. The internal power of the compressor at the jth point of $\mathbf{CM_{M.ip.NG.b}}$ is calculated by formula:

$$N_{ij} = 0{,}001 * \left(\frac{n_j}{n_n}\right)^3 * [N_i / \rho]_{npj} * \rho_{нс},$$

here are:

n_j – it is the **GCU** compressor speed in the jth point of $\mathbf{CM_{M.ip.NG.b}}$;

$[N_i/\rho]_{npj}$ – it is the reduced relative capacity of the compressor in the jth point of $\mathbf{CM_{M.ip.NG.b}}$, taken from the above characteristics on Fig. RPM 7;

the rest – see above.

Calculation example:

For the compressor speed n_{min} = 3710 rpm.

$$N_{i1} = 0{,}001 * \left(\frac{n_1}{n_n}\right)^3 * [N_i / \rho]_{np1} * \rho_{нс} = 0{,}001 * \left(\frac{3710}{5300}\right)^3 * 509{,}171 * 19{,}952 =$$

3,485 MW;

$$N_{i2} = 0{,}001 * \left(\frac{n_2}{n_n}\right)^3 * [N_i / \rho]_{np2} * \rho_{нс} = 0{,}001 * \left(\frac{3710}{5300}\right)^3 * 634{,}149 * 19{,}952 =$$

4,340 MW;

$$N_{i3} = 0{,}001 * \left(\frac{n_3}{n_n}\right)^3 * [N_i / \rho]_{np3} * \rho_{нс} = 0{,}001 * \left(\frac{3710}{5300}\right)^3 * 752{,}608 * 19{,}952 =$$

5,150 MW;

$$N_{i4} = 0{,}001 * \left(\frac{n_4}{n_n}\right)^3 * [N_i / \rho]_{np4} * \rho_{нс} = 0{,}001 * \left(\frac{3710}{5300}\right)^3 * 816{,}202 * 19{,}952 =$$

5,586 MW;

$$N_{i5} = 0{,}001 * \left(\frac{n_5}{n_n}\right)^3 * [N_i / \rho]_{np5} * \rho_{нс} = 0{,}001 * \left(\frac{3710}{5300}\right)^3 * 839{,}055 * 19{,}952 =$$

5,742 MW;

$$N_{i6} = 0{,}001 * \left(\frac{n_6}{n_n}\right)^3 * [N_i / \rho]_{np6} * \rho_{нс} = 0{,}001 * \left(\frac{3710}{5300}\right)^3 * 828{,}843 * 19{,}952 =$$

5,672 MW;

$$N_{i7} = 0{,}001 * \left(\frac{n_7}{n_n}\right)^3 * [N_i / \rho]_{np7} * \rho_{нс} = 0{,}001 * \left(\frac{3710}{5300}\right)^3 * 788{,}339 * 19{,}952 =$$

5,395 MW.

For the compressor speed n_{max} = 5830 rpm.

$$N_{i8} = 0{,}001 * \left(\frac{n_8}{n_n}\right)^3 * [N_i / \rho]_{np8} * \rho_{нс} = 0{,}001 * \left(\frac{5830}{5300}\right)^3 * 509{,}171 * 19{,}952 =$$

13,522 MW;

$$N_{i9} = 0{,}001 * \left(\frac{n_9}{n_n}\right)^3 * [N_i / \rho]_{np9} * \rho_{нс} = 0{,}001 * \left(\frac{5830}{5300}\right)^3 * 634{,}149 * 19{,}952 =$$

16,841 MW;

$$N_{i10} = 0{,}001 * \left(\frac{n_{10}}{n_n}\right)^3 * [N_i / \rho]_{np10} * \rho_{нс} = 0{,}001 * \left(\frac{5830}{5300}\right)^3 * 752{,}608 * 19{,}952$$

= 19,986 MW;

$$N_{i11} = 0{,}001 * \left(\frac{n_{11}}{n_n}\right)^3 * [N_i / \rho]_{np11} * \rho_{нс} = 0{,}001 * \left(\frac{5830}{5300}\right)^3 * 816{,}202 * 19{,}952 =$$

21,675 MW;

$$N_{i12} = 0{,}001 * \left(\frac{n_{12}}{n_н}\right)^3 * [N_i / \rho]_{np12} * \rho_{нс} = 0{,}001 * \left(\frac{5830}{5300}\right)^3 * 839{,}055 * 19{,}952$$

= 22,282 MW;

$$N_{i13} = 0{,}001 * \left(\frac{n_{13}}{n_n}\right)^3 * [N_i / \rho]_{np13} * \rho_{нс} = 0{,}001 * \left(\frac{5830}{5300}\right)^3 * 828{,}843 * 19{,}952$$

= 22,011 MW;

$$N_{i14} = 0{,}001 * \left(\frac{n_{14}}{n_n}\right)^3 * [N_i / \rho]_{np14} * \rho_{нс} = 0{,}001 * \left(\frac{5830}{5300}\right)^3 * 788{,}339 * 19{,}952$$

= 20,935 MW.

4.1.2. The effective power of the compressor at the jth point of **$CM_{M.ip.NG.b}$** is calculated by formula:

$N_{ej} = N_{ij}/\eta_{мех}$;

in which all magnitudes – see above.

Calculation example:

For the compressor speed n_{min} = 3710 rpm.

$N_{e1} = N_{i1}/\eta_{мех}$ = 3,485/0,99 = 3,520 MW;

$N_{e2} = N_{i2}/\eta_{мех}$ = 4,340/0,99 = 4,384 MW;

$N_{e3} = N_{i3}/\eta_{мех}$ = 5,150/0,99 = 5,203 MW;

$N_{e4} = N_{i4}/\eta_{мех} = 5,586/0,99 = 5,642$ MW;

$N_{e5} = N_{i5}/\eta_{мех} = 5,742/0,99 = 5,800$ MW;

$N_{e6} = N_{i6}/\eta_{мех} = 5,672/0,99 = 5,730$ MW;

$N_{e7} = N_{i7}/\eta_{мех} = 5,395/0,99 = 5,450$ MW.

For the compressor speed $n_{max} = 5830$ rpm.

$N_{e8} = N_{i8}/\eta_{мех} = 13,522/0,99 = 13,658$ MW;

$N_{e9} = N_{i9}/\eta_{мех} = 16,841/0,99 = 17,011$ MW;

$N_{e10} = N_{i10}/\eta_{мех} = 19,986/0,99 = 20,188$ MW;

$N_{e11} = N_{i11}/\eta_{мех} = 21,675/0,99 = 21,894$ MW;

$N_{e12} = N_{i12}/\eta_{мех} = 22,282/0,99 = 22,507$ MW;

$N_{e13} = N_{i13}/\eta_{мех} = 22,011/0,99 = 22,233$ MW;

$N_{e14} = N_{i14}/\eta_{мех} = 20,935/0,99 = 21,147$ MW.

4.1.5. The actual current specific fuel consumption in **GCU** is calculated by the formula:

$Gт_{удс} = Gт_c/ N_{ec} = 3641,233 / 16,310 = 223,254$ kg/MW-h,

in which all magnitudes – see above.

4.1.6. Real current conditional variable cost of fuel in the jth point of the **$CM_{M.ip.NG.b}$** of **GCU**, expressed in MW, calculated by the formula:

$Gт_j = N_{ej} * Gт_{удс} * Q_н^р/3600$ MW,

here are:

N_{ej} – it is the effective power of the compressor at the jth point of **$CM_{M.ip.NG.b}$** (see above);

$Gт_{удс}$ – it is the actual current specific fuel consumption in **GCU** (see above Fig. RPM 3).

Calculation example:

For the compressor speed n_{min} = 3710 rpm.

G_{T1} = 3,520 * 223,254 * 49,725/3600 = 10,854 MW;
G_{T2} = 4,384 * 223,254 * 49,725/3600 = 13,518 MW;
G_{T3} = 5,203 * 223,254 * 49,725/3600 = 16,043 MW;
G_{T4} = 5,642 * 223,254 * 49,725/3600 = 17,398 MW;
G_{T5} = 5,800 * 223,254 * 49,725/3600 = 17,886 MW;
G_{T6} = 5,730 * 223,254 * 49,725/3600 = 17,668 MW;
G_{T7} = 5,450 * 223,254 * 49,725/3600 = 16,805 MW.

For the compressor speed n_{max} = 5830 rpm.

G_{T8} = 13,658 * 223,254 * 49,725/3600 = 42,117 MW;
G_{T9} = 17,011 * 223,254 * 49,725/3600 = 52,455 MW;
G_{T10} = 20,188 * 223,254 * 49,725/3600 = 62,254 MW;
G_{T11} = 21,894 * 223,254 * 49,725/3600 = 67,514 MW;
G_{T12} = 22,507 * 223,254 * 49,725/3600 = 69,405 MW;
G_{T13} = 22,233 * 223,254 * 49,725/3600 = 68,560 MW;
G_{T14} = 21,147 * 223,254 * 49,725/3600 = 65,210 MW.

4.1.7. The real total current conditional variable cost of energy for operation of the **GCU** in the jth point of **$CM_{M.ip.NG.b}$** is calculated by the formula:

$D_{C.ip.Vth.b.j} = G_{Tj} + D_{элс}$,

in which all magnitudes – see above.

Calculation example:

For the compressor speed n_{min} = 3710 rpm.

$D_{C.ip.Vth.b.1} = G_{T1} + D_{элс}$ = 10,854 + 0,000636 = 10,854 MW;
$D_{C.ip.Vth.b.2} = G_{T2} + D_{элс}$ = 13,518 + 0,000636 = 13,518 MW;
$D_{C.ip.Vth.b.3} = G_{T3} + D_{элс}$ = 16,043 + 0,000636 = 16,044 MW;
$D_{C.ip.Vth.b.4} = G_{T4} + D_{элс}$ = 17,398 + 0,000636 = 17,399 MW;
$D_{C.ip.Vth.b.5} = G_{T5} + D_{элс}$ = 17,886 + 0,000636 = 17,886 MW;

$D_{C.ip.Vth.b.6}$ = Gт$_6$ + $D_{элс}$ = 17,668 + 0,000636 = 17,669 MW;
$D_{C.ip.Vth.b.7}$ = Gт$_7$ + $D_{элс}$ = 16,805 + 0,000636 = 16,805 MW.

For the compressor speed n_{max} = 5830 rpm.

$D_{C.ip.Vth.b.8}$ = Gт$_8$ + $D_{элс}$ = 42,117 + 0,000636 = 42,118 MW;
$D_{C.ip.Vth.b.9}$ = Gт$_9$ + $D_{элс}$ = 52,455 + 0,000636 = 52,456 MW;
$D_{C.ip.Vth.b.10}$ = Gт$_{10}$ + $D_{элс}$ = 62,254 + 0,000636 = 62,255 MW;
$D_{C.ip.Vth.b.11}$ = Gт$_{11}$ + $D_{элс}$ = 67,514 + 0,000636 = 67,511 MW;
$D_{C.ip.Vth.b.12}$ = Gт$_{12}$ + $D_{элс}$ = 69,405 + 0,000636 = 69,405 MW;
$D_{C.ip.Vth.b.13}$ = Gт$_{13}$ + $D_{элс}$ = 68,560 + 0,000636 = 68,560 MW;
$D_{C.ip.Vth.b.14}$ = Gт$_{14}$ + $D_{элс}$ = 65,210 + 0,000636 = 65,210 MW.

The magnitudes of the $D_{C.ip.Vth.b.j}$ for the other lines bounding the GCU's **CM$_{M.ip.NG.b}$**, is calculated similar including: for lines n_{min} = const, n_{max} = const, $P_{кmax}$ = const, $q_{кс}$ = max, $q_{кс}$ = min, N_{emax} = const, $T_{кmax}$ = const, as well as for the **WP$_c$** point. These calculations are not shown here to reduce the scope of the description.

NM$_{C.ip.Vth.b}$ of the first type are built on the results of calculations – see Fig. RPM 11 which is used for further calculation of the corresponding **Indexed noologistical areas of possible operating modes** (**RPM$_{C.ip.Vth.b}$**).

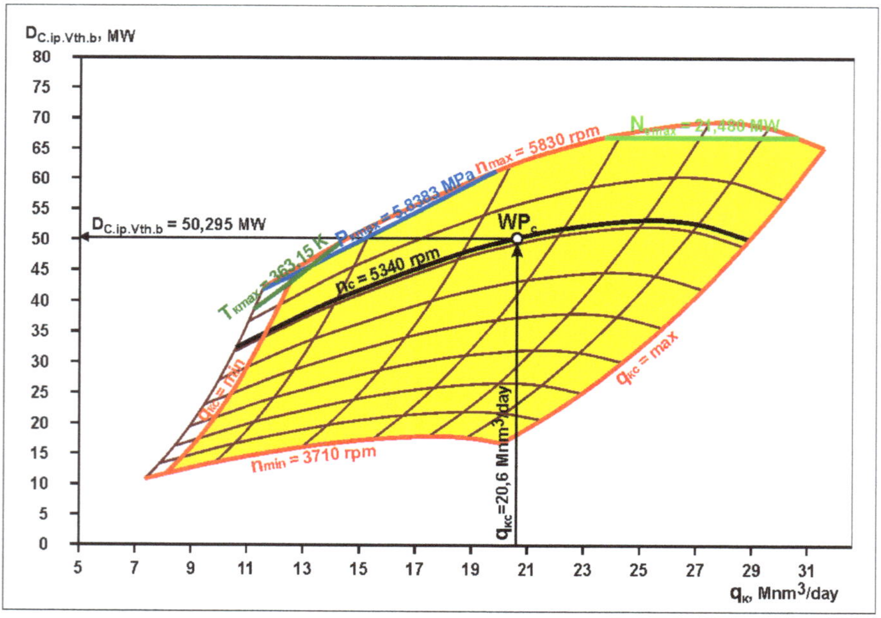

Fig. RPM 11

Calculated **$NM_{C.ip.Vth.b}$** of the first type, painted yellow on Fig. RPM 11, mathematically links **the density of current flow ($F_{M.ip.NG.b}$) of the current noologistical value ($V_{M.ip.NG.b}$)**, that is the **$q_к$** of pumped gas in Mnm³/day, and **the density of the current conditional variable consumption flow ($F_{C.ip.Vth.b}$) of the current noologistical value ($V_{C.ip.Vth.b}$)**, that is its **$D_{C.ip.Vth.b}$** which is expressed in MW.

4.1.8. The real total current conditional fixed energy cost, which is amortized on the functioning of **GCU** in the jth point of the **$CM_{M.ip.NG.b}$** is calculated by the formula:

$FD_{C.ip.Vth.b} = FQ_{элс} / 365 * 24 * T_{Ac} = 18974 / 365 * 24 *6 = 0,361$ MW,

in which all magnitudes – see above.

4.1.9. The real total current energy cost at the jth point of the **$CM_{M.ip.NG.b}$** is calculated by the formula:

$TD_{C.ip.Vth.b.j} = D_{C.ip.Vth.b.j} + FD_{C.ip.Vth.b}$,

in which all magnitudes – see above.

Calculation example:

For the compressor speed $n_{min} = 3710$ rpm.

$TD_{C.ip.Vth.b.1} = D_{C.ip.Vth.b.1} + FD_{C.ip.Vth.b} = 10,854 + 0,361 = 11,215$ MW;
$TD_{C.ip.Vth.b.2} = D_{C.ip.Vth.b.2} + FD_{C.ip.Vth.b} = 13,518 + 0,361 = 13,879$ MW;
$TD_{C.ip.Vth.b.3} = D_{C.ip.Vth.b.3} + FD_{C.ip.Vth.b} = 16,044 + 0,361 = 16,405$ MW;
$TD_{C.ip.Vth.b.4} = D_{C.ip.Vth.b.4} + FD_{C.ip.Vth.b} = 17,399 + 0,361 = 17,760$ MW;
$TD_{C.ip.Vth.b.5} = D_{C.ip.Vth.b.5} + FD_{C.ip.Vth.b} = 17,886 + 0,361 = 18,247$ MW;
$TD_{C.ip.Vth.b.6} = D_{C.ip.Vth.b.6} + FD_{C.ip.Vth.b} = 17,669 + 0,361 = 18,030$ MW;
$TD_{C.ip.Vth.b.7} = D_{C.ip.Vth.b.7} + FD_{C.ip.Vth.b} = 16,805 + 0,361 = 17,166$ MW.

For the compressor speed $n_{max} = 5830$ rpm.

$TD_{C.ip.Vth.b.8} = D_{C.ip.Vth.b.8} + FD_{C.ip.Vth.b} = 42,118 + 0,361 = 42,479$ MW;
$TD_{C.ip.Vth.b.9} = D_{C.ip.Vth.b.9} + FD_{C.ip.Vth.b} = 52,456 + 0,361 = 52,817$ MW;
$TD_{C.ip.Vth.b.10} = D_{C.ip.Vth.b.10} + FD_{C.ip.Vth.b} = 62,255 + 0,361 = 62,616$ MW;
$TD_{C.ip.Vth.b.11} = D_{C.ip.Vth.b.11} + FD_{C.ip.Vth.b} = 67,511 + 0,361 = 67,876$ MW;
$TD_{C.ip.Vth.b.12} = D_{C.ip.Vth.b.12} + FD_{C.ip.Vth.b} = 69,405 + 0,361 = 69,766$ MW;
$TD_{C.ip.Vth.b.13} = D_{C.ip.Vth.b.13} + FD_{C.ip.Vth.b} = 68,560 + 0,361 = 68,921$ MW;
$TD_{C.ip.Vth.b.14} = D_{C.ip.Vth.b.14} + FD_{C.ip.Vth.b} = 65,210 + 0,361 = 65,571$ MW.

The magnitudes of the $TD_{C.ip.Vth.b.j}$ for the other lines bounding the GCU's $\mathbf{CM_{M.ip.NG.b}}$, is calculated similar including: for lines n_{min} = const, n_{max} = const, $P_{кmax}$ = const, $q_{кс}$ = max, $q_{кс}$ = min, N_{emax} = const, $T_{кmax}$ = const, as well as for the $\mathbf{WP_c}$ point. These calculations are not shown here to reduce the scope of the description.

$\mathbf{NM_{C.ip.Vth.b}}$ of the second type are built on the results of calculations – see Fig. RPM 12 which is used for further calculation of the corresponding **Indexed noologistical areas of possible operating modes** ($\mathbf{RPM_{C.ip.Vth.b}}$).

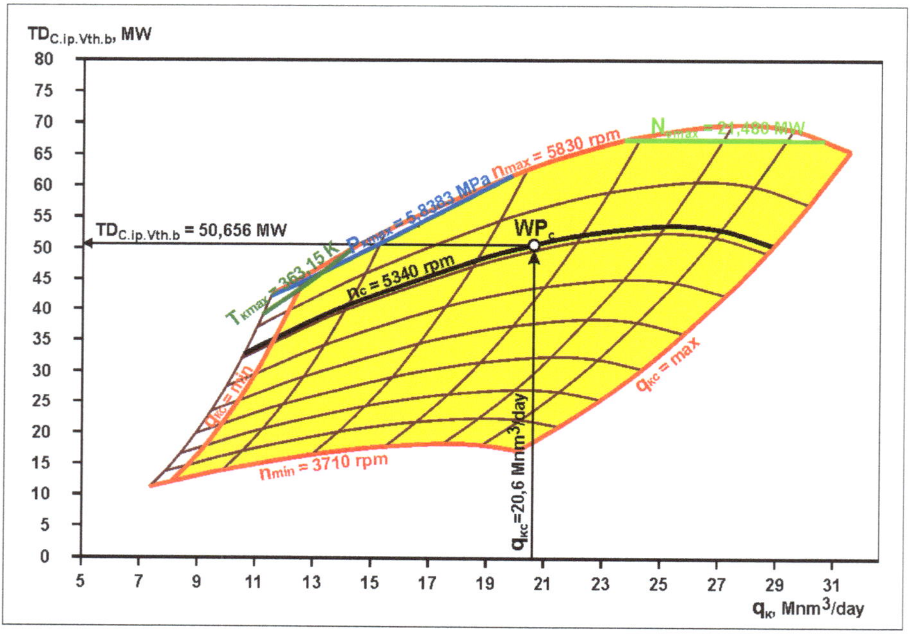

Fig. RPM 12

Calculated $\mathbf{NM_{C.ip.Vth.b}}$ of the second type, painted yellow on Fig. RPM 12, mathematically links **the density of current flow ($\mathbf{F_{M.ip.NG.b}}$) of the current noologistical value ($\mathbf{V_{M.ip.NG.b}}$)**, that is the $\mathbf{q_к}$ of pumped gas in Mnm^3/day, and **the density of the current total consumption flow ($\mathbf{TF_{C.ip.Vth.b}}$) of the current noologistical value ($\mathbf{V_{C.ip.Vth.b}}$)**, that is its $\mathbf{TD_{C.ip.Vth.b}}$ which is expressed in MW.

4.2. The calculation of **the $\mathbf{NM_{C.ip.Mn.b}}$**.

4.2.1. The current conditional variable cost of fuel gas in the jth point of $\mathbf{CM_{M.ip.NG.b}}$ in monetary form is calculated by formula:

$D_{C.ip.G\text{т}.b.j} = N_{ej} * G\text{т}_{\text{удс}} * C_{G\text{т}.c} / \rho_{0c}$,

in which all magnitudes – see above.

Calculation example:

For the compressor speed n_{min} = 3710 rpm.

$D_{C.ip.G\text{т}.b.1} = N_{e1} * G\text{т}_{\text{удс}} * C_{G\text{т}.c} / \rho_{0c} * 1000$ = 3,520 * 223,254 * 172 /0,6804*1000 = 198,639 krub/h;

$D_{C.ip.G\text{т}.b.2} = N_{e2} * G\text{т}_{\text{удс}} * C_{G\text{т}.c} / \rho_{0c} * 1000$ = 4,384 * 223,254 * 172 /0,6804*1000 = 247,396 krub/h;

$D_{C.ip.G\text{т}.b.3} = N_{e3} * G\text{т}_{\text{удс}} * C_{G\text{т}.c} / \rho_{0c} * 1000$ = 5,203 * 223,254 * 172 /0,6804*1000 = 293,610 krub/h;

$D_{C.ip.G\text{т}.b.4} = N_{e4} * G\text{т}_{\text{удс}} * C_{G\text{т}.c} / \rho_{0c} * 1000$ = 5,642 * 223,254 * 172 /0,6804*1000 = 318,419 krub/h;

$D_{C.ip.G\text{т}.b.5} = N_{e5} * G\text{т}_{\text{удс}} * C_{G\text{т}.c} / \rho_{0c} * 1000$ = 5,800 * 223,254 * 172 /0,6804*1000 = 327,334 krub/h;

$D_{C.ip.G\text{т}.b.6} = N_{e6} * G\text{т}_{\text{удс}} * C_{G\text{т}.c} / \rho_{0c} * 1000$ = 5,730 * 223,254 * 172 /0,6804*1000 = 323,350 krub/h;

$D_{C.ip.G\text{т}.b.7} = N_{e7} * G\text{т}_{\text{удс}} * C_{G\text{т}.c} / \rho_{0c} * 1000$ = 5,450 * 223,254 * 172 /0,6804*1000 = 307,549 krub/h.

For the compressor speed n_{max} = 5830 rpm.

$D_{C.ip.G\text{т}.b.8} = N_{e8} * G\text{т}_{\text{удс}} * C_{G\text{т}.c} / \rho_{0c} * 1000$ = 13,658 * 223,254 * 172 /0,6804*1000 = 770,813 krub/h;

$D_{C.ip.G\text{т}.b.9} = N_{e9} * G\text{т}_{\text{удс}} * C_{G\text{т}.c} / \rho_{0c} * 1000$ = 17,011 * 223,254 * 172 /0,6804*1000 = 960,012 krub/h;

$D_{C.ip.G\text{т}.b.10} = N_{e10} * G\text{т}_{\text{удс}} * C_{G\text{т}.c} / \rho_{0c} * 1000$ = 20,188 * 223,254 * 172 /0,6804*1000 = 1139,342 krub/h;

$D_{C.ip.G\text{т}.b.11} = N_{e11} * G\text{т}_{\text{удс}} * C_{G\text{т}.c} / \rho_{0c} * 1000$ = 21,894 * 223,254 * 172 /0,6804*1000 = 1235,614 krub/h;

$D_{C.ip.Gт.b.12} = N_{e12} * Gт_{удс} * C_{\mathbf{Gт.c}} / \rho_{0c} * 1000$ = 22,507 * 223,254 * 172 /0,6804*1000 = 1270,210 krub/h;

$D_{C.ip.Gт.b.13} = N_{e13} * Gт_{удс} * C_{\mathbf{Gт.c}} / \rho_{0c} * 1000$ = 22,233 * 223,254 * 172 /0,6804*1000 = 1254,751 krub/h;

$D_{C.ip.Gт.b.14} = N_{e14} * Gт_{удс} * C_{\mathbf{Gт.c}} / \rho_{0c} * 1000$ = 21,147 * 223,254 * 172 /0,6804*1000 = 1193,435 krub/h.

4.2.2. The real total current conditional variable cost of the operation of the **GCU** in the jth point of the $\mathbf{CM_{M.ip.NG.b}}$ in monetary form is calculated by the formula:

$D_{C.ip.Mn.b.j} = D_{C.ip.\mathbf{Gт}.b.j} + D_{C.ip.T.b}$,

in which all magnitudes – see above.

Calculation example:

For the compressor speed n_{min} = 3710 rpm.

$D_{C.ip.Mn.b.1} = D_{C.ip.\mathbf{Gт}.b.1} + D_{C.ip.T.b}$ = 198,639 + 380,909 = 579,549 krub/h;
$D_{C.ip.Mn.b.2} = D_{C.ip.\mathbf{Gт}.b.2} + D_{C.ip.T.b}$ = 247,396 + 380,909 = 628,306 krub/h;
$D_{C.ip.Mn.b.3} = D_{C.ip.\mathbf{Gт}.b.3} + D_{C.ip.T.b}$ = 293,610 + 380,909 = 674,519 krub/h;
$D_{C.ip.Mn.b.4} = D_{C.ip.\mathbf{Gт}.b.4} + D_{C.ip.T.b}$ = 318,419 + 380,909 = 699,329 krub/h;
$D_{C.ip.Mn.b.5} = D_{C.ip.\mathbf{Gт}.b.5} + D_{C.ip.T.b}$ = 327,334 + 380,909 = 708,244 krub/h;
$D_{C.ip.Mn.b.6} = D_{C.ip.\mathbf{Gт}.b.6} + D_{C.ip.T.b}$ = 323,350 + 380,909 = 704,260 krub/h;
$D_{C.ip.Mn.b.7} = D_{C.ip.\mathbf{Gт}.b.7} + D_{C.ip.T.b}$ = 307,549 + 380,909 = 688,459 krub/h.

For the compressor speed n_{max} = 5830 rpm.

$D_{C.ip.Mn.b.8} = D_{C.ip.\mathbf{Gт}.b.8} + D_{C.ip.T.b}$ = 770,813 + 380,909 = 1151,722 krub/h;
$D_{C.ip.Mn.b.9} = D_{C.ip.\mathbf{Gт}.b.9} + D_{C.ip.T.b}$ = 960,012 + 380,909 = 1340,922 krub/h;
$D_{C.ip.Mn.b.10} = D_{C.ip.\mathbf{Gт}.b.10} + D_{C.ip.T.b}$ = 1139,342 + 380,909 = 1520,251 krub/h;
$D_{C.ip.Mn.b.11} = D_{C.ip.\mathbf{Gт}.b.11} + D_{C.ip.T.b}$ = 1235,614 + 380,909 = 1616,524 krub/h;
$D_{C.ip.Mn.b.12} = D_{C.ip.\mathbf{Gт}.b.12} + D_{C.ip.T.b}$ = 1270,210 + 380,909 = 1651,120 krub/h;

$D_{C.ip.Mn.b.13}$ = $D_{C.ip.Gт.b.13}$ + $D_{C.ip.T.b}$ = 1254,751 + 380,909 = 1635,660 krub/h;
$D_{C.ip.Mn.b.14}$ = $D_{C.ip.Gт.b.14}$ + $D_{C.ip.T.b}$ = 1193,435 + 380,909 = 1574,344 krub/h.

The magnitudes of the $\mathbf{D_{C.ip.Mn.b.j}}$ for the other lines bounding the **GCU's $\mathbf{CM_{M.ip.NG.b}}$**, is calculated similar including: for lines n_{min} = const, n_{max} = const, $P_{кmax}$ = const, $q_{кс}$ = max, $q_{кс}$ = min, N_{emax} = const, $T_{кmax}$ = const, as well as for the $\mathbf{WP_c}$ point. These calculations are not shown here to reduce the scope of the description.

$\mathbf{NM_{C.ip.Mn.b}}$ of the first type are built on the results of calculations – see Fig. RPM 13 which is used for further calculation of the corresponding **Indexed noologistical areas of possible operating modes ($\mathbf{RPM_{C.ip.Mn.b}}$)**.

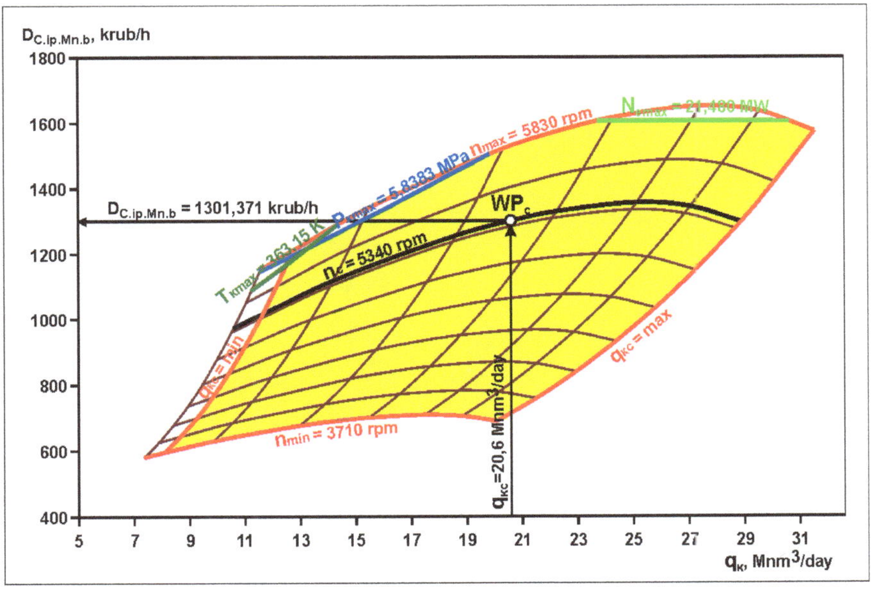

Fig. RPM 13

Calculated $\mathbf{NM_{C.ip.Mn.b}}$ of the first type, painted yellow on Fig. RPM 13, mathematically links **the density of current flow ($\mathbf{F_{M.ip.NG.b}}$) of the current noologistical value ($\mathbf{V_{M.ip.NG.b}}$)**, that is the $\mathbf{q_к}$ of pumped gas in Mnm^3/day, and **the density of the current conditional variable**

consumption flow ($F_{C.ip.Mn.b}$) of the current noologistical value ($V_{C.ip.Mn.b}$), that is its $D_{C.ip.Mn.b}$ which is expressed in krub/h.

4.2.3. The real current conditional fixed cost, which is amortized on the functioning of **GCU** in the jth point of the $CM_{M.ip.NG.b}$ in monetary form is calculated by the formula

$FD_{C.ip.Mn.b} = FQ_{GCU} / 365 * 24 * T_{Ac} = 134428 / 365 * 24 * 6 = 2,558$ krub/h,

in which all magnitudes – see above.

4.2.4. The real total current cost at the jth point of the $CM_{M.ip.NG.b}$ in monetary form is calculated by the formula:

$TD_{C.ip.Mn.b.j} = D_{C.ip.Mn.b.j} + FD_{C.ip.Mn.b}$,

in which all magnitudes – see above.

Calculation example:

For the compressor speed $n_{min} = 3710$ rpm.

$TD_{C.ip.Mn.b.1} = D_{C.ip.Mn.b.1} + FD_{C.ip.Mn.b} = 579,549 + 2,558 = 582.106$ krub/h;
$TD_{C.ip.Mn.b.2} = D_{C.ip.Mn.b.2} + FD_{C.ip.Mn.b} = 628,306 + 2,558 = 630.863$ krub/h;
$TD_{C.ip.Mn.b.3} = D_{C.ip.Mn.b.3} + FD_{C.ip.Mn.b} = 674,519 + 2,558 = 677.077$ krub/h;
$TD_{C.ip.Mn.b.4} = D_{C.ip.Mn.b.4} + FD_{C.ip.Mn.b} = 699,329 + 2,558 = 701.886$ krub/h;
$TD_{C.ip.Mn.b.5} = D_{C.ip.Mn.b.5} + FD_{C.ip.Mn.b} = 708,244 + 2,558 = 710.802$ krub/h;
$TD_{C.ip.Mn.b.6} = D_{C.ip.Mn.b.6} + FD_{C.ip.Mn.b} = 704,260 + 2,558 = 706.818$ krub/h;
$TD_{C.ip.Mn.b.7} = D_{C.ip.Mn.b.7} + FD_{C.ip.Mn.b} = 688,459 + 2,558 = 691.016$ krub/h.

For the compressor speed $n_{max} = 5830$ rpm.

$TD_{C.ip.Mn.b.8} = D_{C.ip.Mn.b.8} + FD_{C.ip.Mn.b} = 1151,722 + 2,558 = 1154.280$ krub/h;
$TD_{C.ip.Mn.b.9} = D_{C.ip.Mn.b.9} + FD_{C.ip.Mn.b} = 1340,922 + 2,558 = 1343.479$ krub/h;
$TD_{C.ip.Mn.b.10} = D_{C.ip.Mn.b.10} + FD_{C.ip.Mn.b} = 1520,251 + 2,558 = 1522.809$ krub/h;

$TD_{C.ip.Mn.b.11} = D_{C.ip.Mn.b.11} + FD_{C.ip.Mn.b} = 1616{,}524 + 2{,}558 = 1619.081$ krub/h;

$TD_{C.ip.Mn.b.12} = D_{C.ip.Mn.b.12} + FD_{C.ip.Mn.b} = 1651{,}120 + 2{,}558 = 1653.677$ krub/h;

$TD_{C.ip.Mn.b.13} = D_{C.ip.Mn.b.13} + FD_{C.ip.Mn.b} = 1635{,}660 + 2{,}558 = 1638.218$ krub/h;

$TD_{C.ip.Mn.b.14} = D_{C.ip.Mn.b.14} + FD_{C.ip.Mn.b} = 1574{,}344 + 2{,}558 = 1576.902$ krub/h.

The magnitudes of the $\mathbf{TD_{C.ip.Mn.b.j}}$ for the other lines bounding the **GCU's** $\mathbf{CM_{M.ip.NG.b}}$, is calculated similar including: for lines n_{min} = const, n_{max} = const, $P_{кmax}$ = const, $q_{кс}$ = max, $q_{кс}$ = min, N_{emax} = const, $T_{кmax}$ = const, as well as for the $\mathbf{WP_c}$ point. These calculations are not shown here to reduce the scope of the description.

$\mathbf{NM_{C.ip.Mn.b}}$ of the second type are built on the results of calculations – see Fig. RPM 14 which is used for further calculation of the corresponding **Indexed noological areas of possible operating modes** ($\mathbf{RPM_{C.ip.Mn.b}}$).

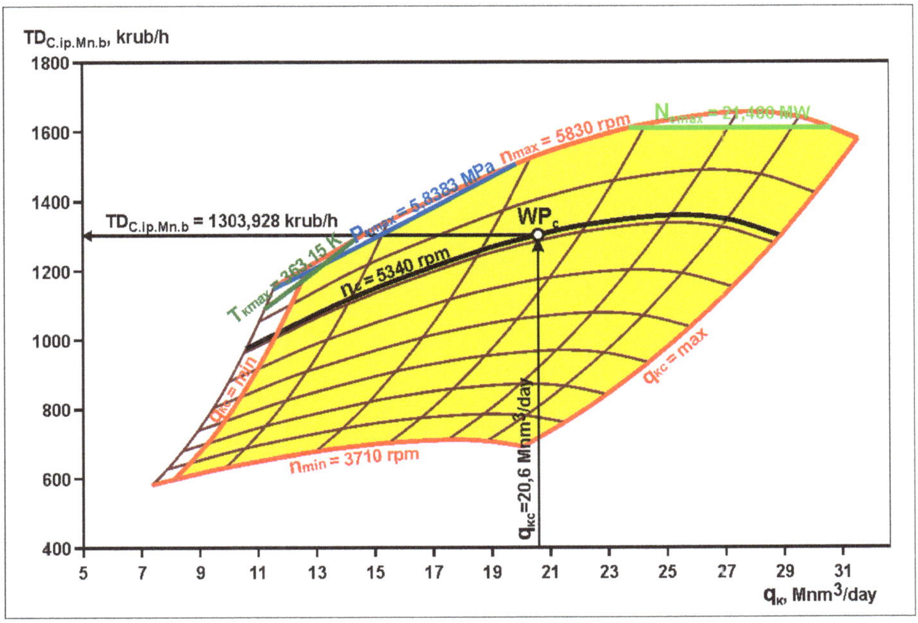

Fig. RPM 14

Calculated $\mathbf{NM_{C.ip.Mn.b}}$ of the second type, painted yellow on Fig. RPM 14, mathematically links **the density of current flow ($\mathbf{F_{M.ip.NG.b}}$) of the current noologistical value ($\mathbf{V_{M.ip.NG.b}}$)**, that is the $\mathbf{q_к}$ of pumped gas in Mnm^3/day, and **the density of the current total consumption flow ($\mathbf{TF_{C.ip.Mn.b}}$) of the current noologistical value ($\mathbf{V_{C.ip.Mn.b}}$)**, that is its $\mathbf{TD_{C.ip.Mn.b}}$ which is expressed in krub/h.

4.3. The calculation of **the $\mathbf{NM_{S.ip.CO2.b}}$**.

4.3.1. The current conditional variable CO_2 emission at the jth point of $\mathbf{CM_{M.ip.NG.b}}$ is calculated by formula:

$D_{S.ip.\mathbf{Gт}.b.j} = N_{ej} * Gт_{удс} * E_{\mathbf{CO2.c}}/1000,$

in which all magnitudes – see above.

Calculation example:

For the compressor speed n_{min} = 3710 rpm.

$D_{S.ip.Gт.b.1} = N_{e1} * Gт_{удс} * E_{\mathbf{CO2.c}}$ = 3,520 * 223,254 * 2,5547/1000 = 2,007 T/h;

$D_{S.ip.Gт.b.2} = N_{e2} * Gт_{удс} * E_{\mathbf{CO2.c}}$ = 4,384 * 223,254 * 2,5547/1000 = 2,500 T/h;

$D_{S.ip.Gт.b.3} = N_{e3} * Gт_{удс} * E_{\mathbf{CO2.c}}$ = 5,203 * 223,254 * 2,5547/1000 = 2,967 T/h;

$D_{S.ip.Gт.b.4} = N_{e4} * Gт_{удс} * E_{\mathbf{CO2.c}}$ = 5,642 * 223,254 * 2,5547/1000 = 3,218 T/h;

$D_{S.ip.Gт.b.5} = N_{e5} * Gт_{удс} * E_{\mathbf{CO2.c}}$ = 5,800 * 223,254 * 2,5547/1000 = 3,308 T/h;

$D_{S.ip.Gт.b.6} = N_{e6} * Gт_{удс} * E_{\mathbf{CO2.c}}$ = 5,730 * 223,254 * 2,5547/1000 = 3,268 T/h;

$D_{S.ip.Gт.b.7} = N_{e7} * Gт_{удс} * E_{\mathbf{CO2.c}}$ = 5,450 * 223,254 * 2,5547/1000 = 3,108 T/h.

For the compressor speed n_{max} = 5830 rpm.

$D_{S.ip.Gт.b.8} = N_{e8} * Gт_{удс} * E_{\mathbf{CO2.c}}$ = 13,658 * 223,254 * 2,5547/1000 = 7,790 T/h;

$D_{S.ip.Gт.b.9} = N_{e9} * Gт_{удс} * E_{CO2.c} = 17{,}011 * 223{,}254 * 2{,}5547/1000 = 9{,}702$ T/h;

$D_{S.ip.Gт.b.10} = N_{e10} * Gт_{удс} * E_{CO2.c} = 20{,}188 * 223{,}254 * 2{,}5547/1000 = 11{,}514$ T/h;

$D_{S.ip.Gт.b.11} = N_{e11} * Gт_{удс} * E_{CO2.c} = 21{,}894 * 223{,}254 * 2{,}5547/1000 = 12{,}487$ T/h;

$D_{S.ip.Gт.b.12} = N_{e12} * Gт_{удс} * E_{CO2.c} = 22{,}507 * 223{,}254 * 2{,}5547/1000 = 12{,}837$ T/h;

$D_{S.ip.Gт.b.13} = N_{e13} * Gт_{удс} * E_{CO2.c\ c} = 22{,}233 * 223{,}254 * 2{,}5547/1000 = 12{,}681$ T/h;

$D_{S.ip.Gт.b.14} = N_{e14} * Gт_{удс} * E_{CO2.c} = 21{,}147 * 223{,}254 * 2{,}5547/1000 = 12{,}061$ T/h.

4.3.2. The real total current conditional variable CO_2 emission in the operation of the **GCU** in the jth point of $\mathbf{CM_{M.ip.NG.b}}$ is calculated by formula:

$$D_{S.ip.CO2.b.j} = D_{S.ip.Gт.b.j} + E_{S.ip.T.b}/1000,$$

in which all magnitudes – see above.

Calculation example:

For the compressor speed $n_{min} = 3710$ rpm.

$D_{S.ip.CO2.b.1} = D_{S.ip.Gт.b.1} + E_{S.ip.T.b}/1000 = 2{,}007 + 4{,}198/1000 = 2{,}012$ T/h;
$D_{S.ip.CO2.b.2} = D_{S.ip.Gт.b.2} + E_{S.ip.T.b}/1000 = 2{,}500 + 4{,}198/1000 = 2{,}504$ T/h;
$D_{S.ip.CO2.b.3} = D_{S.ip.Gт.b.3} + E_{S.ip.T.b}/1000 = 2{,}967 + 4{,}198/1000 = 2{,}971$ T/h;
$D_{S.ip.CO2.b.4} = D_{S.ip.Gт.b.4} + E_{S.ip.T.b}/1000 = 3{,}218 + 4{,}198/1000 = 3{,}222$ T/h;
$D_{S.ip.CO2.b.5} = D_{S.ip.Gт.b.5} + E_{S.ip.T.b}/1000 = 3{,}308 + 4{,}198/1000 = 3{,}312$ T/h;
$D_{S.ip.CO2.b.6} = D_{S.ip.Gт.b.6} + E_{S.ip.T.b}/1000 = 3{,}268 + 4{,}198/1000 = 3{,}272$ T/h;
$D_{S.ip.CO2.b.7} = D_{S.ip.Gт.b.7} + E_{S.ip.T.b}/1000 = 3{,}108 + 4{,}198/1000 = 3{,}112$ T/h.

For the compressor speed $n_{max} = 5830$ rpm.

$D_{S.ip.CO2.b.8} = D_{S.ip.Gт.b.8} + E_{S.ip.T.b}/1000 = 7{,}790 + 4{,}198/1000 = 7{,}794$ T/h;
$D_{S.ip.CO2.b.9} = D_{S.ip.Gт.b.9} + E_{S.ip.T.b}/1000 = 9{,}702 + 4{,}198/1000 = 9{,}706$ T/h;
$D_{S.ip.CO2.b.10} = D_{S.ip.Gт.b.10} + E_{S.ip.T.b}/1000 = 11{,}514 + 4{,}198/1000 = 11{,}519$ T/h;

$D_{S.ip.CO2.b.11} = D_{S.ip.\mathbf{G}T.b.11} + E_{S.ip.T.b}/1000 = 12{,}487 + 4{,}198/1000 = 12{,}491$ T/h;

$D_{S.ip.CO2.b.12} = D_{S.ip.\mathbf{G}T.b.12} + E_{S.ip.T.b}/1000 = 12{,}837 + 4{,}198/1000 = 12{,}841$ T/h;

$D_{S.ip.CO2.b.13} = D_{S.ip.\mathbf{G}T.b.13} + E_{S.ip.T.b}/1000 = 12{,}681 + 4{,}198/1000 = 12{,}685$ T/h;

$D_{S.ip.CO2.b.14} = D_{S.ip.\mathbf{G}T.b.14} + E_{S.ip.T.b}/1000 = 12{,}061 + 4{,}198/1000 = 12{,}065$ T/h.

The magnitudes of the $D_{S.ip.\mathbf{G}T.b.j}$ for the other lines bounding the **GCU's CM$_{M.ip.NG.b}$**, is calculated similar including: for lines n_{min} = const, n_{max} = const, $P_{\kappa max}$ = const, $q_{\kappa c}$ = max, $q_{\kappa c}$ = min, N_{emax} = const, $T_{\kappa max}$ = const, as well as for the **WP$_c$** point. These calculations are not shown here to reduce the scope of the description.

NM$_{S.ip.CO2.b}$ of the first type are built on the results of calculations – see Fig. RPM 15 which is used for further calculation of the corresponding **Indexed noologistical areas of possible operating modes (RPM$_{S.ip.CO2.b}$)**.

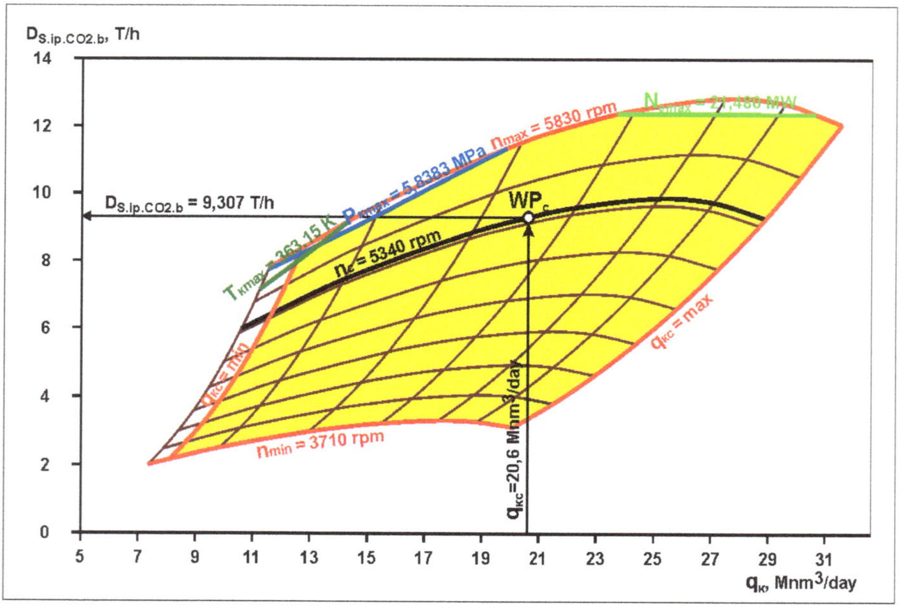

Fig. RPM 15

Calculated **NM$_{S.ip.CO2.b}$** of the first type, painted yellow on Fig. RPM 15, mathematically links **the density of current flow (F$_{M.ip.NG.b}$) of**

the current noological value ($V_{M.ip.NG.b}$), that is the **$q_к$** of pumped gas in Mnm^3/day, and **the density of the current conditional variable emission flow ($F_{S.ip.CO2.b}$) of the current noological value ($V_{S.ip.CO2.b}$)**, that is its **$D_{S.ip.CO2.b}$** which is expressed in T/h.

4.3.3. The real current conditional fixed CO_2 emission, which is amortized on the functioning of **GCU** in the jth point of the **$CM_{M.ip.NG.b}$** in form T/h is calculated by the formula:

$FD_{S.ip.CO2.b} = FQ_{CO2} / 365 * 24 * T_{Ac} = 258273 / 365 * 24 * 6 = 4{,}914$ kg/ч,

in which all magnitudes – see above.

4.3.4. The real total CO_2 emission at the jth point of the **$CM_{M.ip.NG.b}$** is calculated by the formula:

$TD_{S.ip.CO2.b.j} = D_{S.ip.CO2.b.j} + FD_{S.ip.CO2.b}/1000$,

in which all magnitudes – see above.

Calculation example:

For the compressor speed n_{min} = 3710 rpm.

$TD_{S.ip.CO2.b.1} = D_{S.ip.CO2.b.1} + FD_{S.ip.CO2.b}/1000 = 2{,}012 + 4{,}914/1000 = 2{,}017$ T/h;
$TD_{S.ip.CO2.b.2} = D_{S.ip.CO2.b.2} + FD_{S.ip.CO2.b}/1000 = 2{,}504 + 4{,}914/1000 = 2{,}509$ T/h;
$TD_{S.ip.CO2.b.3} = D_{S.ip.CO2.b.3} + FD_{S.ip.CO2.b}/1000 = 2{,}971 + 4{,}914/1000 = 2{,}976$ T/h;
$TD_{S.ip.CO2.b.4} = D_{S.ip.CO2.b.4} + FD_{S.ip.CO2.b}/1000 = 3{,}222 + 4{,}914/1000 = 3{,}227$ T/h;
$TD_{S.ip.CO2.b.5} = D_{S.ip.CO2.b.5} + FD_{S.ip.CO2.b}/1000 = 3{,}312 + 4{,}914/1000 = 3{,}317$ T/h;
$TD_{S.ip.CO2.b.6} = D_{S.ip.CO2.b.6} + FD_{S.ip.CO2.b}/1000 = 3{,}272 + 4{,}914/1000 = 3{,}277$ T/h;
$TD_{S.ip.CO2.b.7} = D_{S.ip.CO2.b.7} + FD_{S.ip.CO2.b}/1000 = 3{,}112 + 4{,}914/1000 = 3{,}117$ T/h.

For the compressor speed n_{max} = 5830 rpm.

$TD_{S.ip.CO2.b.8} = D_{S.ip.CO2.b.8} + FD_{S.ip.CO2.b}/1000 = 7{,}794 + 4{,}914/1000 = 7{,}799$ T/h;

$TD_{S.ip.CO2.b.9} = D_{S.ip.CO2.b.9} + FD_{S.ip.CO2.b}/1000 = 9{,}706 + 4{,}914/1000 = 9{,}711$ T/h;

$TD_{S.ip.CO2.b.10} = D_{S.ip.CO2.b.10} + FD_{S.ip.CO2.b}/1000 = 11{,}519 + 4{,}914/1000 = 11{,}523$ T/h;

$TD_{S.ip.CO2.b.11} = D_{S.ip.CO2.b.11} + FD_{S.ip.CO2.b}/1000 = 12{,}491 + 4{,}914/1000 = 12{,}496$ T/h;

$TD_{S.ip.CO2.b.12} = D_{S.ip.CO2.b.12} + FD_{S.ip.CO2.b}/1000 = 12{,}841 + 4{,}914/1000 = 12{,}846$ T/h;

$TD_{S.ip.CO2.b.13} = D_{S.ip.CO2.b.13} + FD_{S.ip.CO2.b}/1000 = 12{,}685 + 4{,}914/1000 = 12{,}690$ T/h;

$TD_{S.ip.CO2.b.14} = D_{S.ip.CO2.b.14} + FD_{S.ip.CO2.b}/1000 = 12{,}065 + 4{,}914/1000 = 12{,}070$ T/h.

The magnitudes of the $TD_{S.ip.CO2.b.j}$ for the other lines bounding the **GCU's $CM_{M.ip.NG.b}$**, is calculated similar including: for lines n_{min} = const, n_{max} = const, $P_{кmax}$ = const, $q_{кс}$ = max, $q_{кс}$ = min, N_{emax} = const, $T_{кmax}$ = const, as well as for the **WP_c** point. These calculations are not shown here to reduce the scope of the description.

$NM_{S.ip.CO2.b}$ of the second type are built on the results of calculations – see Fig. RPM 16 which is used for further calculation of the corresponding **Indexed noologistical areas of possible operating modes** (**$RPM_{S.ip.CO2.b}$**).

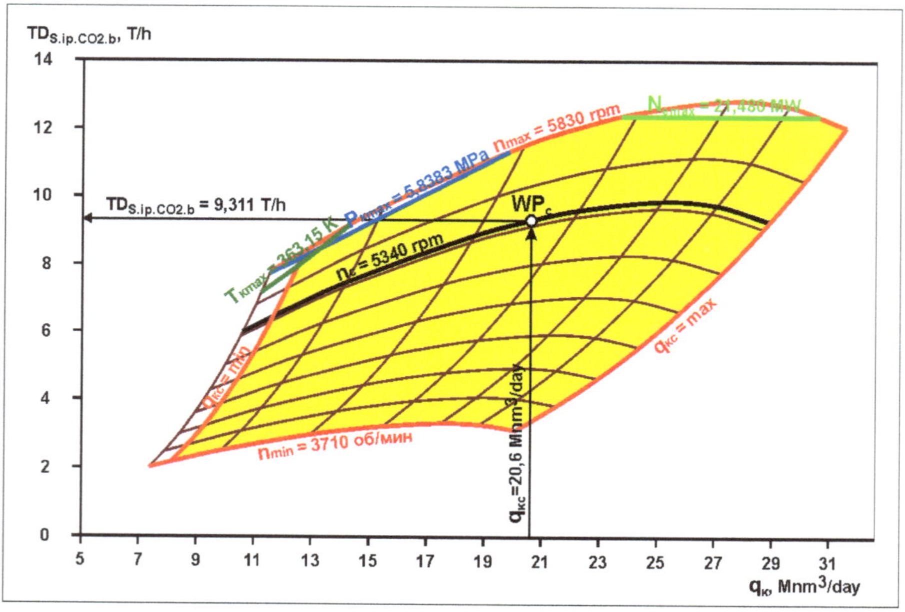

Fig. RPM 16

Calculated $\mathbf{NM_{S.ip.CO2.b}}$ of the second type, painted yellow on Fig. RPM 16, mathematically links **the density of current flow ($\mathbf{F_{M.ip.NG.b}}$) of the current noologistical value ($\mathbf{V_{M.ip.NG.b}}$)**, that is the $\mathbf{q_к}$ of pumped gas in Mnm^3/day, and **the density of the current total emission flow ($\mathbf{TF_{S.ip.CO2.b}}$) of the current noologistical value ($\mathbf{V_{S.ip.Mn.b}}$)**, that is its $\mathbf{TD_{S.ip.CO2.b}}$ which is expressed in T/h.

5. The calculation of **the current noologistical areas of the possible operating modes to specific parameters** (briefly – $\mathbf{NM_{C.ip.Vth.b}}$, $\mathbf{NM_{C.ip.Mn.b}}$ and $\mathbf{NM_{S.ip.CO2.b}}$).

5.1. The current specific energy consumption for **GCU** operation in the jth of the $\mathbf{NM_{C.ip.Vth.b}}$ (see Fig. RPM 11) is calculated by the formula:

$SD_{C.ip.Vth.b.j} = D_{C.ip.Vth.b.j} *24*3600/1000*q_{кcj}$ kJ/nm^3,

in which all magnitudes – see above.

Calculation example:

For the compressor speed n_{min} = 3710 rpm.

$SD_{C.ip.Vth.b.1} = D_{C.ip.Vth.b.1}*24*3600/1000*q_{кc1}$ = 10,854*24*3600/1000*7,362 = 127,385 kJ/nm^3;
$SD_{C.ip.Vth.b.2} = D_{C.ip.Vth.b.2}*24*3600/1000*q_{кc2}$ = 13,518*24*3600/1000*9,851 = 118,560 kJ/nm^3;
$SD_{C.ip.Vth.b.3} = D_{C.ip.Vth.b.3}*24*3600/1000*q_{кc3}$ = 16,044*24*3600/1000*12,945 = 107,080 kJ/nm^3;
$SD_{C.ip.Vth.b.4} = D_{C.ip.Vth.b.4}*24*3600/1000*q_{кc4}$ = 17,399*24*3600/1000*15,464 = 97,212 kJ/nm^3;
$SD_{C.ip.Vth.b.5} = D_{C.ip.Vth.b.5}*24*3600/1000*q_{кc5}$ = 17,886*24*3600/1000*17.471 = 88,451 kJ/nm^3;
$SD_{C.ip.Vth.b.6} = D_{C.ip.Vth.b.6}*24*3600/1000*q_{кc6}$ = 17,669*24*3600/1000*18,809 = 81,160 kJ/nm^3;
$SD_{C.ip.Vth.b.7} = D_{C.ip.Vth.b.7}*24*3600/1000*q_{кc7}$ = 16,805*24*3600/1000*20,082 = 72,303 kJ/nm^3.

For the compressor speed n_{max} = 5830 rpm.

$SD_{C.ip.Vth.b.8} = D_{C.ip.Vth.b.8}*24*3600/1000*q_{кc8}$ = 42,118*24*3600/1000*11,569 = 314,549 kJ/nm^3;

$SD_{C.ip.Vth.b.9} = D_{C.ip.Vth.b.9}*24*3600/1000*q_{\kappa c9} = 52{,}456*24*3600/1000*15{,}481 = 292{,}760$ kJ/nm^3;

$SD_{C.ip.Vth.b.10} = D_{C.ip.Vth.b.10}*24*3600/1000*q_{\kappa c10} = 62{,}255*24*3600/1000*20{,}342 = 264{,}414$ kJ/nm^3;

$SD_{C.ip.Vth.b.11} = D_{C.ip.Vth.b.11}*24*3600/1000*q_{\kappa c11} = 67{,}511*24*3600/1000*24{,}300 = 240{,}049$ kJ/nm^3;

$SD_{C.ip.Vth.b.12} = D_{C.ip.Vth.b.12}*24*3600/1000*q_{\kappa c12} = 69{,}405*24*3600/1000*27{,}455 = 218{,}414$ kJ/nm^3;

$SD_{C.ip.Vth.b.13} = D_{C.ip.Vth.b.13}*24*3600/1000*q_{\kappa c13} = 68{,}560*24*3600/1000*29{,}557 = 200{,}411$ kJ/nm^3;

$SD_{C.ip.Vth.b.14} = D_{C.ip.Vth.b.14}*24*3600/1000*q_{\kappa c14} = 65{,}210*24*3600/1000*31{,}557 = 178{,}539$ kJ/nm^3.

The magnitudes of the $\mathbf{SD_{C.ip.Vth.b.j}}$ for the other lines bounding the **GCU's** $\mathbf{NM_{C.ip.Vth.b}}$, is calculated similar including: for lines n_{min} = const, n_{max} = const, $P_{\kappa max}$ = const, $q_{\kappa c}$ = max, $q_{\kappa c}$ = min, N_{emax} = const, $T_{\kappa max}$ = const, as well as for the $\mathbf{WP_c}$ point. These calculations are not shown here to reduce the scope of the description.

$\mathbf{NS_{C.ip.Vth.b}}$ of the first type are built on the results of calculations – see Fig. RPM 17 which is used for further calculation of the corresponding **Indexed noologistical areas of possible operating modes** ($\mathbf{RPM_{C.ip.Vth.b}}$).

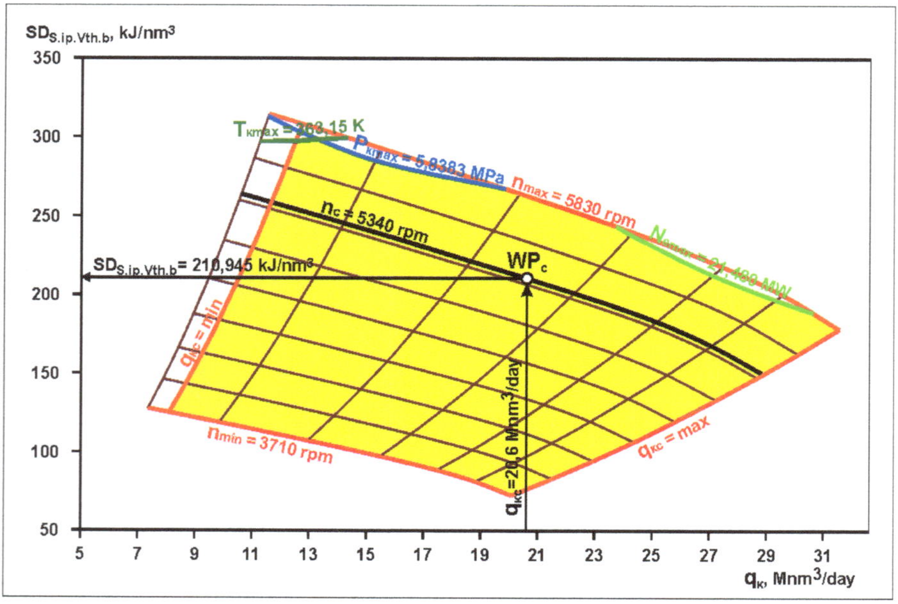

Fig. RPM 17

Calculated $\mathbf{NS_{C.ip.Vth.b}}$ of the first type, painted yellow on Fig. RPM 17, mathematically links **the density of current flow ($\mathbf{F_{M.ip.NG.b}}$) of the current noologistical value ($\mathbf{V_{M.ip.NG.b}}$)**, that is the $\mathbf{q_к}$ of pumped gas in Mnm³/day, and **the specified density of the current conditional variable consumption flow ($\mathbf{F_{C.ip.Vth.b}}$) of the current noologistical value ($\mathbf{V_{C.ip.Vth.b}}$)**, that is its $\mathbf{SD_{C.ip.Vth.b}}$ which is expressed in kJ/nm³.

5.2. **The current specific total energy consumption** for **GCU** operation in the jth of the $\mathbf{NM_{C.ip.Vth.b}}$ (see Fig. RPM 12) is calculated by the formula:

$$STD_{C.ip.Vth.b.j} = TD_{C.ip.Vth.b.j} *24*3600/1000*q_{кcj} \text{ kJ/nm}^3,$$

in which all magnitudes – see above.

Calculation example:

For the compressor speed n_{max} = 3710 rpm.

$STD_{C.ip.Vth.b.1} = TD_{C.ip.Vth.b.1}*24*3600/1000*q_{кc1}$ = 11,215*24*3600/1000*7.362 = 131,621 kJ/nm³;
$STD_{C.ip.Vth.b.2} = TD_{C.ip.Vth.b.2}*24*3600/1000*q_{кc2}$ = 13,879*24*3600/1000*9.851 = 121,726 kJ/nm³;
$STD_{C.ip.Vth.b.3} = TD_{C.ip.Vth.b.3}*24*3600/1000*q_{кc3}$ = 16,405*24*3600/1000*12.945 = 109,489 kJ/nm³;
$STD_{C.ip.Vth.b.4} = TD_{C.ip.Vth.b.4}*24*3600/1000*q_{кc4}$ = 17,760*24*3600/1000*15.464 = 99,229 kJ/nm³;
$STD_{C.ip.Vth.b.5} = TD_{C.ip.Vth.b.5}*24*3600/1000*q_{кc5}$ = 18,247*24*3600/1000*17.471 = 90,236 kJ/nm³;
$STD_{C.ip.Vth.b.6} = TD_{C.ip.Vth.b.6}*24*3600/1000*q_{кc6}$ = 18,030*24*3600/1000*18.809 = 90,236 kJ/nm³;
$STD_{C.ip.Vth.b.7} = TD_{C.ip.Vth.b.7}*24*3600/1000*q_{кc7}$ = 17.166*24*3600/1000*20.082 = 73,856 kJ/nm³.

For the compressor speed n_{max} = 5830 rpm.

$STD_{C.ip.Vth.b.8} = TD_{C.ip.Vth.b.8}*24*3600/1000*q_{кc8}$ = 42,479*24*3600/1000*11.569 = 317,245 kJ/nm³;

$STD_{C.ip.Vth.b.9} = TD_{C.ip.Vth.b.9}*24*3600/1000*q_{кс9} = 52{,}817*24*3600/1000*15.481 = 294{,}774$ kJ/nm^3;

$STD_{C.ip.Vth.b.10} = TD_{C.ip.Vth.b.10}*24*3600/1000*q_{кс10} = 62{,}616*24*3600/1000*20.342 = 265{,}947$ kJ/nm^3;

$STD_{C.ip.Vth.b.11} = TD_{C.ip.Vth.b.11}*24*3600/1000*q_{кс11} = 67{,}876*24*3600/1000*24.300 = 241{,}332$ kJ/nm^3;

$STD_{C.ip.Vth.b.12} = TD_{C.ip.Vth.b.12}*24*3600/1000*q_{кс12} = 69{,}766*24*3600/1000*27.455 = 219{,}550$ kJ/nm^3;

$STD_{C.ip.Vth.b.13} = TD_{C.ip.Vth.b.13}*24*3600/1000*q_{кс13} = 68{,}921*24*3600/1000*29.557 = 201{,}466$ kJ/nm^3;

$STD_{C.ip.Vth.b.14} = TD_{C.ip.Vth.b.14}*24*3600/1000*q_{кс14} = 65{,}571*24*3600/1000*31.557 = 179{,}527$ kJ/nm^3.

The magnitudes of the **$STD_{C.ip.Vth.b.j}$** for the other lines bounding the **GCU's $NM_{C.ip.Vth.b}$**, is calculated similar including: for lines n_{min} = const, n_{max} = const, $P_{кmax}$ = const, $q_{кс}$ = max, $q_{кс}$ = min, N_{emax} = const, $T_{кmax}$ = const, as well as for the **WP_c** point. These calculations are not shown here to reduce the scope of the description.

$NS_{C.ip.Vth.b}$ of the second type are built on the results of calculations – see Fig. RPM 18 which is used for further calculation of the corresponding **Indexed noologistical areas of possible operating modes ($RPM_{C.ip.Vth.b}$)**.

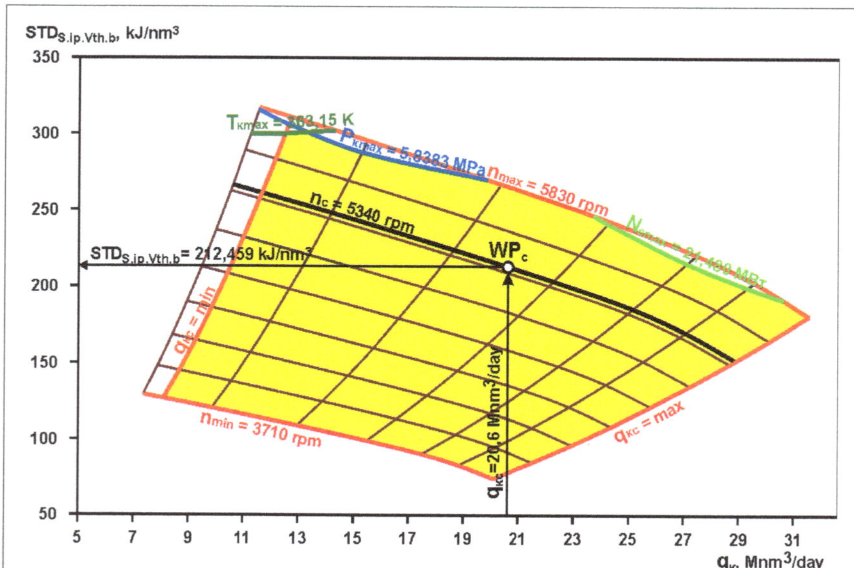

Fig. RPM 18

Calculated $\mathbf{NS_{C.ip.Vth.b}}$ of the second type, painted yellow on Fig. RPM 18, mathematically links **the density of current flow ($\mathbf{F_{M.ip.NG.b}}$) of the current noologistical value ($\mathbf{V_{M.ip.NG.b}}$)**, that is the $\mathbf{q_к}$ of pumped gas in Mnm³/day, and **the specified density of the current total consumption flow ($\mathbf{TF_{C.ip.Vth.b}}$) of the current noologistical value ($\mathbf{V_{C.ip.Vth.b}}$)**, that is its $\mathbf{STD_{C.ip.Vth.b}}$ which is expressed in kJ/nm³.

5.3. The current specific conditional variable cost on the functioning of the **GCU** (current conditionally variable part of the cost of pumping one m³) in the jth point of the $\mathbf{NM_{C.ip.Mn.b}}$ (see Fig. RPM 13) in monetary form is calculated by the formula:

$$SD_{C.ip.Mn.b.j} = D_{C.ip.Mn.b.j}*24*1000/1000000*q_{кcj} \text{ rub/nm}^3,$$

in which all magnitudes – see above.

Calculation example:

For the compressor speed n_{min} = 3710 rpm.

$SD_{C.ip.Mn.b.1} = D_{C.ip.Mn.b.1}*24*1000/1000000*q_{кc1} = 579{,}549*24*1000/1000000*7{,}362 = 1{,}8893$ rub/nm³;
$SD_{C.ip.Mn.b.2} = D_{C.ip.Mn.b.2}*24*1000/1000000*q_{кc2} = 628{,}306*24*1000/1000000*9{,}851 = 1{,}5307$ rub/nm³;
$SD_{C.ip.Mn.b.3} = D_{C.ip.Mn.b.3}*24*1000/1000000*q_{кc3} = 674{,}519*24*1000/1000000*12{,}945 = 1{,}2505$ rub/nm³;
$SD_{C.ip.Mn.b.4} = D_{C.ip.Mn.b.4}*24*1000/1000000*q_{кc4} = 699{,}329*24*1000/1000000*15{,}464 = 1{,}0854$ rub/nm³;
$SD_{C.ip.Mn.b.5} = D_{C.ip.Mn.b.5}*24*1000/1000000*q_{кc5} = 708{,}244*24*1000/1000000*17.471 = 0{,}9729$ rub/nm³;
$SD_{C.ip.Mn.b.6} = D_{C.ip.Mn.b.6}*24*1000/1000000*q_{кc6} = 704{,}260*24*1000/1000000*18{,}809 = 0{,}8986$ rub/nm³;
$SD_{C.ip.Mn.b.7} = D_{C.ip.Mn.b.7}*24*1000/1000000*q_{кc7} = 688{,}459*24*1000/1000000*20{,}082 = 0{,}8228$ rub/nm³.

For the compressor speed n_{max} = 5830 rpm.

$SD_{C.ip.Mn.b.8} = D_{C.ip.Mn.b.8}*24*1000/1000000*q_{кc8} = 1151{,}722*24*1000/1000000*11{,}569 = 2{,}3893$ rub/nm³;

$SD_{C.ip.Mn.b.9} = D_{C.ip.Mn.b.9}*24*1000/1000000*q_{кс9} = 1340,922*24*1000/1000000*15,481 = 2,0788$ rub/nm³;

$SD_{C.ip.Mn.b.10} = D_{C.ip.Mn.b.10}*24*1000/1000000*q_{кс10} = 1520,251*24*1000/1000000*20,342 = 1,7936$ rub/nm³;

$SD_{C.ip.Mn.b.11} = D_{C.ip.Mn.b.11}*24*1000/1000000*q_{кс11} = 1616,524*24*1000/1000000*24,300 = 1,5965$ rub/nm³;

$SD_{C.ip.Mn.b.12} = D_{C.ip.Mn.b.12}*24*1000/1000000*q_{кс12} = 1651,120*24*1000/1000000*27,455 = 1,4433$ rub/nm³;

$SD_{C.ip.Mn.b.13} = D_{C.ip.Mn.b.13}*24*1000/1000000*q_{кс13} = 1635,660*24*1000/1000000*29,557 = 1,3281$ rub/nm³;

$SD_{C.ip.Mn.b.14} = D_{C.ip.Mn.b.14}*24*1000/1000000*q_{кс14} = 1574,344*24*1000/1000000*31,557 = 1,1973$ rub/nm³.

The magnitudes of the $\mathbf{SD_{C.ip.Mn.b.j}}$ for the other lines bounding the **GCU's** $\mathbf{NM_{C.ip.Mn.b}}$, is calculated similar including: for lines n_{min} = const, n_{max} = const, $P_{кmax}$ = const, $q_{кс}$ = max, $q_{кс}$ = min, N_{emax} = const, $T_{кmax}$ = const, as well as for the $\mathbf{WP_c}$ point. These calculations are not shown here to reduce the scope of the description.

$\mathbf{NS_{C.ip.Mn.b}}$ of the first type are built on the results of calculations – see Fig. RPM 19 which is used for further calculation of the corresponding **Indexed noologistical areas of possible operating modes** ($\mathbf{RPM_{C.ip.Mn.b}}$).

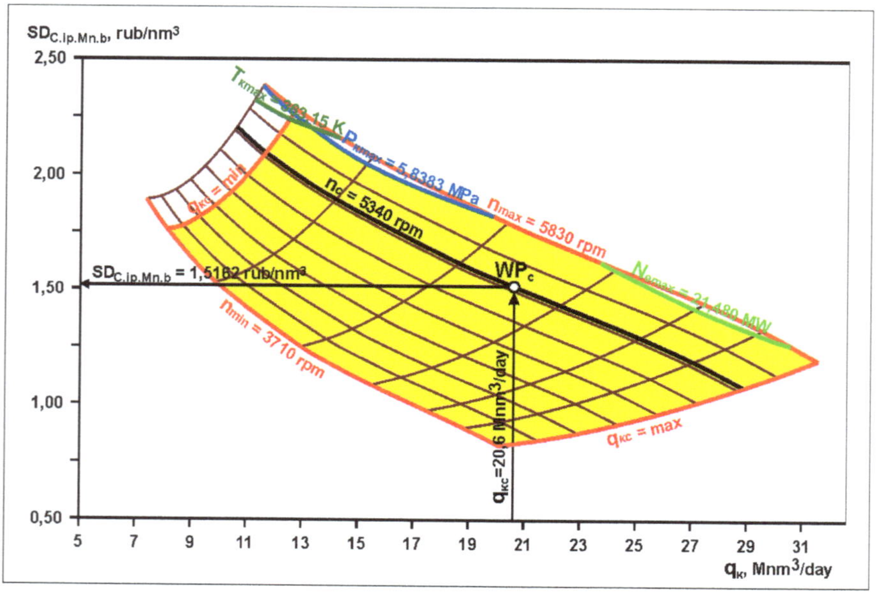

Fig. RPM 19

Calculated **$NS_{C.ip.Mn.b}$** of the first type, **painted** yellow on Fig. RPM 19, mathematically links **the density of current flow ($F_{M.ip.NG.b}$) of the current noologistical value ($V_{M.ip.NG.b}$)**, that is the **$q_к$** of pumped gas in Mnm^3/day, and **the specified density of the current conditional variable consumption flow ($F_{C.ip.Mn.b}$) of the current noologistical value ($V_{C.ip.Mn.b}$)**, that is its **$SD_{C.ip.Mn.b}$** which is expressed in rub/nm^3.

5.4. The current specific total cost on the functioning of the **GCU** (the current cost of pumping one m^3) in the jth point of the **$NM_{C.ip.Mn.b}$** (see Fig. RPM 14) in monetary form is calculated by the formula:

$$STD_{C.ip.Mn.b.j} = TD_{C.ip.Mn.b.j}*24*1000/1000000*q_{кcj} \text{ rub/nm}^3,$$

in which all magnitudes – see above.

Calculation example:

For the compressor speed n_{min} = 3710 rpm.

$STD_{C.ip.Mn.b.1} = TD_{C.ip.Mn.b.1}*24*1000/1000000*q_{кc1} =$ 582,106*24*1000/1000000*7,362 = 1,8976 rub/nm^3;
$STD_{C.ip.Mn.b.2} = TD_{C.ip.Mn.b.2}*24*1000/1000000*q_{кc2} =$ 630,863*24*1000/1000000*9,851 = 1,5369 rub/nm^3;
$STD_{C.ip.Mn.b.3} = TD_{C.ip.Mn.b.3}*24*1000/1000000*q_{кc3} =$ 677,077*24*1000/1000000*12,945 = 1,2553 rub/nm^3;
$STD_{C.ip.Mn.b.4} = TD_{C.ip.Mn.b.4}*24*1000/1000000*q_{кc4} =$ 701,886*24*1000/1000000*15,464 = 1,0893 rub/nm^3;
$STD_{C.ip.Mn.b.5} = TD_{C.ip.Mn.b.5}*24*1000/1000000*q_{кc5} =$ 710,802*24*1000/1000000*17.471 = 0,9764 rub/nm^3;
$STD_{C.ip.Mn.b.6} = TD_{C.ip.Mn.b.6}*24*1000/1000000*q_{кc6} =$ 706,818*24*1000/1000000*18,809 = 0,9019 rub/nm^3;
$STD_{C.ip.Mn.b.7} = TD_{C.ip.Mn.b.7}*24*1000/1000000*q_{кc7} =$ 691,016*24*1000/1000000*20,082 = 0,8258 rub/nm^3.

For the compressor speed n_{max} = 5830 rpm.

$STD_{C.ip.Mn.b.8} = TD_{C.ip.Mn.b.8}*24*1000/1000000*q_{кc8} =$ 1154,280*24*1000/1000000*11,569 = 2,3946 rub/nm^3;

$STD_{C.ip.Mn.b.9} = TD_{C.ip.Mn.b.9}*24*1000/1000000*q_{кс9} = 1343{,}479*24*1000/1000000*15{,}481 = 2{,}0828$ rub/nm^3;

$STD_{C.ip.Mn.b.10} = TD_{C.ip.Mn.b.10}*24*1000/1000000*q_{кс10} = 1522{,}809*24*1000/1000000*20{,}342 = 1{,}7966$ rub/nm^3;

$STD_{C.ip.Mn.b.11} = TD_{C.ip.Mn.b.11}*24*1000/1000000*q_{кс11} = 1619{,}081*24*1000/1000000*24{,}300 = 1{,}5991$ rub/nm^3;

$STD_{C.ip.Mn.b.12} = TD_{C.ip.Mn.b.12}*24*1000/1000000*q_{кс12} = 1653{,}677*24*1000/1000000*27{,}455 = 1{,}4456$ rub/nm^3;

$STD_{C.ip.Mn.b.13} = TD_{C.ip.Mn.b.13}*24*1000/1000000*q_{кс13} = 1638{,}218*24*1000/1000000*29{,}557 = 1{,}3302$ rub/nm^3;

$STD_{C.ip.Mn.b.14} = TD_{C.ip.Mn.b.14}*24*1000/1000000*q_{кс14} = 1576{,}902*24*1000/1000000*31{,}557 = 1{,}1993$ rub/nm^3.

The magnitudes of the $\mathbf{STD_{C.ip.Mn.b.j}}$ for the other lines bounding the **GCU's** $\mathbf{NM_{C.ip.Mn.b}}$, is calculated similar including: for lines n_{min} = const, n_{max} = const, $P_{кmax}$ = const, $q_{кс}$ = max, $q_{кс}$ = min, N_{emax} = const, $T_{кmax}$ = const, as well as for the $\mathbf{WP_c}$ point. These calculations are not shown here to reduce the scope of the description.

$\mathbf{NS_{C.ip.Mn.b}}$ of the second type are built on the results of calculations – see Fig. RPM 20 which is used for further calculation of the corresponding **Indexed noologistical areas of possible operating modes** ($\mathbf{RPM_{C.ip.Mn.b}}$).

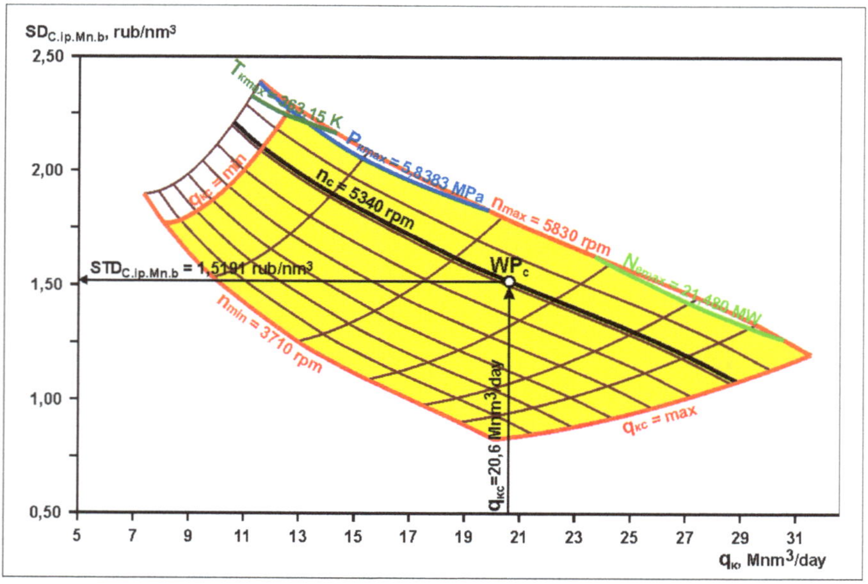

Fig. RPM 20

Calculated $\mathbf{NS_{C.ip.Mn.b}}$ of the second type, painted yellow on Fig. RPM 20, mathematically links **the density of current flow ($\mathbf{F_{M.ip.NG.b}}$) of the current noologistical value ($\mathbf{V_{M.ip.NG.b}}$)**, that is the $\mathbf{q_к}$ of pumped gas in Mnm^3/day, and **the specified density of the current total consumption flow ($\mathbf{TF_{C.ip.Mn.b}}$) of the current noologistical value ($\mathbf{V_{C.ip.Mn.b}}$)**, that is its $\mathbf{STD_{C.ip.Mn.b}}$ which is expressed in rub/nm^3.

5.5. The current specific CO_2 emission in the jth point of the $\mathbf{NM_{S.ip.CO2.b.j}}$ of the **GCU** (see Fig. RPM 15) is calculated by the formula:

$SD_{S.ip.CO2.b.j} = D_{S.ip.CO2.b.j} *24*3600*1000000/1000000*q_{кcj}$ g/nm^3,

in which all magnitudes – see above.

Calculation example:

For the compressor speed n_{min} = 3710 rpm.

$SD_{S.ip.CO2.b.1} = D_{S.ip.CO2.b.1}*24*1000000/1000000*q_{кc1} = 2{,}012*24*1000000/1000000*7{,}362 = 6{,}558$ g/nm^3;

$SD_{S.ip.CO2.b.2} = D_{S.ip.CO2.b.2}*24*1000000/1000000*q_{кc2} = 2{,}504*24*1000000/1000000*9{,}851 = 6{,}101$ g/nm^3;

$SD_{S.ip.CO2.b.3} = D_{S.ip.CO2.b.3}*24*1000000/1000000*q_{кc3} = 2{,}971*24*1000000/1000000*12{,}945 = 5{,}509$ g/nm^3;

$SD_{S.ip.CO2.b.4} = D_{S.ip.CO2.b.4}*24*1000000/1000000*q_{кc4} = 3{,}222*24*1000000/1000000*15{,}464 = 5{,}001$ g/nm^3;

$SD_{S.ip.CO2.b.5} = D_{S.ip.CO2.b.5}*24*1000000/1000000*q_{кc5} = 3{,}312*24*1000000/1000000*17.471 = 4{,}550$ g/nm^3;

$SD_{S.ip.CO2.b.6} = D_{S.ip.CO2.b.6}*24*1000000/1000000*q_{кc6} = 3{,}272*24*1000000/1000000*18{,}809 = 4{,}175$ g/nm^3;

$SD_{S.ip.CO2.b.7} = D_{S.ip.CO2.b.7}*24*1000000/1000000*q_{кc7} = 3{,}112*24*1000000/1000000*20{,}082 = 3{,}720$ g/nm^3.

For the compressor speed n_{max} = 5830 rpm.

$SD_{S.ip.CO2.b.8} = D_{S.ip.CO2.b.8}*24*1000000/1000000*q_{кc8} = 7{,}794*24*1000000/1000000*11{,}569 = 16{,}169$ g/nm^3;

$SD_{S.ip.CO2.b.9} = D_{S.ip.CO2.b.9}*24*1000000/1000000*q_{кc9} = 9{,}706*24*1000000/1000000*15{,}481 = 15{,}047$ g/nm^3;

$SD_{S.ip.CO2.b.10} = D_{S.ip.CO2.b.10}*24*1000000/1000000*q_{кс10} = 11{,}519*24*1000000/1000000*20{,}342 = 13{,}590$ g/nm³;

$SD_{S.ip.CO2.b.11} = D_{S.ip.CO2.b.11}*24*1000000/1000000*q_{кс11} = 12{,}491*24*1000000/1000000*24{,}300 = 12{,}337$ g/nm³;

$SD_{S.ip.CO2.b.12} = D_{S.ip.CO2.b.12}*24*1000000/1000000*q_{кс12} = 12{,}841*24*1000000/1000000*27{,}455 = 11{,}225$ g/nm³;

$SD_{S.ip.CO2.b.13} = D_{S.ip.CO2.b.13}*24*1000000/1000000*q_{кс13} = 12{,}685*24*1000000/1000000*29{,}557 = 10{,}300$ g/nm³;

$SD_{S.ip.CO2.b.14} = D_{S.ip.CO2.b.14}*24*1000000/1000000*q_{кс14} = 12{,}065*24*1000000/1000000*31{,}557 = 9{,}176$ g/nm³.

The magnitudes of the $\mathbf{SD_{S.ip.CO2.b.j}}$ for the other lines bounding the **GCU's** $\mathbf{NM}_{S.ip.CO2.b.j}$, is calculated similar including: for lines n_{min} = const, n_{max} = const, $P_{кmax}$ = const, $q_{кс}$ = max, $q_{кс}$ = min, N_{emax} = const, $T_{кmax}$ = const, as well as for the $\mathbf{WP_c}$ point. These calculations are not shown here to reduce the scope of the description.

$\mathbf{NS_{S.ip.CO2.b}}$ of the first type are built on the results of calculations – see Fig. RPM 21 which is used for further calculation of the corresponding **Indexed noologistical areas of possible operating modes** ($\mathbf{RPM_{S.ip.CO2.b}}$).

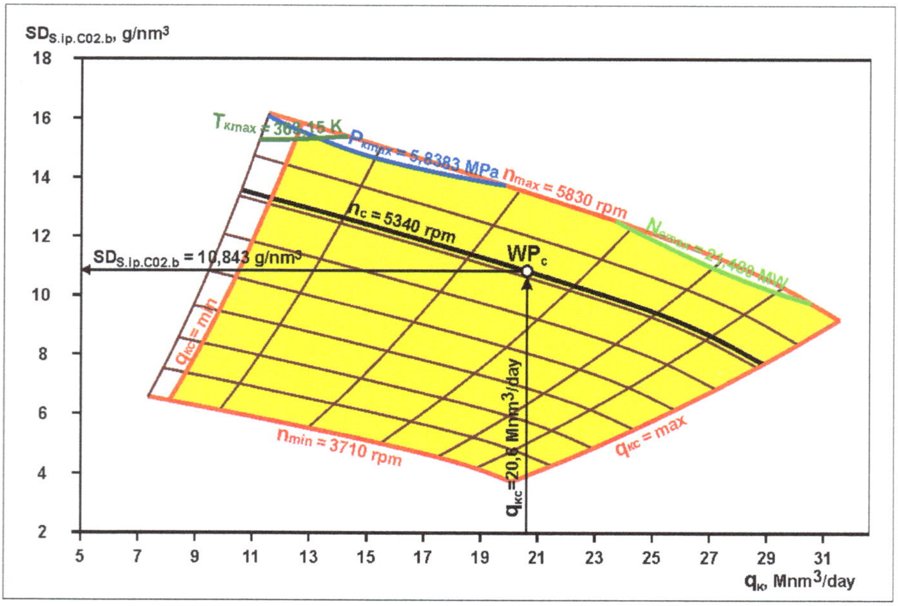

Fig. RPM 21

Calculated $\mathbf{NS_{S.ip.CO2.b}}$ of the first type, painted yellow on Fig. RPM 21, mathematically links **the density of current flow ($\mathbf{F_{M.ip.NG.b}}$) of the current noologistical value ($\mathbf{V_{M.ip.NG.b}}$)**, that is the $\mathbf{q_к}$ of pumped gas in Mnm^3/day, and **the specified density of the current emission flow ($\mathbf{F_{S.ip.CO2.b}}$) of the current noologistical value ($\mathbf{V_{S.ip.CO2.b}}$)**, that is its $\mathbf{SD_{S.ip.CO2.b}}$ which is expressed in g/nm^3.

5.5. The current specific total CO_2 emission in the jth point of the $\mathbf{NM_{S.ip.CO2.b.j}}$ of the **GCU** (see Fig. RPM 16) is calculated by the formula:

$$STD_{S.ip.CO2.b.j} = TD_{S.ip.CO2.b.j} *24*3600*1000000/1000000*q_{кcj} \text{ g/nm}^3,$$

in which all magnitudes – see above.

Calculation example:

For the compressor speed n_{min} = 3710 rpm.

$STD_{S.ip.CO2.b.1} = TD_{S.ip.CO2.b.1}*24*1000000/1000000*q_{кc1} =$ 2,017*24*1000000/1000000*7,362 = 6,574 g/nm^3;
$STD_{S.ip.CO2.b.2} = TD_{S.ip.CO2.b.2}*24*1000000/1000000*q_{кc2} =$ 2,509*24*1000000/1000000*9,851 = 6,113 g/nm^3;
$STD_{S.ip.CO2.b.3} = TD_{S.ip.CO2.b.3}*24*1000000/1000000*q_{кc3} =$ 2,976*24*1000000/1000000*12,945 = 5,518 g/nm^3;
$STD_{S.ip.CO2.b.4} = TD_{S.ip.CO2.b.4}*24*1000000/1000000*q_{кc4} =$ 3,227*24*1000000/1000000*15,464 = 5,008 g/nm^3;
$STD_{S.ip.CO2.b.5} = TD_{S.ip.CO2.b.5}*24*1000000/1000000*q_{кc5} =$ 3,317*24*1000000/1000000*17.471 = 4.557 g/nm^3;
$STD_{S.ip.CO2.b.6} = TD_{S.ip.CO2.b.6}*24*1000000/1000000*q_{кc6} =$ 3,277*24*1000000/1000000*18,809 = 4,181 g/nm^3;
$STD_{S.ip.CO2.b.7} = TD_{S.ip.CO2.b.7}*24*1000000/1000000*q_{кc7} =$ 3,117*24*1000000/1000000*20,082 = 3,725 g/nm^3.

For the compressor speed n_{max} = 5830 rpm.

$STD_{S.ip.CO2.b.8} = TD_{S.ip.CO2.b.8}*24*1000000/1000000*q_{кc8} =$ 7,799*24*1000000/1000000*11,569 = 16,179 g/nm^3;
$STD_{S.ip.CO2.b.9} = TD_{S.ip.CO2.b.9}*24*1000000/1000000*q_{кc9} =$ 9,711*24*1000000/1000000*15,481 = 15,055 g/nm^3;
$STD_{S.ip.CO2.b.10} = TD_{S.ip.CO2.b.10}*24*1000000/1000000*q_{кc10} =$ 11,523*24*1000000/1000000*20,342 = 13,595 g/nm^3;

$STD_{S.ip.CO2.b.11}$ = $TD_{S.ip.CO2.b.11}$*24*1000000/1000000*$q_{кс11}$ = 12,496*24*1000000/1000000*24,300 = 12,342 g/nm^3;

$STD_{S.ip.CO2.b.12}$ = $TD_{S.ip.CO2.b.12}$*24*1000000/1000000*$q_{кс12}$ = 12,846*24*1000000/1000000*27,455 = 11,229 g/nm^3;

$STD_{S.ip.CO2.b.13}$ = $TD_{S.ip.CO2.b.13}$*24*1000000/1000000*$q_{кс13}$ = 12,690*24*1000000/1000000*29,557 = 10,304 g/nm^3;

$STD_{S.ip.CO2.b.14}$ = $TD_{S.ip.CO2.b.14}$*24*1000000/1000000*$q_{кс14}$ = 12,070*24*1000000/1000000*31,557 = 9,180 g/nm^3.

The magnitudes of the **$STD_{S.ip.CO2.b.j}$** for the other lines bounding the **GCU's $NM_{S.ip.CO2.b}$**, is calculated similar including: for lines n_{min} = const, n_{max} = const, $P_{кmax}$ = const, $q_{кс}$ = max, $q_{кс}$ = min, N_{emax} = const, $T_{кmax}$ = const, as well as for the **WP_c** point. These calculations are not shown here to reduce the scope of the description.

$NS_{S.ip.CO2.b}$ of the second type are built on the results of calculations – see Fig. RPM 22 which is used for further calculation of the corresponding **Indexed noologistical areas of possible operating modes** (**$RPM_{S.ip.CO2.b}$**).

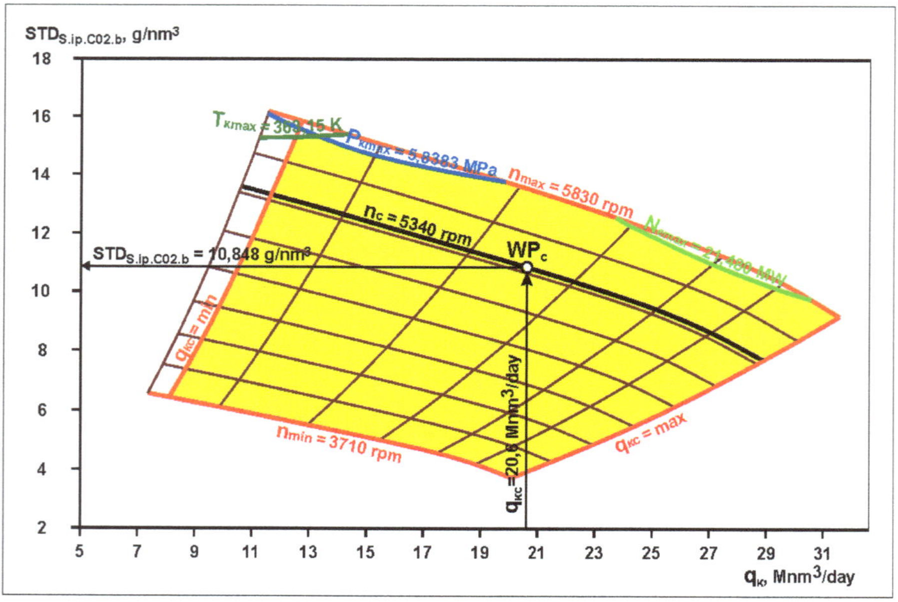

Fig. RPM 22

Calculated **$NS_{S.ip.CO2.b}$** of the second type, painted yellow on Fig. RPM 22, mathematically links **the density of current flow ($F_{M.ip.NG.b}$) of the current noologistical value ($V_{M.ip.NG.b}$)**, that is the **$q_к$** of pumped gas in Mnm^3/day, and **the specified density of the current total emission**

flow ($TF_{S.ip.CO2.b}$) of the current noologistical value ($V_{S.ip.CO2.b}$), that is its **$STD_{S.ip.CO2.b}$** which is expressed in g/nm^3.

6. To calculate **the indexed noologistical areas of the possible operating modes** of **GCU** compressor (briefly – **$RPM_{C.ip.Vth.b}$**, **$RPM_{C.ip.Mn.b}$** and **$RPM_{S.ip.CO2.b}$**).

6.1. Calculate the magnitude of **the index for summation of the current areas of possible modes** of the first type **$Ix_{C.ip.Vth.b}$** of the **GCU** compressor.

The use of **$Ix_{C.ip.Vth.b}$** provides reasonable mode of this **unit of equipment** for working in the same group together to any other **units of equipment** under **the criterion of minimum of the current total conditional variable costs** of energy of all kinds on the functioning of the whole group working together **units of equipment** of the jth points of their **$CM_{M.ip.NG.b}$** - see Fig. RPM 10. The magnitude of **$Ix_{C.ip.Vth.b}$** is calculated by the formula:

$$Ix_{C.ip.Vth.b.j} = Ap_{C.ip.Vth.b.j} * Bp_{C.ip.Vth.b.j} / Cp_{C.ip.Vth.b.j}.$$

The magnitudes **$Ap_{C.ip.Vth.b.j}$**, **$Bp_{C.ip.Vth.b.j}$** and **$Cp_{C.ip.Vth.b.j}$** for this formula are taken from **$NS_{C.ip.Vth.b}$**, which is shown in Fig. RPM 17. Graphic representation of the magnitudes of the first type of **$Ix_{C.ip.Vth.b}$** are built on the results of the calculations in all **$CM_{M.ip.NG.b}$** – see Fig. RPM 23.

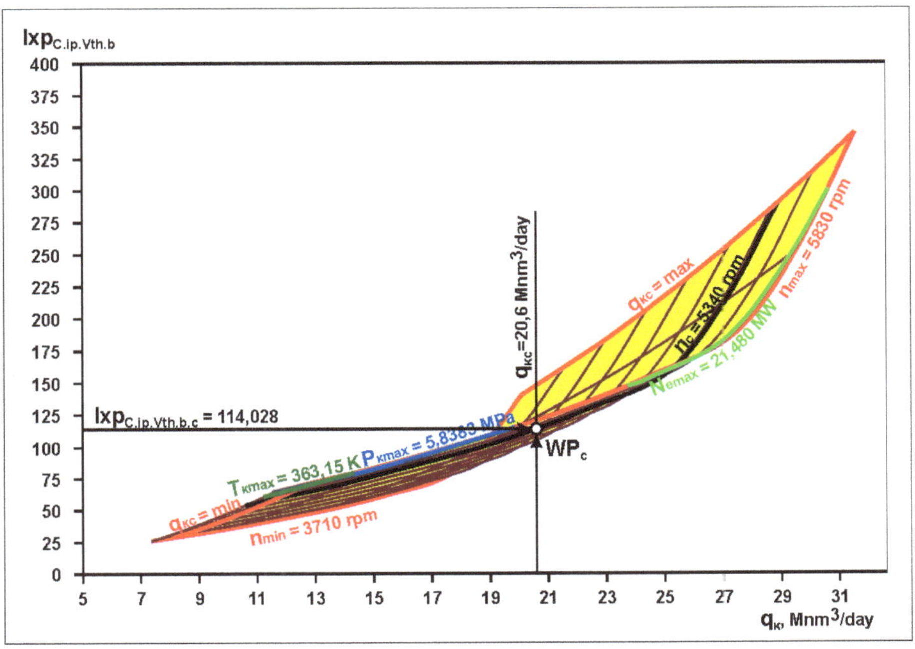

Fig. RPM 23

The contour of the $CM_{M.ip.NG.b}$ take from Fig. RPM 10 and then put into it the lines of a constant magnitude $Ix_{C.ip.Vth.b}$ of the first type from Fig. RPM 23. Its vertical scale translated into the pressure ratio according to the formula $\varepsilon = P_К/P_{НС}$. The lines of a constant **GCU** compressor efficiency and lines of constant frequency of rotation are put into it for useful. Based on the results of calculations, a graphic image of $RPM_{C.ip.Vth.b}$ of the first type is created – see Fig. RPM 24.

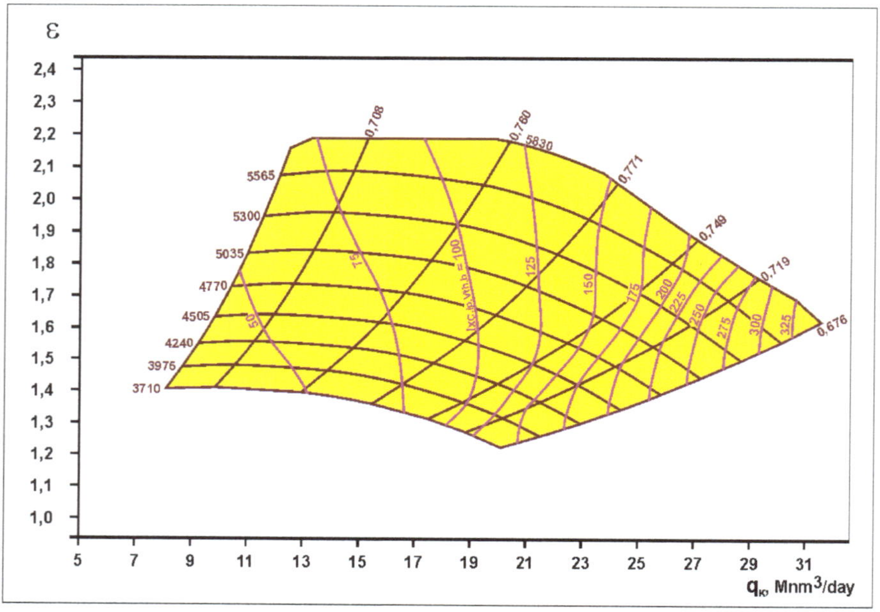

Fig. RPM 24

Calculated **$RPM_{C.ip.Vth.b}$** of the first type, submitted on Fig. RPM 24, mathematically links **the density of current flow ($F_{M.ip.NG.b}$) of the current noological value ($V_{M.ip.NG.b}$)**, that is the $q_К$ of pumped gas in Mnm^3/day, and the minimal conditionally variable specific energy costs of all types, that is the specified conditional variable density **$SD_{C.ip.Vth.b}$** (see Fig. RPM 17) of **current conditional variable consumption flow ($F_{C.ip.Vth.b}$) of the current noological value ($V_{C.ip.Vth.b}$)**, which is expressed in kJ/nm^3, when this **GCU** works in one group with any other **units of equipment**. It is used in **the technology of calculating the upward indexed information pyramid** for summation **$RPM_{C.ih.Vth.b}$** all of **units of equipment** that are working together in the same group. The technology provides calculation of a single **RPM**$_{C.ih.Vth.b}$ the entire group at each point where the combination of their joint work provides they are given the total commercial performance $q_{к\Sigma}$ under **the minimum specific conditionally variable costs of energy** of all kinds, which is a conditionally variable density **SD**$_{C.ih.Vth.b}$, expressed in kJ/nm^3. In addition, it is used in **the technology of calculating the downward indexed information pyramid** for the purpose of assigning a specific reasonable mode of operation of the **GCU** in the group of jointly working **units of equipment**, which will provide a minimum conditionally variable density of **SD**$_{C.ih.Vth.b}$ their **current conditional variable consumption flow (F**$_{C.ih.Vth.b}$**) of the current noologistical value (V**$_{C.ih.Vth.b}$**)** expressed in kJ/nm^3.

6.2. Calculate the magnitude of **the index for summation of the current areas of possible modes** of the second type **Ix**$_{C.ip.Vth.b}$ of the **GCU** compressor.

The use of **Ix**$_{C.ip.Vth.b}$ provides reasonable mode of this **unit of equipment** for working in the same group together to any other **units of equipment** under **the criterion of minimum of the current total costs** of energy of all kinds on the functioning of the whole group working together **units of equipment** of the jth points of their **CM**$_{M.ip.NG.b}$ - see Fig. RPM 10. The magnitude of **Ix**$_{C.ip.Vth.b}$ is calculated by the same formula as given above in paragraph 6.1., for which magnitudes of **Ap**$_{C.ip.Vth.b.j}$, **Bp**$_{C.ip.Vth.b.j}$ and **Cp**$_{C.ip.Vth.b.j}$ are taken from **NS**$_{C.ip.Vth.b}$ shown in figure RPM 18. The image of the second type **RPM**$_{C.ip.Vth.b}$ is built on the results of these calculations. It has visually a small different from of the first type **RPM**$_{C.ip.Vth.b}$ which was shown in figure RPM 24, and for this reason is not shown here to reduce the scope of the description.

Calculated **RPM**$_{C.ip.Vth.b}$ of the second type, mathematically links **the density of current flow (F**$_{M.ip.NG.b}$**) of the current noologistical value (V**$_{M.ip.NG.b}$**)**, that is the $q_к$ of pumped gas in Mnm^3/day, and the minimal total energy costs of all types, that is **the specified total density STD**$_{C.ip.Vth.b}$ (see Fig. RPM 18) of **current total consumption flow (TF**$_{C.ip.Vth.b}$**) of the current noologistical value (V**$_{S.ip.Vth.b}$**)**, which is expressed in kJ/nm^3, when this **GCU** works in one group with any other

units of equipment. It is used in **the technology of calculating the upward indexed information pyramid** for summation $\mathbf{RPM}_{\mathbf{C.ih.Vth.b}}$ all of **units of equipment** that are working together in the same group. The technology provides calculation of a single $\mathbf{RPM}_{\mathbf{C.ih.Vth.b}}$ the entire group at each point where the combination of their joint work provides they are given the total commercial performance $q_{к\Sigma}$ under the minimum total specific costs of energy of all kinds, which is a total density $\mathbf{STD}_{\mathbf{C.ih.Vth.b}}$, expressed in kJ/nm^3. In addition, it is used in **the technology of calculating the downward indexed information pyramid** for the purpose of assigning a specific reasonable mode of operation of the **GCU** in the group of jointly working **units of equipment**, which will provide a minimum density of $\mathbf{STD}_{\mathbf{C.ih.Vth.b}}$ their **total current total consumption flow ($\mathbf{TF}_{\mathbf{C.ih.Vth.b}}$) of the current noologistical value ($\mathbf{V}_{\mathbf{C.ih.Vth.b}}$)** expressed in kJ/nm^3.

6.3. Calculate the magnitude of **the index for summation of the current areas of possible modes** of the first type $\mathbf{Ix}_{\mathbf{C.ip.Mn.b}}$ of the **GCU** compressor.

The use of $\mathbf{Ix}_{\mathbf{C.ip.Mn.b}}$ provides reasonable mode of this **unit of equipment** for working in the same group together to any other **units of equipment** under **the criterion of minimum of the current total conditional variable costs** of all kinds in monetary form on the functioning of the whole group working together **units of equipment** of the jth points of their $\mathbf{CM}_{\mathbf{M.ip.NG.b}}$ - see Fig. RPM 10. The magnitude of $\mathbf{Ix}_{\mathbf{C.ip.Mn.b}}$ is calculated by the formula:

$$\mathbf{Ix}_{\mathbf{C.ip.Mn.b.j}} = \mathbf{Ap}_{\mathbf{C.ip.Mn.b.j}} * \mathbf{Bp}_{\mathbf{C.ip.Mn.b.j}} / \mathbf{Cp}_{\mathbf{C.ip.Mn.b.j}}.$$

The magnitudes $\mathbf{Ap}_{\mathbf{C.ip.Mn.b.j}}$, $\mathbf{Bp}_{\mathbf{C.ip.Mn.b.j}}$ and $\mathbf{Cp}_{\mathbf{C.ip.Mn.b.j}}$ for this formula are taken from $\mathbf{NS}_{\mathbf{C.ip.Mn.b}}$, which is shown in Fig. RPM 19. Graphic representation of the magnitudes of the first type of $\mathbf{Ix}_{\mathbf{C.ip.Mn.b}}$ are built on the results of the calculations in all $\mathbf{CM}_{\mathbf{M.ip.NG.b}}$ – see Fig. RPM 25.

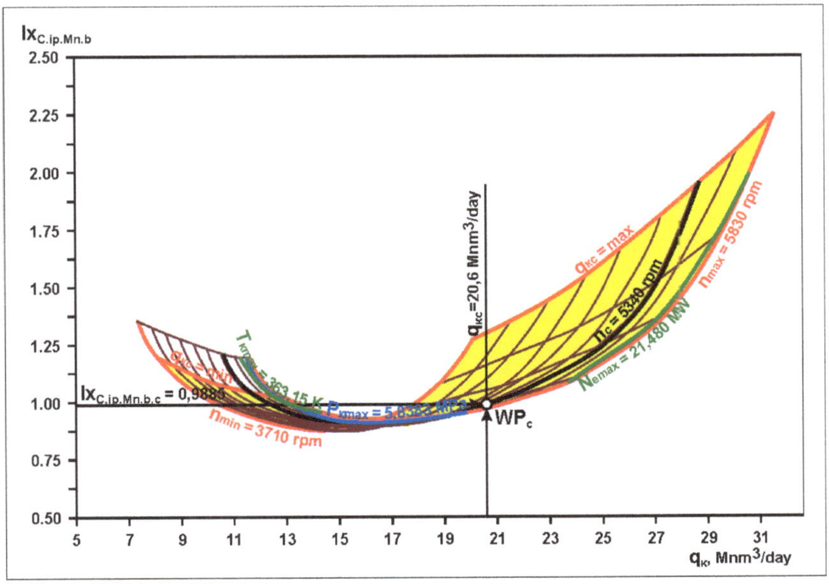

Fig. RPM 25

The contour of the $\mathbf{CM_{M.ip.NG.b}}$ take from Fig. RPM 10 and then put into it the lines of a constant magnitude $\mathbf{Ix_{C.ip.Mn.b}}$ of the first type from Fig. RPM 25. Its vertical scale translated into the pressure ratio according to the formula $\varepsilon = P_K/P_{HC}$. The lines of a constant **GCU** compressor efficiency and lines of constant frequency of rotation are put into it for useful. Based on the results of calculations, a graphic image of $\mathbf{RPM_{C.ip.Mn.b}}$ of the first type is created – see Fig. RPM 26.

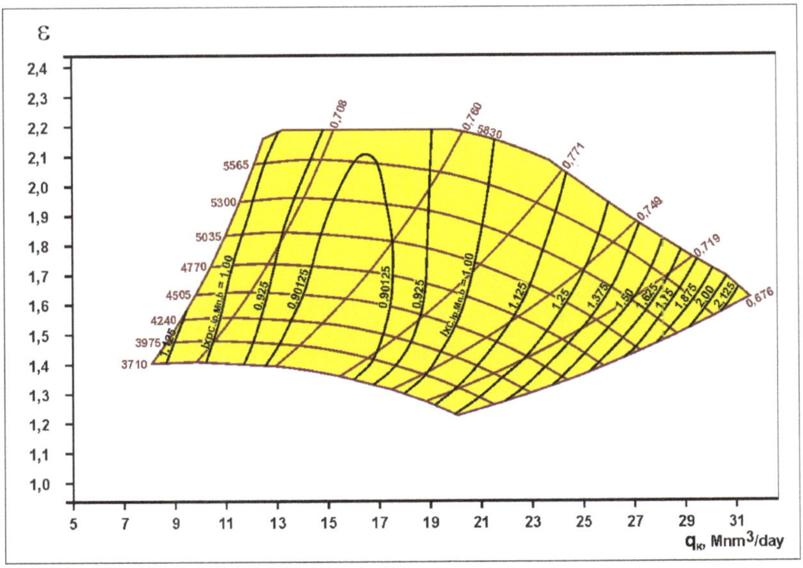

Fig. RPM 26

Calculated **$RPM_{C.ip.Mn.b}$** of the first type, submitted on Fig. RPM 26, mathematically links **the density of current flow ($F_{M.ip.NG.b}$) of the current noologistical value ($V_{M.ip.NG.b}$)**, that is the **$q_к$** of pumped gas in Mnm^3/day, and **the minimal conditionally variable specific costs** of all types in monetary form, that is **the specified conditional variable density $SD_{C.ip.Mn.b}$** (see Fig. RPM 19) of **current conditional variable consumption flow ($F_{C.ip.Mn.b}$) of the current noologistical value ($V_{C.ip.Mn.b}$)**, which is expressed in rub/nm^3, when this **GCU** works in one group with any other **units of equipment**. It is used in **the technology of calculating the upward indexed information pyramid** for summation **$RPM_{C.ih.Mn.b}$** all of **units of equipment** that are working together in the same group. The technology provides calculation of a single **$RPM_{C.ih.Mn.b}$** the entire group at each point where the combination of their joint work provides they are given the total commercial performance $q_{к\Sigma}$ under **the minimum specific conditionally variable costs** of all kinds, which is a conditionally variable density **$SD_{C.ih.Mn.b}$**, expressed in kJ/nm^3. In addition, it is used in **the technology of calculating the downward indexed information pyramid** for the purpose of assigning a specific reasonable mode of operation of the **GCU** in the group of jointly working **units of equipment**, which will provide **a minimum conditionally variable density $SD_{C.ih.Mn.b}$** of their **current conditional variable consumption flow ($F_{C.ih.Mn.b}$) of the current noologistical value ($V_{C.ih.Mn.b}$)** expressed in rub/nm^3.

6.4. Calculate the magnitude of **the index for summation of the current areas of possible modes** of the second type **$Ix_{C.ip.Mn.b}$** of the **GCU** compressor.

The use of **$Ix_{C.ip.Mn.b}$** provides reasonable mode of this **unit of equipment** for working in the same group together to any other **units of equipment** under **the criterion of minimum of the current total costs** of all kinds in monetary form on the functioning of the whole group working together **units of equipment** of the jth points of their **$CM_{M.ip.NG.b}$** - see Fig. RPM 10. The magnitude of **$Ix_{C.ip.Mn.b}$** is calculated by the same formula as given above in paragraph 6.3., for which magnitudes of **$Ap_{C.ip.Mn.b.j}$**, **$Bp_{C.ip.Mn.b.j}$** and **$Cp_{C.ip.Mn.b.j}$** are taken from **$NS_{C.ip.Mn.b}$** shown in figure RPM 20. The image of the second type

RPM$_{C.ip.Mn.b}$ is built on the results of these calculations. It has visually a small different from of the first type **RPM**$_{C.ip.Mn.b}$ which was shown in figure RPM 26, and for this reason is not shown here to reduce the scope of the description.

Calculated **RPM**$_{C.ip.Mn.b}$ of the second type, mathematically links **the density of current flow (F**$_{M.ip.NG.b}$**) of the current noologistical value (V**$_{M.ip.NG.b}$**)**, that is the **q**$_{K}$ of pumped gas in Mnm^3/day, and **the minimal total costs** of all types in monetary form, that is **the specified total density STD**$_{C.ip.Mn.b}$ (see Fig. RPM 20) of **current total consumption flow (TF**$_{C.ip.Mn.b}$**) of the current noologistical value (V**$_{C.ip.Mn.b}$**)**, which is expressed in rub/nm^3, when this **GCU** works in one group with any other **units of equipment**. It is used in **the technology of calculating the upward indexed information pyramid** for summation **RPM**$_{C.ih.Mn.b}$ all of **units of equipment** that are working together in the same group. The technology provides calculation of a single **RPM**$_{C.ih.Mn.b}$ the entire group at each point where the combination of their joint work provides they are given the total commercial performance $q_{K\Sigma}$ under the minimum total specific costs of all kinds in monetary form, which is a total density **STD**$_{C.ih.Mn.b}$, expressed in rub/nm^3. In addition, it is used in **the technology of calculating the downward indexed information pyramid** for the purpose of assigning a specific reasonable mode of operation of the **GCU** in the group of jointly working **units of equipment**, which will provide a minimum density of **STD**$_{C.ih.Mn.b}$ their **total current consumption flow (TF**$_{C.ih.Mn.b}$**) of the current noologistical value (V**$_{C.ih.Mn.b}$**)** expressed in rub/nm^3.

6.5. Calculate the magnitude of **the index for summation of the current areas of possible modes** of the first type **Ix**$_{S.ip.CO2.b}$ of the **GCU** compressor.

The use of **Ix**$_{S.ip.CO2.b}$ provides reasonable mode of this **unit of equipment** for working in the same group together to any other **units of equipment** under **the criterion of minimum of the current total conditional variable** CO_2 **emission** per the functioning of the whole group working together **units of equipment** of the jth points of their

CM$_{M.ip.NG.b}$ - see Fig. RPM 10. The magnitude of **Ix$_{S.ip.CO2.b}$** is calculated by the formula:

$$Ix_{S.ip.CO2.b.j} = Ap_{S.ip.CO2.b.j} * Bp_{S.ip.CO2.b.j} / Cp_{S.ip.CO2.b.j}.$$

The magnitudes **Ap$_{S.ip.CO2.b.j}$**, **Bp$_{S.ip.CO2.b.j}$** and **Cp$_{S.ip.CO2.b.j}$** for this formula are taken from **NS$_{S.ip.CO2.b}$**, which is shown in Fig. RPM 21. Graphic representation of the magnitudes of the first type of **Ix$_{S.ip.CO2.b}$** are built on the results of the calculations in all **CM$_{M.ip.NG.b}$** – see Fig. RPM 27.

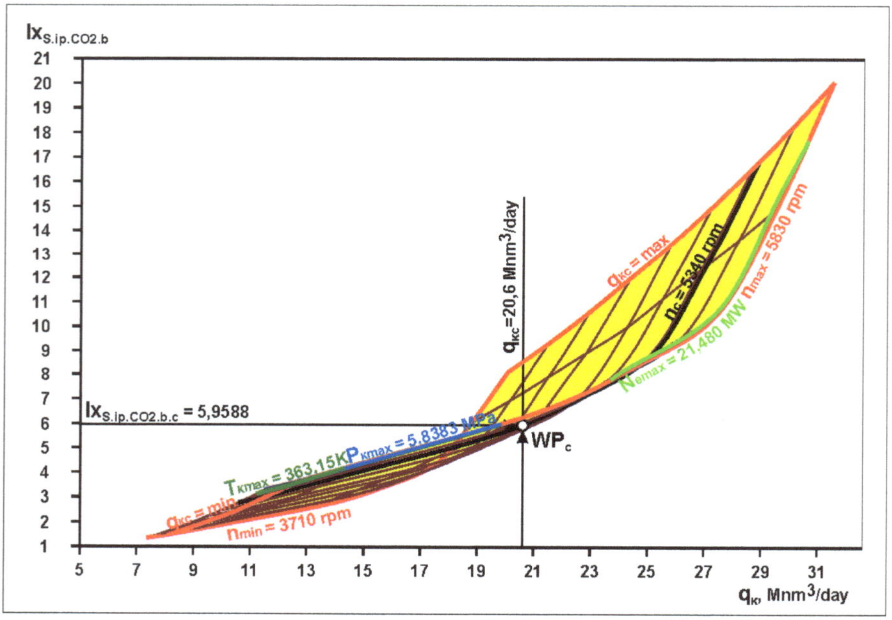

Fig. RPM 27

The contour of the **CM$_{M.ip.NG.b}$** take from Fig. RPM 10 and then put into it the lines of a constant magnitude **Ix$_{S.ip.CO2.b}$** of the first type from Fig. RPM 27. Its vertical scale translated into the pressure ratio according to the formula $\varepsilon = P_{к}/P_{НС}$. The lines of a constant **GCU** compressor efficiency and lines of constant frequency of rotation are put into it for useful. Based on the results of calculations, a graphic image of **RPM$_{S.ip.CO2.b}$** of the first type is created – see Fig. RPM 28.

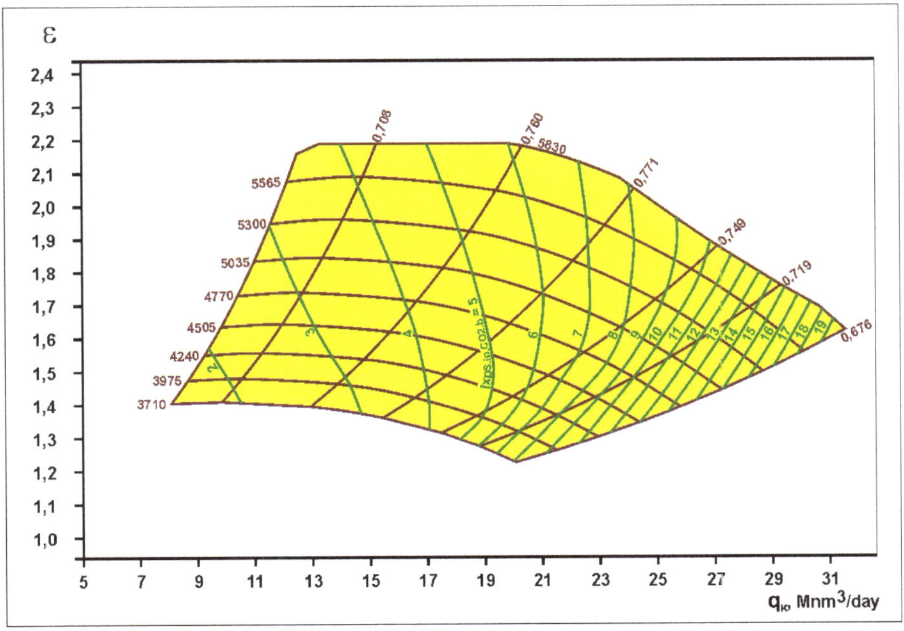

Fig. RPM 28

Calculated **RPM$_{S.ip.CO2.b}$** of the first type, submitted on Fig. RPM 28, mathematically links **the density of current flow (F$_{M.ip.NG.b}$) of the current noologistical value (V$_{M.ip.NG.b}$)**, that is the **q$_к$** of pumped gas in Mnm^3/day, and **the minimal conditionally variable specific CO$_2$ emission**, that is **the specified conditional variable density SD$_{S.ip.CO2.b}$** (see Fig. RPM 21) of **current conditional variable rejection flow (F$_{S.ip.CO2.b}$) of the current noologistical value (V$_{C.ip.CO2.b}$)**, which is expressed in g/nm^3, when this **GCU** works in one group with any other **units of equipment**. It is used in **the technology of calculating the upward indexed information pyramid** for summation **RPM$_{S.ih.CO2.b}$** all of **units of equipment** that are working together in the same group. The technology provides calculation of a single **RPM$_{S.ih.CO2.b}$** the entire group at each point where the combination of their joint work provides they are given the total commercial performance $q_{к\Sigma}$ under **the minimum specific conditionally variable CO$_2$ emission**, which is a conditionally variable density **SD$_{S.ih.CO2.b}$**, expressed in g/nm^3. In addition, it is used in **the technology of calculating the downward indexed information pyramid** for the purpose of assigning a specific reasonable mode of operation of the **GCU** in the group of jointly working **units of equipment**, which will provide a minimum conditionally variable density of $\mathbf{SD_{S.ih.CO2.b}}$ their **current conditional variable rejection flow ($\mathbf{F_{S.ih.CO2.b}}$) of the current noologistical value ($\mathbf{V_{S.ih.CO2.b}}$)** expressed in g/nm^3.

6.6. Calculate the magnitude of **the index for summation of the current areas of possible modes** of the second type $\mathbf{Ix_{S.ip.CO2.b}}$ of the **GCU** compressor.

The use of $\mathbf{Ix_{S.ip.CO2.b}}$ provides reasonable mode of this **unit of equipment** for working in the same group together to any other **units of equipment** under **the criterion of minimum of the current total CO_2 emission** on the functioning of the whole group working together **units of equipment** of the jth points of their $\mathbf{CM_{M.ip.NG.b}}$ - see Fig. RPM 10. The magnitude of $\mathbf{Ix_{S.ip.CO2.b}}$ is calculated by the same formula as given above in paragraph 6.5., for which magnitudes of $\mathbf{Ap_{S.ip.CO2.b.j}}$, $\mathbf{Bp_{S.ip.CO2.b.j}}$ and $\mathbf{Cp_{S.ip.CO2.b.j}}$ are taken from $\mathbf{NS_{S.ip.CO2.b}}$ shown in figure RPM 22. The image of the second type $\mathbf{RPM_{S.ip.CO2.b}}$ is built on the results of these calculations. It has visually a small different from of the first type $\mathbf{RPM_{S.ip.CO2.b}}$ which was shown in figure RPM 28, and for this reason is not shown here to reduce the scope of the description.

Calculated $\mathbf{RPM_{S.ip.CO2.b}}$ of the second type, mathematically links **the density of current flow ($\mathbf{F_{M.ip.NG.b}}$) of the current noologistical value ($\mathbf{V_{M.ip.NG.b}}$)**, that is the $\mathbf{q_{\kappa}}$ of pumped gas in Mnm^3/day, and **the minimal total CO_2 emission**, that is **the specified total density $\mathbf{STD_{S.ip.CO2.b}}$** (see Fig. RPM 22) of **current total consumption flow ($\mathbf{TF_{S.ip.CO2.b}}$) of the current noologistical value ($\mathbf{V_{S.ip.CO2.b}}$)**, which is expressed in g/nm^3, when this **GCU** works in one group with any other **units of equipment**. It is used in **the technology of calculating the upward indexed information pyramid** for summation $\mathbf{RPM_{S.ih.CO2.b}}$ all of **units of equipment** that are working together in the same group. The technology provides calculation of a single $\mathbf{RPM_{S.ih.CO2.b}}$ the entire group at each point where the combination of their joint work provides they are given the total commercial performance $q_{\kappa\Sigma}$ under **the minimum total specific CO_2 emission**, which is a total density $\mathbf{STD_{S.ih.CO2.b}}$, expressed in g/nm^3. In addition, it is used in **the technology of calculating the downward indexed information**

pyramid for the purpose of assigning a specific reasonable mode of operation of the **GCU** in the group of jointly working **units of equipment**, which will provide a minimum density of $\mathbf{STD_{S.ih.CO2.b}}$ their **total current total rejection flow** ($\mathbf{TF_{S.ih.CO2.b}}$) **of the current noologistical value** ($\mathbf{V_{S.ih.CO2.b}}$) expressed in g/nm^3.

6.7. Calculated above $\mathbf{RPM_{C.ip.Vth.b}}$, $\mathbf{RPM_{C.ip.Mn.b}}$ and $\mathbf{RPM_{S.ip.CO2.b}}$ may be combined in a single picture for better visibility because they are based on $\mathbf{CM_{M.ip.NG.b}}$ which was shown on Fig. RPM 10.

$\mathbf{RPM_{C.ip.Vth.b}}$ (see Fig. RPM 24), $\mathbf{RPM_{C.ip.Mn.b}}$ (see Fig. RPM 26) and the $\mathbf{RPM_{S.ip.CO2.b}}$ (see Fig. RPM 28) of the first type are combined on Fig. RPM 29 for any single **GCU**. They are used for the current management of multiple **GCUs** that work the same group.

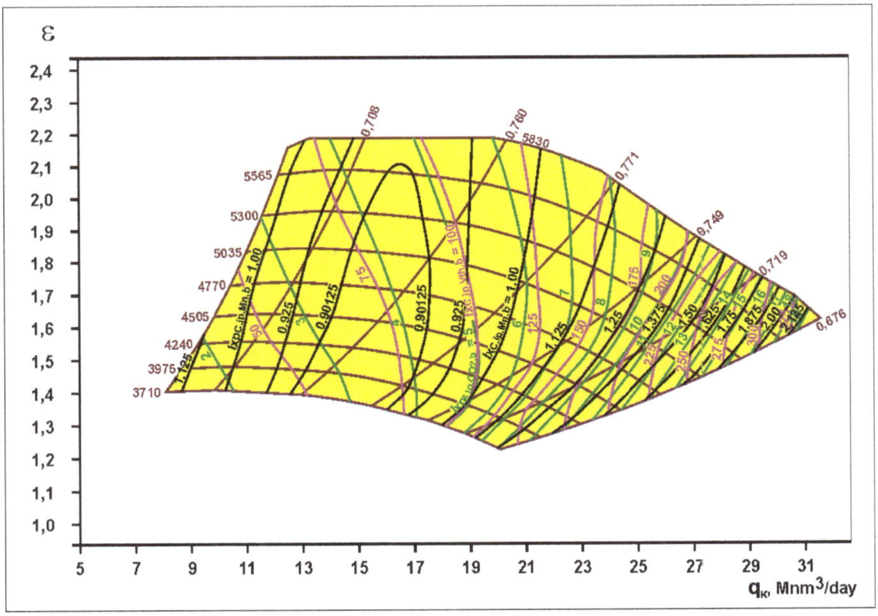

Fig. RPM 29

It follows that in the considered example, for each point of any $\mathbf{RPM_{ip.b}}$ shall be calculated three different index of summation. For example, for the current working point ($\mathbf{WP_c}$), they are: $\mathbf{Ix_{C.ip.Vth.b.c}}$ = 117,480 (see Fig. RPM 23), $\mathbf{Ix_{C.ip.Mn.b.c}}$ = 0.9885 (see Fig. RPM 25) and $\mathbf{Ix_{S.ip.CO2.b.c}}$ = 5,9588 (see Fig. RPM 27). It is also obvious that their number will be increased when increase in the number of criteria of reasonableness of control which **the person** establishes in his **goal**.

All the above about **$RPM_{ip.b}$** the first type, used, for example, in solving current control problems, also applies to **$RPM_{ip.b}$** of the second type, used, for example, in solving problems of modeling, design, planning, forecasting, etc.

The study of the sequence of mathematical operations which was described above in PP. 1 ... 6 gives reason to claim that it consists of two parts.

The first part set out in the PP. 1 ... 5, is preparatory and is a well-known to the relevant professionals a series of calculations based on specific **natural, technical, economic and other Sciences**. Specialists may execute it for each **real object** (**$RO_{ip.l.b}$**) they control which is located at the lowest level of management to any known sequence on the basis of any baseline data and ongoing measurement of **flows of consumption**, **creation** and **rejection** of **noologistical values**, **environment**, etc., which adhere to **the rules** and challenges of management: ongoing management, planning, design, forecasting, etc. The result of these computations should be a mathematical relationship that describes its **current noologistical area of possible operation modes** under specified parameters (**$NS_{C.ip.l.b}$** and **$NS_{S.ip.l.b}$**) - see Fig. RPM 17, RPM 18, RPM 19, RPM 20, RPM 21 and RPM 22. This part is the most time-consuming and requires special knowledge. It is obvious that **the person** using **the technology of Noologistics** may to take mentioned here **$NS_{C.ip.l.b}$** and **$NS_{S.ip.l.b}$** not only by calculation on the basis of the relevant science, as shown above in Example 1 and in **the practical examples of Noologistics implementation**, but also by any other means, which he trusts and which corresponds to the rules observed by him, for example, experimentally on the basis of statistical measurements, intuitively, to receive from the deity, in a dream, etc.

The second part, described in paragraph 6, describes the direct calculation of the **indexed noologistical areas of the possible operating modes** (**$RPM_{ip.b}$**) - see Fig. RPM 24, RPM 26, RPM 28, and 29. This part is the least labour-intensive and may be performed formally through universal mathematical processing.

The possibility of establishing current mathematical dependencies between any types of **values** (**V_v**) in the form of the above-mentioned **indexed noologistical areas of possible modes of operation** is that is the only sign of their classification into the category of **current noologistical values** (V_I): if **the person** is able to calculate them for his **real object**, all related in them **noo values** automatically move into the category of **noologistical values** and may be processed by **the technologies of calculation of indexed information pyramid**. If **the person** is not able to calculate **the indexed noologistical areas of possible modes of operation** for his **real object**, then to control it, he may use only **the technologies of calculation of non-indexed information pyramid**.

From the above it follows that the error control in the application of **the technology of Noologistics** the smaller, the more complete the information used by **the person** in the calculation of **the indexed noologistical areas of possible modes of operation**. An important condition is a pre-agreement from all **persons** by a single set of **criteria of reasonableness of the management** and measurement of all the parameters that will be provided in their **hierarchy**. Such agreement is drawn up in the form of appropriate **rules**, for example, in the form of a law or standard.

Thus, the above-described **indexed noologistical areas of possible modes of operation** are universal and may be used in any current processes of **noo management**. The mathematical apparatus of derivation of the formula used in paragraph 6 in the calculation of any **indices of the summation** (**Ix**) together examples and the necessary consultations will be presented to stakeholders in the composition of a more complete description of **Noologistics** under the special contract.

3.4. The Technology of Calculating Information Pyramids

The concept of **information pyramid** (briefly - **IP**) is widely used in management, where it is used to depict the structure of management of any complex system and its parts.

The use of **information pyramids** in **Noologistics** allowed to solve a known problem of increasing the amount of information that management personnel should take into account when developing a reasonable management solution at each next higher level of management of **the hierarchy of persons of Noologistics** in comparison its previous level. Authors of works on traditional (commodity-money) **Logistics** represent this problem graphically as shown in Fig. IP 1.

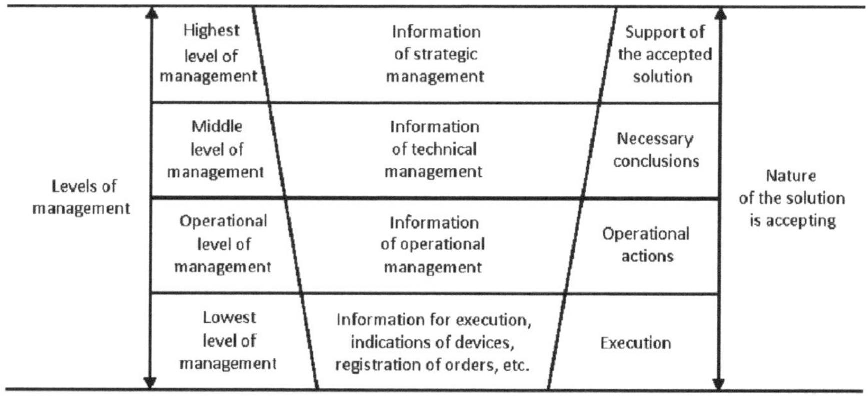

Fig. IP 1

Thus, the amount of information that needs to be processed at the upper levels of **hierarchy** management is usually significantly higher than the physical capabilities of the staff, especially if the set of magnitudes of **the control actions** for all its elements needs to be calculated in **the PRESENT**. This problem in **Noologistics** is solved by the formation of **information pyramids**, an example of which is depicted in Figure IP 2.

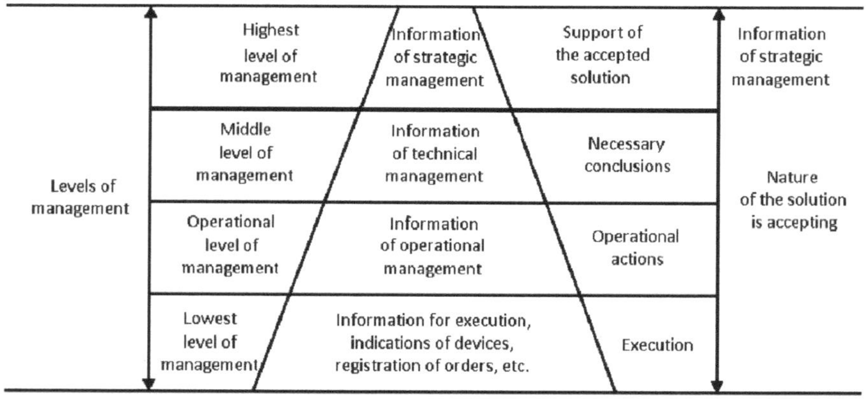

Fig. IP 2

Due to the fact that **the traditional foundations of control theory** do not contain a sufficiently detailed description of **the technology for calculating information pyramids**, it is specifically designed for **Noologistics** and has the following definition:

The technology of calculating the information pyramid in **Noologistics** is the processing of current information flows in accordance the rules of the person, which reduces their total density in the direction from the lower to the upper levels of **the information pyramid** and increases it in the opposite direction.

From the definition of **the information pyramid** it follows that they are distinguished by the direction of processing the current information flows on **Upward Information Pyramids** (briefly - **IP$_U$**) and **Downward Information Pyramids** (briefly - **IP$_D$**).

Noologistics provides the use of **technology of calculating the information pyramids** when managing all types of **hierarchies of persons** and their **real objects** of management. Such a typical scheme, containing four levels of management is showed in Fig. IP 3.

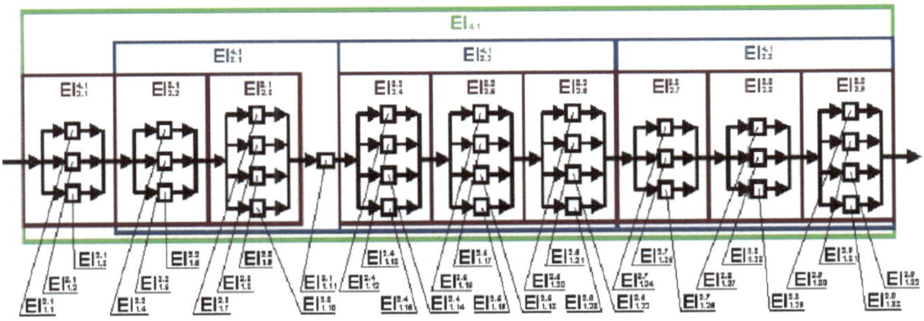

Fig. IP 3

The notation in Fig. IP 3:

The arrows show the direction of the movement of the **ideal objects** of its **persons**, which they control through the considered **grid**, which is their **real object**;

Conventional notations $El_{n.i}^{k.j}$ correspond to the elements of the **grid** are used to manage **the ideal objects** of its **persons** located at different levels of management of them, in which:

n – this is the level number of **the information pyramid**, in which information about the element is located;

i – this is the number of the element into the level of **the information pyramid**, in which information about it is located;

k – this is the number of the higher level of **the information pyramid**, in which is the element with which the element in question is connected through **the current information flows;**

j – this is the number of that element into the higher level of **the information pyramid** with which the element in question is connected through **current information flows.**

Examples of notations for elements of **the information pyramid** (see structure on Fig. IP 4):

$El_{1.1}^{2.1}$, $El_{1.2}^{2.1}$, $El_{1.3}^{2.1}$ – these are the elements, information about which is located in the first (n = 1), the lowest level of **the information pyramid**; they have the numbers i = 1, i = 2, i = 3 in it and are connected by means of **the current information flows** to the element located in the second (k = 2) level of **pyramid**, which has the number j = 1 and is conditionally marked in it by $El_{2.1}^{4.1}$;

$El_{1.4}^{2.2}$, $El_{1.5}^{2.2}$, $El_{1.6}^{2.2}$ – these are the elements, information about which is located in the first (n = 1), the lowest level of **the information pyramid**; they have the numbers i=4, i=5, i=6 in it and are connected by means of **the current information flows** to the element located in the second (k = 2) level of **pyramid**, which has the number j = 2 and is conditionally marked in it by $El_{2.2}^{2.1}$;

$El_{1.7}^{2.3}$, $El_{1.8}^{2.3}$, $El_{1.9}^{2.3}$, $El_{1.10}^{2.3}$ – these are the elements, information about which is located in the first (n = 1), the lowest level of **the information pyramid**; they have the numbers i=7, i=8, i=9, i=10 in it and are connected by means of **the current information flows** to the element located in the second (k = 2) level of **pyramid**, which has the number j = 2 and is conditionally marked in it by $El_{2.3}^{2.1}$;

$El_{1.11}^{3.1}$ – this is the element, information about which is located in the first (n = 1), the lowest level of **the information pyramid;** it has the number i=11 in it and are connected by means of **the current information flows** to the element located in the third (k = 3) level of

pyramid, which has the number j = 1 and is conditionally marked in it by $El_{3.1}^{4.1}$;

$El_{1.12}^{2.4}$, $El_{1.13}^{2.4}$, $El_{1.14}^{2.4}$, $El_{1.15}^{2.4}$ – these are the elements, information about which is located in the first (n = 1), the lowest level of **the information pyramid**; they have the numbers i=12, i=13, i=14, i=15 in it and are connected by means of **the current information flows** to the element located in the second (k = 2) level of **pyramid**, which has the number j = 2 and is conditionally marked in it by $El_{2.4}^{2.2}$;

$El_{1.16}^{2.5}$, $El_{1.17}^{2.5}$, $El_{1.18}^{2.5}$, $El_{1.19}^{2.5}$ – these are the elements, information about which is located in the first (n = 1), the lowest level of **the information pyramid**; they have the numbers i=16, i=17, i=18, i=19 in it and are connected by means of **the current information flows** to the element located in the second (k = 2) level of **pyramid**, which has the number j = 2 and is conditionally marked in it by $El_{2.5}^{2.2}$;

$El_{1.20}^{2.6}$, $El_{1.21}^{2.6}$, $El_{1.22}^{2.6}$, $El_{1.23}^{2.6}$ – these are the elements, information about which is located in the first (n = 1), the lowest level of **the information pyramid**; they have the numbers i=20, i=21, i=22, i=23 in it and are connected by means of **the current information flows** to the element located in the second (k = 2) level of **pyramid**, which has the number j = 2 and is conditionally marked in it by $El_{2.6}^{2.2}$;

$El_{1.24}^{2.7}$, $El_{1.25}^{2.7}$, $El_{1.26}^{2.7}$ – these are the elements, information about which is located in the first (n = 1), the lowest level of **the information pyramid**; they have the numbers i=24, i=25, i=26 in it and are connected by means of **the current information flows** to the element located in the second (k = 2) level of **pyramid**, which has the number j = 2 and is conditionally marked in it by $El_{2.7}^{2.3}$;

$El_{1.27}^{2.8}$, $El_{1.28}^{2.8}$, $El_{1.29}^{2.8}$ – these are the elements, information about which is located in the first (n = 1), the lowest level of **the information pyramid**; they have the numbers i=27, i=28, i=29 in it and are connected by means of **the current information flows** to the element located in the second (k = 2) level of **pyramid**, which has the number j = 2 and is conditionally marked in it by $El_{2.8}^{2.3}$;

$El_{1.30}^{2.9}$, $El_{1.31}^{2.9}$, $El_{1.32}^{2.9}$, $El_{1.33}^{2.9}$ – these are the elements, information about which is located in the first (n = 1), the lowest level of **the information pyramid**; they have the numbers i=30, i=31, i=32, i=33 in it and are connected by means of **the current information flows** to the element located in the second (k = 2) level of **pyramid**, which has the number j = 2 and is conditionally marked in it by $El_{2.9}^{2.3}$;

$El_{2.1}^{4.1}$ – this is the element, information about which is located in the second (n = 2) level of **the information pyramid**; it has the number i=1 in it and are connected by means of **the current information flows** to the element located in the forth (k = 4), the highest level of **pyramid**, which has the number j = 1 and is conditionally marked in it by $El_{3.1}^{4.1}$;

$El_{2.2}^{3.1}$, $El_{2.3}^{3.1}$ – these are the elements, information about which is located in the second (n = 2) level of **the information pyramid**; they have the numbers i=2, i=3 in it and are connected by means of **the current information flows** to the element located in the third (k = 3) level of **pyramid**, which has the number j = 1 and is conditionally marked in it by $El_{3.1}^{4.1}$;

$El_{2.4}^{3.2}$, $El_{2.5}^{3.2}$, $El_{2.6}^{3.2}$ – these are the elements, information about which is located in the second (n = 2) level of **the information pyramid**; they have the numbers i=4, i=5, i=6 in it and are connected by means of **the current information flows** to the element located in the third (k = 3) level of **pyramid**, which has the number j = 2 and is conditionally marked in it by $El_{3.2}^{4.1}$;

$El_{2.7}^{3.3}$, $El_{2.8}^{3.3}$, $El_{2.9}^{3.3}$ – these are the elements, information about which is located in the second (n = 2) level of **the information pyramid**; they have the numbers i=7, i=8, i=9 in it and are connected by means of **the current information flows** to the element located in the third (k = 3) level of **pyramid**, which has the number j = 3 and is conditionally marked in it by $El^{4.1}_{3.2}$;

$El^{4.1}_{3.1}$, $El^{4.1}_{3.2}$, $El^{4.1}_{3.3}$ – these are the elements, information about which is located in the third (n = 3) level of **the information pyramid**; they have the numbers i=1, i=2, i=3 in it and are connected by means of **the current information flows** to the element located in the forth (k = 4), the highest level of **pyramid**, which has the number j = 1 and is conditionally marked in it by $El_{4.1}$;

$El_{4.1}$ – this is the element, information about which is located in the forth (n = 4), the highest level of **the information pyramid**; it has the number i=1 in it.

The structures depicted in Fig. IP 4 a) and b) are proposed as unified structures of the **Upward** (**IP$_U$**) and **Downward** (**IP$_D$**) **Information Pyramids**, which correspond to the typical scheme in Fig. IP 3.

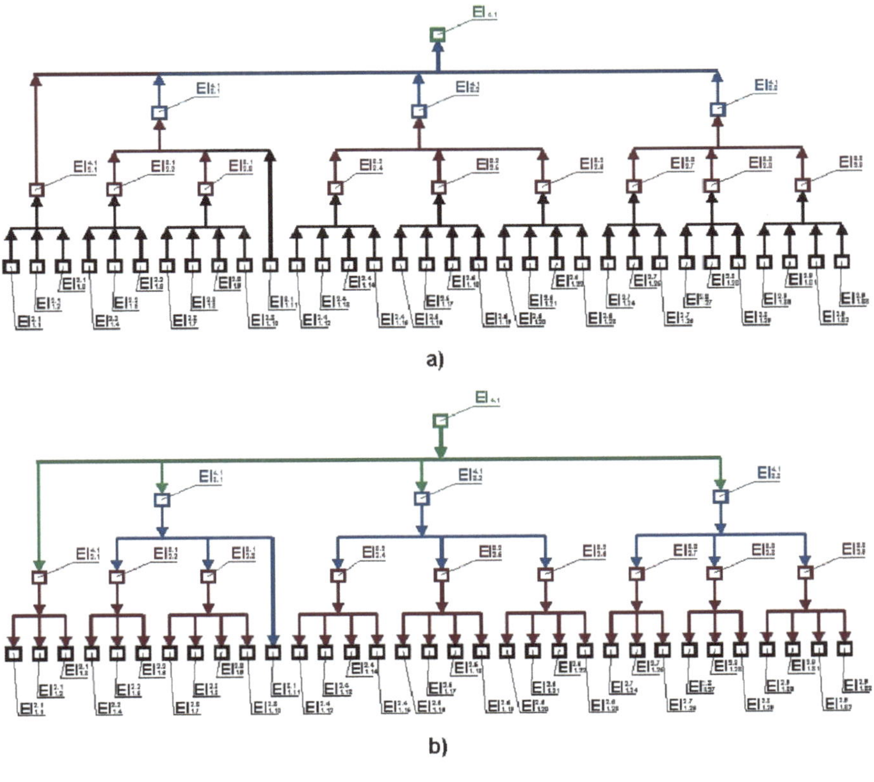

a)

b)

Fig. IP 4

The notation in Fig. IP 4:

The arrows indicate the direction of the current information flows between elements of **the upward** (IP_U, see Fig. IP 3 a)) and of **the Downward** (IP_U, see Fig. IP 3 b)) **Information Pyramids;**

Conventional notations of $El_{n.i}^{k.j}$ correspond to the conventional notations of the elements of the technological scheme, presented in Fig. IP 3.

Obviously, the persons form the structure of each specific information pyramid, respectively, the structure of **the technological scheme of the grid**, **the grid of Noologistics, the hierarchy**, etc.

The operations of arithmetic summation of the magnitudes of the parameters of **noo values** and / or the operation of combining their nomenclatures contained in their formalized descriptions are used in the formation of any **Upward Information Pyramid**.

In the formation of any **Downward Information Pyramid**, the operations of arithmetic subtraction of the magnitudes of the parameters of **noo values** and / or the operation of distribution of their nomenclatures contained in their formalized descriptions are used.

Two types of selection of processed information are used before performing the above operations in **Noologistics**: the first type is in accordance to **the status** of each **person** in the corresponding **hierarchy**, and the second - according to a specially calculated **index** for each **criterion of reasonable management** of the **object** specified in its **goal** in accordance to its **rules**.

From what has been said above, it follows that in **Noologistics** there are four types of technology for calculating information pyramids, including **technology for calculating of**:

Upward Unindexed Information Pyramid, briefly - $\mathbf{IP_{UU}}$ **calculation technology**;

Upward Indexed Information Pyramid, кратко - **IP_{UI} calculation technology;**

Downward Unindexed Information Pyramid, briefly – **IP_{DU} calculation technology;**

Downward Indexed Information Pyramid, кратко - **IP_{UI} calculation technology**.

All parameters, which are indicated as current, are calculated by **The Technology of Forecast Calculation in the PRESENT** and are their trend lines. The result of calculation for all four types of **technology for calculating information pyramids** are trend lines consisting of time-ordered sets of a set of intermediate predictable **information pyramids**. A brief description of the mathematical apparatus, algorithm and result of calculation of one of such intermediate predictable **information pyramids**, each of which is included in the corresponding trend, are shown below in the corresponding examples.

The specific structures of **the information pyramids** may differ from those shown in Fig. IP 4 and have any complexity, any number of levels and elements. Moreover, any upward and downward information pyramid may be placed as an element in any level of another upward and downward pyramid, provided that the same units of measurement are used and the calculated parameter is synchronized, for example, in **the PRESENT**, as well as the same names or codes of **noo values**. This circumstance provides a theoretical opportunity to create a single **information pyramid** of any size, scale and complexity, for example, within any **hierarchy**, **habitat**, **provision of life** (**life support**), **object**, **goal**, **managerial solution**, **environment**, **noosphere**, **noogalaxy**, **noouniverse**, etc.

Graphical images of the results of the calculation of the **upward** and **downward indexed information pyramids**, shown in the examples below, are intended primarily to visualize the results of the software change during its setup. The staff has the possibility to control **the object** in semi-automatic mode after the implementation of **the technology of Noologistics**, that is, to give the command to execute the automatically calculated set of **goal's** management parameters only after a personal analysis of its conformity to the **goal**,

principles and **criteria**. Practice has shown that personnel may use this method of management no more than 15 minutes due to the need to analyze a large flow of information, and then goes to fully automatic control.

The algorithm for calculating **the trend line for a set of control parameters** would be greatly simplified under fully automatic control without synchronous detailed visualization of its results, because the calculation is performed not for a set of points that form the whole image of the current and target areas of possible operating modes and network characteristics, but only for three types of current and target points - operating points and intersection points of network lines by contours of areas of possible operating modes. In addition, the calculation of these points is performed not for all states of **the trend line** of the control object, but only for its two states-its closest and final states. This significantly shortens the calculation time (approximately 5 times) and, consequently, **the trend step in calculating the forecast in the PRESENT** with simultaneous increase in the accuracy of the calculations.

The presented examples of **IP_{UU}, IP_{UI}, IP_{DU}** and **IP_{DI} calculation technologies** show their versatility and simplicity, as well as a real possibility of their application for **noo** and **noologistical** management of **objects** of any type, any size, any complexity, any productivity in any conditions.

All **information pyramids IP_{UU}, IP_{UI}, IP_{DU}** and **IP_{DI}**, which were calculated here based on the current parameters, are trends calculated using **the technology of forecast calculation in the PRESENT**. Therefore, the result of each of the following examples of calculations is one of the set of intermediate states in the trend of the corresponding pyramid.

3.4.1. The Technology of Calculation of the Upward Non-indexed Information Pyramid

The technology of calculating the IP_{UU} consists in arithmetic summation of a bunch of quantities expressed by the same units of measurement and related to the same **noo value**, for example, measured in **the PAST**, measured in **the PRESENT** or projected in **the FUTURE**, and also in the unification of the nomenclature of the quantities of values and / or densities of their flows contained in their formalized descriptions of elements of complex structure, for example, **person**, **hierarchy**, **habitat**, **provision of existence** (**life support**), **object**, **goal**, **managerial solution**, **environment**, **noosphere**, **noogalaxy**, and so on. It is carried out taking into account **the status coefficients** established in the relevant **rules**, starting with the elements of the lowest level of the complex structure mentioned above to the elements of its highest level.

Its main purpose is to calculate a parameter characterizing the total quantity or density of **the flow of noo value**, providing the satisfaction of the total **need** for it of all **persons** in accordance to **the rules** of their **hierarchy**, as well as satisfying their total **need** in the nomenclature of total quantities or densities of flows of **noo values**.

If **the goal** of **the hierarchy**, for example, OJSC Gazprom under the notation $\mathbf{P_{iw}}$, is the supply of natural gas to a number of other **persons**, including exploration of natural gas fields, their development, extraction, preparation for transport, transportation, distribution, transfer, settlements for transferred **natural gas**, etc., under **a compromise** of 50% of the minimum total costs of all types in monetary terms, a 30% minimum of total energy costs of all types expressed in MW and 20% the minimum of the total CO_2 emissions, so for the **noologistical** management of all its **grids** allocates for processing through the $\mathbf{IP_{UU}}$ calculation technology may be used from a multitude of parameters only those that are related to the four types of **current noologistic values**, including:

- **the transported natural gas** (**NG**), which is **the current noologistic creation value**, briefly - $\mathbf{V_{M.iw.NG}}$;
- all kinds of **total monetary costs** (**Mn**), which are **the current noologistic consumed value**, briefly - $\mathbf{V_{C.iw.Mn}}$;
- **the total expenditure of energy of all kinds** (**Vth**), which is **the current noologistic consumed value**, briefly - $\mathbf{V_{C.iw.Vth}}$;
- **the total CO_2 emission** (**CO2**), which is **the current noologistic rejection value**, briefly - $\mathbf{V_{S.iw.CO2}}$.

The parameters of **the current noologistic values** in the example under consideration are:

1. Parameters of **providing the existence** (**life support**) and the current **habitat** in the **PRESENT**, obtained from the means of their measurement by each **person** from each of its b-th **unit of equipment** in the **PRESENT**.

These include:

density of the current creation flow of $V_{M.ip.NG.b}$, briefly - $D_{M.ip.NG.b}$;
density of the current consumed flow of $V_{C.ip.NG.b}$, briefly - $D_{C.ip.NG.b}$;
density of the current consumed flow of $V_{C.ip.Mn.b}$, briefly - $D_{C.ip.Mn.b}$;
density of the current consumed flow of $V_{C.ip.Vth.b}$, briefly - $D_{C.ip.Vth.b}$;
density of the current rejection flow of $V_{S.ip.CO2.b}$, briefly - $D_{S.ip.CO2.b}$;
the current quantity of $V_{M.ip.NG.b}$, briefly – $Q_{M.ip.NG.b}$;
the current quantity of $V_{C.ip.NG.b}$, briefly - $Q_{C.ip.NG.b}$;
the current quantity of $V_{C.ip.Mn.b}$, briefly - $Q_{C.ip.Mn.b}$;
the current quantity of $V_{C.ip.Vth.b}$, briefly - $Q_{C.ip.Vth.b}$;
the current quantity of $V_{S.ip.CO2.b}$, briefly - $Q_{S.ip.CO2.b}$, etc.

The result of their processing using **the IP_{UU} calculation technology** will be the magnitudes of **the densities of the current creation flow** ($D_{M.iw.NG}$), **the consumption flows** ($D_{C.iw.NG}$, $D_{C.iw.Vth}$ and $D_{C.iw.Mn}$) and **the rejection flow** ($D_{S.iw.CO2}$) , and also - **the current quantities** ($Q_{M.iw.NG}$, $Q_{C.iw.NG}$, $Q_{C.iw.Vth}$, $Q_{C.iw.Mn}$ and $Q_{S.iw.CO2}$) in **the PRESENT** at the highest level of management of all **grids** in the entire calculated **hierarchy**. The sequence of their summation operations using **the IP_{UU} calculation technique** is shown in Example 1.

2. Parameters for **providing the existence** (**life support**) and **habitat** from a formalized description of the **goal** in **the FUTURE**, established by each **person** for each of its b-th **equipment units**.

These include:

density of the goal's creation flow of $VA_{M.ip.NG.b}$, briefly - $DA_{M.ip.NG.b}$;
density of the goal's consumed flow of $VA_{C.ip.NG.b}$, briefly - $DA_{C.ip.NG.b}$;
density of the goal's consumed flow of $VA_{C.ip.Mn.b}$, briefly - $DA_{C.ip.Mn.b}$;
density of the goal's consumed flow of $VA_{C.ip.Vth.b}$, briefly - $DA_{C.ip.Vth.b}$;
density of the goal's rejection flow of $VA_{S.ip.CO2.b}$, briefly - $DA_{S.ip.CO2.b}$;
the goal's quantity of $VA_{M.ip.NG.b}$, briefly – $QA_{M.ip.NG.b}$;
the goal's quantity of $VA_{C.ip.NG.b}$, briefly - $QA_{C.ip.NG.b}$;
the goal's quantity of $VA_{C.ip.Mn.b}$, briefly - $QA_{C.ip.Mn.b}$;
the goal's quantity of $VA_{C.ip.Vth.b}$, briefly - $QA_{C.ip.NG.b}$;
the goal's quantity of $VA_{S.ip.CO2.b}$, briefly - $QA_{S.ip.CO2.b}$, etc.

The result of their processing using **the IP_{UU} calculation technology** will be the magnitudes of the densities of **the goal's creation flow** ($DA_{M.iw.NG}$), **the goal's consumption flows** ($DA_{C.iw.NG}$, $DA_{C.iw.Vth}$ and $DA_{C.iw.Mn}$) and **the goal's rejection flow** ($DA_{S.iw.CO2}$) , and also - **the goal's quantities** ($QA_{M.iw.NG}$, $QA_{C.iw.NG}$, $QA_{C.iw.Vth}$, $QA_{C.iw.Mn}$ and $QA_{S.iw.CO2}$) in **the FUTURE** at the highest level of management of all **grids** in the entire calculated **hierarchy**. The sequence of their summation operations using **the IP_{UU} calculation technique** is shown in Example 1.

3. Parameters for **providing the existence** (**life support**) and **habitat** for formalized descriptions of the preparation (simulation of the consequences) of the development and adoption of a management solution in the entire calculated **hierarchy** in **the FUTURE**.

These include:

density of the normative creation flow of $VS_{M.ip.NG.b}$, briefly - $DS_{M.ip.NG.b}$;
density of the normative consumed flow of $VS_{C.ip.NG.b}$, briefly - $DS_{C.ip.NG.b}$;

density of the normative consumed flow of $VS_{C.ip.Mn.b}$, briefly - **$DS_{C.ip.Mn.b}$**;

density of the normative consumed flow of $VS_{C.ip.Vth.b}$, briefly - **$DS_{C.ip.Vth.b}$**;

density of the normative rejection flow of $VS_{S.ip.CO2.b}$, briefly - **$DS_{S.ip.CO2.b}$**;

the normative quantity of $VS_{M.ip.NG.b}$, briefly – **$QS_{M.ip.NG.b}$**;

the normative quantity of $VS_{C.ip.NG.b}$, briefly - **$QS_{C.ip.NG.b}$**;

the normative quantity of $VS_{C.ip.Mn.b}$, briefly - **$QS_{C.ip.Mn.b}$**;

the normative quantity of $VS_{C.ip.Vth.b}$, briefly - **$QS_{C.ip.NG.b}$**;

the normative quantity of $VS_{S.ip.CO2.b}$, briefly - **$QS_{S.ip.CO2.b}$**, etc.

The result of their processing using the **IP_{UU} calculation technology** will be the normative magnitudes of the densities of **the normative creation flow** (**$DS_{M.iw.NG}$**), **the normative consumption flows** (**$DS_{C.iw.NG}$, $DS_{C.iw.Vth}$** and **$DS_{C.iw.Mn}$**) and **the normative rejection flow** (**$DS_{S.iw\ .CO2}$**), and also - **normative quantities** (**$QS_{M.iw.NG}$, $QS_{C.iw.NG}$, $QS_{C.iw.Vth}$, $QS_{C.iw.Mn}$** and **$QS_{S.iw.CO2}$**) in the **FUTURE** at the highest level of management of all **grids** in the entire calculated **hierarchy**. The sequence of their summation operations using **the IP_{UU} calculation technique** is shown in Example 1.

Example 1

The structure of the upward non-indexed information pyramid is shown in Fig. IP 4 a).

1. Summarize the magnitudes of the parameters from the elements of the first lowest level in groups in accordance to the direction of the arrows, forming the magnitudes of the parameters of the elements of the second level.

1.1. Summarize the magnitudes of the parameters from the elements $El_{1.1}^{2.1}$, $El_{1.2}^{2.1}$ and $El_{1.3}^{2.1}$, forming the magnitude of the parameter in group $El_{2.1}^{4.1}$ by the universal formula:

$El_{2.1}^{4.1} = El_{1.1}^{2.1} + El_{1.2}^{2.1} + El_{1.3}^{2.1}$, in which all the conventions are shown in Fig. IP 4 a).

If the magnitudes of $\mathbf{D_{C.ip.NG.b}}$ (see above) are summarized by this formula, then it becomes:

$$D_{2.1}^{4.1} = K_{1.1}^{2.1} * D_{1.1}^{2.1} + K_{1.2}^{2.1} * D_{1.2}^{2.1} + K_{1.3}^{2.1} * D_{1.3}^{2.1},$$

here are:

$K_{1.1}^{2.1}$ - **the status coefficient** determined by **the hierarchy rules** for the element, which in the structure shown in Fig. IP 4 a), conditionally indicated by $El_{1.1}^{2.1}$;

$D_{1.1}^{2.1}$ – the magnitude of $\mathbf{D_{C.ih.NG.b}}$ for the element, which in the structure shown in Fig. IP 4 a), conditionally indicated by $El_{1.1}^{2.1}$;

$K_{1.2}^{2.1}$ – **the status coefficient** determined by **the hierarchy rules** for the element, which in the structure shown in Fig. IP 4 a), conditionally indicated by $El_{1.2}^{2.1}$;

$D_{1.2}^{2.1}$ – the magnitude of $\mathbf{D_{C.ip.NG.b}}$ for the element, which in the structure shown in Fig. IP 4 a), conditionally indicated by $El_{1.2}^{2.1}$;

$K_{1.3}^{2.1}$ – **the status coefficient** determined by **the hierarchy rules** for the element, which in the structure shown in Fig. IP 4 a), conditionally indicated by $El_{1.3}^{2.1}$;

$D_{1.3}^{2.1}$ – the magnitude of $\mathbf{D_{C.ip.NG.b}}$ for the element, which in the structure shown in Fig. IP 4 a), conditionally indicated by $El_{1.3}^{2.1}$.

The status coefficients in **Noologistics** are the magnitudes established by **the hierarchy rules** that are used in the formation of **upward and downward non-indexed information pyramids** and which determine the inequality of the **persons** when they form **the provision of their existence** (**life support**) and **habitat** from the common **providing the existence** (**life support**) of the entire **hierarchy** and from their entire **habitat**.

The status coefficients for the elements $El_{1.1}^{2.1}$, $El_{1.2}^{2.1}$ and $El_{1.3}^{2.1}$ are usually equal to one ($K_{1.1}^{2.1}$ = 1, $K_{1.2}^{2.1}$ = 1 and $K_{1.3}^{2.1}$ = 1) when summing up the magnitudes of the parameters that are measured in them in **the PRESENT**, unless otherwise specified in **the rules** of **the hierarchy**. This provides compliance to **the principle of protecting information from distortion**. In other cases, for example, when forming a **goal**, developing **a noo management solution** and modeling in solving other tasks of managing **a hierarchy**, their magnitudes are determined individually for each **person** or for each type of **persons** corresponds to their **status in the hierarchy**, and reflects the degree of its "fairness", "equality", "democracy", and so on.

Similar substitutions of notations in universal formulas are applied below in the remaining paragraphs of this example when summing the magnitudes of any other parameters.

1.2. Summarize the magnitudes of the parameters from the elements $El_{1.4}^{2.2}$, $El_{1.5}^{2.2}$ and $El_{1.6}^{2.2}$, forming the magnitude of the parameter in group $El_{2.2}^{3.1}$ by the universal formula:

$El_{2.2}^{3.1} = El_{1.4}^{2.2} + El_{1.5}^{2.2} + El_{1.6}^{2.2}$, in which all the conventions are shown in Fig. IP 4 a).

1.3. Summarize the magnitudes of the parameters from the elements $El_{1.7}^{2.3}$, $El_{1.8}^{2.3}$, $El_{1.9}^{2.3}$ and $El_{1.10}^{2.3}$, forming the magnitude of the parameter in group $El_{2.3}^{3.1}$ by the universal formula:

$El_{2.3}^{3.1} = El_{1.7}^{2.3} + El_{1.8}^{2.3} + El_{1.9}^{2.3} + El_{1.10}^{2.3}$, in which all the conventions are shown in Fig. IP 4 a).

1.4. Summarize the magnitudes of the parameters from the elements $El_{1.12}^{2.4}$, $El_{1.13}^{2.4}$, $El_{1.14}^{2.4}$ and $El_{1.15}^{2.4}$, forming the magnitude of the parameter in group $El_{2.4}^{3.2}$ by the universal formula:

$El_{2.4}^{3.2} = El_{1.12}^{2.4} + El_{1.13}^{2.4} + El_{1.14}^{2.4} + El_{1.15}^{2.4}$, in which all the conventions are shown in Fig. IP 4 a).

1.5. Summarize the magnitudes of the parameters from the elements $El_{1.16}^{2.5}$, $El_{1.17}^{2.5}$, $El_{1.18}^{2.5}$ and $El_{1.19}^{2.5}$, forming the magnitude of the parameter in group $El_{2.5}^{3.2}$ by the universal formula:

$El_{2.5}^{3.2} = El_{1.16}^{2.5} + El_{1.17}^{2.5} + El_{1.18}^{2.5} + El_{1.19}^{2.5}$, in which all the conventions are shown in Fig. IP 4 a).

1.6. Summarize the magnitudes of the parameters from the elements $El_{1.20}^{2.6}$, $El_{1.21}^{2.6}$, $El_{1.22}^{2.6}$ and $El_{1.23}^{2.6}$, forming the magnitude of the parameter in group $El_{2.6}^{3.2}$ by the universal formula:

$El_{2.6}^{3.2} = El_{1.20}^{2.6} + El_{1.21}^{2.6} + El_{1.22}^{2.6} + El_{1.23}^{2.6}$, in which all the conventions are shown in Fig. IP 4 a).

1.7. Summarize the magnitudes of the parameters from the elements $El_{1.24}^{2.7}$, $El_{1.25}^{2.7}$ and $El_{1.26}^{2.7}$, forming the magnitude of the parameter in group $El_{2.7}^{3.3}$ by the universal formula:

$El_{2.7}^{3.3} = El_{1.24}^{2.7} + El_{1.25}^{2.7} + El_{1.26}^{2.7}$, in which all the conventions are shown in Fig. IP 4 a).

1.8. Summarize the magnitudes of the parameters from the elements $El_{1.27}^{2.8}$, $El_{1.28}^{2.8}$ and $El_{1.29}^{2.8}$, forming the magnitude of the parameter in group $El_{2.8}^{3.3}$ by the universal formula:

$El_{2.8}^{3.3} = El_{1.27}^{2.8} + El_{1.28}^{2.8} + El_{1.29}^{2.8}$, in which all the conventions are shown in Fig. IP 4 a).

1.9. Summarize the magnitudes of the parameters from the elements $El_{1.30}^{2.9}$, $El_{1.31}^{2.9}$, $El_{1.32}^{2.9}$ and $El_{1.33}^{2.9}$, forming the magnitude of the parameter in group $El_{2.8}^{3.3}$ by the universal formula:

$El_{2.8}^{3.3} = El_{1.30}^{2.9} + El_{1.31}^{2.9} + El_{1.32}^{2.9} + El_{1.33}^{2.9}$, in which all the conventions are shown in Fig. IP 4 a).

2. Summarize the magnitudes of the parameters from the elements of the second level, forming the magnitudes of the total parameters of the elements of the third level.

2.1. Summarize the magnitudes of the parameters from the elements $El_{2.2}^{3.1}$, $El_{2.3}^{3.1}$ and $El_{1.11}^{3.1}$, forming the magnitude of the parameter in group $El_{3.1}^{4.1}$ by the universal formula:

$El_{2.1}^{4.1} = El_{2.2}^{3.1} + El_{2.3}^{3.1} + El_{1.11}^{3.1}$, in which all the conventions are shown in Fig. IP 4 a).

2.2. Summarize the magnitudes of the parameters from the elements $El_{2.4}^{3.2}$, $El_{2.5}^{3.2}$ and $El_{2.6}^{3.2}$, forming the magnitude of the parameter in group $El_{3.2}^{4.1}$ by the universal formula:

$El_{3.2}^{4.1} = El_{2.4}^{3.2} + El_{2.5}^{3.2} + El_{2.6}^{3.2}$, in which all the conventions are shown in Fig. IP 4 a).

2.3. Summarize the magnitudes of the parameters from the elements $El_{2.7}^{3.3}$, $El_{2.8}^{3.3}$ and $El_{2.9}^{3.3}$, forming the magnitude of the parameter in group $El_{3.3}^{4.1}$ by the universal formula:

$El_{3.3}^{4.1} = El_{2.7}^{3.3} + El_{2.8}^{3.3} + El_{2.9}^{3.3}$, in which all the conventions are shown in Fig. IP 4 a).

3. Summarize the magnitudes of the parameters from the elements $El_{2.1}^{4.1}$, $El_{3.1}^{4.1}$, $El_{3.2}^{4.1}$ and $El_{3.3}^{4.1}$ of third level, forming the magnitude of the parameter in group $El_{4.1}$ of forth level by the universal formula:

$El_{4.1} = El_{2.1}^{4.1} + El_{3.1}^{4.1} + El_{3.2}^{4.1} + El_{3.3}^{4.1}$, in which all the conventions are shown in Fig. IP 4 a).

It is obvious that the number of management levels in real **grids**, for example, OJSC Gazprom, may be hundreds of times, and the number of elements in them is millions of times greater than shown in Example 1, but the mathematical apparatus and algorithm for calculation **the upward non-indexed the information pyramid** does not change from this. Moreover, any element calculated in Example 1 may be embedded in another **upward non-indexed information pyramid** of a higher level as one of the numerous elements of any of its levels. Such a multiple input of each calculated **information pyramid** in an **information pyramid** of a higher level will allow to provide the management at the highest level of any **hierarchy, habitat, provision of existence (life support), object, goal, managerial solution, environment, noosphere, noogalaxy** etc.

3.4.2. The Technology of Calculation of the Upward Indexed Information Pyramid

Technology of calculation IP_{UI} is used to calculate the total technical capabilities to achieve the magnitude of a given parameter in **the hierarchy** at the highest level of its management, characterizing the flow or quantity of its certain **noologistical value**, by all its **persons** located at all levels of its management. It is performed according to the algorithm described below by summing a set of **indexed noologistical areas of possible modes of operation** of real **objects** working together in the same group that are previously calculated in the same coordinates with respect to the same current **noologistical values**, beginning with the equipment of the lowest level of the **object** management up to the elements its highest level. Summation is carried out at points in which the magnitudes of **the indices of the criteria of reasonableness** are equal or are the closest in magnitude. Its main goal is to calculate the total technical capabilities of an **object** to meet the total **needs** of the entity at the highest level of management, including the **need** to observe one particular **criterion of management's reasonableness** or to comply with a given trade-off between several **criteria**.

The status coefficients $K_{1.1}^{2.1}$, $K_{1.2}^{2.1}$, $K_{1.3}^{2.1}$, ..., $K_{3.3}^{4.1}$, that are used in forming the IP_{UU} are not used in the formation of the IP_{UI}.

Indexed noologistical areas of possible modes of operation (briefly - $\mathbf{RPM_{C.iw.Mn.b}}$, $\mathbf{RPM_{C.iw.Vth.b}}$ and $\mathbf{RPM_{S.iw.CO2.b}}$) of all the b-th **units of equipment** of the entire **grid** of **person** are summarized by the $\mathbf{IP_{UI}}$ **calculation technology** under **noologistical** management all their **grids**, if the **goal** of **the hierarchy**, for example, OJSC Gazprom conditionally designated $\mathbf{P_{iw}}$, is the supply of natural gas to a number of other **persons** above-mentioned in the description of the $\mathbf{IP_{UU}}$ **calculation technology**, including exploration of natural gas fields, their development, extraction, preparation for transport, transportation, distribution transfer, settlements for transferred natural gas, etc., under a compromise of 50% of the minimum total costs of all types in monetary terms, a 30% minimum of total energy costs of all types expressed in MW, and 20 % minimum of total CO_2 emissions, including:

1. **Indexed noologistical areas of possible modes of operation** (briefly - $\mathbf{RPM_{C.iw.Mn.b}}$, $\mathbf{RPM_{C.iw.Vth.b}}$ and $\mathbf{RPM_{S.iw.CO2.b}}$) of all the b-th **units of equipment** of the entire **grid** of **person** are summarized by the $\mathbf{IP_{UI}}$ **calculation technology** for management in **PRESENT**.

The result of this summation are three **summary indexed noologistical areas of possible modes of operation** of the highest-level control of all **grids** of **the hierarchy**, which are conditionally designated $\mathbf{RPM_{C.iw.Mn}}$, $\mathbf{RPM_{C.iw.Vth}}$ and $\mathbf{RPM_{S.iw.CO2}}$. This set (Σ) of three $\mathbf{RPM_{C.iw.Mn}}$, $\mathbf{RPM_{C.iw.Vth}}$ and $\mathbf{RPM_{S.iw.CO2}}$ is hereinafter conventionally designated $\mathbf{RPM_{iw}}$: $\mathbf{RPM_{iw} = \Sigma(RPM_{C.iw.Mn}, RPM_{C.iw.Vth}, RPM_{S.iw.CO2})}$. The resulting $\mathbf{RPM_{iw}}$ is used to calculate **the current noologistical control actions**.

The sequence of operations using **the** $\mathbf{IP_{UI}}$ **calculation technology** is shown in Example 2.

2. **Goal**'s **indexed noologistical areas of possible modes of operation** (that is, corresponding to the goal set by the person, briefly - $\mathbf{RPMA_{C.iw.Mn.b}}$, $\mathbf{RPMA_{C.iw.Vth.b}}$ and $\mathbf{RPMA_{S.iw.CO2.b}}$) of all b-th goal **units of equipment** of the entire **goal grid** of **the person** are summarized by $\mathbf{IP_{UI}}$ technology in **the goal** setting for **the FUTURE**.

The result of this summation are three **goal's summary indexed noologistical areas of possible modes of operation** of the highest-level control of all **grids** of **the hierarchy**, which are conditionally designated **RPMA**$_{C.iw.Mn}$, **RPMA**$_{C.iw.Vth}$ and **RPMA**$_{S.iw.CO2}$. This set (Σ) of three **RPMA**$_{C.iw.Mn}$, **RPMA**$_{C.iw.Vth}$ and **RPMA**$_{S.iw.CO2}$ is hereinafter conventionally designated **RPMA**$_{iw}$: **RPMA**$_{iw}$ = Σ(**RPMA**$_{C.iw.Mn}$, **RPMA**$_{C.iw.Vth}$, **RPMA**$_{S.iw.CO2}$). The resulting **RPMA**$_{iw}$ is used for modeling in the calculation of **goal** parameters.

The sequence of operations for computing **RPMA**$_{iw}$ using **the IP**$_{UI}$ **calculation technology** is similar to the sequence shown in Example 2, and differs only in the original data.

3. Predicted **indexed noologistical areas of possible modes of operation** (ie, corresponding to the forecast calculated by the **person**, briefly - **RPMS**$_{C.iw.Mn.b}$, **RPMS**$_{C.iw.Vth.b}$ and **RPMS**$_{S.iw.CO2.b}$) of all projected in **the FUTURE** b-th **units of equipment** of the entire projected **grid** of **the person** are summarized according to the **IP**$_{UI}$ **calculation technology** for solving the tasks of developing and adopting a **noologistical management solution** in **the FUTURE**.

The result of this summation are three **predicted summary indexed noologistical areas of possible modes of operation** of the highest-level control of all **grids** of **the hierarchy**, which are conditionally designated **RPMS**$_{C.iw.Mn}$, **RPMS**$_{C.iw.Vth}$ and **RPMS**$_{S.iw.CO2}$. This set (Σ) of three **RPMS**$_{C.iw.Mn}$, **RPMS**$_{C.iw.Vth}$ and **RPMS**$_{S.iw.CO2}$ is hereinafter conventionally designated **RPMS**$_{iw}$: **RPMS**$_{iw}$ = Σ(**RPMS**$_{C.iw.Mn}$, **RPMS**$_{C.iw.Vth}$, **RPMS**$_{S.iw.CO2}$). The resulting **RPMS**$_{iw}$ is used for modeling in the calculation of **rule** parameters.

The sequence of operations for computing **RPMS**$_{iw}$ using **the IP**$_{UI}$ **calculation technology** is similar to the sequence shown in Example 2, and differs only in the original data.

Example 2

1. Background information

1.1. Elements of the technological scheme of **the hierarchy** under consideration.

In the example considered, it is accepted that Fig. IP 3 presents a simplified image of a part of OJSC Gazprom's **grids**, which depicts **the booster compressor station of the Komsomolsk gas field** (**BCS KGF**). This choice is due to the sufficient complexity of **the technological process** (**TP**) in it, the presence of different types of equipment and several levels of management. The successful results of design, creation, installation, commissioning and testing **the system of Noologistics** were the base of that choice also.

A specific element of the real technological scheme of the **BCS KGF** corresponds to each of the elements depicted in Fig. IP 3, including:

Element $El_{2.4}^{3.2}$ simplistically depicts its first compression stage, in which: element $El_{1.12}^{2.4}$ depicts **gas-compressor unit #1** (briefly - **GCU #1**), element $El_{1.13}^{2.4}$ depicts **GCU #2**, element $El_{1.14}^{2.4}$ represents **GCU #3**, element $El_{1.15}^{2.4}$ represents **GCU #4**.

Element $El_{2.5}^{3.2}$ simplistically depicts its first compression stage, in which: element $El_{1.16}^{2.5}$ depicts **GCU #5**, element $El_{1.17}^{2.5}$ depicts **GCU #6**, element $El_{1.18}^{2.5}$ represents **GCU #7**, element $El_{1.19}^{2.5}$ represents **GCU #8**.

Element $El_{2.6}^{3.2}$ simplistically depicts its first compression stage, in which: element $El_{1.20}^{2.6}$ depicts **GCU #9**, element $El_{1.21}^{2.6}$ depicts **GCU #10**, element $El_{1.22}^{2.6}$ represents **GCU #11**, element $El_{1.23}^{2.6}$ represents **GCU #12**.

1.2. Accepted simplifications

Units of equipment totaling 426 units, which are **gas-air coolers** (**GAC**), Mokveld-type bypass valves, which are actually installed in it, are not shown in the image of the **BCS KGF** structure in Fig. IP 3 to reduce the description of **the IP_{UI} calculation technology**.

One Mokveld-type bypass valve is installed behind each **GCU**, which represents the elements $El_{1.12}^{2.4}$, $El_{1.13}^{2.4}$, $El_{1.14}^{2.4}$, $El_{1.15}^{2.4}$, $El_{1.16}^{2.5}$, $El_{1.17}^{2.5}$, $El_{1.18}^{2.5}$, $El_{1.19}^{2.5}$, $El_{1.20}^{2.6}$, $El_{1.21}^{2.6}$, $El_{1.22}^{2.6}$ and $El_{1.23}^{2.6}$, in each compression stage. That is, 12 Mokveld valves are not shown in Fig. IP 3 for simplicity.

A group of **GAC** of the type AVGBS-83P in the amount of 18 pieces, which operate in parallel to each other, is installed in the **BCS KGF** behind the first compression stage, which in Fig. IP 3 represents the element $El_{2.4}^{3.2}$. Each of these **GAC** consists of sections of pipes, cooled by two parallel groups of fans of 3 series-mounted fans, and three types of blinds: input, output and bypass. Therefore, each of these **GAC** should be presented in Fig. IP 3 in the form of a single complex element containing four consecutive elements, one of which contains 2 groups of 3 consecutive elements, and its total number behind the element $El_{2.4}^{3.2}$ is 18 * (3 + 2 * 3) = 162 pieces. That is, a common Mokveld bypass valve, which is installed behind all the **GAC** of this stage's gas, is not shown in Fig. IP 3. The total number of elements actually installed behind the first compression stage, but for simplicity not shown in Fig. IP 3, is 163 pieces.

A group of **GAC** of the type AVGBS-83P in the amount of 22 pieces, which operate in parallel to each other, and one common Mokveld bypass valve are installed in the **BCS KGF** behind the second compression stage, which in Fig. IP 3 represents the element $El_{2.5}^{3.2}$. Therefore, each of these **GAC** should be presented in Fig. IP 3 in the form of a single complex element containing four consecutive elements, one of which contains 2 groups of 3 consecutive elements, and its total number behind the element $El_{2.5}^{3.2}$ is 22 * (3 + 2 * 3) = 198 pieces. The total number of elements actually installed behind the second compression stage, but for simplicity not shown in Fig. IP 3, is 199 pieces.

A group of **GAC** of the type 2AVG-75 “S” in the amount of 21 pieces, which operate in parallel to each other, and one common

Mokveld bypass valve are installed in the **BCS KGF** behind the third compression stage, which in Fig. IP 3 represents the element $El_{2.6}^{3.2}$. Each of these **GAC** consists of pipes, cooled by two series-mounted fans. Therefore, each of these **GAC** should be presented in Fig. IP 3 in the form of a single complex element containing three consecutive elements, and its total number behind the element $El_{2.6}^{3.2}$ is 21 * 3 = 63 pieces. A common Mokveld bypass valve, which is installed behind all the **GAC** of this stage's gas, is not shown in Fig. IP 3 also. The total number of elements actually installed behind the third compression stage, but for simplicity not shown in Fig. IP 3, is 64 pieces.

1.3. Summable areas of possible modes of operation.

Special information set is calculated at **PRESENT** for each of the 12 above-mentioned **GCU**, consisting of three **indexed noologistical total areas of possible modes of operation** (set **RPM**$_{\mathbf{C.iw.Mn.b}}$, **RPM**$_{\mathbf{C.iw.Vth.b}}$ and **RPM**$_{\mathbf{S.iw.CO2.b}}$), which have the appropriate composition and the conventional designation adopted for them:

- for **GCU #1**, designated $El_{1.12}^{2.4}$, it consists of **RPM**$_{\mathbf{C.iw.Mn.1}}$, **RPM**$_{\mathbf{C.iw.Vth.1}}$ and **RPM**$_{\mathbf{S.iw.CO2.1}}$ (this set is briefly denoted by **RPM**$_{\mathbf{iw.1}}$);
- for **GCU #2**, designated $El_{1.13}^{2.4}$, it consists of **RPM**$_{\mathbf{C.iw.Mn.2}}$, **RPM**$_{\mathbf{C.iw.Vth.2}}$ and **RPM**$_{\mathbf{S.iw.CO2.2}}$ (this set is briefly denoted by **RPM**$_{\mathbf{iw.2}}$);
- for **GCU #3**, designated $El_{1.14}^{2.4}$, it consists of **RPM**$_{\mathbf{C.iw.Mn.3}}$, **RPM**$_{\mathbf{C.iw.Vth.3}}$ and **RPM**$_{\mathbf{S.iw.CO2.3}}$ (this set is briefly denoted by **RPM**$_{\mathbf{iw.3}}$);
- for **GCU #4**, designated $El_{1.15}^{2.4}$, it consists of **RPM**$_{\mathbf{C.iw.Mn.4}}$, **RPM**$_{\mathbf{C.iw.Vth.4}}$ and **RPM**$_{\mathbf{S.iw.CO2.4}}$ (this set is briefly denoted by **RPM**$_{\mathbf{iw.4}}$);
- for **GCU #5**, designated $El_{1.16}^{2.5}$, it consists of **RPM**$_{\mathbf{C.iw.Mn.5}}$, **RPM**$_{\mathbf{C.iw.Vth.5}}$ and **RPM**$_{\mathbf{S.iw.CO2.5}}$ (this set is briefly denoted by **RPM**$_{\mathbf{iw.5}}$);

- for **GCU #6**, designated $El_{1.17}^{2.5}$, it consists of $\mathbf{RPM_{C.iw.Mn.6}}$, $\mathbf{RPM_{C.iw.Vth.6}}$ and $\mathbf{RPM_{S.iw.CO2.6}}$ (this set is briefly denoted by $\mathbf{RPM_{iw.6}}$);
- for **GCU #7**, designated $El_{1.18}^{2.5}$, it consists of $\mathbf{RPM_{C.iw.Mn.7}}$, $\mathbf{RPM_{C.iw.Vth.7}}$ and $\mathbf{RPM_{S.iw.CO2.7}}$ (this set is briefly denoted by $\mathbf{RPM_{iw.7}}$);
- for **GCU #8**, designated $El_{1.19}^{2.5}$, it consists of $\mathbf{RPM_{C.iw.Mn.8}}$, $\mathbf{RPM_{C.iw.Vth.8}}$ and $\mathbf{RPM_{S.iw.CO2.8}}$ (this set is briefly denoted by $\mathbf{RPM_{iw.8}}$);
- for **GCU #9**, designated $El_{1.20}^{2.6}$, it consists of $\mathbf{RPM_{C.iw.Mn.9}}$, $\mathbf{RPM_{C.iw.Vth.9}}$ and $\mathbf{RPM_{S.iw.CO2.9}}$ (this set is briefly denoted by $\mathbf{RPM_{iw.9}}$);
- for **GCU #10**, designated $El_{1.21}^{2.6}$, it consists of $\mathbf{RPM_{C.iw.Mn.10}}$, $\mathbf{RPM_{C.iw.Vth.10}}$ and $\mathbf{RPM_{S.iw.CO2.10}}$ (this set is briefly denoted by $\mathbf{RPM_{iw.10}}$);
- for **GCU #11**, designated $El_{1.22}^{2.6}$, it consists of $\mathbf{RPM_{C.iw.Mn.11}}$, $\mathbf{RPM_{C.iw.Vth.11}}$ and $\mathbf{RPM_{S.iw.CO2.11}}$ (this set is briefly denoted by $\mathbf{RPM_{iw.11}}$);
- for **GCU #12**, designated $El_{1.23}^{2.6}$, it consists of $\mathbf{RPM_{C.iw.Mn.12}}$, $\mathbf{RPM_{C.iw.Vth.12}}$ and $\mathbf{RPM_{S.iw.CO2.12}}$ (this set is briefly denoted by $\mathbf{RPM_{iw.12}}$).

The universal subprogram in **the system of Noologistics**, implemented in the **BCS KGF**, calculates these sets for any type of **GCU**. It uses **the passport work characteristics** of each **GCU** and the current measurements of the parameters of their operating modes, automatically obtained from existing control systems. Three other special universal subprograms in **the system of Noologistics** calculate the similar sets for each of its 426 elements, which are not shown in Fig. IP 3, but really installed in the **BCS KGF**. These are universal subprograms for the Mokveld bypass valve, **GAC** of the type AVGBS-83R and **GAC** of the type 2AVG-75 “S”.

1.4. **Priorities of importance** were set (turn-on and turn-off sequence)

Priorities of importance are established for all elements in each group of all levels. They determine the order of use of each element, i.e., its inclusion in operation and shutdown. Each **person** establishes **priorities of importance** in accordance to **the rules** in force for him. The basis for their establish may be, for example, a plan for the withdrawal of equipment for repairs and the need to work out the entire overhaul life by the beginning of the repair. Any change in **priority of the importance** of the element and, consequently, of the sequence of its use is the basis for automatic recalculation of **RPM$_{iw}$**.

In the example considered, it is established that the importance of the element in each group decreases as its number i increases. For example, $El_{1.12}^{2.4}$ has the greatest importance, and $El_{1.15}^{2.4}$ - the smallest one between $El_{1.12}^{2.4}$, $El_{1.13}^{2.4}$, $El_{1.14}^{2.4}$ and $El_{1.15}^{2.4}$ that forming a group under designation $El_{2.4}^{3.2}$. Thus, $El_{1.12}^{2.4}$ is turned on the first and turned off the last, and $El_{1.15}^{2.4}$ is turned on the last and turned off the first in the example in question. And the summation of their **RPM$_{C.iw.Mn.b}$**, **RPM$_{C.iw.Vth.b}$** and **RPM$_{S.iw.CO2.b}$** is performed in the same sequence.

2. **RPM$_{C.iw.Mn.b}$**, **RPM$_{C.iw.Vth.b}$** and **RPM$_{S.iw.CO2.b}$**, calculated for each b-th element of the first lowest level, are summed by groups according to the direction of the arrows in Fig . IP 4 a).

2.1. **RPM$_{C.iw.Mn.b}$**, **RPM$_{C.iw.Vth.b}$** and **RPM$_{S.iw.CO2.b}$** of the first type, previously calculated for $El_{1.12}^{2.4}$, $El_{1.13}^{2.4}$, $El_{1.14}^{2.4}$ and $El_{1.15}^{2.4}$, are summed according to the **priority of the importance** that were set, forming the **RPM$_{C.iw.Mn.\Sigma4}$**, **RPM$_{C.iw.Vth.\Sigma4}$** and **RPM$_{S.iw.CO2.\Sigma4}$** (in set - **RPM$_{\Sigma4}$** of the first type) for $El_{2.4}^{3.2}$ of the second level of control, in the following sequence of operations:

2.1.1. The counters of **RPM$_{C.iw.Mn.b}$**, **RPM$_{C.iw.Vth.b}$** and **RPM$_{S.iw.CO2.b}$** of **GCU #1, #2, #3 and #4** are summarized in accordance to the established sequencing of their turn on.

The circuit for summing the contour of **GCU #1** (see the figure "C1" in Fig. IP 5 **RPM**$_{C.iw.Mn.1}$, **RPM**$_{C.iw.Vth.1}$ and **RPM**$_{S.iw.CO2.1}$ and the contour **RPM**$_{C.iw.Mn.2}$, **RPM**$_{C.iw.Vth.2}$ and **RPM**$_{S.iw.CO2.2}$ (see figure "C2" in Fig. IP 5) for the formation of the contour of their **total current indexed noologistical areas of possible operating modes** (Σ2) is shown in Fig. IP 5.

Summation of their contours is performed by summing the magnitudes of commercial productiveness $q_{к1.j}$ and $q_{к2.j}$ into the j-th points of the corresponding contour lines in which the magnitudes of pressure ratio ε are equal, that is $\varepsilon_{1.j} = \varepsilon_{2.j}$, in that number of:

The magnitude of the total commercial productiveness of **GCUs #1 and #2** at the point $1_{\Sigma 2}$ of their Σ2 contour, conditionally designated $q_{к\Sigma 2.1}$, is calculated by the formula:

$$q_{к\Sigma 2.1} = q_{к1.1} + q_{к2.1} = 10{,}647 + 10{,}721 = 21{,}368 \text{ m. nm}^3\text{/d},$$

here are:

$q_{к1.1}$ – the magnitude of **GCU #1** commercial productiveness at the point 1_1 of the contour of its **RPM**$_{C.iw.Mn.1}$, **RPM**$_{C.iw.Vth.1}$ and **RPM**$_{S.iw.CO2.1}$ at a magnitude of $\varepsilon_{1.1} = 1{,}687$ (see the figure "C1" in Fig. IP 5);

$q_{к2.1}$ – the magnitude of **GCU #2** commercial productiveness at the point 1_2 of the contour of its **RPM**$_{C.iw.Mn.2}$, **RPM**$_{C.iw.Vth.2}$ and **RPM**$_{S.iw.CO2.2}$ at a magnitude of $\varepsilon_{2.1} = 1{,}687$ (see the figure "C2" in Fig. IP 5).

The obtained magnitude of $q_{к\Sigma 2.1} = 21{,}368$ m. nm^3/d is used to construct the point $1_{\Sigma 2}$ of the Σ2 contour contour at the magnitude $\varepsilon_{\Sigma 2.1} = 1{,}687$ (see figure "Σ2" in Fig. IP5).

The magnitude of the total commercial productiveness of **GCUs #1 and #2** at the point $2_{\Sigma 2}$ of their Σ2 contour, conditionally designated $q_{\kappa\Sigma 2.2}$, is calculated by the formula:

$$q_{\kappa\Sigma 2.2} = q_{\kappa 1.2} + q_{\kappa 2.2} = 29{,}273 + 30{,}515 = 59{,}788 \text{ m. nm}^3/\text{d},$$

here are:

$q_{\kappa 1.2}$ – the magnitude of **GCU #1** commercial productiveness at the point 2_1 of the contour of its $\mathbf{RPM_{C.iw.Mn.1}}$, $\mathbf{RPM_{C.iw.Vth.1}}$ and $\mathbf{RPM_{S.iw.CO2.1}}$ at a magnitude of $\varepsilon_{2.1}$ = 2,062 (see the figure "C1" in Fig. IP 5);

$q_{\kappa 2.2}$ – the magnitude of **GCU #2** commercial productiveness at the point 2_2 of the contour of its $\mathbf{RPM_{C.iw.Mn.2}}$, $\mathbf{RPM_{C.iw.Vth.2}}$ and $\mathbf{RPM_{S.iw.CO2.2}}$ at a magnitude of $\varepsilon_{2.2}$ = 2,062 (see the figure "C2" in Fig. IP 5).

The obtained magnitude of $q_{\kappa\Sigma 2.2}$ = 59,788 m. nm³/d is used to construct the $2_{\Sigma 2}$ point of the Σ2 contour_2 contour at the magnitude $\varepsilon_{\Sigma 2.2}$ = 2,062 (see figure "Σ2" in Fig., IP 5).

All points of the figure contour Σ2 contour, which in Fig. IP 5 conditionally designated "Σ2", calculated similarly.

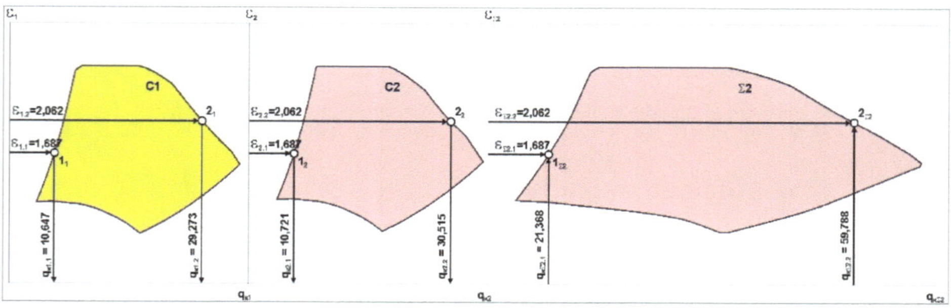

Fig. IP 5

The circuit for summing the contour the Σ2 contour (see the figure "Σ2" in Fig. IP 5 and IP 6) and the contour of **$RPM_{C.iw.Mn.3}$, $RPM_{C.iw.Vth.3}$** and **$RPM_{S.iw.CO2.3}$** of **GCU #3** (see figure "C3" in Fig. IP 6) for the formation of the contour of their **total current indexed noologistical areas of possible operating modes** (Σ3) is shown in Fig. IP 6.

The magnitude of the total commercial productiveness of **GCUs #1, #2 and #3** at the point $1_{\Sigma 3}$ of the Σ3 contour, conditionally designated $q_{\kappa\Sigma 3.1}$, is calculated by the formula:

$$q_{\kappa\Sigma 3.1} = q_{\kappa\Sigma 2.1} + q_{\kappa 3.1} = 21{,}368 + 10{,}550 = 31{,}918 \text{ m. nm}^3/\text{d},$$

here are:

$q_{\kappa 3.1}$ – the magnitude of **GCU #3** commercial productiveness at the point 1_3 of the contour of its **$RPM_{C.iw.Mn.3}$, $RPM_{C.iw.Vth.3}$** and **$RPM_{S.iw.CO2.3}$** at a magnitude of $\varepsilon_{3.1} = 1{,}687$ (see the figure "C3" in Fig. IP 6);

the rest - see above.

The obtained magnitude of $q_{\kappa\Sigma 3.1} = 31{,}918$ m. nm^3/d is used to construct the point $1_{\Sigma 3}$ of the Σ3 contour at the magnitude $\varepsilon_{\Sigma 3.1} = 1{,}687$ (see figure "Σ3" in Fig. IP6).

The magnitude of the total commercial productiveness of **GCUs #1, #2 and #3** at the point $2_{\Sigma 3}$ of the Σ3 contour, conditionally designated $q_{\kappa\Sigma 3.2}$, is calculated by the formula:

$$q_{\kappa\Sigma 3.2} = q_{\kappa\Sigma 2.2} + q_{\kappa 3.2} = 59{,}\ 887 + 28{,}182 = 87{,}970 \text{ m. nm}^3/\text{d},$$

here are:

$q_{к3.2}$ – the magnitude of **GCU #3** commercial productiveness at the point 2_3 of the contour of its **RPM$_{C.iw.Mn.3}$**, **RPM$_{C.iw.Vth.3}$** and **RPM$_{S.iw.CO2.3}$** at a magnitude of $ε_{3.2}$ = 2,062 (see the figure "C3" in Fig. IP 6);

the rest - see above.

The obtained magnitude of $q_{кΣ3.2}$ = 87,970 m. nm^3/d is used to construct the $2_{Σ3}$ point of the Σ3 contour at the magnitude $ε_{Σ3.2}$ = 2,062 (see figure "Σ3" in Fig., IP 6).

All points of the figure Σ3 contour, which in Fig. IP 6 conditionally designated "Σ3", calculated similarly.

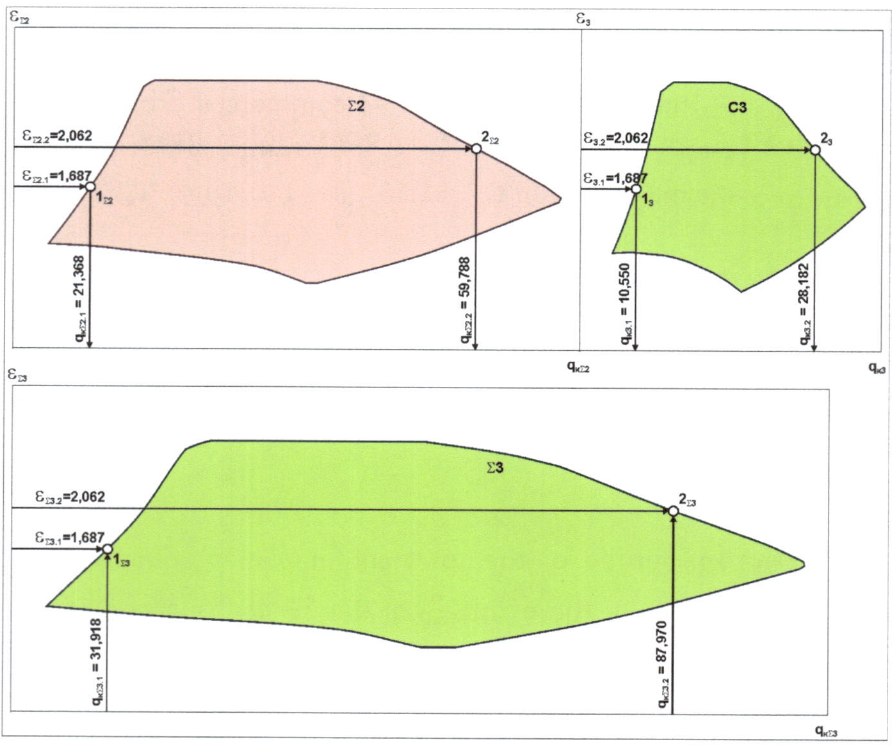

Fig. IP 6

The circuit for summing the Σ3 contour (see the figure "Σ3" in Fig. IP 6 and IP 7) and the contour **$RPM_{C.iw.Mn.4}$**, **$RPM_{C.iw.Vth.4}$** and **$RPM_{S.iw.CO2.4}$** of **GCU #4** (see figure "C4" in Fig. IP 7) for the formation of the contour of their **total current indexed noologistical areas of possible operating modes** (Σ4) is shown in Fig. IP 7.

The magnitude of the total commercial productiveness of **GCUs #1, #2, #3 and #4** at the point $1_{\Sigma4}$ of the Σ4 contour, conditionally designated $q_{\kappa\Sigma4.1}$, is calculated by the formula:

$$q_{\kappa\Sigma4.1} = q_{\kappa\Sigma3.1} + q_{\kappa4.1} = 31{,}918 + 11{,}069 = 42{,}987 \text{ m. nm}^3/\text{d},$$

here are:

$q_{\kappa4.1}$ – the magnitude of **GCU #4** commercial productiveness at the point 1_3 of the Σ4 contour at a magnitude of $\varepsilon_{4.1} = 1{,}687$ (see the figure "C4" in Fig. IP 7);

the rest - see above.

The obtained magnitude of $q_{\kappa\Sigma4.1} = 42{,}987$ m. nm^3/d is used to construct the point $1_{\Sigma4}$ of the Σ4 contour at the magnitude $\varepsilon_{\Sigma4.1} = 1{,}687$ (see figure "Σ4" in Fig. IP 7).

The magnitude of the total commercial productiveness of **GCUs #1, #2, #3 and #4** at the point $2_{\Sigma4}$ of their Σ4 contour, conditionally designated $q_{\kappa\Sigma4.2}$, is calculated by the formula:

$$q_{\kappa\Sigma4.2} = q_{\kappa\Sigma3.2} + q_{\kappa4.2} = 87{,}970 + 30{,}467 = 118{,}437 \text{ m. nm}^3/\text{d},$$

here are:

$q_{K4.2}$ – the magnitude of **GCU #4** commercial productiveness at the point 2_4 of the Σ4 contour at a magnitude of $\varepsilon_{4.2}$ = 2,062 (see the figure "C4" in Fig. IP 7);

the rest - see above.

The obtained magnitude of $q_{K\Sigma 4.2}$ = 118,437 m. nm³/d is used to construct the $2_{\Sigma 4}$ point of the Σ4 contour at the magnitude $\varepsilon_{\Sigma 4.2}$ = 2,062 (see figure "Σ4" in Fig., IP 7).

All points of the figure Σ4 contour, which in Fig. IP 7 conditionally designated "Σ4", calculated similarly.

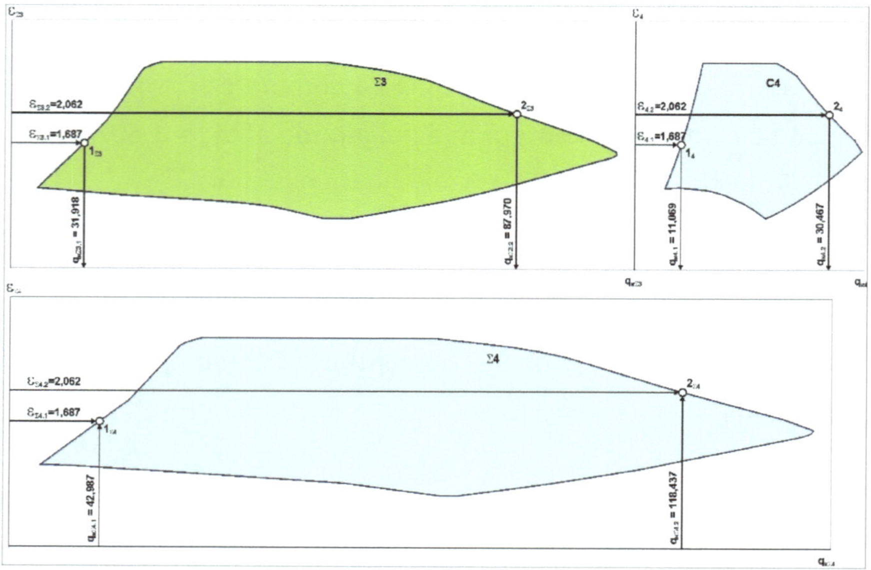

Fig. IP 7

The summation scheme of the above contours, which are shown in Fig. IP 5, IP 6 and IP 7, is shown in Fig. IP 8. They are summed up by overlaying the previously calculated contours with each other, forming a figure under a common contour, inside which the contours are shown with different combinations of working **GCUs #1, #2, #3 and #4**.

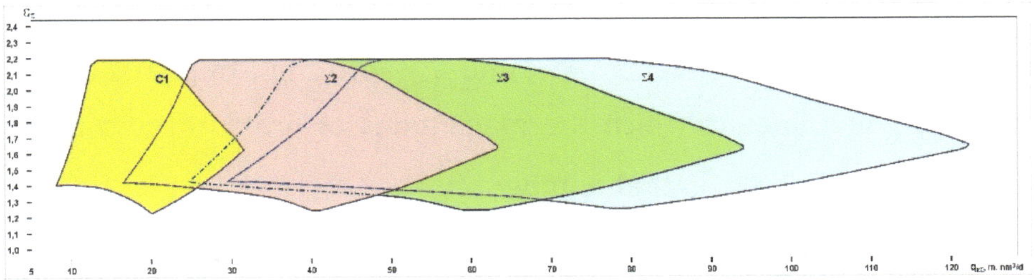

Fig. IP 8

The physical possibility is available in **PRSENT** to reliably and safely operate a group of described **GCUs** through a varies quantities of their turn on within the common contour of all circuits shown in Fig. IP 8. I.e. there is a physical possibility to provide the same total commercial capacity $q_{\kappa\Sigma}$ at the same pressure ratio ε_{Σ} by the work of groups at several numbers of turned on **GCUs** in those places where the contours are superimposed on each other. It is not possible to physically provide reliable and safe operation beyond the limits of the general contour of all the figures shown in Fig. IP 8.

Reliable and safe operation of the **GCU** with the re-entry of the transported gas through the Mokveld bypass valve is physically possible only in the zones to the left of the contours shown in Fig. IP 8. This and other features of the summation process are described in the instructions of the realized **systems of Noologistics** and are not given here to reduce the scope of the description because they are the features of the **GCU** operation.

2.1.2. The lines of the constant values of the summation indices (**$Ix_{C.iw.Mn}$**, **$Ix_{C.iw.Vth}$** and **$Ix_{S.iw.CO2}$**, which are collectively designated **Ix_{iw}**) of **GCUs #1, #2, #3 and #4** are constructed within the contours that were calculated above.

The circuit for summing the line of constant magnitude **$Ix_{C.iw.Vth.1}$** of **GCU #1** (see the figure "C1" in Fig. IP 9) and the line of constant magnitude **$Ix_{C.iw.Vth.2}$** of **GCU #2** (see figure "C2" in Fig. IP 9) for the formation of their total line of constant magnitude **$Ix_{C.iw.Vth.2}$** is shown in Fig. IP 9.

Summation of lines is performed by summing the magnitudes of commercial productiveness $q_{\kappa 1.j}$ and $q_{\kappa 2.j}$ into the j-th points of the corresponding lines in which the magnitudes of pressure ratio ε are equal, that is $\varepsilon_{1.j} = \varepsilon_{2.j}$, in that number of:

The magnitude of the total commercial productiveness of **GCUs #1 and #2** at the point $1_{\Sigma 2}$ on line $\mathbf{Ix_{C.iw.Vth.2}}$ = 50, conditionally designated $q_{\kappa\Sigma 2.1}$, is calculated by the formula:

$$q_{\kappa\Sigma 2.1} = q_{\kappa 1.1} + q_{\kappa 2.1} = 11{,}106 + 11{,}351 = 22{,}457 \text{ m. nm}^3/\text{d},$$

here are:

$q_{\kappa 1.1}$ – the magnitude of **GCU #1** commercial productiveness at the point 1_1 on line $\mathbf{Ix_{C.iw.Vth.1}}$ = 50 at a magnitude of $\varepsilon_{1.1}$ = 1,687 (see the figure "C1" in Fig. IP 9);

$q_{\kappa 2.1}$ – the magnitude of **GCU #2** commercial productiveness at the point 1_2 on line $\mathbf{Ix_{C.iw.Vth.2}}$ = 50 at a magnitude of $\varepsilon_{2.1}$ = 1,687 (see the figure "C2" in Fig. IP 9).

The obtained magnitude of $q_{\kappa\Sigma 2.1}$ = 22,457 m. nm³/d is used to construct the point $1_{\Sigma 2}$ on line $\mathbf{Ix_{C.iw.Vth.\Sigma 2}}$ = 50 at the magnitude $\varepsilon_{\Sigma 2.1}$ = 1,687 (see figure "Σ2" in Fig. IP 9).

The magnitude of the total commercial productiveness of **GCUs #1 and #2** at the point $2_{\Sigma 2}$ on line $\mathbf{Ix_{C.iw.Vth.\Sigma 2}}$ = 150, conditionally designated $q_{\kappa\Sigma 2.2}$, is calculated by the formula:

$$q_{\kappa\Sigma 2.2} = q_{\kappa 1.2} + q_{\kappa 2.2} = 23{,}504 + 24{,}023 = 47{,}527 \text{ m. nm}^3/\text{d},$$

here are:

$q_{\kappa 1.2}$ – the magnitude of **GCU #1** commercial productiveness at the point 2_1 on line **$Ix_{C.iw.Vth.1}$** = 50 at a magnitude of $\varepsilon_{1.2}$ = 2,062 (see the figure "C1" in Fig. IP 9);

$q_{\kappa 2.2}$ – the magnitude of **GCU #2** commercial productiveness at the point 2_2 on line **$Ix_{C.iw.Vth.2}$** = 50 at a magnitude of $\varepsilon_{2.2}$ = 2,062 (see the figure "C2" in Fig. IP 5).

The obtained magnitude of $q_{\kappa\Sigma 2.2}$ = 47,527 m. nm^3/d is used to construct the $2_{\Sigma 2}$ point on line **$Ix_{C.iw.Vth.\Sigma 2}$** = 150 at the magnitude $\varepsilon_{\Sigma 2.2}$ = 2,062 (see figure "Σ2" in Fig., IP 9).

All points of other lines, which in Fig. IP 9 are shown inside the contour conditionally designated "Σ2", calculated similarly.

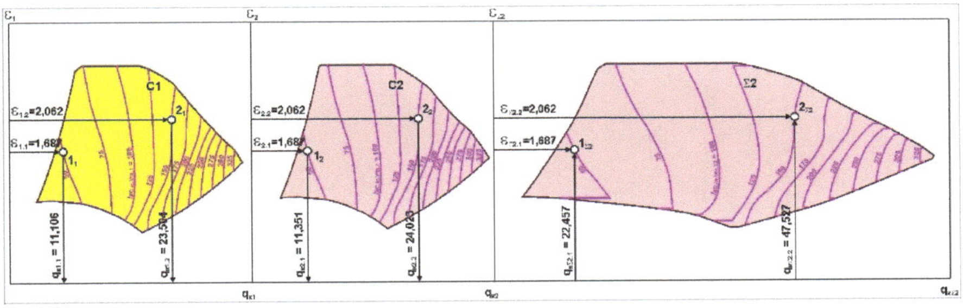

Fig. IP 9

Some of the calculated lines of constant **$Ix_{C.iw.Vth}$**, which are shown in Fig. IP 9 - see, for example, the line **$Ix_{C.iw.Vth.\Sigma 2}$** = 50, have the horizontal segments at the top and bottom. They appear as a result of incomplete overlapping of contours of summable **$RPM_{C.iw.Mn.b}$**, **$RPM_{C.iw.Vth.b}$** and **$RPM_{S.iw.CO2.b}$** of the first type. They show that, due to the partial overlapping of their contours, parts arise in which the decrease in magnitude $q_{\kappa\Sigma 2}$ is provided by a decrease in the magnitude of q_{k1}, and the magnitude of q_{k2} remains unchanged. In this case, the magnitude of **$Ix_{C.iw.Vth.1}$** remains equal to 50, and the magnitude of **$Ix_{C.iw.Vth.2}$** - decreases within its contour. These and other features of the summation process are described in the instructions of the implemented **systems of Noologistics** and are not given here to reduce the scope of the description.

The circuit for summing the line of constant magnitude $\mathbf{Ix_{C.iw.Vth.\Sigma 2}}$ of **GCU #1 and #2** (see the figure "Σ2" in Fig. IP 9 and IP 10) and the line of constant magnitude $\mathbf{Ix_{C.iw.Vth.3}}$ of **GCU #3** (see figure "C3" in Fig. IP 10) for the formation of their total line of constant magnitude $\mathbf{Ix_{C.iw.Vth.\Sigma 3}}$ is shown in Fig. IP 10.

The magnitude of the total commercial productiveness of **GCUs #1, #2 and #3** at the point $1_{\Sigma 3}$ on line $\mathbf{Ix_{C.iw.Vth.\Sigma 3}}$ = 150, conditionally designated $q_{\kappa\Sigma 3.1}$, is calculated by the formula:

$$q_{\kappa\Sigma 3.1} = q_{\kappa\Sigma 2.1} + q_{\kappa 3.1} = 22{,}457 + 10{,}908 = 33{,}365 \text{ m. nm}^3\text{/d},$$

here are:

$q_{\kappa 3.1}$ – the magnitude of **GCU #3** commercial productiveness at the point 1_3 on line $\mathbf{Ix_{C.iw.Vth.\Sigma 3}}$ = 50 at a magnitude of $\varepsilon_{3.1}$ = 1,687 (see the figure "C3" in Fig. IP 10);
the rest - see above.

The obtained magnitude of $q_{\kappa\Sigma 3.1}$ = 33,365 m. nm³/d is used to construct the point $1_{\Sigma 3}$ on line $\mathbf{Ix_{C.iw.Vth.\Sigma 3}}$ = 50 at the magnitude $\varepsilon_{\Sigma 3.1}$ = 1,687 (see figure "Σ3" in Fig. IP 10).

The magnitude of the total commercial productiveness of **GCUs #1, #2 and #3** at the point $3_{\Sigma 3}$ on line $\mathbf{Ix_{C.iw.Vth.\Sigma 3}}$ = 150, conditionally designated $q_{\kappa\Sigma 3.1}$, is calculated by the formula:

$$q_{\kappa\Sigma 3.2} = q_{\kappa\Sigma 2.2} + q_{\kappa 3.2} = 47{,}527 + 23{,}364 = 70{,}891 \text{ m. nm}^3\text{/d},$$

here are:

$q_{к3.2}$ – the magnitude of **GCU #3** commercial productiveness at the point 2_3 on line $\mathbf{Ix_{C.iw.Vth.\Sigma3}}$ = 150 at a magnitude of $\varepsilon_{3.2}$ = 2,062 (see the figure "C3" in Fig. IP 10);

the rest - see above.

The obtained magnitude of $q_{к\Sigma3.2}$ = 70,891 m. nm³/d is used to construct the point $2_{\Sigma3}$ on line $\mathbf{Ix_{C.iw.Vth.\Sigma3}}$ = 150 at the magnitude $\varepsilon_{\Sigma3.2}$ = 2,062 (see figure "Σ3" in Fig. IP 10).

All points of other lines, which in Fig. IP 10 are shown inside the contour conditionally designated "Σ3", calculated similarly.

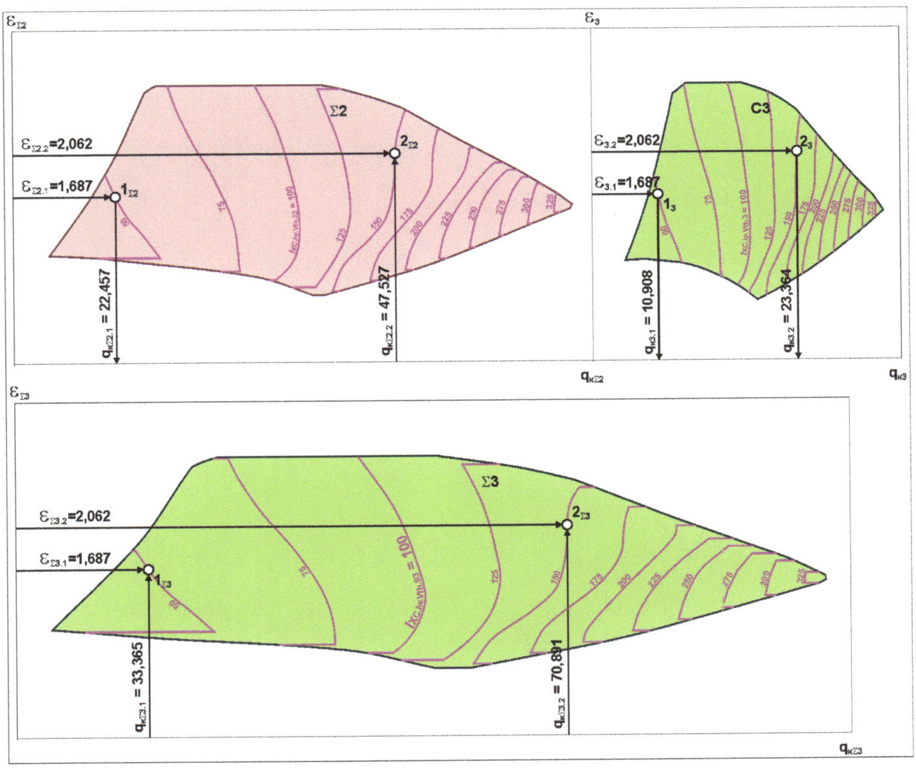

Fig. IP 10

The circuit for summing the line of constant magnitude $\mathbf{Ix_{C.iw.Vth.\Sigma3}}$ of **GCU #1, #2 and #3** (see the figure "Σ3" in Fig. IP 10 and IP 11) and the line of constant magnitude $\mathbf{Ix_{C.iw.Vth.4}}$ of **GCU #4** (see figure

"C4" in Fig. IP 11) for the formation of their total line of constant magnitude $\mathbf{Ix_{C.iw.Vth.\Sigma4}}$ is shown in Fig. IP 11.

The magnitude of the total commercial productiveness of **GCUs #1, #2, #3 and #4** on line $\mathbf{Ix_{C.iw.Vth.\Sigma4}}$ = 50, conditionally designated $q_{\kappa\Sigma4.1}$, is calculated by the formula:

$q_{\kappa\Sigma4.1} = q_{\kappa\Sigma3.1} + q_{\kappa4.1}$ = 33,365 + 11,472 = 44,837 m. nm^3/d,

here are:

$q_{\kappa4.1}$ – the magnitude of **GCU #4** commercial productiveness at the point 1_4 on line $\mathbf{Ix_{C.iw.Vth.\Sigma4}}$ = 50 at a magnitude of $\varepsilon_{4.1}$ = 1,687 (see the figure "C4" in Fig. IP 11);
the rest - see above.

The obtained magnitude of $q_{\kappa\Sigma4.1}$ = 44,837 m. nm^3/d is used to construct the point $1_{\Sigma4}$ on line $\mathbf{Ix_{C.iw.Vth.\Sigma4}}$ = 50 at the magnitude $\varepsilon_{\Sigma4.1}$ = 1,687 (see figure "Σ4" in Fig. IP 11).

The magnitude of the total commercial productiveness of **GCUs #1, #2, #3 and #4** at the point $2_{\Sigma4}$ of their on line $\mathbf{Ix_{C.iw.Vth.\Sigma4}}$ = 150, conditionally designated $q_{\kappa\Sigma4.2}$, is calculated by the formula:

$q_{\kappa\Sigma4.2} = q_{\kappa\Sigma3.2} + q_{\kappa4.2}$ = 70,891 + 24,037 = 94,928 m. nm^3/d,

here are:

$q_{\kappa4.2}$ – the magnitude of **GCU #4** commercial productiveness at the point 2_4 on line $\mathbf{Ix_{C.iw.Vth.\Sigma4}}$ = 150 at a magnitude of $\varepsilon_{4.2}$ = 2,062 (see the figure "C4" in Fig. IP 11);
the rest - see above.

The obtained magnitude of $q_{\kappa\Sigma4.2}$ = 94,928 m. nm^3/d is used to construct the point $2_{\Sigma4}$ on line $\mathbf{Ix_{C.iw.Vth.\Sigma4}}$ = 150 at the magnitude $\varepsilon_{\Sigma4.2}$ = 2,062 (see figure "Σ4" in Fig. IP 11).

All points of other lines, which in Fig. IP 11 are shown inside the contour conditionally designated "Σ4", calculated similarly.

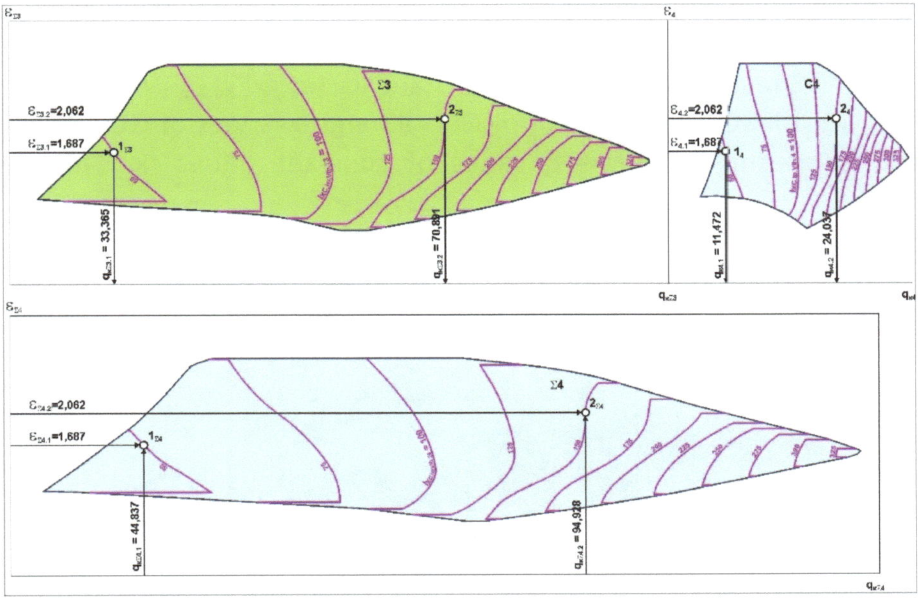

Fig. IP 11

The summation circuit of the above contours together with the lines of constant magnitudes $\mathbf{Ix_{C.iw.Vth.\Sigma4}}$, from Fig. IP 9, IP 10 and IP 11, is shown in Fig. IP 12. Their summation is provided by superimposing the previously calculated contours of C1, Σ2, Σ3 and Σ4 together with the lines of constant magnitudes $\mathbf{Ix_{C.iw.Vth}}$ one on top of the other – see Fig. IP 12.

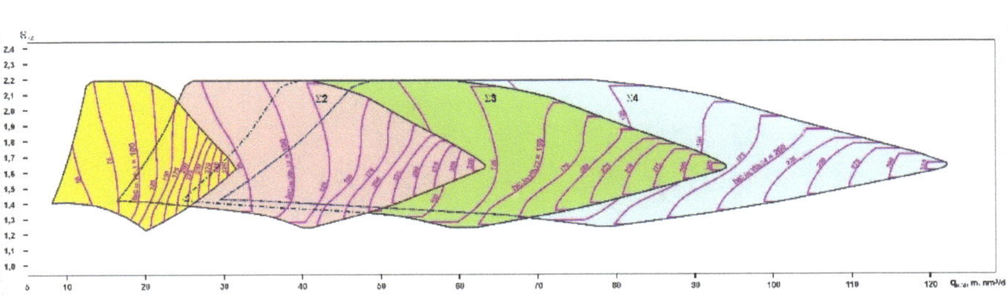

Fig. IP 12

The figure depicted in Fig. IP 12, is a graphical representation of **RPM$_{C.iw.Vth}$** of the first type used in the current control for working together in the same group of **GCUs #1, #2, #3 and #4**, for a minimum of the total current variable consumption of all types power.

Summation of lines of constant values **Ix$_{C.iw.Mn.1}$** of **GCU #1**, **Ix$_{C.iw.Mn.2}$** of **GCU #2**, **Ix$_{C.iw.Mn.3}$** of **GCU #3** and **Ix$_{C.iw.Mn.4}$** of **GCU #4** for the formation of their total lines of constant values **Ix$_{C.iw.Mn}$** are performed within the same contours of C1, Σ2, Σ3 and Σ4 by the same technology as shown above when calculating **RPM$_{C.iw.Vth.Σ4}$** of the first type. Its result (**RPM$_{C.iw.Mn.Σ4}$** of the first type) is shown in Fig. IP 13.

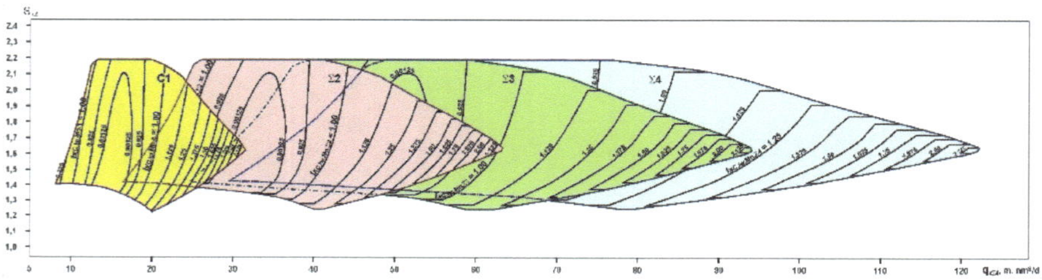

Fig. IP 13

Summation of lines of constant values **Ix$_{S.iw.CO2.1}$** of **GCU #1**, **Ix$_{S.iw.CO2.2}$** of **GCU #2**, **Ix$_{S.iw.CO2.3}$** of **GCU #3** and **Ix$_{S.iw.CO2.4}$** of **GCU #4** for the formation of their total lines of constant values **Ix$_{C.iw.CO2}$** are performed within the same contours of C1, Σ2, Σ3 and Σ4 by the same technology as shown above when calculating **RPM$_{C.iw.Vth.Σ4}$** of the first type. Its result is (**RPM$_{S.iw.CO2.Σ4}$** of the first type) is shown in Fig. IP 14.

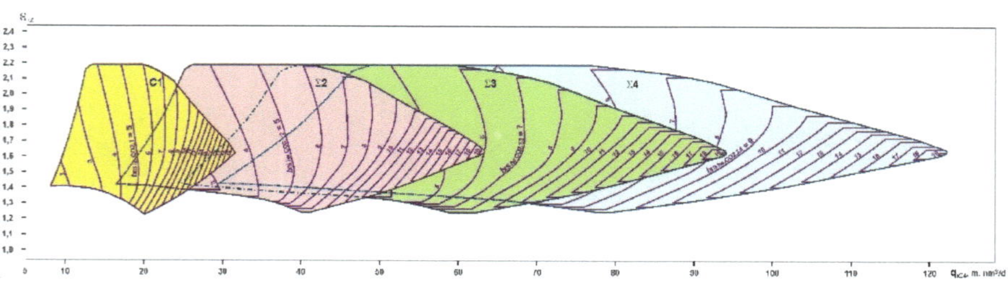

Fig. IP 14

Obviously, there is a technical possibility to combine in one figure all the **RPM**$_{C.iw.Vth.\Sigma4}$, **RPM**$_{C.iw.Mn.\Sigma4}$ and **RPM**$_{S.iw.CO2.\Sigma4}$ of the first type mentioned above - see Fig. IP 15, which are the **the total indexed noologistical area of the possible modes of joint operation** of the first compression stage, which is briefly designated as **RPM**$_{\Sigma4}$.

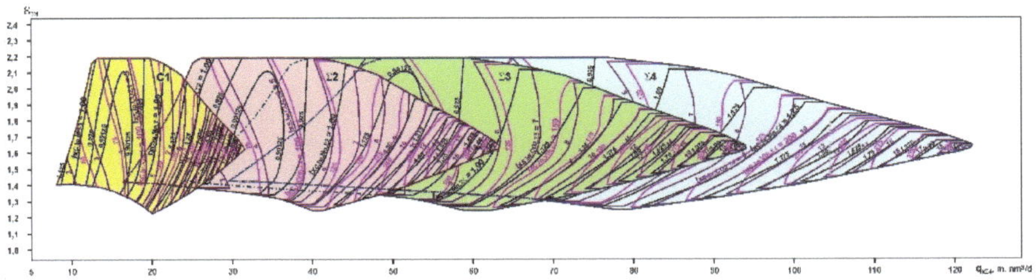

Fig. IP 15

It follows from the foregoing that in the considered example for each point of **RPM**$_{\Sigma4}$ three different types of summation indices (**Ix**$_{C.iw.Vth}$, **Ix**$_{C.iw.Mn}$ and **Ix**$_{S.iw.CO2}$) are calculated as this is shown in Fig. IP 15. It is also obvious that, if necessary, there is a technical possibility to calculate those number of types of **summation indices** that **the person** requires.

RPM$_{\Sigma4}$, calculated above and depicted in Fig. IP 15, refer to the first compression stage of the **BCS KGF**, which has a designation $El_{2.4}^{3.2}$ in accordance to the structure depicted in Fig. IP 3.

2.2. **RPM**$_{C.iw.Mn.b}$, **RPM**$_{C.iw.Vth.b}$ and **RPM**$_{S.iw.CO2.b}$ of the first type, previously calculated for $El_{1.16}^{2.5}$, $El_{1.17}^{2.5}$, $El_{1.18}^{2.5}$ and $El_{1.19}^{2.5}$, are summed according to the **priority of the importance** that were set, forming the **RPM**$_{C.iw.Mn.\Sigma8}$, **RPM**$_{C.iw.Vth.\Sigma8}$ and **RPM**$_{S.iw.CO2.\Sigma8}$ of the first type (in set - **RPM**$_{\Sigma8}$ of the first type) for $El_{2.5}^{3.2}$ of the second level of control, in the following sequence of operations:

These calculations are performed for **GCUs #5, #6, #7 and #8**, similar to the calculations shown in clause 2.1. **GCUs #5, #6, #7 and #8** jointly operate in the second compression stage of the **BCS KGF**, which has designation $El_{2.5}^{3.2}$ in accordance to the structure depicted in Fig. IP 3. These calculations are not given here to reduce the scope of the description. Their result is **the total indexed noologistical area of the possible modes of joint operation** of the first type of the second compression stage, which is briefly conditionally designated **RPM**$_{\Sigma 8}$ (that is, **RPM**$_{C.iw.Vth.\Sigma 8}$, **RPM**$_{C.iw.Mn.\Sigma 8}$ and **RPM**$_{S.iw.CO2.\Sigma 8}$ of the first type combined in one figure), which is presented in Fig. IP 16.

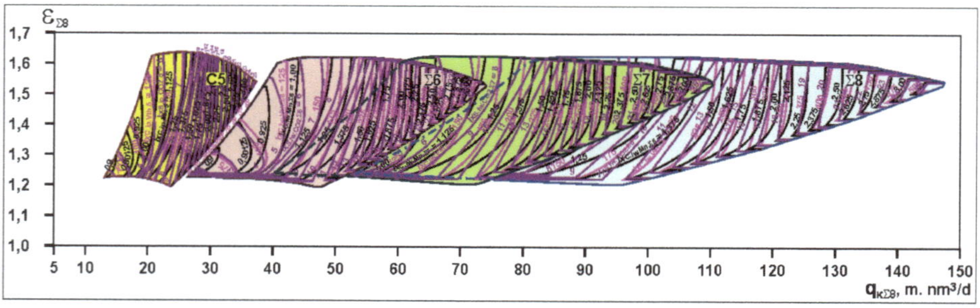

Fig. IP 16

2.3. **RPM**$_{C.iw.Mn.b}$, **RPM**$_{C.iw.Vth.b}$ and **RPM**$_{S.iw.CO2.b}$ of the first type, previously calculated for $El_{1.20}^{2.6}$, $El_{1.21}^{2.6}$, $El_{1.22}^{2.6}$ and $El_{1.23}^{2.6}$, are summed according to the **priority of the importance** that were set, forming the **RPM**$_{C.iw.Mn.\Sigma 12}$, **RPM**$_{C.iw.Vth.\Sigma 12}$ and **RPM**$_{S.iw.CO2.\Sigma 12}$ of the first type (in set - **RPM**$_{\Sigma 12}$ of the first type) for $El_{2.6}^{3.2}$ of the second level of control, in the following sequence of operations:

These calculations are performed for **GCUs #9, #10, #11 and #12**, similar to the calculations shown in clause 2.1. **GCUs #9, #10, #11 and #12** jointly operate in the third compression stage of the **BCS KGF**, which has designation $El_{2.6}^{3.2}$ in accordance to the structure depicted in Fig. IP 3. These calculations are not given here to reduce the scope of the description. Their result is **the total indexed noologistical area of the possible modes of joint operation** of the first type of the third compression stage, which is briefly conditionally designated **RPM**$_{\Sigma 12}$ (that is, **RPM**$_{C.iw.Vth.\Sigma 12}$, **RPM**$_{C.iw.Mn.\Sigma 12}$ and **RPM**$_{S.iw.CO2.\Sigma 12}$ of the first type combined in one figure), which is presented in Fig. IP 17.

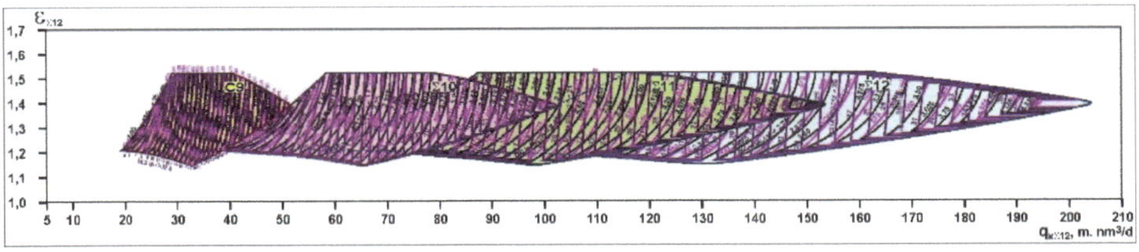

Fig. IP 17

A simple comparison of **RPM$_{\Sigma4}$**, **RPM$_{\Sigma8}$** and **RPM$_{\Sigma12}$**, presented respectively in Fig. IP 15, IP 16 and IP 17, shows that **the person** uses the types of **GCUs** in compression stages that do not provide the best possible load for each of them individually. This is explained by the lack of described here technology at the designer of **BCS KGF**. For example, the maximum possible productivity of the first stage is $q_{\kappa\Sigma 4max}$ = 122,23 m. nm^3/d (see Fig. IP 15) it is less than the maximum possible productivity of the second stage $q_{\kappa\Sigma 8max}$ = 147,339 m. nm^3/d (see Fig. IP 16) by 20.5% and less than the maximum possible productivity of the third stage $q_{\kappa\Sigma 12max}$ = 214,369 m. nm^3/d (see Fig. IP 17) by 75.4%. The maximum possible magnitude of pressure ratio in the first stage is $\varepsilon_{\Sigma 4max}$ = 2,11 (see **the passport characteristics of the compressor NC-16 / 45-1,7**) it is more than the maximum possible pressure ratio in the second stage $\varepsilon_{\Sigma 8max}$ = 1,636 (see **the passport characteristics of the compressor NC -16C / 56-1,44**) by 22,5% and more than the maximum possible pressure ratio in the third stage $\varepsilon_{\Sigma 12max}$ = 1,572 (see **the passport characteristics of the compressor NC-16 / 76-1.44**) by 25.5%.

A **noologistical** comparison of **RPM$_{\Sigma4}$**, **RPM$_{\Sigma8}$** and **RPM$_{\Sigma12}$**, based on the ability to provide a reasonable combination of their current operating mode from the condition of ensuring or minimizing energy costs of all kinds (provided by the use of **Ix$_{C.iw.Vth.\Sigma4}$**, **Ix$_{C.iw.Vth.\Sigma8}$** and **Ix$_{C.iw.Vth.\Sigma12}$**), or the minimum cost of money (provided by the use of **Ix$_{C.iw.Mn.\Sigma4}$**, **Ix$_{C.iw.Mn.\Sigma8}$** and and **Ix$_{C.iw.Mn.\Sigma12}$**), or the minimum CO2 emissions (provided by the use of **Ix$_{S.iw.CO2.\Sigma4}$**, **Ix$_{S.iw.CO2.\Sigma8}$** and

$\mathbf{Ix}_{S.iw.CO2.\Sigma12}$), shows that the selected types of **GCUs** also do not allow using all the possibilities available in them.

3. **RPM**$_{\Sigma4}$, **RPM**$_{\Sigma8}$ and **RPM**$_{\Sigma12}$ of the first type, calculated for elements of the second level, are summed by groups according to the direction of the arrows in Fig . IP 4 a).

3.1. **RPM**$_{\Sigma4}$ of the first stage (see Fig. IP 15) is summed to the **RPM**$_{\Sigma8}$ of the second stage (see Fig. IP 16).

3.1.1. The contours of **RPM**$_{\Sigma4}$ in first-stage are summed to the second-stage **RPM**$_{\Sigma8}$ contours.

The summation scheme for these contours is shown in Fig. IP 18. **RPM**$_{\Sigma4}$, taken from Figure IP 15, shows contours on it, but their horizontal scale is changed in comparison with Fig. IP 15 and equal to the scale of **RPM**$_{\Sigma8}$ in Figure IP 16.

The summation is performed by multiplying the magnitudes of the pressure ratio at those pair points of the contours that have the same productivity magnitude. The points of the total contours are obtained as a result, for example:

The point 1_1 of contour C1, in which the commercial productivity $q_{к1.1}$ = 13,056 m. nm^3/d and the pressure ratio $\varepsilon_{1.1}$ = 1,393, are summed up to the point 1_5 of the contour C5, where the commercial productivity is $q_{к5.1}$ = 13,056 m. nm^3/d day and the pressure ratio $\varepsilon_{5.1}$ = 1,224, according the formula:

$$\varepsilon_{\Sigma1.5.1} = \varepsilon_{1.1} * \varepsilon_{5.1} = 1{,}393*1{,}224 = 1{,}709.$$

The point $1_{\Sigma1.5}$ of contour Σ1.5, depicted in Fig. IP 18, in which the commercial capacity $q_{\Sigma1.5.1}$ = 13,056 m. nm^3/d and the degree of pressure increase $\varepsilon_{\Sigma1.5.1}$ = 1,709, is obtained as a result.

The point 2_1 of contour C1, in which the commercial productivity $q_{к1.2}$ = 13,056 m. nm^3/d and the pressure ratio $ε_{1.2}$ = 2,18, are summed up to the point 1_5 of the contour C5, where the commercial productivity is $q_{к5.1}$ = 13,056 m. nm^3/d day and the pressure ratio $ε_{5.1}$ = 1,224, according to the formula:

$$ε_{Σ1.5.2} = ε_{1.2} * ε_{5.1} = 2{,}18*1{,}224 = 2{,}668.$$

The point $2_{Σ1.5}$ of contour Σ1.5, depicted in Fig. IP 18, in which the commercial capacity $q_{Σ1.5.2}$ = 13,056 m. nm^3/d and the degree of pressure increase $ε_{Σ1.5.2}$ = 2,668, is obtained as a result.

The point $1_{Σ4}$ of contour Σ4, in which the commercial productivity $q_{кΣ4.1}$ = 122,23 m. nm^3/d and the pressure ratio $ε_{Σ4.1}$ = 1,642, are summed up to the point $1_{Σ8}$ of the contour Σ8, where the commercial productivity is $q_{кΣ8.1}$ = 122,23 m. nm^3/d day and the pressure ratio $ε_{Σ8.1}$ = 1,346, according to the formula:

$$ε_{Σ4.8.1} = ε_{Σ4.1} * ε_{Σ8.1} = 1{,}642*1{,}346 = 2{,}211.$$

The point $1_{Σ4.8}$ of contour Σ4.8, depicted in Fig. IP 18, in which the commercial capacity $q_{Σ4.8.1}$ = 122,23 m. nm^3/d and the degree of pressure increase $ε_{Σ4.8.1}$ = 2,211, is obtained as a result.

The point $1_{Σ4}$ of contour Σ4, in which the commercial productivity $q_{кΣ4.1}$ = 122,23 m. nm^3/d and the pressure ratio $ε_{Σ4.1}$ = 1,642, are summed up to the point $2_{Σ8}$ of the contour Σ8, where the commercial productivity is $q_{кΣ8.1}$ = 122,23 m. nm^3/d day and the pressure ratio $ε_{Σ8.1}$ = 1,608, according to the formula:

$$ε_{Σ4.8.2} = ε_{Σ4.1} * ε_{Σ8.2} = 1{,}642*1{,}608 = 2{,}641.$$

The point $2_{\Sigma 4.8}$ of contour Σ4.8, depicted in Fig. IP 18, in which the commercial capacity $q_{\Sigma 4.8.1}$ = 122,23 m. nm³/d and the degree of pressure increase $\varepsilon_{\Sigma 4.8.2}$ = 2,641, is obtained as a result.

The remaining paired points of all the contours depicted in Fig. IP 15 and IP 16 are summed in a similar way and showed the calculated total points in Fig. IP 18, including:

The summation of the paired points of the contours C1 and C5 gives the contour Σ1.5;

The summation of the paired points of the contours C1 and Σ6 gives the contour Σ1.6;

The summation of the paired points of the contours Σ2 and C5 gives the contour Σ2.5;

The summation of the paired points of the contours Σ2 and Σ6 gives the contour Σ2.6;

The summation of the paired points of the contours Σ2 and Σ7 gives the contour Σ2.7;

The summation of the paired points of the contours Σ2 and Σ8 gives the contour Σ2.8;

The summation of the paired points of the contours Σ3 and C5 gives the contour Σ3.5;

The summation of the paired points of the contours Σ3 and Σ6 gives the contour Σ3.6;

The summation of the paired points of the contours Σ3 and Σ7 gives the contour Σ3.7;

The summation of the paired points of the contours Σ3 and Σ8 gives the contour Σ3.8;

The summation of the paired points of the contours Σ4 and C5 gives the contour Σ4.5;

The summation of the paired points of the contours Σ4 and Σ6 gives the contour Σ4.6;

The summation of the paired points of the contours Σ4 and Σ7 gives the contour Σ4.7;

The summation of the paired points of the contours Σ4 and Σ8 gives the contour Σ4.8.

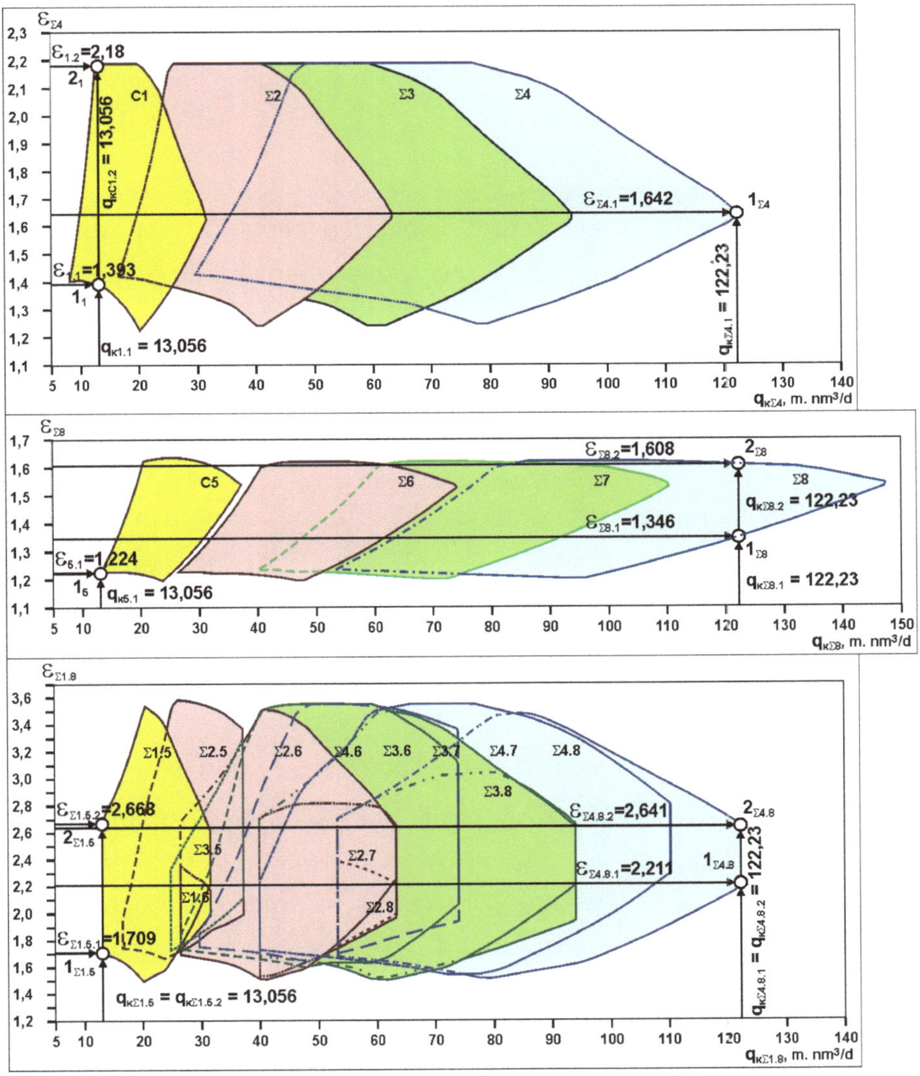

Fig. IP 18

It is obvious that **GCUs** will work together steadily and reliably within each of the corresponding contour calculated and depicted in Fig. IP 18. The fact that the contours are superimposed on each other indicates that there is a technical possibility to provide the same total commercial productivity by a different combination of simultaneously operating **GCUs**, but under different costs of all types of energy (characterized by **the density of the current flow of consumption Vth ($D_{C.iw.Vth.\Sigma 8}$)**), under different costs in monetary terms (characterized by **the density of the current flow of consumption Mn ($D_{C.iw.Mn.\Sigma 8}$)**) and under different CO2 emissions (characterized by **the density of the current flow of CO2 emissions ($D_{S.iw.CO2.\ \Sigma\ 8}$)**). A large number of contours used may give an unnecessary increase in switching of equipment in addition.

Therefore, only those contours are used for the further calculation from the whole set of calculated above, at the points of which the quantities $\mathbf{Ix_{iw.\Sigma 4}}$ and $\mathbf{Ix_{iw.\Sigma 8}}$ are equal or closest to each other. Only contours Σ1.5, Σ2.6, Σ3.6, and Σ4.8 remain for further calculation as a result.

3.1.2. The lines of constant magnitudes $\mathbf{Ix_{iw.\Sigma 4}}$ and $\mathbf{Ix_{iw.\Sigma 8}}$ add up.

The summation scheme for the lines of constant magnitudes $\mathbf{Ix_{iw.\Sigma 4}}$ and $\mathbf{Ix_{iw.\Sigma 8}}$ is shown in Fig. IP 19. The lines of constant magnitudes $\mathbf{Ix_{iw.\Sigma 4}}$, taken from Fig. IP 15, are shown on it, but their horizontal scale is changed in comparison to Fig. IP 15 and is equal to the scale $\mathbf{Ix_{iw.\Sigma 8}}$ in Fig. IP 16.

The lines of constant magnitudes $\mathbf{Ix_{iw.\Sigma 4}}$ and $\mathbf{Ix_{iw.\Sigma 8}}$ add up inside the contours Σ1.5, Σ2.6, Σ3.6, and Σ4.8 by multiplying the magnitudes of the pressure ratio at those pair points of the lines of the same constant magnitudes $\mathbf{Ix_{iw.\Sigma 4}}$ and $\mathbf{Ix_{iw.\Sigma 8}}$, in which the magnitude of commercial productivity is the same ($\mathbf{q_{\kappa\Sigma 4}} = \mathbf{q_{\kappa\ \Sigma 8}}$). The points of the total lines of constant magnitudes $\mathbf{Ix_{iw.\Sigma 4}}$ and $\mathbf{Ix_{iw.\Sigma 8}}$ are obtained as a result, for example:

The point $3_{\Sigma 2}$ of the line $\mathbf{Ix_{C.iw.Vth.\Sigma 2}}$ = 150 within the contour Σ2, in which the commercial productivity $q_{\kappa\Sigma 2.3}$ = 47,334 m. nm^3/d and the pressure ratio $\varepsilon_{\Sigma 2.3}$ = 1,695, are summed up to the point $3_{\Sigma 6}$ on the line $\mathbf{Ix}_{\mathbf{C.iw.Vth.\Sigma 6}}$ = 150 within the contour Σ6, in which the commercial productivity $q_{\kappa\Sigma 6.3}$ = 47,334 m. nm^3/d and the pressure ratio $\varepsilon_{\Sigma 6.3}$ = 1,433 according the formula:

$$\varepsilon_{\Sigma 2.6.3} = \varepsilon_{\Sigma 2.3} * \varepsilon_{\Sigma 6.3} = 1{,}695*1{,}433 = 2{,}429.$$

The point $3_{\Sigma 2.6}$ of the line $\mathbf{Ix}_{\mathbf{C.iw.Vth.\Sigma 2.6}}$ = 150 inside the contour Σ2.6 is obtained as a result. It has the commercial productivity $q_{\Sigma 2.6.3}$ = 47,334 m. nm^3/d and the pressure ratio $\varepsilon_{\Sigma 2.6.3}$ = 2,429. It is depicted in Fig. IP 19.

The point $3_{\Sigma 2}$ of the line $\mathbf{Ix}_{\mathbf{C.iw.Mn.\Sigma 3}}$ = 1,125 within the contour Σ3, in which the commercial productivity $q_{\kappa\Sigma 2.3}$ = 63,907 m. nm^3/d and the pressure ratio $\varepsilon_{\Sigma 2.3}$ = 1,392, are summed up to the point $3_{\Sigma 7}$ on the line $\mathbf{Ix}_{\mathbf{C.iw.Mn.\Sigma 7}}$ = 1,125 within the contour Σ7, in which the commercial productivity $q_{\kappa\Sigma 7.3}$ = 63,907 m. nm^3/d and the pressure ratio $\varepsilon_{\Sigma 7.3}$ = 1,282 according the formula:

$$\varepsilon_{\Sigma 3.7.3} = \varepsilon_{\Sigma 3.3} * \varepsilon_{\Sigma 7.3} = 1{,}392*1{,}282 = 1{,}785.$$

The point $3_{\Sigma 3.7}$ of the line $\mathbf{Ix}_{\mathbf{C.iw.Mn.\Sigma 3.7}}$ = 1,125 inside the contour Σ3.7 is obtained as a result. It has the commercial productivity $q_{\Sigma 3.7.3}$ = 63,907 m. nm^3/d and the pressure ratio $\varepsilon_{\Sigma 3.7.3}$ = 1,785. It is depicted in Fig. IP 19.

The point $3_{\Sigma 4}$ of the line $\mathbf{Ix}_{\mathbf{S.iw.CO2.\Sigma 4}}$ = 7 within the contour Σ4, in which the commercial productivity $q_{\kappa\Sigma 4.3}$ = 87,292 m. nm^3/d and the pressure ratio $\varepsilon_{\Sigma 4.3}$ = 1,964, are summed up to the point $3_{\Sigma 8}$ on the line $\mathbf{Ix}_{\mathbf{S.iw.CO2.\Sigma 8}}$ = 7 within the contour Σ8 (it is closed in Fig. IP 19 by contour Σ7), in which the commercial productivity $q_{\kappa\Sigma 8.3}$ = 87,292 m. nm^3/d and the pressure ratio $\varepsilon_{\Sigma 8.3}$ = 1,695 according the formula:

$$\varepsilon_{\Sigma 4.8.3} = \varepsilon_{\Sigma 4.3} * \varepsilon_{\Sigma 8.3} = 1{,}964*1{,}695 = 3{,}091.$$

The point $3_{\Sigma4.8}$ of the line $\mathbf{Ix_{S.iw.CO2.\Sigma4.8}}$ = 7 inside the contour Σ4.8 is obtained as a result. It has the commercial productivity $q_{\Sigma4.8.3}$ = 87,292 m. nm³/d and the pressure ratio $\varepsilon_{\Sigma4.8.3}$ = 3,091. It is depicted in Fig. IP 19.

The remaining paired points of all the lines of constant magnitudes $\mathbf{Ix_{iw.\Sigma4}}$ and $\mathbf{Ix_{iw.\Sigma8}}$ inside the circuits depicted in Fig. IP 15 and IP 16 are summed similarly and the calculated total points in Fig. IP 19.

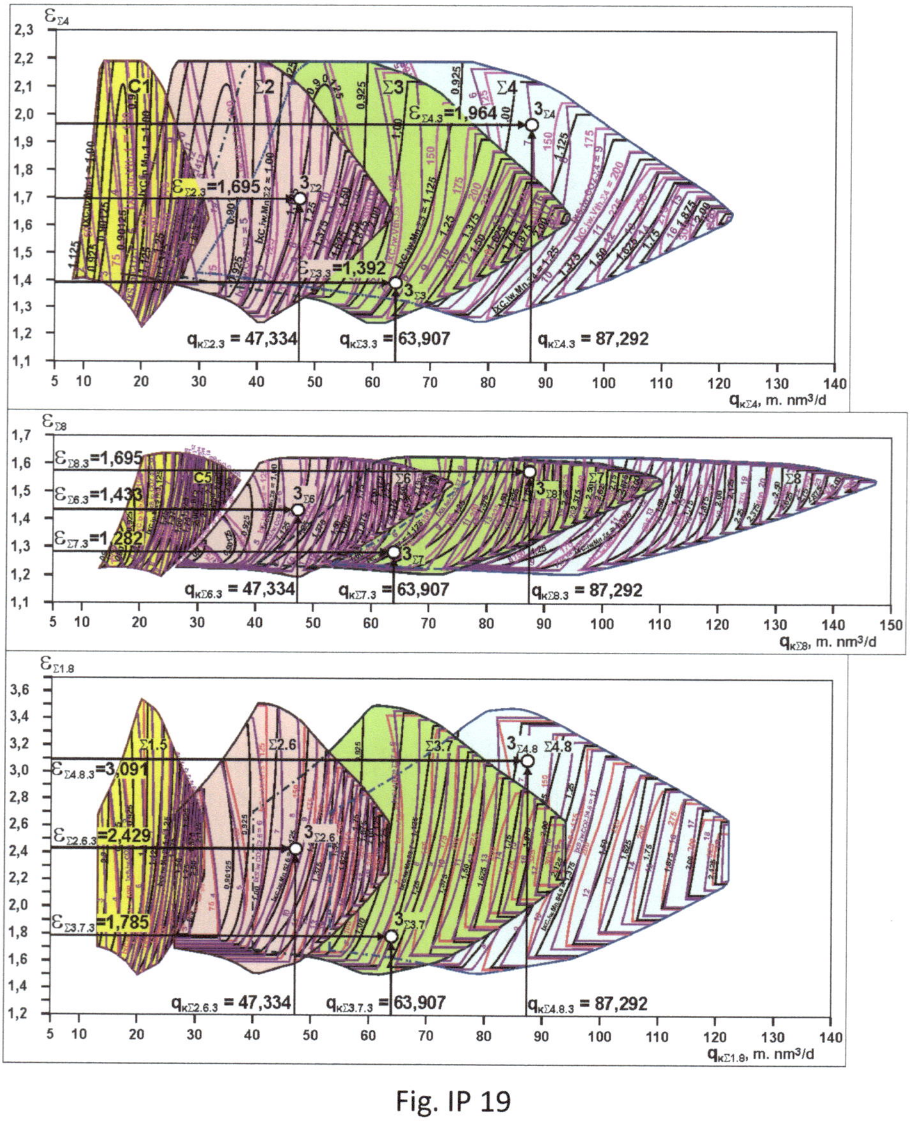

Fig. IP 19

Areas exist within contours in which the lines of constant magnitudes $\mathbf{Ix_{iw.\Sigma4}}$ and $\mathbf{Ix_{iw.\Sigma8}}$ do not have paired points completely corresponding to the summation conditions described above due to unsuccessful selection of **GCUs** types into compression stages in the example considered. Paired points are selected for such parts within the contours by a simple algorithm, which in these circumstances provides the achievement of a given **criterion of reasonableness control**. This algorithm is not described here to reduce the volume of the exposition.

The total current indexed noologistical area of possible modes of joint operation of the first type of the first and second compression stages of the **BCS KGF**, depicted in Fig. IP 19, hereinafter conditionally designated as $\mathbf{RPM_{\Sigma1.8}}$.

3.2. $\mathbf{RPM_{\Sigma1.8}}$ calculated above in paragraph 3.1 (see Fig. IP 19) is summed to the $\mathbf{RPM_{\Sigma12}}$ of the third compression stage (see Fig. IP 17) of the **BCS KGF**.

3.2.1. The contours of $\mathbf{RPM_{\Sigma1.8}}$ are summed up to the $\mathbf{RPM_{\Sigma12}}$ contours of the third stage.

The summation is performed by multiplying the magnitudes of the pressure ratio at those pairs of points of all contours that have the same productivity magnitude in a manner similar to that shown in 3.1.1 above. Then only those contours from the set of contours calculated in this way are left, at the points of which the quantities $\mathbf{Ix_{iw.\Sigma1.8}}$ and $\mathbf{Ix_{iw.\Sigma12}}$ are equal or closest to each other. Only three contours remain for further use as a result, including:

The contour Σ2.9, formed by the summation of the contour Σ2.6 to the contour C9;

The contour Σ3.10, formed by the summation of the contour Σ3.7 to the contour Σ10;

The contour Σ4.11, formed by the summation of the contour Σ4.8 to the contour Σ11.

All the listed summable contours (Σ2.6, C9, Σ3.7, Σ10, Σ4.8 and Σ11) and the result of their summation (Σ2.9, Σ3.10 and Σ4.11) are shown in Fig. IP 20.

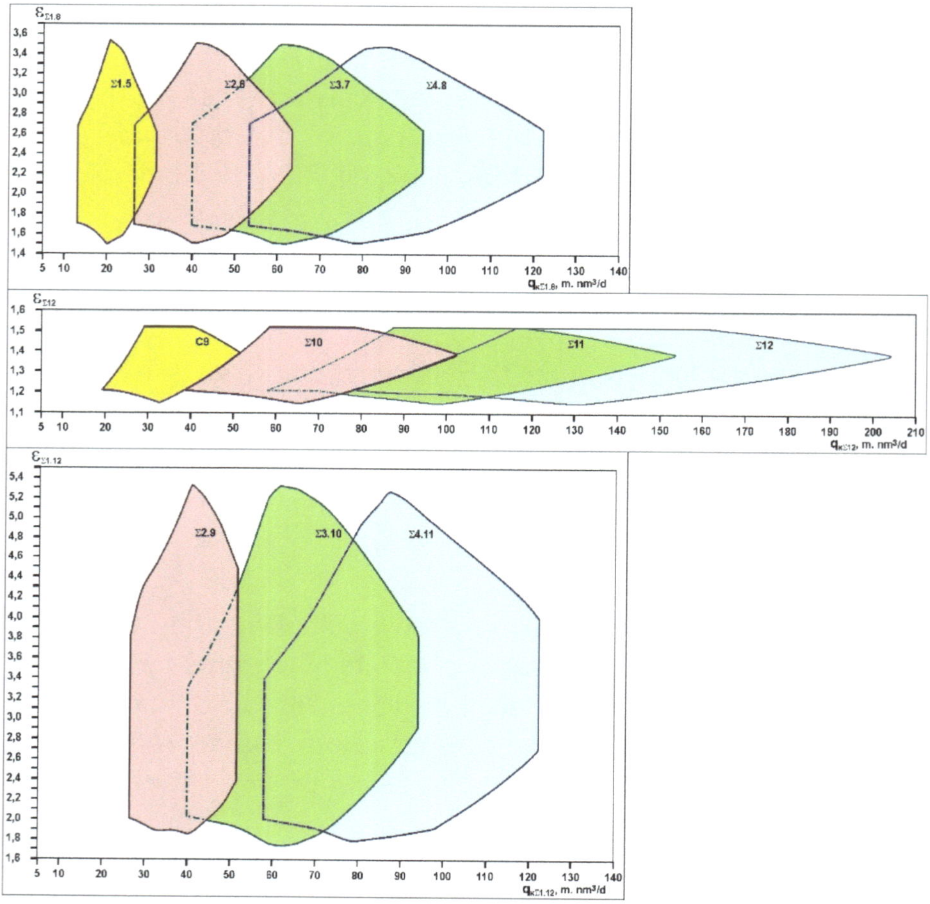

Fig. IP 20

Analysis Fig. IP 20 gives grounds to argue that for normal operation of the **BCS KGF** in its third compression stage, three **GCUs** are sufficient.

3.2.2. The line of constant magnitude $\mathbf{Ix}_{iw.\Sigma1.8}$ is summed to the line $\mathbf{Ix}_{iw.\Sigma12}$.

The lines of constant magnitude $\mathbf{Ix}_{iw.\Sigma1.8}$ and $\mathbf{Ix}_{iw.\Sigma12}$ add up inside the contours Σ2.9, Σ3.10 and Σ4.11 by multiplying the magnitudes of the pressure ratio at those pair points of the lines of the same constant magnitudes $\mathbf{Ix}_{iw.\Sigma1.8}$ and $\mathbf{Ix}_{iw.\Sigma12}$ in which the same magnitude commercial productivity ($\mathbf{q}_{\kappa\Sigma1.8} = \mathbf{q}_{\kappa\Sigma12}$), in the same way as shown in 3.2.1 above. The points of the total lines of constant magnitudes $\mathbf{Ix}_{iw.\Sigma1.12}$ are obtained as a result, which are shown in Fig. IP 21.

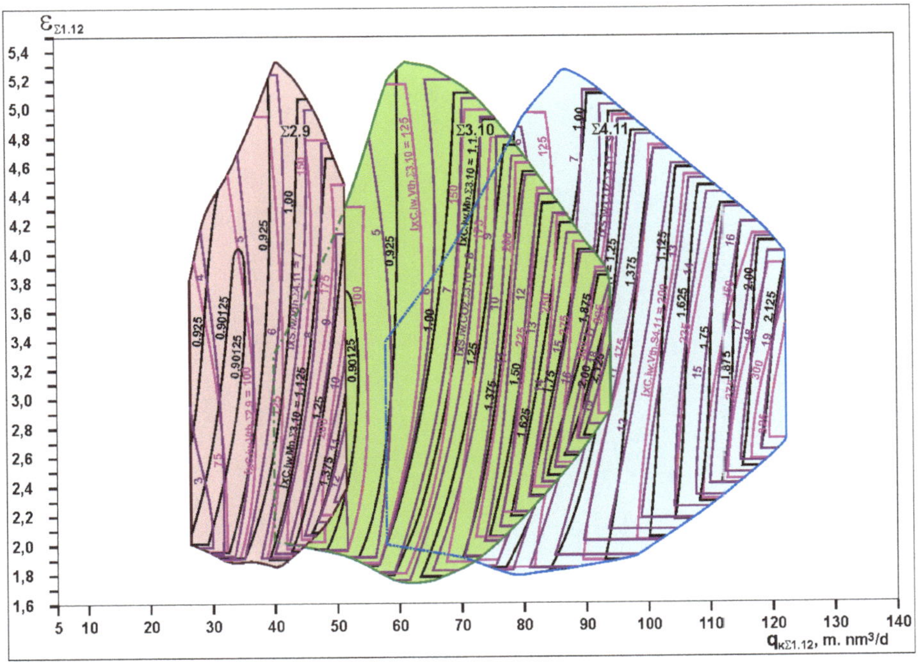

Fig. IP 21

The total current indexed noologistical area of possible modes of joint operation of the first, second and third compression stages of the **BCS KGF**, depicted in Fig. IP 21, hereinafter conditionally designated $\mathbf{RPM}_{\Sigma1.12}$.

4. $\mathbf{RPM_{\Sigma 4}}$, $\mathbf{RPM_{\Sigma 1.8}}$ and $\mathbf{RPM_{\Sigma 1.12}}$, calculated above, are summed up to create the **total indexed noologistical area of possible modes of operation** for the entire **BCS KGF**.

The summation scheme of the above-mentioned $\mathbf{RPM_{\Sigma 4}}$, $\mathbf{RPM_{\Sigma 1.8}}$ and $\mathbf{RPM_{\Sigma 1.12}}$ is presented in Fig. IP 22. Their summation consists in superimposing them on each other in a sequence that corresponds to a specified order of switching on and off the compression stages. The scale of the $\mathbf{RPM_{\Sigma 4}}$ image vertically and horizontally is changed on it in comparison with Fig. IP 15 and equal to the $\mathbf{RPM_{\Sigma 1.8}}$ scales in Fig. IP 19 and $\mathbf{RPM_{\Sigma 1.12}}$ in Fig. IP 22.

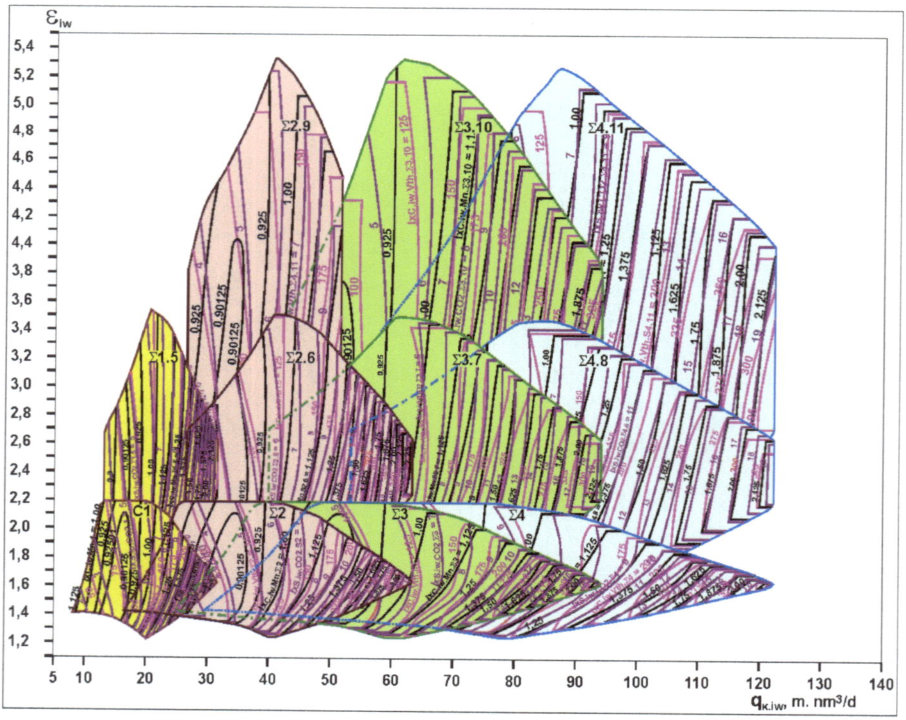

Fig. IP 22

The total current indexed noologistical area of possible modes of operation for the entire **BCS KGF**, depicted in Fig. IP 22, hereinafter conditionally designated $\mathbf{RPM_{iw}}$. It is fully ready for use in the development of **noologistical management solutions** and the calculation of **noologistical control actions** based on the technology of calculating the **downward indexed information pyramid** (**IP_{DI}**), which is described below.

It follows from the calculation technique presented in Example 2, that:

Each j-point within the **RPM_{iw}** contours (see Fig. IP 22) reflects a concrete definite regime of reliable, stable and safe operation of the entire **BCS KGF** at the current time;

The **RPM_{iw}** contours (see Fig. IP 22) are superimposed in order of decreasing **the reasonableness** of the operating modes contained in them from the upper to the lower contour, i.e., the lower contours contain less **reasonable** operating modes compared to the upper ones;

Completely defined lines of constant magnitudes of **the current summation indices**, respectively, **$Ix_{C.iw.Vth.j}$**, **$Ix_{C.iw.Mn.j}$** and **$Ix_{S.iw.CO2.j}$** intersect, at each j-th point within the contours **RPM_{iw}**, by means of which the unambiguous correspondence between reasonable current operating modes of all equipment of the **BCS KGF** are established;

The current number of included compression stages and **GCUs** are assigned within the upper contour of **RPM_{iw}** to provide the minimum energy consumption condition of all types in the form of MW is observed in the entire **BCS KGF** under the current operating conditions under the current commercial productivity $q_{K.iw.j}$, and their operation modes are from conditions of providing their **$Ix_{C.iw.Vth.b}$** magnitudes to be equal to the **$Ix_{C.iw.Vth.j}$** magnitudes;

The current number of included compression stages and **GCUs** are assigned within the upper contour of **RPM_{iw}** to provide the minimum cost conditions of all types in monetary terms is observed in the entire **BCS KGF** under the current operating conditions under the current commercial productivity $q_{K.iw.j}$, and their operation modes are from conditions of providing their $\mathbf{Ix_{C.iw.Mn.b}}$ magnitudes to be equal to the $\mathbf{Ix_{C.iw.Mn.j}}$ magnitudes;

The current number of included compression stages and **GCUs** are assigned within the upper contour of $\mathbf{RPM_{iw}}$ to provide the minimum CO2 emissions is observed in the entire **BCS KGF** under the current operating conditions under the current commercial productivity $q_{K.iw.j}$, and their operation modes are from conditions of providing their $\mathbf{Ix_{S.iw.CO2.b}}$ magnitudes to be equal to the $\mathbf{Ix_{S.iw.CO2.j}}$ magnitudes.

The calculations of the above $\mathbf{RPMA_{iw}}$ and $\mathbf{RPMS_{iw}}$ are based on the $\mathbf{RPM_{iw}}$ calculation sequence described in Example 2, but have their own characteristics.

The calculation of $\mathbf{RPMA_{iw}}$ is performed in the form of a trend of transition to it from $\mathbf{RPM_{iw}}$, which is calculated using **the technology of forecast calculation in the PRESENT**. The purpose of calculating the $\mathbf{RPM_{iw}}$ trend is to provide a constant transition from the current mode of operation of the **BCS KGF**, determined by the parameters of its **point of the current noologistical mode of operation** ($\mathbf{WP_{iw}}$) within the $\mathbf{RPM_{iw}}$ contour, to the goal mode of its operation, determined by the parameters of its point of **the current goal noologistical operating mode** ($\mathbf{WPA_{iw}}$) in limits of the $\mathbf{RPMA_{iw}}$ contour. Результатом этого расчета является постоянно пересчandтанный тренд, состоящandй andз набора j-го состоянandя $\mathbf{RPMA_{iw.j}}$. The recalculation interval for this trend and the number of intermediate j-th states $\mathbf{RPMA_{iw.j}}$ in it are automatically set so that in order to provide a given control accuracy and to limit the rate of change of the operation mode of the entire **BCS KGF** and of each of its elements to the limit of the allowed safe magnitude.

The trend of the j-th state of each parameter used in Example 2 is calculated for each j-th state of $\mathbf{RPMA_{iw.j}}$. Calculation of the trend of j-th states of each parameter for more details see **the technology of forecast calculation in the PRESENT**. The j-th states of $\mathbf{RPMA_{iw.j}}$ are calculated then based on each set of the j-th state of all parameters in the sequence described in Example 2. The set $\mathbf{RPMA_{iw.j}}$ is obtained as a result, which is arranged in the j-th sequence for subsequent use. This sequence of the states of $\mathbf{RPMA_{iw.j}}$ is the $\mathbf{RPMA_{iw.j}}$ trend which is used in the $\mathbf{IP_{DI}}$ described below.

Each j-th point within $\mathbf{RPMA_{iw}}$ contours reflects a certain definite regime of reliable, stable and safe operation of the entire **BCS KGF** at the time moment, determined by the prediction period in **the FUTURE** from the condition of achieving **the goal**;

Completely defined lines of constant magnitudes of **the goal summation indices**, respectively, $\mathbf{Ix_{AC.iw.Vth.j}}$, $\mathbf{Ix_{AC.iw.Mn.j}}$ and $\mathbf{Ix_{AS.iw.CO2.j}}$ intersect, at each j-th point within the contours $\mathbf{RPMA_{iw}}$, by means of which the unambiguous correspondence between reasonable goal operating modes of all equipment of the **BCS KGF** are established;

The goal number of included compression stages and **GCUs** are assigned within the upper contour of $\mathbf{RPMA_{iw}}$ to provide the minimum energy consumption condition of all types in the form of MW is observed in the entire **BCS KGF** under the goal operating conditions under the goal commercial productivity $q_{K.Aiw.j}$, and their operation modes are from conditions of providing their $\mathbf{Ix_{AC.iw.Vth.b}}$ magnitudes to be equal to the $\mathbf{Ix_{AC.iw.Vth.j}}$ magnitudes;

The goal number of included compression stages and **GCUs** are assigned within the upper contour of $\mathbf{RPMA_{iw}}$ to provide the minimum cost conditions of all types in monetary terms is observed in the entire **BCS KGF** under the goal operating conditions under the goal commercial productivity $q_{K.iw.j}$, and their operation modes are from conditions of providing their $\mathbf{Ix_{C.iw.Mn.b}}$ magnitudes to be equal to the $\mathbf{Ix_{C.iw.Mn.j}}$ magnitudes;

The goal number of included compression stages and **GCUs** are assigned within the upper contour of $\mathbf{RPM_{iw}}$ to provide the minimum CO2 emissions is observed in the entire **BCS KGF** under the goal operating conditions under the goal commercial productivity $q_{K.iw.j}$, and their operation modes are from conditions of providing their $\mathbf{Ix_{S.iw.CO2.b}}$ magnitudes to be equal to the $\mathbf{Ix_{S.iw.CO2.j}}$ magnitudes.

The calculation of $\mathbf{RPMS_{iw}}$ is similar to the $\mathbf{RPM_{iw}}$ calculation described in Example 2, but is based on set of source information that

the person took for research in the process of developing **a noological management solution**. The possibility of calculating the trend of j-th states $\mathbf{RPMS}_{iw.j}$ is similar to the one described above for the $\mathbf{RPMA}_{iw}$ trend.

Each j-th point within $\mathbf{RPMS}_{iw}$ contours reflects a certain definite regime of reliable, stable and safe operation of the entire **BCS KGF** at the time moment, determined by the prediction period in **the FUTURE** from the condition of the developed **noologistical management solution**;

Completely defined lines of constant magnitudes of the summation indices, respectively, $\mathbf{Ix}_{SC.iw.Vth.j}$, $\mathbf{Ix}_{SC.iw.Mn.j}$ and $\mathbf{Ix}_{SS.iw.CO2.j}$ intersect, at each j-th point within the contours $\mathbf{RPMS}_{iw}$, by means of which the unambiguous correspondence between reasonable current operating modes of all equipment of the **BCS KGF** corresponding to a modeling **noologistical management solution** are established;

The number of included compression stages and **GCUs** are assigned within the upper contour of $\mathbf{RPM}_{iw}$ to provide the minimum energy consumption condition of all types in the form of MW is observed in the entire **BCS KGF** under the operating conditions under the commercial productivity $q_{K.iw.j}$, and their operation modes are from conditions of providing their $\mathbf{Ix}_{C.iw.Vth.b}$ magnitudes to be equal to the $\mathbf{Ix}_{C.iw.Vth.j}$ magnitudes corresponding to a modeling **noologistical management solution**;

The number of included compression stages and **GCUs** are assigned within the upper contour of $\mathbf{RPM}_{iw}$ to provide the minimum cost conditions of all types in monetary terms is observed in the entire **BCS KGF** under the operating conditions under the commercial productivity $q_{K.iw.j}$, and their operation modes are from conditions of providing their $\mathbf{Ix}_{C.iw.Mn.b}$ magnitudes to be equal to the $\mathbf{Ix}_{C.iw.Mn.j}$ magnitudes corresponding to a modeling **noologistical management solution**;

The number of included compression stages and **GCUs** are assigned within the upper contour of $\mathbf{RPM}_{iw}$ to provide the minimum CO2 emissions is observed in the entire **BCS KGF** under the operating conditions under the commercial productivity $q_{K.iw.j}$, and their operation modes are from conditions of providing their $\mathbf{Ix}_{S.iw.CO2.b}$ magnitudes to be equal to the $\mathbf{Ix}_{S.iw.CO2.j}$ magnitudes corresponding to a modeling **noologistical management solution**.

The calculation technology of $\mathbf{RPM}_{iw}$, $\mathbf{RPMA}_{iw}$ and $\mathbf{RPMS}_{iw}$ for the **BCS KGF**, shown in Example 2, may be used to calculate the total $\mathbf{RPM}_{iw}$, $\mathbf{RPMA}_{iw}$ and $\mathbf{RPMS}_{iw}$ of all gas wells of the **the Kushchevskaya underground gas storage station** (**UGSG**), in the same way as it was used for **UGSG**, and for the workshop for preparing gas to the transport in it. All of them may be recalculated into the total $\mathbf{RPM}_{iw}$, $\mathbf{RPMA}_{iw}$ and $\mathbf{RPMS}_{iw}$ of the entire **UGSG** using the same universal technology. The total $\mathbf{RPM}_{iw}$, $\mathbf{RPMA}_{iw}$ and $\mathbf{RPMS}_{iw}$ may be calculated similarly for other **gas fields** (**GF**) included in Gazprom dobycha Noyabrsk LLC (Gubkinsky, Vyngapurovsky, West-Tarkosalinsky, Muravlenkovsky). $\mathbf{RPM}_{iw}$, $\mathbf{RPMA}_{iw}$ and $\mathbf{RPMS}_{iw}$ of the entire Gazprom dobycha Noyabrsk LLC may be calculated on their basis. $\mathbf{RPM}_{iw}$, $\mathbf{RPMA}_{iw}$ and $\mathbf{RPMS}_{iw}$ of all gas transmission, gas distribution and gas processing enterprises throughout the RF may be calculated similarly regardless of their affiliation.

There is a technical opportunity to calculate $\mathbf{RPM}_{iw}$, $\mathbf{RPMA}_{iw}$ and $\mathbf{RPMS}_{iw}$ in any industry, for example, in the energy sector of any country, the union of countries, the continent, etc. - see **Practical Examples of Noologistics Implementation**.

3.4.3. The Technology of Calculation of the Downward Non-indexed Information Pyramid

The technology of calculating $\mathbf{IP}_{DU}$ consists in the division (distribution) between elements of a complex structure of one magnitude of a certain parameter characterizing the total quantity or total flow density of a certain magnitude defined in **the PAST**, defined in **the PRESENT** or projected in **the FUTURE**, and also in the division (distribution) of one nomenclatures of quantities of **noo values** and / or their flows contained in a formalized description of a complex structure, for example, of **hierarchy**, **habitat**, **provision of existence** (**life support**), **object**, **management solution**, **environment**, **noosphere**,

noogalaxy, **noouniverse**, etc., between the elements of this complex structure. It is carried out, taking into account **the status coefficients** established in the relevant **rules**, starting from the elements of the highest level of the corresponding complex structure to the elements of its lowest level. Its main purpose is to calculate the quantity or density of the flow of **noo value** providing satisfaction of the individual need for it in each **person** in accordance **the rules** of his **hierarchy**, as well as satisfying his individual need for an individual nomenclature of quantities or densities of flows of **noo values** and providing a balance between distributed total and individual magnitudes (that is, observance of the conservation law).

Thus, **the IP_{DU} calculation technology** may be characterized as the process of dividing the total quantity, the total flow density and the composite nomenclature of **noo values** between elements of a complex structure, performed from top-level elements to low-level elements in order to meet the individual **needs** of each **person**, while observing **the rules** of his **hierarchy** and the conservation law. The **IP_{DU} calculation technology** is used for those **noo values** that the **person** has not included in the category of **noologistical values**.

The mathematical apparatus used in the **IP_{DU} calculation technology** is shown below in Example 3.

Example 3

The structure of **the downward non-indexed information pyramid** is shown in Fig. IP 4 b).

1. The magnitude of any total parameter of the element $El_{4.1}$ located in the fourth highest level is divided between the elements of the third level in accordance the direction of the arrows.

1.1. The magnitude of the shared parameter for the element $El_{2.1}^{4.1}$ is calculated by the formula:

$$El_{2.1}^{4.1} = El_{4.1} * K_{2.1}^{4.1} / (K_{2.1}^{4.1} + K_{3.1}^{4.1} + K_{3.2}^{4.1} + K_{3.3}^{4.1}),$$

here are:

$K_{2.1}^{4.1}$, $K_{3.1}^{4.1}$, $K_{3.2}^{4.1}$, $K_{3.3}^{4.1}$ - these are **status coefficients**, the magnitudes of which are indicated in **the rules** of **the hierarchy** according to **the statuses of the elements** in it, and reflect the degree of its "fairness", "equality", "democracy", etc., which are used in the formation of the **IP**$_{UU}$ also;

the rest - see above.

If the total amount of money (**Q**$_{C.iw.Mn}$) is distributed according to this formula, then it becomes:

$$Q_{2.1}^{4.1} = Q_{4.1} * K_{2.1}^{4.1} / (K_{2.1}^{4.1} + K_{3.1}^{4.1} + K_{3.2}^{4.1} + K_{3.3}^{4.1}),$$

here are:

$Q_{4.1}$ – this is the shared magnitude of the total amount of money **Q**$_{C.ih.Mn}$ for the element, which in the structure shown in Fig. IP 4 b), conditionally designated $El_{4.1}$;

$Q_{2.1}^{4.1}$ – this is the distinguished magnitude of **Q**$_{C.ih.Mn.2.1}$ for the element, which in the structure shown in Fig. IP 4 b), conditionally designated $El_{2.1}^{4.1}$;

the rest - see above.

Similar substitutions of conditionally designates to the universal formulas are applied below in the remaining paragraphs of this example when calculating other magnitudes of dividing.

1.2. The magnitude of the shared parameter for the element $El_{3.1}^{4.1}$ is calculated by the formula:

$El_{3.1}^{4.1} = El_{4.1} * K_{3.1}^{4.1} / (K_{2.1}^{4.1} + K_{3.1}^{4.1} + K_{3.2}^{4.1} + Kl_{3.3}^{4.1})$, in which all the symbols are presented above.

1.3. The magnitude of the shared parameter for the element $El_{3.2}^{4.1}$ is calculated by the formula:

$El_{3.2}^{4.1} = El_{4.1} * K_{3.2}^{4.1} / (K_{2.1}^{4.1} + K_{3.1}^{4.1} + K_{3.2}^{4.1} + Kl_{3.3}^{4.1})$, in which all the symbols are presented above.

1.4. The magnitude of the shared parameter for the element $El_{3.3}^{4.1}$ is calculated by the formula:

$El_{3.3}^{4.1} = El_{4.1} * Kl_{3.3}^{4.1} / (K_{2.1}^{4.1} + K_{3.1}^{4.1} + K_{3.2}^{4.1} + Kl_{3.3}^{4.1})$, in which all the symbols are presented above.

2. The magnitude of any total parameter of the elements located in the third level is divided between the elements of the second level in accordance the direction of the arrows.

2.1. The magnitude of the shared parameter for the element $El_{2.2}^{3.1}$ is calculated by the formula:

$$El_{2.2}^{3.1} = El_{3.1}^{4.1} * K_{2.2}^{3.1} / (K_{2.2}^{3.1} + K_{2.3}^{3.1}),$$

here are:

$K_{2.2}^{3.1}$, $K_{2.3}^{3.1}$ - these are **status coefficients**, the magnitudes of which are indicated in **the rules** of **the hierarchy** according to **the statuses of the elements** $El_{2.2}^{3.1}$, $El_{2.3}^{3.1}$;

the rest - see above.

2.2. The magnitude of the shared parameter for the element $El_{2.3}^{3.1}$ is calculated by the formula:

$El_{2.3}^{3.1} = El_{3.1}^{4.1} * K_{2.3}^{3.1} / (K_{2.2}^{3.1} + K_{2.3}^{3.1})$, in which all the symbols are presented above.

2.3. The magnitude of the shared parameter for the element $El_{1.11}^{3.2}$ is calculated by the formula:

$$El_{1.11}^{3.2} = El_{3.2}^{4.1} * K_{1.11}^{3.2} / (K_{1.11}^{3.2} + K_{2.4}^{3.2} + K_{2.5}^{3.2} + K_{2.6}^{3.2}),$$

here are:

$K_{1.11}^{3.2}$, $K_{2.4}^{3.2}$, $K_{2.5}^{3.2}$, $K_{2.6}^{3.2}$ - these are **status coefficients**, the magnitudes of which are indicated in **the rules** of **the hierarchy** according to **the statuses of the elements** $El_{1.11}^{3.2}$, $El_{2.4}^{3.2}$, $El_{2.5}^{3.2}$, $El_{2.6}^{3.2}$;

the rest - see above.

2.4. The magnitude of the shared parameter for the element $El_{2.4}^{3.2}$ is calculated by the formula:

$El_{2.4}^{3.2} = El_{3.2}^{4.1} * K_{2.4}^{3.2} / (K_{1.11}^{3.2} + K_{2.4}^{3.2} + K_{2.5}^{3.2} + K_{2.6}^{3.2})$, in which all the symbols are presented above.

2.5. The magnitude of the shared parameter for the element $El_{2.5}^{3.2}$ is calculated by the formula:

$El_{2.5}^{3.2} = El_{3.2}^{4.1} * K_{2.5}^{3.2} / (K_{1.11}^{3.2} + K_{2.4}^{3.2} + K_{2.5}^{3.2} + K_{2.6}^{3.2})$, in which all the symbols are presented above.

2.6. The magnitude of the shared parameter for the element $El_{2.6}^{3.2}$ is calculated by the formula:

$El_{2.6}^{3.2} = El_{3.2}^{4.1} * K_{2.6}^{3.2} / (K_{1.11}^{3.2} + K_{2.4}^{3.2} + K_{2.5}^{3.2} + K_{2.6}^{3.2})$, in which all the symbols are presented above.

2.7. The magnitude of the shared parameter for the element $El_{2.7}^{3.3}$ is calculated by the formula:

$$El_{2.7}^{3.3} = El_{3.3}^{4.1} * K_{2.7}^{3.3} / (K_{2.7}^{3.3} + K_{2.8}^{3.3} + K_{2.9}^{3.3}),$$

here are:

$K_{2.7}^{3.3}$, $K_{2.8}^{3.3}$, $K_{2.9}^{3.3}$ - these are **status coefficients**, the magnitudes of which are indicated in **the rules** of **the hierarchy** according to **the statuses of the elements** $El_{2.7}^{3.3}$, $El_{2.8}^{3.3}$, $El_{2.9}^{3.3}$;

the rest - see above.

2.8. The magnitude of the shared parameter for the element $El_{2.8}^{3.3}$ is calculated by the formula:

$El_{2.8}^{3.3} = El_{3.3}^{4.1} * K_{2.8}^{3.3} / (K_{2.7}^{3.3} + K_{2.8}^{3.3} + K_{2.9}^{3.3})$, in which all the symbols are presented above.

3. The magnitude of any total parameter of the elements located in the second level is divided between the elements of the lowest first level in accordance the direction of the arrows.

3.1. The magnitude of the shared parameter for the element $El_{1.1}^{2.1}$ is calculated by the formula:

$$El_{1.1}^{2.1} = El_{2.1}^{4.1} * K_{1.1}^{2.1} / (K_{1.1}^{2.1} + K_{1.2}^{2.1} + K_{1.3}^{2.1}),$$

here are:

$K_{1.1}^{2.1}$, $K_{1.2}^{2.1}$, $K_{1.3}^{2.1}$ - these are **status coefficients**, the magnitudes of which are indicated in **the rules** of **the hierarchy** according to **the statuses of the elements** $El_{1.1}^{2.1}$, $El_{1.2}^{2.1}$, $El_{1.3}^{2.1}$;

the rest - see above.

3.2. The magnitude of the shared parameter for the element $El_{1.2}^{2.1}$ is calculated by the formula:

$El_{1.2}^{2.1} = El_{2.1}^{4.1} * K_{1.2}^{2.1} / (K_{1.1}^{2.1} + K_{1.2}^{2.1} + K_{1.3}^{2.1})$, in which all the symbols are presented above.

3.3 The magnitude of the shared parameter for the element $El_{1.3}^{2.1}$ is calculated by the formula:

$El_{1.3}^{2.1} = El_{2.1}^{4.1} * K_{1.3}^{2.1} / (K_{1.1}^{2.1} + K_{1.2}^{2.1} + K_{1.3}^{2.1})$, in which all the symbols are presented above.

3.4 The magnitude of the shared parameter for the element $El_{1.4}^{2.2}$ is calculated by the formula:

$$El_{1.4}^{2.2} = El_{2.2}^{3.1} * K_{1.4}^{2.2} / (K_{1.4}^{2.2} + K_{1.5}^{2.2} + K_{1.6}^{2.2}),$$

here are:

$K_{1.4}^{2.2}$, $K_{1.5}^{2.2}$, $K_{1.6}^{2.2}$ - these are **status coefficients**, the magnitudes of which are indicated in **the rules** of **the hierarchy** according to **the statuses of the elements** $El_{1.4}^{2.2}$, $El_{1.5}^{2.2}$, $El_{1.6}^{2.2}$;

the rest - see above.

3.5 The magnitude of the shared parameter for the element $El_{1.5}^{2.2}$ is calculated by the formula:

$El_{1.5}^{2.2} = El_{2.2}^{3.1} * K_{1.5}^{2.2} / (K_{1.4}^{2.2} + K_{1.5}^{2.2} + K_{1.6}^{2.2})$, in which all the symbols are presented above.

3.6 The magnitude of the shared parameter for the element $El_{1.6}^{2.2}$ is calculated by the formula:

$El_{1.6}^{2.2} = El_{2.2}^{3.1} * K_{1.6}^{2.2} / (K_{1.4}^{2.2} + K_{1.5}^{2.2} + K_{1.6}^{2.2})$, in which all the symbols are presented above.

3.7 The magnitude of the shared parameter for the element $El_{1.7}^{2.3}$ is calculated by the formula:

$$El_{1.7}^{2.3} = El_{2.3}^{3.1} * K_{1.7}^{2.3} / (K_{1.7}^{2.3} + K_{1.8}^{2.3} + K_{1.9}^{2.3} + K_{1.10}^{2.3}),$$

here are:

$K_{1.7}^{2.3}$, $K_{1.8}^{2.3}$, $K_{1.9}^{2.3}$, $K_{1.10}^{2.3}$ - these are **status coefficients**, the magnitudes of which are indicated in **the rules** of **the hierarchy** according to **the statuses of the elements** $El_{1.7}^{2.3}$, $El_{1.8}^{2.3}$, $El_{1.9}^{2.3}$, $El_{1.10}^{2.3}$;

the rest - see above.

3.8. The magnitude of the shared parameter for the element $El_{1.8}^{2.3}$ is calculated by the formula:

$El_{1.8}^{2.3} = El_{2.3}^{3.1} * K_{1.8}^{2.3} / (K_{1.7}^{2.3} + K_{1.8}^{2.3} + K_{1.9}^{2.3} + K_{1.10}^{2.3})$, in which all the symbols are presented above.

3.9. The magnitude of the shared parameter for the element $El_{1.9}^{2.3}$ is calculated by the formula:

$El_{1.9}^{2.3} = El_{2.3}^{3.1} * K_{1.9}^{2.3} / (K_{1.7}^{2.3} + K_{1.8}^{2.3} + K_{1.9}^{2.3} + K_{1.10}^{2.3})$, in which all the symbols are presented above.

3.10. The magnitude of the shared parameter for the element $El_{1.10}^{2.3}$ is calculated by the formula:

$El_{1.10}^{2.3} = El_{2.3}^{3.1} * K_{1.10}^{2.3} / (K_{1.7}^{2.3} + K_{1.8}^{2.3} + K_{1.9}^{2.3} + K_{1.10}^{2.3})$, in which all the symbols are presented above.

3.11. The magnitude of the shared parameter for the element $El_{1.12}^{2.4}$ is calculated by the formula:

$El_{1.12}^{2.4} = El_{2.4}^{3.2} * K_{1.12}^{2.4} / (K_{1.12}^{2.4} + K_{1.13}^{2.4})$,

here are:

$K_{1.12}^{2.4}$, $K_{1.13}^{2.4}$ - these are **status coefficients**, the magnitudes of which are indicated in **the rules** of **the hierarchy** according to **the statuses of the elements** $El_{1.12}^{2.4}$, $El_{1.13}^{2.4}$;

the rest - see above.

3.12. The magnitude of the shared parameter for the element $El_{1.13}^{2.4}$ is calculated by the formula:

$El_{1.13}^{2.4} = El_{2.4}^{3.2} * K_{1.13}^{2.4} / (K_{1.12}^{2.4} + K_{1.13}^{2.4})$, in which all the symbols are presented above.

3.13. The magnitude of the shared parameter for the element $El_{1.14}^{2.5}$ is calculated by the formula:

$$El_{1.14}^{2.5} = El_{2.5}^{3.2} * K_{1.14}^{2.5} / (K_{1.14}^{2.5} + K_{1.15}^{2.5} + K_{1.16}^{2.5}),$$

here are:

$K_{1.14}^{2.5}$, $K_{1.15}^{2.5}$, $K_{1.16}^{2.5}$ - these are **status coefficients**, the magnitudes of which are indicated in **the rules** of **the hierarchy** according to **the statuses of the elements** $El_{1.14}^{2.5}$, $El_{1.15}^{2.5}$, $El_{1.16}^{2.5}$;

the rest - see above.

3.14. The magnitude of the shared parameter for the element $El_{1.15}^{2.5}$ is calculated by the formula:

$El_{1.15}^{2.5} = El_{2.5}^{3.2} * K_{1.15}^{2.5} / (K_{1.14}^{2.5} + K_{1.15}^{2.5} + K_{1.16}^{2.5})$, in which all the symbols are presented above.

3.15. The magnitude of the shared parameter for the element $El_{1.16}^{2.5}$ is calculated by the formula:

$El_{1.16}^{2.5} = El_{2.5}^{3.2} * K_{1.15}^{2.5} / (K_{1.16}^{2.5} + K_{1.15}^{2.5} + K_{1.16}^{2.5})$, in which all the symbols are presented above.

3.16. The magnitude of the shared parameter for the element $El_{1.17}^{2.6}$ is calculated by the formula:

$$El_{1.17}^{2.6} = El_{2.6}^{3.2} * K_{1.17}^{2.6} / (K_{1.17}^{2.6} + K_{1.18}^{2.6} + K_{1.19}^{2.6}),$$

here are:

$K_{1.17}^{2.6}$, $K_{1.18}^{2.6}$, $K_{1.19}^{2.6}$ - these are **status coefficients**, the magnitudes of which are indicated in **the rules** of **the hierarchy** according to **the statuses of the elements** $El_{1.17}^{2.6}$, $El_{1.18}^{2.6}$, $El_{1.19}^{2.6}$;

the rest - see above.

3.17. The magnitude of the shared parameter for the element $El^{2.6}_{1.18}$ is calculated by the formula:

$El^{2.6}_{1.18} = El^{3.2}_{2.6} * K^{2.6}_{1.18} / (K^{2.6}_{1.17} + K^{2.6}_{1.18} + K^{2.6}_{1.19})$, in which all the symbols are presented above.

3.18. The magnitude of the shared parameter for the element $El^{2.6}_{1.19}$ is calculated by the formula:

$El^{2.6}_{1.19} = El^{3.2}_{2.6} * K^{2.6}_{1.19} / (K^{2.6}_{1.17} + K^{2.6}_{1.18} + K^{2.6}_{1.19})$, in which all the symbols are presented above.

3.19. The magnitude of the shared parameter for the element $El^{2.7}_{1.20}$ is calculated by the formula:

$El^{2.7}_{1.20} = El^{3.3}_{2.7} * K^{2.7}_{1.20} / (K^{2.7}_{1.20} + K^{2.7}_{1.21} + K^{2.7}_{1.22})$,

here are:

$K^{2.7}_{1.20}$, $K^{2.7}_{1.21}$, $K^{2.7}_{1.22}$ - these are **status coefficients**, the magnitudes of which are indicated in **the rules** of **the hierarchy** according to **the statuses of the elements** $El^{2.7}_{1.20}$, $El^{2.7}_{1.21}$, $El^{2.7}_{1.22}$;

the rest - see above.

3.20. The magnitude of the shared parameter for the element $El^{2.7}_{1.21}$ is calculated by the formula:

$El^{2.7}_{1.21} = El^{3.3}_{2.7} * K^{2.7}_{1.21} / (K^{2.7}_{1.20} + K^{2.7}_{1.21} + K^{2.7}_{1.22})$, in which all the symbols are presented above.

3.21. The magnitude of the shared parameter for the element $El^{2.7}_{1.22}$ is calculated by the formula:

$El^{2.7}_{1.22} = El^{3.3}_{2.7} * K^{2.7}_{1.22} / (K^{2.7}_{1.20} + K^{2.7}_{1.21} + K^{2.7}_{1.22})$, in which all the symbols are presented above.

3.22. The magnitude of the shared parameter for the element $El_{1.23}^{2.8}$ is calculated by the formula:

$$El_{1.23}^{2.8} = El_{2.8}^{3.3} * K_{1.23}^{2.8} / (K_{1.23}^{2.8} + K_{1.24}^{2.8} + K_{1.25}^{2.8}),$$

here are:

$K_{1.23}^{2.8}$, $K_{1.24}^{2.8}$, $K_{1.25}^{2.8}$ - these are **status coefficients**, the magnitudes of which are indicated in **the rules** of **the hierarchy** according to **the statuses of the elements** $El_{1.23}^{2.8}$, $El_{1.24}^{2.8}$, $El_{1.25}^{2.8}$;

the rest - see above.

3.23. The magnitude of the shared parameter for the element $El_{1.24}^{2.8}$ is calculated by the formula:

$El_{1.24}^{2.8} = El_{2.8}^{3.3} * K_{1.24}^{2.8} / (K_{1.23}^{2.8} + K_{1.24}^{2.8} + K_{1.25}^{2.8})$, in which all the symbols are presented above.

3.24. The magnitude of the shared parameter for the element $El_{1.25}^{2.8}$ is calculated by the formula:

$El_{1.25}^{2.8} = El_{2.8}^{3.3} * K_{1.25}^{2.8} / (K_{1.23}^{2.8} + K_{1.24}^{2.8} + K_{1.25}^{2.8})$, in which all the symbols are presented above.

3.25. The magnitude of the shared parameter for the element $El_{1.26}^{2.9}$ is calculated by the formula:

$$El_{1.26}^{2.9} = El_{2.9}^{3.3} * K_{1.26}^{2.9} / (K_{1.26}^{2.9} + K_{1.27}^{2.9} + K_{1.28}^{2.9} + K_{1.29}^{2.9}),$$

here are:

$K_{1.26}^{2.9}$, $K_{1.27}^{2.9}$, $K_{1.28}^{2.9}$, $K_{1.29}^{2.9}$ - these are **status coefficients**, the magnitudes of which are indicated in **the rules** of **the hierarchy** according to **the statuses of the elements** $El_{1.26}^{2.9}$, $El_{1.27}^{2.9}$, $El_{1.28}^{2.9}$, $El_{1.29}^{2.9}$;

the rest - see above.

3.26. The magnitude of the shared parameter for the element $El^{2.9}_{1.27}$ is calculated by the formula:

$El^{2.9}_{1.27} = El^{3.3}_{2.9} * K^{2.9}_{1.27} / (K^{2.9}_{1.27} + K^{2.9}_{1.27} + K^{2.9}_{1.28} + K^{2.9}_{1.29})$, in which all the symbols are presented above.

3.27. The magnitude of the shared parameter for the element $El^{2.9}_{1.28}$ is calculated by the formula:

$El^{2.9}_{1.28} = El^{3.3}_{2.9} * K^{2.9}_{1.28} / (K^{2.9}_{1.27} + K^{2.9}_{1.27} + K^{2.9}_{1.28} + K^{2.9}_{1.29})$, in which all the symbols are presented above.

3.28. The magnitude of the shared parameter for the element $El^{2.9}_{1.29}$ is calculated by the formula:

$El^{2.9}_{1.29} = El^{3.3}_{2.9} * K^{2.9}_{1.29} / (K^{2.9}_{1.27} + K^{2.9}_{1.27} + K^{2.9}_{1.28} + K^{2.9}_{1.29})$, in which all the symbols are presented above.

3.4.4. The Technology of Calculation of the Downward Indexed Information Pyramid

The technology of calculating IP$_{DI}$ consists in the division (distribution) between elements of a complex structure of one magnitude of a certain parameter characterizing the total quantity or total flow density of a certain magnitude defined in **the PAST**, defined in **the PRESENT** or projected in **the FUTURE the total indexed noologistical area of possible modes of operation**, for example, between elements of a complex **grid** of any **hierarchy**. Division (distribution) is performed on the points of **indexed noologistical areas of possible modes of operation** of elements in which the magnitudes of the indices of **the criteria of reasonableness** are equal or the closest in magnitude, from the elements of the highest level to the equipment of the lowest level in accordance the direction of the arrows in Fig. IP 4 b).

Its main purpose is to calculate the flow density of each **noologistical value** in each **unit of equipment** and the magnitude of the corresponding **control action** on it in **the PRESENT**, the totality of which provides the achieve in **the FUTURE** the individual **goal** of each **person** in accordance the **rules** of its **hierarchy** and its technical capabilities, and providing a balance between distributed total and individual magnitudes (that is, observance of the conservation law).

The status coefficients $K_{1.1}^{2.1}$, $K_{1.2}^{2.1}$, $K_{1.3}^{2.1}$, ..., $K_{3.3}^{4.1}$, defining the statuses of **persons** in **the hierarchy** that are used in the formation of **IP_{UU}** and **IP_{DU}**, are not used in the formation of **IP_{DI}**.

The IP_{DI} calculation technology provides calculation of a set of modeled, current and predicted magnitudes of the parameters of the points of **noologistical operating modes** for each **unit of equipment** of a complex facility in the **PAST**, **PRESENT** or **FUTURE**, as well as the magnitudes of **the noologistical control actions**, the development of **noologistical management solutions**, and the modeling for setting **goals** also. The calculation results are used therein, given above in Examples 1 and 2 in describing the **IP_{UU}** and **IP_{UI} calculation technologies**, respectively, including:

1. The parameters of **providing the existence** (**life support**) and **habitat** in the **PRESENT** (the density of the **total current flow of creation $V_{M.iw.NG}$** (**$D_{M.iw.NG}$**), consumption of **$V_{C.iw.NG}$**, **$V_{C.iw.Vth}$** and **$V_{C.iw.Mn}$** (**$D_{C.iw.NG}$**, **$D_{C.iw.Vth}$** and **$D_{C.iw.Mn}$**), the **$V_{S.iw.CO2}$** (**$D_{S.iw.CO2}$**) rejection, the current magnitude of **$V_{M.iw.NG}$**, **$V_{C.iw.NG}$**, **$V_{C.iw.Vth}$**, **$V_{C.iw.Mn}$**, and **$V_{S.iw.CO2}$** (**$Q_{M.iw.NG}$**, **$Q_{C.iw.NG}$**, **$Q_{C.iw.Vth}$**, **$Q_{C.iw.Mn}$** and **$Q_{S.iw.CO2}$**)), and also - **total current indexed noologistical areas of possible modes of operation** (**RPM_{iw}**), establishing mathematical conformity between them at the highest level of the **object** management.

2. The **goal's** parameters of **providing the existence** (**life support**) and **habitat** in the **FUTURE** (the density of the **goal's total flow of creation $VA_{M.iw.NG}$** (**$DA_{M.iw.NG}$**), **goal's consumption** of **$VA_{C.iw.NG}$**, **$VA_{C.iw.Vth}$** and **$VA_{C.iw.Mn}$** (**$DA_{C.iw.NG}$**, **$DA_{C.iw.Vth}$** and **$DA_{C.iw.Mn}$**), the **$VA_{S.iw.CO2}$** (**$DA_{S.iw.CO2}$**) **rejection**, the **goal's** magnitude of **$VA_{M.iw.NG}$**, **$VA_{C.iw.NG}$**, **$VA_{C.iw.Vth}$**, **$VA_{C.iw.Mn}$** and **$VA_{S.iw.CO2}$** (**$QA_{M.iw.NG}$**, **$QA_{C.iw.NG}$**, **$QA_{C.iw.Vth}$**, **$QA_{C.iw.Mn}$** and **$QA_{S.iw.CO2}$**)), and also - **goal's total indexed noologistical areas of possible modes of operation** (**$RPMA_{iw}$**), establishing

mathematical conformity between them at the highest level of the **object** management.

3. The predicted parameters of **providing the existence** (**life support**) and **habitat** in the **FUTURE** (the density of the total predicted **flow of creation** $\mathbf{VS_{M.iw.NG}}$ ($\mathbf{DS_{M.iw.NG}}$), the consumption of $\mathbf{VS_{C.iw.NG}}$, $\mathbf{VS_{C.iw.Vth}}$ and $\mathbf{VS_{C.iw.Mn}}$ ($\mathbf{DS_{C.iw.NG}}$, $\mathbf{DS_{C.iw.Vth}}$ and $\mathbf{DS_{C.iw.Mn}}$), the $\mathbf{VS_{S.iw.CO2}}$ ($\mathbf{DS_{S.iw.CO2}}$) **rejection**, the predicted magnitude of $\mathbf{VS_{M.iw.NG}}$, $\mathbf{VS_{C.iw.NG}}$, $\mathbf{VS_{C.iw.Vth}}$, $\mathbf{VS_{C.iw.Mn}}$ and $\mathbf{VS_{S.iw.CO2}}$ ($\mathbf{QS_{M.iw.NG}}$, $\mathbf{QS_{C.iw.NG}}$, $\mathbf{QS_{C.iw.Vth}}$, $\mathbf{QS_{C.iw.Mn}}$ and $\mathbf{QS_{S.iw.CO2}}$)), as well as predicted **total indexed noologistical areas of possible modes of operation** ($\mathbf{RPMS_{iw}}$), establishing mathematical conformity between them at the highest level of the **object** management.

The calculation of the above-mentioned values of **noologistical control actions** is carried out in the following universal sequence, which reflects the algorithm of using the mathematical apparatus of the $\mathbf{IP_{DI}}$ **calculation technology**:

1. Define the background information for the calculation.

2. Define the parameters for regulating the current operating modes of all b-th **units of equipment** according to the positions of their **current work points** on all their **current indexed noologistical areas of possible operating modes** - from the $\mathbf{RPM_{iw}}$ of the highest-level **object** management to $\mathbf{RPM_{iw.b}}$ of each **unit of equipment** of the lowest level (briefly - from $\mathbf{WP_{iw}}$ to $\mathbf{WP_{iw.b}}$).

3. Calculate the parameters for regulating **the current goal's (predicted or modeled) noologistical operation mode** of each **unit of equipment** according to the position of its **current goal's noologistical work point** on $\mathbf{RPMA_{iw}}$ (briefly - $\mathbf{WPA_{iw}}$) for the highest management level of **the object**, including the magnitude of those **criterion of management reasonableness** or the amount of **compromise** between them, which corresponds to the accepted **goal**.

4. Calculate the magnitudes of the **current goal's summation indexes**, providing compliance **the criteria for reasonable management**, given by **the person** in his **goal**.

5. Calculate the parameters for regulating **the current goal's (predicted or modeled) in noologistical work points** of the operation modes of each **unit of equipment** on all their **goal**, predictable or modeled **indexed noologistical areas of possible operating modes** - from $\mathbf{RPMA_{iw}}$ or $\mathbf{RPMS_{iw}}$ of the highest level of the management **object** to the $\mathbf{RPMA_{iw.b}}$ or $\mathbf{RPMS_{iw.b}}$ of each lowest-level **unit of equipment** (briefly - from $\mathbf{WPA_{iw}}$ and $\mathbf{WPA_{iw.b}}$ or $\mathbf{WPS_{iw}}$ and $\mathbf{WPS_{iw.b}}$).

6. Use the magnitudes of the parameters of the **goal's** or predicted points of operation modes (**WPA** or **WPS**) obtained in paragraph 5 to develop **noologistical management solutions** and/or to calculate **the noologistical control actions**.

The sequence of processing the information flows using the $\mathbf{IP_{DI}}$ **calculating technology** is shown in Example 4.

Example 4

1. Background information

1.1. Elements of the technological scheme of **the real object** under consideration and their conditional designations are similar to the elements and notations indicated in § 1.1. of Example 2.

1.2. The simplifications adopted are analogous to the simplifications indicated in § 1.2. of Example 2.

1.3. Used $\mathbf{RPM_{iw.1}}$, $\mathbf{RPM_{iw.2}}$, $\mathbf{RPM_{iw.3}}$, ..., $\mathbf{RPM_{iw.12}}$ are similar to those used in Example 2.

1.4. Established priorities of importance (turn-on and turn-off sequence) are the same as those set in Example 2.

1.5. Used $\mathbf{RPM_{\Sigma 4}}$ (see Fig. IP 15), $\mathbf{RPM_{\Sigma 8}}$ (see Fig. IP 16), $\mathbf{RPM_{\Sigma 12}}$ (see Fig. IP 17) and $\mathbf{RPM_{\Sigma 1.12}}$ (see Fig. IP 22) are calculated in Example 2.

1.6. The goal's total commercial productivity of **BCS KGF** q_{kAiw} = 91,940 m. n.m3 / d, has been determined by **the** IP_{UU} **calculation technology** described above in Example 1.

2. Determine the regulating parameters of the current operating modes of all elements of **a real object**.

2.1. Calculate the current performance of **the KGF grid** in which **BCS KGF** operates.

It is obvious that **the KGF grid** in which the **BCS KGF** operates may be represented in the form of an equivalent gas pipeline, which currently has quite certain parameters and performance characteristics. Therefore, to derive a mathematical expression describing the current operating characteristic of **the KGF grid**, a formula known in **the technical literature** that determines the current throughput of any gas pipeline is used, for example:

$$q_{\kappa.iw} = 0{,}326 * 10^{-6} * d^{2,5} * \sqrt{\frac{P^2_{\kappa.iw} - P^2_{н.iw}}{\lambda * \Delta * T_{cp} * z_{cp} * l}},$$

here are:

$q_{к.iw}$ – this is the magnitude of the current commercial productivity of **BCS KGF**, equal to the current throughput of **the KGF grid**, expressed in m. n.m³/d;

d – this is the magnitude of the current internal diameter of the gas pipeline, expressed in mm;

$P_{к.iw}$ – this is the magnitude of the current pressure at the exit from the **BCS KGF** and at the entrance to **the KGF grid**, expressed in kg/cm²;

$P_{н.iw}$ – this is the magnitude of the current pressure at the input to the **BCS KGF** and at the outlet from **the KGF grid**, expressed in kg/cm²;

λ – this is the magnitude of the current coefficient of hydraulic resistance of the pipeline;

Δ – this is the magnitude of the current relative density of the gas through the air;

T_{cp} – this is the magnitude of the average current gas temperature along the length of the gas pipeline, expressed in °K;

z_{cp} – this is the magnitude of the average current compressibility factor of gas along the length of the gas pipeline;

l – this is the magnitude of the current length of the gas pipeline, expressed in km.

Two substitutions were applied to derive the formula used below to calculate the magnitude of the current coefficient K_G, which connects the magnitudes of the pressure ratio $\varepsilon_{iw.j}$ and the commercial productivity $q_{К.iw.j}$ at each j-th point of the current operating characteristic of **the KGF grid**, including:

$\varepsilon_{iw} = P_{К.iw} / P_{Н.iw}$ – this is the magnitude of the current pressure ratio in **BCS KGF**;

$K_G = \frac{\lambda * \Delta * T_{cp} * z_{cp} * l}{(0{,}326 * 10^{-6} * d^{2,5} * P_{н.iw})^2}$ - this is the current coefficient, the magnitude of which connects the magnitudes of $q_{К.iw.j}$ and ε_{iw} in the current operating characteristic of **the KGF grid**.

However, it is not necessary to calculate the magnitude of K_G from the formula used for substitution. The property of the current operating characteristic of **the KGF grid** is used to calculate its magnitude, according to which it necessarily passes through **the current working point (WP_{iw})** of the **BCS KGF**. Therefore, the formula for calculating the current magnitude of K_G was obtained after applying the substitutions in the formula for calculating $q_{К.iw.j}$, and the usual algebraic transformations:

$K_G = \frac{\varepsilon_{iw}^2 - 1}{q_{К.iw}^2}$, in which all the current values ($q_{К.iw}$ and ε_{iw}) appearing in it are known because they are constantly measured in real time by the measuring tools and systems available in the **BCS KGF**. So its magnitude, in the example under consideration, at ε_{iw} = 6,728

MPa / 2,173 MPa = 3,0971 and $q_{к.iw}$ = 79,0132 m. n.m³/d, which were measured on 03.02.2010 at 11:27. 16 seconds, is equal to:

$$K_G = \frac{\varepsilon_{iw}^2 - 1}{q_{к.iw}^2} = \frac{3{,}0971^2 - 1}{79{,}0132^2} = 0{,}0013762.$$

The formula derived from the above formula for the calculation of $q_{к.iw}$ is used to calculate the magnitudes of the pressure ratio $\varepsilon_{iw.j}$ in each j-th point of the current operating characteristic of **the KGF grid** for each magnitude of $q_{к.iw.j}$ in the entire range of possible changes in its commercial productivity into the **RPM$_{iw}$**:

$\varepsilon_{iw.j} = \sqrt{K_G * q_{к.iw.j}^2 + 1}$, in which all the magnitudes are described above.

The parameters of j-th points of the current operating characteristic of **the KGF grid** in the range $q_{к.iw}$ from 10 to 130 m. n.m³/d are calculated below based on this formula - see Fig. IP 22, including:

$$\varepsilon_{iw.1} = \sqrt{K_G * q_{к.iw.1}^2 + 1} = \sqrt{0{,}0013762 * 10^2 + 1} = 1{,}067;$$

$$\varepsilon_{iw.2} = \sqrt{K_G * q_{к.iw.2}^2 + 1} = \sqrt{0{,}0013762 * 20^2 + 1} = 1{,}245;$$

$$\varepsilon_{iw.3} = \sqrt{K_G * q_{к.iw.3}^2 + 1} = \sqrt{0{,}0013762 * 30^2 + 1} = 1{,}496;$$

$$\varepsilon_{iw.4} = \sqrt{K_G * q_{к.iw.4}^2 + 1} = \sqrt{0{,}0013762 * 40^2 + 1} = 1{,}789;$$

$$\varepsilon_{iw.5} = \sqrt{K_G * q_{к.iw.5}^2 + 1} = \sqrt{0{,}0013762 * 50^2 + 1} = 2{,}107;$$

$$\varepsilon_{iw.6} = \sqrt{K_G * q_{к.iw.6}^2 + 1} = \sqrt{0{,}0013762 * 60^2 + 1} = 2{,}440;$$

$$\varepsilon_{iw.7} = \sqrt{K_G * q_{к.iw.7}^2 + 1} = \sqrt{0{,}0013762 * 70^2 + 1} = 2{,}783;$$

$$\varepsilon_{iw.8} = \sqrt{K_G * q_{к.iw.8}^2 + 1} = \sqrt{0{,}0013762 * 80^2 + 1} = 3{,}132;$$

$$\varepsilon_{iw.9} = \sqrt{K_G * q_{к.iw.9}^2 + 1} = \sqrt{0{,}0013762 * 90^2 + 1} = 3{,}485;$$

$$\varepsilon_{iw.10} = \sqrt{K_G * q_{к.iw.10}^2 + 1} = \sqrt{0{,}0013762 * 100^2 + 1} = 3{,}842;$$

$$\varepsilon_{iw.11} = \sqrt{K_G * q_{к.iw.11}^2 + 1} = \sqrt{0{,}0013762 * 110^2 + 1} = 4{,}201;$$

$$\varepsilon_{iw.12} = \sqrt{K_G * q_{к.iw.12}^2 + 1} = \sqrt{0{,}0013762 * 120^2 + 1} = 4{,}563;$$

$$\varepsilon_{iw.13} = \sqrt{K_G * q_{к.iw.13}^2 + 1} = \sqrt{0{,}0013762 * 130^2 + 1} = 4{,}925.$$

The current performance is constructed from the above calculated $q_{к.iw.j}$ and $\varepsilon_{iw.j}$, which is represented as a red line in Fig. IP 23, put over **RPM$_{iw}$**, calculated above in Example 2 (see Fig. IP 22).

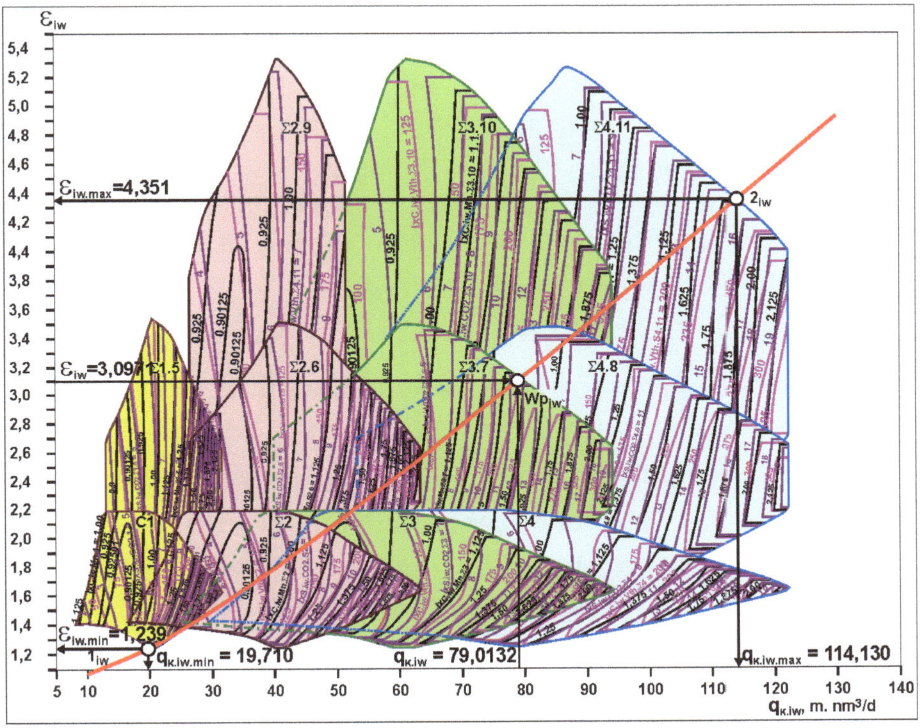

Fig. IP 23

It is obvious for the **BCS KGF** specialists from the above, that:

- **BCS KGF** works without bypass at all points of **RPM$_{iw}$,** which coincide with the current operational characteristics of **the KGF grid**;
- **BCS KGF** may only work with a bypass at all points **RPM$_{iw}$,** which are located to the right of the current performance of **the KGF grid**;
- **BCS KGF** may not physically operate at those **RPM$_{iw}$** points that are located to the left of the current working characteristic of **the KGF grid**;
- The **BCS KGF**, working together **the KGF grid** at the 1_{iw} point, provides the lowest possible current productivity $q_{к.iw.min}$ =

19,710 m. n.m^3/d and the pressure ratio $\varepsilon_{iw.min}$ = 1,239, and at the point 2_{iw} - the maximum possible $q_{к.iw.max}$ = 114,130 m. n.m^3/d and $\varepsilon_{iw.max}$ = 4,351;

- Parameters of the **BCS KGF** operating mode at the point **RPM$_{iw}$** may be provided both by the joint operation of the first and second compression stages, and by the joint operation of all three compression stages, but the joint operation of the first and second stages is more reasonable;
- Parameters of the **BCS KGF** operating mode at the point **RPM$_{iw}$** due the joint operation of the first and second compression stages may be provided by a combination of jointly operating **GCU #1, #2, #3, #5, #6 and #7** forming **RPM$_{\Sigma3.7}$** or by **GCU #1, #2, #3 , #4, #5, #6, #7 and #8**, forming **RPM$_{\Sigma4.8}$**, but the more reasonable of these two options is the combination of **GCU** forming **RPM$_{\Sigma3.7}$**. Thus, the parameters for regulating the current operating modes are rotation frequencies **GCU #1, #2, #3, #5, #6 and #7**, i.e., n_1, n_2, n_3, n_5, n_6 and n_7, which currently measure their systems of aggregate automation.

3. Determine the parameters for regulating **the current goal's noologistical regime** of **the KGF grid**.

3.1. Calculate the current **goal's** performance of **the KGF grid** in which **BCS KGF** operates.

The calculation is performed using the same formulas used in § 2.1 to calculate the j-th points of its current performance:

The **goal's** pressure ratio in **BCS KGF** is calculated by the formula:

$\varepsilon_{Aiw} = P_{к.Aiw} / P_{н.Aiw}$ = 7,768 / 2,159 = 3,5974 – this is the magnitude of the current pressure ratio in **BCS KGF**, here are:

$P_{к.Aiw}$ = 7,768 MPa – this is the magnitude of the current goal's pressure at the exit from the **BCS KGF** and at the entrance to **the KGF**

grid, calculated by **the technology of forecast calculation in the PRESENT**;

$P_{H.Aiw}$ = 2,159 MPa – this is the magnitude of the current goal's pressure at the input to the **BCS KGF** and at the outlet from **the KGF grid**, calculated by **the technology of forecast calculation in the PRESENT**.

3.2. Calculate the current goal's KA_G coefficient, the magnitude of which connects the magnitudes of $q_{к.Aiw.j}$ and $\varepsilon_{Aiw.j}$ in the current goal's operating characteristic of **the KGF grid**, using the formula:

$$KA_G = \frac{\varepsilon_{iw}^2 - 1}{q_{к.Aiw}^2} = \frac{3{,}5974^2 - 1}{97{,}8617^2} = 0{,}0012469,$$

here are:

$q_{к.Aiw}$ = 97,8617 m. n.m³/d – this is the magnitude of the current goal's commercial productivity of **BCS KGF**, calculated by **the technology of forecast calculation in the PRESENT**;

the rest - see above.

3.3. Calculate the parameters of j-th points of **the current goal's operating characteristic** of **the KGF grid**, including:

3.3. Calculate the parameters of j-th points of **the current goal's operating characteristic** of **the KGF grid** in the range of $q_{к.Aiw}$ from 10 to 130 m. n.m³/d, including:

$$\varepsilon_{Aiw.1} = \sqrt{KA_G * q_{к.Aiw.1}^2 + 1} = \sqrt{0{,}0012469 * 10^2 + 1} = 1{,}061;$$

$$\varepsilon_{Aiw.2} = \sqrt{KA_G * q_{к.Aiw.2}^2 + 1} = \sqrt{0{,}0012469 * 20^2 + 1} = 1{,}224;$$

$$\varepsilon_{Aiw.3} = \sqrt{KA_G * q_{к.Aiw.3}^2 + 1} = \sqrt{0{,}0012469 * 30^2 + 1} = 1{,}457;$$

$$\varepsilon_{Aiw.4} = \sqrt{KA_G * q_{к.Aiw.4}^2 + 1} = \sqrt{0{,}0012469 * 40^2 + 1} = 1{,}731;$$

$$\varepsilon_{Aiw.5} = \sqrt{KA_G * q_{к.Aiw.5}^2 + 1} = \sqrt{0{,}0012469 * 50^2 + 1} = 2{,}029;$$

$$\varepsilon_{Aiw.6} = \sqrt{KA_G * q_{к.Aiw.6}^2 + 1} = \sqrt{0{,}0012469 * 60^2 + 1} = 2{,}343;$$

$$\varepsilon_{Aiw.7} = \sqrt{KA_G * q_{к.Aiw.7}^2 + 1} = \sqrt{0{,}0012469 * 70^2 + 1} = 2{,}666;$$

$$\varepsilon_{Aiw.8} = \sqrt{KA_G * q^2_{\kappa.Aiw.8} + 1} = \sqrt{0{,}0012469 * 80^2 + 1} = 2{,}997;$$

$$\varepsilon_{Aiw.9} = \sqrt{KA_G * q^2_{\kappa.Aiw.9} + 1} = \sqrt{0{,}0012469 * 90^2 + 1} = 3{,}332;$$

$$\varepsilon_{Aiw.10} = \sqrt{KA_G * q^2_{\kappa.Aiw.10} + 1} = \sqrt{0{,}0012469 * 100^2 + 1} = 3{,}670;$$

$$\varepsilon_{Aiw.11} = \sqrt{KA_G * q^2_{\kappa.Aiw.11} + 1} = \sqrt{0{,}0012469 * 110^2 + 1} = 4{,}011;$$

$$\varepsilon_{Aiw.12} = \sqrt{KA_G * q^2_{\kappa.Aiw.12} + 1} = \sqrt{0{,}0012469 * 120^2 + 1} = 4{,}354;$$

$$\varepsilon_{Aiw.13} = \sqrt{KA_G * q^2_{\kappa.Aiw.13} + 1} = \sqrt{0{,}0012469 * 130^2 + 1} = 4{,}698.$$

3.4. The **goal's** characteristic is constructed using the $q_{\kappa.Aiw.j}$ and $\varepsilon_{Aiw.j}$ calculated above. It is represented as a blue line in Fig. IP 24, applied over **RPMA$_{iw}$**, calculated above using **the IP$_{UI}$ calculation technology**. The points of the minimum and maximum goal's productivity of **BCS KGF** are applied to this line and their parameters are determined.

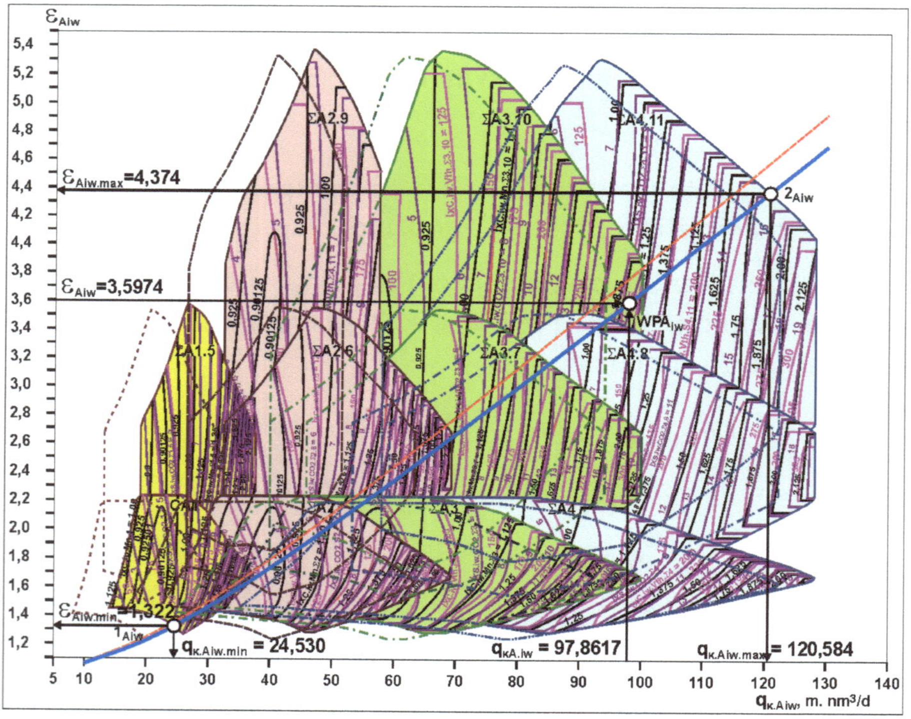

Fig. IP 24

The **RPM_{iw}** contours and the red line of the current characteristic of **the KGF grid**, borrowed from Fig. IP 23, are marked by thin dashed lines for comparison in Fig. IP 24.

It is obvious for the specialists of **BCS KGF** from the above that:

- **$RPMA_{iw}$** differs from **RPM_{iw}**;
- The current **goal's** characteristic of **the KGF grid** differs from its current characteristic;
- The **WPA_{iw}** position and parameters are different from the **WP_{iw}** position and parameters;
- **BCS KGF** will work without bypass at all **$RPMA_{iw}$** points, which coincide the current **goal's** characteristic of **the KGF grid**;
- **BCS KGF** will only work due a bypass at all **$RPMA_{iw}$** points, which are located to the right of the current **goal's** characteristic of **the KGF grid**;
- **BCS KGF** may not physically operate at those **$RPMA_{iw}$** points that are located to the left of the current **goal's** characteristic of **the KGF grid**;
- The **BCS KGF**, working in conjunction **the KGF grid** at the 1_{Aiw} point, will provide the minimum possible current productivity of $q_{к.Aiw.min}$ = 24,5310 m. n.m^3/d and the pressure ratio $\varepsilon_{Aiw.min}$ = 1,322, and at the point 2_{Aiw} - the maximum possible $q_{к.Aiw.max}$ = 120,584 m. n.m^3/d and $\varepsilon_{Aiw.max}$ = 4,374;
- Parameters of the **BCS KGF** operating mode at **WPA_{iw}** point may be provided only by the joint operation of all three of its compression stage;
- Parameters of the **BCS KGF** operating mode at the **WPA_{iw}** point may be provided by a combination of jointly operating **GCU #1, #2, #3, #4, #5, #6, #7, #9 and #10**, forming **$RPMA_{\Sigma3.10}$** or **GCU #1, #2, #3, #4, #5, #6, #7, #9, #10 and #11**, forming **$RPMA_{\Sigma3.11}$**, but the reasonable of these two options is the combination of **GCU** forming **$RPMA_{\Sigma3.10}$**. Thus, the parameters for regulating the

current **goal's** operating modes are rotation frequencies **GCU #1, #2, #3, #5, #6 and #7**, i.e., n_{A1}, n_{A2}, n_{A3}, n_{A5}, n_{A6}, n_{A7}, n_{A9} and n_{A10}. The technology of their calculation is described below.

4. Calculate the magnitudes of the current goal's summation indexes providing compliance **the criteria for reasonable management**, set in the goal entire of the **BCS KGF**, including:

$Ix_{AC.iw.Vth}$ = 293,4 – this is the magnitude of **the current goal's index of summation** at the point **WPA**$_{iw}$ of **RPMA**$_{iw}$, observance of which in all **BCS KGF** elements will provide the minimum energy costs of all kinds in the form of MW in the whole **BCS KGF**;

$Ix_{AC.iw.Mn}$ = 1,954 – this is the magnitude of **the current goal's index of summation** at the point **WPA**$_{iw}$ of **RPMA**$_{iw}$, the observance of which in all **BCS KGF** elements will provide the minimum of all types of costs in monetary terms in the whole **BCS KGF**;

$Ix_{AS.iw.CO2}$ = 16,773 – this is the magnitude of **the current goal's index of summation** at the point **WPA**$_{iw}$ of **RPMA**$_{iw}$, the observance of which in all **BCS KGF** elements will provide the minimum of CO_2 emissions in the whole **BCS KGF**.

The calculation is performed using the mathematical apparatus given in Example 2 above, but which is used to calculate $Ix_{AC.iw.Vth}$, $Ix_{AC.iw.Mn}$ and $Ix_{AS.iw.CO2}$ at only one **RPMA**$_{iw}$ point whose parameters correspond to the parameters **WPA**$_{iw}$ located on the current **goal's** characteristic of **the KGF grid**. It is not shown here to reduce the scope of the description.

5. Calculate the current **goal's noologistical** parameters of regulation at the current **goal's noologistical** points of the operation modes (**WPA**) of all **BCS KGF** elements on all their **RPM**$_{As}$.

5.1. Calculate the current **goal's noologistical** distribution of the pressure ratio over the compression stages.

The **noologistical** combinations of the **goal's** pressure ratio in the **BCS KGF** compression stages are calculated in accordance the magnitudes of calculated above $Ix_{AC.iw.Vth}$, $Ix_{AC.iw.Mn}$ and $Ix_{AS.iw.CO2}$ using the mathematical apparatus given in Example 2 above. It is used only to calculate the pressure ratio at those points in **the current total goal's indexed noologistical areas of the possible modes of joint operation** in the first (**$RPMA_{\Sigma 4}$**), the second (**$RPMA_{\Sigma 8}$**) and the third (**$RPMA_{\Sigma 12}$**) compression stages, in which the following conditions are provided:

Conditions for the first compression stage (**$RPMA_{\Sigma 4}$**):

The magnitude of the current **goal's** summation index **$Ix_{AC.iw.Vth.\Sigma 4}$** = 293,4 at the point **$WPA_{Vth.\Sigma 4}$** on **$RPMA_{\Sigma 4}$** is equal to the magnitude of the current **goal's** summation index **$Ix_{AC.iw.Vth}$** = 293,4 at the point **WPA_{iw}** on **$RPMA_{iw}$**;

The magnitude of the current **goal's** summation index **$Ix_{AC.iw.Mn.\Sigma 4}$** = 1,954 at the point **$WPA_{Mn.\Sigma 4}$** on **$RPMA_{\Sigma 4}$** is equal to the magnitude of the current **goal's** summation index **$Ix_{AC.iw.Mn}$** = 1,954 at the point **WPA_{iw}** on **$RPMA_{iw}$**;

The magnitude of the current **goal's** summation index **$Ix_{AC.iw.CO2.\Sigma 4}$** = 16,773 at the point **$WPA_{CO2.\Sigma 4}$** on **$RPMA_{\Sigma 4}$** is equal to the magnitude of the current **goal's** summation index **$Ix_{AC.iw.CO2}$** = 16,773 at the point **WPA_{iw}** on **$RPMA_{iw}$**;

The magnitude of the current **goal's** commercial productivity is $q_{к.A\Sigma 4}$ = 97,8617 m. n.m^3/d at points **$WPA_{Vth.\Sigma 4}$**, **$WPA_{Mn.\Sigma 4}$** and **$WPA_{CO2.\Sigma 4}$** is equal to the value of the total **goal's** commercial productivity of the entire **BCS KGF** $q_{к.Aiw}$ = 97,8617 m. n.m^3/d.

Conditions for the second stage of compression (**$RPMA_{\Sigma 8}$**):

The magnitude of the current **goal's** summation index **$Ix_{AC.iw.Vth.\Sigma 8}$** = 293,4 at the point **$WPA_{Vth.\Sigma 8}$** on **$RPMA_{\Sigma 8}$** is equal to the magnitude of the current **goal's** summation index $\mathbf{Ix_{AC.iw.Vth}}$ = 293,4 at the point $\mathbf{WPA_{iw}}$ on $\mathbf{RPMA_{iw}}$;

The magnitude of the current **goal's** summation index $\mathbf{Ix_{AC.iw.Mn.\Sigma8}}$ = 1,954 at the point $\mathbf{WPA_{Mn.\Sigma8}}$ on $\mathbf{RPMA_{\Sigma8}}$ is equal to the magnitude of the current **goal's** summation index $\mathbf{Ix_{AC.iw.Mn}}$ = 1,954 at the point $\mathbf{WPA_{iw}}$ on $\mathbf{RPMA_{iw}}$;

The magnitude of the current **goal's** summation index $\mathbf{Ix_{AC.iw.CO2.\Sigma8}}$ = 16,773 at the point $\mathbf{WPA_{CO2.\Sigma8}}$ on $\mathbf{RPMA_{\Sigma8}}$ is equal to the magnitude of the current **goal's** summation index $\mathbf{Ix_{AC.iw.CO2}}$ = 16,773 at the point $\mathbf{WPA_{iw}}$ on $\mathbf{RPMA_{iw}}$;

The magnitude of the current **goal's** commercial productivity is $q_{K.A\Sigma8}$ = 97,8617 m. n.m^3/d at points $\mathbf{WPA_{Vth.\Sigma8}}$, $\mathbf{WPA_{Mn.\Sigma8}}$ and $\mathbf{WPA_{CO2.\Sigma8}}$ is equal to the value of the total **goal's** commercial productivity of the entire **BCS KGF** $q_{K.Aiw}$ = 97,8617 m. n.m^3/d.

Conditions for the third stage of compression ($\mathbf{RPMA_{\Sigma12}}$):

The magnitude of the current **goal's** summation index $\mathbf{Ix_{AC.iw.Vth.\Sigma12}}$ = 293,4 at the point $\mathbf{WPA_{Vth.\Sigma12}}$ on $\mathbf{RPMA_{\Sigma12}}$ is equal to the magnitude of the current **goal's** summation index $\mathbf{Ix_{AC.iw.Vth}}$ = 293,4 at the point $\mathbf{WPA_{iw}}$ on $\mathbf{RPMA_{iw}}$;

The magnitude of the current **goal's** summation index $\mathbf{Ix_{AC.iw.Mn.\Sigma12}}$ = 1,954 at the point $\mathbf{WPA_{Mn.\Sigma12}}$ on $\mathbf{RPMA_{\Sigma12}}$ is equal to the magnitude of the current **goal's** summation index $\mathbf{Ix_{AC.iw.Mn}}$ = 1,954 at the point $\mathbf{WPA_{iw}}$ on $\mathbf{RPMA_{iw}}$;

The magnitude of the current **goal's** summation index $\mathbf{Ix_{AC.iw.CO2.\Sigma12}}$ = 16,773 at the point $\mathbf{WPA_{CO2.\Sigma12}}$ on $\mathbf{RPMA_{\Sigma12}}$ is equal to the magnitude of the current **goal's** summation index $\mathbf{Ix_{AC.iw.CO2}}$ = 16,773 at the point $\mathbf{WPA_{iw}}$ on $\mathbf{RPMA_{iw}}$;

The magnitude of the current **goal's** commercial productivity is $q_{K.A\Sigma12}$ = 97,8617 m. n.m^3/d at points $\mathbf{WPA_{Vth.\Sigma12}}$, $\mathbf{WPA_{Mn.\Sigma12}}$ and $\mathbf{WPA_{CO2.\Sigma12}}$ is equal to the value of the total **goal's** commercial productivity of the entire **BCS KGF** $q_{K.Aiw}$ = 97,8617 m. n.m^3/d.

The following calculated current **goal's** pressure ratios satisfy the conditions described above:

$\varepsilon_{AVth.\Sigma4}$ = 1,6445 – this is the current **goal's** pressure ratio at **WPA**$_{Vth.\Sigma4}$ point of the first stage on **RPMA**$_{\Sigma4}$;

$\varepsilon_{AMn.\Sigma4}$ = 1,5469 – this is the current **goal's** pressure ratio at **WPA**$_{Mn.\Sigma4}$ point of the first stage on **RPMA**$_{\Sigma4}$;

$\varepsilon_{ACO2.\Sigma4}$ = 1,7158 – this is the current **goal's** pressure ratio at **WPA**$_{CO2.\Sigma4}$ point of the first stage on **RPMA**$_{\Sigma4}$;

$\varepsilon_{AVth.\Sigma8}$ = 1,6053 – this is the current **goal's** pressure ratio at **WPA**$_{Vth.\Sigma8}$ point of the second stage on **RPMA**$_{\Sigma8}$;

$\varepsilon_{AMn.\Sigma8}$ = 1,3677 – this is the current **goal's** pressure ratio at **WPA**$_{Mn.\Sigma8}$ point of the second stage on **RPMA**$_{\Sigma8}$;

$\varepsilon_{ACO2.\Sigma8}$ = 1,4547 – this is the current **goal's** pressure ratio at **WPA**$_{CO2.\Sigma8}$ point of the second stage on **RPMA**$_{\Sigma8}$;

$\varepsilon_{AVth.\Sigma12}$ = 1,3627 – this is the current **goal's** pressure ratio at **WPA**$_{Vth.\Sigma12}$ point of the third stage on **RPMA**$_{\Sigma12}$;

$\varepsilon_{AMn.\Sigma12}$ = 1,391 – this is the current **goal's** pressure ratio at **WPA**$_{Mn.\Sigma12}$ point of the third stage on **RPMA**$_{\Sigma12}$;

$\varepsilon_{ACO2.\Sigma12}$ = 1,4412 – this is the current **goal's** pressure ratio at **WPA**$_{CO2.\Sigma12}$ point of the third stage on **RPMA**$_{\Sigma12}$.

The result of calculating all three types of current **goal's** pressure ratios at the **goal's** operating points of all three compression stages of the **BCS KGF** is shown in Fig. IP 25.

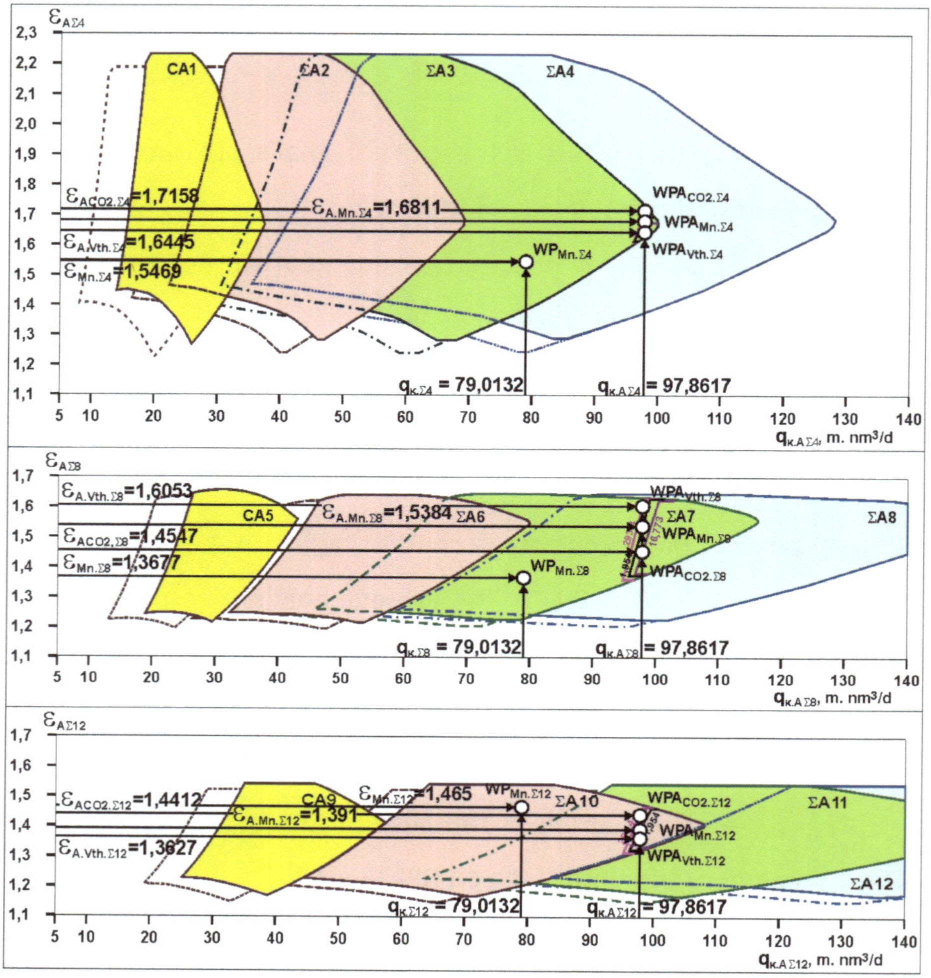

Fig. IP 25

Images of **RPM$_{Σ4}$**, **RPM$_{Σ8}$** and **RPM$_{Σ12}$** and the current **WP$_{Mn.Σ4}$**, **WP$_{Mn.Σ8}$** and **WP$_{Mn.Σ12}$** operating points for all three compression stages of **BCS KGF** and their parameters that are measured at the current time are plotted with dotted lines in Fig. IP 25 for comparison.

It is obvious for the specialists of **BCS KGF** from the above that:

The combination of the operating modes of all three compression stages ensures a minimum of all types of costs in monetary terms entire the **BCS KGF** at the current time;

The accuracy of the calculation of the combination of the pressure ratios is verified by multiplying them, which results in a magnitude must be equal to the total pressure ratio in the entire **BCS KGF**:

$\varepsilon_{AVth.\Sigma4}$ * $\varepsilon_{AVth.\Sigma8}$ * $\varepsilon_{AVth.\Sigma12}$ = 1,6445 * 1,6053 * 1,4412 = 3,5974 = $\varepsilon_{Aiw.j}$,

$\varepsilon_{AMn.\Sigma4}$ * $\varepsilon_{AMn.\Sigma8}$ * $\varepsilon_{AMn.\Sigma12}$ = 1,6811 * 1,5384 * 1,391 = 3,5974 = $\varepsilon_{Aiw.j}$,

$\varepsilon_{ACO2.\Sigma4}$ * $\varepsilon_{ACO2.\Sigma8}$ * $\varepsilon_{ACO2.\Sigma12}$ = 1,7158 * 1,4547 * 1,3627 = 3,5974 = $\varepsilon_{Aiw.j}$,

$\varepsilon_{Mn.\Sigma4}$ * $\varepsilon_{Mn.\Sigma8}$ * $\varepsilon_{Mn.\Sigma12}$ = 1,5469 * 1,3667 * 1,465 = 3,0971 = $\varepsilon_{iw.j}$,

ie, the pressure ratios in the compression stages for each option of providing the criteria of reasonable control, are distributed quite accurately.

5.2. Calculate the current **goal's noologistical** distribution to **GCU** productivity for each compression stage.

Noologistical combinations of goal's productivities in the **GCU** of **BCS KGF** stages are calculated in accordance the magnitudes calculated above $\mathbf{Ix_{AC.iw.Vth}}$ = 293,4, $\mathbf{Ix_{AC.iw.Mn}}$ = 1,954 and $\mathbf{Ix_{AS.iw.CO2}}$ = 16,773 using the mathematical apparatus given above in Example 2. But it is used only to calculate the **GCU** productivity at those points in **the goal's indexed noologistical areas of the possible operating GCU modes** of the first ($\mathbf{RPMA_{C1}}$, $\mathbf{RPMA_{C2}}$, $\mathbf{RPMA_{C3}}$ and $\mathbf{RPMA_{C4}}$), the second ($\mathbf{RPMA_{C5}}$, $\mathbf{RPMA_{C6}}$, $\mathbf{RPMA_{C7}}$ and $\mathbf{RPMA_{C8}}$) and the third ($\mathbf{RPMA_{C9}}$, $\mathbf{RPMA_{C10}}$, $\mathbf{RPMA_{C11}}$ and $\mathbf{RPMA_{C12}}$) compression stages, in which the following conditions are provided:

The conditions for the **GCUs** of first compression stage ($\mathbf{RPMA_{C1}}$, $\mathbf{RPMA_{C2}}$, $\mathbf{RPMA_{C3}}$ and $\mathbf{RPMA_{C4}}$):

The conditions for the **GCU #1** (see area **CA1** in Fig. IP 26)

The magnitude of the current **goal's** summation index $\mathbf{Ix_{AC.iw.Vth.C1}}$ = 293,4 at the point $\mathbf{WPA_{Vth.C1}}$ on $\mathbf{RPMA_{C1}}$ is equal to the magnitude of the current **goal's** summation index $\mathbf{Ix_{AC.iw.Vth}}$ = 293,4 at the point $\mathbf{WPA_{iw}}$ on $\mathbf{RPMA_{iw}}$, and its current goal's pressure ratio $\varepsilon_{\mathbf{AVth.C1}}$ = 1,6445 is equal to the current **goal's** pressure ratio $\varepsilon_{\mathbf{AVth.\Sigma4}}$ = 1,6445 at the point $\mathbf{WPA_{Vth.\Sigma4}}$ on $\mathbf{RPMA_{\Sigma4}}$, which corresponds to its **goal's** productivity $\mathbf{q_{AVth.C1}}$ = 33,9713 m. n.m^3/d at the point $\mathbf{WPA_{Vth.C1}}$ on $\mathbf{RPMA_{C1}}$;

The magnitude of the current **goal's** summation index $\mathbf{Ix_{AC.iw.Mn.C1}}$ = 1,954 at the point $\mathbf{WPA_{Mn.C1}}$ on $\mathbf{RPMA_{C1}}$ is equal to the magnitude of the current **goal's** summation index $\mathbf{Ix_{AC.iw.Mn}}$ = 1,954 at the point $\mathbf{WPA_{iw}}$ on $\mathbf{RPMA_{iw}}$, and its current **goal's** pressure ratio $\varepsilon_{\mathbf{AMn.C1}}$ = 1,6811 is equal to the current **goal's** pressure ratio $\varepsilon_{\mathbf{AMn.\Sigma4}}$ = 1,6811 at the point $\mathbf{WPA_{Mn.\Sigma4}}$ on $\mathbf{RPMA_{\Sigma4}}$, which corresponds to its **goal's** productivity $\mathbf{q_{AMn.C1}}$ = 35,0554 m. n.m^3/d at the point $\mathbf{WPA_{Mn.C1}}$ on $\mathbf{RPMA_{C1}}$;

The magnitude of the current **goal's** summation index $\mathbf{Ix_{AC.iw.CO2.C1}}$ = 16,773 at the point $\mathbf{WPA_{CO2.C1}}$ on $\mathbf{RPMA_{C1}}$ is equal to the magnitude of the current **goal's** summation index $\mathbf{Ix_{AC.iw.CO2}}$ = 16,773 at the point $\mathbf{WPA_{iw}}$ on $\mathbf{RPMA_{iw}}$, and its current **goal's** pressure ratio $\varepsilon_{\mathbf{ACO2.C1}}$ = 1,7158 is equal to the current **goal's** pressure ratio $\varepsilon_{\mathbf{ACO2.\Sigma4}}$ = 1,7158 at the point $\mathbf{WPA_{CO2.\Sigma4}}$ on $\mathbf{RPMA_{\Sigma4}}$, which corresponds to its **goal's** productivity $\mathbf{q_{ACO2.C1}}$ = 32,858 m. n.m^3/d at the point $\mathbf{WPA_{CO2.C1}}$ on $\mathbf{RPMA_{C1}}$.

The conditions for the **GCU #2** (see area **CA2** in Fig. IP 26)

The magnitude of the current **goal's** summation index $\mathbf{Ix_{AC.iw.Vth.C2}}$ = 293,4 at the point $\mathbf{WPA_{Vth.C2}}$ on $\mathbf{RPMA_{C2}}$ is equal to the magnitude of the current **goal's** summation index $\mathbf{Ix_{AC.iw.Vth}}$ = 293,4 at the point $\mathbf{WPA_{iw}}$ on $\mathbf{RPMA_{iw}}$, and its current **goal's** pressure ratio $\varepsilon_{\mathbf{AVth.C2}}$ = 1,6445 is equal to the current **goal's** pressure ratio $\varepsilon_{\mathbf{AVth.\Sigma4}}$ = 1,6445 at the point $\mathbf{WPA_{Vth.\Sigma4}}$ on $\mathbf{RPMA_{\Sigma4}}$, which corresponds to its

goal's productivity $q_{AVth.C2}$ = 32,6226 m. n.m^3/d at the point **$WPA_{Vth.C2}$** on **$RPMA_{C2}$**;

The magnitude of the current **goal's** summation index **$Ix_{AC.iw.Mn.C2}$** = 1,954 at the point **$WPA_{Mn.C2}$** on **$RPMA_{C2}$** is equal to the magnitude of the current **goal's** summation index **$Ix_{AC.iw.Mn}$** = 1,954 at the point **WPA_{iw}** on **$RPMA_{iw}$**, and its current **goal's** pressure ratio $\varepsilon_{AMn.C2}$ = 1,6811 is equal to the current **goal's** pressure ratio $\varepsilon_{AMn.\Sigma4}$ = 1,6811 at the point **$WPA_{Mn.\Sigma4}$** on **$RPMA_{\Sigma4}$**, which corresponds to its **goal's** productivity $q_{AMn.C2}$ = 35,1338 m. n.m^3/d at the point **$WPA_{Mn.C2}$** on **$RPMA_{C2}$**;

The magnitude of the current **goal's** summation index **$Ix_{AC.iw.CO2.C2}$** = 16,773 at the point **$WPA_{CO2.C2}$** on **$RPMA_{C2}$** is equal to the magnitude of the current **goal's** summation index **$Ix_{AC.iw.CO2}$** = 16,773 at the point **WPA_{iw}** on **$RPMA_{iw}$**, and its current goal's pressure ratio $\varepsilon_{ACO2.C2}$ = 1,7158 is equal to the current **goal's** pressure ratio $\varepsilon_{ACO2.\Sigma4}$ = 1,7158 at the point **$WPA_{CO2.\Sigma4}$** on **$RPMA_{\Sigma4}$**, which corresponds to its **goal's** productivity $q_{ACO2.C2}$ = 34,1293 m. n.m^3/d at the point **$WPA_{CO2.C2}$** on **$RPMA_{C2}$**.

The conditions for the **GCU #3** (see area **CA3** in Fig. IP 26)

The magnitude of the current **goal's** summation index **$Ix_{AC.iw.Vth.C3}$** = 293,4 at the point **$WPA_{Vth.C3}$** on **$RPMA_{C3}$** is equal to the magnitude of the current **goal's** summation index **$Ix_{AC.iw.Vth}$** = 293,4 at the point **WPA_{iw}** on **$RPMA_{iw}$**, and its current **goal's** pressure ratio $\varepsilon_{AVth.C2}$ = 1,6445 is equal to the current **goal's** pressure ratio $\varepsilon_{AVth.\Sigma4}$ = 1,6445 at the point **$WPA_{Vth.\Sigma4}$** on **$RPMA_{\Sigma4}$**, which corresponds to its **goal's** productivity $q_{AVth.C3}$ = 31,2678 m. n.m^3/d at the point **$WPA_{Vth.C3}$** on **$RPMA_{C3}$**;

The magnitude of the current **goal's** summation index **$Ix_{AC.iw.Mn.C3}$** = 1,954 at the point **$WPA_{Mn.C3}$** on **$RPMA_{C3}$** is equal to the magnitude of the current **goal's** summation index **$Ix_{AC.iw.Mn}$** = 1,954 at the point **WPA_{iw}** on **$RPMA_{iw}$**, and its current **goal's** pressure ratio

$\varepsilon_{AMn.C3}$ = 1,6811 is equal to the current **goal's** pressure ratio $\varepsilon_{AMn.\Sigma4}$ = 1,6811 at the point $\mathbf{WPA_{Mn.\Sigma4}}$ on $\mathbf{RPMA_{\Sigma4}}$, which corresponds to its **goal's** productivity $\mathbf{q_{AMn.C3}}$ = 27,6725 m. n.m^3/d at the point $\mathbf{WPA_{Mn.C3}}$ on $\mathbf{RPMA_{C3}}$;

The magnitude of the current **goal's** summation index $\mathbf{Ix_{AC.iw.CO2.C3}}$ = 16,773 at the point $\mathbf{WPA_{CO2.C3}}$ on $\mathbf{RPMA_{C3}}$ is equal to the magnitude of the current **goal's** summation index $\mathbf{Ix_{AC.iw.CO2}}$ = 16,773 at the point $\mathbf{WPA_{iw}}$ on $\mathbf{RPMA_{iw}}$, and its current **goal's** pressure ratio $\varepsilon_{ACO2.C3}$ = 1,7158 is equal to the current **goal's** pressure ratio $\varepsilon_{ACO2.\Sigma4}$ = 1,7158 at the point $\mathbf{WPA_{CO2.\Sigma4}}$ on $\mathbf{RPMA_{\Sigma4}}$, which corresponds to its **goal's** productivity $\mathbf{q_{ACO2.C3}}$ = 30,8745 m. n.m^3/d at the point $\mathbf{WPA_{CO2.C3}}$ on $\mathbf{RPMA_{C3}}$.

GCU #4 (see area **CA4** in Fig. IP 26) is switch-off.

The conditions for the **GCUs** of second compression stage ($\mathbf{RPMA_{C5}}$, $\mathbf{RPMA_{C6}}$, $\mathbf{RPMA_{C7}}$ and $\mathbf{RPMA_{C8}}$):

The conditions for the **GCU #5** (see area **CA5** in Fig. IP 26)

The magnitude of the current **goal's** summation index $\mathbf{Ix_{AC.iw.Vth.C5}}$ = 293,4 at the point $\mathbf{WPA_{Vth.C5}}$ on $\mathbf{RPMA_{C5}}$ is equal to the magnitude of the current **goal's** summation index $\mathbf{Ix_{AC.iw.Vth}}$ = 293,4 at the point $\mathbf{WPA_{iw}}$ on $\mathbf{RPMA_{iw}}$, and its current **goal's** pressure ratio $\varepsilon_{AVth.C5}$ = 1,6053 is equal to the current **goal's** pressure ratio $\varepsilon_{AVth.\Sigma8}$ = 1,6053 at the point $\mathbf{WPA_{Vth.\Sigma8}}$ on $\mathbf{RPMA_{\Sigma8}}$, which corresponds to its **goal's** productivity $\mathbf{q_{AVth.C5}}$ = 34,7265 m. n.m^3/d at the point $\mathbf{WPA_{Vth.C5}}$ on $\mathbf{RPMA_{C5}}$;

The magnitude of the current **goal's** summation index $\mathbf{Ix_{AC.iw.Mn.C5}}$ = 1,954 at the point $\mathbf{WPA_{Mn.C5}}$ on $\mathbf{RPMA_{C5}}$ is equal to the magnitude of the current **goal's** summation index $\mathbf{Ix_{AC.iw.Mn}}$ = 1,954 at the point $\mathbf{WPA_{iw}}$ on $\mathbf{RPMA_{iw}}$, and its current **goal's** pressure ratio $\varepsilon_{AMn.C5}$ = 1,5384 is equal to the current **goal's** pressure ratio $\varepsilon_{AMn.\Sigma8}$ =

1,5384 at the point $\mathbf{WPA_{Mn.\Sigma8}}$ on $\mathbf{RPMA_{\Sigma8}}$, which corresponds to its **goal's** productivity $\mathbf{q_{AMn.C5}}$ = 31,7101 m. n.m^3/d at the point $\mathbf{WPA_{Mn.C5}}$ on $\mathbf{RPMA_{C5}}$;

The magnitude of the current **goal's** summation index $\mathbf{Ix_{AC.iw.CO2.C5}}$ = 16,773 at the point $\mathbf{WPA_{CO2.C5}}$ on $\mathbf{RPMA_{C5}}$ is equal to the magnitude of the current **goal's** summation index $\mathbf{Ix_{AC.iw.CO2}}$ = 16,773 at the point $\mathbf{WPA_{iw}}$ on $\mathbf{RPMA_{iw}}$, and its current **goal's** pressure ratio $\varepsilon_{ACO2.C5}$ = 1,4547 is equal to the current **goal's** pressure ratio $\varepsilon_{ACO2.\Sigma8}$ = 1,4547 at the point $\mathbf{WPA_{CO2.\Sigma8}}$ on $\mathbf{RPMA_{\Sigma8}}$, which corresponds to its **goal's** productivity $\mathbf{q_{ACO2.C5}}$ = 32,3294 m. n.m^3/d at the point $\mathbf{WPA_{CO2.C5}}$ on $\mathbf{RPMA_{C5}}$.

The conditions for the **GCU #6** (see area **CA6** in Fig. IP 26)

The magnitude of the current **goal's** summation index $\mathbf{Ix_{AC.iw.Vth.C6}}$ = 293,4 at the point $\mathbf{WPA_{Vth.C6}}$ on $\mathbf{RPMA_{C6}}$ is equal to the magnitude of the current **goal's** summation index $\mathbf{Ix_{AC.iw.Vth}}$ = 293,4 at the point $\mathbf{WPA_{iw}}$ on $\mathbf{RPMA_{iw}}$, and its current **goal's** pressure ratio $\varepsilon_{AVth.C6}$ = 1,6053 is equal to the current **goal's** pressure ratio $\varepsilon_{AVth.\Sigma8}$ = 1,6053 at the point $\mathbf{WPA_{Vth.\Sigma8}}$ on $\mathbf{RPMA_{\Sigma8}}$, which corresponds to its **goal's** productivity $\mathbf{q_{AVth.C6}}$ = 31,8566 m. n.m^3/d at the point $\mathbf{WPA_{Vth.C6}}$ on $\mathbf{RPMA_{C6}}$;

The magnitude of the current **goal's** summation index $\mathbf{Ix_{AC.iw.Mn.C6}}$ = 1,954 at the point $\mathbf{WPA_{Mn.C6}}$ on $\mathbf{RPMA_{C6}}$ is equal to the magnitude of the current **goal's** summation index $\mathbf{Ix_{AC.iw.Mn}}$ = 1,954 at the point $\mathbf{WPA_{iw}}$ on $\mathbf{RPMA_{iw}}$, and its current **goal's** pressure ratio $\varepsilon_{AMn.C6}$ = 1,5384 is equal to the current **goal's** pressure ratio $\varepsilon_{AMn.\Sigma8}$ = 1,5384 at the point $\mathbf{WPA_{Mn.\Sigma8}}$ on $\mathbf{RPMA_{\Sigma8}}$, which corresponds to its **goal's** productivity $\mathbf{q_{AMn.C6}}$ = 35,6127 m. n.m^3/d at the point $\mathbf{WPA_{Vth.C6}}$ on $\mathbf{RPMA_{C6}}$;

The magnitude of the current **goal's** summation index $\mathbf{Ix_{AC.iw.CO2.C6}}$ = 16,773 at the point $\mathbf{WPA_{CO2.C6}}$ on $\mathbf{RPMA_{C6}}$ is equal to the magnitude of the current **goal's** summation index $\mathbf{Ix_{AC.iw.CO2}}$ = 16,773 at the point **WPA**$_{iw}$ on **RPMA**$_{iw}$, and its current **goal's** pressure ratio $\varepsilon_{ACO2.C6}$ = 1,4547 is equal to the current **goal's** pressure ratio $\varepsilon_{ACO2.\Sigma8}$ = 1,4547 at the point **WPA**$_{CO2.\Sigma8}$ on **RPMA**$_{\Sigma8}$, which corresponds to its **goal's** productivity $q_{ACO2.C6}$ = 33,7826 m. n.m^3/d at the point **WPA**$_{CO2.C6}$ on **RPMA**$_{C6}$.

The conditions for the **GCU #7** (see area **CA7** in Fig. IP 26)

The magnitude of the current **goal's** summation index $Ix_{AC.iw.Vth.C7}$ = 293,4 at the point **WPA**$_{Vth.C7}$ on **RPMA**$_{C7}$ is equal to the magnitude of the current **goal's** summation index $Ix_{AC.iw.Vth}$ = 293,4 at the point **WPA**$_{iw}$ on **RPMA**$_{iw}$, and its current **goal's** pressure ratio $\varepsilon_{AVth.C7}$ = 1,6053 is equal to the current **goal's** pressure ratio $\varepsilon_{AVth.\Sigma8}$ = 1,6053 at the point **WPA**$_{Vth.\Sigma8}$ on **RPMA**$_{\Sigma8}$, which corresponds to its **goal's** productivity $q_{AVth.C7}$ = 31,2786 m. n.m^3/d at the point **WPA**$_{Vth.C7}$ on **RPMA**$_{C7}$;

The magnitude of the current **goal's** summation index $Ix_{AC.iw.Mn.C7}$ = 1,954 at the point **WPA**$_{Mn.C7}$ on **RPMA**$_{C7}$ is equal to the magnitude of the current **goal's** summation index $Ix_{AC.iw.Mn}$ = 1,954 at the point **WPA**$_{iw}$ on **RPMA**$_{iw}$, and its current **goal's** pressure ratio $\varepsilon_{AMn.C7}$ = 1,5384 is equal to the current **goal's** pressure ratio $\varepsilon_{AMn.\Sigma8}$ = 1,5384 at the point **WPA**$_{Mn.\Sigma8}$ on **RPMA**$_{\Sigma8}$, which corresponds to its **goal's** productivity $q_{AMn.C7}$ = 30,5389 m. n.m^3/d at the point **WPA**$_{Mn.C7}$ on **RPMA**$_{C7}$;

The magnitude of the current **goal's** summation index $Ix_{AC.iw.CO2.C7}$ = 16,773 at the point **WPA**$_{CO2.C7}$ on **RPMA**$_{C7}$ is equal to the magnitude of the current **goal's** summation index $Ix_{AC.iw.CO2}$ = 16,773 at the point **WPA**$_{iw}$ on **RPMA**$_{iw}$, and its current **goal's** pressure ratio $\varepsilon_{ACO2.C7}$ = 1,4547 is equal to the current **goal's** pressure ratio $\varepsilon_{ACO2.\Sigma8}$ = 1,4547 at the point **WPA**$_{CO2.\Sigma8}$ on **RPMA**$_{\Sigma8}$, which corresponds to its **goal's** productivity $q_{ACO2.C7}$ = 31,7497 m. n.m^3/d at the point **WPA**$_{CO2.C7}$ on **RPMA**$_{C7}$.

GCU #8 (see area **CA8** in Fig. IP 26) is switch-off.

The conditions for the **GCUs** of third compression stage (**RPMA**$_{C9}$, **RPMA**$_{C10}$, **RPMA**$_{C11}$ and **RPMA**$_{C12}$):

The conditions for the **GCU #9** (see area **CA9** in Fig. IP 26)

The magnitude of the current **goal's** summation index **Ix**$_{AC.iw.Vth.C9}$ = 293,4 at the point **WPA**$_{Vth.C9}$ on **RPMA**$_{C9}$ is equal to the magnitude of the current **goal's** summation index **Ix**$_{AC.iw.Vth}$ = 293,4 at the point **WPA**$_{iw}$ on **RPMA**$_{iw}$, and its current **goal's** pressure ratio $\varepsilon_{AVth.C9}$ = 1,4412 is equal to the current **goal's** pressure ratio $\varepsilon_{AVth.\Sigma12}$ = 1,4412 at the point **WPA**$_{Vth.\Sigma12}$ on **RPMA**$_{\Sigma12}$, which corresponds to its **goal's** productivity $q_{AVth.C9}$ = 48,8984 m. n.m^3/d at the point **WPA**$_{Vth.C9}$ on **RPMA**$_{C9}$;

The magnitude of the current **goal's** summation index **Ix**$_{AC.iw.Mn.C9}$ = 1,954 at the point **WPA**$_{Mn.C9}$ on **RPMA**$_{C9}$ is equal to the magnitude of the current **goal's** summation index **Ix**$_{AC.iw.Mn}$ = 1,954 at the point **WPA**$_{iw}$ on **RPMA**$_{iw}$, and its current **goal's** pressure ratio $\varepsilon_{AMn.C9}$ = 1,391 is equal to the current **goal's** pressure ratio $\varepsilon_{AMn.\Sigma12}$ = 1,391 at the point **WPA**$_{Mn.\Sigma12}$ on **RPMA**$_{\Sigma12}$, which corresponds to its **goal's** productivity $q_{AMn.C9}$ = 47,7766 m. n.m^3/d at the point **WPA**$_{Mn.C9}$ on **RPMA**$_{C9}$;

The magnitude of the current **goal's** summation index **Ix**$_{AC.iw.CO2.C9}$ = 16,773 at the point **WPA**$_{CO2.C9}$ on **RPMA**$_{C9}$ is equal to the magnitude of the current **goal's** summation index **Ix**$_{AC.iw.CO2}$ = 16,773 at the point **WPA**$_{iw}$ on **RPMA**$_{iw}$, and its current **goal's** pressure ratio $\varepsilon_{ACO2.C9}$ = 1,3627 is equal to the current **goal's** pressure ratio $\varepsilon_{ACO2.\Sigma12}$ = 1,3627 at the point **WPA**$_{CO2.\Sigma12}$ on **RPMA**$_{\Sigma12}$, which corresponds to its **goal's** productivity $q_{ACO2.C7}$ = 31,7497 m. n.m^3/d at the point **WPA**$_{CO2.C9}$ on **RPMA**$_{C9}$.

The conditions for the **GCU #10** (see area **CA10** in Fig. IP 26)

The magnitude of the current **goal's** summation index $\mathbf{Ix}_{AC.iw.Vth.C10}$ = 293,4 at the point $\mathbf{WPA}_{Vth.C10}$ on $\mathbf{RPMA}_{C10}$ is equal to the magnitude of the current **goal's** summation index $\mathbf{Ix}_{AC.iw.Vth}$ = 293,4 at the point $\mathbf{WPA}_{iw}$ on $\mathbf{RPMA}_{iw}$, and its current **goal's** pressure ratio $\varepsilon_{AVth.C10}$ = 1,4412 is equal to the current **goal's** pressure ratio $\varepsilon_{AVth.\Sigma12}$ = 1,4412 at the point $\mathbf{WPA}_{Vth.\Sigma12}$ on $\mathbf{RPMA}_{\Sigma12}$, which corresponds to its **goal's** productivity $\mathbf{q}_{AVth.C10}$ = 48,9633 m. n.m^3/d at the point $\mathbf{WPA}_{Vth.C10}$ on $\mathbf{RPMA}_{C10}$;

The magnitude of the current **goal's** summation index $\mathbf{Ix}_{AC.iw.Mn.C10}$ = 1,954 at the point $\mathbf{WPA}_{Mn.C10}$ on $\mathbf{RPMA}_{C10}$ is equal to the magnitude of the current **goal's** summation index $\mathbf{Ix}_{AC.iw.Mn}$ = 1,954 at the point $\mathbf{WPA}_{iw}$ on $\mathbf{RPMA}_{iw}$, and its current **goal's** pressure ratio $\varepsilon_{AMn.C10}$ = 1,391 is equal to the current **goal's** pressure ratio $\varepsilon_{AMn.\Sigma12}$ = 1,391 at the point $\mathbf{WPA}_{Mn.\Sigma12}$ on $\mathbf{RPMA}_{\Sigma12}$, which corresponds to its **goal's** productivity $\mathbf{q}_{AMn.C10}$ = 50,0851 m. n.m^3/d at the point $\mathbf{WPA}_{Mn.C10}$ on $\mathbf{RPMA}_{C10}$;

The magnitude of the current **goal's** summation index $\mathbf{Ix}_{AC.iw.CO2.C10}$ = 16,773 at the point $\mathbf{WPA}_{CO2.C10}$ on $\mathbf{RPMA}_{C10}$ is equal to the magnitude of the current **goal's** summation index $\mathbf{Ix}_{AC.iw.CO2}$ = 16,773 at the point $\mathbf{WPA}_{iw}$ on $\mathbf{RPMA}_{iw}$, and its current **goal's** pressure ratio $\varepsilon_{ACO2.C10}$ = 1,3627 is equal to the current **goal's** pressure ratio $\varepsilon_{ACO2.\Sigma12}$ = 1,3627 at the point $\mathbf{WPA}_{CO2.\Sigma12}$ on $\mathbf{RPMA}_{\Sigma12}$, which corresponds to its **goal's** productivity $\mathbf{q}_{ACO2.C10}$ = 47,9723 m. n.m^3/d at the point $\mathbf{WPA}_{CO2.C10}$ on $\mathbf{RPMA}_{C10}$.

GCU #11 (see area **CA11** in Fig. IP 26) and **GCU #12** (see area **CA12** in Fig. IP 26) are switch-off.

Thus, the following calculated current goal's productivities meet the conditions described above:

GCU #1 (see area **CA1** in Fig. IP 26) – $\mathbf{q}_{AVth.C1}$ = 33,9713 m. n.m^3/d; $\mathbf{q}_{AMn.C1}$ = 35,0554 m. n.m^3/d; $\mathbf{q}_{ACO2.C1}$ = 32,858 m. n.m^3/d.

GCU #2 (see area **CA2** in Fig. IP 26) – $\mathbf{q}_{AVth.C2}$ = 32,6226 m. n.m^3/d; $\mathbf{q}_{AMn.C2}$ = 35,1338 m. n.m^3/d; $\mathbf{q}_{ACO2.C2}$ = 34,1293 m. n.m^3/d.

GCU #3 (see area **CA3** in Fig. IP 26) – $\mathbf{q_{AVth.C3}}$ = 31,2678 m. n.m^3/d; $\mathbf{q_{AMn.C3}}$ = 27,6725 m. n.m^3/d; $\mathbf{q_{ACO2.C3}}$ = 30,8745 m. n.m^3/d.

GCU #4 (see area **CA4** in Fig. IP 26) – is switch-off.

GCU #5 (see area **CA5** in Fig. IP 26) – $\mathbf{q_{AVth.C5}}$ = 34,7265 m. n.m^3/d; $\mathbf{q_{AMn.C5}}$ = 31,7101 m. n.m^3/d; $\mathbf{q_{ACO2.C5}}$ = 32,3294 m. n.m^3/d.

GCU #6 (see area **CA6** in Fig. IP 26) – $\mathbf{q_{AVth.C6}}$ = 31,8566 m. n.m^3/d; $\mathbf{q_{AMn.C6}}$ = 35,6127 m. n.m^3/d; $\mathbf{q_{ACO2.C6}}$ = 33,7826 m. n.m^3/d.

GCU #7 (see area **CA7** in Fig. IP 26) – $\mathbf{q_{AVth.C7}}$ = 31,2786 m. n.m^3/d; $\mathbf{q_{AMn.C7}}$ = 30,5389 m. n.m^3/d; $\mathbf{q_{ACO2.C7}}$ = 31,7497 m. n.m^3/d.

GCU #8 (see area **CA8** in Fig. IP 26) – is switch-off.

GCU #9 (see area **CA9** in Fig. IP 26) – $\mathbf{q_{AVth.C9}}$ = 48,8984 m. n.m^3/d; $\mathbf{q_{AMn.C9}}$ = 47,7766 m. n.m^3/d; $\mathbf{q_{ACO2.C9}}$ = 49,8894 m. n.m^3/d.

GCU #10 (see area **CA10** in Fig. IP 26) – $\mathbf{q_{AVth.C10}}$ = 48,9633 m. n.m^3/d; $\mathbf{q_{AMn.C10}}$ = 50,0851 m. n.m^3/d; $\mathbf{q_{ACO2.C10}}$ = 47,9723 m. n.m^3/d.

GCU #11 (see area **CA11** in Fig. IP 26) and **GCU #12** (see area **CA12** in Fig. IP 26) – are switch-off.

The result of calculating the parameters of all three types of current **goal's** work points **WPA** for all **GCUs** in all three compression stages of the **BCS KGF** is shown in Fig. IP 26.

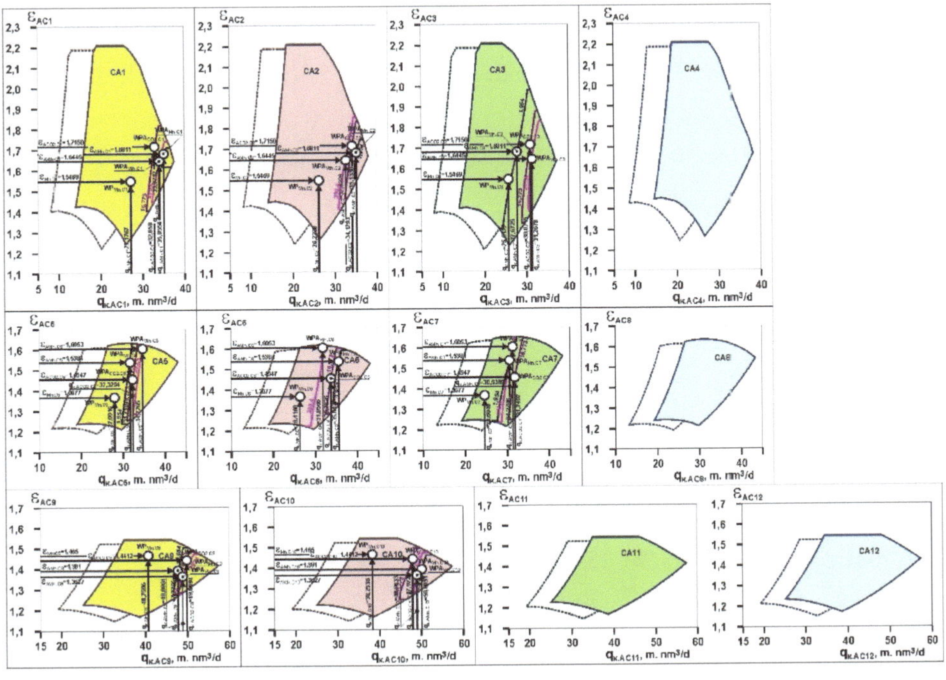

Fig. IP 26

The $\mathbf{RPM_{C1}}$, $\mathbf{RPM_{C2}}$, $\mathbf{RPM_{C3}}$, $\mathbf{RPM_{C5}}$, $\mathbf{RPM_{C6}}$, $\mathbf{RPM_{C7}}$, $\mathbf{RPM_{C9}}$, $\mathbf{RPM_{C10}}$ images and the current work points $\mathbf{WP_{Mn.C1}}$, $\mathbf{WP_{Mn.C2}}$, $\mathbf{WP_{Mn.C3}}$, $\mathbf{WP_{Mn.C5}}$, $\mathbf{WP_{Mn.C6}}$, $\mathbf{WP_{Mn.C7}}$, $\mathbf{WP_{Mn.C9}}$ and $\mathbf{WP_{Mn.C10}}$ for all currently running **GCUs** and their parameters, which are measured at the current time, are plotted in dashed lines on Fig. IP 26 for comparison, including:

$\mathbf{n_{Mn.C1}}$ = 5192,344 rpm, $\mathbf{q_{Mn.C1}}$ = 27,1767 m. n.m³/d, $\boldsymbol{\varepsilon_{Mn.C1}}$ = 1,5469 and $\mathbf{Ix_{C.iw.Mn.C1}}$ = 1,125 – these are the current parameters of the operating mode of **GCU #1** at the point $\mathbf{WP_{Mn.C1}}$ on $\mathbf{RPM_{C1}}$;

$\mathbf{n_{Mn.C2}}$ = 4998,448 rpm, $\mathbf{q_{Mn.C2}}$ = 26,2238 m. n.m³/d, $\varepsilon_{Mn.C2}$ = 1,5469 and $\mathbf{Ix_{C.iw.Mn.C2}}$ = 1,125 – these are the current parameters of the operating mode of **GCU #2** at the point $\mathbf{WP_{Mn.C2}}$ on $\mathbf{RPM_{C2}}$;

$\mathbf{n_{Mn.C3}}$ = 5095,227 rpm, $\mathbf{q_{Mn.C3}}$ = 25,6127 m. n.m³/d, $\varepsilon_{Mn.C3}$ = 1,5469 and $\mathbf{Ix_{C.iw.Mn.C3}}$ = 1,125 – these are the current parameters of the operating mode of **GCU #3** at the point $\mathbf{WP_{Mn.C3}}$ on $\mathbf{RPM_{C3}}$;

$\mathbf{n_{Mn.C5}}$ = 4706,986 rpm, $\mathbf{q_{Mn.C5}}$ = 27,9916 m. n.m³/d, $\varepsilon_{Mn.C5}$ = 1,3677 and $\mathbf{Ix_{C.iw.Mn.C5}}$ – these are the current parameters of the operating mode of **GCU #5** at the point $\mathbf{WP_{Mn.C5}}$ on $\mathbf{RPM_{C5}}$;

$\mathbf{n_{Mn.C6}}$ = 4594,452 rpm, $\mathbf{q_{Mn.C6}}$ = 26,4168 m. n.m³/d, $\varepsilon_{Mn.C6}$ = 1,3677 and $\mathbf{Ix_{C.iw.Mn.C6}}$ = 1,125 – these are the current parameters of the operating mode of **GCU #6** at the point $\mathbf{WP_{Mn.C6}}$ on $\mathbf{RPM_{C6}}$;

$\mathbf{n_{Mn.C7}}$ = 4543,5 rpm, $\mathbf{q_{Mn.C7}}$ = 24,6048 m. n.m³/d, $\varepsilon_{Mn.C7}$ = 1,3677 and $\mathbf{Ix_{C.iw.Mn.C7}}$ = 1,125 – these are the current parameters of the operating mode of **GCU #7** at the point $\mathbf{WP_{Mn.C7}}$ on $\mathbf{RPM_{C7}}$;

$\mathbf{n_{Mn.C9}}$ = 5178,108 rpm, $\mathbf{q_{Mn.C9}}$ = 40,7596 m. n.m³/d, $\varepsilon_{Mn.C9}$ = 1,465 and $\mathbf{Ix_{C.iw.Mn.C9}}$ = 1,125 – these are the current parameters of the operating mode of **GCU #9** at the point $\mathbf{WP_{Mn.C9}}$ on $\mathbf{RPM_{C9}}$;

$\mathbf{n_{Mn.C10}}$ = 5149,083 rpm, $\mathbf{q_{Mn.C10}}$ = 38,2536 m. n.m³/d, $\varepsilon_{Mn.C10}$ = 1,465 and $\mathbf{Ix_{C.iw.Mn.C10}}$ = 1,125 – these are the current parameters of the operating mode of **GCU #10** at the point $\mathbf{WP_{Mn.C10}}$ on $\mathbf{RPM_{C10}}$.

The accuracy of the calculation of the combination of **GCUs** productivities is verified by their addition in each compression stage for each reasonability criterion, which should result in a magnitude must be equal to the total productivity of the entire **BCS KGF**:

$q_{AVth.C1} + q_{AVth.C2} + q_{AVth.C3} = 33,9713 + 32,6226 + 31,2678 = 97,8617$ m. n.m^3/d;

$q_{AMn.C1} + q_{A\ Mn.C2} + q_{AMn.C3} = 35,0554 + 35,1338 + 27,6725 = 97,8617$ m. n.m^3/d;

$q_{ACO2.C1} + q_{A\ O2.C2} + q_{ACO2.C3} = 32,858 + 34,1293 + 30,8745 = 97,8617$ m. n.m^3/d;

$q_{AVth.C5} + q_{AVth.C6} + q_{AVth.C7} = 34,7265 + 31,8566 + 31,2786 = 97,8617$ m. n.m^3/d;

$q_{AMn.C5} + q_{AMn.C6} + q_{AMn.C7} = 31,7101 + 35,6127 + 30,5389 = 97,8617$ m. n.m^3/d;

$q_{ACO2.C5} + q_{ACO2.C6} + q_{ACO2.C7} = 32,3294 + 33,7826 + 31,7497 = 97,8617$ m. n.m^3/d;

$q_{AVth.C9} + q_{AVth.C10} = 48,8984 + 48,9633 = 97,8617$ m. n.m^3/d;

$q_{AMn.C9} + q_{A\ Mn.C10} = 47,7766 + 50,0851 = 97,8617$ m. n.m^3/d;

$q_{ACO2.C9} + q_{ACO2.C10} = 49,8894 + 47,9723 = 97,8617$ m. n.m^3/d;

$q_{Mn.C1} + q_{Mn.C2} + q_{Mn.C3} = 27,1767 + 26,2238 + 25,6127 = 79,0132$ m. n.m^3/d;

$q_{Mn.C5} + q_{Mn.C6} + q_{Mn.C7} = 27,9916 + 26,4168 + 24,6048 = 79,0132$ m. n.m^3/d;

$q_{Mn.C9} + q_{Mn.C10} = 40,7596 + 38,2536 = 79,0132$ m. n.m^3/d.

The verify showed sufficient accuracy of calculations.

5.3. Calculate the current **goal's noologistical** control parameters for the **GCU** in each compression stage.

The magnitudes of the current speed of rotation of the compressors included in their composition are the simplest in the implementation of GCU control parameters in compressor stations. For example, the PID controller was used to control the magnitude of the current commercial productivity of **the Kardam 1 compressor station (Bulgaria)** prior to installation in it the control system using **technology of Noologistics**. He created fluctuations in gas pressure in a network of gas pipelines under a period of 0.5 to 2.5 hours. The reason for these fluctuations was the absence in the PID regulator of a mathematical apparatus for calculating a permanent change in the current operating characteristic of a gas pipeline network, as described in paragraph 3 above. The application the **technology of Noologistics** has eliminated this problem.

The magnitude of the **goal's noologistical** rotational speed of the compressor of each **GCU** is calculated in accordance the magnitudes of the above-estimated **goal's noologistical** productivity and the pressure ratio. **The current goal's real characteristic** ($\mathbf{RM_{M.iw.NG.b}}$) of each compressor that previously was used in the calculation of its $\mathbf{RPMA_{iw.b}}$ is used in these calculation. This calculation is carried out according to the standard procedure outlined in **the usual scientific and technical literature**, and therefore is not presented here to reduce the scope of the description. The result of this calculation is presented below under a division into sets according to **the criteria of reasonable management**, including:

A set of control parameters that provides the minimum energy consumption of all kinds in the entire BCS KGF.

Set of control parameters for **GCU** of the first compression stage:

$\mathbf{n_{AVth.C1}}$ = 5463,108 rpm – current **goal's** rotation speed of the **GCU #1** compressor in point $\mathbf{WPA_{Vth.C1}}$ on $\mathbf{RM_{M.iw.NG.C1}}$ under $\varepsilon_{AVth.C1}$ = 1,6445, $\mathbf{q_{AVth.C1}}$ = 33,9713 m. n.m^3/d and $\mathbf{Ix_{AC.iw.Vth.C1}}$ = 293,4;

$\mathbf{n_{AVth.C2}}$ = 5202,281 rpm – current **goal's** rotation speed of the **GCU #2** compressor in point $\mathbf{WPA_{Vth.C2}}$ on $\mathbf{RM_{M.iw.NG.C2}}$ under $\varepsilon_{AVth.C2}$ = 1,6445, $\mathbf{q_{AVth.C2}}$ = 32,6226 m. n.m^3/d and $\mathbf{Ix_{AC.iw.Vth.C2}}$ = 293,4;

$\mathbf{n_{AVth.C3}}$ = 4888,519 rpm – current **goal's** rotation speed of the **GCU #3** compressor in point $\mathbf{WPA_{Vth.C3}}$ on $\mathbf{RM_{M.iw.NG.C3}}$ under $\varepsilon_{AVth.C3}$ = 1,6445, $\mathbf{q_{AVth.C3}}$ = 31,2678 m. n.m^3/d and $\mathbf{Ix_{AC.iw.Vth.C3}}$ = 293,4.

Set of control parameters for **GCU** of the second compression stage:

$n_{AVth.C5}$ = 5636,213 rpm – current **goal's** rotation speed of the **GCU #5** compressor in point $\mathbf{WPA}_{Vth.C5}$ on $\mathbf{RM}_{M.iw.NG.C5}$ under $\varepsilon_{AVth.C5}$ = 1,6053, $q_{AVth.C5}$ = 34,7265 m. n.m^3/d and $Ix_{AC.iw.Vth.C5}$ = 293,4;

$n_{AVth.C6}$ = 5581,000 rpm – current **goal's** rotation speed of the **GCU #6** compressor in point $\mathbf{WPA}_{Vth.C6}$ on $\mathbf{RM}_{M.iw.NG.C6}$ under $\varepsilon_{AVth.C6}$ = 1,6053, $q_{AVth.C6}$ = 31,8566 m. n.m^3/d and $Ix_{AC.iw.Vth.C6}$ = 293,4;

$n_{AVth.C7}$ = 5522,708 rpm – current **goal's** rotation speed of the **GCU #7** compressor in point $\mathbf{WPA}_{Vth.C7}$ on $\mathbf{RM}_{M.iw.NG.C7}$ under $\varepsilon_{AVth.C7}$ = 1,6053, $q_{AVth.C7}$ = 31,2786 m. n.m^3/d and $Ix_{AC.iw.Vth.C7}$ = 293,4.

Set of control parameters for **GCU** of the third compression stage:

$n_{AVth.C9}$ = 4962,455 rpm – current **goal's** rotation speed of the **GCU #9** compressor in point $\mathbf{WPA}_{Vth.C9}$ on $\mathbf{RM}_{M.iw.NG.C9}$ under $\varepsilon_{AVth.C9}$ = 1,3627, $q_{AVth.C9}$ = 48,8984 m. n.m^3/d and $Ix_{AC.iw.Vth.C9}$ = 293,4;

$n_{AVth.C10}$ = 4845,556 rpm – current **goal's** rotation speed of the **GCU #10** compressor in point $\mathbf{WPA}_{Vth.C10}$ on $\mathbf{RM}_{M.iw.NG.C10}$ under $\varepsilon_{AVth.C10}$ = 1,3627, $q_{AVth.C10}$ = 48,9633 m. n.m^3/d and $Ix_{AC.iw.Vth.C10}$ = 293,4.

A set of control parameters that provides the minimum costs of all types of all kinds in monetary terms in the entire BCS KGF.

Set of control parameters for **GCU** of the first compression stage:

$n_{AMn.C1}$ = 5470,239 rpm – current **goal's** rotation speed of the **GCU #1** compressor in point $\mathbf{WPA}_{Mn.C1}$ on $\mathbf{RM}_{M.iw.NG.C1}$ under $\varepsilon_{AMn.C1}$ = 1,6811, $q_{AMn.C1}$ = 35,0554 m. n.m^3/d and $Ix_{AC.iw.Mn.C1}$ = 1,954;

$n_{AMn.C2}$ = 5615,556 rpm – current **goal's** rotation speed of the **GCU #2** compressor in point $\mathbf{WPA}_{Mn.C2}$ on $\mathbf{RM}_{M.iw.NG.C2}$ under $\varepsilon_{AMn.C2}$ = 1,6811, $q_{AMn.C2}$ = 35,1338 m. n.m^3/d and $Ix_{AC.iw.Mn.C2}$ = 1,954;

$n_{AMn.C3}$ = 5211,667 rpm – current **goal's** rotation speed of the **GCU #3** compressor in point $\mathbf{WPA}_{Mn.C3}$ on $\mathbf{RM}_{M.iw.NG.C3}$ under $\varepsilon_{AMn.C3}$ = 1,6811, $q_{AMn.C3}$ = 27,6725 m. n.m^3/d and $Ix_{AC.iw.Mn.C3}$ = 1,954.

Set of control parameters for **GCU** of the second compression stage:

$n_{AMn.C5}$ = 5327,037 rpm – current **goal's** rotation speed of the **GCU #5** compressor in point $WPA_{Mn.C5}$ on $RM_{M.iw.NG.C5}$ under $\varepsilon_{AMn.C5}$ = 1,5384, $q_{AMn.C5}$ = 31,7101 m. n.m^3/d and $Ix_{AC.iw.Mn.C5}$ = 1,954;

$n_{AMn.C6}$ = 5363,704 rpm – current **goal's** rotation speed of the **GCU #6** compressor in point $WPA_{Mn.C6}$ on $RM_{M.iw.NG.C6}$ under $\varepsilon_{AMn.C6}$ = 1,5384, $q_{AMn.C6}$ = 35,6127 m. n.m^3/d and $Ix_{AC.iw.Mn.C6}$ = 1,954;

$n_{AMn.C7}$ = 5242,744 rpm – current **goal's** rotation speed of the **GCU #7** compressor in point $WPA_{Mn.C7}$ on $RM_{M.iw.NG.C7}$ under $\varepsilon_{AMn.C7}$ = 1,5384, $q_{AMn.C7}$ = 30,5389 m. n.m^3/d and $Ix_{AC.iw.Mn.C7}$ = 1,954.

Set of control parameters for GCU of the third compression stage:

$n_{AMn.C9}$ = 4866,591 rpm – current **goal's** rotation speed of the **GCU #9** compressor in point $WPA_{Mn.C9}$ on $RM_{M.iw.NG.C9}$ under $\varepsilon_{AMn.C9}$ = 1,391, $q_{AMn.C9}$ = 47,7766 m. n.m^3/d and $Ix_{AC.iw.Mn.C9}$ = 1,954;

$n_{AMn.C10}$ = 5005 rpm – current **goal's** rotation speed of the **GCU #10** compressor in point $WPA_{Mn.C10}$ on $RM_{M.iw.NG.C10}$ under $\varepsilon_{AMn.C10}$ = 1,391, $q_{AMn.C10}$ = 50,0851 m. n.m^3/d and $Ix_{AC.iw.Mn.C10}$ = 1,954.

A set of control parameters that provides the minimum CO_2 emission the entire BCS KGF.

Set of control parameters for **GCU** of the first compression stage:

$n_{ACO2.C1}$ = 5664,848 rpm – current **goal's** rotation speed of the **GCU #1** compressor in point $WPA_{CO2.C1}$ on $RM_{M.iw.NG.C1}$ under $\varepsilon_{ACO2.C1}$ = 1,7158, $q_{ACO2.C1}$ = 32,858 m. n.m^3/d and $Ix_{AS.iw.CO2.C1}$ = 16,773;

$n_{ACO2.C2}$ = 5547,424 rpm – current **goal's** rotation speed of the **GCU #2** compressor in point $WPA_{CO2.C2}$ on $RM_{M.iw.NG.C2}$ under $\varepsilon_{ACO2.C2}$ = 1,7158, $q_{ACO2.C2}$ = 34,1293 m. n.m^3/d and $Ix_{AS.iw.CO2.C2}$ = 16,773;

$\mathbf{n_{ACO2.C3}}$ = 5308,256 rpm – current **goal's** rotation speed of the **GCU #3** compressor in point $\mathbf{WPA_{CO2.C3}}$ on $\mathbf{RM_{M.iw.NG.C3}}$ under $\varepsilon_{ACO2.C3}$ = 1,7158, $\mathbf{q_{ACO2.C3}}$ = 30,8745 m. n.m^3/d and $\mathbf{Ix_{AS.iw.CO2.C3}}$ = 16,773.

Set of control parameters for **GCU** of the second compression stage:

$\mathbf{n_{ACO2.C5}}$ = 4963,524 rpm – current **goal's** rotation speed of the **GCU #5** compressor in point $\mathbf{WPA_{CO2.C5}}$ on $\mathbf{RM_{M.iw.NG.C5}}$ under $\varepsilon_{ACO2.C5}$ = 1,4547, $\mathbf{q_{ACO2.C5}}$ = 32,858 m. n.m^3/d and $\mathbf{Ix_{AS.iw.CO2.C5}}$ = 16,773;

$\mathbf{n_{ACO2.C6}}$ = 4954,444 rpm – current **goal's** rotation speed of the **GCU #6** compressor in point $\mathbf{WPA_{CO2.C6}}$ on $\mathbf{RM_{M.iw.NG.C6}}$ under $\varepsilon_{ACO2.C6}$ = 1,4547, $\mathbf{q_{ACO2.C6}}$ = 33,7826 m. n.m^3/d and $\mathbf{Ix_{AS.iw.CO2.C6}}$ = 16,773;

$\mathbf{n_{ACO2.C7}}$ = 4882,203 rpm – current **goal's** rotation speed of the **GCU #7** compressor in point $\mathbf{WPA_{CO2.C7}}$ on $\mathbf{RM_{M.iw.NG.C7}}$ under $\varepsilon_{ACO2.C7}$ = 1,4547, $\mathbf{q_{ACO2.C7}}$ = 31,7497 m. n.m^3/d and $\mathbf{Ix_{AS.iw.CO2.C7}}$ = 16,773;

Set of control parameters for **GCU** of the third compression stage:

$\mathbf{n_{ACO2.C9}}$ = 5140,545 rpm – current **goal's** rotation speed of the **GCU #9** compressor in point $\mathbf{WPA_{CO2.C9}}$ on $\mathbf{RM_{M.iw.NG.C9}}$ under $\varepsilon_{ACO2.C9}$ = 1,4412, $\mathbf{q_{ACO2.C9}}$ = 49,8894 m. n.m^3/d and $\mathbf{Ix_{AS.iw.CO2.C9}}$ = 16,773;

$n_{ACO2.C10}$ = 5106,719 rpm – current **goal's** rotation speed of the **GCU #10** compressor in point $WPA_{CO2.C10}$ on $RM_{M.iw.NG.C10}$ under $\varepsilon_{ACO2.C10}$ = 1,4412, $q_{ACO2.C10}$ = 47,9723 m. n.m^3/d and $Ix_{AS.iw.CO2.C10}$ = 16,773.

6. The sets of **goal's** rotational speeds of the GCU compressors, obtained in paragraph 5, are used to develop **noologistical management solutions** and/or to calculate **the noologistical control actions**.

4. The Practical Examples of Noologistics Implementation

The above-mentioned theory of **Noologistics** and its **technology** were developed based on the results of the creation, installation, commissioning, testing and operation of its **grid** on **the management objects** of several of its **persons**. Their characteristic feature is a relatively simple mathematical apparatus and algorithms for the accurate calculation of **reasonable (noo) management solutions** and **control actions** on **objects** of any kind, of any complexity, of any size, with any number of jointly operating elements of any type in any operating conditions that ensure achievement of the set **goals**, while providing the **principles** and given **criteria of reasonableness**. A list and brief characteristics some of **systems** using the theory of **Noologistics** and its **technology** are below:

Model of reasonable regulation of the compressor station Holowczyce II, Poland, 2002

Compressor station (CS) Holowczyce II is located in Poland near the border of Belarus (52° 17'03.2"N 23° 00'03.2"E). It was equipped with gas-pumping units GPA-C-6.3 in an amount of 3 pcs. and is intended for the distribution of gas from the Yamal-Europe gas main for Poland's consumers.

The Holowczyce II CS was completed in 2002 with one **GCU** consisting of a Dresser-Rand 50P4 compressor driven by an ABB GT10B gas turbine unit (briefly 50P4&GT10B).

GPA 50P4&GT10B significantly differed in technical parameters in comparison to GPA-C-6.3. These differences are visible in comparison of their parameters shown in Table 2.

Table 2

Parameter	GPA-C-6.3	50P4&GT10B
Power, MW	6,3	25
The maximum pressure ratio of the transported gas	1,6	3,2

The purpose of the simulation was to calculate the reasonable modes of joint operation of GPA-C-6,3 and 50P4 & GT10B when they are connected in parallel to each other. Reasonable modes of joint work implied their **safe** and **stable** operation under the provision of a given **productivity**. Provision of any other **principles**, as well as **criteria of reasonableness**, was not included in the notion of reasonable modes of joint work. Therefore, all the other **principles of Noologistics** were provided in the simulation as self-evident, and as a **criterion of reasonableness** the **minimum current density of the conditional variable consumption flow of fuel gas** in the whole CS was chosen. All scientific bases describing the operation of the simulated equipment and the Agreement between the two persons - the Customer and the Contractor - were used as **rules** that needed to be observed when creating the model.

The model of the CS, created on the basis of the conditions described above, made it possible to draw the following main conclusions, which were taken into account in subsequent managerial solutions:

1. The joint operation of gas compressor units GPA-C-6.3 and 50P4&GT10B at their parallel inclusion in one group is possible up to a pressure ratio in them no higher than 1.6. Any attempt to increase the pressure ratio higher than allowed by the instruction manual of GPA-C-6.3, will lead to their accident (surging). Therefore, it is impossible to use the full power of the GPA 50P4 & GT10B at simultaneous operation of it together GPA-C-6.3.

2. The single work of GPA 50P4&GT10B (without the inclusion of GPA-C-6.3 in joint work) is possible up to a pressure ratio not higher than 1.8. The use of a higher pressure ratio in it would be accompanied by an increase in the temperature of the compressed gas at the compressor outlet above 90°C. Thermal insulation of in-station pipelines will be destroyed under the influence of such a high temperature. It is recommended to replace the heat insulation of the in-station pipelines with a more heat-resistant one, for example, withstanding the temperature up to 180 ° C, before using the GPA 50P4&GT10B on the regime with a pressure ratio of 3.2. Therefore, it is impossible to use the full power of the GPA 50P4&ГТ10B without

replacing the thermal insulation of the in-station pipelines with a more heat-resistant one.

System for the reasonable regulation of CS Kardam 1, Bulgaria, 2003

CS Kardam 1 is located in Bulgaria near the border with Romania (43°46'49.13"N, 28°07'27.21"E). The CS is installed on the Balkan Gas Pipeline, which supplies gas from the Ukrainian gas pipelines Ananiev-Tiraspol-Izmail and Shebelinka-Izmail through Moldova and Romania for Bulgaria's consumers. It was equipped with 3 gas compressor units THM-1304 / GGN71B manufactured by HISPANO-SUIZA - France, which have the following parameters:

Power – 9 MW;

The maximum pressure ratio of the transported gas – 1,87.

The goal of creating **the system of Noologistics** was to maintain reasonable regimes for the joint operation of the THT-1304 / GGN71B in the composition of the CS and the entire CS as part of the Balkan Gas Pipeline. Reasonable modes of joint work implied their **safe** and **stable** operation under the provision of a given **productivity**. Provision of any other **principles**, as well as **criteria of reasonableness**, was not included in the notion of reasonable modes of joint work. Therefore, all the other **principles of Noologistics** were provided in the **system of Noologistics** as self-evident, and as a **criterion of reasonableness** the minimum current density of the variable consumption of fuel gas in the whole CS was chosen. All scientific bases describing the operation of the controlled equipment and the Agreement between the two persons - the Customer and the Contractor - were used as **rules** that needed to be observed when creating the **system**.

After commissioning, **the system of Noologistics** provided three control modes:

- manual;
- semi-automatic;
- automatic.

The personnel of the CS used manual control for not more than 2 hours in aggregate. The first reason for the transfer to the semi-automatic control mode was the decision of the person that the system showed a sufficient degree of safety and stability of operation in the mode of manual control. The second reason was staff fatigue due to the need to constantly monitor a large number of parameters of the operating modes THM-1304 / GGN71B and constantly slightly change the frequency of their rotation. The subject used the semi-automatic control mode also in aggregate for no more than 2 hours, after which he transferred the system to automatic control mode. The reasons for the transfer to automatic control are the same.

Pressure fluctuations at the inlet to the compressor station, which occurred in the previous sections of the main gas pipeline, caused the need for frequent changes in the operating modes of the THM-1304 / GGN71B. These oscillations occurred stochastically under a period, the magnitude of which varied from 2 to 4 hours. The dispatcher was forced to compensate for these fluctuations by manually controlling the rotational speed of the THM-1304 / GGN71B. All previous attempts by the person to liquidate fluctuations on outlet of CS using the PID controller of the compressor station for 8 months before the system was started did not produce a result due to the impossibility of its adjustment. The mentioned pressure fluctuations at the output of the CS immediately ceased after the system was switched on to automatic control mode. The reason for their termination is the accurate calculation in **real time of the current characteristics of the main gas pipelines**, in which the entire CS operates, its **noologistical area of possible operating modes** and parameters of the current operating point, as well as - **noologistical areas of possible operating modes** and parameters of **current operating points** of each its **unit of the equipment**.

The model of reasonable management of the gas supply grid of Azerigaz enterprise, Azerbaijan, 2003

The modeling of reasonable management the gas supply grid of Azerigaz enterprise was carried out in 2003 within the framework of a relevant tender. The aim of the simulation was to demonstrate the possibility of using **the technology of Noologistics** in the process of developing management solutions for evaluation:

- reasonable opportunities of the existing pipeline networks of the Azerigas enterprise for gas transportation to consumers inside the country and for export in all seasons;
- reasonable costs of the Azerigaz enterprise for development and operation of the Shah-Deniz gas field;
- reasonable amount of necessary modernization of the existing gas supply system and costs for it at different gas export amounts;
- the possibility of creating **a system of Noologistics** for the Azerigaz enterprise.

The scheme of the gas supply system of Azerigaz enterprise in 2003 is shown in Fig. Ex 1.

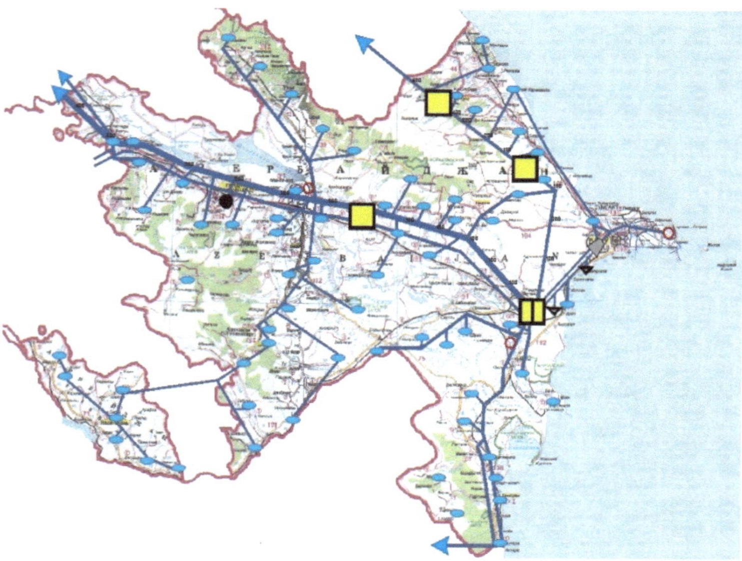

Fig. Ex 1

The model developed for the tender calculated the reasonable modes of joint operation of all elements that make up the Azerigaz gas supply network: sections of main and distribution gas pipelines, underground gas storage facilities, gas distribution stations, compressor stations with centrifugal compressors and gas engines, gas fields, etc., based on ensuring all forecasted needs within the country and the maximum possible amount of gas exports in all possible directions. As a reasonable regime of joint operation of all elements of the gas supply grid of the Azerigaz enterprise implied their safe and stable operation under the provision of a given productivity. Provision of any other **principles**, as well as **criteria of reasonableness**, was not included in the notion of reasonable modes of joint work. Therefore, all the other **principles of Noologistics** were provided in the **system of Noologistics** as self-evident, and as a **criterion of reasonableness** the minimum current density of the variable consumption of fuel gas in the whole grid was chosen. The schemes of existing gas pipelines, information on the equipment of compressor stations, gas distribution stations, gas pipeline grids and other information provided by the Azerigaz were used for the modeling. **All the scientific bases describing the operation of the simulated equipment** and the conditions of participation in the tender that satisfied all **persons** - the Customer, the Investor and each of its Participants were used as **rules** that needed to be observed when creating the model.

One of the options for upgrading the Azerigaz gas supply **grid**, calculated using the developed model, is shown in Fig. Ex 2.

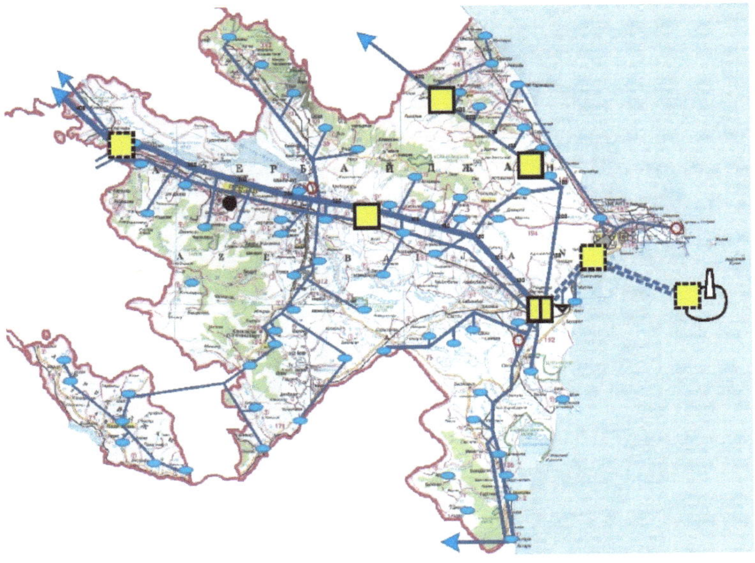

Fig. Ex 2

The model of reasonable management of the Azerigaz gas supply grid was implemented on a Pentium II computer. The duration of the calculation of the set of parameters of a single operating mode of the entire Azerigaz gas supply grid was 1 min. 29 sec. Such speed is due to the use of **technology for calculating information pyramids** and the refusal to process statistical information arrays. **Persons** - the Customer and the Investor - conducted two stages of evaluating the tender participants' proposals by different commissions made up of independent experts. The model described here was recognized by them as the best, but was not realized due to disagreements between the Customer and the Investor that arose later.

System for the reasonable management of a group of wells in the Kushchevskaya underground gas storage station, Russia, 2003

Kushchevskaya underground gas storage station (briefly - **UGSG**) is located in the Krasnodar Territory of Russia (46°31'23.60"N 39°38'223.39"E). It is a branch of the limited liability company KUBANGAZPROM and is designed to compensate for seasonal uneven consumption of gas, reduce peak loads, maintain flexibility and sustainability of gas supplies in the Rostov Region, Krasnodar and Stavropol Territories.

The purpose of the creation of **the system of Noologistics** was the reasonable regulation of a group of jointly operating gas wells. As a reasonable mode of joint work, it was implied their safe and stable operation under the provision of a given sum productivity of extraction or injection. Provision of any other **principles**, as well as **criteria of reasonableness**, was not included in the notion of reasonable modes of joint work. Therefore, as **a criterion of reasonableness** regulating, the reasonable use of underground beds energy was selected. It provided a **minimum current density of the conditional variable consumption flow of fuel gas** in the course of gas extraction and its injection into a controlled group of wells. The remaining **principles of Noologistics** were provided as self-evident.

The main functions of the described **system of Noologistics** are:

- reasonable automatic distribution of the given total amount of gas extraction / injection through the wells of the **UGSG**, based on the current situation, the given form of the surface of the gas-water contact, **the criterion of reasonableness** and the operating mode;
- automatic gas-dynamic studies of wells of **UGSG** without their stopping with determination of the values of current coefficients of

hydro resistivity of loops and boreholes, soil filtration coefficients, and bed pressure;

- graphic visualization of well characteristics;
- the output of information to geoinformation systems to create a volumetric image of the surface of the gas-water contact and the distribution of geological parameters throughout the **UGSG**;
- calculation of **noologistical** magnitudes of depression / repression, bottomhole and wellhead pressure in wells of **UGSG**;
- calculation of the **noologistical** list of wells included in the work of **UGSG**;
- visualization of the process of gas extraction / injection in individual wells, their groups and all of the UGSG in text, tabular and graphical form;
- prevention of waterlogging wells **UGSG** while the extraction and the rupture of the bed in them during injection, etc.

An example of the performance characteristics of vertical and inclined wells of Kuschevskaya **UGSG**, which the **system of Noologistics** automatically calculates, as well as a comparison of their current and **noologistical** operating modes, are shown in Fig. Ex 3.

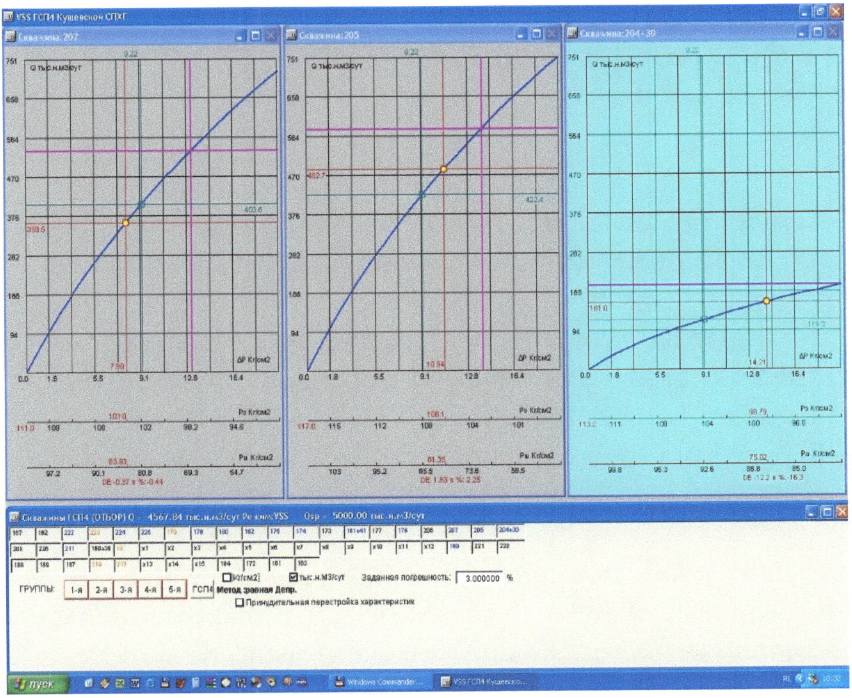

Fig. Ex 3

An example of the common performance characteristics that **the system of Noologistics** automatically calculates when operating in the manual and semi-automatic control mode of Kuschevskaya **UGSG** wells, as well as comparing (on the left) its current and **noological** performance is shown in Fig. Ex 4.

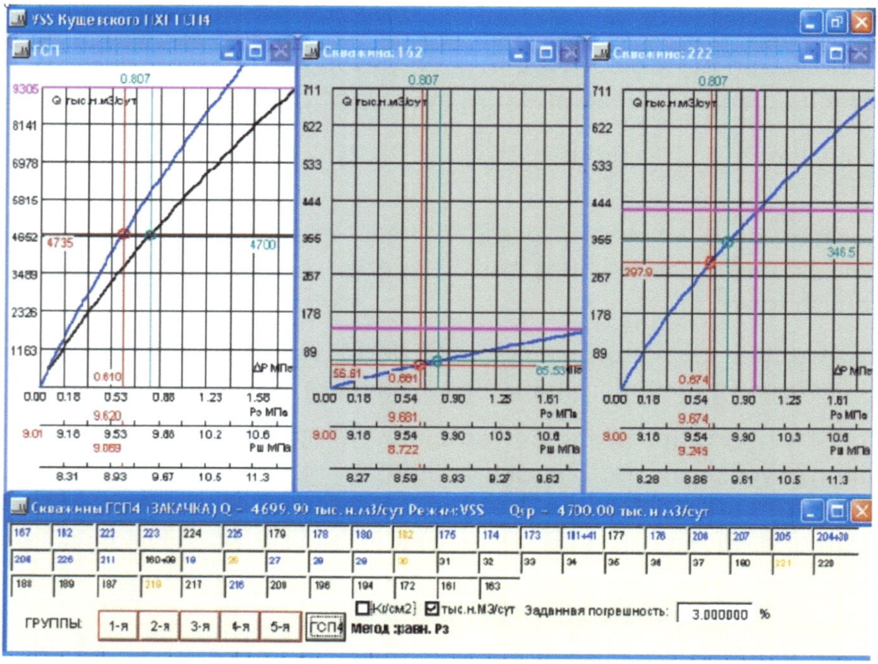

Fig. Ex 4

System for the reasonable regulation of the booster compressor station of the Komsomolsk gas field (BCS KGF), Russia, 2010

The booster compressor station (BCS) of the Komsomolsk gas field (KGF) is located in the Yamalo-Nenets Autonomous District of the Russian Federation (64°19'50.11"N 76°11'48.79"E). It is designed for pumping gas from the Komsomolsk gas field and the Muravlenko gas field to the main gas pipeline. BCS KGF was equipped with:

Gas compressor units of type ГПА – Ц – 16С with a removable flow-through part (RFP) of type 16С/45-1,7-1 manufactured by JSC Kazancompressormash, Kazan, Russia, installed in the first compression stage in the amount of 4 pcs.;

Gas compressor units of type ГПА – Ц – 16С with a RFP of type 16С/41-2,2-1 manufactured by JSC Kazancompressormash, installed in the second compression stage in the amount of 4 pcs.;

Gas compressor units of type ГПА – Ц – 16С with a RFP of type 16С/76-1,7_1 manufactured by JSC Kazancompressormash, installed in the third compression stage in the amount of 4 pcs.;

Apparatuses for air cooling of gas (AAC gas) of the type АВГБС-83Р produced by the Penza Chemical Engineering Plant, Penza, Russia, installed after the first compression stage in the amount of 18 pcs.;

GAC of the type АВГБС-83Р, installed after the second compression stage in the amount of 26 pcs.;

GAC of the type 2АВГ – 75 «С» produced by the Penza Chemical Engineering Plant, installed after the third compression stage in the amount of 21 pcs.;

Anti-surge cocks Mokveld in the amount of 15 pieces installed parallel to each gas compressor unit and each stage of compression according to the technological scheme of the BCS KGF, shown in Fig. Ex 6.

All of the above gas compressor units included gas turbine engines (GTE) of the DG90L2 type with a rated capacity of 16 MW produced by the State Enterprise ZPPG "Zorya" - Mashproekt, Mykolayiv, Ukraine.

Each GAC of the type АВГБС-83Р has 6 fans a capacity of 13 kW each and 3 sets of blinds: input, output and bypass. The total capacity of the fans in each GAC of the type АВГБС-83Р is 78 kW. The total capacity of all 44 GAC of the type АВГБС-83Р installed in the BCS KGF is 3,432 MW.

Each GAC of the type 2АВГ – 75 «С» has 2 fans a capacity of 37 kW each. The total capacity of the fans in each GAC of the type 2АВГ – 75 «С» is 74 kW. The total capacity of all 21 GAC of the type 2АВГ – 75 «С» installed in the BCS KGF is 1,554 MW.

The total nominal power of all gas compressor units installed in the BCS KGF is 192 MW. The total capacity of all GAC installed in the BCS KGF is 4,986 MW.

The purpose of creating **the system of Noologistics** was the calculation of reasonable modes of joint operation of all the above-mentioned **units of equipment** in the BCS and the entire BCS as part of the KGF. As a reasonable mode of joint work, it was implied their **safe** and **stable** operation under the provision of a given **productivity**. Provision of any other **principles**, as well as **criteria of reasonableness**, was not included in the notion of reasonable modes of joint work. Therefore, all the other **principles of Noologistics** were provided in the **system of Noologistics** as self-evident, and as a **criterion of reasonableness** the **minimum current density of the conditional variable consumption flow of fuel gas** in the whole **BCS KGF** was chosen. All scientific bases describing the operation of the controlled equipment and the Agreement between the two persons - the Customer and the Contractor - were used as **rules** that needed to be observed when creating the **system**.

Fig. Ex 5 shows a top view of the KGF in summer:

Fig. Ex 5

Fig. Ex 6 shows the technological scheme of BCS KGF.

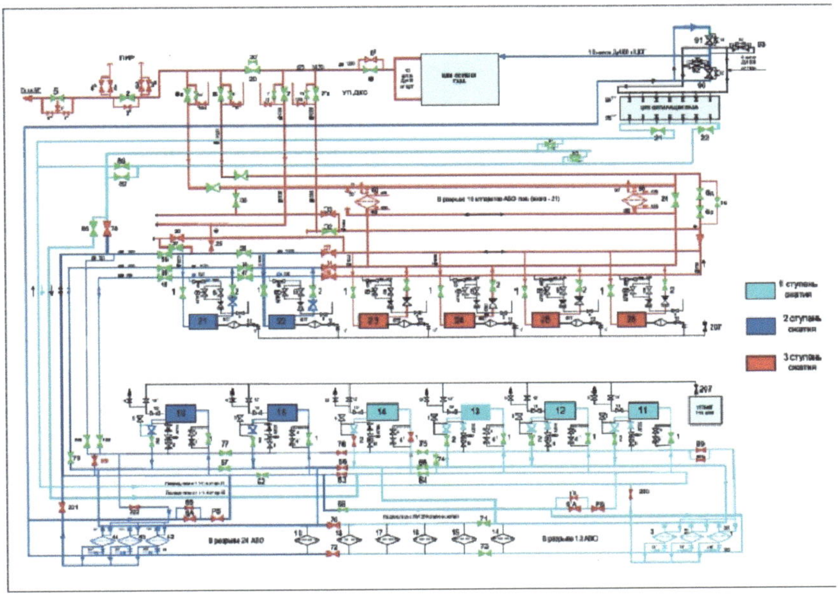

Fig. Ex 6

The system of Noologistics was developed for the BCS KGF in 2010, it processed 2958 analog and 1507 discrete signals that were received from the existing instrumentation and control systems, and calculated a set of 711 **noologistical control actions**. Its main functions are listed below:

- calculation of a reasonable number of compression steps;
- calculation of a reasonable list of gas compressor units, which should be work into each compression stage;
- calculation of the reasonable speed of rotation of the compressor in each operating unit;
- calculation of a reasonable list of **GAC**, which should be work after each compression stage;
- the calculation of a reasonable list of fans that must be work in each working **GAC**;
- calculation of the reasonable position of the input louvers in each working **GAC** of the type АВГБС-83Р;
- calculation of the reasonable position of the output louvers in each working **GAC** of the type АВГБС-83Р;
- calculation of the reasonable position of the bypass louvers in each working **GAC** of the type АВГБС-83Р;

- calculation of the moment of the appearance of the hydrate plug in each working **GAC**;
- calculation of the reasonable position of each antisurge valve of the "Mokveld" type (the preferential position is "closed"), etc.

The noologistic area of possible modes of operation of the entire **BCS KGF** and its calculation are shown in the description of **the technology for calculating the upward indexed information pyramids**.

The software of **the system of Noologistics** provided a perspective for the development of the BCS KGF and provided the possibility for the Customer's specialists to perform the following customizations independently, i.e. without the involvement of the Software Developer, the following settings:

- increase in the number of compression steps up to 4;
- increase in the number of installed gas compressor units in each compression stage up to 5 units;
- connection of the gas pipeline from the Muravlenko gas field to input of any compression stage at the Customer's choice;
- replacement of types of RFP in gas compressor units;
- connection **the system of Noologistics** to the instrumentations and control systems, installed in the BCS KGF;
- operation of **the system of Noologistics** in any of the three control modes: manual, semi-automatic and automatic;
- the work of **the system of Noologistics** in the mode of modeling, etc.

When testing **the system of Noologistics** on the actually operating BCS KGF it was found that it assigns more economical modes of operation in comparison with those established by the technology existing in it. The periods of work were marked, in which the saving of fuel and energy resources exceeded 14%. This was achieved due to a reduction in the number of simultaneous working gas compressor units, by the elimination of gas bypasses via the Mokveld cranes, a reduction in the number of working fans into the **GAC**, a reasonable redistribution of the load between the compression stages and between the gas compressor units into the stages, etc.

Model of reasonable regulation of the power unit of the power plant, Russia, 2011

The aim of the simulation was to demonstrate the universality of **Noologistics** using as its example the large-scale power supply grids. The first step in this direction is to create a model of reasonable regulation for one power unit of a power plant.

There were taken as examples a power unit with a steam boiler P-67 manufactured by JSC ZiO-Podolsk in the Moscow Region, Podolsk and a single-shaft turbine installation K-880-240-5 manufactured by the Leningrad Metal Plant, St. Petersburg (briefly - power unit K-880). The optimal operation mode of the K-880 power unit, was selected to demonstrate the efficiency of reasonable regulation. It was described on pages 148-149 in the book "**94. Рыжкин В. Я. Тепловые электрические станции**".

The technological scheme of the K-880 power unit with the arrangement of characteristic points is shown in Fig. Ex 7.

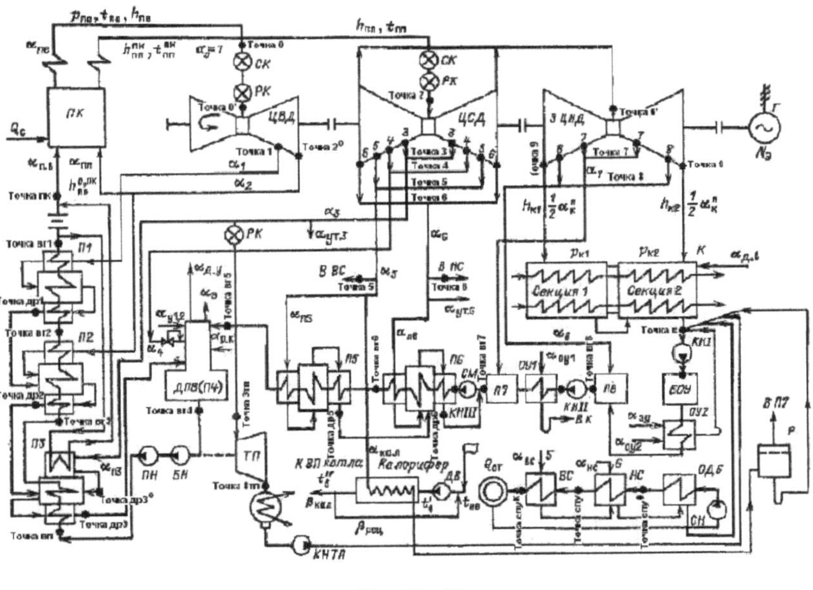

Fig. Ex 7

The notation in Fig. Ex 7 are similar to the ones used in book "**94. Рыжкин В. Я. Тепловые электрические станции**".

The application of reasonable regulation implies compliance with **the principles of Noologistics** and a given **criterion of**

reasonableness. The minimum current density of the conditional variable consumption flow of fuel in the power unit was set as **a criterion of reasonableness** in modeling. And **the principles of Noologistics** were taken for granted.

It is generally accepted in heat and power engineering that it is necessary to maintain the optimal heat distribution between the water heaters in the heat recovery system in the power unit to provide a minimum current density of variable fuel consumption, which is described by a mathematical dependence in the form of a geometric progression, indicator of which is calculated by the formula:

$$\frac{q_3}{q_4} = \frac{q_4}{q_5} = \ldots = \frac{q_{z-1}}{q_z} = m = \sqrt[z-2]{\frac{q_3}{q_\kappa}}$$

This distribution of the load is used everywhere - see, for example, page 44 in the book "**101. Тепловые электрические станции: учебник для вузов**". However, from the point of view of **Noologistics**, in order to minimize the current density of variable fuel consumption, the distribution of heat between the water heaters in the heat recovery system in the power unit must be calculated constantly in the **PRESENT** because it depends on the combination of the magnitudes of the set of current parameters of the unit operating, the technical conditions, the magnitude of the load, and so on. The results of calculating the parameters of the reasonable operation mode of the K-880 power unit under consideration from the condition of **minimum current density of the conditional variable consumption flow of fuel** are shown below under the same initial conditions specified in book "**94. Рыжкин В. Я. Тепловые электрические станции**".

Reasonable parameters in the characteristic points of the technological scheme of the power unit K-880, calculated using **the technology of Noologistics**, are shown in Table 3. The same parameters, which are calculated by the method given in book "**94. Рыжкин В. Я. Тепловые электрические станции**" are shown into parentheses for comparison.

Table 3

The point of the steam process	Thermal circuit element	Steam in turbine outputs			Steam in regenerative heaters					Heated water behind regenerative heaters				
		p MPa	t (x) °C (%)	h kJ/kg	p_r MPa	t_{sr} °C	h'_r kJ/kg	$h_{дr}$ kJ/kg	y_r kJ/kg	θ_r °C	$p_{вr}$ MPa	$t_{вr}$ °C	$h_{вr}$ kJ/kg	x_r kJ/kg
0		23,5 (23,5)	540 (540)	3323 (3323)										
0'		22,8 (22,8)	537 (537)	3322 (3322)										
1	ПВ1	6,14 (6,1)	346,9 (346)	3031 (3029)	5,7	272	1196,8	1100	1929,51	2	31	270	1181,9	121,8
2°	ПВ2	3,83 (3,8)	285,2 (284)	2924,3 (2922)	3,7	245,7	1065,3	939,00	1983,16	2	31,5	243,7	1060,9	168,56
2	ПП	3,37 (3,34)	540 (540)	3542,6 (3543)										
3	ПВ3	2,03 (2,0)	469,5 (469)	3400,1 (3399)	1,9	209,8	896,8	778,00	2621,31	4	32	205,8	891,55	177,08
4	ПВ4	1,043 (1,02)	380,2 (379)	3221,2 (3219)	0,7	164,96	697,1			0	0,7	164,96	697,1	
5	ПВ5	0,523 (0,505)	301,8 (300)	3067,3 (3064)	0,476	150	632,14	531,00	2533,07	2	1,2	148	624,02	73,08
6	ПВ6	0,2216 (0,213)	206,5 (204)	2882,6 (2878)	0,199	120	504,015	404	2473,92	3	1,5	117	491,91	132,11
7	ПВ7	0,0692 (0,0663)	116,6 (114)	2713 (2708)	0,062	86,5	363,106			0	0,062	86,5	362,24	
8	ПВ8	0,01939 (0,0186)	x=97,83 (97,7)	2557,3 (2553)	0,0172	76,45	237,944			0	0,0172	56,8	237,68	
К	К	0,00373 (0,0036)	x=94,24 (94,1)	2411,7 (2407)						0	0,0036	27,149	113,75	

The notation Table 3 are similar to the ones used in book "**94. Рыжкин В. Я. Тепловые электрические станции**" .

Reasonable costs of fresh steam and steam outputs for the regeneration system in the K-880 power unit, calculated using **the technology of Noologistics**, are shown in Table 4. The same parameters, which are calculated by the method given in book "**94. Рыжкин В. Я. Тепловые электрические станции**" are shown into parentheses for comparison.

Table 4

Name	Notation	Unit of measur.	Dimension	
			absolute	the relative
Mass flow of fresh steam	D0	T/h	2524.158 (2551.154)	1 (1)
Mass flow of steam through the 1st output (water heater ПВ1)	D1	T/h	138.65 (162.87)	0.054930242 (0.063841697)
Mass flow of steam through the 2nd output (water heater ПВ2)	D2	T/h	175.79 (204.22)	0.069641199 (0.080050048)
Mass flow of steam through the 3rd output (water heater ПВ3)	D3	T/h	256.38 (283.03)	0.101569531 (0.11094195)
Mass flow of steam through the 4th output (water heater ПВ4)	D4	T/h	40.74 (38.98)	0.01613866 (0.01527936)
Mass flow of steam through the 5th output (water heater ПВ5)	D5	T/h	220.65 (197.18)	0.087413672 (0.077290512)

Mass flow of steam through the 6th output (water heater ПВ6)	D6	T/h	152.95 (124.16)	0.060595905 (0.048668171)
Mass flow of steam through the 7th output (water heater ПВ7)	D7	T/h	91.40 (81.59)	0.036211454 (0.031981605)
Mass flow of steam through the 8th output (water heater ПВ8)	D8	T/h	81.71 (77.04)	0.032369476 (0.030198099)
Mass flow of steam at input of condensator К	Dк	T/h	1352.267 (1367.798)	0.535729863 (0.536148558)

The reasonable process of operation of the K-880 power unit on the h-s diagram, calculated by **technology of Noologistics**, is shown in Fig. Ex 8. The same parameters, which are calculated by the method given in book "**94. Рыжкин В. Я. Тепловые электрические станции**" are shown into parentheses for comparison.

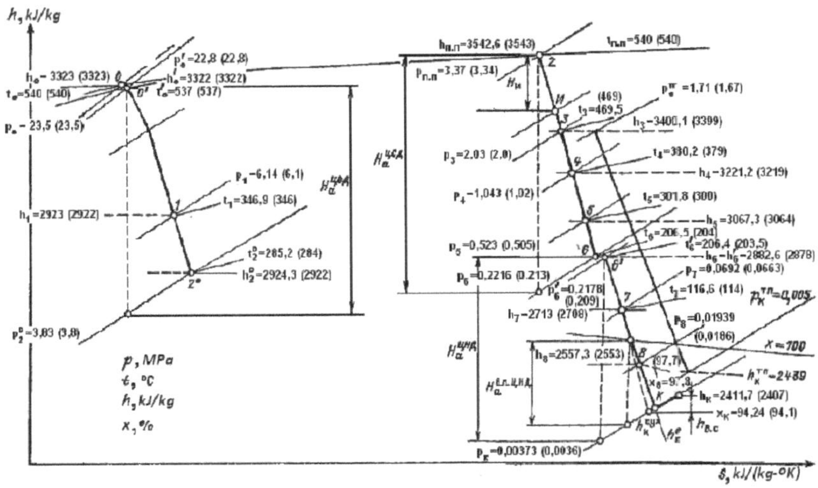

Fig. Ex 8

The reasonable energy equation of the K-880 power unit on the h-s diagram, calculated by **technology of Noologistics**, is shown in Table 5. The same parameters, which are calculated by the method given in book "**94. Рыжкин В. Я. Тепловые электрические станции**" are shown into parentheses for comparison.

Table 5

Turbine Cylinder	The turbine compartment (on the process of expansion of steam)	Share of steam pass through the compartment	Heat drop of steam in the compartment H_{ij}, kJ/kg	Internal work of 1 kg of fresh steam $a_{ij}*H_{ij}$, kJ/kg
ЦВД	0′ - 1	$a_{0'1} = a_0 - a_{с.к} - a^0_{р.к} - a^0_{ср.к} = 1 - 0{,}003 - 0{,}002 - 0{,}0004 = 0{,}9946$ (0,9946)	$H_i^{0'T} = h_0 - h_1 = 3321{,}836 - 3031{,}033 = 290{,}803$ (298)	289,233 (296,391)
	1 - 2^0	$a_{12}0 = a_{0'1} - a_1 = 0{,}9946 - 0{,}054930242 = 0{,}939869758$ (0,930758303)	$H_i^{0T} = h_1 - h_2 = 3031{,}033 - 2924{,}316 = 106{,}717$ (101)	100,3 (94,008)
ЦСД	2 - 3	$a_{12}0 = a'_{пп} = a_{0'1} - a_{у1} - a_{у2} - a_{у3} - a_{у4} - a_2 + a_{с.к} - a^{пп}_{скр} - (a_{о\cdot у2} -$	$H_i^{23} = h_{пп} - h_3 = 3542{,}707 - 3399{,}663 = 143{,}044$ (143)	124,538 (121,682)

		$a^{T}_{д.у1})/3$ = 0,939869758 – 0,0006 – 0,0004 – 0,0006 – 0,0004 - 0,069641199 + 0,003 – 0,0003 – 0,0003 – 0,0002 = 0,870628559 (0,850908255) $a_{пп} = a'_{пп} + a^{пп}_{ск.р} + a^{пп}_{к.р} + a^{пп}_{р.к} - a_{с.к}$ = 0,868228559 (0,850508255)		
	3 – 4	$a_{34} = a'_{пп} - a_3$ = 0,868228559 – 0,101569531 = 0,769059028 (0,739566305)	$H_i^{34} = h_3 - h_4$ = 3399,663 – 3221,23 = 178,433 (180)	137,226 (133,96)
	4 -5	$a_{45} = a_{34} - a_4$ = 0,769059028 – 0,01613866 = 0,75292037 (0,724286945)	$H_i^{45} = h_4 - h_5$ = 3221,23 – 3067,33 = 153,9 (156)	115,879 (113,053)
	5 - 6	$a_{56} = a_{45} - a_5$ = 0,75292037 – 0,087413672	$H_i^{56} = h_5 - h_6$ = 3067,33 – 2882,639 =	122,913 (119,023)

		= 0,6655067 (0,646996433)	184,691 (184)	
ЦНД	6′ - 7	$a_{6'7} = a_{56} - a_6 - a_{y5} - a_{y6} - (a_{o \cdot y2} - a^{T}_{д.y1})/3$ = 0,6655067 – 0,003 – 0,0003 – 0,0003 – 0,0002 = 0,604310792 (0,598328262)	$H_i^{6'7} = h_6 - h_7$ = 2882,639 – 2708,075 = 174,564 (170)	105,491 (101,616)
	7 - 8	$a_{78} = a_{6'7} - a_7$ = 0,604310792 – 0,036211454 = 0,56809934 (0,566346657)	$H_i^{78} = h_7 - h_8$ = 2708,075 – 2557,29 = 150,785 (156)	85,661 (88,29)
	8 - К	$a_{8К} = a_{78} - a_8$ = 0,56809934 – 0,032368476 = 0,535730863 (0,536148558)	$H_i^{8К} = h_8 - h_К$ = 2557,29 – 2411,676 = 150,785 (146)	78,01 (79,829)
$\Sigma(a_i * H_{ij})$ = 1159,246 (1147,187) kJ/kg				

Reasonable energy indicators of the K-880 power unit, calculated by **technology of Noologistics**, is shown in Table 6. The same indicators, which are calculated by the method given in book "**94. Рыжкин В. Я. Тепловые электрические станции**" are shown into parentheses for comparison.

Table 6

#	Name	Notation	Unit of measur.	Dimension
1	Total heat consumption for the turbine unit	$Q_{ту}$	kJ/h	6768505,9 (6835108,8)
2	The effective power of the drive turbine of the feed pump	$N_e^{т.п.п.н}$	kW	29224,96 (29288,2)
3	Heat consumption in air heaters	$Q_{кал}$	kJ/h	176860,7 (183850,0)
4	The heat consumption of the turbine installation for the generation of electricity	$Q_{ту}^{э}$	kJ/h	6526645,2 (6586258,7)
5	Specific heat consumption of the turbine unit for power generation	$q_{ту}^{э}$	kJ/kW-h	7870,78 (7942,06)
6	Efficiency of the power generation plant	$\eta_{ту}^{э}$		0,4573881 (0,4532828)
7	Absolute electrical efficiency of the turbine unit	$\eta_{ту}^{эа}$		0,4255001 (0,4213539)
8	Thermal load of steam boiler	$Q_{пк}$	kJ/h	6807799,4 (6874822,6)
9	Heat transfer efficiency	$\eta_{тр}$		0,9942282 (0,9942233)
10	Quantity of heat of fuel on a steam boiler	Q_c	kJ/h	7357071,6 (7429466,1)
11	Efficiency of the power unit taking into account air heating and heat supply	η_c		0,4025969 (0,3989213)
12	Efficiency of the power unit net	$\eta_c^{н}$		0,3824670 (0,3789752)
13	Unit specific heat consumption of the unit	$q_c^{н}$	kJ/kW-h	9412,58 (9499,30)
14	Hourly fuel consumption	$B_{ут}$	kg/h	251026,1 (253496,2)
15	Hourly consumption of fuel gas	$B_{тг}$	m^3/h	192437,3

				(194330,9)
16	Hourly consumption of coal	B_p	kg/h	469800,2 (474423,1)
17	Specific consumption of conditional fuel net	$q_{ут}^{н}$	kJ/h	321,60 (324,56)

The effect of the application of **technology of Noologistics** for the load distribution between the main turbines of the K-880 power unit is shown in Table 7. The indicators calculated by its application are shown in the column called "Reasonable". The same indicators, but calculated by the method given in the book "**94. Рыжкин В. Я. Тепловые электрические станции**" are shown for comparison in the column with the name "Optimal".

Table 7

Indicator				Effect				
Notation	Unit of measur.	Optimal	Reasonable	Hour	Day	Month	Year	%
D0	T/h	2551,154	2524,15824	26,995761	647,8983	19760,9	236482,8629	1,058178401
Bут	T/h	253,4962	251,026054	2,4701267	59,28304	1808,133	21638,30978	0,974423629
Bтг	T.m³/h	194,3309	192,437331	1,8936066	45,44656	1386,12	16587,99359	0,974423629
Bp	T/h	474,4231	469,80023	4,622891	110,9494	3383,956	40496,52509	0,974423629
bут	g/kW	324,5595	321,596332	2,963124846				0,912968265

The notation in Table 7:

D0 – fresh steam consumption, T/h;
Bут – current conditional fuel consumption, T/h;
Bтг – current fuel gas consumption, T.m^3/h;
Bp – current consumption of coal, T/h;
bут – the current average cost of conditional fuel, g/kW.

It is obvious that the reasonable distribution of heat between the water heaters in the heat recovery system in the power unit, calculated using **the technology of Noologistics**, will not be constant, as is common throughout all known power units, but will change constantly in accordance the change of the current situation. In addition, **noologistical areas of possible operating modes** of other elements of the K-880 power unit: steam boiler, superheater, pumps, calorifiers, etc., were not involved in model calculations to reduce its size. Therefore, the real effect of using **the technology of Noologistics** will be more than calculated above.

The noologistical area of possible operating modes of the K-880 power unit, calculated using **the technology of Noologistics** is shown in Fig. Ex 9.

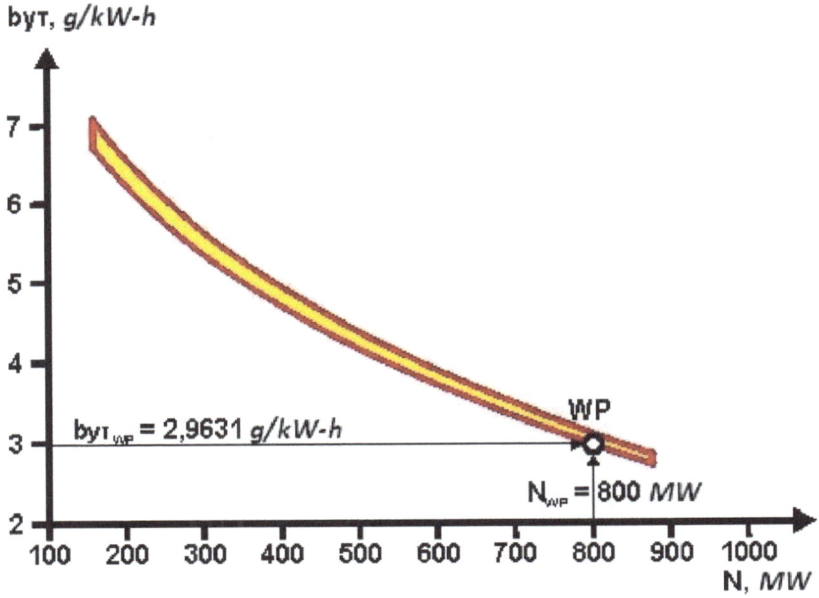

Fig. Ex 9

The notation in Fig. Ex 9:

WP – the **W**ork **P**oint of K – 880;
N – power of K – 880, kW;
Other - see above.

Model of reasonable regulation of power plants, Russia, 2011

The aim of the simulation was to demonstrate the universality of **Noologistics** using as its example the large-scale power supply grids. It was the second step in this direction by creating a model of reasonable regulation a power plant in which several power units are installed.

The power plant, which is adopted for modeling, has a total installed capacity of 3200 MW and contains four K-880 units described above, each of which is operated using **technology of Noologistics**. The four power units mentioned have different degrees of wear, as well as other differences, and, therefore, have **noologistical areas of possible modes of operation** that differ from each other and which have the appearance similar to that shown in Fig. Ex 9 and here are not shown to reduce the scope of the description. The total **noological area of possible operating modes** of the entire power plant with four K-880 power units is calculated in the same way as it is calculated for the entire BCS KGF - see the description of **the technology for calculating the upward indexed information pyramids**. In contrast to the more complex and specialized calculation of **the noologistical area of possible operating modes** of a single power unit, it is a routine repetition of the operations described **in the technology of calculating the upward indexed information pyramids**, and in order to reduce the volume of presentation, it is not shown here, and its result is graphically presented in Fig. Ex 10.

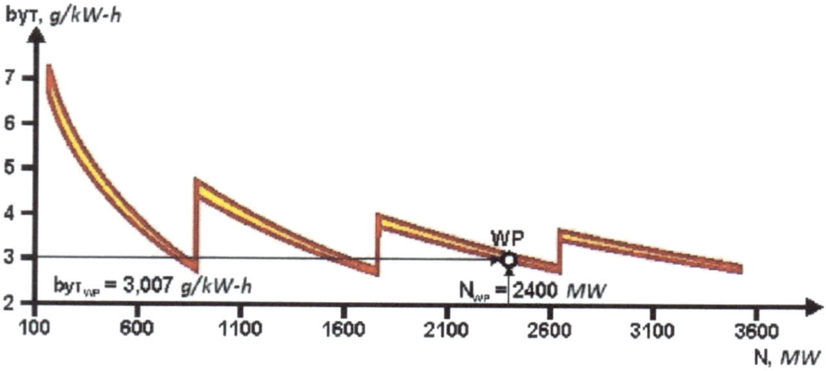

Fig. Ex 10

Model of reasonable regulation of a group of power plants with energy storage, Russia, 2011

The aim of the simulation was to demonstrate the universality of **Noologistics** using as its example the large-scale power supply grids. It is the third step in this direction. A group of three power plants with K-880 power units, similar to the one described above, of a total installed capacity of 9600 MW is adopted for example. The mentioned power stations have different total **noologistical areas of possible operating modes**, which have the appearance similar to that shown in Fig. Ex 10, and operate on electrical grids in conjunction to energy storage. As a energy storage in the model is a reservoir located in a mountainous area, which is equipped with water pumps and hydraulic turbines. Individual **noologistical area of possible modes of operation** was calculated in the model for each element of the energy storage in a manner similar to how they were calculated for each element of the above-mentioned BCS KGF, and then the total **noologistical area of possible modes of operation** of the entire energy storage is calculated on their basis in the same way as it was above is calculated for the whole BCS KGF. These routine calculations are not shown here in order to reduce the volume of description, and their results is graphically presented in Fig. Ex 11.

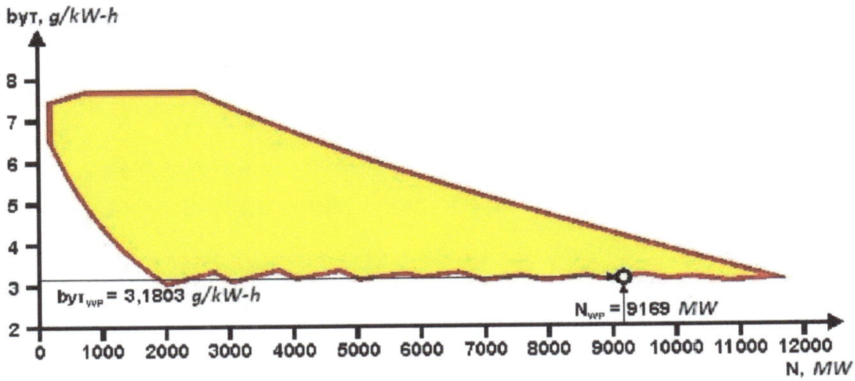

Fig. Ex 11

Modeling of the power unit, power plant with several power units and group of several power stations, working together with the energy storage on a single power supply grid, confirmed the universality of **Noologistics**.

Technology for reducing fuel consumption - energy resources and CO_2 emissions in large-scale gas supply systems

The project under this name was proposed in 2012 for inclusion in the list of EU "Projects of Common Interest " (briefly - PCI) and was registered on 16.07.2012 under the number 047466710491215812.

The project is designed to create a unified **system of Noologistics** for the entire gas infrastructure of the EU and neighboring countries and cover all the priority corridors of its gas supply.

In accordance to **TEN-E Regulation (EU) No 347/2013**, a priority corridor for the EU gas infrastructure, called "**The North-South Gas Interconnection in Central Eastern and Southern Eastern Europe**", was chosen for initial implementation. The project provided for the free creation of a demonstration version for the real object of the gas infrastructure.

Technology for reducing fuel consumption - energy resources and CO_2 emissions in large-scale energy supply systems

The project under this name was proposed in 2012 for inclusion in the list of EU PCI and was registered on 16.07.2012 under the number 773549456101915712.

The project is designed to create a single **system of Noologistics** for the entire energy infrastructure of the EU and neighboring countries and covers all the priority corridors of its energy supply.

In accordance to **TEN-E Regulation (EU) No 347/2013**, a priority corridor for the EU energy infrastructure, called "**North-South electricity interconnections in Central Eastern and South Eastern Europe**", was chosen for initial implementation. The project provided for the free creation of a demonstration version for the real object of the energy infrastructure.

The projects listed above were in the interest of the EU, as reflected in the **DIRECTIVE 2012/27 / EU OF THE EUROPEAN PARLIAMENT AND OF THE COUNCIL of 25 October 2012 on energy efficiency** (**http://eur-lex.europa.eu/LexUriServ/LexUriServ.do?uri = OJ: L: 2012: 315: 0001: 0056: EN: PDF**) and the EU's 2020 energy and climate objective. Both projects claimed the maximum number of points in accordance with the published rules for determining the winners of the competition, but immediately before their accrual, projects were excluded from the review process without any justification. Later, the EU Energy Commissioner Gьnther Oettinger in his letter of July 23, 2013, justified this exception by the lack of actuality (!) of saving fuel-energy resources when selecting projects to the PCI list. The materials of both projects are presented on the Internet on the page of the European Commission.

5. The List of Used Information Sources

1. Агеев А.И., Логинов Е.Л. Нооэкономика: определенная экономика в неопределенном будущем, Журнал Экономические Стратегии № 11, сентябрь 2011.
2. Акимова Т.А., Кузьмин А.П., Хаскин В.В. Экология. Природа-Человек-Техника: учебник для ВУЗов—М: ЮНИТА—ДАНА, 2001 г. — 343 с.
3. Аскар Акаев. Экономика XXI века – это нооэкономика, или экономика справедливости и разума, альманах «Развитие и экономика», № 7, сентябрь 2013 г.
4. Александров А.Г. Оптимальные и адаптивные системы Электронная книга. М., 2003. — 278 с.
5. Банковские информационные системы – Учебник: Университетская серия / под редакцией В. В. Дика. // Москва, Изд. Маркет ДС Корпорейшн, 2006. — 816 с.
6. Бесекерский В. А., Попов, Е. П. Теория систем автоматического регулирования. — СПб.: Профессия, 2004. — 749 с.
7. Бестужев-Лада И. В. Поисковое социальное прогнозирование : перспективные проблемы общества: опыт систематизации / Москва : Наука, 1984. 271 с.
8. Бродецкий Г. Л. Системный анализ в логистике: выбор в условиях неопределенности: учеб. для студ. учреждений высш. проф. Образования — М.: Издательский центр «Академия», 2010. — 336 с.
9. Бродецкий Г. Л., Гусев Д. А., Елин Е. Управление рисками в логистике - М.: Академия, 2010. — 192 с.
10. Бродецкий Г.Л. Экономико-математические методы и модели в логистике: процедуры оптимизации: учебник для студ. учреждений высш. образования / Г.Л. Бродецкий, Д.А.Гусев. — 2-е изд., стер. — М.: Издательский центр «Академия», 2014. — 288 с. — (Сер. Бакалавриат).
11. Вернадский В. И. Биосфера и ноосфера. — М.: Айрис-

пресс, 2004. — 576 с.
12. Власов В.К., Королев Л.Н. Элементы информатики./ Под. Ред. Л.Н. Королева.- М.: Наука, 2008 г. — 512 с.
13. Воробьев В.А., Дьяченко В.В., Вильчинская О.В., Карчагина А.В. Основы природопользования: экологические, экономические и правовые аспекты. Учебные пособие/ под ред. Проф. В.В. Дьяченко. – Ростов н/Д: Феникс, 2007 г. — 97 с.
14. Газоснабжение. СНиП 2.04.08-87, Москва 1995.
15. Геоинформационные системы в менеджменте. Учебное пособие/ С.Г. Казаков, К.Г. Дочева, Г.Н. Сухорукова. - Москва: Изд-во ФГБОУ ВПО «Российский экономический университет им. Г.В. Плеханова», 2015.- 134.С.
16. GOST 12.2.003-91 OSSS. Occupational safety standards system. Industrial equipment. General safety requirements.
17. GOST 13109-97 Electric energy. Electromagnetic compatibility of technical equipment. Power quality limits in public electrical systems.
18. GOST 15150-69 Machines, instruments and other industrial products. Modifications for different climatic regions. Categories, operating, storage and transportation conditions as to environment climatic aspects influence.
19. GOST 15971-90 Information processing systems. Terms and definitions.
20. GOST 24.104-85 Unified system of standards of computer control systems. Computer control systems. General requirements.
21. GOST 24.702-85 Unified system of standards of computer control systems. Efficiency of computer control systems. General principles.
22. GOST 27.004-85 Industrial product dependability. Technological systems. Terms and definitions.

23. GOST 34.201-89 Information technology. Set of standards for automated systems. Types, sets and indication of documents for automated systems making.
24. GOST 8.437-81 State system for ensuring the uniformity of measurements. Systems of information and measurement. Metrological ensuring. General statements.
25. GOST R 50739-95. Computers technique. Information protection against unauthorised access to information. General technical requirements.
26. GOST R 50922-96. Protection of information. Basic terms and definitions.
27. GOST R 51188-98. Information security. Software testing for the existence of computer viruses. The sample manual.
28. GOST R 51275-99. Protection of information. Object of informatization. Factors influencing the information. General outlines.
29. GOST P 51583-2000. Protection of information. The order of creation of the automated systems in the protected design. General outlines.
30. GOST R 51624-2000. Protection of information. Automated systems in a protected design. General outlines.
31. GOST R ИСО 7498-1-99. Information technology. Open Systems Interconnection. Basic Reference Model. Part 1. The Basic Model.
32. GOST R ISO/MEK 15408-1-2002. Information technology. Security techniques. Evaluation criteria for IT security. Part 1. Introduction and general model.
33. GOST R ISO/MEK 15408-2-2002. Information technology. Security techniques. Evaluation criteria for IT security. Part 2. Security functional requirements.
34. GOST R ISO/MEK 15408-3-2002. **Information technology. Security techniques. Evaluation criteria for IT security. Part 3.** Security assurance requirements.

35. GOST RO 0043-001-2010 Protection of information. Information security provision in organization. Basic terms and definitions.
36. GOST RO 0043-003-2012 Protection of information. Certification of information objects. General provisions. National standard of the Russian Federation, limited distribution.
37. GOST RO 0043–004–2013 Protection of information. Certification of information objects. Program and methods of certification tests.
38. Доктрина информационной безопасности Российской Федерации, утвержденная Президентом Российской Федерации 9 сентября 2000 г. № Пр-1895.
39. Дорф Р., Бишоп Р. Современные системы управления Пер. с англ. Б. И. Копылова. – М.: Лаборатория базовых знаний, 2002. – 832 с.
40. Дремов М.В. Формирование региональной логистической системы газообеспечения потребителей [Текст]: автореферат диссертации на соискание ученой степени канд. экон. наук:08.00.06 / М. В. Дремов. - Ростов-на-Дону, 1999. — 23 с.: ил.
41. Журкин И.Г., Шайтура С.В. Геоинформационные системы. (Учебное пособие. Гриф УМО по образованию в области геодезии и фотограмметрии)/ М.:КУДИЦ-ПРЕСС, 2009. — 273 с.
42. Инструкция по предупреждению и ликвидации аварий на тепловых электростанциях. Приказ Минэнерго России от 30.06.03 № 265
43. Инструкция по проведению мероприятий по контролю при осуществлении государственного энергетического надзора за оборудованием, зданиями и сооружениями электрических и тепловых установок, электростанций, котельных, электрических и тепловых сетей энергоснабжающих организаций и потребителей тепловой и электрической энергии. Госэнергонадзор Минэнерго России, 26.11.01 г.

44. Информатика.- / Под ред. Н.В. Макаровой. – М.: Финансы и статистика, 2007. – 768 с.
45. Каталог газодинамических характеристик ЦБК природного газа. ООО «ВНИИГАЗ» пос. Развилка Ленинский р-н, Московская обл.
46. Ким Д.П. Теория автоматического управления (том 1) Том 1. Линейные системы. - М.: Физматлит, 2003. — 288 с.
47. Козаченко А.Н., Лопатин А.С., Никишин В.И., Поршаков Б.П. “Снижение энергозатрат при транспортировании газа”, М.: “Потенциал” Производственно-технический журнал, № 1, 2001. — с. 33-35.
48. NIST Framework and Roadmap for Smart Grid Interoperability Standards, Release 2.0. Февраль 2012. Авторы: NIST (Национальный институт технологий и стандартизации, США), Государственный коммерческий департамент США. (http://www.nist.gov/smartgrid/upload/NIST_Framework_Release_2-0_corr.pdf).
49. Коробкин В.И., Передельский Л.В. Экология: учебник для ВУЗов – Ростов н/Д: Феникс, 2007 г. — 602 с.
50. Корпоративная логистика в вопросах и ответах/ Под общей редакцией: Сергеев В.И. - М.: ИНФРА-М, 2013. — 975 с.
51. Ловцов Д.А., Черных А.М. Геоинформационные системы. - Учебное пособие // Москва, Издательство: Российская академия правосудия 2012. — 192 с.
52. Логистика снабжения: учебник для бакалавриата и магистратуры / В. И. Сергеев, И. П. Эльяшевич ; под общ. ред. В. И. Сергеева. — 2-е изд., перераб. и доп. — М.: Издательство Юрайт, 2014. — 523 с. — Серия: Бакалавр и магистр. Академический курс.
53. Логистика: Основы. Стратегия. Практика / Практическая энциклопедия "Для всех, кто руководит" Под науч. ред. проф. В.И. Сергеева. – М.: Изд. ЗАО "МЦФЭР", 2007. — 1440 с. (Серия "Сменные страницы" с дополнениями 2008).

54. Логистика: учеб. пособие / Б. А. Аникин [и др.]; под ред. Б. А. Аникина, Т. А. Родкиной. – М.: ТК Велби, Изд-во Проспект, 2007. – 408 с.
55. Лонский И.И. Сравнительная оценка возможностей информационных систем// Известия высших учебных заведений. Геодезия и аэрофотосъемка. 2013. № 4. С. 97-99.
56. Лурье И.К. Геоинформационное картографирование. Методы геоинформатики и цифровой обработки космических снимков: учебник для студентов высших учебных заведений, обучающихся по специальности 020501 - Картография, направления 020500 - География и картография / И. К. Лурье. – М.; Изд. Московский гос. ун-т им. М. В. Ломоносова, Географический фак., 2008. — 422 с.
57. Лычкина Н. Н. Имитационное моделирование экономических процессов: учебное пособие. М.: ИНФРА-М, 2011.
58. Матвеев В. В. Информационная пирамида логистической системы с непрерывным технологическим процессом (статья). Логистика, организация и технология перевозок грузов. Сборник научных трудов. Вып. 56. – Калининград: Балтийская государственная академия рыбопромыслового флота. 2003. – С. 33 – 39.
59. Матвеев В. В. Логистика газа. Доклад для 2-ой Международной научно-технической конференции DISCOM 2004, Москва, РГУ нефти и газа имени И.М.Губкина, 2004.
60. Матвеев В. В., Матвеев Вл. В. Ноо Логистика. Краткое описание. ISBN 978-83-949046-0-9. Электронная книга, формат Windows eBook, 15,6 Мб. http://www.noologistics.ru, 04.09.2017. — 401 с.
61. Матвеев В. В. Проблемы энергетической логистики в Калининградской области (статья). Социально – экономическое развитие Калининградского региона (мониторинг, оценка, прогноз). Сборник научных

трудов. – Вып. 52 – Калининград: Балтийская государственная академия рыбопромыслового флота. 2002. – С. 117 – 122.
62. Матвеев В. В. Реализация логистических принципов управления газовой компанией в системе экстремально экономного регулирования и управления крупномасштабными сетями газопроводов (SEER&C). Доклад на 1-й Международной научно-технической конференции DISCOM 2002, Москва, РГУ нефти и газа имени И.М.Губкина, 13.11.2002.
63. Матвеев В. В. Способ регулирования газопровода. Патент РФ № 1755000, 1987 г.
64. Методические рекомендации по техническому расследованию и учету технологических нарушений в системах коммунального энергоснабжения и работе энергетических организаций жилищно-коммунального комплекса (МДК 4 01.2001). Приказ Госстроя России от 20.08.01 № 191
65. Методические указания по допуску в эксплуатацию новых и реконструированных электрических и тепловых энергоустановок. Минэнерго России, 03.04.02 г.
66. Методические указания по составлению энергетических характеристик для систем транспорта тепловой энергии по показателям "разность температур сетевой воды в подающих и обратных трубопроводах" и "удельный расход электроэнергии". Приказ Минэнерго России от 30.06.03 № 278
67. Методические указания по составлению энергетических характеристик для систем транспорта тепловой энергии по показателю "удельный расход сетевой воды". Приказ Минэнерго России от 30.06.03 № 278
68. Методические указания по составлению энергетических характеристик для систем транспорта

тепловой энергии по показателю "потери сетевой воды". Приказ Минэнерго России от 30.06.03 № 278

69. Методические указания по составлению энергетических характеристик для систем транспорта тепловой энергии по показателю "тепловые потери". Приказ Минэнерго России от 30.06.03 № 278
70. Методические указания по устойчивости энергосистем. Приказ Минэнерго России от 30.06.03 № 277
71. МИ 2438-97 Системы измерительные. Метрологическое обеспечение. Основные положения.
72. Мирошник И. В., Никифоров, В. О., Фрадков, А. Л. Нелинейное и адаптивное управление сложными динамическими системами. — СПб.: Наука, 2000. — 548 с. — (Сер.: Анализ и синтез нелинейных систем).
73. Мищенко А. В. Методы управления инвестициями в системах логистики - М.: ИНФРА – М, 2009. — 363 с.
74. Мищенко А. В. Методы управления ограниченными ресурсами в логистике - М.: ИНФРА-М, 2011. — 184 с.
75. Острейковский В.А. Информатика. – М.: Высшая школа, 2007. — 512 с.
76. Панкратов В. С., Вербило А. С. Автоматизированная система диспетчерского управления ГТС. – М.: ВНИИЭгазпром, 2002. — 261 с.
77. Панкратов В. С., Герке В. Г., Сарданишвили С. А., Митичкин С. К. Комплекс моделирования режимов работы ГТС. – М.: ВНИИЭгазпром, 2002. — 56 с.
78. Парахина В.Н., Ушвицкий Л.И. (ред.) Основы теории управления М.: Финансы и статистика, 2003. — 560 с.
79. Smart Grid European Technology Platform (ftp://ftp.cordis.europa.eu/pub/fp7/energy/docs/smartgrids_en.pdf)
80. «Положение о государственной системе защиты информации в Российской Федерации от иностранных технических разведок и от ее утечки по техническим каналам», утверждено постановлением Совета Министров – Правительства Российской Федерации от 15.09.1993 г. № 912-51.

81. Подмарков В.Ю., Герке В.Г. (ОАО «Газпром»), Ефремов В.А. (ВНИИгаз) “Расчетно-оптимизационный комплекс диспетчерского управления ЕСГ”, М.: “Газовая промышленность” № 8, 2001 г., — с. 50-53.
82. Положение об организации и осуществлении контроля за системой оперативно - диспетчерского управления в электроэнергетике и особенностях организации и проведения аттестации лиц, осуществляющих профессиональную деятельность, связанную с оперативно-диспетчерским управлением в электроэнергетике (РД-12-04-2007). Приказ Ростехнадзора от 03.04.07 № 199
83. Положение об оценке готовности электро - и теплоснабжающих организаций к работе в осенне-зимний период. Минпромэнерго России, 25.08.04 г.
84. Поляков А.А., Цветков В.Я. Прикладная информатика: Учебно-методическое пособие: В 2-х частях: Часть.2 /Под общ. ред. А.Н. Тихонова - М.: МАКС Пресс. 2008. - 860с.
85. Порядок организации работ по выдаче разрешений на допуск в эксплуатацию энергоустановок, с изменениями. Приказы Ростехнадзора от 07.04.08 № 212, Минприроды России от 20.08.08 № 182 (зарегистрированы Минюстом России 28.04.08 г., рег. № 11597; 28.08.08 г., рег. № 12197)
86. Порядок согласования с органами государственного энергетического надзора технических условий на разрабатываемое газоиспользующее оборудование. Приказ Минэнерго России от 16.12.02 № 448 (зарегистрирован Минюстом России 04.02.03 г., рег. № 4181)
87. 42 U.S. Code Subchapter IX - SMART GRID. usctc 42 152 IX § 17381 (http://www.law.cornell.edu/uscode/text/42/chapter-152/subchapter-IX)
88. Правила техники безопасности при эксплуатации тепломеханического оборудования электростанций и

тепловых сетей (РД 34.03.201 97). Минтопэнерго России, 03.04.97 г.

89. Правила технической эксплуатации тепловых энергоустановок. Приказ Минэнерго России от 24.03.03 № 115 (зарегистрирован Минюстом России 02.04.03 г., рег. № 4358)
90. Правила устройства и безопасной эксплуатации паровых котлов с давлением пара не более 0,07 МПа (0,7 кГс/см^2), водогрейных котлов и водоподогревателей с температурой нагрева воды не выше 388К (115°С), с изменениями № 1, № 2 и № 3. Приказ Минстроя России от 28.08.92 № 205; Комитет Российской Федерации по муниципальному хозяйству, 12.01.94 г.; Департамент жилищно-коммунального хозяйства, 24.02.95 г.; Госстрой России, 21.01.00 г.
91. Приказ Федеральной службы охраны Российской Федерации от 7.08.2009 № 487 "Об утверждении положения о сегменте информационно-телекоммуникационной сети Интернет для федеральных органов государственной власти и органов государственной власти субъектов Российской Федерации.
92. Пупков К.А., Егупов Н.Д. Методы классической и современной теории автоматического управления (том 1) Учебник в 5-и тт.; 2-е изд., перераб. и доп. Т1: Математические модели, динамические характеристики и анализ систем автоматического управления / Под ред. К.А. Пупкова, Н.Д. Егупова. – М.: Издательство МГТУ им. Н.Э. Баумана, 2004. – 656 с.
93. Рутковский И. П., Швабский В. Л., Дятлов В. В. Автоматизация управления газотранспортными предприятиями и ЕСГ в целом // Газовая промышленность. – 2000. – Октябрь. – С. 8-13.
94. Рыжкин В.Я. Тепловые электрические станции: Учебник для вузов/Под ред. В.Я. Гиршфельда.-3-е изд., перераб. и доп.-М.: Энергоатомиздат, 1987.-328 с.: ил.

95. Савиных В. П. Информационное обеспечение космических исследований // Перспективы науки и образования- 2014. - №2. – с. 9-14.
96. Савиных В.П., Цветков В.Я. Геоданные как системный информационный ресурс //Вестник Российской Академии Наук. 2014. Т. 84. № 9. — с. 826–829.
97. Специальные требования и рекомендации по технической защите конфиденциальной информации. Утверждены приказом гостехкомиссии России от 30 августа 2002 г. № 282.
98. СТП-01-016-2000 СТАНДАРТ ОАО "ЛУКОЙЛ" Автоматизированная система управления электроснабжением. Основные положения и технические требования. ООО «Центр безопасности труда».
99. Стратегия национальной безопасности Российской Федерации до 2020 года, утвержденная Указом Президента Российской Федерации от 12 мая 2009 г. № 537.
100. Стратегия развития информационного общества в Российской Федерации, утверждённая Президентом Российской Федерации 07.02.2008 № Пр-212.
101. Тепловые электрические станции: учебник для вузов. / В.Д. Буров, Е.В. Дорохов, Д.П. Елизаров и др.; под. Ред. В.М. Лавыгина, А.С. Седлова, С.В. Цанева. – 3-е изд., стереот. – М.: Издательский дом МЭИ, 2009. – 466 с.: ил.
102. Требования к оснащенности газоиспользующего оборудования теплоутилизирующим оборудованием, средствами автоматизации, теплотехнического контроля, учета выработки и потребления энергоресурсов. Приказ Минэнерго России от 16.12.02 № 448 (зарегистрирован Минюстом России 04.02.03 г., рег. № 4181)

103. Требования к составлению методик проведения пусконаладочных и режимно-наладочных работ на газоиспользующем оборудовании. Приказ Минэнерго России от 16.12.02 № 448 (зарегистрирован Минюстом России 04.02.03 г., рег. № 4181) и др.
104. Тюкин И. Ю., Терехов В. А., Адаптация в нелинейных динамических системах, (Серия: Синергетика: от прошлого к будущему), Санкт-Петербург: ЛКИ, 2008. — 384 с.
105. Указ Президента Российской Федерации от 17.03.2008 № 351 "О мерах по обеспечению информационной безопасности Российской Федерации при использовании информационно-телекоммуникационных сетей международного информационного обмена".
106. Урлапов В.Е. Геоинформационные системы в экономике: Учебно-методическое пособие. – Нижний Новгород: НФ ГУ-ВШЭ, 2007. – 104 с.
107. Федеральный закон от 27 июля 2006 г. № 149-ФЗ «Об информации, информационных технологиях и о защите и информации»
108. Федеральный закон от 4 мая 2011 г. № 99-ФЗ «О лицензировании отдельных видов деятельности»
109. Федеральный закон Российской Федерации от 3 декабря 2011 г. N 382-ФЗ "О государственной информационной системе топливно-энергетического комплекса", г. Москва.
110. Фель А.В., Стерлигова А.Н. Операционный (производственный) менеджмент. Москва: ИНФРА-М, 2009. — 187 с.
111. ФЗ РФ «О теплоснабжении» (с изменениями на 29 декабря 2014 года) (редакция, действующая с 3 марта 2015 года).
112. ФЗ РФ от 7 декабря 2011 г. № 416-ФЗ «О водоснабжении и водоотведении».

113. Цветков В.Я. Изучение геотехнических систем методами геоинформатики // Международный научно-технический и производственный журнал «НАУКИ О ЗЕМЛЕ». - №3-2012. — с.17-19.
114. Цветков В.Я. Модели и моделирование. - М.: Госинформобр, 2006. - 94с.
115. Цветков В.Я. Системный анализ ГИС // Образовательные ресурсы и технологии. – 2015. - №1(9). – с. 97-103.
116. Цейтлин Е.М. Оптимизация негативного воздействия горного производства с помощью интегрального критерия оценки экологической опасности // Горный информационно-аналитический бюллетень (научно-технический журнал). Отдельная статья (специальный выпуск). — 2013. — № 6. — 16 с.— М.: издательство «Горная книга»
117. Шайтура С.В. Электронно-геоинформационные ресурсы и технологии // Науки о Земле. 2012. № 2. С. 65-68.
118. Экологическая экспертиза: учеб. пособие для студ. учреждений высш. проф. образования / [В. К. Донченко, В. М. Питулько, В. В. Растоскуев, С. А. Фролова] ; под ред. М. Питулько. — 5- изд., перераб. и доп. — М.: Издательский центр «Академия», 2010. — 528 с.
119. Эффективная логистика. / Л.Б. Миротин, И.Э. Ташбаев, О.Г. Порошина – М.: Издательство "Экзамен", 2003. – 160 с.
120. Якубайтис Э.А. Информационные сети и системы: Справочная книга.- М.: Финансы и статистика, 2008. – 368 с.
121. DIRECTIVE 2012/27/EU OF THE EUROPEAN PARLIAMENT AND OF THE COUNCIL of 25 October 2012 on energy efficiency (http://eur-lex.europa.eu/LexUriServ/LexUriServ.do?uri=OJ:L:2012:315:0001:0056:EN:PDF).
122. Draft Regulation on guidelines for trans-European

energy infrastructure and repealing Decision 1364/2006/EC (http://www.publications.parliament.uk/pa/cm201012/cmselect/cmeuleg/428-xlvi/42803.htm).
123. FCCC/CP/1999/7. Review of the implementation of commitments and of other provisions of the Convention. UNFCCC guidelines on reporting and review. UNFCC Conference of the Parties, Marrakech, Fifth session, Bonn, 25 October –5 November 1999.
124. FCCC/CP/2001/20. Guidelines for national systems under Article 5, paragraph 1, of the Kyoto Protocol. UNFCC Conference of the Parties, Seventh session, 10 November 2001.
125. Inventory of U.S. Greenhouse Gas Emissions and Sinks: 1990-1999. U.S. Environmental Protection Agency, 8 April 15, 2001, Washington, DC, USA.
126. SMART GRID, The Office of Electricity Delivery and Energy Reliability (OE) (http://energy.gov/oe/technology-development/smart-grid).
127. The Regulation on Guidelines for trans-European energy infrastructure (TEN-E Regulation (EU) No 347/2013) (http://eur-lex.europa.eu/LexUriServ/LexUriServ.do?uri=OJ:L:2013:115:0039:0075:EN:PDF).
128. Work Programme for implementation of the 'Intelligent Energy - Europe II' programme (http://ec.europa.eu/cip/files/cip/docs/iee-work-programme-2013_en.pdf).

6. About Authors

Matveev Valery Vasilievich,

project Manager, Kaliningrad,

born in 1945, higher education, experience on the published theme for over 30 years.

Matveev Vladimir Valerievich,

Deputy project Manager, Kaliningrad,

born in 1971, higher education, experience on the published theme for over 15 years.

energy_logistics@mail.ru

www.ingramcontent.com/pod-product-compliance
Lightning Source LLC
Chambersburg PA
CBHW041307210926
51847CB00001B/2
* 9 7 8 8 3 9 4 9 0 4 6 1 6 *